GW00362057

7 - SEP. 1995

A 299 FRANCE

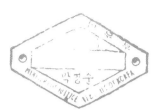

- 6 FEB 1988

DEPARTMENT OF IMMIGRATION
PERMITTED TO ENTER
AUSTRALIA.

24 APR 1986

on

For stay of 12 Month

SYDNEY AIRPORT 54

Person

30 OCT 1989
DEPARTED
AUSTRALIA

SYDNEY 32

I N S I D E R ' S
MEDITERRANEAN
FRANCE
G U I D E

上陸許可
ADMITTED
15. FEB. 1986
Status: 4-1-   4
Duration: 90 days
NARITA(N)
Immigration Inspector

ADMITTED
20 OCT. 1988
Status: 4-1-16
Duration
Port: HANEDA
Signature

№ 011278

THE UNITED STATES
OF AMERICA
NONIMMIGRANT VISA

SSED
Air   Port

U.S. IMMIGRATION
170 HHW 1710

JUL 2 0 1988

HONG KONG
(1038)
- 7 JUN 1987
IMMIGRATION
OFFICER

THE INSIDER'S GUIDES

AUSTRALIA • BALI • CALIFORNIA • CANADA • CHINA • EASTERN CANADA • FLORIDA • HAWAII •
HONG KONG • INDIA • INDONESIA • JAPAN • KENYA • KOREA • MALAYSIA AND SINGAPORE •
MEDITERRANEAN FRANCE • MEXICO • NEPAL • NEW ENGLAND • NEW ZEALAND •
PHILIPPINES • PORTUGAL • RUSSIA • SPAIN • THAILAND • TURKEY •
VIETNAM, LAOS AND CAMBODIA • WESTERN CANADA

Insider's Guide Mediterranean France

© 1996 Kümmerly+Frey AG, Berne

Moorland Publishing Co Ltd
Moor Farm Road, Airfield Estate, Ashbourne, DE61HD, England

published by arrangement with Kümmerly+Frey AG, Berne

ISBN: 0-86190-614-4

Created, edited and produced by Allan Amsel Publishing
53 rue Beaudouin, 27700 Les Andelys, France
Telefax: (33) 32 54 54 50
Editor in Chief: Allan Amsel
Original design concept: Hon Bing-wah/Kinggraphic
Picture editor and designer: Allan Amsel

AUTHOR'S ACKNOWLEDGEMENTS
A small army of people helped me with this book, far more than I can possibly mention, but I
remember and thank them all. My special thanks go to Monique Hamot and her family, Omblyne
Salvy de Richemont, Lucie Peyraud, Tom and Mireille Johnston, Jean-Luc and Sarah Pujol,
Ed Flaherty, Emily Emerson and Arnaud Le Moing, Paule Artillan, Isabelle Forêt, Katia Zeitlin,
my colleague Nik Wheeler and above all my marvelous wife Joanne, whose tireless help and
encouragement from beginning to end were essential to the completion of this book.

PHOTO CREDIT
David Burke: Page 163

Printed by Samhwa Printing Co Ltd, Seoul, Korea

INSIDER'S
MEDITERRANEAN
FRANCE
GUIDE

By David Burke

Photographed by Nik Wheeler

MPC

Contents

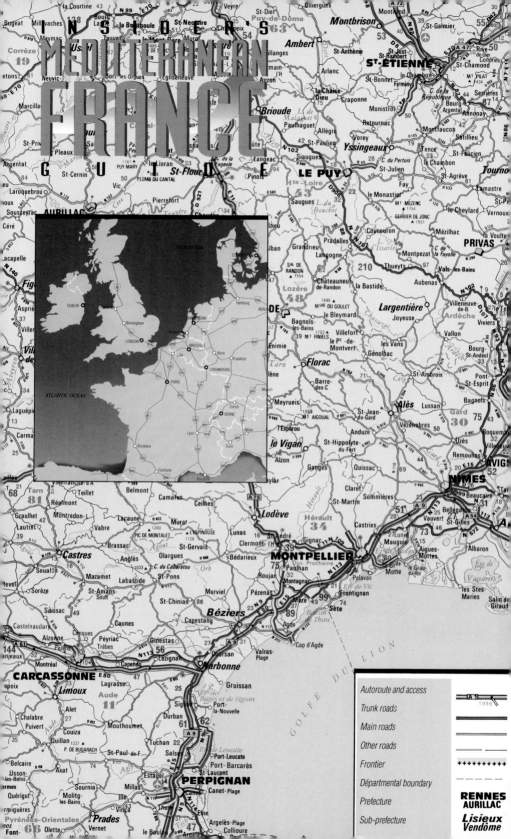

TOP SPOTS

in the Mediterranean. It was built by the Princes of Monaco in the eighteenth century when Roquebrune and Menton were under their rule.

The hard part of the drive is not navigating the *corniches* themselves, which are gently graded, but the steep connector roads between them which zigzag up from the coast or plunge down from high. If you like roller coasters, you'll love this part of the ride.

For other kinds of thrills, be sure to make time for **Monaco**, 19 km (12 miles) east of Nice on the coast road. Its Exotic Garden has 6,000 varieties of cacti and succulents, and the aquarium of its Oceanographic Museum is one of the finest in the world. I recommend staying overnight if you can, to experience the Grand Casino of Monte-Carlo at its most glamorous. You may want to try your luck in its splendid Belle Époque gaming rooms, but if gambling's not for you, relax and watch the high-rollers in action.

Cruise the *Corniches* of the Riviera

YOU DON'T HAVE TO BE A MONTE-CARLO RALLY DRIVER TO TACKLE THE CORNICHES OF THE RIVIERA, but a cool hand at the wheel doesn't hurt. The **Grande Corniche**, the highest of the three parallel roads cut into the slopes of the Maritime Alps between Nice and Menton, presents you with breathtaking drops to the Mediterranean at every turn. On this road built by Napoléon in 1806, you can cruise at an altitude of 550 m (1,800 ft) and peer down dizzily at the Principality of Monaco, which looks like a miniature town in a model train set.

The **Moyenne Corniche**, the middle road built in the late 1920's offers the best views of the classy port towns of Villefranche-sur-Mer and Beaulieu and the Cap Ferrat peninsula, the section closest to Nice. It also provides the only access to the colorful medieval "perched village" of Èze clinging to a sheer, rocky peak overlooking the sea. The Corniche Inférieure, the lower road, snakes in and out of coves along the coast where you can stop and take a dip

The next day visit medieval **Roquebrune** and the flower-filled Italianate port of **Menton** before swinging up onto the Grande Corniche for the 32 km (20 mile) drive back to Nice. At **La Turbie**, at an altitude of 480 m (1,575 ft), pause at the towering sixth century BC monument the Trophy of the Alps that commemorates Emperor Augustus's defeat of the last resisting Ligurian tribes. Another spectacular panorama awaits you — a vast sweep of Riviera coast and Corsica 162 km (100 miles) across the sea.

For non-drivers, several tour operators in Nice offer daily coach excursions. Not as thrilling as driving it yourself, but close enough.

OPPOSITE: Evening on the red rock coast of the Esterel west of Cannes. ABOVE: The Route des Crêtes near Cassis, one of several hair-raising drives you can make along Mediterranean cliffs.

Attack a Fortified City

IF YOU'RE NOT A MEDIEVAL HISTORY BUFF ALREADY, THE MAJESTIC WALLED CITY OF CARCASSONNE IS ALMOST GUARANTEED TO MAKE YOU ONE. Visions of knights in armor, court jesters, damsels in distress, troubadours, jousts and rumbling siege machines leap to mind as you approach this giant fortress in the heart of Languedoc. During the Hundred Years War, Edward the Black Prince brought his army here in hopes of conquering it. Legend has it that he took one look up the hill with the mighty walls looming above him and decided to lay siege somewhere else. Two sets of massive crenelated walls encircle the city, measuring three kilometers (almost two miles) in circumference on the outside, with 52 round towers. Between the two sets of walls is an open space, the *lices* (lists), where any attackers who made it over the outer wall would be killed by defenders raining projectiles down on them from the inner walls. It was this feature more than anything that made the fortress impregnable and earned it the nickname of "The Maid of Languedoc."

As you enter the city through the Porte Narbonnaise, the fortified main gate, you will see meticulously restored medieval houses lining the winding stone streets that have been converted into restaurants, hotels and tourist shops. Regrettably, a lot of shops carry tasteless souvenir junk. But don't let that put you off, because the more you prowl about the Cité, as old Carcassonne is known, the more evocative it becomes.

Be sure not to bypass the **Château Comtal**, the twelfth century castle of the Trencavel family inside the city. They ruled Carcassonne, Béziers and a large part of Languedoc until their downfall during the Albigensian Crusade. Young Viscount Raymond-Roger Trencavel was murdered in this castle in 1209. Frequent guided walking tours start here daily that lead you through the castle and onto ramparts. Your most lasting impressions of this *tour de force* of medieval engineering will be the views from the top of the high walls and towers.

You can take little tourist trains for a 20-minute circuit of the walls, well worth doing if you have the time. But if a choice has to be made, I prefer the defenders' point of view you get from the walking tour, with its marvelous panoramas of the Cité and the vine-covered hills around Carcassonne.

A main stop on the tourist trail, this historical wonder attracts more than 200,000 visitors a year, mostly in the summer. But if you choose to brave the summer crowds, you will see it at its most magical, when it is illuminated
TOP SPOTS

at night. On the 14th of July, there is a tremendous fireworks display, and in August the town explodes with music, dance, crafts shows and jousting tournaments during *Les Médiévales*, a costume pageant which recreates the atmosphere of a medieval fair.

Bouillabaisse by the Sea

IN MEDITERRANEAN FRANCE, WHERE DINING IS AKIN TO A RELIGIOUS EXPERIENCE, HAVING BOUILLABAISSE IS A VERITABLE EPIPHANY. This exuberant Provençal fish soup is made all along the coast, and many places claim to make the best. Maybe it's just the power of suggestion, but I always feel that foods and wines taste best in the place they originally came from — and when it comes to *bouillabaisse*, that place is **Marseille**.

Every morning on the **Vieux Port** (Old Port) of Marseille the fishermen's wives sell their husbands' catch of the previous night on the Quai des Belges. Fronting on this lively scene is the **Miramar Restaurant**, the excellent seafood house of the genial Minguella brothers, Pierre and Jean-Michel. Here you can sit on the outdoor dining terrace and enjoy the view of the harbor and the basilica of Notre-Dame-de-la-Garde topped by a giant golden statue of the Virgin,

At Carcassonne OPPOSITE, the largest fortified city in Europe, little tourist trains make it easy to circle the two miles of mighty walls. ABOVE: Outdoor restaurants at the Cours Saleya Market in Nice.

"*La Bonne Mere*," who watches over all things *Marseillais*, including, clearly, the making of *bouillabaisse*.

The ritual begins with Pierre bringing a tray to your table with six fresh fish for you to inspect. They will be *rascasse* (rockfish), *saint-pierre* (John Dory), *vive* (weever fish), *lotte* (monkfish), *congre* (conger eel) and *rouget* (red mullet), but with a substitution or two possible, depending on the catch of the day. They go back to the kitchen and are boiled by brother Jean-Michel, the chef, in a previously prepared soup made from some of the same kinds of fish already mentioned plus other sea creatures, including *favouilles*, a little green crab that adds a peppery flavor. While you wait expectantly for your meal, Pierre makes sure you have the right wine. A dry white from Cassis is the favorite in Marseille. Domaine du Bagnol 1990 goes down very nicely.

Your first course will be the creamy reddish tan fish soup which you season to your taste with great dollops of *rouille*, a mayonnaise made with garlic, saffron and pepper. You then rub as much fresh garlic as you can stand on some large croutons, add them to the tantalizing soup and dig in. Two or three filling bowls later, the six boiled fish arrive at the table. You know you can't possibly eat this mountain of food, but you make a Herculean effort. And when you finally reach the point where you can't possibly eat another bite, you are amazed to see that all that remains is a pile of cleanly picked bones.

Take a Roman Holiday

IF YOU HAD TRAVELED THROUGH MEDITERRANEAN FRANCE IN THE FIRST CENTURY AD — PROVINCIA ROMANA, AS IT WAS THEN CALLED — YOU WOULD HAVE SEEN ROMAN ARENAS ROCKING TO THE CHEERS OF 20,000 SPECTATORS, parades under triumphal arches, crowded Roman baths, temples, aqueducts and the villas of wealthy Roman landlords. Today as you travel through Provence, you will not only be awed by the powerful architectural legacy left by Rome, but discover that many of these ancient marvels are kept constantly in use. **Nîmes**, the bullfighting capital of France, puts on more *corridas* than any city other than Madrid or Seville in its 20,000-seat Roman arena, along with rodeos, musical performances and — as in the days of the Romans — circuses. In Nîmes's elegant Roman meeting house, the Maison Carrée, you can see the latest in modern art displayed on its two thousand year-old walls, and at the Pont du Gard north of the city, you can take a stroll on top of the magnificent many-arched aqueduct that once carried Nîmes's water supply down from the mountains.

Nîmes calls itself "The Rome of France," but **Arles**, 30 km (19 miles) to the east, lays strong claims to the title as well. For a short time in the early fifth century, Arles even became the capital of the Roman Empire. It also has a 20,000-seat Roman arena that is used for bullfights and other events. Its Roman theater puts on plays in the summer, and you can walk through the moody necropolis of Les Alyscamps, the most important Roman and early Christian burial ground in France. At **Glanum** near **Saint-Rémy**, 24 km (15 miles) north of Arles, you can explore the archaeological site where digs have unearthed the traces of three ancient civilizations — Celto-Ligurian, Greek and Roman, one on top of the other. Take a two minute walk down the road to the Mausoleum, a perfectly preserved monument to Emperor Augustus's grandsons, and admire the vivid bas-reliefs of hunting and battle scenes.

Like Saint-Rémy, **Vaison-la-Romaine**, 69 km (43 miles) to the north, has an active archaeological site to explore, along with a 6,000-seat amphitheater which presents a summer-long program of music, dance and theatrical events.

To complete your circuit of Roman cities in Provence, proceed 27 km (17 miles) to the southwest to **Orange** to see its Arc de Triomphe, the third largest Roman triumphal arch still standing, and especially the magnificent 10,000-seat Théâtre Antique, one of the best preserved Roman theaters anywhere, which

TOP SPOTS

puts on a distinguished series of operas in the summer.

Visit a Vineyard

FROM THE CÔTES DE PROVENCE WINE REGION NORTH OF SAINT-TROPEZ DOWN TO THE PYRÉNÉES, WHERE CÔTES DU ROUSSILLON, BANYULS AND COLLIOURE VINEYARDS RUN INTO THE FOOTHILLS, MEDITERRANEAN FRANCE IS A SEA OF VINES, with only the occasional island of market gardens, orchards and livestock areas interspersed. More than half France's wine comes from its Mediterranean regions, so the opportunities for visiting vineyards are practically unlimited.

The most prestigious wines of Southern France come from Châteauneuf-du-Pape north of Avignon, where the fourteenth century Popes planted their vines on its pebble-covered slopes overlooking the Rhône. The most beautiful vineyard to visit and among the most highly respected is **Château la Nerthe**. This elegant neoclassical mansion in a tree-shaded park is open for visitors weekdays from 8 AM to noon and 2 to 6 PM (90 83 70 11. As you walk through its atmospheric cellars, past hundreds of oak casks and tens of thousands of ageing bottles, you will learn about the thirteen kinds of grape that are blended to make the robust red wines of the area. But you will not learn not how it's done, because each vineyard has its own secret recipe.

This is only one of the many estates you can visit in Châteauneuf-du-Pape. The Tourist Office at Place du Portail in the center of town

ABOVE: The two thousand year-old Roman arena in Arles is used regularly for bullfights, concerts and special events. BELOW: Grapes thrive in most parts of Mediterranean France, making it far and away the nation's largest wine-producing area.

℆ 90 83 71 08, provides a map and a list of estates and their visiting hours. In general, the *caves* are open weekdays, and on Saturdays by appointment only.

The winemakers are generally delighted to welcome you and let you sample their wares, in the hope that you will buy something, of course. But they are also most generous about sharing their deep knowledge with anyone who shows an interest. It's not always easy to meet people when you're on the road, but in Mediterranean France, visiting vineyards is a delightful solution to that problem.

Festive Follies

IN THE SUMMER, FRANCE'S CENTER OF CULTURAL GRAVITY SHIFTS TO THE SOUTH, AND IT IS NO EXAGGERATION TO SAY THAT ALL MEDITERRANEAN FRANCE BECOMES A FESTIVAL. From the month-long international theater festival at Avignon to the opera festivals of Orange and Aix-en-Provence, jazz in Nice and Antibes, classical programs in Prades, Saint-Rémy and Menton and dance, film, photography and folk arts festivals, the region is literally bursting with cultural delights. But no city in the South plays *la carte de la culture*, the culture card, with more vigor than Languedoc's bold, modern capital of **Montpellier**. While other cities content themselves with one major festival a summer, Montpellier puts on three.

Printemps des Comédiens (Springtime for Actors), a three-week festival running from mid-June to early-July, began in 1986 and built a name for itself as a festival of Mediterranean theater. But in 1994, it widened its scope to include the Russian Licedei clown troupe from Saint Petersburg, Shakespeare's "Henry VI" directed by Stuart Seide, an American who lives in Paris, Gogol's *The Nose* by the Lithuanian

State Theater and the Berlin Cabaret featuring transvestite Georgette Dee. The **Festival International Montpellier Danse** is one of the major dance festivals of Europe. Established in 1980, it attracts top companies such as the Béjart Ballet of Lausanne and an eclectic mix of performers from all over the world. The Batsheva Dance Company from Israel, the Contemporary Dance Company of Canton, Michèle Ettori and Michèle Rust appeared in 1994, and a big tango ball concluded the festivities. It is held for two weeks in late June and early July. The largest of Montpellier's festivals is the **Festival de Radio France**, running from mid-July to early August. It features modern classical and contemporary works performed by leading French and international symphony and chamber orchestras, opera companies and jazz and popular artists. Wagner's *Rienzi*, Saint-Saëns's *Etienne Marcel* and Richard Strauss's *Daphné* have been performed in recent years, and jazz and pop artists include the duo of Julia Migenes and Dee Dee Bridgewater, Martial Solal and Leon Redbone.

Further enhancing the high caliber of talent and the bright, often provocative content of its festivals, Montpellier stages its performances in a variety of unusual locales, such as the Cathedral, the courtyard of the Fabre Museum and the Château d'O. This is one of a number of extravagant mansions known as *folies* (follies) that were built in the countryside around Montpellier in the eighteenth century. Its large tree-lined, statue-filled park provides an elegant setting for an evening of music under the stars.

Inside the Papal Palace, only a few of the fourteenth century frescos that decorated the walls remain, but the vastness of the Banquet Hall and other public rooms is something you will never forget. A few hundred yards across the wide square from the Papal Palace, the Petit Palais is a fourteenth century cardinal's mansion which now houses a museum of medieval and early Renaissance painting and sculpture from Italy and from the fifteenth century School of Avignon that emerged as a result of Papal patronage. The collection includes an altarpiece by Enguerrand Quarton, the school's most brilliant painter. His masterpiece, the magnificent "Coronation of the Virgin," can also be seen across the river at the Museé Municipal in Villeneuve-lès-Avignon.

And so, notorious sinners though most of the seven Popes of Avignon were, we not only pardon them, but we thank them for the wealth of artistic and architectural treasures they left us, and for making the City of the Popes one of the most intriguing places in France — an absolute "must" on any traveler's Southern itinerary.

Events are often sold out, so be sure to reserve long in advance. For information and reservations contact the Tourist Office in Montpellier (67 58 67 58.

Pardon the Popes

EARLY IN THE FOURTEENTH CENTURY, IN ONE OF THE MORE BIZARRE TWISTS OF THE MIDDLE AGES, THE CHURCH SUDDENLY DESERTED ROME, THE CAPITAL OF WESTERN CHRISTIANITY, AND MOVED TO A SLEEPY TOWN ON THE EAST BANK OF THE RHÔNE. AND **AVIGNON**, *A BACKWATER OF LITTLE PREVIOUS DISTINCTION, WOKE UP AND FOUND ITSELF ONE OF THE RICHEST AND MOST IMPORTANT PLACES IN THE WORLD* — and soon one of the most corrupt. Petrarch, who worked as a secretary for a cardinal, called Avignon "a sink of vice." About its masters he said, "Prostitutes swarm on the Papal beds." But artists and architects also swarmed to Avignon, attracted by the hefty fees the Popes were willing to pay to transform this town into a city worthy of the princes of the Church.

One look at Avignon today is all that's needed to convince you that they succeeded beyond their wildest dreams. One the most dramatic sights you will encounter in the South will be that of the hulking **Papal Palace** that dominates Avignon. It is one of the best preserved structures of the medieval period, with towers up to 50 m (160 ft) high, and there are four kilometers (two and a half miles) of crenelated walls surrounding the city.

TOP SPOTS

Spend a Day at the Beach

THE ONE THING EVERYONE KNOWS ABOUT MEDITERRANEAN FRANCE IS THAT IT HAS SOME OF THE MOST BEAUTIFUL BEACHES IN THE WORLD — AND SOME OF THE MOST BEAUTIFUL PEOPLE IN THE WORLD ON THEM. Where to find them? Where else but **Saint-Tropez**? — at the **Plage de Pampelonne**,

OPPOSITE BOTTOM: The women of Arles, here in traditional costume, are famed for their beauty. OPPOSITE TOP: The medieval Cathedral of Notre-Dame-des-Doms in Avignon. ABOVE LEFT: Frescos by Matteo Giavonetti at the Papal Palace in Avignon. BELOW: "Lizarding" in the sun at Saint-Tropez.

at the Table du Marché, then dance the night away with your new pals at the "Gayo" — the Papagayo — the hottest disco in town.

Land in an Eagle's Nest

IN LITERALLY HUNDREDS OF DIFFERENT PLACES THROUGHOUT THE REGION, AS YOU ROLL ALONG IN A CAR OR A TRAIN, YOUR EYE WILL CATCH THE OUTLINE OF SOMETHING AT THE TOP OF A STEEP HILL THAT YOU'D SWEAR WAS THE NEST OF A GIGANTIC BIRD. But as you move closer you make out a cluster of houses clinging precariously to the rim, and you see that there's a village up there. These *nids d'aigle* or "eagle's nest" villages are among the most striking features of Mediterranean France. You will find them in all the hilly parts of the region from the Maritime Alps down to the Pyrénées. There are some 400 "perched villages," as they are also known, in the Côte d'Azur and Provence alone.

the five kilometer (three mile) long beach west of town, you can see the most harmoniously shaped individuals you could ever imagine. The women sunbathe topless, of course. It's perfectly natural, no shame attached.

At lunchtime, head for my favorite beach restaurant, Club 55, near the memorial to the 1944 Allied landings. This ethereal eatery started as a canteen to feed Brigitte Bardot and the crew of *And God Created Woman*, and it continues to attract a chic clientele to its tables amid a grove of feathery tamarisk trees.

For a change of pace, take a ten-minute stroll up the beach to the Voile Rouge. There you'll find guys who pump iron gyrating with generously endowed young ladies to loud disco music. This is the most expensive beach club in the area, and proud of it.

After your day at the beach, sip an apéritif at the Café des Arts in Saint-Tropez, where you will recognize, even with their clothes on, many of the people you saw at the beach. Dine

One of the most dramatic — and one of the most convenient to get to — is **Peillon**, daintily balanced atop a 376 m (1,234 ft) spur of rock 19 km (12 miles) northeast of Nice. Like the others, it was built in the Middle Ages, when large bands of bloodthirsty marauders roamed the countryside, and Saracen pirates could appear at any moment. A bird's eye view was as much a matter of survival as a sturdy set of ramparts. Here, as in most medieval hilltop towns, the outer walls of the houses ring the village at the top of a sheer cliff and double as defensive ramparts. They look harsh and forbidding, but once inside the main gate, you will find yourself in a pretty cobblestone square with a fountain, and you will see that this is a delightful village to explore, little changed architecturally since the Middle Ages. The few streets of the town are narrow and very steep, and it's easier to walk up the many flights of steps that lead you through passages under flower-decked stone houses. Visit the Chapelle des Pénitents Blancs (Chapel of the White Penitents) and see the frescos of the fifteenth century School of Nice painter Giovanni Canavesio that depict the Passion of Christ.

If you lunch on the flowery terrace of the Auberge de la Madone, you can enjoy the view of Peillon's deep mountain valley while dining on outstanding Mediterranean cuisine. The inn also has 20 charming and comfortable rooms, all with a view, at rates ranging from 400 to 780 francs. They are much in demand. So if you think you might want to alight in this eagle's nest for a night, be sure to book ahead (93 97 91 17.

Other eagle's nest villages nearby are **Peille**, **Sainte-Agnès**, **Gorbio** and **Roquebrune**, any one of them eminently worth visiting.

Cross Trails with Camargue Cowboys

THE CAMARGUE IS A MAGICAL PLACE THAT KEEPS COMING BACK IN THE DAYDREAMS OF ANYONE WHO'S BEEN THERE — a peaceable kingdom filled with flocks of pink flamingos wading in sun-splashed lagoons, sturdy black bulls tended by Gypsy-like cowboys and acres of grasslands dotted with little white horses. You'll be swept off your feet by this wildlife paradise, where more than 400 species of birds make their home in the nature preserve of this 518 sq km (200 sq mile) delta of the Rhône River. And while you sometimes catch a glimpse of these fine-feathered creatures from your car, the ideal way to observe them is from on top of a horse. On the numerous trails that ring the 13,000 hectare (32,000 acre) wildlife preserve, you can quietly steal close for a view of the nesting areas, and with a little luck have the thrill of finding a nest full of chicks. The horses are docile and know where to go, making any kind of skill

TOP SPOTS

unnecessary. So a **horseback excursion into the Camargue** is an adventure nobody should be afraid of. But if you know how to ride, you can do what my equestrian wife likes to do — take a spirited horse out onto the open ranges of the cattle ranches, or *manades*, that breed bulls for the non-lethal Provençal style of bullfighting.

More than fifty stables in the Camargue rent horses. For information, contact the Office of Tourism in Les-Saintes-Maries-de-la-Mer or the Association des Loueurs des Chevaux (the horse renters' association), Mas des Lys, Route d'Arles (90 97 86 27. I recommend Domaine Paul Ricard, a 600 hectare (1,500 acre) ranch in Méjanes on the northern edge of the Étang de Vaccarès, the large lagoon that is the center of the preserve. Their horses rent for 200 francs for a half-day, 320 francs for a full day (90 97 10 60 or 62.

OPPOSITE: TOP Saint-Jean-de-Buèges, a tiny "perched village" near Saint-Guilhem-le-Désert in Languedoc. BOTTOM *Gardians*, cowboys of the Camargue. ABOVE: A non-lethal Provençal style of bullfighting is practiced in all the towns in and around the Camargue.

YOUR CHOICE

The Great Outdoors

From the high mountain valleys of the Alpes-Maritimes above Nice to the Pyrénées frontier with Spain, Mediterranean France has been blessed with some of the most dramatic scenery in the world, and the most intimate way you can experience it is to walk it. You won't find an easier place to plan your walking trip than in France, because the Comité National des Sentiers de Grande Randonnée (National Committee for Long Rambles), or CNS, has figured it all out for you. The CNS publishes a series of booklets called *Topo-Guides des Grandes Randonnées*, excellently organized guides to the long-distance hiking trails in France with detailed topographical maps and symbols for shelters, water-points, emergency telephones and cultural information on the area. The *Topo-Guides* are in French, but the symbols are explained in English and are easy to follow. You can buy them at bookshops and sporting goods stores throughout France or from the CNS, 64 Rue de Gergovie, 75014 Paris ((1) 45 45 31 02. The average price is about 75 francs. To order them overseas, contact the nearest Maison de la France of the French Government Tourist Office in your country (see TRAVELERS' TIPS, page 324). The book *Walks in Provence*, published by Robinson McCarta, 122 King's Cross Road, London, describes several *grandes randonnées* (*GR's* for short) in the region.

Each *GR* has a number. One of the most popular, *GR-9*, runs from the Alps to the Mediterranean. It comes south from Grenoble in the French Alps and enters Provence north of Mont-Ventoux, crosses the Lubéron National Park and Cézanne's beloved Montagne Sainte-Victoire, descends through the Massif de la Sainte-Baume, where Mary Magdelen is said to have prayed, and the chestnut-covered hills of the Massif des Maures north of Saint-Tropez, and it ends on the shores of the Mediterranean near the marina village of Port-Grimaud.

YOUR CHOICE

Another popular walk, the *GR-10*, starts at Banyuls-sur-Mer on Roussillon's dramatic Côte Vermielle (Vermilion Coast), climbs into vine-covered hills with a huge vista of the Mediterranean and runs westward through the Pyrénées, deep into the Catalan homeland of the Cerdagne, the sunniest region in France, and all the way through the mountains to the Atlantic. The *GR-51*, "the Balcony of the Côte d'Azur," follows the coastal highlands from Castellar by the Italian Border north of Menton to Bormes-les-Mimosas on the Côte des Maures.

If you want to find out where the *GR's* are in any area you're interested in, look at the Kümmerly + Frey/Blay Foldex 1:250,000 map, and you will see faint dotted lines labeled with the *GR* number that indicate the route (see TRAVELERS' TIPS, page 327).

In addition to the *grandes randonnées*, local tourist offices provide maps for *petites randonnées*, short local hikes, some quite spectacular, such as the *Sentier Nietzsche* in Èze, the footpath between the shore and the "perched village," 425 m (1,550 ft) up a steep hill above the Mediterranean. Other marvelous short hikes can be had in the red hills of the Esterel west of Cannes, the Saint-Tropez Peninsula, the Grand Canyon du Verdon, the mountains of La Sainte-Baume northeast of Marseille, the Calanques of Marseille, Montagne-Saint-Victoire near Aix, Mont-Ventoux and the Dentelles de Montmirail in Northern Provence, the Camargue, the Cévennes, the Montagne de la Clape near Narbonne, the Cathar fortresses in the southern Corbières, Collioure and the Côte Vermeille, and a number of places in the Pyrénées.

For dedicated outdoors types who like to rough it in vast tracts of wilderness with nobody else for miles around, Mediterranean France is not likely to be high on their list. To them, its coast would be unthinkably crowded and its national

OPPOSITE: The Grand Canyon of the Verdon River in the Alps of Upper Provence, the largest canyon in Europe.

23

parks too easily accessible to tenderfoots strolling through the woods. On the other hand, if you don't mind seeing a few other people around from time to time while you roam through magnificent scenery, Mediterranean France certainly fills the bill. Mercantour National Park in the Alpes-Maritimes north of Nice has 70,000 hectares (270 sq miles) of protected wildlife area where marmots, partridges, chamois, ibex, wild sheep and other species can be seen. The Vallée des Merveilles (Valley of Marvels) is an enchanting valley in the heart of the Mercantour Park famed for its crystal-clear lakes and the 100,000 designs carved into its rocks by Bronze Age shepherds. Travelers may hike in the park, but no cars, dogs, firearms, fire or camping is allowed (but there is plenty of camping in surrounding areas). For information about the park, contact Parc National du Mercantour, 23 Rue d'Italie, 06000 Nice (93 87 86 10, or the Comité Régional du Tourisme Riviera-Côte d'Azur, 55 Promenade des Anglais, 06000 Nice (93 44 50 59.

Another fine area for rambles is the Park Régional du Lubéron (Lubéron Regional Nature Park) in eastern Provence, a 120,000 hectare (460 sq mile) expanse that includes the heavily wooded Lubéron range, the hilltop ruins of Fort de Buoux dating back to Ligurian times, the abandoned ochre mines of the Colorado de Rustrel, vineyards, farmlands and orchards and 50 rural communities. For information, contact the Parc Naturel Régional du Lubéron, 1 Place Jean-Jaurès, 84000 Apt (90 74 08 55.

Sporting Spree

Mediterranean France is one of the most sports-oriented places in the world. Naturally, water sports leap first to mind, and for sailing, windsurfing, paragliding, water skiing, snorkeling and scuba diving, this is paradise on earth. All are extremely popular and can be found at almost any resort town along the coast.

Sail boats can be rented with or without crews at most ports in the summer, and sailing schools are plentiful. The Fédération Française de Voile (FFV), the national sailing federation, lists 67 approved schools in Mediterranean France. Some of the main ports for sailing are Antibes, Cannes, Saint-Raphaël, Sainte-Maxime, Saint-Tropez, Le Lavandou, Porquerolles, Toulon, Sanary-sur-Mer, Cassis, Marseille, Port-Camargue (the largest pleasure boat port in Europe, with 4,500 berths), La Grande-Motte, Sète, Cap d'Agde and Saint-Cyprien. For information about sailing, contact the local tourist office or the Fédération Française de Voile, 55 Avenue Kléber, 75016 Paris ((1) 44 05 81 00.

The best places for **windsurfing** are Six-Fours-les-Plages west of Toulon, Fos-sur-Mer west of Marseille and the lagoons along the coast of Languedoc and Roussillon.

Experienced **scuba divers** can find plenty of places along the coast to rent gear and beginners to take lessons. The Mecca of *la plongée* (scuba diving) is the Parc National de Port-Cros in the Îles d'Hyères. The entire island is a nature preserve, and it is surrounded by 1,800 hectares (4,320 acres) of protected underwater trails where divers can see a variety of flora and fauna. For information, contact the Parc National de Port-Cros, Castel Sainte-Claire, Rue Sainte-Claire, 83400 Hyères (94 65 32 98 FAX 94 65 84 83; they provide a list of 17 dive clubs in and

convenient to Port-Cros. Other especially active areas for scuba diving are Monaco, Cannes, Cassis, Marseille and on Roussillon's Côte Vermeille (Vermilion Coast), Collioure, Port-Vendres and Banyuls. The central source for information about scuba diving is FFESSM (Fédération Française d'Études et de Sports Sous-marins), 24 Quai de Rive-Neuve, 13007 Marseille (91 33 99 31.

The one active water sport you will not be able to practice, however, is surfing. The waves in the Mediterranean are too mild.

Deep sea fishing is available at many ports. At Sète, the biggest French fishing port in the Mediterranean, you can find charter or regularly scheduled boats to take you out day or night. No permit is necessary as long as your catch is for local consumption.

Fresh water fishing is popular at the large man-made Lac de Sainte-Croix (Lake of Saint

OPPOSITE: Canoeing is popular in the Gorges of the Hérault River in Languedoc. ABOVE: Tennis instruction on one of the forty-three courts of Club Pierre Barthés in Cap d'Agde.

Croix, in the Var and the Alpes-de-Haute-Provence and in mountain streams from the Alpes-Maritimes to the Cévennes to the Pyrénées.

For **white water rafting, canoeing** or **kayaking**, the Verdon River running through the Grand Canyon du Verdon is the most dramatic place for these sports. Here you will barrel along on the swift-moving green water of the Verdon through a string of gorges 21 km (13 miles) long the river has cut into the white limestone plateau of Haute-Provence, with depths ranging from 250 to 700 m (800 to 2,500 ft). Thrill seekers can also pursue these sports in the gorges of the Heérault River near Saint-Guilhem-le-Desert west of Montpellier.

Since **tennis** was invented in France, it's no surprise to find it played everywhere. The main centers are Monte-Carlo, Cannes and Cap d'Agde. The elegant Monte-Carlo Country Club has 23 courts and hosts a number of important tournaments, such as the Monte-Carlo Open in April. Cannes has a vast number of courts, clay and artificial, indoor and outdoor. The biggest tennis village in Europe is Club Pierre Barthés in Cap d'Agde, a highly professional operation with 35 outdoor courts (10 with lights), eight indoor courts, a hotel, furnished apartments and first-rate tennis instruction at all levels. For summer accommodations make your reservations in the early spring. For information, contact Club Pierre Barthés, BP 547, 34305 Cap d'Agde ℰ 67 26 00 26 FAX 67 2677 18. Despite the large number of courts in the region, you may have a difficult time in finding one free in the high season unless you book it in advance.

Though France still lags behind the English-speaking countries in numbers of **golf** courses, the sport has caught on in the past twenty years, and Mediterranean France is one of the best areas in France for it, with forty-four 18-hole courses. Many were built during the

1980's and feature challenging lay-outs by Pete Dye, Ronald Fream, Robert Trent Jones and other leading golf course architects. Golfers who like to tee off twelve months a year will find that the mild Mediterranean climate makes that dream a reality — except when the *mistral* and *tramontane* winds blow too fiercely in Provence and Languedoc, which can make it impossible to play. But the courses in the eastern Côte d'Azur are well-protected from winds. Cannes has the greatest concentration of them, with nine 18-hole links within a half-hour's drive, including the stately, parasol pine-shaded Golf de Cannes-Mandelieu, the Côte d'Azur's oldest, founded by Grand Duke Michael of Russia in 1891. The Lucien Barrière Group owns it, and package tours can be arranged through their Majestic Hotel in Cannes ℰ 92 98 77 00. Golf de Monte-Carlo, started in 1911, is situated on a 900 m (2,950 ft) high plateau overlooking the sea. Prince Rainier is one of the regulars. Package tours can be arranged by its owner, the SBM ℰ 92 16 20 00. In the Var, Golf de Barbaroux in Brignoles is famed for its challenging lay-out by Pete Dye. Another spectacularly lofty course is La Salette in the hills overlooking Marseille ℰ 91 27 12 16. At the Golf de La Grande-Motte on the edge of the Camargue, pink flamingos can be seen taking a dip in the water holes. This challenging lay-out was designed by Robert Trent Jones in 1987. Nîmes and Cap

d'Agde in Languedoc and Saint-Cyprien in Roussillon also have first-rate championship courses. Local tourist offices will help you make arrangements to play. Greens fees range from 150 to 350 francs depending on day of the week and time of the year, with weekends and summer being the most expensive.

The free booklet *Tourisme & Golf* is distributed by the Comité Régional de Tourisme (CRT) Provence-Alpes-Côte d'Azur and *Guide des Golfs* by the CRT Languedoc-Roussillon (see TRAVELERS' TIPS page 327). For a free list of all the golf courses in France, contact the Fédération Française de Golf, 69 Avenue Victor-Hugo, 75783 Paris ((1) 44 17 63 00 FAX (1) 44 17 63 63.

The best way to explore the Camargue is on horseback (see TOP SPOTS, page 21), and there are more than fifty stables to rent you a well-trained horse that knows the nature trails. **Horseback riding** is available in many other parts of Mediterranean France too. Other places where it is particularly popular are the Grand Canyon du Verdon, the "Lavender Alps" of Haute-Provence (so-called because of its vast expanses of lavender fields, blossoming fully in July), the Lubéron, the Cévennes and the Cathar Country of southern Languedoc, where you can explore the hilltop fortress that were the last refuges of the religious sect crushed in the thirteenth century by the Albigensian Crusade. Government tourist offices from the
YOUR CHOICE

local to the regional level provide literature on *randonnées equestres* (equestrian rambles) and addresses of stables (known as *centres equestres* or *centres hippiques*) that rent horses and outfit excursions. For a free booklet on associations involved in equestrian tourism, contact the Association Nationale de Tourisme Equestre, 170 Quai Stalingrad, 92130 Issy-les-Moulineaux ((1) 46 48 83 93.

In the land of the Tour de France, you can be sure the **bicycle** is a well-serviced means of getting around. French Railways (SNCF) has bikes for rent at the baggage counters of most railroad stations. The bikes can be dropped off at another station later. Rental is about 50 francs a day and a deposit or credit card number is required. There are also plenty of private bicycle rental outlets, details of which can be obtained from the local tourist office. Cycling along the crowded coast roads during the summer is not recommended. Back-country roads have much lighter traffic, and the drivers treat bikers with more consideration. The terrain tends to be very steep, though, as you get inland, and strong winds can come up suddenly. So don't do it unless you are in good shape. A helmet is highly recommended.

OPPOSITE BOTTOM: On the *corniches* of the Riviera above Monaco. ABOVE: The best way to view the wildlife of the Camargue, where more than fifty stables rent horses.

27

Again, the Alpes-de-Haute-Provence is popular for cycling. So are the lovely olive, truffle and wine-growing area of La Drôme Provençale around Nyons, the Dentelles de Montmirail, the Lubéron, the Alpilles, the Camargue, the foothills of the Cévennes above Montpellier, the Corbières, and the Conflent, the Cerdagne and the Vallespir in the Pyrénées. For information about cycling and suggested routes, contact Fédération Française de Cyclotourisme, 8 Rue Jean-Marie Jego, 75013 Paris ((1) 44 16 88 88. They have a free introductory booklet in English that has names of local groups that organize biking tours.

Rock climbing is popular in the Calanques of Marseille, the Dentelles de Montmirail and the Grand Canyon du Verdon.

Hang-gliding is popular in the Alpes-de-Haute-Provence and at Pic Saint-Loup near Saint Martin-de-Londres north of Montpellier. In the winter, there is good **skiing** in the Alpes-Maritimes at resorts such as Isola 2000, Valberg and Gréolières-les-Neiges. They are close enough to Nice that in the spring you can easily ski and swim in the Mediterranean on the same day. For information, contact the Comité du Tourisme Riviera–Côte d'Azur, 55 Promenade des Anglais, 06000 Nice (93 50 60 88. There are also numerous skiing stations (*stations de ski*) in the eastern Pyrénées, including Font-Romeu, Eyne 2600 and Bolquère-Pyrénées in the Cerdagne and Les Angles, Formiguères and Puyvalador in the Capcir. For information, contact the Comité Départemental du Tourisme des Pyrénées–Roussillon, 7 Quai de Lattre de Tassigny, BP 540, 66005 Perpignan (68 34 29 94.

For **spectator sports**, football (soccer, as Americans call it) is the most popular, and most cities have professional teams. In Marseille, going to Olympique de Marseille games is virtually a religious event, despite the fact that the club was stripped of its title as European champion in 1994 and demoted to the second division as a punishment for a bribery incident, one of the larger scandals of that year. Rugby is very popular in Languedoc, especially in Béziers, Narbonne and Carcassonne.

The quintessential participatory sport of the region is *pétanque*, the bowling game practiced under the plane trees in town squares in all parts of our region, from Menton on the frontier of Italy to the Côte Vermielle in Roussillon north of Spain. The sport is outwardly quite simple, but requires a great deal of finesse. A little cork ball called a *cochonnet* is tossed onto the playing surface, and the object is to get one of your team's metal balls the closest to it. The game is a social ritual normally indulged in only by men of the region, but women are not excluded if they want to play. *Pétanque* can be a spectator sport also. A big tournament sponsored by the newspaper *Le Provençal* is held in the Parc Borély in Marseille at the end of July.

The Open Road

For an area of its modest size — 525 km (325 miles) along the coast, extending inland 162 km (100 miles) or less in most parts — Mediterranean France offers an astounding diversity of terrains and culturally distinctive places to explore, and the best way to make their acquaintance is by car. The most important thing to remember in the summer is that you have to get off the coast to find anything resembling open roads, and the farther, the better, for unencumbered driving conditions. So put the big *autoroutes* (super highways) behind you, break out your Kümmerly+Frey/Blay Foldex map 1:250 000 for the Provence-Côte d'Azur (Sheet 14) and the Languedoc-Roussillon (Sheet 10), and plunge into the heartlands.

The following itineraries will give you a taste of some of the drives you can make in Mediterranean France:

CÔTE D'AZUR

In the hills directly to the west of Nice is a cluster of small towns and villages made famous by Picasso, Matisse, Renoir, Bonnard, Chagall and others who lived and worked here. The drive starts two kilometers (one and a quarter miles) west of the Nice airport on the coast road. Take a right onto Route D 36 just before reaching the Hippodrome (the race track), and head up to **Cagnes-sur-Mer**. It has a beautifully preserved medieval walled town, Haut-de-Cagnes. Painter Pierre Auguste Renoir spent the last years of his life on his farm east of town, and you can visit his home lovingly maintained as the Renoir Museum. Continue north on D 36 through fields of flowers and orange groves seven kilometers (four miles) to **Saint-Paul-de-Vence**, famed for the many artists and film stars who've stayed here, Bonnard, Picasso, Yves Montand and Simone Signoret among them. The town's star attractions are its sixteenth century ramparts and art museum, the Fondation Maeght, which houses one of the great personal collections of twentieth century painting and sculpture. Vence, a larger medieval walled town four kilometers (two and a half miles) north of Saint-Paul-de-Vence, is where Matisse lived and worked, and it is famed for his Chapelle de la Rosaire. On the edge of a cliff five kilometers (three miles) west of Vence is the village of **Tourrettes-sur-Loup**, once a near-ghost town, brought back to life by weavers, jewelry designers and metal sculptors and potters, many of whose workshops are open to the public. A highly scenic side trip you

can take from here is the 35 km (22 mile) swing along the dramatic **gorges of the Loup River**, with the ancient Saracen stronghold of Gourdon perched 500 m (1,640 ft) above the stream. Resume your circuit of the art villages of the Côte d'Azur by driving down to **Biot**, a hill town a few kilometers in from the coast between Nice and Antibes. There you will find the Musée Fernand Léger (Fernand Léger Museum), filled with his bold paintings, ceramics and tapestries, and the Verrerie de Biot, an outstanding glass-blowing workshop, where artful glassware is created before your eyes, and buy it in the gift shop. In **Vallauris** 12 km (seven and a half miles) south of Biot you can view the huge War and Peace frescoes Picasso painted in an abandoned chapel in 1952, now the Musée National La Guerre et la Paix. This is also the largest ceramics manufacturing center in Southern France, and there are pottery museums and workshops to be visited, with works to suit all tastes, including copies authorized by Picasso of works he created in Vallauris. The entire circuit including the side
YOUR CHOICE

trip through the gorges of the Loup River and back to Nice is about 105 km (65 miles).

From nearby **Cannes** or **Grasse** you can get on the moody **Route Napoléon**, N 85, and head north to the **Grand Canyon du Verdon** (Grand Canyon of the Verdon River). This is the route the fallen Emperor took after escaping exile in Elba in 1815, and is a strange, barren piece of terrain. Once a rough shepherds' trail, today it is a well-paved secondary highway marked by plaques decorated with the Emperor's eagle. At **Castellane**, 80 km (50 miles) north of Cannes, head west to the Grand Canyon, the largest gorge in Europe, 21 km (13 miles) in length, with widths up to 1,500 m (5,000 ft) and depths to 700 m (2,500 ft). The two roads along either side of the Canyon are equally dramatic, with perspectives that take your breath away. But if you only have time to drive one of them, I recommend D 23, the Corniche Sublime, on the

ABOVE: Tourrettes-sur-Loup is one of the finest crafts villages in the hills west of Nice, noted particularly for its weavers, metal workers and jewelry makers.

southern rim because the best hotels and restaurants are on that side. Hiking, rafting and horseback riding are very popular in the Canyon (see SPORTING SPREE, page 25).

For a break from the pace of life on the beaches and in the cafés and discos of Saint-Tropez (see TOP SPOTS page 19), take a drive straight north to the **Massif des Maures**, a range of low mountains densely forested with chestnut, pine and cork oak trees. The foothills are covered by vineyards, and practically every village has its own wine cooperative, where you can sample tasty Côtes de Provence rosés. **La Garde-Freinet**, 20 km (12.5 miles) to the north of Saint-Tropez on D 558, was once a stronghold of Saracen pirates and has retained its medieval atmosphere. If you hike past thousand year-old chestnut trees to the hilltop ruins of the Saracen fortress, you can see what a perfect place it was to watch for merchant ships along the coast. To the west of La Garde-Freinet follow the signs through a winding forest road to **Collobrières**, the chestnut capital, and stop at the Confiserie Azuréenne for *marrons glacés*, mouth-watering candied chestnuts. Nearby you'll find the impressive Chartreuse (Charterhouse) de la Verne. It was founded in the twelfth century, and some vestiges remain, but most buildings date from the seventeenth and eighteenth centuries. They are under restoration by the Bethlehem monastic community. The views of the mountains are magnificent.

PROVENCE

One of my favorite drives is in the **Lubéron**, a 50 km (30 mile) long valley covered with vineyards and fruit orchards and parallel ridge of wooded hills that lies straight north of Aix-en-Provence and straight east of Avignon. It offers everything one could hope for in a drive, a delightful mixture of the beauties of nature and beauties that mankind has contributed to the region. Start your circuit in the picture-perfect hilltop town of **Gordes**, 35 km (22 miles) east of Avignon via N 100, the central road of the Lubéron. In the largely Renaissance Château of Gordes, you can see the works of op-art master Viktor Vasarély, and in the countryside around town, hundreds of strange igloo-shaped huts made of flat stones known as *bories*. A few kilometers outside of Gordes, the exquisite and perfectly preserved twelfth century Cistercian Abbey of Sénanque sits deep in a lavender-filled valley. Concerts are held here in the summer. Drive east from Gordes 10 km (six miles) to the

village of **Roussillon** and discover a town of a different color. The whole town sits on a plateau of ochre which used to be mined in the area, and the buildings are several dozen different shades of oranges and reds. Twenty kilometers (12.5 miles) farther east is the **Colorado of Rustrel**, a huge abandoned open-pit ochre mine covering 15 sq km (10 sq miles), where the action of the weather has sculpted a wonderland of strange, multi-hued shapes. To the south is the Lubéron's central town of **Apt**, where the Saturday market is one of the liveliest and best provisioned in Provence. South of Apt, explore the long, low mountain range of the Lubéron that runs the length of the valley, with a densely forested Parc Naturel Régional du Lubéron (Lubéron Regional Nature Park) on its eastern end. To the west you will find vineyards and lavender farms and the hilltop towns of **Bonnieux**, **Lacoste** and **Oppede-le-Vieux**, which make for pleasant strolling. In the English-speaking world, this has been known as "Peter Mayle country" since 1989, when *A Year in Provence*, his lighthearted satire of this massively gentrified area, became a best-seller.

In **Northern Provence**, where it is the only mountain on the horizon, **Mont-Ventoux** is known as "the Giant of Provence." At 1,912 m (6,265 ft), it has the most stupendous view in all of Provence and is the focus of fascinating drives. To get to Mont-Ventoux, take D 938 southeast from lively **Vaison-la-Romaine** to **Malaucene**, then D 974 along the north slope of Ventoux. The drive to the top takes you from typically Mediterranean vegetation at the bottom through pine forests to bare pebbles above the tree line as you approach the observation point at the **Col des Tempêtes** 21 km (13 miles) from Vaison. The view from the top is enormous — the Cévennes, Montagne-Sainte-Victoire, Marseille and the Mediterranean. On a very clear day right after a *mistral* wind you can see all the way down to Mount Canigou in the Pyrénées. From Mont-Ventoux you can either follow D 974 around the mountain or branch off to the east on D 164 and drive 20 km (12.5 miles) to the lavender-growing capital of **Sault**, sensational in July when the fields are all in bloom. From Sault, the 40 km (25 mile) drive through the Gorge of the Nesque River to **Carpentras** is extremely dramatic.

Another exciting drive you can take from Vaison-la-Romaine is along the **Dentelles de Montmirail**, a chain of limestone hills 16 km (10 miles) long that runs north-south from just below Vaison-la-Romaine on its northern end to Beaumes-de-Venise on the south. The hills are topped by a jagged filigree of white rock that looks something like lace, *dentelles* in French, from a distance. Few of the peaks are higher

than 400 m (1,300 ft), but they look taller because of their cragginess. They are a favorite place of rock climbers. Flat and gently rolling vineyards lie to the west, lovely with the Dentelles as a backdrop. This is the heart of some of the finest wine country in the South. The vigorous reds of Gigondas and Vacqueyras and the delicious sweet aperitif wine Muscat de Beaumes-de-Venise have gained international renown. **Séguret**, 10 km (six miles) south of Vaision-la-Romaine, is a charming town of 714 inhabitants that clings to the western face of the Dentelles. It looks like Bethlehem in a Christmas crib, and in December, that is just what it becomes, when the townspeople dress in Biblical costumes and put on one of the liveliest Christmas pageants in Provence.

LANGUEDOC

In Languedoc, the roads are less traveled than in Provence and the Côte d'Azur, but the same principle holds here: the farther from the coast, the more open the roads. Using **Montpellier** as a base, short drives to the north or the west of the city take you into the foothills of the Cévennes, where there are vineyards practically everywhere, fragrances of wild herbs and flowers, and long stretches of road lined by poplars. **Saint-Martin-de-Londres**, 27 km (19 miles) north of Montpellier on D 986, has a lovely medieval town square and an eleventh century church built by the monks of Saint-Guilhem, and there are interesting drives to nearby **Pic Saint-Loup**, a sharp-peaked

mountain that is a favorite of hang-gliders, and the **Grotte des Demoiselles**, a cave with vast galleries and huge sculpture-like stalagmites and stalactites, 19 km (12 miles) to the north. A few kilometers farther north at Ganges, take D 25 west along the gorges of the Vis to **Saint Maurice-Navacelles** and D 130 north to the **Cirque de Navacelles**, a gigantic crater with an island in the middle that was created by a former course of the Vis River. Straight south of the Cirque de Navacelles via D 25 and D 9, a drive of about 45 km (28 miles), is **Saint Guilhem-le-Désert**, a picturesque medieval village at the entrance the dramatic gorges of the Hérault River, built around its Romanesque abbey. A festival of religious music is held in the village throughout the summer. You can rent kayaks to ride down the rushing Hérault River, and there are exceptionally fine makers of Côteaux de Languedoc wines and *vins de pays* in this area.

The **Corbières** is a sun-blasted range of rugged limestone hills in southern Languedoc famed for its potent red wines, savage beauty and cliff-top fortresses that are almost unbelievably dramatic. These "citadels of vertigo," as they have been dubbed, became the last refuges of the Cathars during the Albigensian Crusade in the thirteenth century. A fascinating driving tour of starts at Carcassonne (see TOP SPOTS, page 15) and takes in the five principal Cathar fortresses of this region, known by the Albigensian Crusaders as "The Five Sons of Carcassonne." **Puilaurens**, the closest, is 68 km (42 miles) south of Carcassonne via D 118 and D 117. This

fortress atop a sheer-cliffed peak 697 m (2,300 ft) high is in excellent condition, with its *donjon* (dungeon), four towers and crenelated walls intact, and there are superb views of Mont-Canigou.

The largest and most dramatic of the "Five Sons" is **Peyrepertuse**. Its outer walls measure two and a half kilometers (over one and a half miles) around, and it is topped by massive Château Saint-Geórges, built by French kings in the late thirteenth century, after the fall of the Cathars. It has a breathtaking panorama of the Corbières, the nearby Château of Quéribus and the Mediterranean. Peyrepertuse towers over the little village of **Duilhac**, 42 km (26 miles) east of Puilaurens via D 117, D 7 and D 14. The smaller but quite impressive fortress of **Quéribus** eight kilometers (five miles) east of Peyrepertuse was the last island of Cathar resistance. It fell to the French in 1255. **Aguilar**, the fourth of the five Cathar fortresses, is in **Tuchan**, 16 km (10 miles) east of Quéribus. The fifth fortress is **Termes**, in the heart of the Corbières. It is the least well-preserved of the Cathar strongholds, but its site overlooking the gorges of the Terminet is very dramatic. Termes is 13 km (eight miles) west of **Villerouge-Termenès** via D 613 and D 40. From Aguilar, it is about 40 km (25 miles), with dramatic roads through the hills of the Corbières all the way.

ROUSSILLON

Roussillon, the relatively un-touristic southernmost part of Mediterranean France, offers the best

chance to get off the beaten track and to explore a splendidly scenic part of France that has managed to hold onto its unique Catalan cultural identity. You will see road signs in Catalan as well as French, see Catalan flags everywhere, and hear the Catalan language being spoken. There are several fine driving itineraries, but to choose one that takes you into the Pyrénées as an example, start from Roussillon's capital of **Perpignan** and head southwest on D 612 toward lofty Mont-Canigou, snow-covered most of the year, to the Aspres, lightly populated foothills of the Pyrénées where the main points of interest are **Castelnou** and the **Prieuré de Serrabone** (Priory of Serrabone). Castelnou is a handsomely-restored medieval walled village of 152 residents, its golden stone houses clustered around an eleventh century fortress on the hill. The village is known for its pottery, ironwork and other handicrafts, and for traditional Catalan food. To get to Castelnou, take D 612 from Perpignan 14 km (nine miles) to Thuir and continue six kilometers (just under four miles) farther southwest on D 48.

The Prieuré de Serrabone is the oldest Augustinian priory in Europe, started in 1082. It is very austere on the outside, but inside contains a dazzling ensemble of sculpted rose marble columns representing fantastic beasts from the *Book of the Apocalypse*, a masterpiece of

The Monastery of Saint Guilhem-le-Désert OPPOSITE TOP was founded by a former companion in arms of Charlemagne. ABOVE: The Gorges of the Hérault River.

Romanesque art. The priory also has a botanical garden with more than a thousand types of Mediterranean plants. It is open daily except public holidays from 10 AM to 6 PM (68 84 09 30. To get there from Castelnou, drive west on the very scenic D 48, heading toward **Canigou**, and two smaller roads jog around to D 618, the road Serrabone is on.

From Serrabone, take D 618 to N 116 and follow it west along the to Têt River Valley to the Conflent, so-named because of the several streams flowing into the River from nearby hills and mountains. Here we are in a peaceful valley of peach orchards and market gardens at the foot of majestic Mont-Canigou, 2,784 (9,140 ft) high, the symbol of the Catalan people. The main town is **Prades**, noted for the Pablo Casals Music Festival held from late July to mid-August, and for its tenth century Abbey of Saint-Michel-de-Cuxa. Six kilometers (nearly four miles) south of Prades on N 116 in a narrow valley where the Têt and Cady rivers flow together is the remarkable town of **Villefranche-de-Conflent**, entirely enclosed within the walls of a seventeenth century fortress designed by Louis XIV's great military architect Sébastien Vauban. Yet despite its stern look from the outside, this little town of less than 300 year-round residents is one of the friendliest places you will ever find, thanks in large part to the bright, young team that runs its tourist and cultural programs, along with the crafts studios and cafés that are in full swing in the summer. Villefranche-de-Conflent is also where you connect with the *Petit Train Jaune* (The Little Yellow Train) to the high mountain plateau of the Cerdagne, the homeland of the Catalan people deep in the Pyrénées. And eight kilometers (five miles) south of Villefranche-de-Conflent via D 116 is the most dramatically situated of all Roussillon's Romanesque abbeys, **Saint-Martin-de-Canigou**, perched on a rocky spur on the very slope of Mont-Canigou. Hikers can reach it by a steep, rugged trail, about half an hour's climb each way. It is not accessible by car, but Garage Villaceque in Vernet-les-Bains provides jeep rides to the abbey for 150 francs per person (68 05 51 14.

Backpacking

The Côte d'Azur is one of the most famously expensive places in the world, particularly during the peak summer season, and for that reason, some cost-conscious travelers may think they should avoid Mediterranean France altogether. If so, they are mistaken. There are plenty of ways to keep costs down, even on the Côte d'Azur, and as you move onto the *arrière pays*, the back country, prices go down. They

also drop noticeably as you travel from the east to the west along the Mediterranean crescent.

In general, food and lodging cost about a third less in Languedoc and Roussillon than they would in restaurants and hotels of comparable quality on the Côte d'Azur. And as an additional benefit, the little hotels, youth hostels or camping grounds you choose to stay in to save money may be more relaxed and informal than expensive hotels, making it easier for you to meet hospitable French people and fellow travelers.

Camping is tremendously popular in Mediterranean France. Practically every town in this book has at least one camping ground. Most operate their own *camping municipal*, which can range from a modest site with basic sanitary facilities to deluxe spreads with swimming pools, tennis courts, restaurants, bars, supermarkets, laundromats and plenty of shade trees. In addition to the municipal camp sites, there are at least a thousand privately owned camping grounds in the region. Like hotels, camp sites are rated by stars by the Ministry of Tourism, from one to four, depending on location, facilities and attractiveness of the site. The ones near the shore are generally the most expensive, and they tend to be *complet* (full) in the summer, so you should reserve as long as possible in advance. Four-star camp sites run about the same price as a cheap hotel. On the Côte d'Azur, the most expensive place, a first-class site for a car and a caravan will cost about 165 francs, for a car and a two-person tent about 100 francs, and for a tent alone about 90 francs. Some especially popular areas for

on 54 camp sites in the Alpes-Maritimes, with color photos, text in French and English, but no prices specified. Or you can pick it up at the Tourist Office in Nice. Michelin also publishes *Camping Caravaning France*, a selective guide to 3,500 camping sites nationwide (62 francs).

Inexpensive accommodations are to be had at *auberges de jeunesse* (youth hostels), which offer single-sex dormitory accommodations to people of any age for 40 to 47 francs for a bed alone, and 66 francs in the most luxurious ones, with breakfast included. Many have kitchen facilities or serve inexpensive meals. Some take reservations, but most don't. They give out rooms between 8 AM and 10 AM, and to get one, you have to go early, particularly in the summer. Other drawbacks are that they have curfews in the evening and are often located far from the center of town. For information, contact the national youth hostel association in your home country or the Fédération Unie des Auberges de Jeunesse (FUAJ), 27 rue Pajol, 75018 Paris ((1) 44 89 87 27 FAX (1) 44 89 87 10, which has nineteen youth hostels in Mediterranean France, or the Ligue Française des Auberges de la Jeunesse (LFAJ), 38 Boulevard Raspail, 75007 Paris ((1) 45 48 69 84 FAX 45 44 57 47, which has seven. You must become a member of one of the youth hostel organizations, which you can do in your home country or at any youth hostel. The fee is 70 francs if you are under 26, 100 francs if you are 26 or over. The membership card entitles you to discounts on museum visits, excursions and shopping in some places. For people who are traveling alone, a youth hostel is the least expensive place to stay. But if there are a few of you, sharing an inexpensive hotel room can be as cheap or cheaper.

Though Bed and Breakfasts are not nearly as common in France as in the British Isles, La Fédération Nationale des Gîtes de France has a program called *Chambres & Tables d'Hôtes* (guest rooms), which are rooms and apartments you can rent by the night in peoples homes. They are located mainly in rural villages and on working farms and vineyards. This is a very pleasant and comfortable way to enter into the life of a family and a community. Prices are generally in the 200 to 300 franc range for two people with a copious breakfast included. About a third of the guest houses will also serve you a modestly priced meal upon request. French and English language versions of a booklet entitled *Chambres & Tables d'Hôtes*, broken down by different regions, can

camping are **Cagnes-sur-Mer** and **Villeneuve-Loubet-Plage** west of Nice, **Saint-Aygulf** west of Fréjus, the **Camargue** and the **whole coast of Languedoc and Roussillon**, with vast numbers of camping grounds along the beaches in and around **Cap d'Agde** and along the coast near **Béziers**, **Narbonne** and **Perpignan** (where **Argelès-sur-Mer** has 56 camping grounds with several thousand of emplacements). In the backcountry, the **Alpes-de-Haute-Provence** and the area of the **Grand Canyon du Verdon** have important concentrations of camp sites, and they are also sprinkled liberally throughout the **foothills of the Cévennes and the Pyrénées**. Campers who want to rough it in the open countryside are strongly urged to get permission from the landowners so as to avoid possible bad feelings or worse. Information on camping grounds can be obtained from government tourist offices on all levels. For the addresses of regional and departmental tourist offices (which cover an area roughly equivalent to an English or American county), see TRAVELERS' TIPS, page 324. The central source is the Fédération Française de Camping et Caravaning, 78 rue de Rivoli 75004 Paris ((1) 42 72 84 08. Their annual *Guide Officiel Camping/Caravaning* lists all camp sites in France with their government ratings, facilities and prices. It is sold in most bookshops in France and at Maisons de France overseas (72 francs). *Camping Caravaning Riviera Côte d'Azur*, available from the Comité du Tourisme Riviera-Côte d'Azur (see TRAVELERS' TIPS, page 324 for their address), is a free map-brochure with information

YOUR CHOICE

Informal styles of life prevail at Les Saintes-Maries-de-la-Mer in the Camargue OPPOSITE TOP and along the Languedoc coast's one hundred miles of fine sand beaches ABOVE, which have plenty of camping grounds on them.

be bought or ordered from the Maison des Gîtes de France, 35 rue Godot-de-Mauroy, 75009 Paris ((1) 47 42 25 43. It costs 95 francs. French language booklets entitled *Vacances en Gîtes de France*, which have an explanation of the symbols in English, can also be purchased there or at any large French bookstore, at prices that vary according to the length of the booklet.

If you are a family or group, you may want to rent a *gîte*, a fully furnished and equipped country cottage or house in a village, which the Maison des Gîtes de France can also help you locate, and you can save money by doing your own cooking. *Gîtes* can be rented for a week-end, a week or several weeks at a time. *Gîte* owners are generally local people who try to make you feel right at home in their community. Prices vary greatly depending on the size of the *gîte*, its location and the season. There is an extra charge for linens.

It goes without saying that the *gîtes* closest to the Mediterranean tend to be the most expensive. Regional booklets for *gîtes* in Provence-Alpes-Côte d'Azur and Languedoc-Roussillon are available, in French only. Renting a *gîte* takes planning and must be done early. To do so, buy one of the guides, which have photos and written descriptions, and after you have chosen a *gîte*, you contact the owner directly. Tourist offices will also have their own lists of rental properties in the area.

For reasonably-priced hotels, you would be wise to lay out 70 francs for the annual guide of the Logis de France group, a federation of

family-run hotel-restaurants of which there are dozens throughout Mediterranean France. They range in price from inexpensive to moderate, normally between 200 and 350 francs for a double room depending on their location, classification and facilities. You can buy the guide in most book or newspaper shops in France or you can order it from the Fédération Nationale des Logis de France, 83 Avenue d'Italie, 75013 Paris ((1) 45 84 70 00 FAX (1) 45 83 59 66. For more information about hotels, see ACCOMMODATION, page 328.

Getting around Mediterranean France by public transportation is not very expensive to start with, and substantial discounts are available. People under 26 and over 60 are eligible for discounts of up to 50 percent on main line trains, and a program called "*Joker*" that is open to everyone gives people who make a reservation 30 to 60 days in advance a 60 percent discount, and eight to 30 days in advance a 40 percent discount. Train service along the coast is excellent. You could easily and inexpensively hop from town to town there and rent bikes at the train station to get around locally (see SPORTING SPREE, page 25). Getting inland on public transportation is another story. There are buses, and they are not too expensive, but their service is very irregular. Most local people here drive their own cars. If you're tempted to hitch hike on the big highways, don't. Instead you should choose secondary and smaller roads. Presentable young people usually don't have too much trouble getting a ride, though my teen-age son tells me he's had the best luck hitching in the South of France when accompanied by a girl.

Living It Up

THE EXCEPTIONAL HOTELS
Cannes, Nice, Cap d'Antibes, Cap-Ferrat, Monte-Carlo — their very names set your head spinning with visions of the high life — Cary Grant and Grace Kelly wheeling along the Riviera, Onassis-sized yachts draped with Beautiful People, a *croupier* pushing a tottering stack of chips across the table, hopefully in your direction. The Côte d'Azur is where luxury tourism was invented in the extravagant *belle époque* of the late nineteenth century, and for people who demand palatial hotels, gourmet restaurants and elegant boutiques and the have the deep pockets to afford them, this area remains one of the most satisfying places on earth. But even if you don't happen to be a millionaire, you may want to have a splurge. While there are plenty of places to do it elsewhere in Mediterranean France, on the Côte d'Azur, there is truly an embarrassment of choices.

Take hotels: we could easily name two dozen between Monaco and Saint-Tropez whose splendid location, architecture, gorgeous decor and lavish and impeccable service put them not only in the luxury category, but breathtakingly so.

Among them are the Hôtel de Paris and its sister-hotel the Hermitage in Monaco, the Château de la Chèvre d'Or in Èze, the Voile d'Or and the Bel-Air Cap-Ferrat in Cap-Ferrat, the Negresco in Nice, the Hôtel du Cap in Cap d'Antibes, the Carlton and the Martinez in Cannes, the Villa de Belieu in Gassin, the Byblos and Bastide de Saint-Tropez in Saint-Tropez, to name just a dozen. Here we are talking about hotels that run 1,500 francs a night and up.

Away from the Côte d'Azur, there are few such supremely deluxe hotels. In Avignon, the Hôtel de l'Europe and the Mirenda fill the bill, as does Aix's elegant Villa Gallici, and Marseille has its marvelous Petit Nice. In Languedoc and Roussillon, there are few hotels in the deluxe category (four stars in the official government ratings), and only one of them, the Hôtel de la Cité in Carcassonne, could hold its own with the best of the ones on the Côte d'Azur. However, sophisticated inns of grand rustic elegance abound in the countryside in Provence as well as the Côte d'Azur. The famous Oustaù de Baumanière in Les Baux is the prototype of the luxury rural inn, and its fellow members in the prestigious Relais & Châteaux group are well represented in Mediterranean France. There are 25 of them in Provence and the Côte
YOUR CHOICE

d'Azur and two in Languedoc-Roussillon (which illustrates the disproportionately large number of luxury establishments to the east of the Rhône compared to the west). A heavy concentration of upscale country inns is found amid the hills of the Alpilles, a popular resort area northeast of Arles, where the Oustaù de Baumanière is located. Other rural hostelries of great comfort and rustic elegance are the Château de Trigance, an eleventh century castle near the Grand Canyon du Verdon, and the Mas du Langoustier, a rambling pink ochre hotel on its own private cove in a remote corner of the island of Porquerolles in the Îles d'Hyères, one of the most serenely restful spots you are ever likely to find.

EXCEPTIONAL RESTAURANTS

Gourmets will have no trouble finding culinary pleasure in Mediterranean France, and as with hotels and *le luxe* in general, the Côte d'Azur leads the way. Mediterranean France's current temple of *gourmandise* is Alain Ducasse's Louis XV Restaurant at the Hôtel de Paris in Monte-Carlo. But Maître Ducasse is far from the only extraordinarily fine chef in the region. Just to mention some of the others who have gained international fame, there are Roger Vergé in

Belle époque flair on the Côte d'Azur: OPPOSITE at the Grand Casino of Monte-Carlo, ABOVE, LEFT at La Rotonde at Nice's Hôtel Negresco and RIGHT at Monaco's Hôtel Hermitage , with a winter garden by Gustave Eiffel.

37

Mougins, Dominique Le Stanc in Nice, Jacques Chibois in Cannes and Grasse, Christian Willer and Francis Chauvenau in Cannes, Francis Cardaillac in Saint-Tropez, Guy Gedda in Bormes-les-Mimosas, Jean-Paul and Gérald Passédat in Nice, Jean-André Charial in Les Baux, Christian Étienne in Avignon, Pierre and Jany Gleize in Château-Arnoux, Jean-Pierre Cazals in Port-Camargue, Jacques and Laurent Pourcel in Montpellier, and Michel del Burgo in Carcassonne. This is a far-from-exhaustive list. A dozen or more first-rate chefs could easily be added. The point is that, if you can afford it, cuisine of the highest quality is within your reach in practically all parts of Mediterranean France, but especially to the east of the Rhône. For information on Mediterranean cuisine, see GALLOPING GOURMETS page 50.

NIGHTLIFE

Nightlife is generally linked to the casino, and often the casino *is* the night life. Menton is an example, where the Club 06 at the Casino de Menton puts on the only floor show in town.

The big, famous casinos are in Monte-Carlo, which has three operating in the winter and four in the summer, Nice with one, Juan-les-Pins with one and Cannes with three, including the Casino Croisette, the most active of all, with up to 10,000 visitors a day in the height of the season in summer. Casinos can be found practically everywhere along the coast. They may not all have roulette, baccarat and chemin de fer, but wherever you go, you'll never be far from the klink and whirr of *machines à sous*, as slot machines are called, or electronic draw poker, which is the rage now. Little Port-Barcarès in Roussillon, in its desperation to have a casino, ran an old cruise ship up onto its beach and converted it into one. Casinos are not confined to the racy cities along the coast. Even dignified cities inland have them, such as Digne-les-Bains and Aix-en-Provence.

On the Côte d'Azur, for nightclubs, discos and musical bars, the leading towns are Monaco, Nice, Cannes and Saint-Tropez, and Antibes's beach and entertainment quarter of Juan-les-Pins deserves special mention for its seven discos and innumerable music bars and cafes that are jumping until three or four o'clock in the morning.

Marseille also has a very active night life, with a number of musical bars and discos on the east side of the Vieux Port.

In the big university towns of Aix-en-Provence and Montpellier, each with about 50,000 students, and there are good discos and music clubs in both cities that are geared to the young scholars' tastes.

Family Fun

In some places, taking a trip with children in tow can be an ordeal, but in Mediterranean France, there is no end of activities to keep the little nippers amused. The numerous beaches along the 525 km (325 miles) of coastline are the most obvious kid-pleasers, and the facilities for water sports and most other sports are staggering (see SPORTING SPREE, page 25). But there are lots more activities than sports and sand castles that are exciting for children, and luckily most of them are fun for parents as well.

FUN ON THE WATER

In a number of places, there are short **ferry-boat rides to islands**, such as the Îles de Lérins off

ABOVE: The Hôtel Majestic, one of Cannes's "palaces."
LEFT: A folklore festival in Fontvieille near Arles.
RIGHT: A Catalan barbecue in Céret, a town in the cherry tree-covered Vallespir foothills of the Pyrénées.

Cannes, the Îles d'Hyères and the Château d'If, the island fortress where Alexandre Dumas's fictional Count of Monte-Cristo was kept prisoner. It is a short trip from the Vieux Port (Old Port) of Marseille. For kids, the boat ride is a thrill, the idea of being on an island is exciting, and you can make a complete experience of it with a picnic and a swim. From Marseille or Cassis, you can also take a **boat ride to the Calanques de Marseille**, a string of dramatic fjords cut into white limestone cliffs along the coast between Cassis and Marseille. In the Camargue, you can take **barge tours of wildlife areas** every day in the summer from Les Saintes-Maries-de-la-Mer and Aigues-Mortes, and in Languedoc there are **barge cruises** on the restful, tree-shaded Canal du Midi and connecting bodies of water. They can be taken from Sète, Agde, Béziers and Narbonne. You could also **rent a house boat** and pilot it yourself.

SCENIC TRAIN RIDES
Short train trips can be taken from Nice to the Alpes-de-Haute-Provence on the colorful *Train des Pignes* (Pine Cone Train), from Narbonne to Bize-Minervois on the *Autorail Touristique du Minervois* with stops at a Gallo-Roman potter museum and an olive-oil cooperative on the way, and in the Pyrénées the *Petit Train Jaune* takes you from Villefranche-de-Conflent through the magnificent mountain scenery of the Cerdagne. It has open cars in the summer.

FUN IN THE WILD
A must for any family is the **Camargue**, the wide delta of the Rhône River. Its wetlands are home to huge flocks of pink flamingos and 400 other species of birds and its ranges are trod by little white horses and black bulls that are bred for non-lethal Provençal style bullfighting, herded by cowboys (see TOP SPOTS, page 21). You can rent horses to explore the nature trails or rent bicycles to ride along the sea dike that runs for 20 km (12.5 miles) between the large central pond of the wildlife reserve, the Étang de Vaccarès, and the Mediterranean. There are also 60 km (40 miles) of fine sand beaches in the Camargue.

Another place were you are sure to see plenty of wildlife is the **African Reserve of Sigean** south of Narbonne. It has 2,400 African animals of 157 species including lions, elephants, hippos and giraffes, living on a simulated African plain on the Languedoc coast.

SEE LIFE UNDERWATER
To see undersea creatures, be sure to visit the aquarium of the Oceanographic Museum in Monaco, one of the world's finest. It has 90 tanks with 450 different species of fish, a truly hypnotic experience. The Arago Laboratory in Banyuls-sur-Mer on the Côte Vermielle (Vermilion Coast) in Roussillon also has a first-rate aquarium. It has 39 tanks containing 250 species of creatures from the waters off the Languedoc coast. Marineland in La Brague on the coast road just east of Antibes puts on the biggest **marine aquatic animal show** in Europe, and next door is a large fairground with water slides, miniature golf and other kid-pleasing pastimes.

OUTDOOR PURSUITS IN THE GRAND CANYON DU VERDON
For natural wonders, a drive along the Grand Canyon du Verdon in the Alpes-de-Haute-Provence offers spectacular views of the largest canyon in Europe. For the more adventurous members of the family, there are **kayak and white water rafting trips** down the river, and for the younger or less adventurous ones, the large Lake of Sainte-Croix at the western end of the canyon offers swimming and boating. Horses can be rented for rides in and around the canyon. For information about the Grand Canyon du Verdon, check with the tourist office at Castellane or Moustiers-Sainte-Marie or ADRI-CIMES, 19 Rue Docteur Honnorat, 04000 Digne-les-Bains (92 37 07 01, which provides information on all sports in the Alpes-de-Haute-Provence area.

Caves are fascinating places for children to explore, and two of the largest and most mysterious are to be found in the foothills of the Cévennes above Montpellier, the **Grotte des Demoiselles** near the medieval town of Saint-Martin-de-Londres, which has huge galleries 50 m (165 ft) high, and the **Grotte de Clamouse** near the medieval monastery of Saint Guilhem-le-Dessert. At Fontaine de Vaucluse east of Avignon, you will find the **Underground World of Norbert Casteret**, a series of caves with underground rivers and waterfalls and chambers filled with stalagmites and stalactites collected by the famed speleologist. The Fontaine de Vaucluse is a mysterious spring at the foot of a steep cliff from which water gushes downhill to form the River Sorgue. Despite numerous scientific explorations, including three by Commander Cousteau, nobody has been able to determine the source of this water.

CASTLES AND FORTRESSES
The most original trained-animal show is the Eagles of Beaucaire, a full-costume medieval pageant featuring free-flying eagles, falcons and vultures that is held four times a day in the summer at the Château de Beaucaire, the imposing shell of an eleventh century castle on the west bank of the Rhône.

People of all ages love medieval castles, and one of the most dramatic and best-preserved examples, Good King René's Château de Tarascon, sits directly across the river from Beaucaire on the east bank of the Rhône. Its interior gives you a good sense of what it was like to live in a castle.

Even more dramatic fortresses are to be found in Languedoc. They include Carcassonne, the largest medieval fortress city in Europe with two rings of high crenelated walls (see TOP SPOTS page 15), and Peyrepertuse, a huge ruined Cathar fortress atop a steep hill in the rugged Corbières (see THE OPEN ROAD, page 33). No child will ever forget these places. In Roussillon, the Fortress of Salses near Perpignan is a massive, sinister-looking fort with walls 15 m (almost 50 ft) thick that was built by the Spanish in the late sixteenth century. It is well-preserved and fascinating to explore. Villefranche-de-Conflent is a completely walled town in a Pyrénées valley, its ramparts designed in the seventeenth century

by Louis XIV's famed military engineer Sébastien Vauban. There is a 1,000-step tunneled staircase to hilltop Fort Liberia that the kids will enjoy climbing. Two other impressive walled cities are Aigues-Mortes, a perfectly preserved thirteenth century port on the western edge of the Camargue that was built for the Crusades, and Avignon, whose ring of crenelated ramparts was built by the Popes of Avignon in the fourteenth century, along with their gigantic Papal Palace.

VIEW PRE-HISTORY

Two places where children can have fascinating glimpses into prehistory are at the **Terra Amata Museum** near the old port in Nice, where the actual shelters of Paleolithic men who hunted here 400,000 years ago have been incorporated into the museum and true-to-life tableaus show the way they lived, and the **Centre Européen de la Préhistoire** in Tautavel near Perpignan. This is a modern museum of prehistory that contains the oldest human skull found in Europe, that of a nomadic hunter know as Tautavel Man. It is 450,000 years old.

GETTING AROUND WITH CHILDREN

Traveling with children doesn't have to cost you a fortune. In France hotel rooms are generally rented by the room, not the number of people staying in it, though there will be a small extra charge for additional cots. For information on camping, youth hostels and other budget accommodations, see BACKPACKING, page 34.

A wonderful side-benefit of traveling as a family is that, as everywhere, French people warm up to strangers with children.

Cultural Kicks

Though the first images of Mediterranean France that leap to mind are of sunny beaches, palm-lined avenues and the high life, you could have a thoroughly rewarding trip through the region without setting foot on a beach or in a deluxe restaurant, four-star hotel or casino. After Paris and the Île de France, no other part of France — and few places of comparable size anywhere — are as rich in cultural attractions as this.

THE ARCHITECTURAL LEGACY

The Mediterranean region was the first part of France to be exposed to Western Civilization, thanks to the Greeks who established a colony in Marseille in the seventh century BC and spread out to Arles, Toulon, Nice, and Agde in succeeding centuries. The Greek towns were eventually taken over by the Romans, whose architectural legacy is very rich in the Cimiez

section of Nice, in Fréjus and particularly the Rhône Valley, where Nîmes, Arles, Orange, Saint-Rémy-de-Provence and Vaison-la-Romaine have extensive Roman remains, including large arenas and theaters that are still in regular use (see TOP SPOTS, page 16). There are archaeological museums with important collections from the Roman period in all these places and in Marseille, Agde and Narbonne, the original capital of the Roman province.

From the middle ages, there is an even more extensive artistic and architectural legacy, with Romanesque churches and abbeys in every part of the region, from Côte d'Azur to the Pyrénées. Some of the most important Romanesque churches are the cathedrals and basilicas of Saint-Victor in Marseille, Saint-Sauveur in Aix, Saint-Trophime in Arles, Notre-Dame-de-Nazareth in Vaison-la-Romaine, Saint-Nazaire in Carcassonne and Sainte-Eulalie-et-Sainte-Julie in Elne. Among the most aesthetically distinguished abbeys are Le Thoronet in the Var, Sénanque and Silvacane in Provence, Saint-Gilles near Camargue, Saint-Guilhem-le-Désert west of Montpellier, Fontfroide near Narbonne, Lagrasse in the Corbières and Serrabone, Saint-Michel-de-Cuxa and Saint-Martin-du-Canigou in the Pyrénées in Roussillon. Carcassonne, Aigues-Mortes and Avignon are the quintessential medieval cities of Mediterranean France, the latter possessing an important museum of medieval paintings as well as its architectural treasures. There are also medieval hilltop villages, so-called "perched villages," by the

hundreds with fascinating buildings, sculptures and paintings from the period. In fact, other than the new beach resorts created since the 1960's, there are few towns of any size that don't have Romanesque remains of some kind.

The Gothic style came late to the South, but left the largest ecclesiastical structures in the region —the Basilica of Saint-Maximin-la-Sainte-Baume and the cathedrals of Saint-Just in Narbonne and Saint-Jean in Perpignan.

Other architectural periods that are well-represented in the region are the Baroque in Menton, Nice, Grasse, Marseille, Aix, Avignon, Uzès, Montpellier and Pézenas, the Belle Époque "wedding cake" style in Monaco, Nice and Cannes, and contemporary (i.e., post World War II) styles in Marseille, Nîmes and Montpellier. For more information on all these periods, see BUILDINGS OLD AND NEW, page 77.

MUSEUMS

The art museums of the region are also remarkably rich, particularly in twentieth century art, since many of the greatest painters of the century settled here and saw fit to lavish their works on the area, including such giants of modern painting as Picasso, Matisse and Chagall. Nice has the most art museums, and they are of extraordinarily high quality. The Matisse

OPPOSITE: The Jardin de la Fontaine TOP in Nîmes, Boating BOTTOM on the Canal du Midi. ABOVE: "Baigneuses" at the Renoir Museum in Cagnes-sur-Mer, the last home of Pierre-Auguste Renoir.

Museum, the Chagall Museum, MAMAC (the Museum of Modern and Contemporary Art) and the Museum of Naïve Art are especially worth visiting. In Saint-Paul-de-Vence, the Fondation Maeght has a dazzling collection of modern painting (Matisse, Chagall, Bonnard, Kandinsky) and sculpture (Calder, Giacometti, Miro), and Matisse's famous Chapel of the Rosary is just up the road in Vence. The Renoir Museum is in nearby in Cagnes-sur-Mer, the Léger Museum is in Biot, and Picasso's huge "War and Peace" fresco in Vallauris. A short distance away is the Picasso Museum in Antibes's Château Grimaldi, which has many important works not only by Picasso, but by Léger, De Staël, Klein, Alechinsky and numerous other modern painters and sculptors. Saint-Tropez's Annonciade Museum has a superb collection of Pointillist, Nabi and Fauve paintings, and the Granet Museum in Aix has eight small paintings by native son Paul Cézanne. Marseille's Cantini Museum and Arles's Réattu Museum have prestigious collections of modern art, and in Montpellier, the Fabre Museum has several paintings by native son Frédéric Bazille, one of the founders of Impressionism, and by Veronese, Poussin, David, Delacroix, Courbet and others. Perpignan's Hyacinthe Rigaud Museum, named for the Perpignan native who was the leading portrait artist of Louis XIV's court, has a fascinating and highly eclectic collection ranging from medieval Catalan altarpieces to work by contemporary Catalan painter Antoni Tàpies, along with three sketches by another Catalan artist who worked in this very building, Pablo Picasso. This prolific genius is abundantly represented in one of the most remarkable small art museums you will ever see, the Museum of Modern Art of Céret. This little town in the eastern foothills of the Pyrénées is known as the "Mecca of Cubism" because of the critical work Picasso and Braque did in that style in Céret, and its museum contains works from the Cubist Period to the present, including paintings by Chagall, Dufy and Miro, drawings by Matisse and sculptures by Maillol, a native of Roussillon, and 53 items by Picasso, including a delightful series of ceramic bowls decorated with bullfighting scenes. For more information on art see PAINTING under LIFE AND ART, page 80.

THE PERFORMING ARTS

Classical music, opera, dance and theater are alive and well in Nice, Monaco, Marseille and Montpellier off-season. For the schedule of events, check with the tourist office in each locale. But the big season for the performing arts is the summer, and for information on that, refer to MAJOR FESTIVALS AND EVENTS on page 333.

Shop Till You Drop

TOWN AND COUNTRY MARKETS

The most fun to be had shopping in Mediterranean France is in the open air markets. These can be food markets, antique and bric-a-brac markets or Provençal markets, in which food, handicrafts, household products and clothing are sold. All towns have at least one market a week, and no matter how sleepy it may be the rest of the week, the town wakes up on market day.

Nice has a big, colorful, tremendously lively food and flower markets six mornings a week on the Cours Saleya amid the pastel Baroque buildings of Old Nice, and on Mondays the antique and bric-a-brac dealers take over the space. Antibes is another city with an extremely lively market, this being a Provençal one held every morning except Monday in its large market pavilion and nearby streets by the walls of the medieval town. Cannes has one of my favorite food markets, the Marché Forville, a jolly pink stucco pavilion exuding the happy flavors and aromas of Provence — fresh herbs, olives, cheeses, honey, fruits and vegetables, flowers — likewise open every morning except Monday. Other towns and cities with especially lively markets are Saint-Tropez, Aix-en-Provence — which has three — and Apt, Arles, Saint-Rémy-de-Provence, Vaison-la-Romaine, Nyons, Uzès (the loveliest of all Provençal markets, in my opinion), Narbonne and Céret.

HANDICRAFTS

For handicrafts, the main towns in the hills west of Nice are Vence and Saint-Paul-de-Vence, where you can find a wide range of crafts — pottery, jewelry, weaving, metal sculpture — Tourrettes-sur-Loup, known particularly for its weavers, Biot for blown glass and Vallauris for pottery. Another creative center for pottery and for chinaware is Moustiers-Sainte-Marie in the Alpes-de-Haute-Provence.

Marseille and Aix are noted for their santons, "little saints" in Provençal, small sculpted figures of Provençal peasants used in Christmas cribs. They are seen everywhere in markets and souvenir shops.

Another distinctive product of the region is the bright colored block-printed fabric in paisley, floral or geometrical patterns that you will see in all Provençal markets, either as yard goods or made into tablecloths and napkin sets, dresses, skirts, pocket books and other products. The leading maker of these traditional Provençal fabrics and products is Souleiado. The company is located in Tarascon and has retail shops in Nice, Cannes, Saint-Tropez, Toulon, Marseille, Aix, Arles, Les Baux, Saint-Rémy, Avignon,

Orange, Nîmes, Montpellier and other towns in the region.

ANTIQUES

For antiques, **Isle-sur-la-Sorgue** east of Avignon is the leading purveyor. You will also find good antique shopping in **Marseille**, **Aix**, **Avignon**, **Nice**, **Antibes**, **Saint-Tropez**, **Toulon**, **Montpellier** and **Perpignan**.

PERFUME AND LUXURY GOODS

The perfume capital of France is **Grasse**, where you can buy scents directly from Molinard, Galimard, Fragonard and other manufacturers. For luxury goods of all kinds, your best hunting grounds will be **Monte-Carlo**, **Cannes** and **Saint-Tropez**.

Short Breaks

Mediterranean France is an ideal place to take a long weekend or short holiday. No matter what you crave — cultural kicks, sporting sprees (golf, tennis, scuba diving, a boat trip), the great outdoors (a short walking, bicycling or horseback trip through exciting countryside), living it up in playgrounds of the rich or simply relaxing in exquisitely restful surroundings —this area is likely to have what it takes to give you a memorable and uplifting escape from the routine.

There are a dozen towns and cities that are easy to get to by plane or train where you could spend a richly rewarding short break, culturally,
YOUR CHOICE

gastronomically and otherwise. For the high life, you need only go to Monte-Carlo and Cannes. For high life, art and architectural treasures and a real city to explore, there is the Côte d'Azur's capital of **Nice**. The peaceful old port of **Menton** has particular charm to those who love gardens. A very satisfying break could be spent in the art-rich hill towns of **Vence**, **Saint-Paul-de-Vence** or **Cagnes-sur-Mer**, all of which have superb cuisine and lodging, with visits to the nearby crafts towns of Tourrettes-sur-Loup, Biot and Vallauris. The old port of **Antibes**, its luxurious cape and its beach and nightlife mecca of Juan-les-Pins make a lively combination of historical, nostalgic and nocturnal fun. For a mixture of gastronomy, historical treasures and the spectacular scenery of the Calanques of Marseille, a weekend in **Marseille** and **Cassis** would be hard to beat. Other excellent destinations for short breaks are **Aix-en-Provence**, **Avignon** and its neighbors of Villeneuve-lès-Avignon and Châteauneuf-du-Pape, **Arles** and the neighboring Camargue, **Nîmes**, the nearby Pont du Gard and **Uzès**, **Montpellier**, **Narbonne**, **Carcassonne**, and **Perpignan**. Any one of these places offers a memorable experience in itself and has surrounding areas that are well worth exploring.

If you'd like a more rural escape, I suggest the Lubéron, easily reached from Avignon, where **Gordes** has the most to offer in the way

ABOVE There's no shortage of art on the Côte d'Azur: on the port at Saint-Tropez LEFT and in the pottery capital of Vallauris RIGHT.

of food and accommodations, or **Vaison-la-Romaine** in Northern Provence, with excursions to the olive capitol of Nyons, Mont-Ventoux and the wine-rich Dentelles de Montmirail. This area is most easily reached from Montélimar or Orange.

As previously mentioned, two spots where you can totally unwind from the pressures of life are the Mas du Langoustier, a cheerful hotel with exceptionally fine Provençal cuisine on a remote little cove on the delightful island of **Porquerolles**, and the medieval **Château de Trigance**, a storybook castle perched atop the village of the same name in a wide, quiet valley near the dramatic Grand Canyon du Verdon, beautifully converted into a Relais & Châteaux hotel and restaurant.

For art lovers, the excellent collections in the museums in Nice, Cagnes-sur-Mer, Saint-Paul-de-Vence, Vence and Antibes make them obvious options for aesthetically intense breaks. A weekend in "Cézanne Country" is another idea. Here you will base yourself in Paul Cézanne's native city of **Aix-en-Provence** and see the important places of his childhood, the last studio he worked in, perfectly preserved, his beloved Montagne-Sainte-Victoire and the red earth landscape around it, and, of course, the eight paintings by Cézanne in the Granet Museum. The Aix Tourist Office has their itinerary carefully mapped out for you. The Arles Tourist Office has done the same for "Van Gogh Country," which includes the places he frequented and painted in Arles and in the Camargue and the Crau, and in nearby Saint-Rémy, where Van Gogh had himself committed in a mental hospital for a year, Tourist Office has mapped out an itinerary of the places he painted — orchards of gnarled olive trees, rows of cypresses, instantly recognizable from paintings. Unfortunately, however, there are no works of Van Gogh in the region.

A less-known, but exciting area for lovers of Modern Art is the delightful medieval port of Collioure south of Perpignan, known as "The Cradle of Fauvism" because of the work Matisse and Derain did there in 1905 and 1906, and the nearby Pyrénées hill town of **Céret**, dubbed "The Mecca of Cubism" because of the work Picasso and Braque did there a few years later. Céret's Museum of Modern Art has a first-rate collection of art from Cubism to the present. Both towns are easily reached from Perpignan by either car or public transport.

For an extended break of four or five days, you could take in the impressive concentration of Roman vestiges in an around **Nîmes**, **Arles**, **Saint-Rémy**, **Vaison-la-Romaine** and **Orange** (see TOP SPOTS, page 16).

You could also tailor your short break around a special event or holiday, such as the **Gypsy Pilgrimage** to the **Camargue** in late May or one of the big **bullfighting festivals** in Nîmes, Arles or Béziers, or for that matter, any of the festivals or special events listed in FESTIVE FLINGS, following section. There's no end of marvelous short trips that can be made in this region.

Festive Flings

The Mediterranean has always been a festive part of the world, going back at least to the days of the ancient Greeks, with their Dionysian revels, and the French corner of the Mediterranean is certainly no exception. Celebrations here fall into four different categories — traditional, arts, modern special events and bullfighting *ferias*.

TRADITIONAL FESTIVALS

Festivals of tradition are fêtes of long standing, usually associated with a religious holiday, a local saint's day, a celebration of a local hero or heroic event, a harvest or wine festival. The most important religious festivals take place in winter and spring, following the Christian calendar, from Christmas to Easter.

The **Christmas season** is celebrated with special fervor in Provence, where Christianity first came to France. In December, Marseille has a market for *santons*, the sculpted "little saints" used in *crèches*, or Christmas cribs, that are a specialty of the region. The town of Séguret in the Vaucluse transforms itself into a living *crèche*, with the whole town in costume. On Christmas eve, the traditional Shepherd's Mass takes place at Allauch near Marseille. Midnight masses are held at the grotto at La Sainte-Baume, where Mary Magdalene is said to have prayed, and many other places throughout the region. The **Fête du Citron**, the lemon festival, is held in Menton in early February, when citrus fruits by the thousands are used to decorate parade floats. **Carnival** in Nice, France's Mardi Gras, soon follows, a two-week blast of parades, music, theater and dancing in the streets, culminating in a massive fireworks display. On Good Friday, there are processions by several religious brotherhoods in Roussillon. The **Procession of the Penitents of the Sanch** in Perpignan ("*sanch*" being Catalan for *sang*, or blood), is the most dramatic because of the red hoods they wear.

Pentecost at the end of May brings the **Fête des Gardians** at Arles, a big rodeo with cowboys from the Camargue, held at the Roman Arena. Nearby Saint-Rémy puts on the **Fête de la Transhumance**, a shepherds' festival in which thousands of sheep are driven through the center of the old town.

The Eagles of Beaucaire, a medieval-style birds of prey show at the Château de Beaucaire on the Rhône.

Saint-Tropez has its two **Bravades** in mid-May and in mid-June, the first to honor their patron saint, Torpes, the second to celebrate a heroic defense of the town against the Spanish in the seventeenth century, with parades in fanciful sailors' uniforms and firing of noisy muskets.

The most exciting religious event of the year is the **Gypsy Pilgrimage** to Les-Saintes-Maries-de-la-Mer in the Camargue on May 24 and 25, when Gypsies from come from all over Europe to carry a statue of their patron saint, the Black Saint Sara, down to the sea. There is lots of Gypsy music and dancing. The **Fête de Saint-Pierre** honoring Saint Peter, the patron saint of fisherman, is celebrated in many ports in early July, nowhere more vigorously than in Sète, where water jousts are the featured events.

On July 14, Cannes celebrates **Bastille Day** with a tremendous fireworks display on the Croisette. The same day, the mighty walled city of Carcassonne explodes with light, sound and fireworks, and in the first two weeks in August follows it up with **Les Médiévales**, a program of medieval pageants, jousting, crafts shows and musical events. Late in August, Aigues-Mortes, another walled city, celebrates the **Fête de Saint-Louis** with a medieval pageant and nearby Sète with another round of water jousting.

Arles's **Fête des Prémices du Riz**, the rice harvest festival, is held the second week of September.

In the fall, every town and village that makes wine has its **Fête du Vin** with music, dancing in the village square and, of course, lots of wine-tasting. The wine capital of Béziers puts on its **Fête du Vin Nouveau** the third Sunday in October on the grand tree-shaded Allées Paul Riquet that reminds everyone of Las Ramblas in Barcelona.

ARTS FESTIVALS

Arts festivals are held the year round, but the big season is clearly the summer, when music, theater, dance, folk and visual arts programs abound in our Mediterranean region. If you look at arts sections of *Libération*, *Le Monde* or one of the other national newspapers, you will find twenty festivals or big musical events to choose from here on an average summer day. Montpellier is the most active city, with one major theater, music and dance festival after another. It starts with **Printemps des Comédiens**, a French and European theater festival, in early June. A huge dance festival, the **Festival International de Danse**, follows for two weeks in late June and early July, presenting leading companies from America and all over the world. For the rest of the summer, every suitable setting for music from the cathedral to the city's ultra-modern music halls is taken over by the eclectic programs of classical and avant-garde music, opera, chamber music and jazz of the **Festival International de Radio France**. Many of the concerts are broadcast live by Radio France (see TOP SPOTS, FESTIVAL FOLLIES, page 18).

48

Meanwhile, starting in early July, at the month-long **Festival d'Avignon**, the City of the Popes cuts loose with performances by hundreds of theater companies, dance troupes and orchestras from all over the world and street entertainers on the cafe-lined Place de l'Horloge. An hour away, Aix presents it prestigious **Festival International d'Art Lyrique et de Musique** for opera and classical music. On the Côte d'Azur, the **Nice Jazz Festival** takes over the Roman Arena in Cimiez for two weeks in early July, and **Jazz à Juan** at Juan-les-Pins follows it right away, with the greatest names in jazz, blues and R&B at both places. **L'Été Vaison** features dance, music and theater in the Roman theater of Vaison-la-Romaine, and at the 10,000-seat Roman Théâtre Antique in Orange, the **Chorégies d'Orange** is one of the world's top opera events. **Organa**, an international organ festival, takes place at Saint-Rémy from July through September, and La Roque d'Anthéron's **Festival International de Piano** is held at the Abbeye de Silvacane the first three weeks of August.

MODERN SPECIAL EVENTS

Many of the modern festive events are associated with sport. Monte-Carlo figures heavily in this category with its **car rally** in January, **circus festival** in February, **tennis open** in April and **Grand Prix de Monaco Formula-1** car racing in May. The other leading place for special events is Cannes. The **Cannes Film Festival** in May gets most of the attention, but that's just the tip of the iceberg. Festivals and major trade shows are going on practically all the time.

The **Nioulargue** is a tremendous international sailing event at Saint-Tropez at the end of September. Huge old yachts, former America's Cup champions and challengers and racers of other classes participate. There are races between boats of different ages and classes.

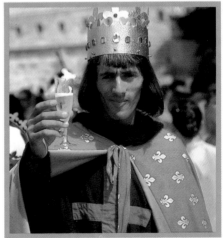

Every town and village has at least one big festival a year. OPPOSITE TOP: The *sardana*, the traditional Catalan dance, at a *sardana* festival in Collioure. ABOVE: A rustic local festival in tiny Saint-Etienne-des-Grès in the Alpilles. BELOW: King Saint Louis on his feast day of August 25 at Aigues-Mortes.

BULLFIGHTING

Bullfighting needs a category all of its own. It is the rage in southern Provence and Languedoc, where Nîmes, Arles and Béziers are the great centers of *la tauromachie*. Only Madrid and Seville have more *corridas* than Nîmes, where the **Feria de Pentecote**, held in the Roman arena in late May, is France's biggest bullfighting event. There is music and street dancing and partying around the clock, with impromptu *bodegas* set up all over town. Nîmes revels in *la tauromachie* all over again the third week of September at the **Feria des Vendanges**, the harvest festival. Arles has its big **Corrida de Pâques** at Easter and, like Nîmes, plenty of normal bullfights throughout the summer. Most of the bullfighting is Spanish style, with all the colorful pageantry, where they kill the bull at the end. But a Provençal style of bullfighting is also practiced in this part of France. Here young men dare death by trying to pluck a rosette, *la cocarde*, from between the bull's horns. But at the end of the match, the bull stays alive and is allowed to go back home to the Camargue.

There are bullfights in both styles in Saint-Rémy, the Camargue and many other places. Béziers has its **Feria**, Spanish style, on August 14 and 15, with the running of the bulls through the streets, parades, the *corrida* and partying all night.

For a more complete listing of the various festivals and special events, see TRAVELERS' TIPS, page 333.

Galloping Gourmets

In the sixteenth century, Alonso Vasquez, a Mediterranean man, traveled to Flanders and was dismayed by what he discovered about what people ate and didn't eat there. It was "the land where there grows neither thyme, nor

lavender, figs, olives, melons, or almonds; where parsley, onions and lettuce have neither juice nor taste; where dishes are prepared, strange to relate, with butter from cows instead of olive oil."

Sr. Vasquez's manner of expression may have a quaint ring, but the idea behind it is strictly contemporary. A 1994 *Gault-Millau Magazine* called our present moment in culinary history *"L'Heure du Midi"* ("The Hour of the South") and said "Long eclipsed by the 'values' of the North where butter, cream and meat in abundance reigned, fish, tomatoes and olive oil have little by little regained their place… in the sun."

In 1994 also, the *Wine Spectator* named Alain Ducasse the best chef in the world. He is the chef of Monte-Carlo's Louis XV Restaurant and the most highly regarded practitioner of Mediterranean cuisine.

The food is delicious, but what brought it into vogue, particularly in America, were the health benefits associated with "the Mediterranean Diet." When it was scientifically demonstrated that the mixture of bread, olive oil and tannic wine acts as a magic potion against cardiovascular disease, the stampede to olive oil and French red wine was on.

Alain Ducasse, a serene man, completely unfazed by the kingly position into which his cooking has thrust him, rejects the notion that this is a fad. "Mediterranean cuisine is not a phenomenon of fashion," he says. "It has always seduced everyone, as it seduced me, because it is real, essential, universal, and because it was born — and it is not just by chance — in the cradle of Western civilization."

The essentials of Mediterranean cuisine are simple, and that is part of its charm. They are olive oil, wine, garlic, tomatoes and herbs from Provence — thyme, rosemary, sage, savory, marjoram, oregano, basil, and parsley — fresh Mediterranean fish, fresh Provençal vegetables

and, from time to time, meat. The key to success is judicious application of the oil, herbs, garlic and wine to subtly flavor the fish and vegetables without obliterating their own natural savor.

VEGETABLES

In the cuisine of the leading chefs of the region, Ducasse, Roger Vergé, Dominique Le Stanc and others, the vegetable is the star of the show. *Petits farcis* are stuffed tomatoes, peppers, onions, eggplants, zucchinis and even the blossoms of zucchinis, *fleurs de courgettes*. Various fillings are used, depending on the season and the imagination of the chef. Colorful as well as delicious. *Beignets de fleur de courgette* are deep-fried zucchini-blossom fritters. *Ratatouille* ("ra-ta-tweee," not "ra-ta-too-ey" as it is sometimes mispronounced) is a cooked dish of sliced eggplant, zucchini, tomatoes, peppers and onions seasoned with garlic and herbs. It is normally served cold in the summer. *Soupe au pistou* is a popular vegetable soup with basil, garlic, and olive oil. *Mesclun*, also spelled *mesclum*, is a mixture of several tender salad greens, grown mainly in the back country of Nice. The Cours Saleya market in Nice is the best place to find it. *Salade Niçoise*, the famous salad of tuna, anchovies, black olives and lettuce, is sold everywhere. *Truffles* come mainly from the Tricastin in Northern Provence, where Valréas is its big market town. Since the lower Rhône Valley and the Durance Valleys are the leading vegetable producing areas of France, you are sure to find and abundance of fresh Provençal legumes.

SEAFOOD

Because of over-fishing of the Mediterranean, the local fish has become quite expensive, and much of the seafood you find in the markets and restaurants is actually trucked in from the

Atlantic. But Mediterranean people are willing to pay the higher price, because their seafood has more flavor, they claim. The important Mediterranean fish to look out for are *rouget* (red mullet), *saint-pierre* (John Dory), *loup de mer* (sea bass), *requin* (shark, a local variety, very tender), *turbot*, *rascasse* (scorpion fish of the rockfish family, essential for *bouillabaisse*), *chapon de mer* (a rockfish-like cousin of the *rascasse*). The biggest French fishing port on the Mediterranean is Sète on the Languedoc coast. Most shellfish come from this coast too. The *moules* and *huîtres* (mussels and oysters) from Bouzigues are especially well-known. You will also find local *crevettes* (shrimp), *langoustines* (large crayfish), *tourteaux* (crabs) and at outlandish prices, the occasional **langouste**, a clawless spiny lobster. *Encornet* or *seiche* squid, cuttlefish) and *poulpe* (octopus) are widely available. Restaurants often have *"Petite Friture"* on the menu as an *entrée* (the French term for first course). This is a heaping platter of little deep-fried whitebait, enough for a light lunch with bread and a green salad.

Bouillabaisse is the classic Mediterranean fish soup. It originated in the Marseille area, but is available all along the coast, generally at very hefty prices. The dish was created to give fishermen's families a way to eat the fish of little value in the catch that otherwise would have been thrown away. But now that there is no such thing as a cheap Mediterranean fish, you will not find the real thing for less than about 200 francs per serving. But it is an enormous feast and an unforgettable experience, especially when served right at the port or with a view of the coast.

The flavors of the South, shellfish in Saint-Tropez OPPOSITE BOTTOM, Provençal herbs, sausages from Arles, and olives OPPOSITE TOP, ABOVE LEFT and RIGHT at the Saturday morning market in Uzès.

Bourride is a soup of white fish, onions, tomatoes, garlic, herbs and olive oil, seasoned with *aïoli* (garlic mayonnaise) that is generally much cheaper than *bouillabaisse*, but delicious too, and served all along the coast. It is a specialty of Sète.

Soupe des Pêcheurs (fishermen's soup) is a general term for fish stews also found on the menu.

Brandade de morue, a mousse of salted cod with garlic and cream or olive oil, is another reasonably-priced dish that is widely available. It is a specialty of Nîmes.

The different areas all have their own local specialties, and none more than Nice, whose famous *salade Niçoise* is just the tip of the iceberg (not iceberg lettuce, fortunately). The great Niçois fish dish you will see on the menu is *stockfish*, also called *stocaficada* or *estoficado*. This can be either a flattened dried codfish or a purée of codfish with olive oil, tomatoes, black olives, peppers, potatoes, onions, garlic and herbs. (Recommendations about where to find local specialties will be found in the travel chapters).

The beautiful Catalan port of Collioure is famous for its anchovies (*anchois*), which are grilled right on the beach.

Before moving on to the meat, let me put in a word for a personal favorite, grilled sea bass with fennel (*loup de mer grillé au fenouil*), a naturally delicious fish, so simple to prepare that only a very careless chef could go wrong.

MEAT

Roast lamb (*agneau*) is a great favorite, lamb from Sisteron in the Alpes-de-Haute-Provence being the most highly prized. Chicken (*poulet*) is usually served roasted or cooked in a tomato sauce (*à la Provençale*). *Pintade* (guinea hen) is another favorite bird. *Daube*, a stew of braised chunks of meat, usually beef, with various vegetables, is common in most of the region. Some local specialties are *saucisson d'Arles*, a salami-like dried pork and beef sausage, *gardiane*, a stew made from the meat of bulls in the Camargue and upper Languedoc (sometimes from bulls killed in the bull ring), and in Marseille and the lower Rhône, *pieds et paquets*, sheep's feet cooked in tomatoes, olive oil and wine, and with little packets of sheep's entrails, which is much more savory than it sounds. During hunting season, especially as you get into the mountains, many restaurants feature *gibier* (game) — *sanglier* (wild boar), *marcassin* (young boar), *chevreuil* (venison), *lièvre* (hare), *faisan* (pheasant), *perdrix* (partridge), *caille* (quail). *Cassoulet* is not really part of the Mediterranean cuisine, but since our boundaries extend as far west as Carcassonne, one of the main cities for this dish, we include it. It

is a casserole of baked white beans and a combination of meats, such as duck, goose, mutton, pork, and sausage, very hearty and filling. In Roussillon the traditional Catalan dish is *cargolade*, a mixed grill of snails, lamb, and sausage cooked over vine clippings, a complicated meal to prepare, rarely made today.

SAUCES, DRESSINGS AND DIPS

Aïoli is garlic mayonnaise. *Anchoïade* is an anchovy, garlic and olive oil sauce. *Pistou* is a basil, garlic and olive oil sauce. *Rouille* is a mayonnaise of olive oil, garlic and hot peppers, served with bread, normally with *bouillabaisse* and fish soups. *Tapenade* is a paste of black olives, olive oil, garlic, anchovies, capers and lemon juice, served either with bread as an appetizer or used in cooking.

CHEESES

The cheeses of Mediterranean France come mainly from the ring of mountains surrounding the region and can be purchased fresh from their makers in the wonderful outdoor markets at Apt, Aix, Carpentras, Uzès and other places. **Annot** and **Banon** in the Alpes-de-Haute-Provence are noted for their sheep and goat cheeses. *Picodon* is a small, hard, flat, disc of goat cheese aged in brandy from northern Provence.

Pélardon is a little disc of goat cheese from the Cévennes, often sold in a blend of olive oil and *eau-de-vie*. **Tomme Arlésienne**, also called **Tomme de Camargue**, is made from a blend of cow and goat milk flavored with savory, popular in upper Languedoc and Arles.

PASTAS AND BREADS

Pasta is popular everywhere, especially in Old Nice, where delicious *gnocci*, pizza and their own local onion pizza called *pissaladière* can be found at every turn, as well as *pan bagnat* (*salade Niçoise* on a roll) and *socca* (crêpes made from chick-pea flour). *Fougasse*, a flat, latticed, pizza crust-like bread flavored with olives, onions, anchovies, herbs or spices, is available in most *boulangeries* in Provence. Great for picnics.

DESSERTS, SWEETS AND PASTRIES

Provence being France's largest fruit-growing area, a big candied fruit-making business has developed. The leading places for *fruits confits* (candied fruit) are Apt in the Lubéron, Saint-Rémy and the Nice area. Nice also makes a tart called a *tourte aux blettes* filled with raisins, Swiss chard and pine nuts. Saint-Tropez has its famous *Tarte Tropézienne*, a tart filled with confectioners cream. *Calissons d'Aix* are little flat biscuits of almond, honey and melon paste

made in Aix. *Navettes de Saint-Victor* are tubular orange-flavored biscuits made by a famous eighteenth-century bakery in Marseille. The great chocolate candy-maker is **Puyricard** near Aix, whose products are sold throughout the region. There are many kinds of **honey** available, but to put in a word for my personal favorite, lavender honey is fantastic.

WINE

As with Mediterranean cooking, these have been exciting years for the area's wines. Since the 1960's, there has been a revolution in wine-making in the South. With only a few prestigious exceptions before that revolution — Châteauneuf-du-Pape, Bandol, Fitou — the area was known mainly for the vast quantities of "plonk," cheap red wine, it produced. The other main product of Southern vineyards was rosés, a whole category of wine once sneered at by wine connoisseurs. That situation has changed over the past twenty-five years, as the South has responded to the affluent French public's increasing demand for quality wines and a corresponding drop in the market for plonk. The wines have of the South have improved drastically, as its wine makers have followed a strategy of high quality and low yields. Both their red wines and that formerly despised category of rosés have gained a good deal of respect.

Mediterranean France has been making wine since the sixth century BC, when the Greeks taught the local Ligurians that there was something else that could be done with grapes

YOUR CHOICE

besides eat them. It is the oldest wine-making area in France and by far the largest. By the time of the *Pax Romana*, when the Empire's bread and circuses needed prodigious quantities of wine, the whole sweep of Provincia Gallia Narbonensis was planted in vines, except for the eastern flank, where the land was not suitable. Today, other than the Alpes-Maritimes, where there are only two very small wine-growing areas, the high mountains, and a few sections where there are only orchards, rice fields or cattle ranches, there are vineyards just about everywhere. In most places, the soil is so poor and the climate so hot and dry that the hardy grape vine is the only plant that can survive.

Since individual wine-growing areas will be discussed as we come upon them, we will only give a brief geographical overview here.

There are three major wine-growing regions in Mediterranean France. In Northern Provence, the Rhône Valley is known mainly for its **Côtes du Rhône** wines, most of them reds, of which **Châteauneuf-du-Pape** is the best known *Appellation d'Origine Contrôlée (AOC)*, and in fact was the first *AOC* ever created. (The *AOC* is a strict set of government standards that guarantees a wine's place of origin, the varieties of grapes used and production methods and quantities allowable; it tends to promote quality, but is not in itself a guarantee of quality). Newer *AOC*'s in Northern Provence

ABOVE: A vineyard in the Hérault, France's most productive wine-making *département*.

are **Côteaux du Tricastin** and **Côtes du Ventoux**, similar wines to Côtes du Rhône. West of the Rhône, the villages of **Tavel** and **Lirac** are famed for their rosés.

The second major region consists of the mainly rosé-producing western part of the Côte d'Azur, the Var, where the *AOC* is **Côtes de Provence**, and the area around Aix, where **Côteaux d'Aix-en-Provence** wines are grown, also mainly rosés. In 1995, a former sub-area of Côteaux d'Aix-en-Provence in the hills of the Alpilles that produces mostly red wines gained the right to an *AOC* of its own, **Baux de Provence**. Côtes de Provence and Côteaux d'Aix-en-Provence produce more than half of France's *AOC* rosés. Within this area are three smaller, but very prestigious *AOC's* — **Bandol**, famed for its vigorous reds, **Cassis** known for its dry whites, and **Palette**, a tiny *AOC* area south of Aix with only two vineyards.

The third major region is Languedoc-Roussillon, the largest and currently the most dynamic wine-producing region in France. It makes mostly reds. Moving from north to south, its main *AOC* table wines are **Costières de Nîmes** in the area around Nîmes, followed by **Côteaux de Languedoc**, covering a large area along the coast and up into the foothills of the Cévennes, with twelve different locally labeled areas (**La Clape, Faugères, Picpoul de Pinet**, etc.). Continuing southward, we come to the **Minervois**, the overlapping **Corbières** and **Fitou** areas and **Côtes du Roussillon**.

Most areas in Languedoc and Roussillon have graduated to *AOC* status since the 1960's, some in very recent years.

Languedoc and Roussillon wine makers have also put great effort into improving their *vins de pays*, pleasant little country wines without all the regulations of the *AOC's*. **Vin de Pays d'Oc** from the Hérault department of Languedoc has built a large following France in the past few years. You should not hesitate to try it.

In Roussillon, the predominant *AOC* table wine is **Côtes du Roussillon**, but there are two small, highly prestigious *AOC's* you should know about — **Collioure** from vineyards on the steep hillsides of the Côte Vermeille, which produce some of the most subtly flavorful reds of Southern France, and **Blanquette** et **Crémant de Limoux**, sparkling white wines from the charming town of Limoux in the hills west of the Corbières. Sparkling wines were made here before the process of putting bubbles in wine made its way up to Champagne.

Languedoc and Roussillon also produce a number of *vins doux naturels*, or sweet aperitif wines, most notably those of **Rivesaltes** and **Banyuls**.

For the tourist, the existence of thousands of vineyards presents a unique opportunity to enrich his or her travels. Wine makers are more than happy to have people visit their caves. You will have the chance to experience what wine writer Hugh Johnson calls "the unique complex of sensual, aesthetic and intellectual rewards that only wine of all products can offer: it is a perfect expression of modern civilization at its best. There is simply nothing that so perfectly encapsulates pleasure, social well-being, and aesthetic exploration at the same time."

Special Interests

There are many special interests that can be pursued in the region, either by stopping in one place to participate in an educational program or by pursuing your particular passion as you travel along.

CULINARY LESSONS

Given the enormous interest that Mediterranean cuisine has generated in recent years, many travelers may welcome a chance to learn how to prepare it. Guy Gedda, dubbed "The Pope of Provençal cooking" by his fellow chefs of the region, happily reveals all to small groups in his Jardin des Perlefleurs restaurant in flowery Bormes-les-Mimosas on a hill overlooking the Îles d'Hyères. In his kitchen and garden, he teaches one full Provençal menu per day, five days a week, and you can go for one class or as many as you please. Sessions start at 9:30 AM and end at about 3 PM. The **Jardin des Perlefleurs** is at 100 Chemin de l'Orangerie, 83230 Bormes-les-Mimosas (94 64 99 23. The cost is 400 francs on weekdays, 500 francs on Saturday or Sunday. Another fine place to study Provençal cooking is at famed chef Roger Vergé's **École du Moulin** in Mougins near Cannes. Classes are held in a specially designed teaching kitchen upstairs at M. Vergé's other restaurant, L'Amandier. Here the sessions are about two and a half hours long and cost 300 francs per day or 1,350 francs for a series of five. Classes are held Tuesday through Saturday. For information or bookings, write to the school at Restaurant l'Amandier, 06250 Mougins, or call or fax them at (93 75 35 70 or FAX 93 90 18 55.

VISITING VINEYARDS

As noted, vineyards abound in the region, and stopping in to visit them is one of the most enjoyable things you can do. The most dynamic wine-making area at the moment is Languedoc, and if you would like to have an organized tour there, a group of eight leading vineyards has banded together as the **Club des Grands Vins** de **Châteaux de Languedoc**, and they make all the land arrangements (hotels, meals and ground transportation, everything first-class) for visitors to tour their *châteaux*. They include the Abbaye de Valmagne, a breathtaking medieval abbey in the vicinity of Meze on the Basin de Thau, where prestigious Côteaux du Languedoc wines are made, and the distinguished Château de Lastours in the Corbières south of Narbonne. A three-day tour costs 3,480 francs, a four-day tour 4,415 francs. For information, contact Jean Viennet at the Château de Raissac, 34500 Béziers (67 28 15 61 FAX 67 28 19 75.

HOUSEBOATING

Houseboating is available in the canals to the west of the Rhône. From Beaucaire, you can cruise along the northern edge of the Camargue on the Canal du Rhône à Sète past the medieval

walled city of Aigues-Mortes and the ancient island cathedral of Maguelone to the bustling fishing port of Sète. From there you can continue south through the Bassin de Thau and enter the Canal du Midi that wends its peaceful, tree-lined way by Béziers, the Oppidum d'Ensérune and Carcassonne. There are several places where you can rent houseboats, principally **Beaucaire**, **Saint-Gilles**, **Port-de-Colombiers** near **Béziers**, **Argens-Minervois** and **Castelnaudary**. Addresses and phone numbers of companies that rent them can be found in the chapter on Languedoc. For more information, contact the Comité Régional du Tourisme du Languedoc-Roussillon, 20 Rue de la République,

34000 Montpellier (67 22 81 00. To make boat rental arrangements in the United States before coming to France, get in touch with Le Boat, P.O. Box E, Maywood NJ 07607 ((201) 342-1838 FAX (201) 342-7498 or toll-free 1-800-992-0291, which represents the Crown Blue Line, or in Great Britain, Andrew Brock Travel Ltd, 54 High Street East, Uppingham, Rutland LE15 9PZ ((0572) 821 330 FAX 821 072. Ask for their helpful booklet called *French Country Cruises*.

NUDIST COLONIES

Nudism, or *naturisme* as *naturistes* prefer to call it, is very popular in Mediterranean France, both at the shore and in the mountains. **Héliopolis** on the Île du Levant in the Îles d'Hyères is the granddaddy of French nudist colonies. It started in the 1930's and is still going strong. But by far the largest is **Port Ambonne** at Cap d'Agde, where 25,000 to 30,000 nudists are in residence in mid-summer, and there are hotels, camping grounds, restaurants, banks

ABOVE LEFT: The bells of the fortified church of Les Saintes-Maries-de-la-Mer. ABOVE RIGHT: A plumed escort at the African Reserve of Sigean near Narbonne. LOWER RIGHT and FOLLOWING PAGES: Cruising on the Canal du Midi.

and supermarkets for nudists. For information, contact the Fédération Française de Naturisme, 65 Rue Toqueville, 75015 Paris ((1) 47 64 32 82 FAX 47 64 32 63. They will send you a free brochure on all the nudist resorts and camps in France in any of the five major European languages. To get it sent to you overseas, you must mail them three international mail coupons, which are available in post offices in your country.

HEALTH SPAS
You will notice that many towns in the region have the suffix *les bains* added to their names, as in **Digne-les-Bains, Amélie-les-Bains, Molitg-les-Bains**, and so forth, many of them in the Pyrénées. These and many others without *les bains* in their names are natural springs where treatment facilities have been established to take advantage of the minerals in the spas' waters to cure various medical conditions — respiratory, arthritic, urinary, and so forth. Some of the mineral springs have been in use since the time of the Romans. For information, contact the Fédération Thermale et Climatique Française, 16 Rue Estrapade, 75005 Paris ((1) 43 25 11 85.

Another kind of water treatment available in several places along the coast is *thalassothérapie*, which uses salt water, massage, mud baths with algae solutions and exercises for its curative and stress-relieving ends. These include treatments for a wide range of conditions, from rheumatism to smoking to the stresses of the modern world to simply getting in shape. There are modern centers at the Marina Baie des Anges in **Villeneuve-Loubet** near Nice, **Antibes, Saint-Raphaël, Fréjus, Port-Camargue**, and **La Grande-Motte**. For information, contact the Maison de la Thalassothérapie, 230 Rue du Faubourg Saint-Honoré, 75008 Paris ((1) 45 63 16 15 FAX (1) 45 63 07 54.

LANGUAGE COURSES
If you'd like to study French, the **Institut de Français**, 06230 Villefranche-sur-Mer (93 01 88 44 FAX 93 76 92 17, offers intensive courses for adults in two to four week cycles. In Avignon, you can study French at the **Centre de Recherche et d'Études**, 35 Rue Joseph Vernet (90 82 68 10.

GARDEN VISITS
For those with a special interest in horticulture, the most important gardens are the **Tropical Garden** and the **Colombières Garden** in **Menton**, the **Exotic Gardens** in **Monaco** and **Èze**, the gardens of the **Ephrussi de Rothschild** in **Cap-Ferrat**, the **Thuret Garden** in **Cap**

d'Antibes, **Princesse Pauline's Garden** and the **Noailles Gardens** in **Grasse**, and the **Olbius Riquier Gardens** in **Hyères**.

THE RELIGIOUS HERITAGE
Christianity first established itself in France in the Mediterranean area, and important remains of Gallo-Roman and very early medieval churches and monasteries are to be found in the Îles-de-Lérins, Fréjus, Marseille and Arles in Provence, and in Elne and Serrabone in Roussillon. The Romanesque results of the full flowering of the medieval monastic movement can be found as you travel throughout the region (see ROMANESQUE, page 78).

Mediterranean France also played a crucial role in Jewish history in France, particularly during the Middle Ages, when the Kingdom of France expelled the Jews and they took refuge in the Papal lands of the Comtat Venaissin in what is now the Vaucluse. The oldest synagogue in France is in Carpentras, and there are other vestiges of the medieval Jewish presence in Cavaillon, Avignon and other places in the Comtat. For a fascinating free brochure on the subject entitled *The Road of Jewish Heritage in the South of France*, contact the Comité Départemental du Tourisme de Vaucluse, Place Campana, 84000 Avignon (90 86 43 42.

Taking a Tour

For people who prefer to let the travel professionals lay out their itineraries and handle all the logistics, a number of companies offer package deals in Southern France. Because of their bargaining power with airlines and hotels, the arrangements they make are often less expensive than they would be if you made the same bookings on your own.

"VISIT FRANCE" ORGANIZED TOURS
The organization with the most extensive array of programs is Visit France, a subsidiary of Air Inter, the domestic airline of Air France. The trips run from simple air travel-hotel-auto rental arrangements in dozens of cities and towns throughout the region to more focused stays, including a cruise on the Rhône, gastronomic visits to Marseille, the birthplace of *bouillabaisse*, Castelnaudary, the home of *cassoulet*, and the *haute cuisine* center of Cannes, a Camargue safari, a deluxe golf weekend in Monaco, tennis at the Club Pierre Barthés in Cap d'Agde, skiing at Isola 2000, *thalassothérpie* (salt water-oriented health programs) at a number of centers along the coast, and attending Nice's Carnival and its Jazz Festival.

The selection of hotels is excellent. So is their colorful and informative brochure, which I highly recommend your ordering or picking up at a travel agency. In France, Visit France's packages can be booked by any travel agent. In the United States, they are represented by Jet Vacations, 1775 Broadway (Suite 2405), New York, N.Y. 10019 ((212) 474-8740 FAX 586-2069; in Canada, Jet Tours Canada, 2000 Mansfield (Suite 1410), Montreal, Quebec H3A 3A2 ((514) 847-5099 FAX 285-1843; in Great Britain, by Air France Holidays, Gable House, 18-24 Turham Green Terrace, London W4 1RF ((44-81) 242-0808 FAX 742-3445; in Australia, by Eurovacations, 4/62 Clarence Street, Sydney NSW 2000 ((02) 262-6398 FAX 262-6301; in New Zealand, by General Travel New Zealand, Dataset House, 143 Nelson Street, Auckland 1 ((64-9) 377-1764 FAX 309-4167; in South Africa, by Thomsons, P.O. Box 41032, Craighall 2024 ((011) 788-0810 FAX 788-2664. In foreign countries, Visit France's trips are marketed under the name of the local representative.

AMERICAN EXPRESS
Another organization that can arrange just about anything for you is American Express. For information on their services, call them in your local area or from anywhere in the United States at 900-990-0400 (there is a phone charge of 50 cents a minute). Their offices and correspondents in Mediterranean France can book local sightseeing trips, coach excursions, boat trips, rental and chauffeur-driven cars on an *à la carte* basis. Their main office in the region is American Express-Daro Voyages, 11 Promenade des Anglais, 06000 Nice (93 16 53 53 FAX 93 16 53 42.

ALLEZ FRANCE
This friendly British outfit that offers a wide range of trips — golf holidays, wine tours, canal boat rentals, mobile and home holidays, short breaks in Nice, Antibes, Juan-les-Pins, the Grand Canyon du Verdon — and a large selection of rental apartments, cottages and villas, with color photos of them in their brochure. Allez France is at 27 West Street, Storrington, West Sussex RH20 4DZ ((01903) 742 345 FAX 745 044.

GOLF TOURS
InterGolf offers golfing tours of the French Riviera from the United States. For information, get in touch with them at P.O. Box 500608, Atlanta GA 31150-0608 ((404) 518-1250 FAX 518-1272, United States toll-free number (800) 468-0051. Another United States company offering golf tours on the Riviera is the Holiday Emporium, 12044 Ventura Boulevard, Studio City CA ((818) 985-2814, and in England, Par-Tee Tours,

Fairway House, North Road, Chorleywood WD3 5LE ((0923) 284 558. There is a fax at this number too.

ORGANIZED BIKING AND WALKING TOURS
For outstanding biking and walking trips in Provence, get in touch with Butterfield & Robinson in Canada. The group leaders are bright and knowledgeable, the food and accommodations top-of-the-line, and their brochure is a work of art. It goes without saying that these trips are not cheap. They also rent country homes in Provence and the Côte d'Azur. Their address is 70 Bond Street, Toronto, Ontario M5B 1X3 ((416) 864-1354 FAX 864-0541. Their toll-free number in the United States is (800) 678-1147 and in Canada (800) 268-8415.

CULTURAL AND EDUCATIONAL PROGRAMS
For information on the full range of cultural and educational programs available in Mediterranean France — crafts workshops, art and music classes, studies of the French language and culture, and so forth — contact the Cultural Service of the French Embassy or Consulate closest to you.

There are always plenty of archaeology projects under way in Provence and Languedoc that need summer volunteers. To find out what these projects are, write to the Direction des Antiquités Préhistoriques et Historiques, 21 Boulevard du Roy René, 13617 Aix-en-Provence, or 5 bis Rue de la Salle l'Évêque, 24000 Montpellier.

ABOVE: A biking tour in Provence.

Welcome to Mediterranean France

IF YOU COME TO THE south of France in the long, hot days of summer, you will hear a shrill rasping chant in the background wherever you go: the ceaseless song of the cicada. *"Le soleil me fait chanter"* chirps the noisy insect — "The sun makes me sing." Provençal children smile. They know what many Northerners have been thrilled to discover later in life — Van Gogh, Matisse and Chagall among them: In Mediterranean France, the sun makes everything sing.

And this is clearly the sun's country. It's hot and dry in the summer and, like the rest of the Mediterranean basin, warm the year round. In all four of its regions, the Côte d'Azur, Provence, Languedoc, and Roussillon, you will find 3,000 hours of sunshine a year, and temperatures that rarely drop below 11° C (52° F) even in the winter, a stark contrast to Paris and the rest of Northern France known for its cold and overcast days. Geography and climate have conspired to make this ten percent of France's surface a paradise for nature lovers, sports enthusiasts and sun worshipers who come south to "lizard themselves," as the French say, on the beaches.

Mediterranean France is shaped like a giant Greek amphitheater, ideally oriented south and east, facing the sun and sea. Nine chains of mountains wall in this crescent-shaped arena, flanked on either side by the two greatest ranges in Europe, the Alps and the Pyrénées. The seven other ranges, including the Alpes-de-Haute-Provence and the Cévennes, with heights up to 1,700 m (5,580 ft), are only 200 km (125 miles) or less from the shore in most places. The nearly unbroken rampart 700 km (440 miles) long locks in the Mediterranean warmth and provides a barrier against the cold drafts of the North.

But the Mediterranean Sea, the region's other boundary, has always provided a gateway to the outside world through the dozens of ports scattered along 520 km (325 miles) of coastline between Italy and Spain. Since this region fronts on the sea that was the Cradle of Western Civilization, it has a cultural heritage as brilliant as its weather.

The seeds were planted by Greek seafarers who arrived in the seventh century BC with the vine, the olive tree and Ionian ideas. They established towns along the coast and a style of eating, drinking and making merry that characterizes Mediterranean France to this day. To them we must add the other peoples who brought their influences to the area — Romans, early Christians, Catalans, Italians, Cathars from the Balkans, Protestants from Switzerland and Germany and the Gauls, Celts and Franks from what is now Northern France.

The other main route of travel between the Mediterranean coast of France and the outside world has always been the Rhône River and its valley, the only corridor between North and South. The Greeks used it for trade, the Romans to conquer Northern Europe, and the Northern French to invade the South.

The valley also acts as a massive ventilating system, for it is down the Rhône that the *Mistral*, the "Master Wind" hurls itself from the North. This wind can be fierce and sometimes dangerous. But it is also responsible for the famed sparklingly clear days and nights that Van Gogh captured so brilliantly in his sunflower paintings and his "Starry Night."

While I can't hope to fully convey all the human dimensions of an area that has been

shaped by 2,600 years of evolution and cross-cultural pollination, I have tried to point out the major influences that have created the distinctive cultures of the the Côte d'Azur, Provence, Languedoc and Roussillon. I think of Mediterranean France as a gigantic tapestry with its threads of history woven into the fabric of today. Where else can you watch a modern dance program in the courtyard of the fourteenth century Palace of the Popes, wine and dine in a beautifully restored Romanesque abbey, or attend a bullfight in a 2,000 year-old Roman Arena? To me, this area's greatest appeal has always been the relaxed, natural Mediterranean blend of the very old and the very new. My travels in this part of the world have given me some of the most pleasurable moments in my life, and I hope, as historian Fernand Braudel puts it, that "a little of this joy and a great deal of Mediterranean sunlight will shine from the pages of this book."

OPPOSITE: Entrevaux in the Alps of Upper Provence, fortified by Louis XIV to defend France's Var River frontier with the Duchy of Savoy.
ABOVE: Collioure, a magnet for painters since the days of Matisse.

The Country and its People

AS THE CROSSROADS between Italy and Spain, the Mediterranean basin and Northern Europe, this region had no choice but to have a tumultuous life. Since the days of the Greeks and Romans, the main currents of Western European history have swept back and forth through here — Charlemagne, the Albigensian Crusade, the Popes of Avignon, Napoléon, the World War II Allied landings, the European Union today. This is by no means a simple story. But if it seems at times too crowded with actors and events, it may help you to keep in mind that only a few important powers have dominated the region over its three thousand years of history. They were the Greeks, the Romans, three houses of medieval lords, and, from the thirteenth century onward, the Kingdom, Empire and Republic of France. To these we should add the pervasive influence of the Roman Catholic Church, a major factor in art and architecture, politics and all aspects of social behavior from the latter years of the Roman Empire to the present.

THE FIRST MILLION YEARS

The first human beings to set foot in Europe crossed the Straits of Gibraltar from Africa a million years ago. Not surprisingly, they wasted no time getting up to the Côte d'Azur. Stone tools and bone fragments from 950,000 years ago found in a cave at Roquebrune-Cap-Martin are the oldest evidence of human presence in Europe. 500,000 years later, Tautavel Man hunted in the valleys north of Roussillon, where his skull, the oldest discovered in Europe, was found in a cave north of Perpignan, along with bones of the elephants, woolly rhinoceroses and deer that were his prey. Similar refuse from Stone Age hunters' feasts was found in a cave at Terra Amata at the foot of Mount Boron in Nice. Though other hunters undoubtedly roamed the hills and valleys of Mediterranean France over much of the period, no evidence of their presence during the next few hundred thousand years has surfaced. But in 1985 the next important trace of prehistoric man's activities in the area came to light — cave drawings skillfully depicting penguins, seals and land animals that were discovered in a grotto near Marseille. These paintings from 18,000 to 27,000 years old are the oldest European artwork ever found, predating those at Lascaux in the Périgord by up to 13,000 years. The paintings were discovered by scuba diver Henri Cosquer in a cave that was submerged when the level of the Mediterranean rose after the last Ice Age.

In December 1994, another astounding discovery was made at Combe d'Arc in the Ardèche northwest of Avignon: four large caves containing over three hundred clear, extremely skillful paintings of mammoths, rhinos, lions, oxen, a red hyena and the only panther and owls recorded in prehistoric cave paintings. These are believed to be 20,000 years old. This area was the northernmost part of Europe inhabited by humans in those chilly times.

Around 6,000 BC, sheep were domesticated in southwest Provence, and hunting gave way to pastoral life. The oldest pottery yet discovered in Western Europe also appeared in Provence at this time. But the strangest reminder of early Man's presence is to be found in Vallée des Merveilles in the Alpes-Maritimes, where more than 100,000 complex abstract designs were scratched into the rocks by Bronze Age shepherds.

By 1,000 BC, Ligurian tribes from northern Italy were farming and raising animals throughout Provence, and living in fortified hilltop settlements known as *oppida*. West of the Rhône, native Iberians followed the same pattern, always settling well in from the coast, partly for practical reasons — staying away from malarial swamps and pirates — but also from a deep-seated peasant distrust of the sea. "*Lauso la mare e tente'n terro,*" goes an old Provençal saying — "Praise the sea and stay on land." The Ligurians' *oppidum* of Entremont near Aix and the Iberians' *oppidum* of Ensérune between Béziers and Narbonne, now well-excavated archaeological sites, grew into large towns. In the seventh century BC, Celts from northern Germany migrated south, married Ligurians and joined them in their bucolic lifestyle. But the next group to arrive came by the sea. They were an adventurous lot with a Dionysian outlook who introduced the characteristic Mediterranean spirit that permeates the region to this day.

THE GREEKS

Around 600 BC, Greek seafarers from Phocaea in Asia Minor came upon a magnificent harbor framed by white limestone hills so reminiscent of the Ionian coast that it must have made their hearts leap. Legend has it that the Phocaeans — not to be confused with the Phoenicians who were a Semitic people from Lebanon — landed in the middle of a ceremony in which Gyptis, the daughter of the area's Ligurian chief, was in the process of choosing a husband. But when she saw the handsome Greek leader Protis, she looked no farther. Not only did her father give his consent to the marriage, but he threw in the harbor as her dowry. The Greeks named the harbor Massalia, which later became known as Marseille. It is the oldest city in France. The only other French cities close to it in age are the colonies Massalia founded in the next two centuries:

Nikaia (Nice), Monoikos (Monaco), Antipolis (Antibes), Athenopolis (Saint-Tropez), Telunion (Toulon), and Agathe (Agde). The Greeks set up trading posts, comptoirs, in the lower Rhône at Arles, Avignon and Orange to barter with local Celto-Ligurians. But more importantly, the Greeks introduced two farm products from back home that would become essential elements in the diet, the economy and the character of the region. "From the first millennium before Christ," writes historian Fernand Braudel, "the civilization of the vine and the olive tree spread westwards from the eastern part of the sea. This basic unity was established far back in time, nature and man working to the same end."

THE ROMANS

In 124 BC, at Massalia's instigation, a Roman army attacked the Celto-Ligurian *oppidum* on the plateau of Entremont, home to a tough bunch of warriors who used to chop off the heads of their enemies and hang them on their front doors. But they were no match for the disciplined Roman legions, who plowed Entremont under. The following year, Consul Caius Sextius Calvinus built the first full-scale Roman settlement in Gaul on the plain below Entremont at the site of a thermal spring. Originally called "Aquae Sextiae" (the waters of Sextius), over the years its name shrank to Aix.

During the Punic Wars in the third century BC, the Massalian Greeks united with the up-and-coming Romans against Carthage, Massalia's principal trade rival, but the Celto-Ligurians did not. They allowed Hannibal to pass freely through their lands as he marched his army and elephants from Spain to Italy in 214 BC. When Carthage went down to defeat in 201 BC, Rome annexed its former colonies in Spain. But since some of the Celto-Ligurian tribes continued to be troublesome, securing a reliable overland route between Italy and Spain turned out to be a thorny problem for the Romans. While their Greek allies were better positioned to crack down on the troublemakers from their settlements along the coast, they had little interest in military matters and preferred to let the Romans come in and handle the tribes, a bit of negligence they would pay for dearly one day.

Within the next few years, the Romans moved permanently into Vaison-la-Romaine, Narbonne and Carcassonne, and in 102 BC, the Roman general Marius wiped out a vast horde of Teutonic invaders in a battle near Aix where an estimated 100,000 men, women and children were killed and another 100,000 taken prisoner. The victory gave its name to the ridge from which Marius observed the battle, Montagne Saint-Victoire, and the name Marius has been a Provençal favorite ever since.

In 49 BC, the cat finally swallowed the canary. Marseille made the mistake of supporting Julius Caesar's rival general Pompey in their civil war,

Portrait of Hadrian in the Roman quarter of Puymin in Vaison-la-Romaine ABOVE LEFT and Roman friezes at the Glanum archeological site in Saint-Rémy-de-Provence ABOVE RIGHT, mementos of five centuries of Roman rule.

and in revenge, Caesar stripped Marseille of its colonies and transferred Rome's trade to the ports that had sided with him. Narbonne, Fréjus and Nice profited handsomely, but the greatest beneficiary was Arles, which supplanted its mother city of Marseille as the dominant port linking the Rhône and the Mediterranean. Narbonne, Rome's main port on the western sweep of the Mediterranean, became the capital of the newly created *Provincia Romana Narbonensis*, and when Augustus (Caesar) wiped out the last Celto-Ligurian tribe that had failed to capitulate in 14 BC, *Provincia Romana Narbonensis* was seamlessly integrated into the economy and culture of the Italian peninsula.

Under the *Pax Romana*, the Golden Age of security and prosperity (golden, that is, for the lucky half who didn't happen to be slaves), the frontiers of the Roman Empire stretched from Scotland to Armenia, and the Romans could truly call the Mediterranean *Mare Nostrum*, "our sea." Though much of what they built in *Provincia Romana* has disappeared, enough remains to give a picture of their style of living during the first two centuries AD. The large arenas of Arles and Nîmes, the theaters of Cimiez in Nice, Vaison-la-Romaine and Orange, and the Pont du Gard aqueduct that fed the baths of Nîmes testify to the paramount role of sensual enjoyment and entertainment in their daily lives, and since they only worked half-days, they had plenty of time to indulge these tastes. Towns such as Vaison-la-Romaine and Glanum near Saint-Rémy grew wealthy from agriculture, while cities at main crossroads prospered from trade, most notably Aix, situated at the intersection of the Aurelian and Decumanus Ways, and Nîmes at the northern end of the Domitian Way to Spain. Nîmes was colonized by ex-legionnaires, as were Narbonne and Orange. The former soldiers were given land grants as a reward for past services and as a way to keep them from getting involved in revolts.

Whatever modest inroads Christianity might have made in the first three centuries AD, it was not until the conversion of Emperor Constantine in the early fourth century that the religion really caught on. Provençal legend has it that Constantine was on his way from Arles to Rome to try to put down a revolt when he had a vision at La Croix-Valmer near Saint-Tropez: a cross in the sky and a sign that said, *"in hoc signo vinces"* ("in this sign you will conquer"). He went on to victory, then converted, and many a Provençal followed suit. In 314, he presided over the first council of bishops held in France at his palace at Arles, one of his favorite cities. In the early fifth century the first Christian monastery, Saint-Victor, was built in Marseille. But even as early as Constantine's time, dry rot had set into the top-heavy, inefficient, slave-based economy, and barbarians were

nibbling at the outer edges of the Empire. Constantine shifted the capital from Rome to Constantinople, and in 395 the Empire split permanently into East and West. The Visigoths, Ostrogoths and Huns put Rome to sack several times in the following century, and in 476, the date marking the fall of the empire, the last Western Roman emperor, one Romulus Augustulus, was chased out of Rome by the Goths, bringing five centuries of political unity in *Provincia Romana* to an end.

THE MIDDLE AGES

The Middle Ages is the thousand-year period from the fall of the Roman Empire to the end of feudalism and the rise of the absolute monarchy in the late fifteenth century. In some parts of Europe, this was a time of almost unmitigated chaos. Mediterranean France would experience its greatest period but also its most tragic defeat at this time.

Unfortunately, the history of this period unfolds in untidy ways, with trails that crisscross and go in many directions. But they all come together eventually with the emergence of the Kingdom of France, Europe's first nation-state, as the dominant power in the South.

After Rome's collapse, one barbarian tribe after another crossed the Alps and rampaged through Provence. Without Roman protection, the region found itself shattered into hundreds of city states and smaller localities, all trying to defend themselves from the hordes. By the sixth century, Caius Sextius Calvinus's once-thriving town of Aix was reduced to a pile of rubble.

The attacks from the east eventually ran their course, only to be replaced by a new cycle of invasions starting in the eighth century, when the Saracens, Spain's Moslem conquerors, crossed the Pyrénées. Their seemingly invincible armies swept a wide path of devastation across Languedoc and Provence and advanced northward until they were finally stopped by Charles Martel and the Franks at the Battle of Poitiers in 732. As Martel and his army pursued the Saracens south, the people of the *Midi* became acquainted with their fellow Christians from the North. It was not a happy experience. Martel sacked the cities of the South so brutally that the people of Arles begged the Saracens to come back and save them.

Charles Martel's son Pepin the Short made himself king in 751 and maintained Frankish domination of the South. His son Charlemagne expanded the kingdom into an empire covering most of Western Europe that he ruled with an iron hand from his capital, Aix-la-Chapelle (Aachen in today's Northern Germany). Charlemagne's influence was such that he had himself crowned Emperor by the Pope personally in Rome in

800 AD, in order to symbolize the union of Church and Empire.

After Charlemagne's death, the empire was divided into three kingdoms — one in France, one in Germany, and a short-lived middle kingdom between them that was soon carved up and absorbed by the French and German kingdoms. Lords owning land to the west of the Rhône became vassals of the king of France and those to the east of it vassals of the king of Germany, who later took the title of Holy Roman Emperor. But as the feudal system developed, a number of the vassals grew richer and more powerful than the kings themselves and ruled their lands with de facto independence. Such was the case with the two powerful ruling houses that emerged in the South — the Counts of Toulouse and the Counts of Barcelona.

The Counts of Toulouse, who had been granted their fief by Charlemagne himself, extended their sway over all of Languedoc from the Garonne to the Rhône, and, by the eleventh century, a large part of northern Provence as well. The Counts of Barcelona started from scratch. After making their fortune from iron mining and advanced metal-working techniques in their Catalan homeland in the Pyrénées, they established themselves as the Counts of Barcelona and Roussillon, and by the early twelfth century had themselves crowned Kings of Aragon. They oversaw a sea trading empire with ports in Barcelona, Majorca, Collioure, Perpignan and Montpellier that rivaled those of Venice and Genoa. And when Count Raimond Bérenger I married Douce de Gévaudan, the daughter of the Count of Provence in 1112 and added the ports of Provence to his holdings, the western Mediterranean became known as "a Catalan lake."

THE AGE OF THE TROUBADOURS

The rule of the Counts of Toulouse and Barcelona ushered in a period of political stability, the economy came to life, and with the support of rich lords and the burgeoning monastic movement, the region launched into a glorious artistic period, with churches and monasteries going up everywhere. Architects studied the Roman models around them, and proceeding from the medieval axiom, "Architecture is applied geometry," created the sublime southern Romanesque style which is seen in Saint-Michel-de-Cuxa in Roussillon, Fontfroide in the Corbières, the Cistercian Abbeys of Silvacane, Sénanque and Le Thoronet in Provence and the Church of Saint-Trophime in Arles. There are hundreds of lesser-known gems from the period also stretching from the Pyrénées to the remote valleys of the Alpes-Maritimes. From the eleventh to the thirteenth centuries "The Age of the Troubadours" developed at the open-

minded courts of the South. Toulouse, Barcelona, Carcassonne, Aix-en-Provence and Les Baux welcomed poets and applauded the ingenious lyrics they sang to the high-born ladies there. The Southern "Courts of Love" reached a level of cultural refinement never before approached in Western Europe, and the troubadour singing in the mellow accents of the *Midi* replaced the warrior as the popular hero of the day. While the official language of the clergy and upper classes remained Latin, three vernaculars, all closely related, developed in Southern France. They were Provençal, Catalan, and the Langue d'Oc, so-called because the word for "yes," was "*oc*," from the Latin "*hoc*" (as opposed to the Langue d'Oïl spoken in Paris, in which "yes" was "*oïl*," from the Latin "*ille*"). So widely accepted were these vernaculars as the languages of poetry that Dante, who traveled in Provence, considered writing his *Divine Comedy* in Provençal.

These new cultural centers in the South created cultural links not only among themselves, but also with Italy and Spain and with Arab and Jewish thinkers, who were far more advanced in science and medicine than the Europeans. This rich exchange intensified when the Crusades began in 1095 and traffic between east and west increased dramatically. Montpellier, the great medical school of the Middle Ages, got its head start through its Arab cultural contacts.

The "what ifs" of history are always stimulating to speculate about — and the great one of this region's history is "What if the Catalan-Occitan-Provençal culture had continued to knit together and ended up by forming a nation?" Imagine a country stretching from Catalonia to the Maritime Alps, with Barcelona, Montpellier, Toulouse, Marseille and Nice as its centers of production, commerce and culture. But that was not to be. And ironically, it was the very quality we admire most about this Southern culture — its openness to new ideas and different people — that would become its undoing. Because this openness also extended to new ideas about religion, and that was a realm the Church of Rome considered its exclusive jurisdiction.

At the end of the twelfth century, the Church, which had become so rich and self-involved that it had lost touch with the people, suddenly woke up to the fact that it had a full-blown "heresy" on its hands in Languedoc.

THE ALBIGENSIAN CRUSADE

The heretics were called Cathars, from *cathari*, meaning "pure" in Greek, and were also known in France as Albigensians, because Albi in northern Languedoc was one of the religion's main centers. A dualistic religion that grew out of the

Manichaean belief in two divine forces, one good and the other evil, the Cathar movement developed in the Balkans in the eleventh century and spread rapidly through Languedoc in the twelfth century, due in large part to the interest of ladies of noble families, since in the Cathar religion, women were seen as equals to men in the eyes of God. The religion advocated Bible study in the vernacular, direct personal communication with God, and austerity — ecclesiastical wealth and power being especially evil — all of which were extremely threatening ideas to Rome. The Church tried but failed in its efforts to persuade the lords of Languedoc to root out the "heretics" (often the lords' own wives and relatives), and when the papal legate dealing with the heresy was murdered at the door of the Abbey of Saint-Gilles in 1208 by a follower of the Count of Toulouse, Pope Innocent III seized on the incident to enlist the Northern nobility in a crusade. He offered them the same incentives that they were offered in the crusades against the Moslems in the Holy Land — the right to any lands taken from the heretics or their defenders and entry into Heaven for any who died in the process. In the cold light of history, the Albigensian Crusade has gone down as a cynical land grab by the northern aristocracy and a political power play by the Church.

In 1209 an army of 50,000 Northerners (some estimates go much higher) invaded Languedoc. It was led by "God's Madman," Simon de Montfort, perhaps the most hate-inspiring man in all of French history, though Arnaud-Amaury, the Crusade's Papal Legate, may be even worse. He is reported to have said when asked how to distinguish the heretics from the faithful during the siege of Béziers, "Kill them all. God will recognize His own."

Béziers fell in 1209, Carcassonne next, and year after year, de Montfort and his men murdered and burned their way through Languedoc. King Pedro II of Aragon finally broke away from a crusade of his own against the Moslems in Spain to come to the aid of his relation by marriage, Count Raymond VI of Toulouse. But in 1213 King Pedro was killed at the Battle of Muret, and the Southerners went down to catastrophic defeat. While all hope of victory ended that day for the Cathars, many took to the dramatic hilltop fortresses in the Corbières known as the "Five Sons of Carcassonne," which did not fall until mid-century. To track down individual heretics, put them on trial and send them to the stake if convicted, the Church created an new agency that would later to go to greater fame in Spain — the Inquisition.

After the defeat of the Cathars, Aragon signed the Treaty of Corbeil in 1258 giving up its claims to all lands north of Roussillon, and the Kingdom of France took title to the Count of Toulouse's lands. Further extending France's presence in the

South, in 1241, King Louis IX (later canonized as Saint Louis), purchased a piece of land on the western shore of the Camargue from a local monastery and built the port of Aigues-Mortes for his Crusades to the Holy Land. This was the Kingdom of France's first foothold on the Mediterranean coast, and a signal, if another one was needed, that the North had come South to stay.

THE FLOWERING OF PROVENCE

Five years later in 1246, King Louis's crafty younger brother, Charles of Anjou, made himself Count of Provence by marrying Count Raimond Bérenger V's daughter Beatrice, a sister of Louis's wife Marguerite. (To give an idea of how much prestige the Count of Provence enjoyed, his two other daughters married King Henry III of England and the Holy Roman Emperor). Two decades

later, through arms and Papal intrigue, Charles of Anjou made himself King of Naples, and for the better part of the next two centuries, the Angevin dynasty would be far more occupied with holding onto its hotly-contested kingship of Naples than in governing the lands in Provence.

In 1274, ever solicitous of good relations with the Pope, Charles entered into an agreement with his nephew King Philip III (the Bold) of France to transfer to the Papacy most of the rural lands in Northern Provence formerly owned by the Count of Toulouse, as a delayed reward for the Church's role in the Albigensian Crusade. In 1309, Philip IV (the Fair) persuaded French-born Pope Clement V to leave Rome, then in the throes of anarchy, and move to the Comtat Venaissin, the Church's property in Provence where the French could offer him protection with their strongholds across the Rhône. So, in the greatest shock of the Middle Ages, the Papacy moved from the Eternal City to

this hitherto unnoticed corner of the world. Later Popes moved into Avignon and built its huge Papal Palace, and in 1348, the year of the plague that killed half the population of Southern France, Pope Clement VI "purchased" the city of Avignon from the beautiful, flamboyant Queen Jeanne of Naples, the Countess of Provence. In fact, this was her bargain with the Papacy to buy her way out of the charge of murdering her husband, Andrew of Hungary. The Church never paid for its purchase, but Queen Jeanne went back to Naples relieved of her immediate problem.

This sort of cynical merchandising of divine pardon infuriated poet Francesco Petrach, who worked for a cardinal in Avignon. He called the city "a sink of vice" and said, "Everything there

The Papal Palace in Avignon, the seat of the Catholic Church when the Popes abandoned Rome in the fourteenth century.

The Country and its People

71

breathes a lie — the air, the earth, the houses, and especially the bedrooms." Venal souls though they were, one can't help being grateful to the Popes of Avignon for their palace, the ramparts around the city, and the fine body of fourteenth century paintings that they commissioned.

Seven Popes reigned during the "Babylonian Captivity" from 1309 to 1377, followed by two anti-Popes, the last one leaving Avignon in 1409. The Church would continue to own Avignon and the Comtat Venaissin, however, for another three centuries until the French Revolution took them over in a peaceful transition in 1791.

In 1382, Queen Jeanne of Naples ended her scandal-ridden life true to fashion by being murdered by one of her cousins. A struggle for power broke out in the House of Anjou, and Duke Amadeus VII of Savoy took advantage of it for his own ends. In 1388, he persuaded Jean Grimaldi, the Angevin governor of Provence's County of Nice, to bring Nice under the protection of the House of Savoy, thus giving the landlocked duchy in the Italian Alps the port on the Mediterranean it coveted. Nice's five centuries of Savoyard rule before joining France in 1860 would give it the distinctively Italian flavor it has to this day.

The last Angevin Count of Provence was the colorful "Good King" René, who presided over the most artistic court in Europe in Aix-en-Provence from 1434 to 1480. His title of "king" came from his claim to the throne of Naples, which had been lost by the House of Anjou before his time. As for "good," taxpayers in Provence found that a questionable title, too. They grumbled about the tax money he squandered on schemes to recover the lost throne and his lavish spending on the arts. René was a poet, a painter, a composer, a scientist, adept in all the classical languages and several modern ones — a throwback to the great days of the troubadours and a precursor of the Renaissance man. A body of myth later credited him with painting the famous "Burning Bush" triptych (Nicholas Froment actually painted it), in which the sleek, well-fed king appears in one of the side panels. He did however, introduce the silkworm and the muscat grape to Provence, and they created prosperity for years to come. We can still savor his grapes in Muscat de Beaumes-de-Venise, the delicious aperitif wine.

René also built mighty Tarascon castle on the Rhône facing the French King's castle across the river at Beaucaire. As Count of Provence, René was still a vassal of the Holy Roman Emperor, and the Rhône was, as it been had since the break-up of Charlemagne's realm, the frontier between the Kingdom of France and the Holy Roman Empire, one of the last remaining vestiges of the feudal period.

Good King René died in 1480, and the glory days of Provençal culture with him. His nephew

and heir Charles of Maine died without heirs the following year and willed Provence to the Kingdom of France. Reinvigorated by their triumph over the English in the Hundred Years War, which had ended thirty years earlier, the French kings were in the process of unifying the country under strong centralized royal authority. The feudal system was over.

THE FRENCH IN THE SOUTH

Under French rule, Provence was governed by a viceroy but had its own local assembly, the Parliament of Aix, which had powers of taxation.

Provençals had traditionally bemoaned two local scourges, the blustery *mistral* and the flood-prone Durance. Now they added a third — the tax-prone Parliament of Aix. In 1539, the death of Provençal and Languedoc culture was put into law by the Edict of Villers-Cotterêts. It established French, the *Langue d'Oil*, as the only language to be used in official communications — a blatant act of Northern cultural imperialism that automatically reduced Southerners to second-class citizenship.

At the same time, Protestantism took root in the South, always France's most fertile ground for "heresy." It spread rapidly in Provence and Languedoc, and as in the time of the Albigensian Crusade, repression was not long in coming. The Wars of Religion were a series of intermittent wars between Catholics and Protestants in many parts of France in the late sixteenth century. They started in 1542 with the massacre of the Vaudois sect in the Lubéron, 2,000 executed and 800 sold as galley slaves in this crack-down by the crown and the Parliament of Aix. As in the time of the Cathars, the violence in Languedoc was especially grave. Appalling acts of brutality were committed by both sides, but the Protestants, who were greatly outnumbered, got the worst of it, and thousands died in their strongholds of Nîmes, Aigues-Mortes and Montpellier. Tens of thousands went into exile or took to the Cévennes Mountains for refuge. The violence finally ended in 1598 when King Henry IV, a Protestant who had tactically converted to Catholicism, issued the Edict of Nantes, which guaranteed toleration of

In 1659, France and Spain settled on the Pyrénées as their border. Catalonia was split in two, Roussillon going to France, the rest remaining under Spanish rule. The Catalans had supported France in the war, hoping to be rewarded with all of Catalonia as a buffer state between France and Spain. But their hopes were betrayed for France's geopolitical aims.

"The Great Century," as the seventeenth century is known, was a time for grand projects, the Palace of Versailles being the grandest, but from an engineering point of view, the great project of the South was more than its equal. In 1666, Louis XIV and his chief minister Colbert gave Baron Pierre-Paul Riquet of Béziers authorization

Protestantism and allowed Protestants to keep several fortified places as safeguards.

In the seventeenth century, Cardinal Richelieu reactivated the persecutions. As secretary of state and then chief minister to Louis XIII from 1616 to 1642, he worked obsessively to impose the power of the crown over all areas of French life, and since the Huguenots were seen as per se disloyal to the Catholic king, they had to be brought to heel. In 1622, Louis XIII invaded Montpellier, the leading center of Protestantism in the South, and once more it became the scene of terrible bloodshed. Territorial expansion was another of Richelieu's priorities, and in the South, he focused on Roussillon. In a war with Spain in the 1640's, Louis XIII led a long siege against Perpignan in which the defenders earned the nickname of "rat eaters." Hearing that Perpignan had finally fallen, the Cardinal died a happy man in 1642.

The Country and its People

to go ahead on the construction of the Canal du Midi, a barge canal linking the Atlantic and the Mediterranean by way of Toulouse and the Garonne. It had been a dream since the time of the Romans, but the mountains had defied all previous plans. After fifteen years of construction with up to 10,000 workers at a time, the largest and most ingenious engineering feat of the century was completed in 1681, bringing new prosperity to Languedoc, since it could now ship its wine and grain to any place in the world.

But only a few years later Louis XIV visited destruction on the land. In 1685, he revoked the Edict of Nantes, and once again Montpellier and Nîmes were under attack. Many took refuge in the Cévennes, and countless Protestants left France

Aigues-Mortes, the Kingdom of France's first port on the Mediterranean.

for good — a loss to the country of many of its most industrious people.

In his long reign from 1643 to 1715, Louis XIV led France into one foreign war after another, most with little to show at the end. But his last war brought France a valuable property in the South, the Principality of Orange, which had been owned by the Dutch royal family since the early sixteenth century. It was ceded to France by the Treaty of Utrecht in 1713.

The Sun King also put his brilliant military architect Sébastien Vauban to work on a vast fortress-building program. Vauban's forts and ramparts dot Mediterranean France from Antibes and Entrevaux on France's eastern frontier with

Savoy to the far south along France's recently acquired Pyrénées border with Spain at Ville-franche-de-Conflent, Mont-Louis and other key spots in the mountains. Along with Roman ruins, Romanesque abbeys and walled hilltop villages, Vauban's constructions rank as the most dominant architectural features of Mediterranean France.

The military projects of Louis XIV cost a fortune, however, and the ruinous state in which he left France at his death in 1715 would be one of the main causes of the downfall of the Kingdom in 1789.

Despite religious and other wars and several plagues, including one that killed more than half Marseille's population in 1720, Provence and Languedoc prospered under French rule in the seventeenth and eighteenth centuries. Marseille became France's main commercial port, while Montpellier, after losing its shipping business to Marseille, went on to new prosperity in textile manufacturing. Toulon prospered as France's main naval base and Antibes as France's eastern-most port. But the greatest beneficiary of *La Paix Française* was the Provençal capital of Aix, whose dozens of elegant seventeenth- and eighteenth-century residences speak volumes about the sweetness of life before the Revolution.

REVOLUTION AND EMPIRE

The French Revolution brought on considerable bloodshed and destruction of the Church and nobles' property in Aix, where an estimated 8,000 clergy and aristocrats lost their lives. But while there were isolated incidents of violence elsewhere, compared to many other parts of France, the level of destructiveness was relatively mild. In the cities, the "reds" of the urban proletariat welcomed the Revolution, but the rural majority showed little enthusiasm for it, remaining "whites" — royalists — in their hearts. Administratively, the Revolution brought far-reaching changes. In 1790, the large historical provinces of France — Brittany, Aquitaine, Provence and the rest — were abolished and divided into a number of smaller, county-sized administrative units called *départements* with directors, *préfets*, appointed by the central government in Paris. The aim was to keep political power out of the hands of the land-owning aristocrats who had formerly controlled the regions. By weakening regional authority, the Revolutionary government gave itself more of a stranglehold over the country than the kings had had. Provence was divided into two parts, once-proud Aix was stripped of its capital status and proletarian Marseille became the capital of the newly created *département* (county) of Bouches-du-Rhône. In 1791 the Revolution further extended its grip on southern France by taking control of the papal properties of Avignon and the Comtat Venaissin. With Orange and the Lubéron added to it, this became the *département*, or county, of the Vaucluse.

In 1792 a troupe of 500 volunteer militiamen, "reds" from Marseille, marched to Paris to join the Revolution. Waving tri-colored flags, they sang a new tune called "The Song of the Army of the Rhine," whose melodramatic and bloodthirsty words caught the spirit of the times. By the time they reached Paris people were calling the song *La Marseillaise*.

With the execution of the King, an armed rebellion against the Revolution broke out in the South, and French royalists joined with the British to seize the military port of Toulon. A 23 year-old artillery officer named Napoléon Bonaparte distinguished himself in 1793 by his brilliant tactics in the retaking of Toulon, and was promoted to brigadier general. This was one of the Corsican's few happy associations on the mainland of Mediterranean France. Other than General Masséna, his *"enfant chéri de la victoire"* ("beloved child of victory"), who was from Nice, Napoléon had little use for Southerners. As fighting men, they lacked the level of zest he required, and as royalists, they were not to be trusted by a man who wanted to be Emperor. The people of the South had little use for Napoléon either. In 1815, after escaping his exile in Elba and landing at Golfe-Juan between Cannes and Antibes, he had to sneak through the mountains of Provence on a shepherd's trail for fear of being betrayed to the royal authorities.

THE NINETEENTH CENTURY

In the 1830's, France, which had lost most of its original colonies to the English during the late eighteenth century, made itself a colonial power again, first in Algeria, then expanding into Africa and the Far East. As "The Gateway to Africa and the Orient," Marseille thrived as never before, especially after the opening of the Suez Canal in 1869.

France's last major territorial expansion in Europe came in 1860, when Napoléon III made a deal with the House of Savoy to provide French military forces to help Savoy dislodge Austria from northern Italy in exchange for Savoy giving France its rights to the County of Nice. In a referendum held the same year, Nice voted to join France, much to the chagrin of Nice-born Italian patriot Giuseppe Garibaldi, and Menton and Roquebrune, former possessions of Monaco, followed suit. This was one of Napoléon III's few foreign policy successes. Had it failed, Nice would probably be the westernmost city in Italy today.

By the time Nice and Menton joined France, they were already popular wintering places for the English upper classes, as was Cannes. After the original casino in Monte-Carlo was built in the 1860's, royalty and the rich flocked to the gaming tables. And the Riveria launched into the extravaganza of luxurious living known as *la belle époque*. The age of mass tourism was born on the Côte d'Azur.

The late nineteenth century also saw the emergence of a serious literary movement in Provence, where Poet Frédéric Mistral and his followers were struggling to revive the grand tradition of Southern poetry. Centered in Arles, the Félibrige was a literary group that started creating works in the Occitan languages, Langue d'Oc and Provençal, dialects of the great days of the troubadours. Mistral won the Nobel Prize for Literature 1904 and left a legacy of renewed pride in the Occitan culture that had been systematically suppressed since the Edict of Villers-Cotterêts.

In the 1870's phylloxera, a virulent infestation of plant lice from vines imported from America, devastated most of the vineyards throughout France. Provence and Languedoc suffered tremendous losses. In 1874 there were two-and-a-half million hectares (six million acres) of vineyards under cultivation in Languedoc-Roussillon, but by 1900 only one-and-a-half million hectares (four million acres) remained. Resistant root stock from America brought a slow recovery,

but for the growers the disruption of the market was devastating. By the time the vines recovered in the early part of the century all the power was in the hands of middlemen, *négociants*, who squeezed the growers so unmercifully that a general revolt broke out in Languedoc in 1907. The widespread development of wine cooperatives in Languedoc and throughout the region dates from this troubled period.

THE WAR YEARS

In World War I, the South shared the tragedy of the rest of France, losing twenty-five percent of its

young men in the conflict, but was spared the devastation suffered by the Northeastern area. As France's largest port and a major industrial city, Marseille continued to prosper, but on the Côte d'Azur the war put an end to the lavish *belle époque* period. The biggest spenders, Czar Nicholas and the Russian aristocracy, were lost to the Russian Revolution, and other royal visitors stayed away for the duration. In the 1920's, celebrity artists and writers such as Matisse, Cocteau and Scott Fitzgerald set the tone. The new vogue of sunbathing became the rage, along with the old habit of spending money, until the Great Depression put a damper on those wild and carefree days.

During the first three years of World War II, Mediterranean France suffered no physical damage, but after the Germans occupied the South in November, 1942, extensive destruction followed. It started with the French Navy scuttling their own fleet in the harbor of Toulon to keep it from falling into German hands, and the region's ports and industrial cities were bombed extensively by the Allies. The Germans dynamited Marseille's Panier quarter, a casbah-like immigrant

OPPOSITE: Louis XIV in an unlikely pose at the Promenade du Peyrou in Montpellier. ABOVE: *Belle époque* splendor at the Grand Casino of Monte-Carlo.

neighborhood that harbored *Résistance* fighters, and just before the Allied landings in Provence, blew up the port of Saint-Tropez. In Arles, the two houses Van Gogh had lived in were leveled by allied bombs. On August 15, 1944, the Allies made Normandy-style landings on the beaches of Saint-Tropez and the coast of the Maures and, with strong support from the *Résistance* in Marseille, Toulon and Nice, quickly drove the Germans and Italians out.

TODAY'S MEDITERRANEAN FRANCE

The post-War period has seen a radical transformation of Mediterranean France, touching every aspect of the way people live. The population of the region, now six-and-a-half million, has doubled in the towns and cities along the coast. A huge building boom that started in the 1960's on the Côte d'Azur and spread along the coast has resulted in tens of thousands of new structures going up, and unfortunately, aesthetics has been the last thing most of their builders have had in mind. The area east of the Rhône, including the large cities of Nice, Marseille and Toulon, has become one of the most densely populated areas in France. But within it there are enormous discrepancies between the built-up coastal areas and the inland rural areas. After the War, *désertification* — the abandonment of villages set in as the population migrated to the cities. Once-thriving villages became ghost towns and have only been saved from extinction by crafts people who settled there from the 1960's onward (in Tourettes-sur-Loup near Vence, for example) or by purchasers of second homes (*à la* Peter Mayle in the chic Lubéron).

To the west of the Rhône, a De Gaulle and Pompidou government program to develop the coast resulted in two dozen modern middle-class beach resort towns springing up, but there is still much more open space between them than on the Côte d'Azur. The inland areas of Languedoc-Roussillon are also more open because of the volume of agriculture in the region. The population density there is far below the national average.

Mediterranean France has also seen tremendous economic growth and change since the 1960's, with 70 percent of today's work force now employed in service occupations. With 240 million overnight stays registered each year in the Provence-Alpes-Côte d'Azur region and 85 million in Languedoc-Roussillon, tourism supplies the most jobs and income, and Cannes, Nice, Monaco and Montpellier have developed major convention centers and other facilities to attract business tourism to compensate for the seasonal nature of vacation tourism. The many high-tech-nology operations that have installed themselves in the region, drawn by the prestigious universities in Montpellier, Aix-Marseille and Nice, have also become a major factor in the region's economy. Sophia-Antipolis, the large, modern technology park in a pine forest between Nice and Antibes, bills itself as "the Silicon Valley of France," and formerly staid Montpellier has become one of the liveliest cities in France, thanks to its computer, telecommunications and medical technology businesses. These sectors are very vulnerable to economic fluctuations, however, and unfortunately the business downturn of the 1990's gave Montpellier one of the highest unemployment rates in France.

Besides the more modern industries, Mediterranean France continues to support itself by its traditional occupations. The Côte d'Azur grows vast amounts of flowers for its perfume industry and the florist trade, and Provence is France's leading producer of fruit and rosé wines. Languedoc and Roussillon remain France's largest wine producer. Almost 10 percent of the work force there cultivates the land. While Marseille's traditional industries of shipping and heavy industry have declined since the War, it remains Southern Europe's main port, and its huge steel plants and petrochemical zones west of the city are major employers.

Politically, Mediterranean France is in stronger shape than it has been in centuries in relation to central government as a result of the move to decentralization. In 1982 the French government established regional governments in which several departments were grouped together to form larger administrative units with locally elected leadership. In the Mediterranean area two regional governments were created, Provence-Alpes-Côte d'Azur comprising six departments with its capital in Marseille, and Languedoc-Roussillon with five departments and its capital in Montpellier. Paris still has most of the power, but decentralization has given the regions considerably more control over their own cultural and economic directions.

The wave of the economic future in both Mediterranean regions is toward the formation of economic mini-states capable of competing effectively in the European Union business environment in the "post-tourist" economy of the twenty-first century. In the Nice-Antibes area, the first building block is already in place with the Sophia-Antipolis complex, and plans are being drawn up to link the economy of the eastern Côte d'Azur with that of Northern Italy. In Languedoc, a high-tech axis between Montpellier and Nîmes was formed in the 1960's and has spread south to Perpignan. Plans for the future call for a link-up with the economies of Marseille and Aix, which have also become centers for high technology. A high-technology Age of the Troubadours may be in the offing for the twenty-first century.

Yet for all the changes, some for the better and some for the worse, the Mediterranean remains the Mediterranean. *Mare nostrum* is "our sea" not just for the Romans, but for anyone who has shared in the great, ancient culture born on these shores. And if the coast has gotten annoyingly modern in places, all you need to do is go a short distance inland where vineyards and olive orchards fan out from little hilltop villages and the timeless quality of the Mediterranean remains.

LIFE AND ART

Any notions you might have about the supposed distinction between Life and Art will evaporate quickly as you stroll through a market in Mediterranean France, where the ramble itself becomes an aesthetic experience. The light of the region — "soft and tender, in spite of its brilliance," as Matisse termed it — gives an extraordinary luminosity to the colors of fruits and vegetables raising them to the level of artistic delight. Add the aesthetic pleasure of medieval houses or neoclassic arcades surrounding the market and the artistry of a local craftsman whose work you pause to admire, and you start to understand why, given a atmosphere such as this, this region has nourished so much artistic achievement over the past two thousand years.

BUILDINGS OLD AND NEW

French people call their old buildings *vieilles pierres*, or "old stones," and in most places treat them somewhat solicitously, like feeble senior citizens of distinction. But not in Mediterranean France. Here the "old stones" are expected to pull their weight. They are kept in constant use as museums, of course, but also as sites for public events and performances, wine showrooms, tourist offices, and even, in the case of Perpignan's fourteenth century maritime tribunal the Loge de la Mer, the most elegant fast food outlet you'll ever see.

There have been four outstanding periods for architecture in Mediterranean France — Roman, medieval, the seventeenth and early eighteenth century, and modern times — corresponding to the region's moments of greatest prosperity. And in each period, the society of the day left a vivid self-portrait in stone.

Roman

In the arenas, temples, forums, baths, water systems, highways and other vast public works projects the Romans built wherever they settled, they

The Country and its People

created an image of unshakable self-confidence, as was perfectly appropriate for the masters of the known world. By the first century AD, *Provincia Romana Narbonensis*, covering an area equivalent to today's Mediterranean France, seemed to historian Pliny the Elder "more than a province, another Italy." You can find Roman remains intact in all parts of the region from Augustus's impressive Trophy of The Alps overlooking Monaco to a 29-arch irrigation aqueduct watering vineyards in the foothills of the Pyrénées. But the place that really shows you what Pliny meant by "another Italy" is the area of the lower Rhône Valley in and around Nîmes, Arles and Orange (SEE A ROMAN HOLIDAY, page 16). They've got arenas, theaters,

baths, aqueducts, residential neighborhoods, triumphal arches, temples —the works. The Romans were the masters of stone construction, here you will see them at their best. Archaeology buffs may want to stop at Fréjus, an important port in the early days of the Empire. While none of its original buildings remain intact, the foundation stones of the old port and its 10,000-seat amphitheater and some sections of walls can be seen. Cimiez, the Roman town of Cemenelum in a park overlooking Nice, on the other hand, has a well-preserved 5,000 seat theater still in use, extensive baths and other Roman vestiges and a Museum of Archaeology with exhibits on the Roman presence in the Maritime Alps. Emperor Augustus's 50 m (160 ft) tall Trophy of the Alps is perched

Place Richelme in Aix-en-Provence, where a food market has been held daily since the middle ages.

high above Monaco on the Grande Corniche in La Turbie. It was built to commemorate the final defeat of the Ligurians. There's no question who was the boss here.

Romanesque

The region's second great period for architecture started in the tenth century and extended into the thirteenth, and the lovely churches, abbeys and cloisters built during this period are touching expressions of the deep religious faith of medieval society. The style is known as "Romanesque" because the architects were inspired by the Roman buildings they saw around them. Barrel vaults and rounded arches became characteristic features.

The Counts of Barcelona were important patrons of the burgeoning monastic movement, and thanks to them, Roussillon has an especially large number of Romanesque masterpieces. The most dramatically situated is the eleventh century abbey of Saint-Martin-du-Canigou high on the slopes of Mont-Canigou in the Pyrénées. The tenth century abbey of Saint-Michel-de-Cuxa in nearby Prades has delightfully sculpted floral patterns on the capitals of its cloister, and the Priory of Serrabone is known for the vivid depiction of monsters from the Book of the Apocalypse on the capitals of its pink marble columns. The Cathedral at Elne has a large, handsome cloister built between the twelfth and fourteenth centuries whose sculptures show the evolution of the Southern Romanesque style, one with a peculiarly Southern sensuality quite distinct from the austere medieval styles one finds in the North.

As cultural historian Fernand Benoît points out, "In the face of the abstract art of the North, the knowledge of Humanism, that is to say, of the human figure, is an essentially Mediterranean fact." This can be seen in the touching faces of the saints and angels, of the chosen people and especially of the damned, on the main portal of the church of Saint-Trophime at Arles.

Other fine examples of Romanesque art and architecture abound throughout Mediterranean France. They include the Abbey of Fontfroide near Narbonne, Saint-Guilhem-le-Désert north of Montpellier, the elaborately sculpted portals of the church of Saint-Gilles on the western edge of the Camargue, and the twelfth century Cistercian abbeys of Le Thoronet, Silvacane and Sénanque, known as "The Three Sisters of Provence."

Baroque

The worldly societies of the seventeenth and early eighteenth centuries built cities with Baroque flair. In the Quartier Mazarin of Aix-en-Provence, there are entire streets of honey-colored stone mansions, some with balconies supported by statues of giant muscle men known as *"Atlantes"* and all with grand interior staircases decorated with intricate wrought iron railings in a style peculiar to Aix. The Pavilion de Vendôme is an especially elaborate summation of Aix's Baroque characteristics. The leading sculptor of Atlantes and more importantly the greatest Southern architect of the period was Marseille-born Pierre Puget. He designed Marseille's elegant Vieille Charité, originally a large workhouse, now home to art museums and exhibition centers. In Vieux Montpellier, the old part of the city has many fine homes from the period, and in the surrounding countryside, there are several wildly fanciful residences of the period known as "Follies." Nearby Pézenas, which was the co-capital of Languedoc with Montpellier in the seventeenth century, is a living museum of "Great Century" architecture. Here you can visit the Hôtel d'Alfonce, where Molière and his company used to perform, and Gély's barber shop (now the Tourist Office), where he used to gather material for his comedies by eavesdropping on the conversations of the nobles.

Nice developed a very Italian version of the Baroque, and in a stroll through Old Nice, built almost entirely in this period, you will see many examples, including the Cathedral of Sainte Repérate, whose interior is lavishly decorated with gilded plaster and marble, and the Lascaris Palace, with its sweeping main staircase and airy mythological paintings on the ceilings. Menton's Parvis Saint-Michel, the Baroque main square of the old city, is a model of taste and discretion. Drive north from Menton into the Alpes-Maritimes, and you will find exquisite Baroque churches in Sospel, Briel-sur-Roya and Saint-Martin-Vésubie.

Modern

Unlike the structures of the earlier periods, late twentieth century architecture is more likely to be built of concrete, steel and glass than limestone and marble. And unlike the serenely monolithic ensembles of the earlier styles, the modern approach is one of diversity. Instead of one universal style, you will find a variety of disparate personal styles, as is appropriate to the Age of Anxiety. Le Corbusier launched the Post-War period with the most controversial building of its time, L'Unité d'Habitation in Marseille. Built in the late 1940's,

spaces designed by Jean Nouvel, Philippe Starck, Michel Wilmotte, Martial Raysse and Sir Norman Foster, whose classically proportioned modern art center and library the Carré d'Art was completed in 1993. In Montpellier, grandiose projects have been the order of the day. They include Claude Vasonti's bunker-like concert hall, the Corum, and Ricardo Bofill's Antigone, an expanse of residential and business structures that are monumental in their vastness and their updated neoclassic style.

The modern buildings of Nîmes and Montpellier may not please one and all. But this much is sure: they have made these cities more interesting to look at. Not many can make that claim.

the cantilevered seventeen-storey glass and bare concrete box was a self-contained living unit with duplex apartments, shops and schools all in the same building. It was the first of a projected six-building residential complex called La Cité Radieuse, but it stirred up such a such storm that Le Corbusier never got the financing to build the other five. In sunny Marseille, the objectors called it a crime to put people inside a concrete container sitting off the ground. They called it "*La Maison du Fada*", "The House of the Madman." Nevertheless, young architects loved it, and few buildings of the twentieth century have been more influential.

The most active cities for contemporary architecture in the 1980's and 1990's have been Nîmes and Montpellier. Their mayors have sought out top modern architects for major public works projects, and the results are striking. Nîmes now has a large array of imaginative buildings and public

Other Monuments

The four major styles mentioned may be the most abundant in the region, but there are many unique, exciting buildings to be seen from other periods as well. For dramatic medieval fortresses go to Languedoc, where you'll find the huge walled city of Carcassonne and the sun-blasted Cathar fortress of Peyrepertuse, a "citadel of vertigo" sitting on a jagged cliff in Corbières. Along the coast in the Camargue and Languedoc there are medieval fortified churches, menacing structures designed to double as strongholds. In Avignon is the ultimate in fortified religious establishments, the fourteenth century Papal

OPPOSITE: The Cloisters of Saint-Trophime in Arles, one of many Romanesque gems in Mediterranean France. ABOVE: Twentieth century art in a fourteenth century setting, a Botero exhibit at the Papal Palace in Avignon.

Palace, a vast walled ensemble of buildings and courtyards protected by battle towers over 50 m (160 ft) high. Gothic architecture is rare in the region. The most outstanding example is Narbonne's powerful Cathedral of Saint-Just, whose 41 m (135 ft) tall nave is the third tallest in France. Renaissance buildings are rare too. Most are medieval castles that were converted into Renaissance palaces. The *châteaux* of Grignan, Gordes and Cagnes-sur-Mer are good examples.

In the nineteenth century, a heavy, pompous Romanesque-Byzantine style developed in Marseille. Its prime examples are the basilica of Notre-Dame-de-la-Garde at the highest point in the city and the Cathédrale de la Major overlooking the main docks. For light pompous architecture, the Côte d'Azur's ultra-elaborate *belle époque* style can't be beat. It blossomed in the late nineteenth century, a time when the rich were not the slightest bit embarrassed about displaying their wealth. Landmarks of the style are Monte-Carlo's Grand Casino, Hôtel de Paris and Hôtel Hermitage and Queen Victoria's sprawling Regina Palace in Cimiez. The *belle époque*'s last two landmarks were constructed just before World War I brought the period abruptly to an end: the Hôtel Negresco in Nice and the "wedding cake" to end all wedding cakes, the Hôtel Carlton in Cannes.

PAINTING

So powerful is the artistic charisma of Van Gogh, Cézanne, Matisse and Picasso that they throw the rest of the region's artists into the shadows. Travelers tend to follow "in the footsteps" of those famous four, along with perhaps a few other stars of the modern period such as Chagall and Dufy, and often miss out on exciting works by artists who are not so well-known. The many works of Matisse and Picasso in the region may be its most outstanding art treasures, but they are by no means the only ones. The museums of the region offer many happy surprises for those who look around — works by Charles Camoin or Paul Guigou, for example, excellent painters with whom most travelers are unacquainted. The churches and abbeys contain many art treasures from the earlier periods, often hiding in obscure corners.

Early Painting
The Popes of Avignon were the first to stimulate painting in the region by hiring distinguished Italian painters such as Simone Martini and Matteo Giovannetti to decorate the Papal Palace in the early fourteenth century, and luckily some of the many frescoes they and their teams of artists painted on the walls of the palace have survived. After the Popes went back to Rome late in the century, art remained an important activity

in Avignon, and in the fifteenth century, a full-fledged School of Avignon emerged. There are fine examples of this work at the Musée du Petit Palais near the Papal Palace, including an altarpiece by the most talented member of the school, Enguerrand Quarton. His masterpiece, "The Coronation of the Virgin," dating from 1453, is in the Musée Municipal Pierre de Luxembourg across the Rhône in Villeneuve-les-Avignon. I urge you to see this painting, for many reasons, including Quarton's unusual depiction of the Father and the Son as mirror images, but especially for his sensitivity to the clarity of Mediterranean light. The other great painting of this period, which you must ask the guardian to show you, because it is encased in a protective cabinet, is at the Cathedral of Saint-Sauveur in Aix, the triptych "The Burning Bush," painted the 1476 by Nicholas Froment, under the patronage of "Good King" René, whose portrait can be seen in the left hand panel.

The other important movement in painting during the transition to the Renaissance in Mediterranean France was that of the late fifteenth to mid-sixteenth century School of Nice. Its leader was Ludovico Bréa, whose finely drawn figures and personal approach to light and shadow can be admired in his triptychs in the Franciscan church in Cimiez and Monaco's Cathedral. Bréa has been labeled "the Fra Angelico of Provence." The comparison is just in that the two artists share a gentle sensibility, but unfair to Ludovico Bréa in that it robs him of his individuality. Other works by Bréa and other School of Nice artists can be found in little churches in the Alpes-Maritimes north of Menton and in Biot and other hill towns between Nice and Antibes.

Baroque Era Painters
Hyacinthe Rigaud was the most successful portrait artist of Louis XIV's time. One of his three famous (and enormous) portraits of the Sun King can be seen in the main salon of the Hôtel Negresco in Nice. The Hyacinthe Rigaud Museum in Perpignan has a self-portrait of the benign-looking artist.

The great Southern-born painter of the late eighteenth century was Jean-Honoré Fragonard from Grasse. The Villa-Musée Fragonard has a large collection of his lighthearted rococo sketches, wash drawings, engravings and paintings.

Nineteenth Century Realism
In 1854, Gustave Courbet, "The Father of French Realism," made a trip to Montpellier and worked in the Languedoc countryside.

His painting "La Rencontre," better known as "Bonjour, Monsieur Courbet," had an enormous influence on young Southern painters and awakened them to the power that could be achieved through the meticulous analysis of the Mediterranean light.

Two painters who fell under that influence were Frédéric Bazille from Montpellier and Paul Guigou from the Vaucluse. Bazille became one of founders of Impressionism and painted outdoors with Renoir and Monet, but his career was cut short at the age of 29 when he died in the Franco-Prussian War. The Musée Fabre in Montpellier has nine of his sunny, vivacious early-period Impressionist paintings.

Paul Guigou was more traditional in style, but also an artist of exceptional sensitivity to the light of the South. His tender landscapes can be seen at the Musée des Beaux Arts in Marseille and the Musée Granet in Aix. Guigou died at 37.

Modern Art

The work done by painters in Mediterranean France from the late nineteenth century to the mid-twentieth century and the influence it had on the rest of the art world can only be described as explosive. It started in the 1880's with the return of Paul Cézanne to his native Aix and the arrival of Vincent Van Gogh in Arles, and it continued with the arrival of Signac, Matisse, Derain, Renoir, Bonnard, Dufy, Picasso, Braque, Léger, Chagall, Cocteau, de Staël and numerous others.

From Menton on the Italian border to Collioure and Céret in French Catalonia, there seems to be hardly a place along the coast where one of these artists did *not* work. It would take far more space than we have here to give this subject even a cursory treatment. The travel itineraries include information about these artists, where they painted, and where you can see their works. The principal modern art collections are at the Cocteau Museum in Menton; the Matisse, Chagall and Dufy museums in Nice; the Fondation Maeght in Saint-Paul-de-Vence; the Picasso Museum in Antibes; the Annonciade in Saint-Tropez; the Réattu in Arles; the Fabre in Montpellier; the Hyacinthe Rigaud Museum in Perpignan; and the Museum of Modern Art in Céret. There are two museums devoted to op-art master Victor Vasarély. One is in Aix-en-Provence, the other one in Gordes.

As for Cézanne and Van Gogh, who are ultimately responsible for all this, they were not understood in their time by the people of Aix and Arles. Now they are, but more for their commercial than their artistic value. Posters, post cards, souvenir books, Van Gogh tee-shirts, Cézanne coffee mugs, et cetera, et cetera. It doesn't matter. The sunflowers and olive trees and starry nights that Van Gogh painted in the fields around Arles and Saint-Rémy are still there, as beautiful as ever — even better, in fact, because of what he showed us. The same could be said about Cézanne and his beloved Montagne-Sainte-Victoire.

There are no paintings by Van Gogh in the area, but eight small paintings by Cézanne can be seen in the Musée Granet in Aix.

Contemporary Art

The history of art in Mediterranean France does not end with the passing of Matisse and Picasso. In the 1960's a group of artists called the New School of Nice or Nouveaux Réalistes, emerged, with Nice-born Yves Klein as their leader. They reacted against the French modern art establishment much the same way American Pop artists reacted against Abstract Expressionism, by basing much of their art on surprising and often comical treatment of everyday objects. The

sculptors Arman and Martial Raysse, also from Nice, were early partners of Klein, and their fellow Mediterranean artists César and Ben share their satirical bent. Their temple is MAMAC, Nice's Musée d'Art Moderne et d'Art Contemporain, which opened in 1990. It also has a large collection of American works from the 1960's on.

Other museums where contemporary art is on display are the Fondation Maeght, the Picasso Museum in Antibes, the Musée Cantini in Marseille, the Carré d'Art in Nîmes and the Museum of Modern Art in Céret, where the Catalan and Languedocian side of the contemporary art world is represented by Tàpies, Viallat, Jean and Jacques Capdeville and others.

The Picasso Museum in Antibes ABOVE is one of many museums in Mediterranean France where you can see works by outstanding artists who have lived and worked here.

The
Côte
d'Azur

EASTERN CÔTE D'AZUR

IF THERE'S ONE PLACE in the South that would seem to need no introduction, it's the eastern end of Mediterranean France, the fabled Côte d'Azur. We've been so bombarded with media coverage of the Cannes Film Festival, Monaco's princely family and the hype of glamour there in general, that it's easy to become jaded. But this place is full of surprises, and the first is that those clichés we've been fed about elephantine yachts draped with golden-tanned beauties and fabulous mansions overlooking the azure sea are all true — and more excessively true than we could have possibly imagined. Stroll along the yacht basin in Cannes or drive past the estates of Cap d'Antibes, and you'll be exposed to a level of sybaritic living that is staggering. And it's hard to imagine as you gape at the cathedral of luxury, the Grand Casino of Monte-Carlo, that little more than a century ago, the Côte d'Azur was a poor, backward region, and the priceless real estate upon which the Grand Casino now stands was a rocky goat pasture owned by a Prince of Monaco who was practically down to his last franc.

In *Côte d'Azur, the Inventing of the French Riviera*, Mary Blume describes the area before the development of tourism as "a raised and spectacularly beautiful sea front strip which... consisted of villages sharing poverty, brilliant sunshine and inaccessibility. A fringe, a liminal space, waiting to be invented."

What made it all possible was the arrival of the railroad in the 1860's. Suddenly it became easy to get to this isolated strip, and when Queen Victoria, Czar Nicholas II and the other crowned heads of Europe decided to make sunny Nice, Cannes and Monte-Carlo their winter headquarters, the rich and the well-to-do swept along in their wake. Modern mass tourism was born on the Côte d'Azur and quickly became its major source of income, as it remains to this day. And this is no bagatelle we're talking about. Twenty-four million visitors spend 40 billion francs a year (roughly eight billion dollars) on their travels in this region.

The catchy term "Côte d'Azur" created by poet Stephen Liégeard in 1887 originally applied to the 60 km (38 mile) stretch of coast between Menton and Cannes, where *belle époque* tourism flourished, but in the twentieth century its has been broadened to cover the 200 km (125 miles) of coastline between Menton and Bandol and a good deal of countryside inland. On the coast, this adds another 140 km (87 miles) of lovely, twisting shore line to the west of Cannes along with many resort towns, including swinging Saint-Tropez, and the three delightful islands of the Îles d'Hyères. The big naval port of Toulon and the prestigious wine-growing area of Bandol are at the western end of the coast. Moving inland, the Côte d'Azur extends northward into the Maritime Alps (Alpes-Maritimes) and the Alps of Upper

Provence (Alpes-de-Haute-Provence). Exactly how far it goes into the mountains is open to debate, but for the purpose of our travels, it extends as far north as the "Lavender Alps" of Upper Provence, where fields of lavender stretch out as far as the eye can see, and Digne-les-Bains, the lively main town, is the perfect base for exploring the area. It lies 152 km (95 miles) northwest of Nice and is easily reached by road or the colorful *Train des Pignes*, the "Pine Cone Train," up the Var River Valley.

Today's view of the Côte d'Azur points up the wide range of attractions it has to offer beyond the classic flesh pots of the coast. And in the summer, when the narrow, two-lane coast road

is normally crowded, trips to the interior offer welcome relief.

Besides the "Lavender Alps," the beauties of nature include the Vallée des Merveilles (Valley of Marvels) in the Mercantour National Park of Alpes-Maritimes, where Stone Age shepherds carved enigmatic designs in the rocks, and the Grand Canyon du Verdon, the largest canyon in Europe, 700 m (2,500 ft) deep, where hiking, white-water rafting and horseback excursions are popular. The Côte d'Azur is peppered with fortified medieval hilltop villages, "perched villages," from the coastal highlands far up into the mountains. In one cluster where Matisse, Bonnard and Picasso and many other artists lived, you can now visit potters, glass blowers, weavers, sculptors and other crafts persons at work in their studios. The Var district in the western Côte d'Azur is a vast sea of vineyards, producing Côtes de Provence and Bandol wines, and there is no end of wine-making *châteaux* to be visited.

Taking advantage of the whole Côte d'Azur can add a great deal of enjoyment to your trip. But let's face it, what draws us here is the fleshpots.

And that brings us to Nice.

The Grand Canyon of the Verdon River, one of the scenic treasures awaiting those who venture in from the coast.

NICE

Nice is *the* big city of the Côte d'Azur, the one place you can't avoid, and you shouldn't. It is everything the main city of an area should be — its capital, its commercial center, its transportation hub and a fully functioning metropolis 365 days a year, the only one on this end of the coast. It is also one of the most delightful cities in Europe to visit, and the main reason is that Nice is a city made for walking. There are formal promenades such as the famed Promenade des Anglais along the grand sweep of the Baie des Anges (Bay of Angels) and the flowery, fountain-filled Promenade du Paillon through the center of the city. But the narrow, winding streets of Vieux Nice (Old Nice) present a different kind of walking experience. Italianate houses, Baroque churches, lively markets and shops will reward you with a discovery a minute. And snacking on Nice's unique cuisine is an irresistible part of the fun.

Thanks to the sheltering crescent of high hills behind the city, Nice has fine weather the year round. In the Spring, you can take a dip in the Mediterranean and be on a ski slope in the Alpes-Maritimes an hour later. Because of its mild winters, Nice has a high percentage of retirees. But young people choose to live here too, drawn by the University of Nice and job opportunities in tourism and high-technology. Along with the old Niçois families, who provide Nice with its distinctly Italian flair, the cross-section of young and old people makes for an interesting mix. The verve of this city of 350,000 is such that despite the importance of tourism to its economy, it gives you the feeling that life would go on even if the tourists stopped coming.

While Nice delivers sun, sea, palm tree-lined promenades and high living to those who seek it, this city is also is treasure chest of art. You can find religious paintings by the medieval School of Nice, individual museums devoted to long-time residents Matisse, Chagall and Dufy, and works by the artists of the contemporary New School of Nice. Nice has more museums genuinely worth visiting than any other city in the South of France. And practically all of them are free.

BACKGROUND

The first known inhabitants of Nice were nomadic Stone Age hunters who stalked hippos and elephants in the area of the Port 400,000 years ago. They camped in caves at the foot of Mount Boron, where their bone-littered shelters were unearthed during a construction project in 1966 at Terra

OPPOSITE: The beach of Nice and the city's landmark, the domed Hôtel Negresco.

Amata just east of the Port. But permanent settlement did not come until four thousand centuries later, in the fourth century BC, when the Greeks from Marseille established a port for their coastal shipping and built an acropolis on top of the Colline du Château (Castle Hill) overlooking the port and Baie des Anges. They named the town Nikaia, most likely in honor of Nike, the Goddess of Victory. The Romans preferred to set themselves up on the heights of Cimiez three kilometers (two miles) inland, where they established an army post on the Julian Way. After Augustus crushed the last independent Ligurian tribes in the Alps in 14 BC, they made Cemenelum the capital of the Alpes-Maritimes district. By the second century AD, it had grown to a city of 20,000, and extensive ruins remain from this period, including a 5,000-seat theater still in use.

The Italian flavor so conspicuous in Nice comes from its five centuries of rule by the House of Savoy. In 1388, Duke Amadeus VII, in need of a port for his landlocked Alpine duchy, took advantage of a split in the House of Anjou, Provence's rulers, and talked Jean Grimaldi, their governor in Nice, into betraying the County of Nice to Savoy. Except for occasional periods of French occupation, Nice would remain under Savoyard rule until 1860, when Napoléon III made an arrangement with the Italian minister Cavour that brought Nice and its county under French sovereignty, to the horror of Giuseppe Garibaldi, who yearned to see his native city become the westernmost port of a unified Italy.

In 1763, Dr. Tobias Smollett, the British physician and novelist, spent the winter in Nice and wrote that it was as warm in December as London was in May, so the British upper classes started to come here to winter. By the time Nice became French a century later, there was already a well-established British colony and a Promenade des Anglais. With the arrival of the railroad in 1864, the well-to-do English started coming in numbers, and when Queen Victoria wintered in Cimiez in the 1890's, Nice's fortune in upscale tourism was made. *Belle époque* palaces sprouted from the Promenade des Anglais up to Queen Victoria'a Regina Palace in Cimiez. In 1890, 22,000 people wintered in Nice. By 1910, there were more than 150,000 winter residents. The Russian nobles were the most extravagant of all. In 1912 they built Nice's Russian Orthodox Cathedral. But World War I put an abrupt end to the *belle époque* period and the Russian Revolution to its biggest spenders. While The Jazz Age brought a resurgence of tourism to the Côte d'Azur in the 1920's, sunbathing came into vogue, and Nice lost its cachet because of its pebbly beaches. Towns down the coast with sandy beaches such as Juan-les-Pins and Cannes became more attractive to vacationers, who now

One way street
Pedestrian area
Public building
Park or garden
Parking
Taxis

started coming more in the summer than in the winter.

In the post-World War II era, Nice's image has suffered from political corruption, charges of organized crime in the casinos and the flight of Jacques Médecin, its disgraced long-time mayor. Nevertheless, it has moved actively into high-tech, modern service industries and business-related tourism, with its mammoth new Acropolis convention center, and is the second most visited city in France. The Promenade des Anglais has lost most of its *belle époque* palaces, but the landmark Negresco is still there. And Old Nice, the seventeenth and eighteenth century Baroque section of town, a crime-ridden slum twenty years ago that we were told to avoid, has been renovated and is now one of the stellar attractions of the Côte d'Azur.

GENERAL INFORMATION

As everywhere in Mediterranean France, your first stop should be the **Tourist Office**, where you will find mountains of maps and booklets on hotels, camping grounds, restaurants and cultural attractions in French and English and well-informed personnel eager to help. There are three offices in Nice. One is at the Nice Airport (93 83 32 64, another is at the SNCF, the train station on Avenue Thiers, between the Boulevard Gambetta and Avenue Malausséna (93 87 07 07, and the third is near the Méridien Hotel at 5 Avenue Gustave V (93 87 60 60. Walking tours of Old Nice and *belle époque* Nice are led by passionate and erudite guides. For a booklet on the moderate and inexpensive hotels of the Logis de France association, ask at the Tourist Office or pick it up at the Logis de France desk at the Gare Routière, the bus station, on the Esplanade du Paillon (93 80 80 40. They have about 100 inns and hotels in the Alpes-Maritimes area, but not in Nice itself.

The following contacts may be helpful to you during your visit:

Nice-Côte d'Azur Airport (93 21 30 30.

Gare SNCF (main railway station) (93 87 50 50, for information on the *grandes lignes* (main lines) and regional Métrazur service between Saint-Raphaël and Menton. **Chemins de Fer de la Provence** (Train des Pignes) (93 82 10 17. **Gare Routière** (bus station) on the Esplanade du Paillon (93 85 61 81, for bus service along the coast and to hill towns inland. **Navette Bus Aéroport-Riviera**, is the **airport bus service** (93 96 31 51.

Taxi (93 80 70 70.

Car Rental: Avis (93 21 36 33; **Budget** (93 16 24 16; **EuropCar** (93 21 36 44; **Hertz** (93 21 36 72; **Thrifty** (93 89 71 10.

The **Automobile Club de Nice et Côte d'Azur** is on Rue Massenet (93 87 18 17.

Guided **coach tours** to Monaco and the *corniches* of the Riviera and other day-trips are offered by **Phocéen Cars** at 2 Place Masséna (93 85 66 61, at 11 Avenue Jean Médecin (93 85 46 81, and **Sun Riviera Tours** at 14 Rue François Guisol (93 26 59 50.

Boat excursions to Monaco and points along the Riviera and to the Îles de Lérins are operated by **Bateaux Gallus**, 24 Quai Lunel, on the west side of the port (93 55 33 33.

For **Health emergencies: S.O.S. Médecin** (93 85 01 01, or dial 15 for SAMU (emergency medical service).

Little **Tourist Trains** are a good way to get your bearing. They make a 45-minute circuit of

the Old City, the Château and the Promenade des Anglais, leaving the corner of the Promenade des Anglais and Jardin Albert Ier every 15 minutes from 10 AM to 7 PM in season, less often the rest of the year (25 francs). They can be combined with a boat trip to Villefranche (45 francs) (93 71 44 77. Tourist passes for unlimited rides on **Sunbus**, Nice's excellent bus system cost 22 francs per day, 80 francs for five days (93 16 52 10.

FESTIVALS

Carnaval is two weeks of parades with lavish floats, dancing in the streets, masked balls, theater, and the Battle of Flowers centered on Place Masséna, but spilling out everywhere into the city.

A wine festival in Cimiez, where the Romans settled on the hilltop overlooking Nice.

It starts 12 days before Ash Wednesday and culminates in fireworks over the Baie des Anges the night of Shrove Tuesday (Mardi Gras).

The **Nice Jazz Festival** is another two-weeks of partying, this one up the hill in the Park of Cimiez, featuring top names in jazz, blues and R&B, with picnics, concerts in the Roman theater and relaxed conversations between musicians and fans. This was Dizzy Gillespie's favorite festival, and I have warm memories of the time I spent with him and other musicians here. Formerly called **La Grande Parade du Jazz**, it takes place early to mid-July.

WHAT TO SEE

The best place to start exploring Nice is on top of the **Colline du Château** (Castle Hill), the rock towering above the east end of the Promenade des Anglais. This is where the Greeks had their acropolis and the House of Savoy built the fortress that gave the hill its name. Unfortunately, Louis XIV had the fortress demolished during the War of the Spanish Succession in 1706 and the Dukes never got around to rebuilding it when they recovered the city. From the observation platform you can see the entire panorama of Nice. To the west is the blue and turquoise **Baie des Anges** with Nice's three and a half miles of pebbly beach and the palm-lined **Promenade des Anglais** and **Quai des États-Unis** running along it. Directly below the Château is **Le Vieux Nice** (Old Nice), the triangle of red tiled roofs of Baroque-era churches and houses between the foot of the Colline du Château, the Quai-des-États-Unis and the wide garden esplanade built over the bed of the Paillon River that cuts through the city. This is the boundary between seventeenth and eighteenth century Old Nice, with its narrow winding streets, and the nineteenth and twentieth century part which is laid out in a grid. The esplanade, which changes names a few times along its way, begins at the bay with the Jardin Albert 1er, followed by **Espace Masséna, Promenade du Paillon** and **Promenade des Arts,** where the new theater, modern art museum and Acropolis convention center are located.

Looking down from the east side of the Château, you see **Port Lympia**, the inner harbor cut into the gap between the Château and Mount Boron, and the outer harbor where the ferries for Corsica dock. Cupping the city is a natural amphitheater of steep hills and beyond them to the north, the Alpes-Maritimes, usually topped by snow. Few cities have been blessed with a natural setting as perfect as this.

To get up to the Château, there is an elevator at the end of Rue des Ponchettes open 9 AM to 7:30 PM all year which costs five francs. Or you can walk up the 300 steps.

Vieux Nice

Old Nice is a city-within-a-city with narrow winding streets, bright Baroque squares in pastels, rust and ochre, and visual surprises and tantalizing aromas at every turn. The only way to explore it is by foot, which is easy enough, since all of Vieux Nice has been made a pedestrian zone. The heart of the old city is **Cours Saleya** a few minutes by foot down Rue des Ponchettes from the Château. The long rectangular courtyard was the promenade for Nice's high society in the eighteenth century, and now is the site of a flower market every morning except Mondays, when the antique and bric-a-brac dealers take over. The greenhouses of the Riviera are among Europe's main producers of roses, carnations and other cut flowers, so visitors to the **Cours Saleya Flower Market** are treated to a dazzling array of color and aroma all year round. Adjoining is a fruit and vegetable market, where the food stall of **Thérèse** is abuzz with activity. Customers are lined up for *soccas* (chick pea crepes) and *pissaladières* (onion pizzas) cooked and served sizzling hot by a crew of jovial and tireless Niçoises. They don't sell beverages, those you buy from **La Cambuse**, the café across the street. A cool glass of Côtes de Provence rosé washes these Niçois treats down very nicely.

A few steps away is the **Chapelle de la Miséricorde**, a 1740 Baroque gem designed by Bernardo Vittone. It is open only for mass on Sunday mornings and by special arrangement with the Tourist Office which organizes tours. The **Musée Raoul Dufy** (see MUSEUMS, page 93) is a few steps outside the Cours Saleya on the Quai des États-Unis.

Those with a sweet tooth should pop into **Pâtisserie-Confiserie Auer** at 7 Rue Saint-François-de-Paule across from the Nice Opéra House to sample the delicious chocolates and candied-fruit that have made it an institution since 1820.

At N° 14 is the retail store of the olive oil mill **Alizari**, selling cured olives *à la Niçoise*, olive oil, lavender honey and herbs. Just breathing in the sweet Provençal aromas is intoxicating.

From the Cours Saleya, take Rue Sainte Réperate one block to the Rue de la Préefecture. At N° 17, photographer **Jean-Louis Martinelli** sells his exquisite post cards and posters of Nice. Across the street at N° 16 is the cavernous **Grandes Caves Caprioglio** which has a huge selection of Provençal wines, including Château de Bellet and Château de Crémat from the tiny Bellet wine-producing area north of Nice. (There is very little wine produced in the eastern Côte d'Azur, unlike the rest of Mediterranean France, which produces vast quantities).

OPPOSITE: The Monday antiques market at the Cours Saleya. RIGHT: All of Old Nice has been converted to vehicle-free walking streets.

The Côte d'Azur

Baroque **Sainte-Repérate Cathedral** on Place Rossetti is dedicated to Nice's patron saint, a 15-year old virgin martyred in Palestine whose body floated to Nice on a flower-decked boat towed by Angels (hence the name Baie des Anges). Also on Place Rossetti you can try the delicious home-made ice cream and sherbet at **Fenocchio**, in more than eighty flavors.

Palais Lascaris at 15 Rue Droite is a Genoese-style mansion built by the Count of Ventimiglia in the seventeenth century. It has a grand balustraded staircase and richly decorated apartments with frescoes of mythological themes on the vaulted ceilings. Closed on Monday.

Continue up Rue Droite past artists' boutiques and vendors of savory food (see WHERE TO EAT, page 96) to **Place Garibaldi**, where the lively **Grand Café de Turin** takes up one corner of the handsome yellow ochre arcaded square named for the Nice-born Italian patriot.

The Port

A few minutes by foot to the east of Place Garibaldi on Rue Cassini will take you to **Port Lympia**, the protected inner harbor used by fishing boats and pleasure craft and lined by seafood restaurants and cafés. On the lower slope of Mont-Boron just to the east of the inner harbor, you will find **Terra Amata**, where the nomadic Stone Age hunters' shelters were discovered in 1966 (see MUSEUMS, page 94). Continue around Port Lympia to the commercial port, where the **Gare Maritime** (Maritime Station) is located. It handles ferry service to Corsica and boat trips along the coast.

Place Masséna and the Promenade du Paillon

One block west of Place Garibaldi is the Promenade du Paillon, the flowery, fountain-dotted esplanade that divides Old Nice from the modern city. (Note the Gare Routière, the station from which buses leave to all parts of the Côte d'Azur and Provence). The central point of Nice straddling the esplanade is Place Masséna, the wide square framed by red-ochre Italianate buildings with vaulted arcades. Rue Masséna leads to a pleasant walking area of fashionable boutiques, bars and cafes and ice-cream parlors.

The Promenade des Anglais

The Promenade des Anglais got its start in 1822 as a public works project funded by a wealthy English clergyman, Reverend Lewis Way. Originally a six-foot wide footpath along the Baie des Anges called La Strada del Littorale, it was widened and renamed the Promenade des Anglais in 1844. In its *belle époque* heyday, the upper classes of all Europe strolled past its domed white wedding-cake palaces. Today a busy six-lane roadway disrupts the former leisurely pace, and most of the palaces have given way to modern high-rises. A

McDonald's and the crude Las Vegas-style Casino Ruhl further detract from the air of elegance. But reminders of grandeur remain — the turn-of-the-century **Westminster** and **West End** hotels, the **Musée Masséna**, the facade of the Art Deco **Palais de la Méditerranée**, saved from demolition a few years ago, and above all, the mythic 1912 **Hôtel Negresco**, whose jolly pink and green dome has become as much a symbol of Nice as the Eiffel Tower has in Paris. Take a stroll through this splendid hotel even if you don't plan to check in. It is a registered National Historic Monument with more art treasures than many museums, including one of Hyacinthe Rigaud's famous full-figure portraits of Louis XIV showing off his legs, and the largest Aubusson carpet in the world. This is the hotel where the celebrities stay, and to see them and touch up with the *belle époque* ghosts, have a drink at the bar, unchanged in style since the day it opened. The brasserie and the restaurant of the

Negresco are also the finest in Nice (see WHERE TO EAT, page 96 and 97).

The Museums of Nice

The **Musée d'Art Moderne et d'Art Contemporain** (MAMAC) (Museum of Modern and Contemporary Art) has an extensive collection of late twentieth century art including De Kooning, Stella, Warhol, Haring and particularly the New School of Nice — Arman, Martial Raysse and Yves Klein, with more than 20 of that Nice-born innovator's works. Go up to the roof for Klein's Garden of Eden installation and the fine view of the city. On Fridays at 9:30 PM, the weekly lighting of Klein's "Wall of Fire" takes place.

MAMAC's building, four massive white marble towers linked by thick arched steel beams around a glassed-in core, sparked controversy when it opened in 1990. Designed by Yves Bayard and Henri Vidal, it forms an architectural unit with the

hexagonal white marble **Théâtre de Nice** across the **Esplanade des Arts**, an open walkway between the buildings lined with sculptures by Calder, Barry Flanagan, Marc de Suvero and others. Looking out on the sculptures from the ground floor of the museum is the fashionable but affordable Café des Arts. The Museum is closed Tuesdays.

The **Musée des Beaux Arts**, the fine arts museum, is an Italian Renaissance-style mansion with a formal staircase and winter garden and has works by Fragonard, Degas, Monet, Renoir, Sisley, Rodin, Braque, Picasso, Bonnard and Van Dongen. There are also areas devoted to Nice's Van Loo family of Rococo painters and pioneering *belle époque* poster artist Jules Chéret. It is at

---

MAMAC, Nice's museum of modern and contemporary art, whose collection is as bold as its design.

33 Avenue des Baumettes, a five-minute walk west of the Negresco. The museum is closed Mondays.

The **Musée Raoul Dufy** has 28 paintings, 16 watercolors and dozens of drawings and graphics by the long-time Nice resident, including several of his airy scenes of the Côte d'Azur. It is at 77 Quai des États-Unis near the Cours Saleya market and is closed Sunday mornings and Mondays.

The **Musée International d'Art Naïf** (International Museum of Naïve Art) has 600 works by naïve artists from all over the world from the eighteenth century to today in the Château Sainte-Hélène, the grand *belle époque* mansion built by François and Marie Blanc, the Monte-Carlo casino bosses. It is on Avenue du Val-Marie in the Fabron quartier west of downtown Nice and closed on Tuesdays.

The **Musée Masséna** is the former mansion of Marshal Masséna's grandson, and now Nice's historical museum. It has artifacts from the Roman era through the nineteenth century. The lavish Second Empire rooms are worth the visit in themselves. The museum is at 35 Promenade des Anglais next to the Negresco and closed on Mondays.

The **Musée de Terra Amata**, built on the site of the shelters of nomadic Early Paleolithic Acheulean hunters who lived here 4,000 centuries ago, has true-to-life tableaus of their mode of living. The museum is at 25 Boulevard Carnot by the northeastern corner of the Port. It is closed Mondays.

Cimiez's Museums

Cimiez is the hill overlooking Nice where the Romans built their city of Cemenelum. It is now home to an archaeological museum at the Roman site, a monastery with important School of Nice art works and two exciting modern art museums. To get to Cimiez by bus from downtown Nice, take the N° 17 bus from the Promenade du Paillon. As you mount the Boulevard de Cimiez you can't miss the sprawling white *belle époque* Regina Palace where Queen Victoria spent the last several winters of her life. She enjoyed riding around Nice in a little donkey cart and was loved by the Niçois, who erected a statue of her in front of the Regina Palace, which is now an apartment house. Henri Matisse also spent his last years at the Regina where he died in 1954. He is buried in the cemetery at Cimiez.

The **Musée Matisse** is a handsome red-ochre Italianate seventeenth century villa set amid the Roman ruins of Cimiez's park at the crest of the Boulevard de Cimiez. The collection includes 236 of Matisse's drawings, 218 engravings, 59 sculptures including *Nus vus de Dos*, his four cast bronze studies of female nude backs done between 1909 and 1930, each one more abstract than

its predecessor. It is on the far wall of the lobby. There are colored paper cut-outs for the Chapel of the Rosary at Vence, 68 paintings, including *Portrait de Madame Matisse* (1905), *Nu au Fauteuil*, *Plante Verte* (1936-37), and *Nature Morte aux Grenades* (1947), as well as many photos and items from the master's personal art collection. The museum is closed Tuesdays.

The main points of interest at the Roman archaeological site of **Cemenelum** are the **Baths**, the largest in all Gaul, which reminds us how very advanced the Mediterranean peoples were then in comparison to Northerners, and the **Arena**, the 5,000-seat amphitheater used for combats of gladiators, which reminds us how bloodthirsty they were. The Arena is now used for concerts, including those of the delightful Nice Jazz Festival. The **Musée d'Archéologie**, opened in 1989, contains objects from the Iron Age to the Middle Ages, and especially the Roman period at Cemenelum and the Alpes-Maritimes. It is closed Sunday mornings, Mondays, and the month of November.

The **Franciscan Monastery of Cimiez** which is also located in the park, has a lovely cloister and two masterpieces of the School of Nice, a 1475 Piéta and a 1512 Crucifixion by Ludovico Bréa, in its church of **Notre-Dame-de-l'Assomption**.

Musée National au Message Biblique Marc Chagall (National Museum of the Biblical Message) features the 17 huge canvases of Chagall's happy ecumenical vision of the books of Genesis and Exodus, "The Biblical Message," in glowing Chagallian blues, greens, yellows, purples and reds. "The Song of Songs," a group of six large red-toned paintings, is a touching love song to his wife Vava. Be sure not to miss the recital hall. It has the magnificent blue, blue, blue stained glass windows of "The Creation." The Chagall Museum is downhill from the park on Avenue Docteur Ménard, just to the west of Boulevard de Cimiez. This is one of the few museums in Nice that has an admission charge, 35 francs. The museum is closed Tuesdays.

NOTE: All Nice's museums close for lunch, normally from 12 PM to 2 PM.

Russian Orthodox Cathedral

Slightly off-beat but none the less interesting, the Russian Orthodox Cathedral, is the largest Russian church outside Russia. It has five colorful glazed tile onion domes and a splendid array of gold icons. Funded by Czar Nicholas II, the church was completed in 1912, five years before his overthrow. It is open daily but closed Sunday morning to sightseers. However, visitors who wish to attend a Russian mass are welcome. Mass starts at 10:30 AM and lasts about two and a half hours. It is a magnificent ceremony. The cathedral is at 17 Boulevard du Tzarewich in a quiet residential district west of the railway station.

The Beaches of Nice

Nice has one of the most beautiful waterfronts you will ever see, but because its beaches are made of pebbles, many sunbathers prefer the sandy beaches of the towns to the west. I find the rustle of pebbles rolling in the waves very soothing as I soak up the sun on the less crowded beaches here, and a pair of plastic sandals solves the problem of walking on the hot stones. The large **Plage Publique des Ponchettes** on the Quai des États-Unis is a free public beach with fresh water showers. For an inexpensive day at the beach, pick up the makings of a picnic at the nearby Cours Saleya market. But if you want to be pampered, 15 private beaches along the Quai des États-Unis and the Promenade des Anglais have restaurants and snack bars and rent mattresses and beach umbrellas. The fee for a changing room and mattress is 40 to 65 francs. I like the **Plage Beau Rivage** on the Quai des États-Unis. It has a festive open air grill, moderate to moderately expensive, and a modestly priced snack bar. Reed mats are put on the pebbles to make it easy for you to get to the water, and windsurfing, water skiing, and parascending (flying behind a speed boat) are available. At night you can dine here under the stars (93 80 75 06. **Castel Plage** at the eastern end of the Quai des États-Unis, is another beach I enjoy. This is where Nice's young artistic crowd goes (93 85 22 66.

WHERE TO STAY

There are 230 classified hotels in Nice, and you should have no problem getting a room of your choice except during Carnaval or the month of July and the first three weeks of August, for which you should book long in advance. But Nice is a big convention city, and there's always a possibility of your hitting one. So to be on the safe side, book ahead if you can. Many hotels reduce their prices off-season, and a number of them offer two nights for the price of one on weekends. The Tourist Office has a list.

Luxury/Very Expensive

All the great names have stayed at the **Negresco****, 37 Promenade des Anglais (93 88 39 51 FAX 93 88 35 68, from Scott and Zelda Fitzgerald to Queen Elizabeth II, who must have felt right at home in the palatial surroundings. The 150 rooms and suites are little museums in themselves, with antiques chosen by the owner, Mme. Augier. There are two restaurants, the Chantecler, Nice's leading gourmet eatery, and the delightful Rotonde for lighter fare (see WHERE TO EAT, page 96), and the bar is the most glamorous in town. A private beach is across the Promenade. The **Palais Maeterlinck****, 30 Boulevard Maurice Maeterlinck, Cap de Nice (93 56 21 12 FAX 93 26 39 91, is

splendidly isolated on a sea-side cliff between Nice and Villefranche-sur-Mer. This cypress-studded estate of the famed Belgian playwright is now a classy hotel (26 rooms and suites) with a colonnaded pool, beach and gourmet restaurant, Le Mélisande.

Expensive

Built into a cliff of the Château's hill, **La Pérouse****** at 11 Quai Rauba-Capéu (93 21 34 63 FAX 93 62 59 41, is 65 room hotel with a cozy, private club atmosphere, a rooftop pool and garden, intimate bar and restaurant, and a superb view of the Nice shore front and Baie des Anges. At 875 francs for a sea view double, our least expensive choice

and my favorite in this category. The **Beau Rivage****, at 24 Rue Saint-François-de-Paule (93 80 80 70 FAX 93 80 55 77, is a fashionable address where Matisse, Chekhov, and Nietzche stayed. It has 120 elegant rooms, down the street from the Cours Saleya and a block from its own private beach. The **Abela****, at 223 Promenade des Anglais (93 37 17 17 FAX 93 71 21 71, has 333 modern rooms, a rooftop pool, piano lounge and good buffet lunches. Jazz artists in town for the festival stay here.

Moderate

There are many good choices in this category. The most imaginative is the **Windsor***** at 11 Rue Dalpozzo (93 88 59 35 FAX 93 88 94 57, a hotel with a Zen ambience. It has an oriental lobby, tropical garden with a small pool and recorded jungle bird calls, a gym, wood-paneled bar and restaurant, and all 65 rooms are decorated by contemporary artists. It is three blocks in from the Promenade des Anglais. The Mercure chain has three of its comfortable, well-run modern hotels centrally located in Nice, with rates in our moderate range

The Hotel Negresco, one of the "domed wedding-cake palaces" which evoke the nineteenth century heyday of the Promenade des Anglais.

except for a few weeks, mainly in August. They are the **Mercure Masséna****** 58 Rue Gioffredo near Place Masséna (93 85 49 25 FAX 93 62 43 27, the **Mercure Opéra***** at 91 Quai des États-Unis (93 85 74 19 FAX 93 13 90 94, and the **Mercure Baie des Anges***** on the Promenade des Anglais upstairs from the Casino Ruhl, entrance at 2 Rue Halevy (93 82 30 88 FAX 93 82 18 20. The **Primotel Suisse***** 15 Quai Rauba-Capéu (93 62 33 00 FAX 93 85 30 70, has 40 plain, modern rooms, half of them with the same marvelous Baie des Anges view as its more glamorous next-door neighbor, La Pérouse. For a hotel in a quiet setting with a view of the whole city, try the **Petit Palais*****, actor-director Sacha Guitry's former mansion at 10 Avenue Emile-Bieckert in Cimiez (93 62 19 11 FAX 93 62 53 60, convenient to the Chagall and Matisse Museums and the Roman ruins. It has 25 tasteful rooms and a terrace overlooking all of Nice.

Inexpensive

At the **Acanthe**** 2 Rue Chauvain (93 62 22 44 FAX 93 62 29 77, you will find 50 cheerful, newly-renovated rooms, many with views of the Espace Masséna, and the warm Southern hospitality of owner Patrice Duchesne, a transplanted Northerner. Ask for one of the four round rooms overlooking the fountain. At 280 francs for a double, this is one of the best bargains in town. Another friendly hotel is the **Dante**** at 12 Rue Andrioli (93 86 81 00 FAX 93 97 27 17, with 30 spotlessly clean, renovated rooms 200 m from the Promenade des Anglais. The **Régence**** 21 Rue Masséna (92 87 75 08 FAX 93 82 41 31, in the pedestrian shopping area west of Place Masséna, has 40 neat, simple rooms. Like the more costly hotels, these all have baths or showers, TV and direct-dial phones.

Camping

There are no camping grounds in Nice itself, but there are many in the outlying communities. Cagnes-sur-Mer just west of Nice Airport has eight and Villeneuve-Loubet-Plage, the next town, has nine. The Nice Office of Tourism has information on camping sites, including a free map-brochure published by **L'Hôtellerie de Plein Air des Alpes Maritimes**, an association representing sixty camps in the Alpes-Maritimes. For more details, you can go to their office at the **Parc des Maurettes**, 730 Avenue du Docteur Lefevbre, Villeneuve-Loubet-Plage (93 20 91 91. If you are driving, it's in back of the big Intermarché shopping center on N 7, or if you go by Métrazur train, a 15-minute ride from Nice that costs 30 francs round-trip, it is 400 m north of the Villeneuve-Loubet-Plage station. The Parc des Maurettes is an attractive camp in a wooded setting a 15-minute walk from the beach, open mid-January to mid-November. Also in Villeneuve-Loubet-

Plage, **La Vielle Ferme** on Boulevard des Groules (93 33 41 44 is open all year. It has a large indoor-outdoor pool in use 10 months of the year and is located less than a mile from the beach. In general, a site for a medium-sized car and caravan sites rents for about 165 francs, 100 francs for a car and a two-person tent and 90 francs for space for a two-person tent alone.

WHERE TO EAT

Good food at all prices is easy to find in Nice, from the gourmet cuisine of the Negresco's Chantecler to the *Niçois* treats that you buy in the street — *socca* (chick pea crêpes), *pissaladière* (onion pizza), *salade Niçoise* and *pan bagnat* (*salade Niçoise* in a big roll). You can have a filling lunch of *pan bagnat*, beer or wine and coffee for about 30 francs. If you still have room, try a *tourta de bléa*, a pie made of raisins, Swiss chard and pine nuts, an odd-sounding combination, but somehow it works. Vieux Nice has lots of little restaurants and stands specializing in fast food *à la Niçoise* such as this. Some of my favorites are bustling **Thérèse** at the Cours Saleya market, **Nissa Socca** at 5 Rue Sainte-Réperate and **Chez René** at 2 Rue Miralheti, just off Boulevard Jean Jaurès. This busy spot has two outlets facing each other across an alley and families sit elbow to elbow at long outdoor tables making no secret of the good time they are having. At Chez René, along with your *pissaladière*, you get a slice of the real life of Old Nice. But go early. It closes at 9 PM. The maestro of *socca* is **Pipo** at 13 Rue Bavastro near the Port. He makes it just the way I like it — slightly crisp on the outside, soft but not mushy inside. A big plate of socca and a half bottle of rosé will run you 40 francs. Pipo is open evenings only.

For a full Niçois meal in a lively bistro ambiance, try **Barale** at 39 Rue Beaumont north of the Port (93 89 14 94. You sit at your table, and the legendary Mme. Barale starts dishing out her delicious seven course fixed-price menu — every specialty we have mentioned plus a main course of sautéed veal, all for 200 francs, wine included. As you can imagine, the restaurant is always full. Reservations are a must. Barale is closed for the month of August. **Merenda**, a tiny hole-in-the-wall at 4 Rue de la Terrasse near the Cours Saleya, serves *beignet de fleur de courgette* (zucchini blossom fritters), *potage au pistou* (vegetable soup), the Niçois cod fish specialty *stockfish*, *daube* (Provençal stew) and *mesclum* (tender mixed salad greens). A meal will run you 150 to 200 francs. There's no phone, and they don't take reservations, so come early. Merenda is also closed in August.

Expensive

For gourmet restaurants the **Chantecler** in the Negresco (93 88 39 51, is in a class by itself. Here talented young chef Dominique le Stanc serves his interpretation of classic Provençal cuisine (full-flavored vegetables, fresh Mediterranean fish, Sisteron lamb), while his gracious wife Daniele makes sure that all goes well in the Regency dining room. The Chantecler is expensive, but offers a three-course luncheon menu for 200 francs, 250 francs with wine and coffee included. I have rarely eaten as well as I have here, and I urge you to take advantage of this chance to sample the best of the region's cuisine at a more than reasonable price. The Chantecler has an illustrious Michelin two-star rating. **Don Camillo**, 5 Rue des Ponchettes (93 85 67 95, serves upscale Italian-Niçois cuisine by Frank Cerruti, a former assis-

tant of Alain Ducasse. The **Grand Pavois (Chez Michel)** at 11 Avenue Meyerbeer (93 88 77 42, makes the best *bouillabaisse* in town, along with a full range of fish and lobster dishes, and veteran Côte d'Azur restaurateur Jacques Marquise and his vivacious wife Joianna, a Californian, maintain a relaxed ambiance, with most of the clientele regular customers. Another first-rate seafood house is **Dents de la Mer**, 2 Rue Saint François de Paule (93 80 99 16, a colorful eatery with an open terrace on the Cours Saleya and a pirate ship dining room with aquariums built into the walls.

Moderate
La Rotonde at the Hôtel Negresco (93 88 39 51, is a domed room decorated with brightly painted wooden merry-go-round horses that serves French bistro cuisine and Nice specialties under the supervision of Dominique le Stanc. One of the most

animated spots in town is the **Grand Café de Turin**, 5 Place Garibaldi (93 62 29 53, where fresh shellfish is served under the arcades, open to 11 PM. For solid brasserie fare try **Flo**, a member of the renowned Flo chain, at 4 Rue Sacha Guitry near Place Masséna (93 13 38 38. Here you eat in a former theater that has been converted into a spectacular dining space where the kitchen is on stage. Late supper specials served after 11 PM include a fresh seafood platter and white wine for 95 francs.

For light fare **L'Avion Bleu**, 10 Rue Alphonse Karr (93 87 77 47, serves salads, sandwiches and grilled meat and fish. The restaurant is decorated with Art Deco aeronautical posters and airplane models and stays open late.

NIGHTLIFE

For serious music, the **Opéra de Nice** presents classical concerts and a season of opera. For information contact the Opéra de Nice at 4-6 Rue Saint-François de Paule near the Cours Saleya market (93 80 59 83 FAX 93 80 34 83. Many concerts are held in churches. The Office of Tourism has a full schedule of programs. For a taste of the life in the fast lane, **Casino Ruhl**, 1 Promenade des Anglais (93 87 95 87, offers slot machines, table games, a Vegas-style floor show and a disco. The **Bar des Oiseaux** at 5 Rue Saint-Vincent, Vieux Nice (93 80 27 33, is a lively jazz club and café-theater with birds flying around the room. **Pam-Pam Masséna** at 1 Rue Desboutin (93 80 21 60, offers live Caribbean music in a tropical setting near Place Masséna. **Chez Wayne** at 15 Rue de la Préfecture (93 13 46 99, has rock music and British beer. **Frog** at 3 Rue Milton Robbins (93 85 85 65, has rock music, Tex-Mex food, steak and ribs.

HOW TO GET THERE

At the large, modern **Nice-Côte d'Azur Airport**, there are nine direct flights per day from London (Air France, British Airways, British Midland, Air UK) and one direct flight a day each from New York and Atlanta on Delta. There are 37 flights per day from Paris (Air France, Air Inter, AOM), and hundreds from 32 other cities in France and 40 cities in other European countries, as well as Africa and the Middle East.

There is bus service every 20 minutes on **Navette Bus Aeroport-Riviera** from the airport to Nice's Gare Routière (bus terminal), with stops along the Promenade des Anglais on its 15-minute route. The cost is 21 francs. If you want to take a **taxi**, be sure you have agreed on a price with the driver before you set off from the airport (the Tourist Office will tell you what a fair price to your

ABOVE: *Al fresco* dining is common virtually year-round in the balmy climate of Nice.

The Côte d'Azur

destination should be). Most of Nice's taxi drivers are honest, but there are enough bad eggs to have given them a bad reputation.

Nice is also well-served by **SNCF**, the national rail service. It has four direct trains a day from Paris and five more with connections in Marseille or Toulon. By high-speed trains (*trains à grande vitesse*, or *TGV*'s), the trip from Paris takes seven hours. These trains also stop at the major cities along the coast. In addition, the SNCF runs a regional service for the Côte d'Azur called Métrazur that makes all the local stops between Saint-Raphaël and Menton, with trains approximately every half hour.

For international bus service, **Eurolines** runs coaches from London and other non-French European cities, and the regional bus company **Phocéen Cars** runs buses from main points in Provence and the Côte d'Azur. There is no bus service to Nice from Paris or other French cities out of the region. (For more information on plane, train and bus service, see GETTING TO MEDITERRANEAN FRANCE), page 321.

Regionally, Nice's excellent train and bus service along the coast and inland make it the only practical base for exploring the eastern end of the Côte d'Azur. And for people traveling by car, all roads in the area lead to and from Nice.

EXCURSIONS INLAND

There are fascinating excursions to be made in every direction from Nice, but many are in directions in which travelers often fail to look — inland. The few I have selected will give you a sample of the variety available to those who can divert their gazes from the beguiling coast and cast them toward the mountains. These journeys are a ride on the "The Pine Cone Train" to the Alpes-de-Haute-Provence, a trip to a "perched village" near Nice. See also pages 117 to 118 for rambles in the magnificent and mysterious Vallée des Merveilles (Valley of Marvels) in the Alpes-Maritimes.

THE PINE CONE TRAIN

The Pine Cone Train (*Le Train des Pignes*) runs from Nice along the dramatic Var River Valley to Digne-les-Bains in the Alpes-de-Haute-Provence, a quiet refuge from the intensity of the coast. The train got its nickname in the nineteenth century because it was so slow-moving that people could hop off and on to gather pine cones. The distance from Nice to Digne is 152 km (95 miles), and the trip takes three hours. You can get off at any of the colorful hill towns along the way to poke around

Entrevaux, a stop on the route of the "Pine Cone Train" from Nice to the Alpes-de-Haute-Provence.

The Côte d'Azur

or have lunch, then get on another train and continue your journey. On summer Sundays, you can take a marvelous old steam train that only runs on the section between **Puget-Théniers** and **Annot**. One place to get off and explore is **Entrevaux**, a tiny town in the middle of nowhere with incongruously massive ramparts and fortifications running up a steep hill. This was once the frontier of France, and the fort and walls were built by Vauban to confront the Duchy of Savoy.

ANNOT AND DIGNE-LES-BAINS

Annot is a gracious medieval walled town of 1,100 in a bright mountain valley with a broad main street shaded by large plane tree and strange caves in the hills where ancient troglodytes once lived.

Digne-les-Bains (population 16,000) is a lively spa town, a center of lavender and fruit growing, with first-rate restaurants and hotels. It is the perfect base for exploring the Alpes-de-Haute-Provence. Be sure to visit **Samtzer Dzong**, a touch of Shangri-la in Provence. This is a the home of intrepid world traveler Alexandra David-Neel, the first Western woman to visit Tibet, who died here in 1969 at the age of 101. It is now a Tibetan meditation center which has been visited twice by the Dalai Lama.

General Information
The **Nice Tourist Office** can help you with train schedules and information, but note that the *Train des Pignes* does not leave from the Gare SNCF. It is operated by **Chemins de Fer de la Provence (** 93 82 10 17, and it leaves from the **Gare du Sud** at 4 Rue Alfred Binet, a few blocks north of the Gare SNCF. This is where you buy your ticket. There are five trains a day in the summer, and the Nice to Digne round-trip fare is 198 francs.

The town of **Annot** has a particularly helpful **Tourist Office**, located on the main square **(** 92 83 23 03. For information in **Digne-les-Bains** the efficient team at the large, modern **Tourist Office** at the main traffic circle, the Rond Point, can probably tell you anything you want to know about the town or the surrounding area **(** 92 31 42 73 FAX 92 32 27 24. For further information on hiking, horseback excursions, white water rafting, hang-gliding and other outdoors activities in the Alpes-de-Haute-Provence, contact ADRI-CIMES, 19 Rue Dr Honnorat, Digne-les-Bains **(** 92 31 07 01.

Where to Stay and Where to Eat
For a stay in a restful country town, **Annot** is the best choice, and the **Hôtel de l'Avenue**** just off the main square **(** 92 83 22 07 FAX 92 83 22 07, is pleasant and inexpensive. In **Digne-les-Bains**, the

OPPOSITE: Villefranche-sur-Mer on the Corniches of the Riviera, one of the finest natural harbors in the Mediterranean.

Hôtel Restaurant du Grand Paris*** 19 Boulevard Thiers **(** 92 31 11 15 FAX 92 32 32 82, is a seventeenth century monastery, now a charming hotel with 26 recently renovated, moderately priced rooms and the top restaurant in town. Owner-chef Jean-Jacques Ricaud's mastery of lamb, pigeon, game and other local ingredients has earned him a Michelin star. But the meal is expensive. **Origan**, an easy-going restaurant at 6 Rue Pied de Ville **(** 92 31 62 13, has tables on a pedestrian street in the summer and features snails, lamb with truffle butter and foie gras and other classic regional fare at moderate prices.

Twenty five kilometers (15 miles) west of Digne is **La Bonne Étape****** in **Château-Arnoux (** 92 64 00 09 FAX 92 64 37 36, a former coach house, now a handsomely decorated Relais & Châteaux inn, with 11 plush moderately-priced rooms and seven expensive suites, a pool and a restaurant that is the gourmets' first choice in Upper Provence. Here you can savor subtle delights prepared by the renowned father and son team of Pierre and Jany Gleize — zucchini blossoms stuffed with vegetables, duck with lavender honey and lemon, Sisteron lamb, a remarkable assortment of local cheeses, lemon and chocolate tart, and an exceptional wine list featuring the vintages of the South. La Bonne Étape is expensive.

THE PERCHED VILLAGE OF PEILLON

Peillon is one of the most dramatically perched of all "perched villages," 376 m (1,234 ft) up on the tip of a spur of rock overlooking the narrow valley of the Paillon River, its geometrical cluster of houses looking like the work of a Cubist painter. But the austerity is a facade. Once you get into the village, you find a charming square with a fountain, a medieval chapel with school of Nice frescoes and flowers everywhere. Despite its being only 19 km (12 miles) from Nice, Peillon has managed to remain one of the most authentic of all the medieval villages. (See LAND IN AN EAGLES' NEST, page 20).

Peillon is one of the 400 or so medieval "eagles' nest" villages in the Côte d'Azur and Provence region. They are built on the top of steep hills and surrounded by walls or arranged in such a way that the outer walls of houses form ramparts encircling the town, as in the case of Peillon. Today, these places look quaint, but they are vivid reminders of how dangerous life was in the Middle Ages, when Saracen pirates or roving bands of marauders known as "les grandes compagnies" could appear at any moment. It gave the inhabitants daunting defensive positions, and most importantly, the chance to spot the brigands trying to sneak up on them before it was too late. Inside a perched village, the streets are steep and narrow, with steps cut into the rock in places to get from one level to the next, and alleys run underneath

the houses. The local lord's castle was usually built at the highest point, but in many cases, it was replaced in more peaceful times by a church, as it was in Peillon in the eighteenth century.

Where to Eat

For lunch or dinner, the clear choice is the flowery, olive tree-shaded terrace of the **Auberge de la Madone** overlooking the valley at the foot of the village. The quality of the cooking, strictly seasonal and regional, matches the charm of the setting. Fixed-price menus start at 130 francs for a weekday lunch. This is a popular spot, so book in advance (93 97 91 17. The Auberge has 20 newly renovated rooms in bright Provençal decor and is an extremely restful place to stay. It is closed from late October to late January except at Christmas and New Year.

How to Get There

To get there by car from Nice, head out of town from Place Masséna on Boulevard Jean-Jaurès and Boulevard Risso following the signs for Sospel and follow D 2204 and D 21 to Peillon. The drive takes half an hour. The TRAM bus line runs three coaches a day from Nice's Gare Routière, in the early morning, at noon and in the late afternoon. The price is 12 francs.

ALONG THE COAST

The **Corniches of the Riviera** are three parallel roads that run 32 km (20 miles) across the face of the mountainous coast between Nice and the Italian border. The two upper roads offer such spectacular views of the Mediterranean and the shore line that they would be worth driving for the scenery alone. But the *corniches* also offer several exciting towns to visit, and even have a small foreign country tucked into their craggy folds, the Principality of Monaco.

The **Grande Corniche**, the highest, was built in 1806 by Napoléon and runs along Via Julia Augusta, the Roman route from Genoa to Cimiez. It has quasi-aerial views of the coast and sea. From the **Moyenne (Middle) Corniche** you get the best views of the Villefranche-Beaulieu-Cap-Ferrat section, and it provides the only access to the "perched village" of Èze. The **Corniche Inférieure**, built by the Princes of Monaco in the eighteenth century, twists along the coast, where Monaco and most of the towns are situated (see CRUISE THE CORNICHES OF THE RIVIERA, page 13).

Tour operators in Nice offer daily bus excursions to the towns of the *corniches* (see GENERAL INFORMATION, page 89), but if you can do it, I urge you to drive it yourself, to control your own pace and shift up and down from corniche to corniche at will.

The first town you come to is Villefranche seven kilometers (four miles) to the east of Nice, separated from it by Mount Boron.

VILLEFRANCHE-SUR-MER, BEAULIEU-SUR-MER AND CAP-FERRAT

Villefranche-sur-Mer, its next-door neighbor Beaulieu and the little Cap-Ferrat peninsula poking out into the sea, between them form one of the most exclusive areas in France, with estates by the dozens, luxury hotels, classy restaurants and yacht-filled harbors shielded by steep olive-wooded

hills. Incongruously, you will often find gun-sprouting warships in Villefranche, whose deep water port is used by the French, British and United States navies.

Since these towns form a unit, we have grouped their hotels and restaurants together to give you a better picture of the range that is available in the area.

BACKGROUND

Villefranche was founded at the beginning of the fourteenth century by the Count of Provence, Charles II of Anjou, as a free port, hence its name. Later in the century it fell into the hands of the Dukes of Savoy, who began fortifying Villefranche, one of the finest natural harbors in the Mediterranean, as their main naval base. Vauban so admired the Citadel, built in 1560, that he talked

Louis XIV into sparing it from demolition, a fate that the Château in Nice did not escape. Much of the harbor front and lower village date from the seventeenth and eighteenth century, when the Savoyard navy was a power to reckon with and was kept busy in wars against France.

In the 1920's, Jean Cocteau and his surrealist crowd stayed at the Welcome Hôtel on the waterfront, where they wrote, painted and composed music in the day and hobnobbed with sailors at night.

General Information

The **Tourist Office** is at Place François Binon on the Corniche Inférieure (93 01 73 68. The train and bus stations are to the east of the port overlooking the town beach. There are tourist offices at St-Jean-Cap-Ferrat, on the central street of the peninsula at 59 Avenue Denis-Séméria (93 76 08 90, and in Beaulieu-sur-Mer at Place Georges Clémenceau (93 01 02 21.

WHAT TO SEE

The **waterfront** is colorful, with houses painted in cheerful pink and pastel tones, busy cafés and restaurants and a small public beach to the east of the port. The **old town** rises almost vertically from the shore, and if you have good legs its winding old streets are fascinating to explore. It's so steep that in some places they've had to use stairs. Look for **Rue Obscure**, a street that tunnels under a row of houses in back of the harbor, parallel to the waterfront.

In 1957, Cocteau came back to Villefranche to portray the life of Saint Peter in frescoes and ceramics on the walls of the abandoned Chapelle Saint-Pierre. "It is beautifully done," noted Noel Coward in his diary. "Lovely craftsmanship and pale colors, but I had no idea all the apostles looked so like Jean Marais." Nearby in the **Citadel** is a museum of the late sculptor Volti, a long-time resident and ardent admirer of the female form.

Cap-Ferrat is the small, wooded peninsula directly to your left as you look out from the waterfront of Villefranche. To drive there from Villefranche, take the Corniche Inférieure east out of town, then take the first right you come to, and you are there. Or you can take the local bus to the little port of Saint-Jean-Cap-Ferrat. The Cap-Ferrat peninsula has dozens of lavish estates, Somerset Maugham's Villa Mauresque among them, but most are hidden from view by high walls, and trying to catch a glimpse of the lifestyles of the rich and famous is an exercise in frustration. But the **Villa Ephrussi de Rothschild**, the pink and white mansion constructed by Baroness Rothschild at the beginning of this century, is open to the public and displays her exquisite collection

of eighteenth century paintings, tapestries and furniture. There are also seven hectares (17 acres) of gardens with views of Villefranche and Beaulieu that should not be missed. It is closed on Mondays.

The view from **Pointe de Saint-Hospice** on the east side of the peninsula takes in the Gulf of Saint-Hospice, Èze, Monaco and Cap-Martin, with the Alpes-Maritimes soaring up from the sea. The old fishing port of **Saint-Jean-Cap-Ferrat**, also on the east side, now bulges with yachts and sailboats. It's a pleasant place to stop for a sandwich or a drink and watch the boats, and if you want to take a dip, there are several little beaches, including a sandy one — rare on this end

of the coast — the **Plage de Passable** on the west side of the peninsula.

Beaulieu, "beautiful place," so named by Napoléon, lies immediately to the east of Cap-Ferrat on the Baie des Fourmis (Bay of Ants), which got its name from the cluster of black rocks in the water. This flowery town is shielded by a ridge of high hills in back of it, which gives it one of the gentlest winter climates in France. **Villa Kerylos** sits on a bluff overlooking the east end of the bay. It is a lavish reproduction of an ancient Greek estate with a number of authentic Greek mosaics, statues, amphoras and vases, and its magnificent setting gives it views of Cap-Ferrat, the Gulf of Saint-Hospice and the "perched village" of Èze.

OPPOSITE: Villa Kerylos in Beaulieu-sur-Mer.
ABOVE: Villa Ephrussi de Rothschild in Cap-Ferrat.

The villa is open afternoons only, closed Mondays and the month of November.

WHERE TO STAY

For these who want to indulge themselves, some of the ritziest hotels on the Côte d'Azur are found in these towns. But good choices are to be found in moderate and inexpensive hotels too.

Luxury and Very Expensive

Grand Hôtel du Bel-Air-Cap Ferrat**** sits right on the tip of Cap-Ferrat, (93 76 50 50 FAX 93 76 13 02, in a 15 acre park with a funicular to its pool on the sea and 59 sumptuous rooms and suites.

It is a Relais & Châteaux member. Perched above the yacht harbor of Saint-Jean-Cap-Ferrat is the **Voile d'Or******, an elegant 50 room and five suite hotel with a view toward Èze and Monaco and a pool built into a rock shelf by the sea (93 01 13 13 FAX 93 76 11 17. The **Metropole******, 15 Boulevard du Maréchal Leclerc, Beaulieu-sur-Mer, (93 01 00 08 FAX 93 01 18 51, is a sunny, cream-colored nineteenth century Italianate palace now a 50-room, 3-suite Relais & Châteaux hotel with a large pool on the sea facing Cap-Ferrat. You can come for lunch and enjoy the pool facilities at all three of these hotels.

Moderate

At the **Welcome***** Quai Colbert, Villefranche-sur-Mer (93 76 76 93 FAX 93 01 88 81, you'll find 32 comfortable rooms at this lively hotel on the port where Cocteau and company stayed in the 1920's. In Saint-Jean-Cap-Ferrat, the **Brise Marine*****, Avenue Jean-Mermoz (93 76 04 36 FAX 93 76 11 49, has 16 pleasant, spacious rooms, a quiet garden and a view of the Gulf, convenient to the port and Pointe-Sainte-Hospice, but no pool or restaurant. The **Belle Aurore***** closer to the port at 49 Avenue Denis-Séméria (93 76 04 59 FAX 93 76 15 10, has 19 restful rooms, a pool and a garden restaurant.

Inexpensive

Coq Hardi** at 8 Boulevard de la Corne d'Or (Moyenne Corniche), Villefranche (93 01 71 06, a Logis de France inn, has 20 rooms, a restaurant and a pool with a view. **Costière*** at Avenue Albert 1er, Saint-Jean-Cap-Ferrat (93 76 03 89, has 15 neat, simple rooms, a garden and pretty views from the center of the cape.

WHERE TO EAT

All the four-star hotels mentioned above have excellent gastronomic restaurants which have earned them one Michelin star, and are quite expensive. **Le Provençal**, chef Jean-Jacques Jouteux's elegant restaurant at 2 Avenue Denis-Séméria overlooking the port of Saint-Jean-Cap-Ferrat (93 76 03 97, also sports a Michelin star and is noted for its fish and fowl dishes (the duckling in cinnamon crust is my favorite). There is a 200 franc luncheon menu. Down the street on the Port de Plaisance, **Le Sloop** serves imaginative seafood and pasta dishes at somewhat more modest prices (93 01 48 63. For a casual culinary experience, try lively **Cate's Place** (formerly Langoustine) at 10 rue du May, in Villefranche (93 01 91 86. It serves tapas, empanadas, ribs and hamburgers on red and white oilcloth tables.

HOW TO GET THERE

The *Métrazur* service has trains from Nice's Gare SNCF roughly every half hour in season, barely a five-minute trip.

There is also frequent bus service from Nice's Gare Routière. If you are driving from Nice, you have two choices. You can come via the Corniche Inférieure, which you pick up by taking Boulevard Carnot (N 98) east from Port Lympia and follow the coast around the base of Mount Boron to Villefranche, or, as I recommend, take the Moyenne Corniche (N 7), which winds up behind Mount Boron and gives you marvelous high angle views of Villefranche and Cap-Ferrat before you descend to Villefranche via Avenue du Général Leclerc. To get onto the Moyenne Corniche from Nice, take Rue Barla, four blocks north of Port Lympia. You can get to Beaulieu by *Métrazur* train or by bus.

ÈZE

From Èze-Bord-de-Mer, the beach town three kilometers (two miles) east of Beaulieu on the Corniche Inférieure, you can drive up to the "perched village" of Èze, sitting a rocky spur 427 m (1,400 ft) above the sea. Èze is located on the Moyenne (Middle) Corniche, and this is one of the few spots where there is an access road between *corniches*. Alternately, you can park your car at sea level and walk up the **Sentier Nietzsche** (Nietzsche's Path). This footpath that winds its way up to the village was the favorite promenade of the German philosopher when he vacationed here, and the philosopher is said to have thought out parts of *Thus Spake Zarathustra* when he took his walks. You'll see as the philosopher did, that the views of the coast get more and more powerful as you ascend, and from the top they nothing short of super. On a clear day you can see Corsica 100 miles away.

Èze is a typical medieval hilltop village in most ways, but unlike the others that normally have a castle or a church at the top, this perched village is crowned by a garden of cactus.

Hikers can pick up a map called *Èze Randonnées* (Èze Rambles) which will point out the many footpaths in this rugged area.

WHAT TO SEE

There is a fourteenth century **White Penitents' Chapel** with a strange thirteenth century Catalan crucifix in which Christ is seen smiling. The highest point of the village has the **Jardin Exotique**, an exotic garden with dozens of varieties of cacti and succulents built around the ruins of the castle. Spring is the best time to see the cacti, as they put out their psychedelic yellow, orange and blood red blossoms then.

BACKGROUND

Èze was originally a Celto-Ligurian *oppidum* that, due to its superb defensive and look-out position, was valued by the Greeks, Romans, Saracens, Counts of Provence and various medieval lords after Èze fell under Savoyard rule in 1388. Èze used to have a castle at the top of the town, but it was demolished by Louis XIV in 1706 during a war against Savoy.

As a monument in the village states, 100 percent of Èze's voters opted to join France in the County of Nice plebiscite of 1860.

GENERAL INFORMATION

The **Tourist Office**, is at Place du Général de Gaulle by the main gate of the village (93 41 26 00.

The Côte d'Azur

WHERE TO STAY

Èze has two exquisite small luxury hotels within the old village, the **Château Eza****** (93 41 12 24 FAX 93 41 16 64, and the **Château de la Chèvre d'Or****** (93 41 12 12 FAX 93 41 06 72. Both have breathtaking Riveria views. The Eza has eight rooms and suites. The Chèvre d'Or, a Relais & Châteaux member, has 19 rooms and suites and a small pool overlooking the sea. Both hotels are very expensive. An inexpensive alternative on a hill above the village is the **Hermitage du Col d'Èze**** on the Grande Corniche (93 41 00 68. This cheerful 14-room Logis de France inn has a pool,

The Grand Hotel Cap-Ferrat OPPOSITE and the Château de la Chèvre d'Or in the perched village of Èze ABOVE, two of the Riviera's many supremely elegant hotels.

sea and mountain views and a good, moderately priced restaurant. It is reached by taking D 46 from the village. Closed from mid-November to mid-January.

Camping
Les Romarins on the Grande Corniche is a wooded 50-place campsite with modest facilities (hot showers and a snack bar) and a magnificent panorama of the Alps, Cap-Ferrat and the sea (93 01 81 64. It is open from mid-April to the end of September. Be sure to reserve long in advance for the summer months.

WHERE TO EAT

At the **Château Eza**, the accent is on Provençal and Niçois cuisine, while the **Château de la Chèvre d' Or** specializes in more classically French fare, and both restaurants are very expensive. At his garden restaurant **Borfiga** on Place du Général de Gaulle at the entrance to the village, Chef Richard Borfiga serves refined Provençal fare and offers a special luncheon menu at 190 francs (93 41 05 23. All three restaurants have one Michelin star.

HOW TO GET THERE

The Métrazur train stops at Èze-Bord-de-Mer. Seven buses a day from Nice's Gare Routière stop at Èze's Place du Général de Gaulle and continue on to Monaco. By car, Èze can be reached directly from Nice by the Moyenne Corniche, or by the Corniche Inférieure to Èze-Bord-de-Mer and the access road up to the village, or by the Grande Corniche and D 46 from Col d'Èze down to the village.

THE PRINCIPALITY OF MONACO

Though the skyline has become cluttered with tax-sheltered banking and business high-rises, and Somerset Maugham, who called it "a sunny place for shady people," may be more right today than ever before, no visitor to the Côte d'Azur should think of bypassing Monaco. It is the best place on the Riveria to get a taste of the way the crowned heads of Europe lived during the "banquet years" of the late nineteenth century, thanks to the Grand Casino of Monte-Carlo and the other grandiose *belle époque* buildings clustered around it. They were frequented by kings, princes, emperors and legendary courtesans such as Caroline Otéro, "La Belle Otéro," whose perfect *poitrine* several Côte d'Azur hotels claim as the model for their domes. That ravishing creature was covered with jewels by the likes of King Edward VII, Czar Nicholas II, King Leopold II, King Alfonso XIII and William K. Vanderbilt, but when she eventu-

ally went broke, "La Belle Otéro" took it in stride. She said, "What does one come to Monte-Carlo for if not to lose?"

Besides its casinos and *belle époque* attractions, Monaco has one of the world's finest oceanographic museums, the world's largest exotic garden, the oldest and second-most publicized ruling family in the world, public safety second to none and a level of excellence in its hotels and cuisine that has set the standards for the world for more than a century. And with its illustrious Opera, Ballet and Philharmonic Orchestra and a first-rate line-up of pop stars at the Salle des Étoiles, Monaco's cultural agenda is remarkably rich for a country with only 28,000 residents.

BACKGROUND

In 1297, Francesco ("the Clever") Grimaldi disguised himself as a monk, coaxed the guards into

letting him into the palace, took out a sword and killed them, opened the gate to his associates and made himself master of Monaco. To this day, the Grimaldi coat of arms features two monks with swords in their hands.

In the mid-nineteenth century, after his citrus producing possessions of Roquebrune and Menton had broken away, and his remote little realm was threatened with bankruptcy, Prince Charles III took a plunge into casino gambling in the hope of reviving the economy. He built a gaming house on a goat-grazing rocky promontory called Spélugues and renamed it Monte-Carlo—Mount Charles. The railroad arrived a few years later, and with it the rich and demimonde from all over the world. Prince Charles's bet paid off so well that he exempted Monaco's residents from taxes in 1869, a status they have enjoyed ever since.

As Grimaldi rulers have been doing for seven centuries, Prince Rainier III, *"Le Patron"*

("the boss"), as his subjects call him, has redirected the economy of his little nation since coming to power in 1949. Aware that the gambling-based luxury tourism could no longer support the economy, he has focused on international banking and business tourism. At the same time, he has worked to maintain Monte-Carlo's image of glamour, a juggling act helped greatly by his 1956 marriage to the elegant Hollywood queen Grace Kelly.

In 1987, worried that the "Hong Kong of Europe" label was tarnishing Monte-Carlo's reputation for luxury, the Société des Bains de Mer (Sea Bathing Society), the major hotel, restaurant and casino-owning company in Monaco, whose largest shareholder is the Prince, hired an up-and-coming young chef to run its flagship Louis XV

For the daily changing of the Guard at the Prince's Palace in Monaco, be there by 11:55 AM.

MONACO AND MONTE-CARLO

Restaurant at Monte-Carlo's Hôtel de Paris. The SBM gave Alain Ducasse *carte blanche* and 20 million francs ($3.5 million) for renovations, and — haute cuisine being what is in French culture — pinned their hopes for refurbishing their aura on him. In 1990, at the age of 33, Alain Ducasse became the youngest chef ever to win three Michelin stars and has gone on to become one of the most influential chefs of the 1990's (food critics write about the "Generation Ducasse"). The Louis XV is one of a handful of the world's most highly regarded restaurants, and thanks to this success the star quality missing from Monte-Carlo since the tragic death of Princess Grace in 1982 has come back.

Riviera are the Airport-Riviera Shuttle Buses (93 21 30 83.

Take **Heli Air Monaco**, for helicopter trips between Nice Airport and Monaco and aerial tours of the region (92 05 00 50.

Taxi (93 50 56 28; 24-hour radio taxi (93 15 01 01.

Health emergencies, The Princess Grace Hospital Center (93 25 98 69.

PRINCIPAL EVENTS

The **Monte-Carlo Open**, the first big clay court tennis tournament of the year, is held at the Monte-Carlo Country Club in April.

GENERAL INFORMATION

No visa is needed to enter Monaco from France. Monaco uses French currency, but has its own postal system and issues colorful stamps.

The **Tourist Bureau** is at 2A Boulevard des Moulins, Monte-Carlo (93 30 87 01, and has superlative tourist literature and service. Pick up their map of Monaco's excellent public transportation system. If you are coming by private car, I suggest parking it (the big "P" indicates public parking) and getting around by foot, bus and the numerous public elevators that have been installed to take you from level to level in this steep town.

Other information that may be of use to you: The **Gare SNCF** (train station), on Avenue Prince Pierre is centrally located in the Condamine (93 25 54 54. The **Navettes Bus Aéroport-**

The Formula 1 auto race, the **Grand Prix de Monaco**, whose course runs through the city streets, takes place the weekend of Ascension (40 days after Easter); the town is jammed, so unless you're a fan, I suggest that you stay away. The **Festival International de Feux d'Artifice** is a fireworks festival held several evenings in July and August, when the world's leading pyrotechnics specialists put on shows. Check with the Tourist Bureau for the exact dates.

WHAT TO SEE

With only 195 hectares (468 acres) — half as big as New York's Central Park, two percent the size of

The Rock of Monaco, where the Prince's Palace, the Cathedral and the Oceanographic Museum are located.

The Côte d'Azur

Paris — Monaco is small enough to explore by foot. But to save time, take the N° 1 bus between Monaco ("the Rock," where the Palace and the Oceanographic Museum are) and Monte-Carlo, and to save leg muscles, the N° 2 to the Exotic Garden, high on a hill.

Small as it is, the Principality has seven distinct areas. From west to east, they are **Fontvieille**, a new business district with a heliport, a new harbor, and the football stadium; the **Exotic Garden** on a hill overlooking the sea and coastline; **Le Rocher**, the Rock of Monaco, a sheer-cliffed promontory on which the Prince's Palace, Cathedral, and Oceanographic Museum sit; the **Condamine**, which has the train station, market, and yacht

harbor; **Monte-Carlo**, where the casinos and de luxe hotels are; **Larvotto**, where the public beach and Monte-Carlo Sporting Club are; **Monte-Carlo Beach**, with the beach hotel and tennis courts, is located in neighboring Roquebrune. The **Monte-Carlo Golf Club** is on Mont-Agel 900 m (3,000 ft) above the sea.

For our sightseeing purposes, we will explore four of these areas, the Condamine, the Rock, the Exotic Garden and Monte-Carlo.

The Condamine

The Condamine is the center of Monaco, where the port cuts a swath between the steep promontories of the Rock and Monte-Carlo. Multimillionaires keep their Onassis-sized yachts in the **harbor**, and you can ogle them from the promenade or a café along the Boulevard Albert 1er. A colorful food and flower market is held mornings in and around the nineteenth century **Marché de la Condamine** a few blocks in from the harbor facing the Gare SNCF, the train station.

The Rock

The Rock of Monaco lies immediately to the west of the Condamine. This is where the Palace, the Cathedral and the Oceanographic Museum are located. The Prince's Palace (Palais Princier) is a large rambling, cream-colored Renaissance building on a wide square where the main event of the day is the changing of the guard at 11:55 AM. The Palace's seventeenth century Grand Apartments are sumptuous and there is a fine collection of Napoléonic memorabilia, thanks to Prince

Louis II's fascination with the Emperor. Guided visits are available daily.

The somber late nineteenth century neo-Romanesque **Cathedral** in the center of the Rock has several fine School of Nice paintings, including Ludovico Bréa's subtle 18-panel Saint Nicholas altarpiece, which will show you why he is known as "the Fra Angelico of Provence." To the left of the altar is the austere tomb of Princess Grace, touchingly decorated by bouquets from her admirers.

The **Musée Océanographique** atop the western face of the Rock was built in 1910 by Albert I, the Scientist Prince, for the collections he and his teams brought back from their pioneering oceanographic voyages in the early twentieth century. It has grown under the direction of Jacques-Yves Cousteau from 1957 to 1988 and under François Doumenge since then, and is one of the two sights

The Côte d'Azur

you absolutely must see in Monaco (the other being the Grand Casino). The aquarium is one of the world's finest, with 90 large bright modern tanks filled with 4,500 fish of 450 different species. The colors are dazzling, the movement hypnotic. This is a place you have to drag yourself away from. The upper floors contain scientific exhibits, including whale skeletons and a 13 m (43-ft) giant squid. There is a 60 franc entrance fee.

The Exotic Garden

The **Jardin Exotique** is a garden of cacti and succulents that grows up a protected rocky hillside overlooking the Condamine. In this warm, dry, windless micro-climate, many of these strange

machines-à-sous (slot machines) off to one side in the Salle Blanche. To get into the gaming rooms, you must show your passport and pay a 50 franc fee. No tie is required for the first rooms, where the minimum stakes are low, but to enter the *salons privés*, the private rooms where stakes start at 100 francs, there is an additional 50 franc entrance fee, and men must wear jackets and ties. (There's an even more private room where stakes start at $50,000, but you need to be known by the management to get in there). Even if you don't gamble, it's a thrill to wander through these incredibly ornate rooms and watch the high-rollers scatter their chips on the tables, like being in a James Bond movie. The **Opéra de Monte-Carlo** is located off

plants do better than in their African and American homelands. There are Mexican candelabras over 40 ft (12 m) tall, bigger than any in Mexico, and a 135 year-old *Echinocactus Grusonnii* sent back by Emperor Maximillan to Napoléon III. The garden is open daily and is most easily reached by the N° 2 bus from the Rock.

Monte-Carlo

The huge ornate *belle époque* **Grand Casino** on the Place du Casino is the focus of everything in Monte-Carlo. Designed by Charles Garnier, the famed architect of the Paris Opéra, in the 1870's, it is visited by more than a million people a year, though only six to seven percent actually try their luck in the vast rococo gambling rooms where roulette, chemin de fer, blackjack and baccarat are played. Finally yielding to popular demand several years ago, the Grand Casino installed

The Côte d'Azur

main the lobby of the Grand Casino. You can't always get in to see it, but it doesn't hurt to ask. It is a smaller but more opulent version of Garnier's Opéra de Paris. In the summer, the private gambling rooms move down from the Grand Casino to the Sporting Club at the beach in Larvotto.

Loews Casino is a Las Vegas-style gaming house in the Loews Hotel on the seafront of Monte-Carlo that brought the one-armed bandit to town in the 1970's. It also has craps, poker, punto banco and American roulette, and many people prefer its more easy-going American ambiance.

The **Café de Paris** on the Place du Casino has no gaming tables, but an impressive array of slot machines, and here there are no entry fees or dress requirements. Its lively outdoor terrace is the best

OPPOSITE LEFT: A street in old Monaco. OPPOSITE RIGHT: The Exotic Garden. ABOVE: The Café de Paris at the Place du Casino in Monte-Carlo.

spot in town for the other popular game in Monte-Carlo, people-watching.

Across the square is the glittering **Hôtel de Paris**, where the *belle époque* high rollers stayed. Notice the small equestrian statue of Louis XIV in the lobby. The horse's right knee is shiny because rubbing it is said to bring good luck. Be sure to look into **Louis XV-Alain Ducasse Restaurant** to the right of the entrance. It is one of most beautiful as well as one of the finest restaurants in the world (see WHERE TO EAT).

The **Musée National de Monaco** (Doll Museum), a short walk down the hill east of the Place du Casino at 17 Avenue Princesse Grace, has a huge collection of minutely detailed nine-

teenth century dolls, their furnishings and possessions, including printed books you'd need a magnifying glass to read. There are 80 automated figures with movements so human that they are eerie, Pierrot writing a letter, in particular. The museum is open daily.

WHERE TO STAY

Monaco has 2,258 hotel rooms, three-quarters of them in palaces or four-star hotels where prices run from 1,000 and 3,000 francs for a double. But there are a few comfortable, modestly priced rooms to be found here too.

Luxury/Very Expensive

The glamorous **Hôtel de Paris****** on Monte-Carlo's Place du Casino, (92 16 30 00 FAX 93 25 59 17, where Edward VII and other *belle époque* high-rollers stayed, has 129 supremely elegant rooms, 69 suites, a deluxe indoor-outdoor pool with a terrace overlooking the harbor and a health club with sauna, steam bath and massage. Its sister hotel, the Hermitage, in which the pool complex is actually located, shares this facility. The **Hermitage****** on quiet Square Beaumarchais (92 16 40 00 FAX 93 50 47 12, a few steps away from the Place du Casino, is a more discreetly elegant *belle épo-*

que masterpiece. It has a winter garden with a stained glass cupola designed by Gustave Eiffel, 220 rooms and 16-suites, many overlooking the harbor. This is my favorite hotel in Monaco. The **Monte-Carlo Beach Hotel***** Route du Beach, Monte-Carlo (93 28 66 66 FAX 93 78 14 18, is a 46 room Art Deco resort hotel on a lovely Mediterranean cove with a private beach, Olympic swimming pool, gourmet restaurant, rustic buffet-grill on a pier and snack bar. The 23 tennis courts of the Monte-Carlo Country Club are right up the hill. This is a very fashionable address, with designer Karl Lagerfeld the next-door neighbor.

Expensive

The **Abela***** 23 Avenue des Papalins, Fontvieille (92 05 90 00 FAX 92 05 91 67 is an up-to-date 192 room hotel built in 1989 and a member of the highly professional Abela chain.

Moderate

Hôtel le Siècle*** 10 Avenue Prince Pierre, Monaco (93 30 25 56 FAX 93 30 03 72 has 35 comfortable air-conditioned rooms near the train station.

Inexpensive

Hôtel de France** 6 Rue de la Turbie (93 30 24 64 FAX 92 16 13 34 has 26 simple rooms with showers. **Helvetia*** 1 *bis* Rue Grimaldi in the Condamine (93 30 21 71 FAX 92 16 70 51, has 25 modest rooms, 21 with a bath or shower.

WHERE TO EAT

One of the great restaurants in the world is the **Louis XV-Alain Ducasse**, in the Hôtel de Paris (92 16 30 01, where you will eat like a king, but healthier, on the sophisticated Provençal-Ligurian cuisine of Alain Ducasse. Here amid the glowing Louis XV period decor, you may choose your wine from among the 250,000 bottles in the cellar. Plan on 1,000 francs à la carte for dinner, but there is a three-course luncheon special on weekdays at 390 francs. The room only seats 50, so be sure to reserve well in advance. **Le Grill** (92 16 30 02, is the Hôtel de Paris's penthouse restaurant where you will dine overlooking the Grand Casino and the sea and savor the bright Provençal offerings of Ducasse protegé Bruno Caironi, whose talent has earned him a Michelin star. Expect to pay 600 to 700 francs for a meal. The **Saint-Benoît** at 10 Avenue de la Costa, Monte-Carlo (93 25 02 34, is an excellent fish restaurant overlooking the port with prices less than half those of the Grill. Still more modestly priced are the **Café de Paris** on the Place du Casino (92 16 20 20, for brasserie food on a large, busy terrace in the heart of Monte-Carlo's action, and **Pinocchio**, 30 Rue Comte Felix Gastaldi, Monaco-Ville (93 30 96 20, for good Italian fare in the old city. **Sam's Place**, 1 Avenue Henri

The Côte d'Azur

Dunant, Monte-Carlo (93 50 89 33, is a very relaxed place, good for grilled fish or meat. **Le Texan**, 4 Rue Suffren Reymond, Monaco (93 30 34 54, is a lively spot in the Condamine up the street from the port featuring Tex-Mex cuisine. Princess Stephanie comes here often.

NIGHTLIFE

The fashionable disco of the Principality is **Le Jimmy'Z** at the Monte-Carlo Sporting Club (93 24 14 14. **Stars and Bars** at 6 Quai Antoine 1er (93 50 95 95, has an American-style sports bar downstairs and a blues bar upstairs with live bands most nights. Here you'll find buffalo chicken

wings, baked potato skins, burgers, draft beer by the bucket and the occasional vocal by Prince Albert. Unquestionably the most relaxed place in town.

HOW TO GET THERE

From the Nice Airport, **Navettes Bus Aéroport-Riviera** (Airport–Riviera Shuttle Buses) depart every hour, and the 22 km (14 mile) trip takes 45 minutes. It costs 80 francs. **Heli Air Monaco** has **helicopter shuttles** every 20 minutes from Nice Airport and Monaco, a spectacular seven-minute trip, 350 francs one-way (which is 25 to 50 francs cheaper than a taxi). They also offer exciting aerial tours starting at 220 francs. There are **trains** from Nice's Gare SNCF train station every half hour in summer, somewhat less frequently off-season, a 15 minute trip. Travelers arriving by

train will find themselves in the heart of Monaco at the Gare SNCF in the Condamine. There are frequent **regional buses** from the *gares routières* (bus stations) of Nice or Menton that stop at a number of places along the Corniche Inférieure in Monaco. Coming by **car**, Monaco is most easily reached by the Corniche Inférieure (N 98), its main through street. For those who aren't daunted by the steep, twisting roads, D 53 winds down from both the Grande Corniche (D 2564) and the Moyenne Corniche (N 7).

MENTON

The contrast is striking. While Monaco races toward the twenty-first century, Menton is content to amble along in the nineteenth, which gives it its charm. This faded but still graceful Italianate seaside town of 29,000 (the same size as Monaco) on the frontier with Italy is known for its lemon trees, flower gardens and high proportion of retirees — almost a third of the population. Lemon trees produce fruit the year round, and a colorful Lemon Festival is held during Mardi Gras, with extravagant parade floats decorated in citrus fruits by the hundreds of thousands. Menton rivals Beaulieu as the warmest place on the Côte d'Azur.

BACKGROUND

Menton became a property of the Grimaldis of Monaco in 1346, and its citrus farming provided the bulk of the Principality's income until Menton and neighboring Roquebrune-Cap-Martin broke free of Monaco's rule in the great democratic upheaval of 1848. In 1860, the same year as Nice's plebiscite, Menton and Roquebrune-Cap-Martin voted to join France. Like Monaco, Menton (or "Mentone," as it was still known at the time) became a prosperous winter resort in the late nineteenth century, favored particularly by the English, as the large number of British-named hotels indicates. But they came for health reasons, not the high life, under the influence of Dr. J. Henry Bennet's best-seller, *Mentone and the Riviera as a Winter Retreat*, which promoted Menton's climate as a panacea against tuberculosis.

GENERAL INFORMATION

There are two **Tourist Offices** in Menton, the main one at the Palais de l'Europe, 8 Avenue Boyer on the Jardin Biovès (93 57 57 00, and a smaller one at the Pinède du Bastion near the town market just west of the port (93 28 26 27. They can give you

OPPOSITE: The lobby of the Hôtel de Paris. ABOVE: *Belle époque* facade on the Grand Casino of Monte Carlo, designed by Charles Garnier.

the dates of the **Chamber Music Festival** that is held in August.

For train information call **Gare SNCF** (93 87 50 50. The **Gare Routière**, the bus station, is on Route de Sospel (93 35 93 60. **Hippocampe**, a boat line based at Quai Napoléon III at the port (93 35 51 52, runs ninety-minute **boat trips** around the harbor and along the Riviera coastline from the beginning of April to the end of October. The fare is 50 francs.

WHAT TO SEE

La Vieille Ville is the pink and pastel old town winding up the hill overlooking the harbor, its

narrow streets lined with tall Genoese-style houses from the seventeenth century. At the top is the **Parvis Saint-Michel**, a Baroque square paved with gray and white stones with a mosaic of the coat of arms of town's former owners, the Grimaldi family. Two Baroque churches, the large **Église Saint-Michel**, and the **Chapelle des Penitents Blancs**, and several mansions of the period front on the square. Chamber music festival concerts are held here in August.

The **Promenade du Soleil** is a pleasant beach-front walk that intersects at the **Casino de Menton** with the **Jardin Biovès**, the flowery, palm and lemon tree-lined main esplanade of the new (nine-teenth century) town that runs diagonally inland from the shore.

The **Salle des Mariages**, the wedding hall in the Hôtel de Ville (City Hall) on Rue de la Répub-lique, has fanciful historical-mythological murals on the theme of love by the multi-talented Jean Cocteau. It is open weekdays. The **Musée Coc-teau** is in a small fort on the Quai Napoléon III at the east end of the Promenade du Soleil built by

Honoré II of Monaco in the seventeenth century. Here there are more love scenes by Cocteau in a series of paintings called "Innamorati" and an amusing animal series, "Animaux Fantastiques." Admission is free. The museum is closed Tues-days. The colorful town market **is held daily across the street.**

Besides the Jardin Biovès, two other gardens to see in Menton are **Jardin des Colombières** and the **Jardin Botanique Exotique** in the luxurious Garavan section in the hills to the east of the old town. The former is a six-hectare (15-acre) garden designed by Ferdinand Bac, a jack-of-all-arts and illegitimate son of Napoléon III, and features Mediterranean vegetation growing in seemingly wild profusion. The garden is open daily. The Jardin Botanique Exotique, also known as Val Rahmeh, the name of the villa it surrounds, be-longs to the Natural History Museum of Paris and has more than 700 varieties of plants, many from the Mediterranean, but others from tropical and subtropical areas as well. The gardens are terraced and offer lovely views of the sea and the town. The garden is closed Tuesdays. If you'd like a horticultural bonus, you can easily nip into Italy to visit the ravishing **Hanbury Gardens** at Mortola Inferiore, which is outside Ventimi-glia, four kilometers (two and a half miles) to the east. It has 2,000 varieties of plants from all four corners of the world. Hanbury Gardens is closed Wednesdays.

WHERE TO STAY

After the overwhelmingly luxurious hotel scene in Monaco, Menton is a real come-down. Its for-mer grand hotels have been converted into apart-ment buildings, and our recommendation here is to stay at one of the town's modest, but pleasant small hotels such as the **Hôtel de Londres**** at 15 Avenue Carnot (93 35 74 62 FAX 93 41 77 78. It has 21 neat rooms and is only 25 m from the beach.

WHERE TO EAT

Again, Menton's restaurants can't compare with Monaco's, but **Le Saint-Michel** has good fresh seafood in a number of intriguing fixed-price menus ranging from 75 to 250 francs with wine included. There is service with a smile by owner-chef Robert Guillou and his team. The restaurant is at 23 Rue Saint-Michel (93 35 55 44.

NIGHTLIFE

The **Casino de Menton**, built in 1934 and operated by the Lucien Barriere Group, is Menton's only real entertainment center, offering the full range of games, including slot machines which were

ABOVE: The quiet life in Menton, a haven for retired people. OPPOSITE: A popular resort for affluent English people in the last century, Menton retains a bit of the old *très British* charm.

installed in 1993, and a floor show at the Club 06. It is open daily all year (92 10 16 17.

HOW TO GET THERE

To get to Menton, take the Corniche Inférieure from Monaco and follow it along the coastal lowland 16 km (10 miles) to the east. There is Métrazur train service from Nice every half hour in the summer and frequent coach service by the **Rapides Côte d'Azur** (RCA) bus line.

ROQUEBRUNE-CAP-MARTIN

The town of Roquebrune-Cap-Martin has two distinct parts. Cap-Martin is a cape with a sea-level community, Roquebrune is on a hill town overlooking it, reached by the Grande Corniche. Before returning to Nice via the Grande Corniche, you may want to take a swing through **Cap-Martin**, a little peninsula directly west of Menton that we bypassed when we drove in from Monaco. Cap-Martin is one of the rare verdant spots in the area, with woodlands and magnificent, flowery estates. The road along the east side of the cape offers expansive views of Menton and the Italian Riviera, and on the west side, there are footpaths through the pines and cypresses. The coastal path to the west, the Promenade Le Corbusier, named in honor of the architect, who drowned here in 1965, reveals dramatic vistas of Monaco, the steep hills behind it and the castle of Roquebrune.

The road through Cap-Martin leads you to the Grande Corniche (D 2564). Follow it up into the bare, rocky hills overlooking the coast to the medieval village of **Roquebrune**, whose narrow streets, many of them vaulted, lead to the castle at the top.

BACKGROUND

Roquebrune's castle, one of the oldest in France, was built at the end of the tenth century by Count Conrad I of Ventimiglia as a defense against Saracen pirates. Like most properties of value around here, it eventually fell into the hands of the Grimaldis, who owned it for several centuries and rebuilt it to make it suitable for artillery. Originally the whole village of Roquebrune was part of the castle, but in the fifteenth century, the keep at the top was isolated from the rest of the buildings, and the village became a separate entity.

GENERAL INFORMATION

The **Tourist Office** is in the modern part of Roquebrune below the Grande Corniche at 20 Avenue Paul-Doumer (93 35 62 87.

WHAT TO SEE

Despite its souvenir and crafts shops, old Roquebrune has managed to conserve its medieval character, and prowling its steep, winding cobblestone streets, staircases and vaulted passageways is intriguing. Rue Moncollet leads to the top of the village, where you can't miss the **castle** with its massive walls 3.5 m (11.5 ft) thick. In the *donjon*, the castle's keep, the fully furnished and surprisingly small apartment of the medieval lord can be visited on the third floor. However cramped the lord of the castle may have felt in his quarters, the vast panorama from the fourth floor artillery platform more than makes up for it — the red roofs of the old village, Cap-Martin, Monaco, the sea and the mountains. Another sight to pause for is the 1,000 year-old olive tree just outside the village on the Route da Menton, 10 m (33 ft) around the middle.

Every August 5th, a large religious procession takes place in the afternoon in which scenes from the Passion of Christ are re-enacted at different places between the village and the Chapel of La Pausa, fulfilling a vow villagers made to the Virgin in 1467 after being spared from the plague.

WHERE TO STAY

At Vistaero Point 1,000 ft (300 m) up on the Grande Corniche in Roquebrune, the **Vista Palace Hôtel****** has the most spectacular view of any hotel. All of Monaco is at your feet to the west and Menton and the Italian Riviera in the other direction (92 10 40 00 FAX 93 35 18 94. Rooms in this elegantly modern hotel are expensive off-season and very expensive in-season, when standard doubles go for 2,400 francs. A much more modest choice, but cozy atmosphere is the 31-room **Westminster**** at 14 Avenue Louis Laurens, Roquebrune (93 35 00 68 FAX 93 28 88 50, a Logis de France member with a garden, sea views and doubles at 400 francs.

WHERE TO EAT

Le Vistaero, the Vista Palace's gourmet restaurant, serves refined French and Mediterranean cuisine against a panoramic backdrop at appropriately lofty prices. In contrast, at **Le Piccolo Mondo**, a warm little family restaurant in old Roquebrune, there is nothing remotely approaching elegance. You park yourself at a table, and Tony gives you all the good, inexpensive Italian food you can eat. It is at 15 Rue Grimaldi (93 35 19 93.

LA TURBIE

Heading toward Nice on the Grande Corniche, the next town to the west of Roquebrune is La Turbie seven and a half kilometers (four and a half miles) away, where you should stop for one more sensational panorama of the Riviera. Here you can see from Italy to the Esterel Mountains west of Cannes and on most days Corsica across the sea. You can also visit the **Trophée des Alpes** (Trophy of the Alps), the 50-m/165-ft high monument erected in 6 BC to celebrate Emperor Augustus's final triumph over the last independent tribes of Ligurians in the Alps. Though

miles). At 750 m (2,450 ft), **Sainte-Agnès** is the highest of all the Côte d'Azur's villages. It is 13 km (eight miles) north of Menton on D 22. **Castellar,** also the same distance from Menton on D 24, is where the *GR-51*, the *Grande Randonnée* hiking trail "the Balcony of the Côte d'Azur," begins. There are buses from Menton's Gare Routière to all three of these villages.

Another route north from Menton, D 2566 in the direction of Sospel, leads to the Roya Valley and the Vallée des Merveilles (Valley of Marvels).

THE VALLEY OF MARVELS

La Vallée des Merveilles is called that for two

mostly in ruins, four of its original columns remain standing.

EXCURSIONS INLAND

PERCHED VILLAGES

While you're on the eastern end of the *corniches*, there are three other dramatically perched villages you may want to see. All of them are at the dead end of narrow valleys leading in from the coast. **Gorbio** sits on a particularly savage rocky site, but in contrast, the houses are richly landscaped with flowers, olive trees and pines. It can be reached from Roquebrune by the narrow, twisting nine kilometers (five and a half mile) back road through the hills, or from Menton on the equally twisting D 23, a distance of 13 km (eight

reasons — the 100,000 designs scratched into its rocks by Bronze Age shepherds and the particularly magical quality of its scenery. In the summer, this bright mountain valley in the heart of the 70,000 hectare (270 square mile) Mercantour National Park is carpeted in grass and wildflowers, and there is a chain of crystal-clear lakes running north and south along the nine kilometers (five and a half miles) of the valley. Tall peaks surround it, and rugged Mont Bégo, 2,872 m (9,423 ft) high, dominates the scene. The valley was a site of pilgrimage for the Ligurians, and strange ancient inscriptions in stone enhance its aura of mystery. There are shapes that can be made out in the pictures — human figures, spears, axes, heads of

The grassy valleys, trails and mountain vistas of Mercantour National Park are only 50 km (30 miles) inland from Menton.

cattle, half moons — but also abstract designs whose meanings are unknown. Though the drawings are numerous, they are not easy to find, and first-time visitors are strongly advised to go accompanied by a professional guide. The valley can be visited safely from June through September, otherwise the weather can be a problem.

There are no roads in the Vallée des Merveilles. It can reached only by walking, but approved off-road vehicles can take you right up to its entrances. The access tracks lead in from the parallel valleys on either side, the dramatic **Valley of the Vésubie**, "Little Switzerland," to the east on Route D 2565 and the equally dramatic **Roya Valley** to the west on Route N 204 near the Italian frontier.

The principal towns for organizing trips into the Vallée des Merveilles are **Saint-Martin-Vésubie** to the west and **Tende** to the east. The **Association des Guides et Accompagnateurs des Alpes Méridionales** in Saint-Martin-Vésubie (93 03 26 60, or in Tende (93 04 69 22 can help you make your plans. In Nice, you can get help from the **Comité Régional du Tourisme Riviera-Côte d'Azur**, 55 Promenade des Anglais, Nice (93 44 50 59. Or, to make it really easy on yourself, you can take a combined bus and jeep tour from Nice. **Santa Azur** at 11 Avenue Jean Médecin (93 83 46 81, runs two all-day trips per week in the summer via the Roya Valley. The fare is 300 francs.

If you go up there from Menton, the Tourist Office on the Jardin Biovès can give you all the information you need.

NICE TO CANNES

As you head west out of Nice on the Promenade des Anglais, just past the Nice-Côte d'Azur Airport you cross the wide, pebbly, usually dry bed of the Var River, the former frontier between France and the Duchy of Savoy. And immediately across the river starts the most artistically rewarding cluster of towns and villages in France —

Cagnes-sur-Mer, Saint-Paul-de-Vence, Vence, Biot and Vallauris. Renoir, Matisse, Picasso, Chagall and Léger lived and worked here, and the area remains a prime *lieu* for artists, potters, glass blowers, weavers, sculptors and jewelry makers, many of whose workshops are open to the public. The first town you come to is Cagnes-sur-Mer.

CAGNES-SUR-MER

Cagnes-sur-Mer, directly west of the Var River, is made up of three different parts: Cros-de-Cagnes on the coast, the modern town of Cagnes-Ville on the hill and the walled medieval village of Haut-de-Cagnes at the town's highest point. Driving along the N 98 coast road from Nice, you will first pass through the cluttered sea-level beach and port area of **Cros-de-Cagnes**, where the **Hippodrome de la Côte d'Azur**, the race track, is located. You can go to daytime horse races here from December through March and evening races in July and August. For information call (93 20 30 30. But the main attractions in Cagnes-sur-Mer are to be found two kilometers (one and a quarter miles) in from the coast in hilltop Haut-de-Cagnes.

BACKGROUND

As in many places along this coast, the Grimaldi name figures heavily in this town's history. The Château Grimaldi was built as a fortress in 1309 by Rainier Grimaldi, Lord of Monaco and Admiral of France. A later member of this branch of the family, Henri Grimaldi, gained the favor of Cardinal Richelieu and Louis XIII by influencing his cousins in Monaco to ally themselves with France. The riches heaped upon Henri Grimaldi by France enabled him to transform the old fortress into an opulent Renaissance château in 1620 and financed several generations of notoriously high-living descendants until the people of Cagnes threw them out of town during the Revolution.

GENERAL INFORMATION

The **Tourist Office** is on the hill in the modern part of town at 6 Boulevard Maréchal Juin (93 20 61 64.

WHAT TO SEE

Enter the thirteenth century main gate of **Haut-de-Cagnes** and wind your way up the steep streets to the castle at the top of the hill. The **Grimaldi Château and Museum** has a bright Renaissance patio and banquet hall contrasting with the heavy vaulted medieval rooms on the ground floor. On the second floor is the **Museum of Modern Medi-**

terranean Art, with paintings by Chagall, Dufy, Fujita, Kisling and other artists who worked on the Côte d'Azur. The **Suzy Solidor Bequest**, also on the second floor, is a group of 40 portraits of the popular French musical star of the early twentieth century by well-known artists of the period, including Cocteau, Dufy, Picabia and Marie Laurencin. The château-museum is closed Tuesdays and from June 10 to 30 and the beginning of October to mid-November.

The **Musée Renoir** on Route des Collettes east of Haut-de-Cagnes is the house where Pierre-Auguste Renoir moved to in 1908 at the age of 67 in hopes that the Mediterranean climate would enable him to keep painting. Though assistants had to fix his brush between his crippled arthritic fingers, Renoir's twelve final years turned out to be among his most productive (the Musée d'Orsay's "Les Grandes Baigneuses" is an example), and ten canvases from this period are on display in the museum. Renoir also took up sculpture for the first time, by proxy, through a young sculptor who followed his instructions. His large bronze statue "Vénus Victrix" stands in the garden, amid flowers, lemon, orange and olive trees. The museum is closed Tuesdays and from October 15 to November 15.

WHERE TO STAY

The deluxe hotel is **Le Cagnard***** on Rue Pontis-Long in Haut-de-Cagnes (93 20 73 21 FAX 93 22 06 39, a fourteenth century mansion within the town walls converted to a Relais & Châteaux hotel with 18 rooms and 10 suites. A moderately priced choice is **Les Collettes**** at 38 Chemin des Collettes (93 20 80 86, a 13-room modern hotel with a pool facing the Renoir Museum.

Camping

There are eight camping grounds in Cagnes-sur-Mer, nine in the neighboring town of Villeneuve-Loubet-Plage and numerous others in other parts of this area. For information, ask at the Tourist Office or contact L'Hôtellerie de Plein Air des Alpes-Maritimes at the Parc des Maurettes, 730 Docteur Lefèvbre, Villeneuve-Loubet-Plage (93 20 91 91.

WHERE TO EAT

Le Cagnard has the most glamorous restaurant in town, serving inventive dishes such as John Dory with fresh pasta in octopus ink and lamb with fresh coconut, rating one Michelin star, quite expensive. It is closed at lunch Thursdays and from the beginning of November to mid-December. At the **Restaurant des Peintres**, 71 Montée Bourgade au Haut-de-Cagnes (93 20 83 08, young chef Alain Llorca, trained by Alain Ducasse and Dominique Le Stanc, has also earned himself one Michelin

star. He serves Provençal cuisine with menus starting at 200 francs including wine. Closed Wednesday and mid-November to mid-December. At **Josy-Jo**, 4 Place Planastel, Haut-de-Cagnes (93 20 68 76, you'll dine on fish or meat grilled on a wood fire served on the lively terrace by the Bandecchi family, delicious, but also expensive. It is closed at lunch on Saturday, all day Sunday, and from mid-July to mid-August. **La Bourride** in Cros-de-Cagnes (93 31 07 75, is a small, elegant eatery in a pine grove facing the port with seafood at honest prices (menus from 150 francs). It is a good place to try the savory Mediterranean fish stew after which it is named. Closed Wednesday and two weeks in February.

HOW TO GET THERE

By train, take the Métrazur line to the station at Cagnes-sur-Mer, which is in the lowland part of town. There are frequent buses from the train station to Haut-de-Cagnes. There are also frequent buses from Nice's Gare Routière. Tour operators in Nice run daily tours excursions to Cagnes-sur-Mer, Saint-Paul-de-Vence and the other artistic villages of this area (see GENERAL INFORMATION, NICE, page 89. If you are driving, take the N 98 coast road west from Nice, turn right onto D 36 at the Hippodrome and drive two kilometers (one and a quarter miles) north to Haut-de-Cag-

ABOVE: Renoir's studio at the Renoir Museum in Cagnes-sur-Mer, where the artist spent the last twelve years of his life. OPPOSITE: The Marina Baie des Anges, a modern luxury apartment complex west of Nice.

nes. The old town is open to pedestrians only. So park you car at the underground parking area by the main gate (look for the big letter "P").

SAINT-PAUL-DE-VENCE

Built on the slopes of an especially graceful hill, Saint-Paul-de-Vence, seven kilometers (four miles) north of Cagnes-sur-Mer, is another medieval walled village that has had an exceptional involvement in the arts.

BACKGROUND

Saint-Paul-de-Vence was one of the fortified villages guarding Provence's frontier with Savoy, and it owes its sixteenth century ramparts to King François I, who built them to ward off aggression by his perennial rival Emperor Charles V. The town declined in the nineteenth century, but became a favorite of artists such as Bonnard, Modigliani and Picasso in the 1920's and was adopted by film celebrities such as Yves Montand and Simone Signoret, who were married on the terrace of the **Colombe d'Or**, the hotel and restaurant the artists made their clubhouse.

GENERAL INFORMATION

The **Tourist Office** is inside main gate of the walled village, on the right side of Rue Grande ℂ 93 32 86 95.

WHAT TO SEE

Inside the imposing fourteenth century portal, the steep, narrow streets of the village are lined with handicrafts shops and souvenir boutiques, since this is a prime stop for tourist buses, especially in the summer. But no matter how crowded it gets, the view from the top of the sixteenth century ramparts, with fields of flowers and orange groves in the valleys and the Alps towering in the distance, makes a visit worthwhile. The **Church**, which dates from the early thirteenth century, but was largely redone in Baroque style, has a rich treasury of twelfth to fifteenth century silverwork and a painting of Saint Catherine of Alexandria attributed to Tintoretto.

The **Colombe d'Or** has one of the finest personal art collections in France, with works by Bonnard, Picasso, Matisse, Dufy et al, that owner Paul Roux amassed as payment of artists' hotel and restaurant bills. You can see it for the price of a meal. The Colombe d'Or is opposite the main portal of the village.

One kilometer north-east of the village, idyllically set in a pine forest, is the museum of the **Fondation Maeght**. It was built in 1960 to house the dazzling collection of the husband and wife team of modern art dealers, Aimé and Marguerite Maeght. It is one of the museums I enjoy most in France. Sculptures by Calder, Arp and Miro greet you as you cross the green lawn to the entrance, and inside Architect Jose-Luis Sert's sweeping pavilion are paintings by Bonnard, Matisse, Chagall, Braque, Léger, Kandinsky and De Staël. In a grassy inner courtyard you will find a cluster of Giacometti's lanky figures, and Miro has a playful sculpture garden all his own. Be aware that in the summer much of the permanent collection is loaned out or put in storage to make room for exhibits by contemporary artists. The museum is open daily but closed at lunch time off-season.

WHERE TO STAY

Expensive
The famous **Colombe d'Or*** is outside the main gate of the medieval village ℂ 93 32 80 02 FAX 93 32 52 94. It has 15 very attractive, expensive rooms and 10 very expensive suites, a pool, and modern art. Just west of town on the route to Colle-sur-Loup is the **Mas d'Artigny**** ℂ 93 32 84 54 FAX 93 32 95 36, a Relais & Châteaux member, with 52 deluxe rooms and 29 suites amid 20 acres of pines and private pools with 25 of the living units.

Moderate
At the **Orangers*** Chemin des Fumerates, Saint-Paul-de-Vence ℂ 93 32 80 95 FAX 93 32 00 32, you'll find six charming rooms in an orange grove with fresh juice at breakfast. To get there from the

village of Saint-Paul, take the Route de la Colle for one kilometer (six-tenths of a mile) and turn right onto Chemin des Fumerates. The **Hostellerie de l'Abbaye*** is on Route de Grasse in **La Colle-sur-Loup**, the residential village next door to Saint-Paul-de-Vence (93 32 66 77 FAX 93 32 61 28. This medieval residence of the Saint-Honorat monks has 13 pleasant rooms and a pool, with rooms in both the moderate and expensive price range. **Marc Hely*** is on Route de Cagnes D 6) in La Colle-sur-Loup (93 22 64 10 FAX 93 22 93 84, and has 15 modern rooms in a countrifed setting.

WHERE TO EAT

The food is good at the **Colombe d'Or**, but it is the delightful atmosphere on the large terrace restaurant overlooking the countryside that makes this expensive place worth the money. The **Mas d'Artigny**'s veranda restaurant also has a panoramic view, and its sophisticated regional cuisine has earned it one Michelin star. At the **Hostellerie de l'Abbaye** you'll dine in the cloister on noted chef Stephane Bensherif's Provençal cooking with menus from 190 francs. It's very popular in the summer so be sure to reserve early.

HOW TO GET THERE

There are frequent local buses from Cagnes-sur-Mer. By car, take D 6 from Cagnes-sur-Mer to Saint-Paul-de-Vence via La Colle-sur-Loup, a distance of seven kilometers (four miles).

VENCE

Vence is a large walled medieval hill town of 15,000 on a plateau 10 km (six miles) from the Mediterranean with a open view of the sea and the mountains. It lies four kilometers (two and a half miles) north of Saint-Paul-de-Vence and is considerably less crowded than its neighbor. Its most noted attraction is Matisse's Chapelle du Rosaire.

BACKGROUND

Vence was founded by the Ligurians and later became an important Roman town. It was one of the early centers of Christianity, and from the fourth century until the Revolution, its destiny was guided by a series of powerful bishops. The most remarkable of the bishops was Godeau in the seventeenth century, an ugly dwarf-like man, but a brilliant wit, poet, man of letters and favorite of aristocratic ladies. Cardinal Richelieu made him the first member of the Académie Française. But Godeau renounced the worldly life at the age of 30, took holy orders and was appointed Bishop of Vence the following year. He devoted himself

to improving the town, introducing the industries of tanning, perfume-making and pottery and rebuilding the Cathedral for the next 36 years of his life until his death in 1672.

GENERAL INFORMATION

The **Tourist Office** is in the center of town at Place Grand-Jardin (93 58 06 38.

WHAT TO SEE

Matisse considered his decoration of the **Chapelle du Rosaire**, completed in 1951, the culmination of everything he had been striving to achieve. He designed the stained glass windows of the chapel simply and in three colors — lemon yellow for God and sunlight, grass green for vegetable life and blue for the Mediterranean sea. His famous biblical figures on the walls are done in bold black outlines, baked into white ceramic tiles. The soft light from the windows gently colors the figures on the surrounding walls, creating an otherworldly effect. Matisse also designed the boldly patterned priests' robes, the paper cut-outs of which can be seen at the **Musée Matisse** in Nice.

The Chapel is on Route D 2210 about a kilometer (six-tenths of a mile), north of town (the street is named Avenue des Poilus in town and changes to Avenue Henri Matisse as you approach the Chapel). From the outside the chapel is a little white box that you could easily drive past without noticing. The chapel is open Tuesdays and Thursdays from 10:00 to 11:30 AM and 2:30 to 5:30 PM, closed November 1 to December 14. (93 58 03 26.

La Vieille Ville, the old part of Vence within the walls, has preserved its medieval character. If you enter the town on the west side by the fortified **Porte de Peyra**, you find yourself in the **Place du Peyra** where the Romans had their forum and there is now a pretty eighteenth century fountain. A market is held here every morning, and there are many crafts boutiques. The **Cathedral** was built over several centuries from the Romanesque to the Baroque periods, and there are even some Roman stones with Latin inscriptions to be seen. You may also visit the **tomb of Bishop Godeau**.

WHERE TO STAY AND WHERE TO EAT

The magnificent **Château Saint-Martin****** on Avenue des Templiers is a former Knights Templar residence in a 32-acre private park with views of Vence and the coast. Its 14 rooms and 10 suites are richly furnished with antiques, and its Michelin one-star restaurant is known for superb Provençal cuisine. This Relais & Châteaux mem-

OPPOSITE: An installation by Miro in the sculpture garden of the Fondation Maeght in Saint-Paul-de-Vence.

ber is open from mid-March to mid-November
(93 58 02 02 FAX 93 24 08 91. To reach it, take the
D 2 north in the direction of Coursegoules two
and a half kilometers (one and a half miles). It is
very expensive. For a moderately-priced hotel,
La Roseraie**, a Logis de France member, is a
peaceful 12-room country house with a pool in a
garden setting on Avenue des Templiers, direction
Coursegoules (400 m or 1,300 ft from the center of
town) (93 58 02 20 FAX 93 58 99 31. La Roseraie is
closed the month of January. It has no restaurant.
For an inexpensive hotel and restaurant, try the
Auberge des Seigneurs** on Place Frene (93 58
04 24 FAX 93 24 08 01. This quaint old stone inn in
La Vieille Ville has 10 pleasant rooms at a top room
rate of 330 francs and serves hearty regional food
in the medium price range.

HOW TO GET THERE

There are frequent local buses from Saint-Paul-de-
Vence, Cagnes-sur-Mer (where you can connect
with the Métrazur train line) and Nice, and three or
four shuttle buses a day from Nice Airport to Place
Grand-Jardin. By car, take D 2 from Saint-Paul-de-
Vence, four kilometers (two and a half miles).

TOURRETTES-SUR-LOUP

The cliffside village of **Tourrettes-sur-Loup** five
kilometers (three miles) west of Vence became a
virtual ghost town after World War II, but was
brought back to life by the artisans who settled
here. It is now one of the leading handicrafts villages of the Côte d'Azur and for its mixture of
quality and ambiance, the one I like best. It is much
less touristy than Saint-Paul-de-Vence and much
more authentically artisanal. The countryside
around Tourrettes is a major producer of violets,
and during the Fête des Violettes in March, all the
houses are decked with the flowers.

GENERAL INFORMATION

The **Tourist Office** is on the main square, Place de
la Libération (93 24 18 93.

WHAT TO SEE

The main attraction here is the **handicrafts workshops**. The town is especially noted for its weavers, but Tourrettes also has fine potters, jewelry-
makers, wood-carvers and metal sculptors, many
of whom you can watch as they work. Almost all
are on Grande-Rue, the little horseshoe-shaped
main street that follows the line of the town's cliff,
entered by either of the gates on the main square.
The fifteenth century **church** has a School of Nice
triptych, and the Chapelle Saint-Jean at the en-

trance to the village is decorated with charming
naïve frescoes done by Ralph Soupault in 1959.

HOW TO GET THERE

Tourrettes can be reached easily by bus from
Vence, as it is on the line between Vence and
Grasse. Ask at the Tourist Office in Vence for the
schedule. By car, it is five kilometers (three miles)
west of Vence on D 2210.

FURTHER AFIELD

THE GORGES OF THE LOUP RIVER

West of Tourrettes-sur-Loup, the Loup River cuts
a deep gorge into the Pre-Alps of Grasse, presenting a chance for a drive through some of the most
spectacular scenery in the South of France.

The distance is only 35 km (22 miles), but you should figure on a good two hours to make this drive. To explore the gorges of the Loup River you will need a car or some other form of self-locomotion. The **Tourist Office** in Tourrettes-sur-Loup has information on the entire area, but there is also a tourist office in Bar-sur-Loup, in the Donjon of the Château (93 42 72 21.

Bar-sur-Loup

Bar-sur-Loup is a handsome hilltop village 16 km (10 miles) west of Tourrettes-sur-Loup on D 2210 where Americans can pay homage to of one of the great heroes of their Revolution, Admiral Count François de Grasse, whose family seat this was. His naval blockade of Chesapeake Bay in 1781 prevented Lord Cornwallis and his Redcoats from escaping by sea, thus enabling Washington, Rochambeau and Lafayette to close the trap at Yorktown, the turning point of the war. A life-size bronze of Admiral De Grasse is in the main square by the church.

At the **Église Saint-Jacques**, put a franc in the coin-operated timing device to light up the 14-panel **altarpiece** by School of Nice master Ludovico Bréa. On the rear wall of the church is the haunting Danse Macabre, a primitive work painted on a wood panel by an unknown fifteenth century artist. It shows a death-figure firing arrows into the thighs of dancers to punish them for dancing during Lent, after which their little naked souls leave their bodies through their mouths. They are then weighed on a scale by Saint Michael who is seated at the foot of Christ, before being hurled into the mouth of a Hieronymus Bosch-like monster representing Hell.

The eagle's nest village of Gourdon high above the gorges of the Loup River, a Saracen stronghold in the Middle Ages.

The Côte d'Azur

For lunch, **L'Amiral** is a bright, spacious restaurant in an eighteenth century house on the Place du Château that once belonged to the Admiral. It serves tasty menus from 80 francs.

Bar-sur-Loup to Gourdon
Continuing the circuit, head north from Bar-sur-Loup to Pont-du-Loup and take D 6 north along the crest of the dramatic **gorges of the Loup** where you will find a lovely waterfall a few kilometers farther along the road. At Bramafan, cross the river and wind southward on D 3 for the best views of the deep gorge this little river has cut, especially dramatic from the eagle's nest village of **Gourdon**. This old Saracen stronghold sits on

a rocky spur 500 m (1,640 ft) above the river, 765 m (2,510 ft) above sea level, and offers a vast panorama of the valley, the coast and the mountains. With its winding streets and restored houses, this perched village of only 230 year-round inhabitants has a wonderful atmosphere off-season. During the summer, however, it tends to get crowded with tourists and vendors selling carved olive wood pieces, honey and nougat. The thirteenth century **Château** was built on the foundations of the original Saracen fortress, and architectural features of the original one were retained. There is a **Historical Museum** on the ground floor with a disturbing collection of ancient weapons and a prison with a torture table. Seven rooms on the second floor contain the **Museum of Naïve Painting**, with a fine collection of naïve art by international artists from the period 1925–1970 and a portrait by Henri Rousseau. The Château has three levels of terraced **gardens by Le Notre**, the designer of Versailles's gardens, and from the top level you get the same grand panorama as from the square by the church.

A cheerful, moderately-priced lunch spot with a view is the **Taverne Provençale** at Place Église Grandure.

ABOVE: The colorful Fernand Léger Museum in Biot.
OPPOSITE: A pottery workshop in Vallauris.

BIOT

Back on the coast road, you'll find Biot, a pleasant and remarkably tranquil old town in the heart of prime tourist country between Cagnes-sur-Mer and Antibes. Biot has been known since antiquity for its earthenware jars made from the rich local deposits of clay, and while a few potters carry on the tradition, the town was supplanted as the area's main ceramics producer in the nineteenth century by the booming potteries of Vallauris. It is the glass-blowers who now draw people to Biot.

GENERAL INFORMATION

The **Tourist Office** is at Place de la Chapelle in the center of town (93 65 05 85.

WHAT TO SEE

At the **Verrerie de Biot**, you can watch master glass blowers at work, a magical process resulting in the tasteful vases, glasses and pitchers in pale shades of blue, green and purple bubble glass that you can buy at the retail shop. The Verrerie is open daily from 8 AM to 7 PM (93 65 03 00. It is across from the Léger Museum.

The **Musée Fernand Léger** with its football field-sized (500 sq m) mosaic facade of sports scenes in primary reds, blues, yellows and greens is one of Biot's major attractions. The museum is southeast of the village, just off D 4, watch for the signs. Léger lived and worked in Biot and bought the site in 1955 to create a sculpture garden, but died shortly thereafter. Madame Léger oversaw the construction of the museum, which opened in 1960 and was enlarged in 1989. It has 348 of Léger's paintings, ceramics and tapestries featuring his chunky people at work and play in the industrial age and the world of the circus. The museum is closed Tuesdays.

The **Église-Sainte-Madeleine-Saint-Julien** has two School of Nice altarpieces, the eight-panel "Retable du Rosaire" (Virgin of the Rosary) attributed to Ludovoco Bréa and the four-panel "Ecce Homo" by Giovanni Canavesio.

The winding narrow streets and colonnaded **Place des Arcades** have great charm, especially in the evening after the day-trippers have gone back to Nice or Cannes.

Marineland
The largest marine zoo in Europe is **Marineland** in La Brague, on the coast road four kilometers (two and a half miles) from Biot. The show features porpoises, orcas, seals and other trainable creatures of the sea (93 33 49 49.

Next to Marineland there is a permanent **fairground** with large water slides, a farm with animals of Provence, miniature golf, and a jungle walk filled with thousands of butterflies.

WHERE TO STAY

The **Hostellerie du Bois Fleuri***** 199 Boulevard de la Source (93 65 68 74 FAX 92 94 05 85, has 12 spacious rooms in a pink Provençal inn in the woods which are moderately priced. The **Hôtel des Arcades*** (93 65 01 04 has 12 pleasant rooms at inexpensive to moderate prices.

Camping

There are numerous camping grounds in neighboring Villeneuve-Loubet-Plage. For information, again, contact **L'Hôtellerie de Plein Air des Alpes-Maritimes** at the Parc des Maurettes, 730 Docteur Lefevbre, Villeneuve-Loubet-Plage (93 20 91 91, or contact the Office of Tourism in Biot.

WHERE TO EAT

The charming **Auberge du Jarrier** at 30 Passage de la Bourgade (93 65 11 68, serves the refined Provençal cuisine of Christian Metral, with fixed-price menus starting at 200 francs. It rates one Michelin star. This is a very popular restaurant, so be sure to reserve. It is closed Tuesday at lunch in July and August. **Terraillers** on 11 Route du Chemin Neuf at the foot of the village (93 65 01 59, is a sixteenth century pottery workshop, now an elegant restaurant with Claude Jacques's gourmet Provençal cuisine. It also boasts one Michelin star and has menus starting at 160 francs. Closed Thursday at lunch in July and August and every Wednesday, and from November 1 to the beginning of March. For good food in a vivacious setting, I head straight for the **Galerie-Café-Hôtel des Arcades**, 16 Place des Arcades (93 65 01 04, the Brothier family's bistro in the arcades of old Biot. Here you will find *pistou*, *pieds de porc*, *tripes à la Niçoise* (vegetable soup, pigs knuckles and Nice-style tripes) and other Provençal specialties. The copious 160 franc menu is an excellent value. Be sure to reserve early, as the 15 tables are usually packed. The family also runs the hotel and has an interesting contemporary art gallery.

HOW TO GET THERE

To get to Biot by train, take the Métrazur line to La Brague on the coast where the station is located. There is a bus every hour from the station to Place des Arcades in Biot. To come by bus, there is also frequent local bus service along the coast road. If you are driving, take D 4 from La Brague, four kilometers (two and a half miles).

VALLAURIS

Pottery has been made at since the time of the Romans. In 1501, after the population had been wiped out by the plague, 70 Genoese families were brought in to re-populate the village, potters among them. These families reconstructed the town and laid it out in the checkerboard pattern we see today.

In 1946 Picasso, who was then living nearby in Golfe-Juan, met the potters Georges and Suzanne Ramié, who invited him to their studio, Madoura, in Vallauris. Picasso fell in love with the process, moved to Vallauris and started

working with the Ramiés, turning out as many as 25 pieces a day. Picasso's work in ceramics brought Vallauris great fame. In 1952 he returned to Vallauris and painted the huge "War and Peace" fresco in an abandoned chapel.

Today Vallauris, two kilometers (one and a quarter miles) inland from Golfe-Juan, is a bland, semi-industrial town of 25,000 which makes a living from the mass production of ceramics. But you can find some independent potters here and many ceramics boutiques that carry the full gamut of quality from the sublime to the dreadful.

GENERAL INFORMATION

The Tourist Office is in the center of town on Square du 8 Mai 1945 (93 63 82 58. To arrange visits to potters' workshops, contact **L'Association Vallaurienne d'Expansion Céramique**, which is in the heart of town at 15 Rue Sicard (93 64 66 58.

WHAT TO SEE

The **sixteenth century Château** is a sixteenth century priory of the Îles de Lérins monks and one of the few examples of Renaissance architecture in Provence, and it houses two museums. The **Musée National de la Guerre et de la Paix** is an abandoned chapel with Picasso's huge frescoes on its walls. On the left are the horrors of war, on the right the joys of peace, and on the rear the brotherhood of Man, with the four races shaking hands and holding aloft the dove of peace. The other museum is the **Musée Municipal de Céramique et d'Art Moderne**. It has a collection of droll Picasso ceramics and six rooms on the second floor devoted to Italian-born painter Alberto Magnelli (1888–1971), who worked most of his life in France.

You can see potters working at the **Musée de la Poterie** on Rue Sicard or simply walk along Avenue Georges Clémenceau, Rue du Plan or Rue Sicard where you can find plenty of shops to drop in on. Alain Ramié runs **Galerie Madoura** where Picasso worked with his parents George and Suzanne, and this studio has the exclusive right to sell reproductions of Picasso's pottery. It is on Avenue des Anciens-Combattants-d'Afrique-du-Nord (93 64 66 39.

HOW TO GET THERE

By local bus service, you can reach Vallauris from Place Charles de Gaulle in Antibes or from the Gare SNCF in Cannes, the train station there. If you are driving from Biot, take D 504 west for eight kilometers (five miles), then left on D 103 for two kilometers, then right (west) on D 435 for the last two kilometers.

ANTIBES

Antibes is one of the oldest, most attractive port towns of the Côte d'Azur with a wide, sheltered harbor filled with yachts, ramparts along the sea front, and the star-shaped Fort Carré perched on a steep hill. Antibes, its ritzy peninsula of Cap d'Antibes and its nightlife oasis of Juan-les-Pins all have good beaches. Antibes is famed for the many varieties of roses created here (one-third of all varieties sold in the world), though less and less are grown because of the high price of real estate. In addition, this growing metropolis of 70,000 has Sophia-Antipolis, the large new high technology complex in the hills nicknamed the "Silicon Valley of the Côte d'Azur." This blend of the very old and the very new makes Antibes, perhaps more than anywhere else, the epitome of today's South of France.

BACKGROUND

The name Antipolis, "the city opposite," was given to the town by the Greeks from Massalia who founded the port in the fifth century BC. But opposite what? Most scholars say Nice, but others say Corsica. In the civil war between Caesar and Pompey, Antibes sided with the winner and was rewarded with special status, prospering under Roman rule, unlike its mother city of Marseille which lost all. But the Visigoths and Ostrogoths reduced it to rubble after the fall of the empire,

and plagues and Saracen pirates almost finished it off. By the year 1,000, the city was practically a ghost town. Under the Angevin Counts of Provence and local ownership by yet another branch of the Grimaldi family, Antibes returned to prosperity, particularly after 1388, when Nice defected to Savoy and Antibes became Provence's easternmost port. A century later it became the Kingdom of France's easternmost port, which was a mixed blessing, since the town was bombarded time and again by the navies of the Dukes of Savoy, Emperor Charles V and the British.

GENERAL INFORMATION

Tourist Office is at 11 Place du Général de Gaulle in the center of town (92 90 53 00.

The **train station, Gare SNCF** is near the port on Avenue Robert-Soleau (93 99 50 50.

The **Gare Routière**, the **bus terminal**, is located at Place Guynemer just east of Place du Général de Gaulle (93 34 37 60.

For **taxis**: Gare SNCF (93 33 93 97; Place du Général de Gaulle (93 34 03 47.

There are numerous **auto rental agencies**: **Avis** (93 34 65 15; **Budget** (93 34 36 84; **Côte d'Azur Auto** (93 67 81 81; **EuropCar** (93 34 79 79; **Fun Location** (93 67 66 94; **Hertz** (93 61 18 15; **Midi Location** (93 34 48 00.

Bike and motorbike rental can be found at **Holiday Bikes**, 2 Rue des Frères Garbero (93 74 50 25.

Le Petit Train, the little motorized tourist train, makes a 50-minute circuit of Antibes and Juan-les-

inscriptions, sometimes upside-down, that show how the successive masters of Antibes re-worked the materials left by their predecessors.

Picasso left the mark of his genius in many places in Mediterranean France, but nowhere more powerfully than in the Château Grimaldi. In the autumn of 1946, he was living in Golfe-Juan, and desperately in need of a studio, and Dor de la Souchère, the director of the modest local museum in the Château, offered him the use of some empty rooms. This was during the early period of Picasso's relationship with Françoise Gilot, one of the most joyous periods of his life, as evident in *La Joie de Vivre*, his large painting of a voluptuous nymph dancing on the seashore, centaurs tooting

Pins, leaving Place des Martyrs de la Résistance in downtown Antibes every hour on the hour from 10 AM to 11 PM in the summer. The fare is 30 francs.

WHAT TO SEE

La Vieille Ville is the walled old city that centers on the medieval **Château Grimaldi** and **Cathedral**, with mighty **ramparts** on the sea side that were designed by Vauban in the late seventeenth century. The Greeks built here first, followed by the Romans and later the Grimaldi, who built their château in the twelfth century on top of Roman ruins. Its watch tower dates from medieval times too, as does the matching Saracen tower nearby, so-named because it was used to watch out for the pirates. As you wander about, look carefully at the stones of the buildings and you will see Latin

flutes and smiling goats prancing. Picasso departed Antibes after six months and left his enormous output of the period to the Château Grimaldi museum, and it became the core of the **Musée Picasso**. Two years later he added a dazzling selection of his ceramics from Vallauris. The museum later added Picasso prints from different periods and also acquired first-rate works by other twentieth century artists — Léger, Ernst, Klein, Arman, Raysse, Alechinsky, César, Germaine Richier and ten works by Nicholas de Staël, including his last work, the huge, partially unfinished canvas *The Big Concert*, painted in Antibes in 1955 the week before he took his own life. The museum is closed on Tuesdays, major holidays and from early November to early December.

Sculptures by Germaine Richier on the sea wall of the Picasso Museum in Antibes.

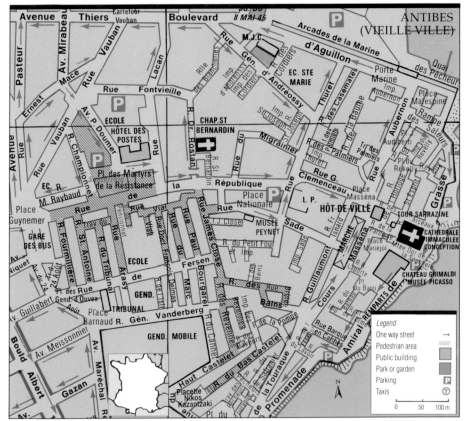

Antibes's **Provençal market**, one of the best on the Côte d'Azur, is held every morning except Mondays in the open pavilion on the Cours Masséna and around it, outside the walls of the old city. **Veziano**, the *boulangerie-pâtisserie* on 2 Rue de la Pompe near the market, makes deservedly famous *pissaladière*, the Nice-style onion pizza.

The eastern Côte d'Azur is not wine country, but **Domaines Ott**, the prestigious maker of Côtes de Provence and Bandol wines, has a retail outlet in Antibes. For a preview of wine-tasting visits to their vineyards in the Var, sample some of their distinctive wines at 4 Avenue Edmond Salvy, Antibes (93 34 38 91.

WHERE TO STAY

Very Expensive

The **Hôtel du Cap****** at the tip of Cap d'Antibes (93 61 39 01 FAX 93 67 76 04, is a vast, sumptuous palace built in 1870 with acres of gardens and a private beach facing the Îles de Lérins. Masters of the universe come here to unwind. Your fellow guests will be the likes of the Marvin Davises, who had $10 million in jewels with them until they were robbed in their limousine on the way to the Hôtel du Cap in 1992. It is the most expensive

hotel in the area, and no credit cards are accepted. Open April through October.

Moderate

The **Miramar***** at the Plage de la Garoupe, Cap d'Antibes (93 61 52 58 FAX 93 61 60 01, is a relaxed beach hotel with 31 moderately priced rooms and a restaurant for guests only. Open March through November. The **Royal***** Boulevard Maréchal **Leclerc, Antibes** (93 34 03 09 FAX 93 34 23 31, is an old-fashioned 38-room hotel situated south of the ramparts of Old Antibes near the beach of La Salis with its own restaurant, the Dauphine. Closed from the second week of November to mid-December. The **Mas de la Pagane**** 15 Avenue du Mas Ensoleillé (93 33 33 78 FAX 93 74 55 37, is an eighteenth century country house a short walk from Old Antibes with five spacious, comfortable guestrooms, a garden restaurant and a peaceful, country-like ambiance.

Inexpensive

Relais du Postillon** 8 Rue Championnet (93 34 20 77, has 14 pleasant rooms in downtown Antibes. The **Auberge Provençale*** at 61 Place Nationale (93 34 13 24, has five simple rooms with baths two blocks from the market.

WHERE TO EAT

Le Bacon at Cap Bacon on Cap d'Antibes (93 61 50 02 is my first choice in this area. It serves delicious *bouillabaisse*, rated the best on the Côte d'Azur, and that and their other fresh seafood dishes have earned the Sordello brothers a Michelin star. The dining terrace is delightful with a magnificent view over the Baie des Anges. It is very expensive, but very popular, so reserve early. **Aux Vieux Murs**, Promenade Amiral de Grasse (93 34 06 73, is a sunny restaurant with vaulted ceilings built into the ramparts of old Antibes with a beautiful view of the port. It serves a delicious four-course Provençal menu with such choices as young rabbit pie, *pissaladière* made with fresh cod flakes, mixed fish casserole with *ratatouille* sauce and stuffed saddle of lamb for a reasonable 200 francs. The **Mas de la Pagane** serves good, fresh regional cuisine in its restful garden with a view of the sea or in the dining room of the handsome old country house. Menus start at 140 francs. Closed Sunday evenings and at lunch time in the summer.

CAP D'ANTIBES

Cap d'Antibes is the small peninsula that starts just to the south of Vauban's ramparts and extends some two and a half kilometers (about a mile and a half) into the sea, with the Baie des Anges to the east and Golfe Juan to the west. This lovely cape is studded with majestic umbrella pines, covered with elegant estates and ringed by pretty beaches, one of which, La Garoupe, became the setting for the famous opening scene of Fitzgerald's "Tender is the Night." Scott and Zelda spent a good deal of time here in the 1920's visiting Gerald and Sara Murphy at their Cap d'Antibes estate, the Villa America. The novel's palatial hotel was modeled on the Hôtel du Cap. The views are marvelous from everywhere.

The **Jardin Thuret** on Boulevard du Cap is a botanical garden that has been introducing plants from other warm climates to the Côte d'Azur environment since 1857. Some 3,000 species of exotic trees and plants are represented in the four hectare (10 acre) spread, including the eucalyptus, now very common on the Côte d'Azur, which the garden brought in from Australia. The Jardin Thuret is open weekdays and entrance is free.

The **Sanctuaire de la Garoupe** is a sailors' shrine with a large collection of marine ex-votos, naïve paintings that have been offered as thanks to Notre-Dame-de-Bon-Port (Our Lady of Safe Homecoming), the patron saint of sailors, for saving their lives in storms, shipwrecks and other accidents. On either the first or second Sunday of every July there is a solemn procession in which the gilded wooden statue of Notre-Dame-de-Bon-Port, which has been brought down to the Cathedral in Antibes a few days earlier, is returned to the Sanctuary by the seamen. The **Musée Naval et Napoléonien**, is a former gun battery, is a museum with a collection of Napoléonic memorabilia. It has a fine panorama of the Îles de Lérins.

JUAN-LES-PINS

Stretched out on the gentle curve of a fine sandy shore immediately to the west of Cap d'Antibes, Juan-les-Pins has something no other town on the Côte d'Azur can boast of: a jumping night life

area. Cafés, bars, discos and pizzerias are jammed to all hours, which makes Juan-les-Pins a great place for the young.

Background

It was here in 1921 that restaurateur Edouard Baudoin came up with the revolutionary idea of launching a summer season on the Riviera, which up until then had been strictly a winter vacation land. Millionaire Frank Jay Gould, son of the "Mephistopheles of Wall Street" Jay Gould, came up with the financing, and they built the first casino here. It was a great success, but a bitter one for Baudoin, because a few years later, Gould, true to his robber baron genes, aced him out of it. But Baudoin has not been forgotten by Juan-les-Pins: the most prestigious street for nightlife, where the

A beachful of youth at Antibes.

modern Eden-Casino is located, is named Boulevard Edouard-Baudoin. The vogue of sunbathing first caught on in Juan-les-Pins in the 1920's, and its pine-lined shore remains one of the best on the Côte d'Azur.

General Information
Tourist Office is on the waterfront at 51 Boulevard Charles Guillaumont (92 90 53 05. Bikes and motorbikes can be rented at **Antibes Cycles**, 33 Boulevard Guillaumont (93 76 80 61. For **taxis** call (93 61 14 08 or 93 61 09 39.

What to See
The action is basically the beach and the night life, but from the middle to the end of July, **Jazz à Juan**, one of Europe's premier jazz festivals, which started here in 1960, is held in the Pinède, the pine grove in the center of town. Information about the Jazz Festival can be obtained from the Tourist Office.

Where to Stay
Juan-les-Pins is essentially a summer resort. Except as noted, the following hotels are open from April through October. If you are planning to stay for a week or more, a number of modern apartment complexes rent out furnished studios and apartments which can be less expensive than hotels. The Tourist Office has a list.

VERY EXPENSIVE

The **Juana****** on Avenue Gallice (93 61 08 70 FAX 93 61 76 60, is an elegant 1930's resort with an easygoing ambiance. It has 45 rooms, a pool complex amid palms and flowers and a private beach across the Pinède. The **Belles Rives****** on Boulevard Edouard-Baudoin (93 61 02 79 FAX 93 67 43 51, was the Fitzgeralds' favorite. This 41-room Art Deco hotel is directly on its own private beach and has recently been restored to the way Scott and Zelda liked it.

MODERATE

The **Sainte-Valérie***** at Rue de l'Oratoire (93 61 07 15 FAX 93 61 47 52, a few steps from the Pinède has 30 comfy, well-equipped rooms with prices in both the moderate and expensive categories. The **Pré Catelan**** at 22 Avenue des Lauriers, Juan-les-Pins (93 61 05 11 FAX 93 67 83 11, is a pleasant 18-room hotel in a palm garden a few minutes walk from the beach and is open all year.

CAMPING

There are ten camping grounds in Juan-les-Pins with more than 1,600 places. For information, ask the Tourist Office.

Where to Eat
La Terrasse at the Hôtel Juana is the leading gourmet table in the Antibes area, and chef Christian Morriset has earned two Michelin stars with his Provence-accented cuisine. The 250 franc luncheon menu is more than worth it. A legend among

Côte d'Azur chefs, Jacques Maximin has created a Provençal menu for the **Restaurant du Casino** that is prepared by his talented young assistant Olivier Gouin and served on the terrace overlooking the beach, with a luncheon menu at 200 francs. The restaurant is in the Eden-Casino on Boulevard Edouard-Baudoin (92 93 71 71. **Bijou Plage**, on Boulevard Charles Gillaumont (93 61 39 07, has a seafood restaurant on the beach with a good luncheon menu at 100 francs. Neighboring **Moorea Plage** has live Brazilian music and modestly priced food and is popular with the young professional crowd (93 61 58 68. **Vesuvio** and **La Bodega** in the heart of the entertainment district make good pizzas.

Nightlife
Every night is Carnival in Rio at the main intersection of the nightlife area, as the Brazilian bands at the open-air **Pam-Pam** and **Le Festival** clubs fire salvos of samba across the street at each other. The Pam-Pam is at 137 Boulevard Wilson (93 61 11 05, Le Festival is at 146 Boulevard Wilson (93 61 04 62. One block away, rock bands from the **Mezza Rock Café** at 16 Avenue Dautheville (93 61 60 70 blast their sounds into the street. The **Madison Piano Bar** at 6 Avenue Alexandre III (93 67 83 80 features jazz. In the summer, the seven discos and numerous bars are hopping until three or four in the morning. More adult-type pursuits, such as gambling your life's savings away, are focused on the **Eden Casino** on Boulevard Baudoin (92 93 71 71.

Trompe l'oeil at the ultra-deluxe Hôtel du Cap on Cap d'Antibes.

HOW TO GET THERE

There are several trains a day from Paris, Marseille, Toulon and Italy that arrive at the Gare SNCF in Antibes. The local Métrazur train also makes frequent stops there. Buses from Cannes and Nice, including the Nice Airport shuttle bus, stop at Place du Général de Gaulle. All other buses stop at the Gare Routière. By car, Antibes is easily reached by the A 8 *autoroute* or the N 98 coast road. Access Juan-les-Pins by car from Antibes, taking Boulevard Wilson west from Place Charles de Gaulle, a five minute drive. Juan-les-Pins has its own SNCF train station on Avenue de l'Esterel. There are also local buses along the coast.

GOLFE-JUAN

Golfe-Juan is an uninspiring little beach town that neighbors Juan-les-Pins to the west. It is known mainly as the place where Napoléon landed on March 1, 1815, after escaping from exile on Elba. This marked the beginning of the Hundred Days, when Napoléon rallied the country to his banner and led it to Waterloo. There is a suitably gravestone-like monument by the beach at the spot where the Emperor landed. This is where the Route Napoléon starts, the modern road that follows the trail Napoléon took to the north. Golfe-Juan is also the place where Robert Capa took the wonderful photograph of Picasso following Françoise Gilot on the beach holding a big umbrella over her head.

CANNES

In December 1834, Lord Brougham, the former Chancellor of the Exchequer and one of the best-connected men in England, was on his way to Italy for the winter, but his coach was stopped at the Var frontier by the Savoyard health authorities because of a cholera quarantine. Unable to proceed, Lord Brougham returned west along the coast until he came to a little fishing village in a magnificent natural setting with reeds (*cannes*) fringing its pretty harbor. He fell completely under the charm of the place, bought land and started building a villa. His upper class friends came from England to visit and started building villas of their own. And so, by this twist of fate, Cannes was launched on its upscale trajectory. Gourmet restaurants, fine shops and luxury

hotels soon followed. The Prince of Wales gave his weighty stamp of approval. Grand Duke Michael of Russia financed the Cannes-Mandelieu golf club. The Hôtel Carlton went up in 1912 and became the touchstones of Cannes's aura of wealth and glamour.

On the level of permanent cultural attractions, Cannes is no Nice or Antibes. But it makes up for this lack by putting on festivals and conventions practically non-stop. The Cannes Film Festival in May is the most famous, and the hype it generates is a key factor in maintaining Cannes's image of glamour, but there are literally dozens of other trade shows and festivals, and even if they don't interest you directly, they keep the city's hotels, restaurants, casinos and nightspots hopping most of the year. "Life is a Festival," Cannes says, and it means it.

BACKGROUND

The earliest traces of habitation in Cannes are from a Celto-Ligurian settlement on Mount Chevalier, the hill of the Suquet district overlooking the harbor. The Romans followed and set up a military post there, Castrum Marsellinum. In the eleventh century, the monks of Saint-Honorat, who owned Cannes, built the square tower you see on the highest point of the hill. It was needed to watch for Saracen pirates, for whom the monks' island monastery just off the coast was a juicy target. The monastery became very wealthy during the Middle Ages as one of France's most popular sites of pilgrimage. Ultimately the pirates and various foreign navies made life too difficult for the monks, and they abandoned the Island of Saint-Honorat, leaving the fisherfolk of Cannes to fend for themselves.

Lord Brougham introduced Cannes's new lifestyle and economy in the nineteenth century. But he also helped the local fishermen by getting his friend King Louis Philippe to clean up the harbor, which had become overgrown with reeds.

In 1939 the Cannes Film Festival tried to hold its first session, but was annulled by the outbreak of World War II. It resumed in 1946, and its success has been a big factor in Cannes's overall success in tourism. Cocteau, Bardot, Truffaut, Goddard, Belmondo, Deneuve and Delon set a sophisticated European tone in the 50's and 60's, but from the 70's on, the Festival has gone more and more Hollywood. Today's pilgrims to Cannes are movie producers who flock to the Festival in May and devote themselves to business pursuits with more-than-religious zeal. The Freudian quest for fame, power, riches and the love of women reverberates everywhere, and people-watching on the Croisette, amusing the rest of the year, becomes more and more frenzied as the Festival goes on, with all eyes darting about for a glimpse of a Star. But even in the era of Stalone

---

Inhibitions evaporate on the beaches of Southern France OPPOSITE, as here in Cannes. OPPOSITE BOTTOM: The Old Port of Cannes, which Lord Braugham came upon by chance in December, 1834.

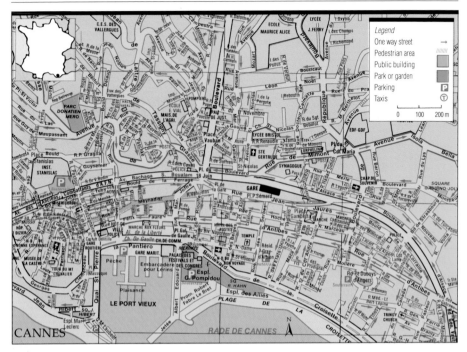

and Schwartzenegger, Cannes has somehow managed to maintain its image of class.

GENERAL INFORMATION

There are **two Tourist Offices**. The main one is at the central landmark of the city, the **Palais des Festivals** (locally known as *"Le Bunker"*) (93 39 24 53, and the other one is at the **Gare SNCF** (train station) (93 99 19 17. The staff will make hotel reservations for you, provide you with free local maps and brochures and help you with festival bookings.

Transportation Contacts

The **Gare SNCF** is centrally located on Rue Jean Jaurès, which parallels the Croisette five blocks in from the beach. For train information call (93 99 50 50 (main line trains or the local Métrazur line).

There is a **bus terminal** at the Gare SNCF for buses to the neighboring hill towns such as Mougins, Grasse and Vallauris (93 39 31 37. The **Gare Routière** bus station by the Hôtel de Ville has buses that run along the coast (93 39 11 39. There you can also get the **bus to Nice-Côte d'Azur Airport** (93 31 30 30. For **long-distance trips**, the **CTM station** across from the Palais des Festivals at Square Prosper Merimée has buses for Marseille, Aix, and Avignon (93 39 79 40.

Bus Azur is the city's bus line, and its terminus is by the Hôtel de Ville (93 39 18 71.

At the **Gare Maritime**, the maritime terminal is next to the Palais des Festivals, you can get boats to the Îles de Lérins.

For **taxis**: **Hôtel de Ville** (93 39 60 80; **Hôtel Majestic** (93 99 52 10; **Gare SNCF** (93 38 30 79; **Hôtel Carlton** (93 38 09 76. Car rental: **Avis** (93 94 15 86; **Budget** (93 99 44 04; **Europcar** (93 39 75 20; **Euro Dollar** (93 94 10 99; **Hertz** (93 99 04 20.

You can **rent bikes** at the **Gare SNCF baggage counter** (93 38 20 10. **Bike and motorcycle** rental can also be found at: **Cannes Location Rent**, 5 Rue Allés between Rue d'Antibes and the Gambetta parking garage (93 39 46 15; **Location Mistral**, 4 Rue Georges Clémenceau to the west of the Vieux Port (93 39 33 60.

Medical emergencies: dial 15 for SAMU (emergency medical service).

FESTIVALS

Festivals, congresses and large business gatherings keep Cannes active forty weeks of the year. The biggest, the **Cannes Film Festival**, is held the second and third weeks of May. Other large entertainment industry gatherings are MIDEM for the music business in January and MIP-TV in April and MIPCOM in October for television. **Guitares Passion**, a festival of all styles of guitar music, is held in April. Summer is very active for musical events, with **Nuits Musicales du Suquet**, a classical music festival in mid-July, and about fifty jazz, pop and rock concerts run at the outdoor **Théatre de la Mer** throughout the summer. Three dates to note in your travel agenda are July 14, August 15 and August 24. This is when Cannes stages its **Pyro-Musical Evenings**, fireworks displays scored to music over the Croisette. They are fabulous. In November, there is the **Cannes International Dance Festival**. For schedules and details, contact the Tourist Office.

WHAT TO SEE AND WHAT TO DO

Modern Cannes

There are two different Cannes, really, one old and one new. The one the whole world knows is the modern Cannes. It centers on the palm-lined **Boulevard de la Croisette** with its palatial hotels and cafés and luxury shops fronting on the long crescent of beach to the east of the Palais des Festivals, the dividing point. For beach lovers,

and in the evening stop at the lounge of the Art Deco Martinez, where you will find genial Jimmy McKissic entertaining at the piano. The serene **Majestic** and the ultra-modern **Noga Hilton** are also well worth a visit.

Upscale **shopping** is a main activity in Cannes, whose Golden Triangle of luxury boutiques is comparable to Rodeo Drive in Beverly Hills or Rue du Faubourg Saint-Honoré in Paris. The shopping course runs from the mall of the Noga Hilton along the Croisette to the Galleries of the Gray-d'Albion and on to Rue d'Antibes, the city's main shopping street. Haute couture, men's fashions, jewelry, perfume, leather work, shoes and other luxury products can all be found

the long sandy curve of the Croisette is lined with beach clubs, each with a restaurant, open for lunch only, except for special holiday nights (see WHERE TO EAT, page 137). The palatial hotels all have elegant beach clubs open to one and all, for a price. There are free public beaches in Cannes too, but only one small one in this costly part of town, in the sea-side of the Palais des Festivals. (The best public beaches are at **Gazagnaire** on the east side of Pointe de la Croisette, which gets the best sun in the morning, and the **Plages du Midi** west of the Vieux Port, which gets it in the afternoon).

The *"palaces,"* as the palatial hotels of the Croisette are called, play a large part in keeping the feeling of glamour alive in Cannes, and to get in touch with that glamour, you should visit the lobbies of these stunning establishments. Pause for a drink on the legendary terrace at the **Carlton** where the movie crowd gathers at Festival time,

here, often with the words "and Cannes" added to New York, London and Paris on the label.

But the greatest fun in this part of Cannes is **people-watching** along the Croisette, and that doesn't have to cost you a franc.

The natural setting could hardly be better — a mile-long crescent of sandy beach along the Croisette, the Îles de Lérins across the water in front of it, the rust-colored peaks of the Esterel range off to the right and the amphitheater of hills shielding the city from behind. The bulky **Palais des Festivals** at the beginning of the the Croisette is where the movie stars mount the famed red-carpeted steps in May. The **Tourist Office** is here too, along with the most active casino on the Côte d'Azur, the **Casino Croisette**.

Night on the Boulevard de la Croisette, where Cannes's palatial hotels, chic cafés and luxury shops and casinos are.

Old Cannes

To the west of the Palais des Festivals lies the **Vieux Port** and **Le Suquet**, the old part of Cannes that existed before Lord Brougham first set foot here in 1834. A statue of the elegant gentleman surveys the old fishing port from the plane tree-shaded Allées de la Liberté, where the main activity is *pétanque*, Provençal bowling. In back of the **Hôtel de Ville** (city hall) at the western end of the Allées, turn right on Rue Louis Blanc and walk two blocks to the place I love best in Cannes — the big pink stucco pavilion of the **Forville Market**. It bursts with the colors, flavors and aromas of the region — roses, carnations, fresh fruit and vegetables, locally caught fish, olives, herbs from

Provence. This is where you meet the real *Cannois*, the people of Cannes, a world apart from the high life of the Croisette. The market is open every morning except Mondays.

Behind the Hôtel de Ville you will also find **Rue Saint-Antoine**, which winds its way up Mont Chevalier to the **Suquet**, the old town built on the site of the Roman military camp. The narrow street is lined so solidly with eating places that it looks like one long restaurant that keeps changing cuisines. Some of the best food bargains in Cannes are to be found here (see WHERE TO EAT). Bear left at the top, and you will see the sixteenth century church of **Notre-Dame-d'Es-pérance** where classical concerts are held in the summer. Nearby is the **Musée de la Castre**, a medieval castle, now an eclectic archaeological museum. Its square tower, the highest point in Cannes, is the one that was built by the monks of Saint-Honorat in the eleventh century to watch for the Saracen pirates. The panorama gives you views of the Esterel, the Isles de Lérins, the Riviera, the Vieux Port, the Palais des Festivals, the Croisette and Cannes's hills. The view from the top of the Suquet is especially dramatic at night, when the palaces of the Croisette are illuminated.

If you go back to the Hôtel de Ville and go one block up Rue Louis Blanc then turn right onto **Rue**

Meynadier you will find the liveliest food shopping street in town. **Ceneri** at N° 22 is the most respected cheese shop on the Côte d'Azur. For gifts, look into **Cannolive** at 16 Rue Venizelos, the block that runs between Rue Meynadier and the railway station. It has a large, tasteful selection of Provençal fabrics, ceramics, little saints, olive products, honey, and regional wines and liqueurs, including Lérina, a liqueur made from honey by the monks of Saint-Honorat Island.

WHERE TO STAY

Cannes is one of the top places in the world to indulge in lavish living, and rooms at the palatial hotels of the Croisette are staggeringly expensive. But there are plenty of modestly-priced one and two-star establishments among the 112 classified hotels, and out of season, the luxury hotels offer special rates. The Tourist Office will be happy to help you find a room that you can afford and also make your reservation for you.

Luxury/Very Expensive

There are four hotels on the Croisette known as "the palaces," and the term is no exaggeration. The marble bathrooms in these hotels are larger than most bedrooms in others, and taking a bath is a transcendental experience. These hotels are generally fully booked in high season, so reserve early. And if you want a room at Film Festival time, you will have to book years in advance.

Since each one of the palatial hotels has its own distinct personality and all are at the pinnacle of quality and in the same price range, the choice of where to stay is mainly a matter of aesthetic taste. The **Carlton****** 58 La Croisette (93 68 91 68 FAX 93 38 20 90, is a dazzling 1912 "wedding cake" with 345 luxurious, luminous rooms and is the cornerstone of Cannes's *belle époque* period. In front of the hotel is the famous outdoor cafe, the Terrasse, where the movie moguls go to be seen. The **Majestic****** at 14 La Croisette (92 98 77 00 FAX 93 38 97 90, was built in 1926 in *belle époque* style, with 287 elegant rooms, a pool in a grassy lawn, and a piano lounge. An Art Deco hotel built in 1929, the **Martinez****** 73 La Croisette (92 98 73 00 FAX 93 39 67 82, is nothing less than stunning. This is the largest hotel in Cannes, with 430 spacious, recently restored rooms. The **Noga Hilton****** 50 La Croisette (92 99 70 00 FAX 92 99 70 11, is an ultra-modern 225 room hotel built in 1992 at a cost of $100 million on the site of the former Palais des Festivals. It has a piano lounge in its soaring white marble lobby, a modern rooftop pool and a sun deck with magnificent views.

In season, a night will run you $250 to $750 for a standard double, depending on the location of the room.

Expensive
The **Gray d'Albion****** at 38 Rue des Serbes (92 99 79 79 FAX 93 99 26 10, is an attractive modern 186-room hotel a few steps from the Croisette. It has a lively atmosphere, lots of shops and its own beach.

Moderate
The **Splendid***** at 4 Rue Felix Faure, fronting on the Allées de la Liberté (93 99 53 11 FAX 93 99 55 02, is a tastefully renovated 64-room *belle époque* beauty overlooking the the port and the Palais des Festivals. It is also close to the Forville market, and many rooms have kitchenettes, an advantage if you are staying for any length of time. I like this

hotel very much and consider it the best deal in town. **Hôtel de Paris***** 34 Boulevard de l'Alsace (93 38 30 89 FAX 93 39 04 61, is an elegant early twentieth century hotel with 50 up-to-date rooms and a pool in its palm-lined courtyard. It's close to the train station and about a ten minute walk from the Croisette. **Olivier***** 5 Rue Tambourinaires (93 39 53 28 FAX 93 39 55 85, is a charming old inn in the Suquet with a swimming pool, convenient to the public beaches of the Plages du Midi. Thirteen of its 24 pleasant rooms have baths.

Inexpensive
Albert 1er** 68 Avenue de Grasse (93 39 24 04 FAX 93 38 83 75, has 11 cozy rooms with baths in a hotel in back of the Suquet. A number of inexpensive modern chain hotels are also located out by the Cannes-La Bocca Aérodrome to the west of the city. The **Campanile**** group has one of its well-

run hotels with 95 rooms at the Aérodrome (93 48 69 41 FAX 93 90 40 42, and there is a **Balladins*** hotel with 129 bare-bones modern rooms, very modestly priced at 204 Avenue Francis Tonner (93 48 21 00 FAX 93 48 23 00.

Camping
The camping grounds most convenient to the city are to be found in the area of the Cannes-La Bocca Aérodrome. **Le Grand Saule** on Boulevard de la Frayère (93 47 07 50 is open from March to October. **Bellevue Caravaning** at 67 Avenue Maurice Chevalier (93 47 28 97 is open from April to the end of October. For more information, contact the Tourist Office.

WHERE TO EAT

There is a heavy concentration of expensive gourmet restaurants in Cannes, but there are plenty of good reasonably-priced eateries too, especially in the Suquet. Note too that a number of top gourmet restaurants have introduced fixed-price luncheon menus that give you a chance to sample the *haute cuisine* of the region at reasonable prices.

Very Expensive
Christian Willer's refined Provençal cuisine at the airy **Palme d'Or** in the Hôtel Martinez (92 98 74 14, has made this one of the most illustrious restaurants in Southern France, with two Michelin stars. **La Belle Otéro**, with the same lofty Michelin rating, features Francis Chauveau's delicate touch with regional cuisine. It is at Carlton Casino Club, a deluxe English-style gaming club on the seventh floor of the Carlton Hotel (93 39 69 69. If you feel like a splurge, try the 270 franc fixed-price luncheon menu, wine included. Also in the Carlton, on the ground floor, is the hotel's own distinguished restaurant, **La Côte**, another refined Provençal table where you can't go wrong. The other two "palaces" have good restaurants too. The Majestic Hotel's **Sunset** offers an excellent luncheon buffet in its restful garden setting, and **La Scala** at the Noga Hilton serves savory Mediterranean Italian specialties on its flowery mezzanine terrace directly overlooking the Croisette.

Expensive
The **Royal Gray** in the Hôtel Gray d'Albion (92 99 79 79, was long the most prestigious restaurants in Cannes under maître Jacques Chibois. He left the Royal Gray in 1994 to open his own place in Grasse, but remains the restaurant's consultant, and his assistant Michel Bigot has

Two of Cannes's "palaces," the Majestic OPPOSITE and the Carlton ABOVE, where movie moguls gather on its famed terrace during the Cannes Film Festival.

taken over as chef. The quality remains excellent. The fare is traditional French and Provençal, and there is a Gourmet Menu with seven or eight choices of appetizers, main courses and desserts for 175 francs. There are several restaurants on the beach worth mentioning, though they're only open at lunch. On the **Plage Gray d'Albion**, the menu is also supervised by Jacques Chibois. The **Carlton** is very good too. The **Miramar** and the **Lido** beaches serve excellent lunches at somewhat lower prices, about 200 francs, wine included.

Moderate

A cluster of three excellent restaurants of different styles can be found on the lower end of Suquet's restaurant row, at prices that are moderate to expensive, depending on what you order. **L'Echiquier**, at 14 Rue Saint-Antoine (93 39 77 79, serves traditional French food in a cozy atmosphere. The **Maschou** at 15 Rue Saint-Antoine (93 39 62 21, serves charcoal grilled meats and fish in a candlelight setting. The **Mesclun** at 16 Rue Saint-Antoine (93 99 44 19, is noted for seafood. Down the hill on the Vieux Port **Gaston et Gastounette** at 6 Quai Saint-Pierre (93 39 47 92, is a lively, folksy eatery serving fish, *bouillabaisse* and other Provençal fare. The **Corsaire Croisette** is a sidewalk restaurant with a large outdoor terrace at 62 La Croisette (93 43 09 54, where you can dine on fish and seafood platters in the heart of the Croisette's action.

Inexpensive

La Cave, at 9 Boulevard de la République (93 99 79 87, serves *legumes farcis, beignet de fleurs de courgette, rougets grillés* (stuffed vegetables, deep fried zucchini blossoms and grilled rockfish) and the whole range of Provençal dishes. The restaurant is very popular, and service can be slow. **La Brouette de Grand Mère**, 9 Rue d'Oran (93 39 12 10, is an old-style bistro that serves rabbit, beef stew and other bistro fare. **La Moule Rit** at 13 Rue Saint-Antoine (93 39 19 99, has mussels, fries and beer. At the **Taverne de Lucullus** on the south side of the Forville market pavilion, you'll find a hearty regional menu for 42 francs, lunch only.

NIGHTLIFE

As elsewhere along the Côte d'Azur, nightlife centers on the casinos, and in Cannes there are three. The **Casino Croisette** in the building of the Palais des Festivals is the busiest on the Côte d'Azur, attracting up to 10,000 players a day to its tables and machines at the height of the season. Most people play *machines-à-sous*, the slot machines. The **Carlton Casino Club** on the seventh floor of the Hôtel Carlton and the **Casino Riviera**

in the Noga Hilton are smaller, more discreet casinos for traditional games. No special dress code is required to play the slot machines, but to enter any of the gambling rooms, gentlemen must wear jackets and ties, and everyone must show a passport or an identity card of a European Union member country.

To dance the night away, go to **Le Jane's Club** at the Hôtel Gray d'Albion (92 99 79 59, which is open from 10:30 to dawn, or to **Le Jimmy'Z de Regine** at the Casino Croisette (93 68 00 07, which carries on from 11 PM to dawn. **La Chunga**, 72 La Croisette (93 94 11 29, is a lively café with recorded rock music that rocks from 8:30 PM to dawn. Across the street at the **Amiral Lounge** of

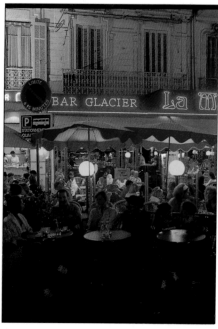

the Martinez, versatile Jimmy McKissic is at the piano.

HOW TO GET THERE

To come by plane, you fly to the Nice-Côte d'Azur Airport and take the airport bus to Cannes. The Airport-Riveria Navette Bus leaves every hour and takes 45 minutes. The fare is 70 francs. There are four direct trains a day from Paris and five more with connections at Marseille or Toulon, and the local Métrazur train stops at Cannes's Gare SNCF. By bus, there are numerous coaches serving the coast road and the hill towns of the interior. Coming by car you can take the A-8 *autoroute*, the N 98 along the coast, or the N 85 from the Alpes-de-Haute-Provence.

One of the lively cafés near the Old Port in Cannes.

THE ÎLES DE LÉRINS

For a delightful excursion from Cannes, take a boat ride to the Îles de Lérins, the two islands just off the coast, where you can swim, visit the fortress where the mysterious "The Man in the Iron Mask" was kept prisoner, stroll through the pine and eucalyptus covered hills, or simply enjoy the change of pace. The good restaurants on the islands are fairly expensive, so you may want to buy the ingredients for a picnic on Rue Meynadier or at the Forville Market before you leave. This is strictly a day trip. There are no hotels on the islands.

There are frequent boats from the Gare Maritime in Cannes. The 15-minute trip to Île Sainte-Marguerite costs 40 francs, the 30-minute trip to Saint-Honorat 45 francs, and a combined trip to both 60 francs.

ÎLE SAINTE-MARGUERITE

The closer and larger of the two islands, Île Sainte-Marguerite, is three kilometers (two miles) long and a kilometer (two-thirds of a mile) wide. It offers a number of nature walks through the hills, and there are groves of giant eucalyptus on the southeastern side. **Fort Sainte-Marguerite** (also called Fort Royal or Fort Vauban), is a sixteenth century fortress on a steep cliff, guarding the narrow passage between the island and Pointe Croisette. From this vantage point you will have another dramatic view of Cannes. Enter the **Musée de la Mer** in the fort to visit the cell of "The Man in the Iron Mask" *Masque de Fer*, who was kept here from 1687 to 1698, then transferred to the Bastille, where he died in 1703. Scores of theories continue to circulate about the identity of this man who got on the wrong side of Louis XIV. Was he Louis's illegitimate older brother? Was he Louis's wife Maria Theresa's African page boy and lover? To this day his identity remains a mystery. The one thing we do know is that the mask was velvet, not iron. The museum also has items salvaged from ancient shipwrecks, including ones from a first century BC Roman vessel and a tenth century AD Arab wreck. The museum is closed on Tuesdays.

The best restaurant on Île Sainte-Marguerite is **La Guérite** (93 43 49 30, serving seafood at fairly expensive prices. To get there, follow the sign for *Sentier Botanique*, the botanical trail that leads up the hill from the main pier.

ÎLE SAINT-HONORAT

The smaller island, Île Saint-Honorat, is 1,500 m (about one mile) long and 400 m (1,300 ft) wide. It is owned by the Cistercian order, which has a monastery and farm fields, but they allow you to

walk about the island freely. They will also sell you a bottle of Lerina, the delicious liqueur they make from honey.

The original monastery was founded at the end of the fourth century by Saint-Honorat, one of the pioneers of the monastic movement in France. During the Middle Ages, it grew wealthy from revenue from pilgrims and extended its holdings to the mainland. At one time the Monastery of Saint-Honorat owned Cannes, Mougins and Vallaurius. Incessant raids by pirates and foreign navies eventually led to the monastery's abandonment, but it was brought back to life in 1869 by the Cistercians of the Abbey of Sénanque.

Be sure to visit the eleventh century fortified **monastery** built on a little point of land surrounded by water on three sides. The only entrance is a doorway cut into the wall four m (13 ft) above the ground. It looks bizarre, but it had its purpose — to protect the monks from Saracen raiders. They would climb to the door by ladder, then pull the ladder inside and slam the door.

Chez Frédéric serves excellent, fish, lobster and bouillabaisse on a terrace overlooking the sea (93 48 66 88.

MOUGINS

Mougins, one of the former properties of the monks of Saint-Honorat, is a hill town built around a medieval bell tower seven kilometers (four and a half miles) north of Cannes. All the land around here used to be covered by olive groves and fields of roses. Some remain, but residential development has gobbled up much of it. The town itself has kept the atmosphere of a Provençal village, and its little houses are decked with flowers. So a visit here may come as a welcome relief to the high-intensity life at the shore. It is also one of the prime spots to explore the gastronomy of the region, made world-famous by chef Roger Vergé and his Moulin de Mougins. But M. Vergé is by no means alone. With only one-seventh the population of Cannes, little Mougins has almost as many outstanding restaurants as the glamorous city it overlooks.

The **Tourist Office** is on Avenue Jean-Charles Mallet (93 75 87 67.

WHAT TO SEE AND WHAT TO DO

Roger Vergé and his staff hold Provençal **cooking classes** designed for amateur chefs in small groups, 15 maximum, in a special kitchen upstairs at L'Amandier, M. Vergé's restaurant in the village. The two and a half hour sessions are built around one theme or one menu. Classes are held Tuesdays through Saturdays, 300 francs per session, 1,350 francs for a series of five. Reservations must be made 48 hours in advance. For information, call or write L'École du Moulin, Restaurant L'Amandier, 06250 Mougins Village (93 75 35 70 FAX 93 90 18 55.

For a taste of the Côte d'Azur when it was the playground of only the rich, visit the **Musée de l'Automobiliste** which has a large fleet of magnificent antique cars — Bugattis, Hispano-Suzas, Rolls Royces, and old racing cars, with 70 kept on display at one time. It is five kilometers (three miles) east of Mougins at the Nord de Bréguières parking area on the A 8 *autoroute*. The museum is open from 10 AM to 7 PM April through September, to 6 PM the rest of the year (93 69 27 80.

WHERE TO EAT

The famous **Moulin de Mougins** is an elegant old mill in the Quartier Notre-Dame-de-Vie in the countryside outside Mougins (93 75 78 24. It remains a highly prized destination for the well-healed gourmet. But to make his cuisine more available to people of ordinary means, M. Vergé has introduced a sumptuous three-course Mediterranean-Provençal luncheon menu at 245 francs. In town, Mme. Vergé oversees the running of the **Bistro de l'Amandier** at Place du Commandant Lamay (93 90 00 91, a cafe-restaurant with specials of the day such as *bouillabaisse* or *brochettes* of lamb at 82 francs and wine by the *pichet*. Another favorite of mine is **Feu Follet**, Place de la Mairie (93 90 00 91 FAX 92 92 92 62, Jean-Paul Battaglia's restaurant by the fountain in the heart of the old village. In this sunny, fun-filled terrace, waitresses in Provençal dress will bring you fresh pasta, fish, lamb and bright little regional wines at reasonable prices. Fixed-price menus start at 148 francs.

HOW TO GET THERE

There is regular bus service from the SNCF station in Cannes. You can get a bus schedule there or from the Tourist Office. If you are driving from Cannes, take Boulevard Carnot north, then bear left onto Avenue de Campon (the *autoroute* connector), which is Route N 285. You pass under the *autoroute*, then follow the signs to Mougins.

GRASSE

Sitting high on a limestone plateau overlooking flower fields 17 km (11 miles) north of Cannes, Grasse is the perfume capital of the world, and most visitors come here to see how its most famous product is made and to buy some right at the source. Grasse is a large, rather cluttered-looking town of 42,000 inhabitants, but if you take the time to explore it you will find some surprises.

BACKGROUND

The perfume industry was introduced in the sixteenth century by the Queen of France, Catherine de Medici, who encouraged the Grasse's traditional glove-making industry to perfume its gloves, as was done in refined circles in Italy. With the Revolution, elegant gloves went out of fashion, and the companies simply switched to perfume alone. They perfected the techniques for extracting the essence of a flower's scent, the base element for perfume, and the sweet smells of some thirty factories continue to bring success to the area today.

GENERAL INFORMATION

There are two **Tourist Offices**, the main one on the large public promenade at 22 Cours Honoré Cresp (93 36 66 66, the other at the top of the town at Place de la Foux (93 36 03 56, opposite the Centre International, a large modern conference center on Boulevard du Jeu-de-Ballon. For ease of touring, park your car at the top of the town in the big public parking lot directly north of the Centre International and pick up your maps and information at the Tourist Office at Place de la Foux. Bookings for guided tours of Villa de Noailles gardens must be made at the Tourist Office.

FESTIVALS

There is a **rose festival** the second weekend in May and a **jasmine festival** the first Sunday in August. Check with the tourist office for information.

WHAT TO SEE

To see the old part of Grasse, the **Vieille Ville**, start at the Place de la Foux, and descend the double set of steps with a fountain in the middle to wend your way to the long, narrow **Place aux Aires**. Try to get here in the morning, when the **market** is held daily except Mondays, and you will be plunged into the spirit of old Provence. There is a fountain in the square and on the north side, a tall, handsome arcaded mansion, the **Hôtel Isnard** which was built in 1781. The **Cathedral of Notre-Dame-du-Puy**, started in the Romanesque style in the twelfth and elaborated with Gothic and Baroque elements, should not be missed. The main points of interest there are three early paintings by Rubens, "Christ Crowned with Thorns," "The Crucifixion" and "Saint Helena," and one of Fragonard's rare ventures into religious art, his "Washing of the Feet." There is also a touchingly sincere School of Nice triptych of Saint Honorat, Saint Clement and Saint Laurent which has been attributed to Ludovico Bréa.

At the **Musée de l'Art et de l'Histoire de Provence** (Museum of Provençal Art and History), a handsome eighteenth century residence at 2 Rue Mirabeau built by Count Mirabeau's sister Louise, there is an excellent collection of pottery from Biot and Vallauris and china from Moustiers, Apt and Castellet along with rooms furnished in the styles of Louis XIII, Louis XIV and Louis XV. The museum is closed Mondays and Tuesdays, the month of November and the first week of December.

The **Musée de la Parfumerie** nearby at 8 Place du Cours, an elegant, terraced promenade, has many exhibits illustrating the history and manufacturing processes of perfumes from antiquity to the present. It is also closed Mondays and Tuesdays, the month of November and the first week of December.

The **Musée de la Marine** (Naval Museum) around the corner on Boulevard du Jeu-de-Ballon has five rooms of exhibits relating mainly to the career of Admiral De Grasse, including a model of his flagship, *La Ville de Paris,* on which he received Generals Washington, Rochambeau and La Fayette in Chesapeake Bay during the Yorktown campaign. This museum is closed on Sundays and during the month of November.

The **Villa-Musée Fragonard** at 23 Boulevard Fragonard is the seventeenth century mansion of Jean-Honoré Fragonard, the darling of Louis XVI's court, in which the Grasse native took refuge in 1791 to escape the fate of many of his aristocratic clients. The museum has an extensive collection of his sketches, engravings, wash drawings, oils and five well-executed copies of an especially lighthearted series of panels he painted for Madame du Barry (the originals are in the Frick Museum in New York). It is called, *"Le Progrès de l'Amour dans le Coeur d'Une Jeune Fille"* (The Progress of Love in the Heart of a Young Girl). The museum keeps the same hours as the Musée d'Art et d'Histoire.

The most popular tourist attractions in Grasse are the **perfume factories**, and the three largest and most prestigious, Fragonard, Galimard and Molinard offer free tours. Here you can see how the fragrances are extracted from the vast quantities of roses, mimosa, lavender and jasmine grown in the region (it takes six tons of rose petals to make one quart of essence) and how the master perfume makers exercise their ancient craft. Naturally, each tour ends in the gift shop. Fragonard is located at 20 Boulevard Fragonard near the Musée Fragonard (93 36 44 65. Galimard is at 73 Route de Cannes (93 09 20 00 and Molinard is at 60 Boulevard Victor Hugo (93 36 03 91. They are open all day in the summer from 9 AM to 6:30 or 7 PM. In the winter they close from noon to 2 and in the evening at 6 PM.

Not surprisingly, Grasse is one of the Côte d'Azur's best spots for **gardens. Princess Pauline's Garden**, constructed by Napoléon's sister Pauline Borghese on a high point overlooking the town, offers a fine panorama of Grasse and the coast. In the Saint-François district, the sumptuous gardens designed by **Viscount Charles de Noailles** in the 1930's have been reopened to the public after extensive restoration. Guided visits are given on Fridays or by special arrangement with the Tourist Office.

An interesting detour in the vicinity is to the **Huilerie de la Brague**, an olive oil mill in **Opio** seven kilometers (four miles) east of Grasse. To get there take D 2085 to Châteauneuf de Grasse,

then D 3 to Opio. It is at the bottom of the valley at 2 Route de Châteauneuf (93 77 23 03. This ancient mill, some of whose walls date from the fifteenth century, has been in the same family for six generations, and during the harvest season from November through March, visitors can observe the manufacturing process, from the washing of the olives, to the crushing by huge stone wheels, to the various methods used to prepare the oil and the paste. Owner Roger Michel often guides the visitors himself. Besides its high-quality olive oil and every other olive product imaginable, the mill's excellent gift shop sells a wide range of other Provençal products, including honey, jams and jellies and Provençal fabrics.

WHERE TO STAY

The **Hôtel des Parfums*** *** offers tranquillity, a swimming pool, 60 moderate-priced rooms and 11 expensive duplex suites. It is on Boulevard Eugène Charabot near Place de la Foux in the upper part of Grasse (93 36 10 10 FAX 93 65 35 48. The **Hôtel du Panorama**** is at 2 Cours Ho-

ABOVE: Picking flowers in the perfume capital, Grasse.

noré Cresp (93 36 80 80 FAX 93 36 92 04, convenient to the Fragonard Museum. It has 36 comfortable modern rooms in the inexpensive and moderate price range, all with balconies and fine views.

WHERE TO EAT

Oddly, for a town that has made its living off the olfactory senses, Grasse is not noted for gourmet cooking. However, one of the master chefs of the Côte d'Azur, Jacques Chibois, the long-time master of the ovens at the Royal Gray in Cannes, has recently opened his own place in Grasse, **La Bastide Saint-Antoine,** (93,09 16 48,

at 45 Avenue Henri Dunant, and it is sure to bring luster to the restaurant scene here. Very fine meals are also to be had at **Maître Boscq** at 13 Rue de la Fontette (93 36 45 76, in the heart of La Vieille Ville, which features local Grasse specialties such as garlic soup, snails with basil sauce and *fassum grassois* (cabbage stuffed with meat and vegetables) on a charming outdoor terrace at reasonable prices (menus from 125 francs). **Amphitryon** is at 16 Boulevard Victor-Hugo at the bottom of the Cours Honoré Cresp (93 36 58 73. Here you can feast on such imaginative dishes as wild mushroom ravioli, fisherman's stew with red wine and hot apple tart loaded with cinnamon and nuts. Menus start at 98 francs, and there is an excellent selection of wines.

OPPOSITE AND ABOVE: Views of the village of Aiguines on the Grand Canyon of the Verdon.

HOW TO GET THERE

There are frequent buses from the Gare SNCF in Cannes. If you are driving, take Route N 85 north from Mougins.

FURTHER AFIELD

THE GRAND CANYON OF THE VERDON

While not nearly as gigantic as its namesake on the Colorado, the Grand Canyon du Verdon is the largest gorge in Europe, 21 km (13 miles)

long, with widths varying from 200 to 1,500 m (650 to 5,000 ft) and depths from 250 to 700 m (800 to 2,500 ft) cut by the green waters of the Verdon River into the white limestone plateau of Haute-Provence. Remarkably, this vast natural wonder was unknown to the world until the early twentieth century, when Edouard-Alfred Martel, the explorer, mountain climber and father of speleology in France, began surveying the gorges in 1905.

The key town for the Grand Canyon du Verdon is **Castellane,** 63 km (40 miles) north of Grasse on the Route Napoléon, N 85. It sits on the north bank of the Verdon River a few miles east of the start of the Grand Canyon du Verdon.

General Information

Stop at the **Tourist Office** on Rue Nationale in downtown Castellane (92 83 61 14, and they will provide all the information you need on hotels, camping grounds and sports facilities and detailed maps for hikers indicating emergency phones and shelters on the trails through the canyon.

Boats and canoes can be rented at **Pont du Galetas** at the west end of the canyon where the Verdon River empties into big Lac de Sainte-Croix. For **river rafting**, contact Verdon Animation Nature. They have offices at La Palud-sur-Verdon (92 77 30 15, and in Moustiers (92 74 66 94. A number of stables in the area offer **horseback tours**. Information on all sports in the area is provided by ADRI-CIMES, 19 Rue Docteur Honorat, 04000 Digne-les-Bains (92 31 07 01.

along the northern rim. Both sides are very dramatic, with perspectives that take your breath away. But if you only have the time see one side, I recommend the Corniche Sublime, because the best hotels and restaurants are on that side. From Castellane take D 952 12 km (seven and a half miles) to Pont-de-Soleils and turn left onto D 955 south, which will lead you around to D 71, which is the Corniche Sublime. The most vertiginous points along this drive are the **Balcons de la Mescla**, a sheer drop 230 m (750 ft) to the Mescla, where the raging waters of the Artuby meet the equally fast-flowing waters of the Verdon. Further along is the **Falaise des Cavaliers** (the Knights' Cliff), the start of a three kilometers (two miles)

In the summer, the Castellane Tourist Office runs a shuttle bus two or three times as a day to the Grand Canyon, dropping people off at the start of the various hiking trails and picking them up later in the day. On Tuesdays, there is a guided tour (in French) that makes a circuit of the Grand Canyon and gives the customers two hours in Moustiers-Sainte-Marie for lunch and visiting the pottery studios.

You can make a day trip from the coast (see HOW TO GET THERE, page 144), but it is a very long day. I strongly recommend that you spend a night up here to give yourself enough time to really experience the area.

What to See and What to Do

There are two roads for touring the Grand Canyon by car, the **Corniche Sublime** along the southern rim and **Route des Crêtes** (Crest Road)

stretch of gorge with depths ranging from 250 to 400 m (800 to 1,300 ft). For motorists, walkers and bikers, the *corniches* along the rim of the cliffs offer sensational views, while hikers, horseback riders and white water rafters can enjoy their sports thousands of feet below. Hiking trails are well-marked, but very rugged, and only experienced hikers with good boots and emergency supplies should consider it. At the western end of the Grand Canyon, is the large **Lac de Sainte-Croix**, an artifical lake covering 2,500 hectares (6,000 acres), where swimming and sailing are popular.

Where to Stay and Where to Eat

My favorite place in the area is unquestionably the **Château de Trigance***** in **Trigance** (94 76 91 18 FAX 94 47 58 99, an eleventh century castle with round towers and crenelated battlements on a hill above its tiny village eight kilometers (five miles) south of the Grand Canyon. It has been beautifully converted into 10-room Relais & Châteaux hotel and restaurant where you can enjoy tranquillity and dine like a lord on fine Provençal cooking in its vaulted stone dining hall decorated with medieval pennants and armor. It is somewhat expensive, 530 to 700 francs demi-pension (per person, breakfast and one meal included in the price of the room). It is closed from mid-November to mid-March. **Le Viel Amandier**** also in Trigance (94 76 92 92 FAX 94 47 58 65, is a pleasant 12-room Logis de France inn down the hill from the Château and half the price. Closed mid-December to mid-February. The **Hôtel-Restaurant du Grand Canyon**** in **Aiguines** (94 76 91 31 FAX 94 76 92 29, is at the Falaises des Cavaliers 39 km (24 miles) west of Castellane on D 71. This modern hotel is the only one directly on the Grand Canyon. It is built at the top of the cliffs 275 m (900 ft) up with a dining terrace extending out over the edge — a sensational place to have lunch, at moderate prices. It has 16 moderately-priced rooms, and there are footpaths into the canyon, hang-gliding, rock-climbing, horseback riding, canoeing and rafting nearby. Open from May to mid-October.

CAMPING

The area around the Grand Canyon du Verdon and the Lac de Sainte-Croix is tremendously popular for camping. Castellane has 14 camping grounds with 1,571 individual places, La Palud-sur-Verdon on the north side of the Canyon has seven grounds with 82 places and there are numerous others. The best bet is to inquire at the Tourist office in Castellane.

How to Get There

Castellane can be reached by bus daily from the Gare Routières in Nice, Cagnes-sur-Mer or Grasse by the **VFD** bus company. For information call VFD in Grenoble (76 47 77 77 or check with the Tourist Offices in any of those towns. The **Société des Autocars Girieud** of Colmars-les-Alpes runs bus tours of the Grand Canyon from Cannes and Nice in the summer. For information call (92 83 40 27. **Santa Azur** also offers day trips by bus from Nice (93 85 46 81.

If you are driving, the best way to get to the Grand Canyon du Verdon from the coast is on N 85, the Route Napoléon. This is the route, a shepherd's path in his day, that the fallen Emperor took with his little column of supporters after landing at Golfe-Juan on March 1, 1815. It is marked with plaques in the shape of an eagle, a reference to Napoléon's boast, "The eagle will fly from bell tower to bell tower to the towers of the Notre Dame de Paris." The route was inaugurated in 1932, and it starts at the gravestone-like monument in Golfe-Juan where he landed, follows the

N 7 to Cannes, skirts the city (too many royalists), and heads north to Mougins and Grasse on N 85. North of Grasse, Napoléon made his way through barren, rocky terrain into the mountains. The route, now a well-surfaced secondary highway, winds up through appropriately ominous countryside, with the Alpes-de-Haute-Provence in the distance. The Route Napoléon continues all the way up to Grenoble in the Alps, but for our purpose, we only go as far as Castellane, the eastern gateway to the Grand Canyon.

MOUSTIERS-SAINTE-MARIE

At the western end of the canyon is one of Europe's most renowned pottery centers, Moustiers-Sainte-Marie, an attractive village in a craggy mountain setting with a waterfall pouring down from the rocks above it, and a long iron chain with a star in the middle strung between two peaks

above the town. The chain was installed in fulfill-ment of a vow by a knight from the area taken prisoner during the Crusades, who swore to put it there if he ever saw Moustiers again. The town became an important china-making center in the seventeenth century thanks to a secret glaze given to it by a monk from Faenza in Italy, which is the origin of the word *faïence*. The **Musée de la Faïence** has a large selection of the white table-ware with delicate blue or yellow decorations that made Moustiers famous.

This is a very creative little town, and a number of workshops sell their hand-made ceramics. If you are thinking of buying, be sure the piece has the label of the Moustiers-Sainte-Marie artisans association stamped on it. **L'Atelier Ségriès**, Route de Riez (92 74 66 69, sells copies of eighteenth century Ségriès classics as well as modern crea-tions (closed in August). **JMV Fine** on the Place de l'Église (92 74 69 92, is the Fine family's work-shop, where classical and original designs are made and decorated entirely by hand (closed January and February). But these are by no means the only studios doing good work, as an hour of poking around in this atmospheric town will make abun-dantly clear. The **Tourist Office** is in the town hall, the Mairie (92 74 67 84.

Where to Stay and Where to Eat

If you care to stay here, two modest but comfort-able inns are the 22-room **Colombier**** on the Route de Castellane just outside town (92 74 66 02, which is open all year, but has no restaurant, and the **Bonne Auberge**** in town (92 74 66 18 FAX 92 74 65 11, with 16 rooms and a restaurant, open mid-February to mid-November.

Moustiers-Sainte-Marie at the western end of the Grand Canyon, one of France's most creative centers for ceramics.

There are also eight camping grounds in Moustiers with a total of 762 places. For information, contact the Tourist Office.

For dining, **Santons** on Place de l'Église (92 74 66 48, is a top gourmet restaurant with specialties such as fresh noodles with foie gras and truffles, turbot with artichokes and roast pigeon casserole with sausage created by chef André Albert, a native of the area, whose delicate touch has earned him one Michelin star. It is a cozy place with a vine-covered dining terrace, expensive, but very popular, so be sure to make reservations.

How to Get There

There is regular bus service between Castellane

and Moustiers only one day a week, on Saturday. You really need a car up here.

CANNES TO FRÉJUS

From Cannes to Fréjus, there are 42 km (28 miles) of remarkably varied coast line. The drive starts with a grand sweep of sandy beach as you head west from Cannes on N 98 — the **Plages du Midi**, the **Plages de la Bocca** and the beach of **La Napoule** dominated by a bizarre gothic castle built in the 1920's by Henry Clews, a rich American eccentric and self-styled sculptor overlooking the gentle curve of the Gulf of Napoule. Then you arrive at the **Massif de l'Esterel**, a craggy range of rust-red

ABOVE: A shepherd moving his sheep to pasture in the Alpes-de-Haute-Provence.

volcanic rock 19 km (12 miles) long by 11 km (seven miles) wide that looms up to the west of La Napoule, and here starts a lovely, winding drive along tiny turquoise bays niched into sheer-cliffed inlets where the blue of the sea contrasts boldly with the red of the rock.

At the resort town of **Le Trayas** eight kilometers (five miles) west of La Napoule, you enter the **Var**, the western part of the Côte d'Azur. Continuing along the Esterel corniche (N 98), the lofty observation points at **Pic de Cap Roux** (452 m or 1,484 ft) at Le Trayas and the **Sémaphore du Dramont**, the lighthouse near Agay, offer grand panoramas of the sea and the mountains. The beach towns of **Miramar**, **Anthéor**, **Agay** and others lie along this road, and in summer, the traffic can be murder. It is 22 km (14 miles) from Le Trayas to Fréjus.

FRÉJUS AND SAINT-RAPHAËL

BACKGROUND

The name Fréjus is derived from "Forum Julii," "The Forum of Julius." It was founded as a naval port by Julius Caesar in 49 BC and became an important base under his nephew Octavius. The light, fast galleys that carried the day against Antony and Cleopatra at Actium in 31 BC were built here. During the first and second centuries AD the town boomed and is believed to have reached a population of 40,000, about the same as today. It was an active naval and commercial port with an aqueduct, baths, an arena and all the other accouterments of a prosperous Roman city. But in the declining years of the Empire and afterwards, the harbor was neglected, and silt from the Argens River started filling the Roman port.

Fréjus was an important early center of Christianity, and in the fourth century, became the see of a bishop. Like the other towns along this coast, Fréjus was invaded time and again by Saracen pirates, who reduced it to rubble in the tenth century. In the twentieth century, the development of the Fréus Plage and neighboring Saint-Raphaël beach resorts have brought the area back to prosperity as a vacation spot for the French middle classes. But the area has not abandoned its military roots. Fréjus is the home of the French Navy's largest air base.

Fréjus is one of the larger towns of the Var with 41,500 inhabitants, and urban sprawl has linked it with Saint-Raphaël, a town of 26,500 to the east, a key place for rail and bus connections (see HOW TO GET THERE, page 147).

GENERAL INFORMATION

The **Tourist Office** in Fréjus is near the Cathedral at 325 Rue Jean-Jaurès (94 17 19 19. Saint-Raphaël

The Côte d'Azur

has its own Tourist Office by the train station at Place de la Gare (94 95 16 87. For information about train schedules, contact the **Gare SNCF station in Saint-Raphaël** (94 91 50 50. For bus information, get in touch with **Sodétrav** at the Gare Routière bus station, Square Docteur Régis, Saint-Raphaël, just up the street from the train station (94 95 24 82. There are frequent trains and buses between downtown Fréjus and downtown Saint-Raphaël, a distance of three kilometers (two miles).

WHAT TO SEE

While not nearly as impressive or well-preserved as the Roman ruins of Cimiez and certainly not those of Nîmes or Arles, **La Ville Romaine** (The Roman City) merits a visit. The **arena**, some of whose walls and vaulted passageways remain, seated 10,000 and is now used for occasional bullfights and rock concerts. There are bases of stone walls that outline the **Roman port**, now filled in and grassed over. Adjoining the Roman City to the south is the **Quartier Episcopal**, where the **Cathedral** has a late fourth or early fifth century octagonal **Baptistry** that is one of the oldest Christian structures in France. In the Cathedral, note the "Retable de Sainte-Marguerite," a mid-fifteenth century altarpiece painted on wood by School of Nice artist Jacques Durandi. There is also a handsome two-storey cloister from the thirteenth century to the side of the Cathedral, and upstairs is the interesting **Archaeological Museum**, with a perfectly preserved Roman mosaic tile floor, a double-faced marble bust of Hermes and other statuettes in marble and bronze that were unearthed at Forum Julii.

WHERE TO STAY

A peaceful hotel near the Ville Romaine and the Quartier Episcopal is **L'Aréna***** at 139 Rue du Général de Gaulle (94 17 09 40 FAX 94 52 01 52, a converted bank with 30 very comfortable rooms in Provençal decor at moderate rates. The **Auberge du Vieux Four**** at 57 Rue Grisolle (94 51 56 38, has eight cozy, inexpensive rooms. For a hotel right on the beach, try the **Excelsior***** on its Promenade René Coty in Saint-Raphaël, with its street entrance at 193 Boulevard Félix Martin (94 95 02 32 FAX 94 95 33 82. It has 36 bright rooms that open onto the main beach and the Gulf of Fréjus, with room rates in the moderate range.

Camping

There are 22 camping grounds in Fréjus and the neighboring beach town of Saint-Aygulf with 7,300 places, 1,600 in the largest, Camping de Saint-Aygulf (94 17 62 49 FAX 94 81 03 16, open

June to mid-September. **Holiday Green** is a plush camping ground with 740 places in wooded terrain with a huge swimming pool six kilometers (nearly four miles) from the beach on the Route de Bagnols in Fréjus (94 40 88 20 FAX 94 51 49 59, catering to a mainly British clientele. It is open from April to the end of September. For the summer, you must book long in advance. For a full list camping grounds in this area, contact the Tourist Office of Fréjus or Saint-Raphaël. The Comité Départemental du Tourisme du Var publishes a fee list of 250 camping grounds throughout the Var. You may phone or fax for it at (94 09 00 69 FAX 94 62 90 55 or write to 5 Avenue Vauban (BP 5147), 83000 Toulon.

WHERE TO EAT

Lou Calen at Place de la Mairie near the Fréjus Cathedral (94 52 36 87 serves sea bass terrine with basil, *rouget* with *tapenade* (red mullet with black olive, anchovy and caper sauce) and other Provençal treats with fixed-price menus from 150 francs. In the same area, the rustic restaurant of the **Auberge du Vieux Four** has a full range of well-prepared regional fare at moderately expensive prices. For a delightful Provençal lunch by the sea, take a run down to **L'Orangerie**, Promenade René Coty on the beach in Saint-Raphaél (94 83 10 50, for stuffed *sardines à la Niçoise, bourride* (fish soup) and fillet of lamb with rosemary-flavored gnocchi. Luncheon menus here start at 98 francs. A lively inexpensive restaurant with a delightful living terrace is **L'Equipe** at 10 Boulevard Gallieni in Frejus Plage, (94 51 12 62. It is noted for its deserts. Try the *crème brûlée* (custard tipped with carmelized sugar). Delicious.

HOW TO GET THERE

Fréjus and Saint-Raphaël are both stops on the main SNCF train line. Saint-Raphël is the western terminus of the Métrazur line, the local train service that stops at all the towns along the coast between Saint-Raphaël and Menton. To the west of Saint-Raphaël and Fréjus, the rail line swings inland north of the Massif des Maures, and there are no train stations along the coast for the next 93 km (58 miles) until the line rejoins the coast at Toulon.

Transportation to and from the coastal towns in between Fréjus-Saint-Raphaël and Toulon is by the buses of Sodétrav (Société Départementale des Transports du Var), whose headquarters is in Hyères Z 94 65 21 00, and whose schedules can be obtained by contacting them directly or by checking with local tourist offices or bus stations.

Coming from the east by car, take N 98, the coast road, or N 7 from La Napoule to Fréjus. From the west, you can take the A 8 *autoroute*, N 7 or N 98.

FRÉJUS TO SAINT-TROPEZ

As you leave Fréjus, the N 98 runs through a string of beach towns sprinkled along a pretty 19 km (12 mile) stretch of undulating coast, with the cork, oak and the pine-wooded hills of the **Massif des Maures** inland. It takes you to **Sainte-Maxime** on the Gulf of Saint-Tropez. This is a middle-class family resort where female sunbathers wear not only the bottoms of their bathing suits but the tops, while across the gulf shimmers the town that invented toplessness, Sainte-Maxime's polar opposite, Saint-Tropez.

SAINT-TROPEZ

Guy de Maupassant discovered Saint-Tropez while cruising the Côte d'Azur in 1887 in his sailboat *Bel Ami*, and described it as "one of those charming and simple daughters of the sea, those nice little modest towns, bred in the water like a shellfish, that produce sailors."

A few years later, painter Paul Signac fell under its spell and settled here, which influenced his friends, Matisse, Bonnard, and other artists to come (Matisse painted his seminal "Luxe, Calme et Volupté" in Saint-Tropez). By the 1930's, when Collette joined the small army of writers and artists in residence, Saint-Tropez had become "Montparnasse on the Sea."

In 1955, Bardot and Vadim blew the town's mildly bohemian image wide open with their film *Et Dieu Créa la Femme* (*And God Created Woman*), and Saint-Tropez became France's epitome of fashionable sun-baked sex. "Saint-Trop" (*trop* means "too much" in French) introduced the Bikini in the 1950's and the first topless sunbathing in public at Tahiti Beach twenty years later. For those seeking action, there's still more of that here than anywhere else on the coast except perhaps Juan-les-Pins, but at a level of chic incomparably higher. Insufferable or amusing? That's for you to decide. Saint-Tropez is the acid test.

Saint-Tropez is the name of a peninsula as well as the famous port town, and we will be exploring this land of vineyards and quaint villages too. But first, we will plunge into the belly of the beast.

It is reached by Route D 98, a five-kilometer or three-mile-long branch of the coastal road N 98 that dead ends at the port of Saint-Tropez.

BACKGROUND

Athenopolis to the Greeks, Heraclea to the Romans, Saint-Tropez takes its name from Torpes, a

---

The port of Saint-Tropez is the prettiest on the Côte d'Azur.

Christian martyr whose body floated in on a boat. According to legend, Torpes was a Roman centurion during the reign of Nero who declared his Christianity and was beheaded. The headless body was set adrift from Pisa in a boat with a cock and a dog put there to devour it, but out of respect for the holy martyr, they kept their appetites in check. The saint's body was preserved by the locals but disappeared during the Saracen raids in the eighth century.

The port of Saint-Tropez prospered under the Counts of Provence, but its wealth and isolated position made it a tempting target for pirates and the navies of England and Spain, and for centuries the people of Saint-Tropez resisted one raid after another.

Admiral Pierre-André de Suffren, known as the Bailli (Bailiff), was Saint-Tropez's eighteenth century hero. He fought the English in Indian Ocean and in the Caribbean during the American Revolution, and his image in bronze surveys the Port. In August 1944, the Germans blew up most of the buildings on the port side of Saint-Tropez before surrendering to the invading Allies. The charming pink and ochre houses that now line the quays are mostly reproductions.

GENERAL INFORMATION

The main **Tourist Office** of Saint-Tropez is on Avenue du Général de Gaulle (94 97 41 21 and is open all year. In season, the annex on the port at Quai Jean-Jaurès is open April through mid-October (94 97 45 21. This is a highly professional staff that can help you with any inquiries. They have a reservation service that will book rooms for you in hotels or in residences with furnished rooms and apartments (*meublés*), which can cost much less than hotels during longer stays.

The following contacts may be helpful:

The **Gare Routière** (bus station) is on Avenue du Général de Gaulle at the entrance to town near the Tourist Office. All **bus service** to Saint-Tropez is by **Sodétrav** (94 97 88 51.

Car rental: **Avis**, Avenue du 8 Mai 1945 (94 97 03 10; **Europcar**, Residence du Port (94 97 15 41; Hertz, Rue Nouvelle Poste (94 97 22 01.

With the volume of car traffic in the summer, **bikes or motor scooters** make a lot of sense. They can be rented at **Etablissements Mas-Louis**, 5 Rue Joseph Quaranta, down from the Place des Lices (94 97 00 60, or at Easy Biker, 12 Avenue du Général Leclerc (94 97 73 79.

The **taxi stand** is in front of the Annionciade Museum on the Port (94 97 05 27.

Boat services: Vedettes Bleues has regular summer service between Saint-Raphaël and Saint-Tropez (50 minutes) (94 95 17 46; **MMG** has regular summer service between Sainte-Maxime and Saint-Tropez (20 minutes) (94 96 51 00.

Medical emergency, Saint-Tropez Hospital, Avenue Foch (94 79 47 30.

FESTIVALS

There are two local celebrations known as *bravades* every year. The first, the **Bravade de Saint-Tropez** is of religious origin, with parades and ceremonies on the 16th, 17th and 18th of May in honor the town's patron saint, Saint-Tropez. The second, the **Bravade des Espagnols**, on June 15 is in honor of a heroic defense the town put up against the Spanish fleet in 1637, with parades in fanciful red, white and blue sailors' uniforms. There is much firing of noisy muskets at both celebrations.

The last event of the season is the **Nioulargue**, a sailing event that started as a friendly challenge between two skippers in 1980 and now attracts hundreds of classic and modern racing vessels of all sizes from all over the world, including a number of America's Cup boats and their famous captains. It is normally held the last week of September or the first week of October.

WHAT TO SEE AND WHAT TO DO

The Port

The port of Saint-Tropez is the prettiest on the Côte d'Azur and in summer the liveliest. The harbor is packed with elephantine motor yachts moored with their sterns to the dock. In the evening, onlookers stand and gawk at the wealthy owners and their guests taking cocktails on the deck and supping in their open cabins, much like the courtiers at Versailles did when Louis XIV dined on a platform to allow his lessers to watch. As at Cannes during the Film Festival, all eyes are constantly darting around for celebrities (who never show up). The waterfront is animated in the morning, swarming in the late afternoon and evening and when the discos get going, rocking until the wee hours.

For the best people-watching in this part of town go to the **Café de Paris** near the statue of the Bailli de Suffren. The century-old **Sénéquier** remains popular too, with its three-legged red tables and excellent *tarte tropézienne*, a tart filled with confectioners cream. Unlike Nice, Cannes and the other ports along the Côte d'Azur, which face

south and east and get their best sun in the morning, the port of Saint-Tropez is on a hook of land that faces north and west and gets its most direct sun in the late afternoon.

The extraordinary quality of Saint-Tropez's light has attracted many painters, as you will see at the **Musée de l'Annonciade** on the east side of the port, a sixteenth century chapel converted into a museum to house the art collection of industrialist Georges Grammont. Mainly Pointilist, Nabi and Fauve, the collection includes Matisse's "La Gitane," Bonnard's "Nue Devant la Cheminée and works by Seurat, Vuillard, Dufy, Vlaminck, Derain, Braque, Manguin and Maillol, and there are a number of paintings of Saint-Tropez. Two evocative scenes of the town are Signac's rosy pointillist "Vue de Saint-Tropez Coucher du Soleil au Bois de Pins" of 1896 and Charles Camoin's 1939 "Place des Lices," with village men playing

pétanque under the plane trees on the sun-dappled town square. The museum is open from 10 AM to Noon and 3 PM to 7 PM from June through September, from 2 PM to 6 PM the rest of the year. It is closed Tuesdays and the month of November.

Place des Lices

At the **Place des Lices** a five minute stroll from the Port up Rue Georges Clémenceau you'll see the sons and grandsons of Camoin's players pitching *boules* on the same spot. The tree-shaded, bare-earthed Place de Lices (*lices* means lists, where the jousts were held in the Middle Ages) is the heart of Saint-Tropez and my favorite part of the town. It is the best place to learn the rules and strategies of the Provençal bowling game of *pétanque*, as the Tropéziens are an amiable bunch, glad to elucidate the fine points of the game. The food market is held here on Tuesday and Saturday morning, the clothing and bric-a-brac market on Saturday.

Saint-Tropez is fine town for **shopping**, and its two supremely stylish general stores are near the Place des Lices. **Fred Prysquel** at 34 Boulevard Louis Blanc has the best in pottery, home furnishings, shoes and mens' clothing with a real flair. The impeccable **Galeries Tropéziennes** at 56 Rue Gambetta has espadrilles, wicker baskets, yard goods and everything for the house and pool. **Rondini** at 16 Rue Georges Clémenceau down the street from the Place des Lices has been making top-quality, extremely comfortable leather sandals for three generations, and at pretty **Place de la Garonne** one block away, you'll find several classy couturiers' boutiques.

Old Saint-Tropez

The **Quartier de la Ponche** is the old section of town with narrow, cobbled boutique-and-restaurant-lined streets interspersed with tiny squares that wind up the hill from the port to the Citadel's park. A sixteenth century hilltop fortresses, the **Citadel** has a commanding view in all directions from the roof of its donjon — the port, the gulf, the Maures, the Esterel, even the Alps after an air-clearing blast of the Mistral. Its **Musée Naval** has scale models of ships from the days of the Greeks and the Romans and celebrates the exploits of Saint-Tropez's local hero the Bailai de Suffren. There are also exhibits on the Allied landings in August 1944 at Saint-Tropez and the Côte d'Azur.

The Beaches

There are some small beaches to either side of the port, but the main beaches lie to the west. The **Plage des Salins** is three kilometers (two miles) straight west of town on the Route des Salins, and

Saint-Tropez has been an important sailing town since the days of the ancient Greeks OPPOSITE, and has fascinating old back streets to explore ABOVE.

The Côte d'Azur

Tabu Plage and Tahiti Plage, scandalous in their day and still very sexy, are about the same distance to the southwest, reached by the Route de Tahiti. But the best beaches are along the **Plage de Pampelonne**, a five kilometers (three mile) sweep of fine sand that actually lies in the neighboring town of Ramatuelle. It is reached by the Route des Plages (D 93). There are some thirty beach clubs here where you can rent mattresses, umbrellas and windsurfers, have lunch or refreshments at their restaurants and snack bars.

My favorite is **Club 55**, which started as an informal canteen for the cast and crew of *And God Created Woman* in 1955 (hence the name). If you want to spend a day surrounded by people who all look like they stepped out of the pages of *Town and Country* magazine, this is the place. It is directly to the left of the Allied Landing memorial at the foot of Boulevard Patch, the connector road from D 93. Those who like vulgar displays of the flesh (and who doesn't?) should check out the **Voile Rouge**, a ten minute walk up the beach toward town. There you will find beefy guys with pony-tails and bulging babes of *Penthouse* proportions undulating to loud thumping music.

Topless sunbathing is the norm on these beaches. Nude sunbathing is officially prohibited, but there are isolated beaches north of the Plage des Salins and from Cap Camarat at the southern end of the Plage de Pampelonne to La Croix-Valmer where sunbathing in the altogether is legally tolerated and commonly practiced.

WHERE TO STAY

Saint-Tropez has the most imaginatively extravagant small hotels in Mediterranean France, with prices to match — 1,500 to 4,000 francs for a double room in season and suites up to 5,500 francs. A quarter of the hotels are in the four-star category and more than a third are three-star establishments. The following hotels are in the town of Saint-Tropez. For other options in the surrounding area, see the listing for the Saint-Tropez Peninsula (see page 154).

Luxury/Very Expensive

Byblos**** Avenue Paul Signac (94 97 00 04 FAX 94 97 40 52, is a simulated Mediterranean village built around a large pool on the hillside of the Citadel with a generous view of the town and the gulf. Its 59 individually decorated rooms and 48 duplex suites are all gorgeous. Ursula Andress's favorite, room 245, has a circular Jacuzzi in the loft bedroom and a private sunning terrace (yours for 4,200 francs). Open April through October. As you enter Saint-Tropez on D 98, look for the **Résidence de la Pinède****** on Plage de la Bouillabaisse (94 97 04 21 FAX 94 97 73 64. This 35-room, seven-suite Relais & Château hotel,

more traditional in decor, is the town's only luxury hotel-restaurant right on the water, *pieds dans l'eau*, as they say. Open April through mid-October. The **Bastide de Saint-Tropez****** on Route des Carles, (94 97 58 16 FAX 94 97 21 71, is a refined country estate in a lovely garden setting with 15 gorgeous rooms and 11 suites. Closed the month of January.

Expensive

Sube*** Quai Suffren (94 97 30 04 FAX 94 54 89 08 has 31 bright rooms and a big ship's bar and lounge overlooking the port. Open all year. Centrally located at the top of la Ponche facing the park of the Citadel, **Hôtel Le Barron**** 23 Rue

de l'Aioli, (94 97 06 57 FAX: 94 97 58 72, is a friendly 12-room hotel which is open all year.

Moderate

Two small, spotless, hostelries in the 400 franc range, not far from the Place des Lices are **Lou Cagnard**** (94 97 04 24, with 19 plain rooms on a quiet garden watched over by Eve, the most serious-faced dog in the world, and **Le Colombier**** (94 97 05 31, on the Impasse des Conquettes with 13 rooms in a town house with a flowery courtyard. Both are open all year, but no credit cards are accepted.

Inexpensive

You have come to the wrong place.

ABOVE: Tahiti Beach, still swinging after all these years. OPPOSITE: A café on the port in Saint-Tropez.

WHERE TO EAT

For Provençal classics in a delightful garden setting, **L'Olivier**, the gourmet restaurant of the Bastide de Saint-Tropez, is my first choice, featuring the imaginative touch of François Cardaillac, the most respected chef of the area, with one Michelin star. For gourmet dining on the water, the Provençal-Mediterranean restaurant of **La Pinède** is tops, also with a Michelin star. Byblos also has a fine gourmet restaurant, **Les Arcades**. Just down the street from the Place des Lices, Gerald Leroy, the young former star chef of the Château de La Messardière has opened his own place, **La Table du Marché**, at 38 Rue Clémenceau (94 97 85 20, and his contemporary bistro-style restaurant has become the most popular in the area. Expensive, but not ruinous, if you choose carefully. Upstairs is the **Salle à Manger**, an intimate, expensive dining room where guests can watch through large windows into the kitchen as the young master and his staff prepare their meals in the magnificent kitchen. The **Brasserie de la Renaissance**, on the Place des Lices (94 97 02 00, is a chic terrace where you dine on subtly prepared local specialties, packed at meal times, fairly expensive. **Hôtel Le Barron** has a friendly, moderately priced restaurant on the front porch looking up at the Citadel, open all year. The **Auberge des Maures** on Rue de Boutin, a tiny alley off 43 Rue Allard, has solid food at modest prices in a tree-shaded courtyard (94 97 01 50.

NIGHTLIFE

The disco for suave adults to be seen at is the **Caves du Roy** at the Byblos (94 97 00 04. The Beautiful People, mostly young (of course), go to dance at **Papagayo** ("Le Gayo") on Rue du 11 Novembre 1918 at the Port (94 97 07 56. Empty at midnight, it starts to fill up at 1 AM, is throbbing by 3 AM and blasting full tilt until 5 AM. On crowded nights you'll need "*un look*" to get in. Study the chosen to find out what works. For men of all ages, clip-on pony tails are highly recommended. 90 franc entrance fee with one drink. **L'Ocatve** on Place de la Garonne is a cheerful lounge with live music nightly (94 97 22 56.

HOW TO GET THERE

There is no train to Saint-Tropez, so if you're not driving, your choices are bus, boat or helicopter. All bus services from other coastal towns of the Var is provided by Sodétrav (94 97 88 51.

If you are arriving in the region via the Toulon-Hyères Airport, Sodétrav will take you to Saint-Tropez (see GENERAL INFORMATION, page 164).

There is a regular **boat service** from Sainte-Maxime and Saint-Raphaël in the summer (see GENERAL INFORMATION, page 150). There are seven **helicopter flights** per day in the summer from the Nice-Côte d'Azur Airport, **Heli Inter** (93 80 41 70.

By **bus from the Nice Airport**, Aviabus has four trips a day to Saint-Raphaël, a one hour ride (94 51 43 98, and you can take the Sodétrav bus from there to Saint-Tropez.

THE SAINT-TROPEZ PENINSULA

Besides its beaches, the hilly, 10 km (six mile)

square Saint-Tropez Peninsula has magnificent umbrella pines, vineyards, several interesting old villages to explore and outstanding choices of hotels and restaurants. The **Tourist Office** for the Gulf of Saint-Tropez and the Pays des Maures is located at the big intersection of the Saint-Tropez Peninsula, the **Carrefour de la Foux** in **Gassin**, five kilometers (three miles) from Saint-Tropez. This office furnishes travel information on the Saint-Tropez Peninsula and the Maures mountains directly to the north (94 43 42 10. They will also book accommodations for you. Their reservation desk has a separate number (94 43 40 70.

WHAT TO SEE AND WHAT TO DO

Port-Grimaud

This mini-Venice, where boats tie up in front of the houses, was built in 1968 but has aged, as architect François Spoerry intended, to look like a Mediterranean fishing village that has been there forever. It is very pleasant to stroll along the canals and stop for a pastis in one if the cafés. To get there from Saint-Tropez go north on D 98 and N 98 about seven kilometers (four and a half miles). It is nestled in the crook of the Gulf of Saint-Tropez.

Ramatuelle

An old perched village on a plateau overlooking Pampelonne Beach, Ramatuelle can be reached by taking Route D 93, the Route des Plages, south from Saint-Tropez for six kilometers (three and three quarter miles) then D 61 west. The village was occupied in the ninth century by Saracen pirates until dislodged in 972 by Count William I of Provence. There is an important **jazz festival** here in the middle of July (94 79 26 04.

Moulins de Paillas is the peninsula's highest point. From 326 m (1,070 ft), you can see all the way from the Îles d'Hyères to the Italian Riviera a distance of more than a hundred miles. To get there from Ramatuelle, take the D 89 for four kilometers (two and a half miles) to the north.

Gassin

The pretty hill town of Gassin can be reached by driving through rolling vineyards and is two and a half kilometers (about a mile and a half) away from Moulins de Paillas on D 89. A number of outstanding winemakers are here (see WINE TASTING below).

WHERE TO STAY

Luxury/Very Expensive

The **Villa de Belieu****** in Gassin (94 56 40 56 FAX 94 43 43 34, is a handsome ochre country mansion on the grounds of the Bertaud-Belieu vineyards whose 15 rooms and five suites range from mere opulence to the near-kinky, and its public rooms are a Renaissance Italian fantasy. It has tennis courts, an outdoor pool and a sybaritic fitness center with indoor pool, sauna, hammam (Turkish bath), Jacuzzi and massage. The hotel is open all year. The **Château de la Messardière****** Route de Tahiti, Ramatuelle (94 56 76 00 FAX 94 56 76 01, is a medieval-style nineteenth century *château* on a hilltop between Saint-Tropez and the beaches with the most spectacular views of any hotel in the area, large swimming pool and 69 plush rooms and 24 suites. **La Giraglia****** is a pretty ensemble of Provençal style houses integrated into the "little Venice" of Port-Grimaud, right on the beach with a big swimming pool looking across the bay at Saint-Tropez and 48 extremely comfortable rooms (94 56 31 33 FAX 94 56 33 77.

Expensive

La Ferme d'Augustin*** Plage de Tahiti, Ramatuelle (94 97 23 83 FAX 94 97 40 30, is a 33 room inn, a Relais de Silence member, situated in a park full of flowers 100 yards from Tahiti Beach with it's own restaurant. Open Easter to October. The **Hostellerie le Baou***** Avenue Gustave Etienne, Ramatuelle (94 79 20 48 FAX 94 79 28 36, sits on the edge of an this ancient perched village and has 41 tasteful rooms wit h

balconies and terraces overlooking the sea. Open March 1 through November 15. **Les Bergerettes***** Route des Plages, Ramatuelle (94 97 40 22 FAX 94 97 37 55, is a 29 room Provençal-style villa shaded by umbrella pines on six hectares (15 acres) of rolling woodlands overlooking vineyards and Pampelonne Beach. Open April to October.

Camping

There are numerous camping grounds on the Saint-Tropez Peninsula. The closest to Saint-Tropez on the Plage de Pampelonne and the most cramped for space are **La Toison d'Or** (94 79 83 54 and **Kon Tiki** next door (94 79 80 17, open from Easter to the end of September. Both are right on the beach, always full July and August. The camp sites at the other end of Pampelonne Beach are less cramped. **Les Tournels** on a pine-covered hill on the road to the Cap Camarat lighthouse is very pleasant and is open all year (94 79 80 54. In Gassin, **Camping Moulin de la Verdagne**, in the middle of vineyards, is open in season (94 79 78 21. You must reserve long in advance for July and August at any of these camps. For information and assistance, contact the Gulf of Saint Tropez Tourist Office at the Carrefour de la Foux in Gassin (94 43 40 70.

WHERE TO EAT

The off-again, on-again **Château de la Messardière**, formerly one of the area's best restaurants under chef Gerald Leroy, is back on again under Jean-Louis Vosgin, whose imaginatively spiced dishes, such his salmon steak with olive oil, coarse salt and Sechuan pepper or his squid ravioli on a bed of light vegetable curry, make a meal in this spectacular hilltop eatery a thoroughly rewarding experience. At the **Villa de Belieu**, you can dine in Renaissance splendor on menus of traditional French gourmet food featuring the wines of the Domaines Bertaud-Belieu, which are included. These two restaurants are very expensive. For a change of pace and somewhat more modest prices, try **Port Diffa** for *couscous, tagine* (a spicy meat stew) and other Moroccan specialties prepared and served to perfection on a cheerful terrace overlooking the boat-filled River Giscale at Cogolin Plage on the Gulf of Saint-Tropez. It is at Les-Trois-Ponts-sur-la-Giscale on Route N 98 just south of Port Grimaud and immediately to the east of the big Carrefour de la Foux traffic circle (94 56 29 07.

WINE TASTING

Driving through the Saint-Tropez Peninsula, you will see vineyards practically everywhere. This is prime Côtes de Provence wine country, and you have the perfect opportunity to start learning about the region's vintages in **Gassin**. **Château Minuty** is the most distinguished winemaker of the peninsula, and one of only 23 wine-making estates of the Côtes de Provence area to be designated a *cru classé*, an extremely prestigious rating. The Côtes de Provence area is especially noted for its delicate, dry rosés, and Château Minuty excels in them. But it also makes outstanding whites and, what is relatively rare in this area, a deep-colored, flavorful red, Cuivée de l'Oratoire. Château Minuty is set in a magnificent valley in the hills overlooking the Gulf of Saint-Tropez with tall plane trees, palms and rose bushes around its handsome Second Empire *château*. It is on the Route de Ramatuelle in Gassin (94 56 12 09. Open Monday to Friday, 9:15 AM to noon and 2 PM to 6:30 PM, year round.

Also on the Route de Ramatuelle is **Château Barbeyrolles** (94 56 33 58, a small vineyard with a 12 hectares (29 acres) of vines whose diaphanous and delicately flavorful "Pétale de Rose" ("Rose Petal") rosé, made by Régine Sumeire, one of the rare female winemakers, is highly prized by the *sommeliers* and wine connoisseurs and of the area. Château Barbeyrolles is open daily from 9 AM to 7 PM in season.

The oldest of the Saint-Tropez Peninsula's vineyards is **Domaines Bertaud-Belieu**, again on the Route de Ramatuelle (94 56 16 83, a 50 hectare (120 acre) spread that was owned by the Charterhouse of La Verne monastery in the Middle Ages. It produces 300,000 bottles of wine a year, rosé, white and red, and has a glamorous hotel and restaurant on its property, the Villa de Belieu (see WHERE TO STAY and WHERE TO EAT on page 154). It is open daily in season.

HOW TO GET THERE

Sodétrav runs the occasional local bus between the towns of the Saint-Tropez peninsula, but to explore the area, you need a car or some other means of getting around on your own. Bikes or mopeds can be rented in Saint-Tropez. For reasonably presentable individuals, hitchhiking is a viable alternative.

FURTHER AFIELD

Some travelers in southern France find that what they like most about the area are the sophisticated pleasures of the Côte d'Azur. If you are one of them, you will not want to budge from the Saint-Tropez Peninsula. But for those who tire of hot sand, bare flesh and voluptuous living, or who simply want to see some other, quite different places, two refreshing jaunts to the north may be in order.

THE MASSIF DES MAURES

The Maures is a strange place, a solitary island of crystalline rock covered by pine, cork-oak and chestnut forests in an area that is otherwise all limestone covered by vineyards. Along with Corsica, Sardinia and the Balaeric Islands, this range of low, rounded mountains, which runs 40 miles long by 20 miles wide between Fréjus and Hyères, is a remnant of a primitive land mass called Tyrrhenia that once covered practically all the western Mediterranean basin. It lies directly north of the Saint-Tropez Peninsula.

For more than two centuries, these hills were occupied by Saracen pirates. They were descendents of Moorish warriors defeated by Charles Martel at Poitiers in 732 who established themselves here and used it as a land base to raid towns in Provence. They were finally driven out by Count William of Provence in 973.

The name Maures is not derived from Moors, however, but from the Provençal word *maouro* meaning dark, because of the dense forests that used to cover the area. The forest is not as dense as it used to be, because of fires in the late 1980's. Much of it has grown back as scrub. But there are still plenty of cork oaks, which are used to make corks for bottles, a technique taught to the natives by the Saracens, and the chestnuts are used to make the delicious candies known as *marrons glacés*. The foothills are covered with vineyards, and practically every village has its cooperative and estates producing wines of all levels from *vins de table* to *AOC* Côtes de Provence.

General Information
Tourist Offices: 1 Boulevard des Aliziers, Grimaud, (94 43 26 98; Chapelle Saint-Éloi, Route de Grimaud, La Garde-Freinet, (94 43 67 41.

What to See and What to Do
A swing through some interesting towns in the Maures starts at **Grimaud** five kilometers (three miles) north of the big traffic circle of the Carrefour de la Foux. The name Grimaud derives from Grimaldi, another branch of the enterprising Genoese family that has made such a mark along this coast. This Grimaldi was a knight who came to help Count William chase out the Saracens.

Grimaud is a lively town of 3,300 that has managed to keep its medieval look. The town has good handicrafts workshops and boutiques centering around arcaded Rue des Templiers. From the impressive ruins of a castle at the top of the hill there is a grand vista of the Maures and the Gulf of Saint-Tropez. There is an outstanding Provençal restaurant, **Les Santons** (94 43 21 02, and a modestly-priced café with a dining terrace outside its vine-coverd old house, the **Café de France**.

On your way to Collobrières 20 km (12.5 miles) west of Grimaud on woodsy Route D 14, keep an eye out for the sign for the **Chartreuse de la Verne** on the left six kilometers (three and three quarters miles) before you reach Collobrières. Take the narrow winding access road through the cork-oaks, pines and chestnuts to the **Chartreuse (Charterhouse) de la Verne**, a monastery founded in the twelfth century and expanded several times over the centuries. In the Middle Ages, it established the vineyards that now cover the Saint-Tropez Peninsula. The impressive buildings date mainly from the seventeenth and eighteenth centuries. They were abandoned during the Revolution and are in a semi-ruined state. But the Bethlehem monastic community, which moved here in 1983, is renovating them little by little. Closed Tuesdays, October and main religious holidays. There are splendid views of the mountains.

The pretty, shaded village of **Collobrières** is the *marron glacé* capital, and the **Confiserie Azuréenne** on Boulevard Koenig makes a delicious version of the chestnut candies and other mouth-watering treats, such as jellies made from roses, violets, rosemary and (of course) chestnuts. There is also good local wine at the **Cave des Vigernons**, and for lunch, **La Petite Fontaine** on the main square, Place de la République, serves tasty Provençal home cooking at modest prices. From Collobrières, drive north on the wooded mountain roads through the attractive village of **Notre-Dame-des-Anges** and continue west to **La Garde-Freinet**, the Saracens' chief stronghold until they were expelled by Count William. The village, which lies 10 km (six miles) north of Grimaud on D 558, has also kept its medieval atmosphere. It makes corks and its own brand of *marrons glacé*, Marrons de Luc. From town you can hike past chestnut trees dating back almost to the time of the Saracens to the hilltop ruins of their fortress, a climb of about half an hour. There you can see what a perfect vantage point this was to watch for ships along the coast. When the look-out spotted a prize, he would signal the pirate ships waiting in the Gulf of Saint-Tropez, and the chase was on. Looking north, you will see the wide, vineyard-covered plain of the central Var.

There is little public transportation the Maures. Sodétrav has a daily bus from Le Lavandrou to Cogolin, Grimaud and La Garde-Freinet, but there is no bus service from Saint-Tropez. You need a car or a scooter to get around here.

THE HEART OF THE VAR

North of the Maures you descend into the flat semi-arid central plain of the Var where the Aurelian Way ran in Roman times and the big east-west

roads run today, the bland, but speedy A 8 *autoroute* and good old Nationale 7 celebrated by Charles Trenet's song. This is the oldest wine-making region in France, dating from the arrival of the Greeks. Rosé, its specialty, is sometimes thought of as a recently created wine, but in fact the ancient Greeks and Egyptians made it, and in the fifteenth century, Good King René, who governed this area as Count of Provence, was a great fan of rosé.

General Information
Tourist Offices are located at Place du Général de Gaulle in **Les Arcs-sur-Argens** (94 73 37 30, at Place d'Entrechaud in **Lorgues** (94 73 92 37, and on Grand Rue in Le Thoronet (94 73 87 11. The Maison des Vins des Côtes de Provence is on Route Nationale 7, Les Arcs (94 73 33 38.

What to See and What to Do
Les Arcs-sur-Argens is a rich wine-growing area 26 km (16 miles) west of Fréjus is home to the **Maison des Vins des Côtes de Provence**, a large, attractive information center on Route N 7 operated by the wine growers' association. Its wine-tasting cellar is open daily from 10 AM to 7 PM, to 8 PM between July and September, and there is a Provençal restaurant where special care is given to matching the cuisine and the wine, open every day except Monday. Long stigmatized as a wine that was not serious, rosé has gained respect in the past few decades as wine-makers of the area worked hard to improve quality, and in 1977 succeeded in earning their *Appellation d'Origine Controlée* (AOC). 18,000 hectares (43,000 acres) are under cultivation in *AOC* Côtes de Provence approved vines. 75 percent of the production is rosé, and the dry, light rosés of the Côtes de Provence now account for 40 percent of France's *AOC* rosé wine. Good reds and whites are also made. Do not hesitate to give them a try.

The Maison des Vins will help you map out a wine route. Some vineyards I recommend visiting in the vicinity are Domaines Ott's **Château de Selle** at **Taradeau** near Les Arcs (94 68 86 86 (one of Domaines Ott's three vineyards in the Var, all marvelous), **Château Sainte-Roseline** in Les Arcs (94 72 32 57, the fourteenth century **Domaine de Castel Roubine** in Lorgues (94 73 71 55, and in Le Luc, thirteenth century **Commanderie de Peyrassol** (94 69 71 02 and **Domaine de Brigue** (94 60 74 38. These are all excellent winemakers with very atmospheric *châteaux* to visit.

Besides visiting vineyards, there are cultural attractions to be aware of. In **Les Arcs**, the medie-

---

OPPOSITE TOP: Along the Route Napoléon north of Grasse. OPPOSITE: Mercantour National Park in the Maritime Alps.

val quarter of **Le Parage** is dominated by the ruins of the castle of the Villeneuve family, with its beautifully restored **watch tower**. In the **church**, there is a 16-panel **altarpiece** of the Virgin and Child surrounded by Provençal saints by Ludovico Bréa and an odd *crèche animée*, a mechanical crib, with a decor of the old village of Les Arcs. Four kilometers (two and a half miles) to the east of Les Arcs is the **Chapelle Sainte-Roseline** (Saint Roseline's Chapel), on the site of the Charterhouse of which Saint Roseline, a member of the Villeneuve family, was prioress from 1300 to 1328. The body of the saint lies in a remarkably well-preserved state in a shrine to the right of the nave. There is a handsome early

Baroque altarpiece and there are several interesting modern pieces, including a large mosaic by Chagall on the life of Saint Roseline.

The **Abbaye du Thoronet** is a Romanesque gem built in the late twelfth century on land donated by Raimond Bérenger III, the Count of Barcelona and Provence. It lies in **Lorgues** 28 km (17.5 miles) west of Les Arcs via D 10 and D 562. This is the oldest and smallest of the "Three Sisters of Provence," exquisite Cistercian abbeys all built within a few years of one another. The other two are Silvacane north of Aix and Sénanque near Gordes in the Lubéron (see THE LUBERON pages 212 to 219). The code of the order called for simplicity and disdain of all decoration, and the architecture certainly reflects that. But the loveliness of the natural settings (an isolated niche amid wooded hills in this case) and the stone they are made of (here a slightly reddish stone from the Esterel) soften the severity of the design. Because of that and of many pleasing design details — the fountain in the little vaulted hexagonal pavilion in Le Thoronet's cloister, for example — each of the three "sisters" has its own personality. Open all year.

ABOVE: Restaurant signs in the northern Var's Alpes de Provence announce that the wild boar has arrived.

Where to Stay and Where to Eat

Compared to the Saint-Tropez Peninsula, excellent choices in hotels and restaurants in this area are few and far between. And because most of the best restaurants in this area are in hotels, we deal with food and lodging together, with the exception of Chez Bruno in Lorgues, which serves food only.

As you move in from the coast, you will notice that the cuisine changes, with more emphasis on lamb as the main course and a greater use of truffles in the cooking. That magical root may be the most unique food ingredient native to Provence, but there are no ifs or buts about where to try it: **Chez Bruno** in Lorgues (94 73 92 19, three kilometers (two miles) south of town on the road to Les Arcs. Hefty Bruno Clement's truffle-laced cuisine has made it a prized stop on every gastronome's Southern itinerary. The pigeon pie with foie gras and truffles is much in demand. Prices are far from low here, but for quality and originality, Chez Bruno's 270 franc fixed-price menu is more than fair. Very popular, must reserve.

The **Logis du Guetteur***** at the Place du Château in Les Arcs (94 73 30 82 FAX 94 73 39 95, is a picturesque hotel-restaurant in the fortress of the medieval village with a swimming pool and 10 very comfortable rooms at moderate rates. *Demi-pension* is required in season (that is, breakfast and one other meal included in the price of the room), 480 francs per person. The excellent restaurant features regional dishes with plenty of truffles, with fixed-price menus starting at 125 francs.

Two moderately-priced little country inns I heartily recommend for their charm and tasty regional food are **Lou Calen***** 1 Cours Gambetta, Cotignac (94 04 60 40 FAX 94 04 76 64, which is 23 km (14 miles) west of Lorgues, and the **Auberge du Vieux Fox**** on the Place de l'Eglise in Fox-Amphoux (94 80 71 69 FAX 94 80 78 38, 10 km (six miles) north of Cotignac.

Le Calalou*** in **Moissac-Bellevue**, near Aups (94 70 17 91 FAX 94 70 50 11, is a delightful country resort on an old estate amid olive groves with a swimming pool, tennis courts and fine Provençal restaurant, open mid-March to mid-November. *Demi-pension* is required in season, 500 to 700 francs per person, depending on the season, and fixed-price menus start at 140 francs. It lies only 28 km (18 miles) south of the western end of the Grand Canyon du Verdon, which makes it a perfect base for exploring that natural wonder, see GRAND CANYON DU VERDON, page 142).

CAMPING

On the outskirts of Les Arcs, **Camping L'Eau Vive** (94 47 40 66, is open from March to the beginning of November, but it is near the *autoroute* and somewhat noisy. For a small quiet site, head north to

Camping des Prés on the Route de Tourtour at Aups (94 70 00 93. It is open all year. Also at Aups are **Camping Saint-Lazare** (94 70 12 86 and **International Camping** (94 70 06 80 on the road to Fox-Amphoux, both open from April to the end of September. For a more information on camping, contact the local Tourist Office.

How to Get There

Les Arcs is on the main SNCF line. By TGV, the trip takes about six hours from Paris with connections at Marseille or Toulon. From Saint-Raphaël or Fréjus it is a trip of half an hour. For train information in the Var call (94 91 50 50.

Rapides Varois (94 47 05 05 has a few buses a day between Les Arcs and Lorgues and a few other towns, and there are a few other small bus lines whose schedules you can get at the Tourist Office at Les Arcs, but frankly, unless you have all kinds of time to waste, you need a car to get around here.

THE SAINT-TROPEZ PENINSULA TO TOULON

The town of **La Croix-Valmer** at the western edge of the Saint-Tropez Peninsula is where Emperor Constantine is said to have had his vision of the cross (*In hoc signo vinces*), and there is a stone cross commemorating the event. It is also the start of the **Corniche des Maures**, Route D 559, which hugs the ins and outs of the seaside cliffs along a verdant stretch of coast running 20 km 12.5 miles between La Croix-Valmer and Bormes-les-Mimosas. A new turquoise bay is revealed at every turn, and across the water sit the Îles d'Hyères. Most of the little towns along the Corniche des Maures have preserved a good deal of their natural beauty, **Le Rayol** on the coast, for example, and **Bormes-les-Mimosas**, a hill town as flowery as its name. But sadly, some have buried it in concrete. The once-charming port of **Le Lavandou** is an example of that.

GENERAL INFORMATION

The **Tourist Office** at Bormes-les-Mimosas is at Place Gambetta (94 71 15 17. At Le Lavandou it is at Quai Gabriel Péri, (94 71 00 61.

WHAT TO SEE AND WHAT TO DO

At **Le Rayol** in the middle of the *corniche*, the **Domaine du Rayol** is a *belle époque* estate by the sea that had fallen into ruin, but to conserve its rich plantings was taken over by the Conservatoire du Littoral in 1989 to be turned into a botanical garden. It is still partly abandoned, which adds to its poetry. There are tours seven times a day

from July to September, less often the rest of the year (94 05 50 06.

In **Bormes-les-Mimosas**, you are in the land of **Guy Gedda**, the genial chef his fellow chefs of the region call "the Pope of Provençale Cuisine." He not only prepares savory specialties of the Midi at his superb **Jardin des Perlefleurs** restaurant (open July through September only), but teaches you how to make them in courses held at the restaurant all year. One six-course meal is taught per day Wednesday through Sunday (400 francs on weekdays, 500 francs on Saturday and Sunday). 100 Chemin de l'Orangerie, 83230, Bormes-les-Mimosas (94 64 99 23.

WHERE TO STAY

Les Roches**** 1 Avenue des Trois-Dauphins in **Aiguebelle**, four and a half hilometers east Le Lavandou (94 71 05 07 FAX 94 71 08 40, has everything a seaside luxury hotel should have — a pool and private beach, gardens, 42 deluxe rooms with big terraces with view of the sea and the Îles d'Hyèers and an outstanding restaurant. It is very expensive. Open Easter to the beginning of November. In the moderate price level, the **Palmiers***** is quiet country hotel a five minute walk from the sea with 21 pleasant rooms, *demi-pension* required in season, open all year. It is on Chemin du Petit Fort in **Cabasson**, eight kilometers (five miles) west of Le Lavandou on Cap de Brégançon (94 64 81 94 FAX 94 64 93 61. The **Paradis**** is an unassuming paradise in a big, flower-filled hillside garden with 20 neat, cheerful, inexpensive rooms and sea views. It is on Mont-des-Roses in Bormes-les-Mimosas (94 71 06 85. Open April through the end of September.

Camping

There's only one camping grounds right on the beach, **Camp du Domaine de la Favière** at the Plage de la Favière in Bormes (94 71 03 12 (two kilometers west of Le Lavandou on Route 559). It has 25 hectares (60 acres) of pine groves on a fine sand beach. To be sure of getting a place in the summer, you should book a good six months in advance. Other sites half a mile (800 m) or less from the beach in the towns along the Corniche du Maures are: **Camping Manjastre**, Route de Cogolin, (N 98), Bormes-les-Mimosas (94 71 03 28; **Camping les Mimosas** at Cavaliére (94 05 82 94; **Parc-Camping de Pramousquier** at **Pramousquier** (94 05 83 95; two sites in **Cavalaire-sur-Mer** — **Camping de la Baie**, Boulevard Pasteur (94 64 08 15 and **Camping de la Pinède**, Chemin des Mannes (94 94 11 14. They are open from March to mid or late October. Reserve as early as possible for mid-summer. If you want to contact them by mail, add "Var" (the name of district they are in) when you address on the enevelope.

WHERE TO EAT

At **Les Roches** in Aiguebelle, Laurent Tarridec, a Breton, has established himself as one of the masters of Mediterranean cuisine at this luxurious Michelin one-star restaurant, where fixed-price menus run from 455 to 635 francs. Open Easter to the beginning of November. In Bormes-les-Mimosas, at the **Jardin des Perlefleurs**, where cooking lessons are given all year (see above), you can dine on Guy Gedda's delightful cooking from July through September. A four-course Provençal feast goes for 220 francs (wine not included). Another fine place to eat in Bormes-les-Mimosas is the **Tonnelle des Delices** at Place Gambetta (94 71 06 85, Guy Gedda's old restaurant, where his worthy disciple Alain Gigant carries on the tradition. It is open from March to late October. In both restaurants, figure on about 300 francs *à la carte* on the average.

WINE TASTING

La Londe-les-Maures between Bormes-les-Mimosas and Hyères has only one distinction, and what a delightful distinction to have: it makes some of the best Côte de Provence wines. Three of the top châteaus are **Domaine du Galoupet** (94 66 40 07, **Domaine Saint-André-de-Figuières** (94 66 92 10, and **Clos Mireille** (94 66 80 26, one of Domaines Ott's superlative vineyards. You can visit their caves daily except Sunday.

HOW TO GET THERE

There are no trains. All these towns are serviced by the buses of Sodétrav that run between Toulon and Saint-Raphaël. For information call **Sodétrav** in Hyères at (94 65 21 00. By car, the towns are all on Route D 559.

HYÈRES

Hyères is a pleasant little city of 48,000 on a well-sheltered slope overlooking the sea with lots of flowers and palm trees. It is one if the oldest settlements on the coast. It started as a trading post called Olbia set up by the Greeks from Marseille on the shore at Almanarre, which later became the Roman port of Pomponiana. In the Middle Ages, the town moved up onto Castéou hill for the protection of the castle built there by the Lords of Fos. Hyères is the ancestor of all modern Côte d'Azur resorts. It was the first town the upper-class English started coming to in Mediterranean

France, as early as the late eighteenth century. With nineteenth century regulars like Queen Victoria and Robert Louis Stevenson, it became the place to be in the winter until the center of luxury tourism shifted to Nice, Cannes and Monte-Carlo at the end of the century. Today Hyères is the center of a prosperous fruit, vegetable, and wine-growing area.

GENERAL INFORMATION

The **Tourist Office** is at Rotonde Jean-Salusse, Avenue de Belgique, in modern Hyères just below the old city (94 65 18 55.

The main **airport** for this part of the coast is here, **Toulon-Hyères Airport** (94 22 81 60.

Trains, Gare SNCF (92 22 39 19 (for service to Toulon and points west; there is no train service east from Hyères).

Sodétrav Bus Line, Place Joffre (94 65 21 00.

Ferries leave from **Hyères Plage** (the Port of Hyères) and the port of **La Tour Fondue** on the Giens Peninsula, the main ports for ferries to the Îles d'Hyères. See HOW TO GET THERE, page 162.

WHAT TO SEE

Place Massillon is the heart of **La Vieille Ville**, the medieval part of town, and a lively market is held there daily. The ruins of the twelfth century **Tour Saint-Blaise** can be seen in the park up the hill. Nearby in the park is a showplace of modern architecture, the austere **Villa de Noailles**, also known as the Château Saint-Bernard, built by Robert Mallet-Stevens in 1924 for the patron of Surrealist artists, Charles de Noailles. The villa has been renovated by the city and is used as an exhibition center. It has grand panoramas of the sea and the islands. South of La Vieille Ville is the **Jardins Olbius-Riquier**, one of the finest gardens on the Côte d'Azur, six and a half hectares (16 acres) planted with many species of palms, cacti and other exotic plants and a pond for aquatic birds.

The narrow **Giens Peninsula** extends south of the Toulon-Hyères Airport for seven kilometers (four miles). Here sea salt is evaporated in pans, and there are good sandy beaches along the east coast, leading to the tiny town of **Giens** at the tip. This hill was an island as recently as Roman times, and like the Îles d'Hyères, is geologically part of the Massif des Maures. At the end of the road is **La Tour Fondue**, where ferries leave for Porquerolles.

WHERE TO STAY AND WHERE TO EAT

The best hotel is the **Mercure***** at 19 Avenue Thomas, a few blocks south of the center of town (94 65 03 04 FAX 94 35 58 20. This is a friendly,

OPPOSITE TOP: Porquerolles, the main island of the Îles de Hyères. OPPOSITE BOTTOM: The ferry between the Giens Peninsula and the Îles de Hyères.

                        The Côte d'Azur

attractive modern hotel with 84 spacious, well-appointed rooms, palm trees, a grassy lawn, a swimming pool, and a grill. Room and food prices are moderate. For more ambitious eating, try the **Jardins de Bacchus** nearby at 32 Avenue Gambetta (94 65 77 63 or **La Colombe** two and a half kilometers (about a mile and a half) west of town on N 98 (Ancienne Route de Toulon) (94 65 02 15, both serving well-tempered Provençal fare at moderate prices.

Camping

There are more than 30 camping grounds in Hyères and the Giens Peninsula. Three sites close to the beach are **Domaine du Ceinturon** at the Plage d'Ayguade near the Airport (94 66 32 65 and **Clair de Lune** (94 58 20 19 and **L'International** (94 58 20 25 on the beach at La Madrague in Giens. For a complete list, contact the Hyères Tourist Office.

HOW TO GET THERE

There are five flights a day from Paris to Toulon-Hyères Airport. There are nine connexions a day from Paris to the Gare SNCF in Hyères, changing trains at either Marseille or Toulon, a trip of six to seven hours depending on the connection. By bus, Phocéen Cars connects Hyères with the main places of the Côte d'Azur and Provence, including Marseille, Aix, Saint-Tropez, Saint-Raphaël, Nice, etc., and Sodétrav links it with all the stops along the coast between Toulon and Saint-Raphaël. By private car, there are numerous routes from the east, west and north.

THE ÎLES D'HYÈRES

The three islands one sees from Hyères and the Corniche des Maures are the Îles d'Hyères, **Porquerolles**, **Levant** and **Port-Cros**, also known as the "Îles d'Or" — the Golden Isles — because of the glow given off in certain light by mica in their rocks. The islands have been fought over by everyone from the ancient Ligurians, Greeks and Romans, the monks from Saint-Honorat, the Saracens, French, Turks, Spanish and the English down to the Germans and the Americans in World War II.

Much of the land on these islands is now protected, and no cars may be brought to them by non-residents.

GENERAL INFORMATION

Porquerolles has its own **tourist office** by the ferry dock on the island (94 58 33 76. For information about Port-Cros and Île du Levant, call or go to the Tourist Office in Hyères (94 65 18 55. For infor-

mation about boating and scuba diving, popular on all three islands, contact the Tourist Offices.

For information about the **nature reserve** on the Île de Port-Cros, contact **Parc National de Port-Cros**, Castel Sainte-Claire, Rue Sainte-Claire, 83400 Hyères (94 65 32 98 FAX 94 65 84 83. They also provide a list of dive clubs in the area.

For information about **Héliopolis**, the nudist colony on the Île du Levant, contact the **Tourist Office in Hyères** or write to the Association des Amis de l'Île du Levant, 203 *bis* Rue Saint-Martin, 75003 Paris, for a brochure in French, English, German and Italian.

ÎLE DE PORQUEROLLES

In 1971 the French Government, showing admirable foresight, bought most of the western Island of Porquerolles, the largest of the three, to preserve it in its natural state. Otherwise it might well be bristling with condos today. The hills are covered with pine, eucalyptus and underbrush of many shades of green and 200 hectares (about 500 acres) of vineyards. Environmental controls on this wooded island of seven and a half by two kilometers (four and a half by one and a quarter miles) are very strict. Since forest fires are a real menace, no smoking is allowed except in the town, with fines ranging up to 5,000 francs. The town of **Porquerolles** is the very image of the small Mediterranean port, with its little **Fort Sainte-Agathe** on the hill, red-roofed houses around the boat-filled harbor, palm trees and sunshine practically every day.

In short, Porquerolles is a paradise. But it's a paradise that is easy to get to, and in the summer, ferry-load after ferry-load of nature-lovers pour onto the island. 10,000 to 15,000 visitors per day join the 3,500 summer residents (the winter population is 400) to roam the countryside and seek out the dozens of little sandy beaches that ring the shore. Nevertheless, if you only have time for one boat trip on your travels through southern France, I recommend that it be to Porquerolles. Even if you only have a short time on the island, try to take the approximately two-and-a-half-kilometer (about a mile and-a-half miles) walk across the middle of the island from the port to the Lighthouse (*Phare*), the high point on the south side of the island, which has magnificent views in all directions. Allow about ninety minutes from the port and back.

Where to Stay and Where to Eat

Most hotels on Porquerolles require *demi-pension* (breakfast and one meal included in the price of the room) in season. Hotel restaurants are open to the general public.

My first choice on the Mediterranean coast to unwind in is the **Mas du Langoustier***, a rambling pink-ochre hotel with 57 very spacious and comfortable rooms on its own sandy cove on a remote point amid 40 hectare (96 acres) of eucalyptus, parasol pines and vineyards. It positively exudes serenity. And chef Michel Sarran gets the most savory tastes out of stuffed zucchini blossoms, sea bream with a mousse of burnt eggplant or grilled tuna that melts in your mouth. The fixed-price menu costs 300 francs, wine from Mas's fine vineyard included. *Demi-pension* runs 550 to 1,100 francs per person, depending on the month and type of room. The Mas is open from the beginning of May to the beginning of October (94 58 30 09 FAX 94 58 36 02. The moderately-priced **Auberge des Glycines***** is a pretty inn

maps follow nature trials leading through a marvelous variety of sea plants and colorful fish you can swim close to, because they are used to people who come with no lethal intentions. The place to stay on Port-Cros is **Le Manoir**** (94 05 90 52 FAX 94 05 90 89, an old-fashioned 19-room hotel that is run like a family resort from the last century. When the dinner bell rings, the meal is served, and if you miss it, you're out of luck. Open mid-May to early October.

ÎLE DU LEVANT

The Île du Levant, the easternmost island, is most famous for **Héliopolis**, the original French

on Place d'Armes, Porquerolles's main square (94 58 38 36 FAX 94 58 35 22. It has 13 tastefully decorated rooms, a shaded patio and fresh, tasty Mediterranean cuisine. Open mid-April to mid-October.

The inexpensive **Sainte-Anne**** on Place d'Armes (94 58 30 04 FAX 94 58 32 26 is a friendly, old-fashioned family-style hotel with 15 rooms and hearty, uncomplicated fare in the restaurant. Open early February to November 11.

The ÎLE DE PORT-CROS

The whole of the middle island of Port-Cros is a nature reserve, the **Parc National de Port-Cros**, with well-marked botanical trails to follow. The reserve includes an 1,800 hectare (4,320 acre) underwater park around the island too, where divers and snorkelers armed with plastic-coated

naturiste (the preferred term for nudist) gathering place, founded in 1931. It is very casual, not formal enough to be called a colony. On a day trip, just go, and where you notice that people aren't wearing clothes, you can take yours off too. Cameras are strongly discouraged. There are three hotels on the island, the 18-room **Héliotel**** (94 05 90 63, the 15-room **Gaëtan*** (94 05 91 78 and the 23- room **Brise Marine*** (94 05 91 15. There are three little camping grounds, eight guesthouses, rental apartments, bungalows, restaurants, shops and w6ater sports facilities. For information, see GENERAL INFORMATION, page 162.

Mas du Langoustier, a supremely restful resort hotel on the island of Porquerolles.

HOW TO GET THERE

There is regular **ferry service** to the Îles d'Hyères from six ports along the coast: **Cavalaire-sur-Mer**, **Le Lavandou**, **Port-de-Miramar**, **Hyères-Plage** near the Hyères-Toulon airport, **La Tour Fondue** at the tip of the Giens Peninsula and **Toulon**.

The **TLV** line runs boats to Porquerolles from La Tour Fondue every half hour in the summer, 67 francs for the 20 minute ride (94 58 21 81. TLV also runs boats to Port-Cros and Île du Levant from Hyères-Plage (Port d'Hyères) (94 57 44 07 and offers all-day trips to the three islands from both ports in the summer.

Vedettes Îles d'Or (94 71 01 02 has boats from Cavalaire, Le Lavandou and Port-de-Miramar to Port-Cros, Levant and Porquerolles. Three companies in Toulon offer circuits of the three islands, **SNRTM** (94 93 07 56, **Transmed 2000** (94 92 96 82, and **Bateliers de la Rade** (94 46 24 65.

TOULON

If there's one place that doesn't fit the Côte d'Azur's image, it's Toulon, a big navy and proletarian city singularly lacking in architectural merit. Much of its downtown was leveled by bombing in World War II, and the city was rebuilt helter-skelter, with no thought for aesthetics. It now has more than 400,000 inhabitants in the metropolitan area, 167,000 in the inner city.

Yet for all its apparent drawbacks, this is not a place you should bypass. It has a magnificent natural harbor, the largest in the Mediterranean. It also has some very interesting museums. And who knows, after overindulging in *le luxe* in Saint-Tropez, a blast of relatively gritty reality may be refreshing.

Toulon lies 18 km (11 miles) west of Hyères.

BACKGROUND

Like the other main towns and cities of the coast, Toulon was founded by the Greeks from Marseille, who called it Telonion. Under the Romans, who called it Telo Martus, it became important because of a rich purple dye, much prized by the Roman upper classes, extracted from conches living in its waters.

Despite its superb natural harbor, Toulon didn't become a military port until the sixteenth century, after Provence was absorbed by France. In the seventeenth century, Louis XIV made it his main naval port and set Vauban to strengthening its defenses, which had plenty of opportunity to prove their worth in Louis's endless wars. It was during this period that slaves were used to

row the infamous royal galleys. They were common criminals, political prisoners, prisoners of war, fifty four-man teams of slaves to a galley hefting fifty-foot long oars. People entertained themselves by watching the galley slaves at the Vieille Darse (the old port). This system of punishment was abolished in 1748 and replaced by the *bagne*, the system of prison camps from which Victor Hugo had Jean Valjean escape in *Les Misérables*.

During the French Revolution, Toulon's royalists turned the city over to the British in 1793, and in the campaign to retake it, Napoléon, then a 23 year-old artillery officer, first made a name for himself. In the fall of that year, he led a six-week siege of a seemingly impregnable complex of British forts known as "Little Gibraltar" in La Seyne on the west side of the harbor, and dislodged the British. In appreciation, the Convention promoted him to brigadier general.

In the nineteenth century, as the French built their colonial empire, their main naval base of Toulon grew rapidly and became almost exclusively a naval town.

In World War II, when the Germans occupied Southern France, the French Navy scuttled its own fleet in Toulon harbor in December 1942, sending 60 ships to the bottom to prevent their falling into German hands. Toulon was liberated from the Nazis in August, 1944.

GENERAL INFORMATION

The **main Tourist Office** is at 8 Avenue Colbert (94 22 08 22. In the summer, there are branch offices at Toulon-Hyères Airport (94 57 45 72 and Toulon's Gare SNCF (94 62 73 87.

Flight Information, Toulon-Hyères Airport (94 38 57 57. Airport shuttle bus (94 22 81 00.

Train station, Gare SNCF, Avenue Toesca (94 91 50 50.

The **bus station** is next to the train station. **Sodétrav** serves Hyères and the coastal towns to the east, including Saint-Tropez (94 65 21 00, and **Phocéen Cars** at the same phone number serves Cannes and Nice; **Littoral Cars** (94 74 01 35 and **Sociéte Varoise de Transports** (42 70 28 00 serve towns to the west; **Transvar** (94 28 93 28 and **Autocars Blanc** (94 92 97 41 serve towns to the north. For information on the web of bus lines that cover the area, contact the Tourist Office.

Taxis, 24-hour service (94 93 51 51.

Boat tours of the harbor: Transports Maritimes Toulonnais (TMT) (94 31 10 73; **Bateliers de la Rade** (94 46 24 65; **Vedette Alain** (94 46 29 89. All are open all year. **Boat tours to the Îles d'Hyères, SNRTM** (94 93 07 56; **Transmed 2000** (94 92 96 82; **Bateliers de la Rade** (94 46 24 65.

Health emergencies: SAMU (94 27 07 07; **SOS Médecins** (91 31 33 33.

WHAT TO SEE AND WHAT TO DO

Several companies offer boat rides around **the harbor** (see above), very impressive when the aircraft carrier Clémenceau and other big French warships are in port. The harbor has two parts, **La Petite Rade**, the perfectly sheltered inner harbor, and **La Grande Rade**, the larger outer harbor, which is also well-protected by the Saint-Mandrier Peninsula.

On the waterfront **Quai Stalingrad**, look out for the **Atlantes**, the colossal twin muscle-men sculpted in the seventeenth century by Pierre Puget, said to have been modeled on suffering galley slaves, and themselves the models for the many Atlantes straining to hold up balconies in Aix and elsewhere in Provence. At the west end of Quai Stalingrad, the **Musée Naval** has an excellent collection of scale models of ships, figureheads by disciples of Puget, statues of admirals by Puget himself, paintings and drawings of old Toulon, including scenes of its notorious *bagne*. Closed Tuesday.

La **Vieille Ville** is the one part of Toulon that escaped the World War II bombings. It is reached by **Rue d'Alger** that leads you up from Quai Stalingrad. A little section of the rough old sailor-bar district remains. It is so pungently realistic with its flop-houses, neon signs and street-walkers that you'd swear you had walked onto the set of a 1930's waterfront movie. It lies to the west of Rue d'Alger. Get there fast before the urban developers beat you to it.

You can also take the **Téléferique**, the cable car, up to **Mont Faron** for one of the best panoramas on the Côte d'Azur (which is saying a lot). From a height of 584 m (1,917 ft), it takes in all of Toulon, the huge harbor and roadstead, Cap Sicié to the west, and the mountains in back of the city. The **Musée-Mémorial du Débarquement en Provence** near the top of the Téléferique is a moddern museum with electronic displays, films and memorabilia relating to the Allied landing on the cost of Provence in August 1944. Closed Mondays.

West of Toulon is **La Seyne**, a promontory with good views of Toulon and the harbor from **Fort Balaguier**. The fort has a **museum** with Napoléon memorabilia, naval models and artifacts made by prisoners in the *bagne*. Closed Mondays and Tuesdays.

Farther out on this peninsula is **Cap Sicié**, from which there are views along the coast from Îles d'Hyères to the Calanques de Marseille 32 km (20 miles) away. The view is best from the hilltop church of **Notre-Dame-du-Mai**, 358 m (1,175 ft) high. The church is a place of pilgrimage for sailors and contains a number of ex-voto artworks.

WHERE TO STAY

The **New Hôtel Tour Blanche***** Avenue de Vence (at the foot of the Télépherique) (94 24 41 57 FAX 94 22 42 25, has views of the harbor from all 92 comfortable modern rooms and from the terrace of the restaurant, and there is a pool and a *pétanque* surface. The **Corniche***** at 1 Littoral Frédéric Mistral (94 41 35 12 FAX 94 41 24 58, is an attractive, modern 22-room hotel close to the main beach. Both these hotels are moderately priced. The **Dauphiné**** 10 Rue Berthelot (94 92 20 28 FAX 94 62 16 69, is a well-maintained older hotel with 57 inexpensive rooms on the edge of La Vieille Ville. It has no restaurant.

Camping

The camping grounds in the Toulon are mainly at **La Seyne-sur-Mer** on the west side of the port. **Camping Beauregard** 300 m (1,000 ft) from the beach in **La Garde** is open all year (94 20 56 35. For a complete list of camps in the area contact the Tourist Office.

WHERE TO EAT

The **Bistrot** at the Hôtel Corniche has an outdoor restaurant built around huge pine trees that serves first-rate Provençal fare at inexpensive prices (lunch 99 francs, drinks included). The **New Hôtel Tour Blanche** features grilled shrimp and fish, good but expensive. The **Dauphin**, 21 *bis* Rue Jean Juarès (94 93 12 07, is a cosy restaurant near the Place d'Armes with fresh fish *à la Provençale* and an exceptional selection of Bandol wines, with menus from 90 francs. Chef Alain Bilès also organizes wine-tasting visits to vineyards in the region with meals served at the *châteaux*.

HOW TO GET THERE

There are five flights a day from Paris to Toulon-Hyères Airport and four direct trains a day from Paris, a five-hour trip, along with another half-dozen trains with connections at Marseille, which adds a half-hour to an hour to the trip. The trains continue on to Saint-Raphaël, Cannes and Nice. By bus, several lines connect Toulon with the other towns and cities of the Côte d'Azur and Provence (see GENERAL INFORMATION, page 166). By car, Toulon is easily reached by highway.

TOULON TO BANDOL

On the western shore of Cap Sicié, 12 km (seven and a half miles) directly west of Toulon, starts a sports-oriented stretch of beach towns and there are some interesting little islands owned by *pastis* baron Paul Ricard. The **Îles des Embiez** off **Le Brusc** have an oceanographic park and a sports center, and the **Île de Bendor** off Bandol has scuba diving, a marine museum, an art gallery and a wine and liqueur exposition. The stretch of coast from Le Brusc through Six-Fours-les-Plages to **Sanary-sur-Mer** is one of the leading spots for windsurfing in France. **Sanary** and **Bandol** are active pleasure boat ports. **Bandol** is famed for its wine (see WINE, page 166).

GENERAL INFORMATION

Tourist Offices: Six-Fours, Plage de Bonnegrâce, the main beach (94 07 02 21; Quai Saint-Pierre, **Le Brusc** (summer only) (94 34 15 50; **Sanary**, Jardins de Ville, the beachfront promenade (94 74 01 04; **Bandol**, Allées Alfred Vivien, by the pleasure port (94 29 41 35. These Tourist Offices can supply information on hotels, camping, bicycle rental and sports. A couple of places where you can rent **bikes** in Bandol are **Hookipa Sport** (94 29 53 15 and **Gallia Sports** (94 29 60 33. There are **ferries** to the Île de Bendor every half hour from the Port of Bandol in the summer, an eight-minutes ride. There is a **market** every morning on Place de la Liberté in the center of Bandol.

WHERE TO STAY

There are plenty of hotels to chose from. Bandol has 23, Sanary-sur-Mer 11 and Six-Four has seven. I like the **Hôtel de la Tour**** Quai du Général de Gaulle, Sanary (94 74 10 10 FAX 94 74 69 49, a charming old-fashioned 26-room hotel on the port with a flowery terrace restaurant, moderate prices for both. A very enjoyable place to stay is the **Coin Azur*** Rue Raimu, Bandol (94 29 40 93 FAX 94 32 51 93, a rambling villa overlooking the beach at the Plage de Renécros with 15 spacious, inexpensive rooms and a warm, easy-going atmosphere. On the Île de Bendor, **Délos Palais***** (94 32 22 23 FAX 94 32 41 44, is the ideal spot on this waters sports Mecca, but it is expensive.

Camping

In **Sanary**, the main camping grounds are **Les Girelles** (94 74 13 18 and **Le Mogador** (94 74 10 58. In **Bandol** it is **Vallonge** (94 29 49 55. They are open from Easter to the end of September.

WHERE TO EAT

The **Auberge du Port**, 9 Allées Jean Moulin, Bandol (94 29 42 63, is an extraordinarily good seafood restaurant right on the waterfront with menus from 105 francs. The **Coin Azur** has good shellfish and grilled fish in its modestly-priced restaurant and a snack bar on the beach. In Six-Fours-les-Plages, **La Brise** at the Port de la Coudoulière offers simply prepared, delicious seafood with fixed-price menus from 98 francs (94 34 61 27. Open Easter to mid-October.

WINE TASTING

Bandol is one of the most prestigious wine regions of Southern France, noted especially for its vigorous reds. It was one of the South's pioneers in the movement from low-quality, high-quantity inexpensive wines to high-quality expensive ones. In Bandol's case, this was a return to high quality, because its wines had enjoyed a great reputation during the *Ancien Régime* (it was Louis XV's favorite wine). And because it traveled well by sea, Bandol wines were prized all over the world. After the phylloxera epidemic wiped out the vineyards in the 1870's, however, for practical and marketing reasons, the growers replanted their fields in higher-yield grapes than the Mourvèdre traditionally used to make Bandol. The long road back to quality started in the 1920's. It was pursued in the 1930's by a small group of visionaries who went back to the traditional vines. Their efforts were rewarded with an AOC for Bandol in 1941.

The vineyards of Bandol extend over an area of 2,700 hectares (6,500 acres) though only half of it is planted with the Mourvèdre, Grenache and Cinsaut grapes that are used to make the wine. They include the coastal towns of **Bandol** and **Sanary**, and inland the attractive medieval perched villages of **Le Castellet** and **La Cadière d'Azur** and the market town of **Le Beausset**, gently hilly countryside to drive through with vineyards practically everywhere. The winemakers are especially easygoing and enjoyable to visit.

Domaine Tempier in **Plan-du-Castellet** north of Bandol has long been recognized as one of the area's finest producers. Lucien Peyraud, the patriarch of the family, led the movement to quality wines in the 1930's, with the support of his spirited wife Lucie, née Tempier, a famous cook and one of the most beloved individuals in the South of France. Their sons Jean-Marie and François now run the vineyard. It can be visited weekdays except at lunchtime and Saturday mornings. Closed Saturday afternoon and Sunday (94 98 70 21.

Other top producers of Bandol are Comte de Saint-Victor's **Chateau de Pibarnon** in **La Cadiére d'Azur** (94 90 12 73, **Domaine de Terre-Brune** in **Ollioules** (94 74 01 30 and **Domaines Ott's Chateau Romassan** in **Castellet** (94 98 71 91. But these are not the only producers of fine Bandol wines by any means. For information on Bandol wines and caves to visit, contact the **Association de Vins de Bandol** in **Le Beausset** (94 90 29 59.

HOW TO GET THERE

Bandol is a stop on the main SNCF train line. Sanary and Six-Fours can be reached by regular bus service from Toulon.

MASSIF DE LA SAINTE-BAUME

Continuing inland from the Bandol wine area, you come to one of the most mysterious places in Southern France, the **Massif de la Sainte-Baume** and **Saint-Maximin-la-Sainte-Baume**.

Baoumo is Provençal for cave, and **La Sainte-Baume** is the cave where Mary Magdalen is said to have spent the last thirty-three years of her life in prayer. The cave, now converted into a chapel, is on the slope of **Saint-Pilon**, a mountain in the heavily wooded **Massif de la Sainte-Baume** about 40 km (25 miles) north of the Bandol wine country. It has been an important place of pilgrimage since the Middle Ages. For the legend of how Mary Magdalen came to France, see THE CAMARGUE section, page 239. On July 21 and 22 and on Christmas Eve a midnight mass is celebrated in the chapel. The cave is reached by a not-too-difficult 30-minute hike on well-marked paths up Saint-Pilon from either the village of **Plan-d'Aups-Ste-Baume** on D 80 or the **Carrefour des Chênes** at the intersection of D 80 and D 95. Real hikers can continue another three-quarters of an hour to the top of Saint-Pilon 994 m (3,260 ft) high with a panoramic view of the Mediterranean, Montagne Sainte-Victoire and Mont-Ventoux. The north slope of the mountain has a cool, damp Northern European microclimate. Maples, beeches and lime trees grow here amid a dense, leafy underbrush of ivy, yew, holly and privet. On the southern side of Saint-Pilon, there is a complete change of ecology, with only Mediterranean plants and trees.

Long before Mary Magdalen's time, even before the Greeks, Sainte-Baume was a place of pilgrimage. Ligurians came to pray to fertility goddesses. All civilizations have considered it holy. To this day, though the Var has as rapacious a bunch of real estate predators as can be found anywhere, this area has been left free of commercial exploitation, in contrast to much of the Var's coast.

Two hotels stand on either side of Saint-Pilon, both are elegant eighteenth century country houses with outstanding restaurants, the **Domaine de Châteauneuf****** to the north in **Nans-les-Pins**, a Relais & Châteaux hotel with its own 18-hole golf course (94 78 90 06, and the **Relais de la Magdeleine****** to the south in **Gémenos** ((42 32 20 16). **Le Parc**** also in Gémenos is a pleasant little hotel (42 32 20 38. There is a hostel for pilgrims at Plan d'Aups-Ste-Baume ((42 04 50 21). For information contact the Tourist Office in Gémenos (42 82 07 29.

To get to this area from Bandol wine country, take N 8 northwest from Le Beausset to Gémenos, 28 km (17.5 miles), then wind up little D 2 another 12 km (7.5 miles) to Plan d'Aups-Ste-Baume.

SAINT-MAXIMIN-LA-SAINTE-BAUME

Saint-Maximin-la-Sainte-Baume 20 km (12.5 miles) north of La Sainte-Baume is a depressing town that looks like some dusty forgotten corner of Mexico. Bulging up like a whale on the surface of the ocean, visible for miles around, is the **Basilica of Saint-Maximin**. Millions of pilgrims have come over the centuries, including such notables as Louis XIV. What brought them are relics claimed to be those of Mary Magdalen. Her remains were said to have been hidden in the eighth century to prevent them from falling into the hands of the Saracens, but disappeared. In the thirteenth century Charles of Anjou, Count of Provence and brother of King Louis IX (Saint Louis), launched a search for the missing relics, and lo and behold, in 1279 they were found. Charles built a crypt which was elaborated over the next two and a half centuries into the largest Gothic church in Provence. A cranium said to be Mary Magdalen's is on display in a gold reliquary in the crypt. The crypt also contains relics of Saint Maximinus and Saint Suedonius, two of her companions on the boat to the Camargue. The relics of Mary Magdalen are taken out for a procession on her feast day, July 22.

The Basilica has one of the largest and finest pipe organs in France, built in 1773, with almost 3,000 pipes. They were saved from being melted down for guns during the Revolution by Lucien Bonaparte, Napoléon's clever younger brother, who was in charge of the warehouse the basilica had been converted to. He saved it, the story goes, by having *La Marseillaise* played on it at critical moments. The adjoining **Ancien Couvent Royal** (Old Royal Convent), started at the same time as the Basilica and finished in the fifteenth century, has a large cloister with 32 bays. There are organ recitals at the Basilica on 4 PM Sundays in the summer. Orchestral concerts of religious music are held in the cloister of the Ancien Couvent Royal and in the Basilica in July and August. For information, contact the **Tourist Office** at the Hôtel de Ville (94 78 00 09.

By car, Saint-Maximin can be reached by D 80 and N 560 from Plan d'Aups 20 km (12.5 miles) to the south, and it is about 40 km (25 miles) east of Aix-en-Provence on the A 8 *autoroute* and roughly the same distance from Marseille. Three bus lines come here from Marseille and Aix, **Phocéen Cars** (93 85 66 61, **Blanc** (94 69 08 28 and **Lombard** (94 78 00 32. Phocéen's buses also come from Nice, Fréjus-Saint-Raphaël and other points east, and Blanc has two buses a day from Toulon.

The Côte d'Azur

Provence

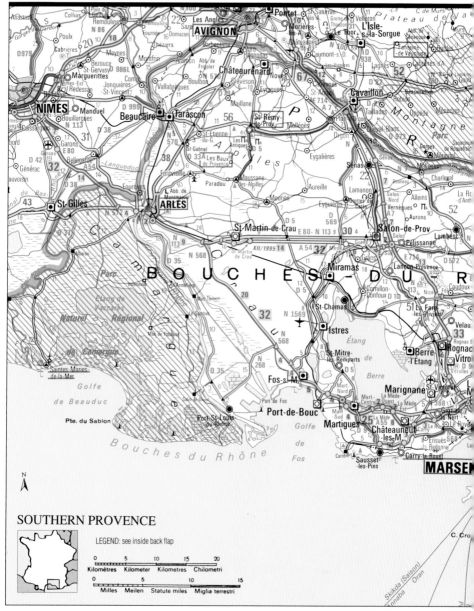

SOUTHERN PROVENCE

LEGEND: see inside back flap

0   5   10   15   20
Kilométres Kilometer Kilometres Chilometri

0   5   10   15
Milles Meilen Statute miles Miglia terrestri

PEOPLE GET MISTY-EYED when they talk about Provence. And why not? It is the heart of historical Provinicia Romana with legendary cities such as Arles, Nîmes, Avignon, Aix and Marseille. It has mountains and vineyard-covered valleys, a great river flowing the length of it and a dramatic coastline from the soaring cliffs of Cassis and the *calanques* of Marseille to the moody wetlands of the Camargue. In Provence, there is a fine equilibrium between the beauties of nature, the riches of culture and the pleasures of the flesh. There are music, dance and theater festivals galore in the

summer and cuisine, wine and lodging of the highest order all year round.

In the Côte d'Azur, the coastline is the focus of everything. But in Provence, although the coast is certainly important, the axis is its river, the Rhône. The towns and cities of Orange, Avignon, Tarascon, Beaucaire and Arles are on it, and Marseille, though it fronts on the Mediterranean, owes its development as a great port to its position near the mouth of the Rhône. The Rhône Valley has been the main route between the North and the South from the times of the Greeks and Romans

Papal city of Avignon, the Roman towns of Orange and Vaison-la-Romaine, and the Côtes du Rhône wine country.

Readers who have been following our east to west itinerary through the Côte d'Azur may continue with the sections that follow CASSIS, MARSEILLES, page 174, AIX-EN-PROVENCE, page 183.

The distances between places are short. It takes half an hour to drive each leg of the Nîmes–Arles–Avignon triangle, half an hour from Marseille to Aix, and it is only 160 km (100 miles) from the Drôme Provencale in the north to Marseille in the south.

BANDOL TO CASSIS

From Bandol, take the coast road D 559 west toward Marseille through **Les Lecques**, the last town of the Côte d'Azur, and enter Provence at **La Ciotat**. This town, half beach resort, half shipyard, is where the first motion picture was shot in 1895 by the Lumière brothers. They filmed a head-on scene of a train entering La Ciotat station, and when they projected it in a theater, the audience panicked and ran out. It is also the town where the rules for the Provençal bowling game of *pétanque* were devised.

Following the curve of the shore, drive through the center of La Ciotat, turn right onto Route D 141 and climb to the 13 km (eight mile) **Route des Crêtes** (crest road) along the cliffs of Cap Canaille. It is 399 m (1,310 ft) down to the sea from its highest point at **Grande Tête** — the loftiest cliff in France. The view from the headland just east of Cassis, with vineyards running down steep slopes to the shore, sailboats on the sparkling sea and the little port in the crook of the bay is a marvelous mental postcard.

Be warned, though: if it's windy and you're driving a light car, the gusts on the Route des Crêtes can be dangerous. As an alternative, stay on D 559, the main road inland from La Ciotat to Cassis.

CASSIS

Few small ports in the Mediterranean could compete with Cassis in a beauty contest. The harbor is filled with boats and lined with cafés, a tree-shaded square where the villagers play pétanque, and its town beach poking out into the sea on a finger of land. But what makes Cassis unique is the grandeur of the high ridge in the background and the mighty cliffs of Cap Canaille to the east — not close enough to overwhelm it, as the Maritime Alps do the little ports east of Nice, but framing the town perfectly.

What also makes Cassis unique is its wine.

to our days. The main north-south rail line runs through the Rhône corridor, as does the Autoroute du Soleil, the six-lane highway most cars and trucks use, carrying southern fruit, vegetables and wine to the cold north and armies of northern vacationers to the sunny south.

Travelers driving down from the north will enter Mediterranean France in the sunny olive, truffle and wine-growing region south of the Drôme River nicknamed "La Drôme Provençale," or directly south of it, the Vaucluse, home of the

GENERAL INFORMATION

The **Tourist Office**, on Place Baragnon one block in from the *pétanque*-playing square in the port (42 01 71 17, offers a list of 14 Cassis vineyards that can be visited besides information on restaurants, accommodations and sports facilities.

WHAT TO SEE AND WHAT TO DO

Cassis is the most popular and most convenient place for visiting the **Calanques de Marseille**. This is a string of dramatic fjords (*calanques*) with sheer white limestone cliffs and amazingly translucent turquoise and blue water that filigrees the coastline for 17 km (11 miles) to the west of Cassis. Most lie within the city limits of Marseille, hence the name. Boats run frequently from the port of Cassis to the *calanques* daily all summer. The hour-long trip to the three closest ones, **Port-Miou**, **Port-Pin** and **En-Vau** is well worth the price of 45 francs. Boat trips are also available to more remote *calanques*.

They can also be explored from the land. From Cassis, drive to Port-Miou, the boat-lined *calanque* west of town, and park in the lot, where you will find a clearly marked trail to the next calanque, Port-Pin, with a pretty little beach. Allow one hour round-trip for the hike. For En-Vau, the prettiest, allow two and a half hours.

WHERE TO STAY AND WHERE TO EAT

The **Plage du Bestouan***** on Avenue Dardanelles, a kilometer west of town (42 01 05 70 FAX 42 01 34 82, is a peaceful 30-room hotel overlooking a small beach with a good restaurant, **Le Bestouan**. Room prices are moderate to somewhat expensive. Open late March to late October. The **Liautaud**** at 2 Rue Victor Hugo (42 01 75 37 FAX 42 01 12 08, is a pleasant, inexpensive 32-room hotel on the port. It has no restaurant. Closed from mid-November to the beginning of January. The top restaurant is **La Presqu'île**, two kilometers (one and a quarter miles) from town on the road to Port-Miou (42 01 03 77, offering impeccably prepared seafood and a magnificent view of the sea and Cap Canaille. It is expensive. Open early March to mid-October.

Camping

Les Cigales is a 300-place camping ground on three shaded hectares (eight and a half acres) on the Route de Marseille, D 559, one kilometer from the port of Cassis (42 01 07 34, open March 15 to

November 15. It is one of the closest camping sites to Marseille 22 km (13.5 miles) away.

WINE TASTING

Cassis is one of South's most prestigious wine-making areas. Its dry whites are the only beverage the *Marseillais* would think of drinking with *bouillabaisse* (not be confused, by the way, with black currant *cassis* liqueur from Burgundy used to make *kirs*). The most beautiful of Cassis's vineyards to visit is the **Clos Sainte-Madeleine**, which has a handsome mansion overlooking the sea and 12 hectares (28 acres) of vines running up to the Cap Canaille cliffs. The proprietors,

M. and Mme. Sack, will be happy to let you taste their excellent whites and rosés (42 01 70 28. **Domaine de Bagnol**, another outstanding Cassis vineyard, also makes reds as well as whites and rosés (42 01 78 05.

HOW TO GET THERE

There are trains every hour from Gare Saint-Charles in Marseille. However, the train station in Cassis is located three kilometers (two miles) from town. Buses operated by the S.C.A.C. line also run every hour from Marseille, from either the Gare Saint-Charles or Place Castellane, and drop you at the Casino in Cassis, which is a short walk to the port. By car, Cassis is 23 km (14 miles) from downtown Marseille on D 559 and four kilometers (two and a half miles) from the A 50 *autoroute* between Marseille and Toulon.

The Route des Crêtes ABOVE between La Ciotat and Cassis has the highest seaside cliffs in France. The *calanques* of Marseille OPPOSITE, the chain of dazzling white limestone fjords between Cassis and Marseille, are most easily reached by boat from Cassis.

MARSEILLE

Marseille is the most surprising city in Mediterranean France, and the most astonishing discovery many visitors make is that they can walk about freely with little danger of being robbed or gunned down in the street. Unfortunately, most people's image of Marseille is right out of *The French Connection*, where the hit man shoots his victim, coolly breaks off a chunk of the dead man's *baguette*, and saunters off up the street munching it. But in fact, though the noxious influence of the Mafia has indeed been strong, Marseille, which is France's second city with 800,000 people, ranks well below Paris in crimes against persons and only ninth among French cities. And compared to any American big city, its crime rate is laughably low. Except in one or two rough neighborhoods you have no reason to visit anyway, the ordinary precautions one would take in any big city are all that are needed.

What does Marseille have going for it other than safe streets? Plenty: a spectacular natural setting, Greek island weather kept bright by the mistral, the ever-lively Vieux Port and fascinating urban corners to explore, a rich panoply of cultural attractions, and easy access to the beach-studded coast and islands. Marseille also has one of the most exciting cuisines of France, starting with *bouillabaisse*. To this should be added the cuisines of the immigrant populations of Italians, Armenians, Greeks, Turks, Spaniards, North Africans, West Africans, Vietnamese, Thai and Chinese, all represented in substantial numbers. The nightlife is active too, mainly in the many clubs, discos, bars and cafés around the Vieux Port.

To learn to appreciate this city, give yourself time and poke around. Marseille will reward you in unexpected ways.

BACKGROUND

Marseille is the oldest city in France, founded in the seventh century BC by Greek sea traders from Phocaea in Asia Minor who named it Massalia. They brought the olive tree and the secret of wine-making and set up trading posts along the coast and up the Rhône. Marseille prospered for centuries until it made the mistake of going against Julius Caesar in 49 BC, and he and his successors cut Marseille out of the profits for the rest of the Pax Romana. A thousand years later, the Crusades to the Holy Land, which started in 1095, brought Marseille fully back to life, when it became their main port. And despite wars, plagues and frequent pirate raids, it continued to prosper, particularly after Provence joined the Kingdom of France. The discovery of America and the opening up of the ocean route to Asia via the Cape of Good

Hope, which gave the Atlantic ports the advantage in world trade, undermined Marseille's dominance. In 1720, a plague that came in on a merchant ship from Syria killed more than half the population of 90,000. But by the time of the Revolution, the city had grown to its pre-plague level, and the economy was doing well.

Habitually at odds with all central governments, Marseille welcomed the Revolution. In 1792, a company of 500 volunteer soldiers from Marseille stirred people with their singing of a new song called "The War Song of the Army of the Rhine," and it became known as the *"La Marseillaise."*

In the 1830's, Marseille became the gateway to France's developing colonial empire in North and

Equatorial Africa, and a period of fabulous prosperity ensued, especially after the opening of the Suez Canal in 1867, linking the Mediterranean with the Far East. Locally manufactured products such as soap added to the city's affluence. Prosperity continued until the Great Depression of the 1930's and the disaster of World War II, in which Marseille was heavily bombed by the Allies. On top of that, German occupation forces dynamited a large part of the Panier, the immigrant neighborhood on the west side of the Vieux Port, which was a hotbed of Résistance activity.

The collapse of the French colonial empire in the 1950's and 1960's brought further economic disaster to the city. Though the Port of Marseille remains the second largest port in Europe for cargo after Rotterdam, and a million passengers a year still pass through it, its economic vitality is nowhere near what it once was. Nor have the huge steel mills developed in Fos-sur-Mer provided the economic stimulus hoped for. High technology and clothing manufacture hold promise, and Marseille has belatedly started to see itself as a place for cultural tourism, after the chance discovery in 1967 of the ancient Greek port of Massalia awakened a new sense of the city's archaeological riches.

GENERAL INFORMATION

The **Tourist Office** is easy to find at 4 Canebière, Marseille's main street that starts at the Vieux Port. It is open daily, until 8 PM in summer (91 13 89 00. There is also a small office at the Gare Saint-Char-

67 28; **Hertz** (91 79 22 06; **Rent-a-Car** (91 91 23 24; **Thrifty** (91 05 92 18.

The **bus and subway lines** of the local RTM are modern and simple to use. A *carnet* of six tickets costs 39 francs.

Little **Tourist Trains** from the Quai des Belges to Notre-Dame-de-la-Garde or the Panier run frequently all summer, 25 francs. (The N° 60 city bus also runs between the Vieux Port and Notre-Dame-de-la-Garde).

Boat Excursions: tour boats (*navettes*) to the Château d'If run every hour in the summer from the Quai des Belges, 40 francs. There are also trips to the *calanques* of Marseille at various prices, depending on the length of the trip.

les, the railway station. The Tourist Office offers excellent brochures; practical assistance and cultural tours by passionate, well-informed guides, some in English. Its monthly magazine, *Marseille Atout*, lays out the city's cultural attractions (in French only, 20 francs). A seven-day tourist pass to all the museums in the city can be purchased here or in any museums for 30 francs.

These phone numbers may be useful:

Marseille-Provence International Airport at Marignane (42 78 21 00. Gare Saint-Charles, the **SNCF train station** (91 08 50 50. The **bus station, Gare Routière**, Place Victor-Hugo (91 08 16 40, in back of the train station.

Taxis: Marseille Taxi (91 02 20 20; **Taxis Phocéens** (91 06 15 15; **Eurotaxis** (multi-lingual) (91 97 12 12.

Car rental: Avis (91 08 41 80; **Budget** (91 71 75 00; **EuroDollar** (91 37 07 08; **EuropCar** (91 49

Medical Emergencies: SOS Médecin (91 52 91 52.

WHAT TO SEE AND WHAT TO DO

Vieux Port
The focal point of the city is the Vieux Port (Old Port), a long natural harbor indented into the city and surrounded by hills. It was Marseille's main port until the mid-nineteenth century, when the large-scale shipping activities were shifted to the new port of La Joliette to the west. The Vieux Port is now filled with pleasure and fishing boats, and a funny little ferry boat crosses it from the **Hôtel de Ville** to the **Place aux Huiles**. Don't miss the open-air **fish market** held every morning on the

Marseille's island fortress of the Château d'If and the Frioul Islands.

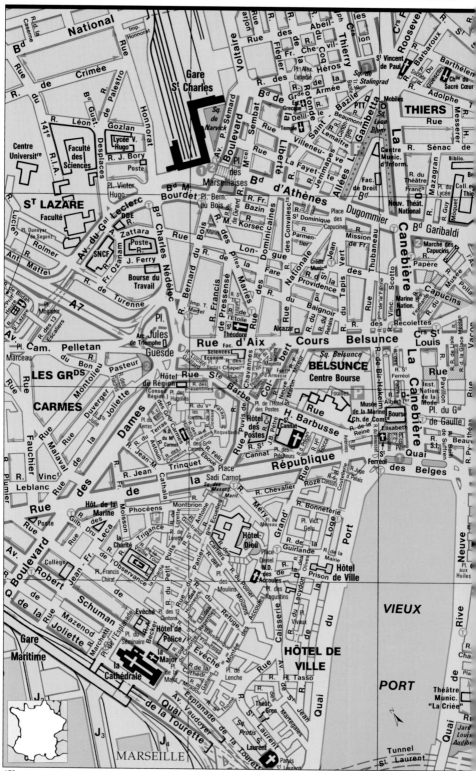

MARSEILLE

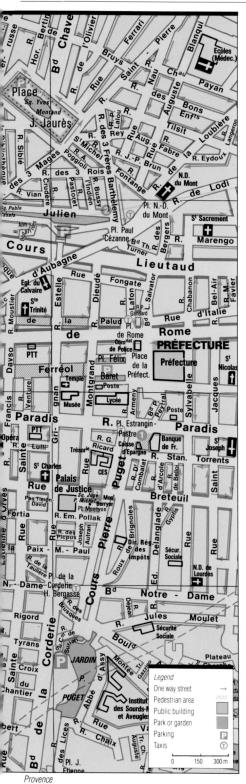

Quai des Belges at the foot of Marseille's main street, the Canebière. Here fishermen's wives sell their husbands' catch of the previous night. It is a very animated scene. Walk over to the Jardin des Vestiges, where Greek and Roman ruins unearthed in 1967 during excavations for a commercial center have been preserved in a garden setting as an archaeological site (it is two minutes from the port, at the back of L'Église Saint-Ferréol). There are walls dating from the second century BC, and the shape of Lacydon, the ancient port, is clear. The modern Musée d'Histoire de Marseille, which fronts on it, has scale models of the port as it was in antiquity and ancient artifacts that include the remains of a Roman ship. It is open from 12 PM to 7 PM, closed Sundays.

In the nineteenth century, when the port of Marseille was bursting with activity, the cafés that lined the Canebière were where the traders did all their business. Napoléon III considered this undignified and had a splendid Bourse built for them. The traders never used it. They stayed in their coffee shops and kept doing business Marseille style. All the old cafés and grand hotels are closed now, and the Canebière has lost its luster. But in 1994, the city opened Espace Mode, a large new fashion institute, museum and exhibition space, at 11 La Canebière in hopes of revitalizing this once-proud thoroughfare. It is open from 12 PM to 7 PM, closed Monday and holidays. On the east side of the Vieux Port, to your left as you look out to the sea, along the Quai de Rive Neuve and the pedestrian streets in back of it, there are dozens of restaurants and cafés on the streets intersecting at Place Thiers and on the long, wide, Italian-looking square, the Cours d'Estienne d'Orves. This square used to be covered by a huge, ugly above-ground parking garage, but a campaign by local business people succeeded in having it torn down. Suddenly the Vieux Port shed its rough sailor ambiance and became a bright, cheerful, safe, but still colorful, place for tourists to relax and enjoy the many outdoor cafés and restaurants on the Cours. Take a look at Les Arcenaulx, a big stone loft building that was part of the seventeenth century arsenal complex, and is now an attractive modern book store with a restaurant. Its owner, publisher Jeanne Laffitte, led the campaign to renovate the square and subsequently became the President of the Marseille Tourist Office.

The Musée Cantini, Marseille's museum of twentieth century art, is nearby at 19 Rue Grignan. Its permanent collection is particularly strong on surrealism and contemporary paintings and sculptures, with works by César, Arman, Alechinsky, Hartung, Bacon, Balthus, Tàpies, Viallat and others. It also has a fine collection of French china from the seventeenth and eighteenth centuries, including examples of tableware from Marseille. It is open from 11 AM to 6 PM June through September, 10 AM to 5 PM the rest of the year, closed Monday and holidays.

Notre-Dame-de-La-Garde

From the highest point in the city on a hill to the east of the Vieux Port, "La Bonne Mère," the huge gilded statue of the Virgin on top of the basilica of Notre-Dame-de-la-Garde, casts her protective gaze over the city and acts as a beacon to sailors out at sea. The basilica's observation point is the best place for visitors to get the geographical sense of Marseille — the Vieux Port, the islands, the corniches and the mountains.

The basilica itself is lugubrious mid-nineteenth century neo-Byzantine structure designed by Espérandieu, who also built the Cathedral of the Major on the other side of the Vieux Port. It is filled with votive offerings, including ex-voto paintings given by sailors saved from shipwrecks.

Down the hill is the fortress-like eleventh century **Basilica of Saint-Victor**. Its deep, vaulted **crypt** is the remains of the first monastery in France, built by Saint Cassien in the fifth century. *Chandeleur*, an all-night vigil with green candles and a procession of the Black Madonna of Saint-Victor is held on February 2. The bishop blesses the *navettes de Saint-Victor*, biscuits in the shape of little boats like the one that, legend has it, carried Mary Magdalene, Lazarus and their fellow saints to Provence. They are made from a secret recipe in a 1781 oven by the **Four des Navettes** at 136 Rue Sainte up the street from the Basilica. The tasty orange-flavored *navettes* are sold the year round.

Château d'If

As the Statue of Liberty is to New York, the Château d'If is to Marseille. No trip would be complete without a boat ride to it. The sixteenth century fortress, most famous as the prison of Dumas's fictional Count of Monte Cristo, sits on a barren white limestone island surveying the roadstead of Marseille. The trip including a visit to the Château takes an hour and a half.

Vieille Charité and the Panier

The Vieille Charité is a beautifully restored seventeenth century neoclassical gem designed by Marseille architect and sculptor Pierre Puget, who deserves to be much better known than he is. The spacious former workhouse has three levels of arcaded walkways and wraps around a courtyard with an elegant oval-domed chapel in the middle. The complex is used for expositions and houses a **Museum of Mediterranean Archaeology**, with a rich Egyptian collection, and a new **Museum of African, Oceanic and Amerindian Art** (MAAOA). They are open from 11 AM to 6 PM June through September, 10 AM to 5 PM the rest of the year, closed

Monday and holidays. To walk there from the Vieux Port, you traverse the narrow, twisting, colorful, formerly sinister streets of the **Panier**, a quarter that has hosted wave after wave of immigrants. In the twentieth century, they have been Armenians, Italians and now North Africans. But gentrification is well under way.

Other Sights

The **Palais Longchamp** is a twin-winged wedding cake palace with a huge, ornate fountain in the middle built by Espérandieu in the 1860's to celebrate the arrival of the water from the Durance via Montrichier's Canal de Marseille. The **Musée des Beaux Arts** is in the west wing of the palace

and has works by Marseille natives Pierre Puget and Honoré Daumier, Paul Guigou from the Vaucluse and Gustave Courbet, his mentor. It is open from 11 AM to 6 PM June through September, 10 AM to 5 PM the rest of the year, closed Monday and holidays. The **Musée d'Histoire Naturelle** is in the east wing of the building, and there is a shady park and a small zoo. To get to the Palais Longchamp from the Vieux Port, take the N° 80 bus up the Canebière or the Metro to Longchamp-Cinq-Avenues.

On an esplanade with fountains and trees, pedestrian **Cours Julien** on the hill north of the Vieux Port is lined with antique and curiosity shops, fascinating for browsing in the daytime, and its cafés, restaurants and little theaters and cabarets make for lively evenings. You can walk up the hill or go by Metro. The stop is Cours Julien.

Unité d'Habitation, Le Corbusier's 17-storey concrete and glass building cantilevered on sculptural concrete pillars, is one of modern architecture's most controversial landmarks. It is a self-contained living unit for 1,600 people with a shopping center, elementary school, hotel and recreational areas built into it. Le Corbusier planned six of them for his Cité Radieuse, but only this one, completed in 1952, went up. It is at 280 Boulevard Michelet, one mile east of the Vieux Port, on the N° 21 bus line. The stop is called "Corbusier".

The **Musée des Arts et Traditions Populaires**, a museum devoted to the area's popular arts and traditions, has fully furnished nineteenth century rooms, pottery, kitchenware, china, traditional cos-

que (fjord surrounded by rocky cliffs) in the city that is an active fishing port, very colorful, with restaurants. You can swim off the rocks at the entrance to the Vallon des Auffes or at the beach club of the **Restaurant de la Corniche Bistrot Plage** a few steps west of the Monument overlooking the Château d'If. Farther east on the Corniche, you come to the **Plage du Prado**, the main public beach, and the *château* and large grassy park of the **Parc Borély**. The N° 83 bus from the Vieux Port follows the Corniche Kennedy to the beaches.

The Calanques de Marseille

Follow the coast road another six kilometers (four miles) to the east to **Cap Croisette**, and you will

tumes, and a fine collection of *santons*, the handmade "little saints." The museum is in the Provençal estate house of Julien Pignol, a disciple of Mistral, at 5 Place des Héros in **Château-Gombert**, one of the 110 villages that make up Marseille that has best retained its small-town identity. The museum is open from 2:30 PM to 6:30 PM, closed Tuesday. To get there, take the Metro to La Rose and the N° 5 S or 5 T bus to Château-Gombert.

The Corniche

Corniche Président J.F. Kennedy starts just past the **Parc du Pharo**, the lighthouse park on the east side of the mouth of the Vieux Port, and winds eastward for five kilometers (three miles) along the shore. Look for the big **Monument aux Morts d'Orient** on your right. Park there if you can and walk down to the **Vallon des Auffes**, a tiny *calan-*

Provence

see why the Greeks liked it here. The burning white rock islands just off the cape are more typically Cycladic than most of the Cyclades. The road ends at **Les Goudes**, a little port at the start of the *calanques* of Marseille (reached ed by the N° 19 and N° 20 buses from the Plage du Prado). From here hikers can set off into the limestone hills called the **Marseilleveyre** along the *calanques*. Trails lead to Cassis about 17 km (11 miles) away.

The dramatic **Calanque de Sormiou** can be reached by car, but in the summer only if you know people there or a have reservation at one of its restaurants (see WHERE TO EAT, page 180).

OPPOSITE: The Château d'If, where Dumas's Count of Monte Cristo was imprisoned. ABOVE: The Palais Longchamp, where Marseille's Museum of Fine Arts and Museum of Natural History are located.

WHERE TO STAY

There are good hotels at all prices, and the Tourist Office will help you find one. Ask about the two-nights-for-the-price-of-one weekend program that many Marseille hotels take part in. Because the city is so spread-out geographically, we deal separately with hotels in downtown Marseille and ones along the *corniche*.

Downtown hotels

In the **expensive** category, the **Pullman Beauvau****** at 4 Rue Beauvau (91 54 91 00 FAX 91 54 15 76, is a handsome old antique-furnished 71-room hotel at the most central of all possible locations, the foot of the Canebière fronting on the Vieux Port. At the other end of the Vieux Port is the **Sofitel Vieux Port****** 36 Boulevard Charles-Livon (91 52 90 19 FAX 91 31 46 52, a modern, impersonal 127-room hotel by the Parc du Pharo that has a panoramic view of the city from the mouth of the Vieux Port and has a swimming pool.

Among the **moderately-priced** hotels, the **Mercure Centre***** Rue Neuve-Saint Martin (91 39 20 00 FAX 91 56 24 57, overlooking the Jardin des Vestiges has 199 tasteful modern rooms and a fine restaurant, L'Oursinade. The **Hôtel Tonic***** 45 Quai des Belges (91 55 67 46 FAX 91 55 67 56, is a bright new hotel on the Vieux Port, with Jaccuzis in all the rooms.

In the **inexpensive** range, **Saint-Ferréol's Hotel**** at 19 Rue Pisançon (91 33 12 21 FAX 91 54 29 97, three blocks from the Vieux Port, has 19 newly renovated rooms, each decorated with the works of one artist, Cézanne, Van Gogh, Gauguin and big marble bathrooms, a pleasant lounge and warm personal service. Rooms with Jaccuzis are in the moderate range. **Chambres d'Hôtes Gilles et Pia Schaufelberger**, 2 Rue Saint-Laurent (91 90 29 02, are two impeccable bed-and-breakfast rooms rented by a marvelous couple in their spacious fourteenth-floor apartment overlooking the Vieux Port. At 200 francs, this is an unbeatable deal.

The Corniche

Le Petit Nice**** at Anse Madlormé, a little *calanque* at 160 Corniche Kennedy (91 59 25 92 FAX 91 59 28 08, is the Passédat family's delightful 13-room, 3-suite mansion, splendidly perched on a shelf of rock on the sea. This is one of my favorite hotels anywhere. It's like being on a luxurious yacht. A Relais & Châteaux member. It is expensive. In the moderately priced category, the **New Hotel Bompard***** is perched high above the Corniche at 2 Rue Flots-Bleu off Boulevard Bompard (91 52 10 93 FAX 91 31 02 14, in its own peaceful park with a swimming pool. But be sure to get a room with a view.

Camping

As of this writing there are no camping grounds operating within the city limits of Marseille. The closest ones are **Les Cigales** in Cassis (see CAMPING page 172) or La Verdière, a 45-place site in Septèmes-les-Vallons 10 km (six miles) north of Marseille on N 8 in the directions of Aix. It is open all year (91 65 59 98.

WHERE TO EAT

The Vieux Port

There's no need to leave the Vieux Port for your *bouillabaisse*, because the hefty Minguella brothers make a magnificent one and serve it to perfection at the **Miramar** at 12 Quai du Port (91 91 10 40. It is expensive, but well worth it, and dining on the terrace of this lively Michelin one-star restaurant with its view of the harbor is a pleasure in itself. Closed Sundays, the first

three weeks of August and Christmas through to New Year. At **Patalain**, 49 Rue Sainte (91 55 02 78, vivacious chef Suzanne Quaglia serves imaginative Marseillaise cuisine in her charming yellow arabesque restaurant up the steps from the Cours d'Estienne d'Orves. Menus from 150 francs (weekday lunch) to 330 francs. Closed Saturday lunch, Sunday, and late July to late August. **Les Arcenaulx**, 25 Cours d'Estienne d'Orves (91 54 77 06, is a refined modern restaurant in a book store and art gallery that once was an arsenal. **Les Mets de Provence**, 18 Quai Rive Neuve (91 33 35 38, serves the famed Provençal menu created by chef Maurice Brun, a full evening of feasting, 335 francs.

In the **moderate** price range, **Bistro Gambas** at 29 Place aux Huiles (91 33 26 44, serves grilled shrimp, curries and *ratatouille*. Closed Saturday lunch and Sundays. **L'Atelier Chocolat** at 45 Cours d'Estienne d'Orves (91 33 55 00, is an

art gallery and luncheon spot with a cozy club-like ambience. **Bar de la Marine** at 15 Quai de Rive Neuve (91 54 95 42, serves hearty food and drinks in a bar modeled after the one in Pagnol's "Marius" or at tables on the port, near the place where the ferry crosses from the Place aux Huiles to the Hôtel de Ville.

The Panier

The **Panier des Arts** at 3 Rue des Petits-Puits (91 56 02 32, serves savory Provençal bistro meals at reasonable prices, down the street from the Vieille Charité. **L'Art et les Thés** is a pleasant tea room in the courtyard of the Vieille Charité (91 56 01 39, serving light lunches. At **Chez Etienne** on 43 Rue de Lorette (no phone), Etienne Cassaro, a

The port of Martigues west of Marseille, whose special light made it a favorite subject of Provençal painters.

legendary figure in the Panier, makes the best pizzas in Marseille.

The Corniche

At **Passédat**, the superb restaurant of the **Petit Nice Hôtel**, the father-and-son team of Jean-Paul and Gérald Passédat come up with the astonishing Provençal-Marseillais inventions that have made them a legend and earned them their two Michelin stars. It is expensive, but a real gastronomic thrill. A 300 franc luncheon menu is offered on weekdays, beverage included. In good weather you dine on the terrace overlooking the sea. For succulent seafood and lots of atmosphere, a colorful old eatery that I enjoy enormously is **Chez**

Fonfon in the tiny *calanque* the Vallon des Auffes (91 52 14 38. Prices are moderate to expensive. Nearby, the **Restaurant de la Corniche Bistrot Plage** at 60 Corniche J.F. Kennedy (91 31 80 32, is a big, airy restaurant and beach club overlooking the Château d'If, good for fresh fish, grilled meats and salads at moderate prices.

The *Calanques*

La Grotte is at the Calanque de Callelongue in **Les Goudes**, where the coast road dead-ends at Cap Croisette (91 73 17 79. They serve pizzas and seafood in a pleasant garden at moderate prices (closed evenings October to May, except Saturday). **Le Château** at the Calanque de Sormiou (91 25 08 69 serves excellent seafood, moderately priced, on a terrace overlooking this remote, dramatic *calanque*. After lunch you can enjoy a walk or a swim. You could easily spend a whole day here. In the summer, the road to Sormiou is closed to all cars except those of residents or people who have booked a table at a restaurant. So be sure to book ahead.

Nightlife

For highbrow entertainment, Marseille has the **Opéra Municipal** (91 55 00 70, which puts on an

ambitious season of operas and classical music in its handsome Art Deco opera house, the famous **Ballet National de Marseille Roland Petit** (91 71 03 03 and a prestigious French national theater, the **Théâtre National Marseille la Criée** (91 54 70 54. The Tourist Office can provide information on their programs.

For lighter entertainment, **Le Trolley-Bus** at 24 Quai de Rive Neuve (91 54 30 45, has four vaulted caves, three with jazz, rock and Latino music, the last an art gallery and wine bar, open Thursday, Friday and Saturday from 11 PM. **Le Pèle Mèle** at 45 Cours d'Estienne d'Orves (91 54 85 26 has live jazz. **Le Bar de la Marine** at 15 Quai de Rive Neuve (91 54 95 42 has a warm Pagnol-like ambiance and is a relaxed place to have a drink on the Vieux Port. For a taste of Marseille in its Golden Age, try the **Café de Paris** at 42 Rue Saint-Saëns (91 33 52 74, the last of the grand pre-War cafés. **Le Perroquet Bleu** at 72 Boulevard des Dames (91 91 11 18, off Rue de la République, is a delightful place to sip a pastis or a glass of rosé and listen to recorded music in landmark Art Nouveau decor. **Il Caffe** at 63 Cours Julien (91 42 02 19, is a popular watering place. **O'Stop** at 1 Place de l'Opéra (91 33 85 34, directly across the street from the opera house, has a lively clientèle of night creatures. Open all night.

How to Get There

There is one flight per hour on average from Paris's Orly Airport to Marseille-Provence International Airport from 6:30 AM to 9:55 PM on Air Inter or Air France. From London there are three flights a day on British Airways and one on TAT and AOM. There are shuttle buses (navettes) from the airport to Gare Saint-Charles, Marseille's railway station, every 20 minutes. The trip takes 25 minutes and costs 39 francs. By train from Paris's Gare de Lyon, there are 11 TGV's (high-speed trains) a day from Paris, a four-and-three-quarter-hour trip. There are also train connections to most other southern cities.

Eurolines has a bus service to Marseille from London and most other major European cities. Phocéen Cars and other companies have buses between Marseille and the main towns of the Côte d'Azur, Provence and Languedoc.

By car, the A 7 *autoroute* down the Rhône Valley leads directly to its terminus in Marseille, and numerous highways lead to the city from the east. Driving in Marseille can be confusing. I suggest parking your car at the big underground garage at the Cours d'Estienne d'Orves near the Vieux Port and exploring the downtown on foot, Little Tourist Train and local bus, and save the car for trips to the outlying areas.

AIX-EN-PROVENCE

The old Provençal capital of Aix lies only half an hour inland from Marseille, but you would be hard pressed to find two cities more different than these — Marseille, the big, flamboyant nineteenth century port in a dramatic sun-bleached setting, teeming with immigrant masses and fanatical fans of the Olympique de Marseille football team and Aix, the calm, aristocratic, tree-shaded, very French (Caucasian, that is) city of modest size with gurgling fountains and honey-colored seventeenth century neoclassical mansions. Aix doesn't even have a football team.

This is an old city with young people. Almost one-third of its 170,000 area residents are students at its university's faculty of law and letters (the more modern subjects such as science and medicine are taught in Marseille). But far from closing itself off from the modern world, Aix has moved into computer and high-tech industries, and in the past 40 years its population has doubled. Most of the growth has taken place in the bland new suburbs that ring the city, leaving the elegant old center intact. Aix is modest in size, but large in cultural attractions, a nice combination. Not surprisingly, Aix comes out tops in the public opinion polls rating the cities French people would most like to live in.

BACKGROUND

The first settlement at Aix was on the plateau of Entremont north of the present city, where the Celtic-Ligurian Salyen tribe established an *oppidum*. They traded with the Greeks from the sixth century BC and were much influenced by them artistically. But the Greeks and the Saylens had a falling-out in the second century BC, and the Greeks asked the Romans for help. Consul Caius Sextius and his legions destroyed Entremont in 124 BC and cleared the Celtic-Ligurians out, but the Romans stayed and set up a colony at the hot springs on the plain below. They called it Aquae Sextiae (the waters of Sextius), the origin of the name Aix. With its key position at the intersection of the roads from Rome to Spain and from upper Provence to Marseille, Aix flourished during the Pax Romana. But it was reduced to rubble and all but deserted during the barbarian invasions.

Under the Church, which made it a bishopric, and the Counts of Provence, who made it their capital, Aix recovered from the Dark Ages, and a rich, artistic court life developed under the Angevin dynasty. The University of Aix was founded in 1409, and the last Angevin Count of Provence, "Good King" René, a lover of poetry, music, art and good living, had the most sophisticated court in Europe in the mid-fifteenth century.

When the Angevin line died out in the late fifteenth century, Provence passed under the rule of the King of France. Aix remained the regional capital under a viceroy and the Parliament of Aix. In the seventeenth century, an extremely rich period for Aix, the elegant Quartier Mazarin went up, under the aegis of Archbishop Michel Mazarin, the Cardinal's brother. Prosperity continued until the French Revolution, in which one of its native sons, the scandalous Count Mirabeau, played an early role, but he died in 1791 of apparently natural causes before the guillotine could get him. Aristocratic Aix took the full brunt of the Revolution. Nobles and clergy were killed by the thousands, and Aix lost its position as a capital,

reduced to a mere sub-prefecture in the new Bouches-du-Rhône department, of which proletarian Marseille became the capital. While Marseille boomed in the nineteenth century, Aix stagnated. By World War I its population had dropped to 30,000.

Only since World War II has Aix has fully recovered its morale and become the universally admired city it is today.

GENERAL INFORMATION

Aix's large **Tourist Office** is on the main traffic circle at the Fontaine de la Rotonde, the big wedding cake of a fountain with the three Graces on

OPPOSITE: A café on the Old Port of Marseille.
ABOVE: The Tour de l'Horloge, built in 1510, in the ancient Vieil Aix section of Aix-en-Provence.

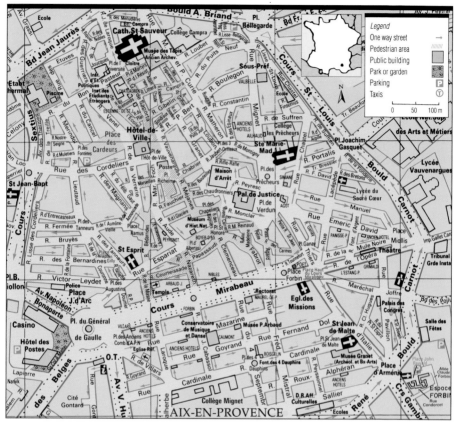

top, naked boys riding swans and jets of water
shooting every which way. The thoroughly professional staff of the Tourist Office will help you
with all reservations and provide excellent maps
and documents in all major languages. They also
offer guided tours of Vieil Aix (Old Aix), the Quartier Mazarin and "Cézanne Country." The office
is at 2 Place du Général de Gaulle (42 16 11 61.

Here are some useful contacts in Aix:

**Airport: Marseille–Provence International
Airport** (42 89 09 74. **Railway station, Gare SNCF**
(91 08 50 50. **Bus station, Gare Routière** (42 27 17 91.

Taxis: Les Artisans (42 26 29 30; **Mirabeau** (42
21 61 61; **Taxi-Radio Aixois** (6 AM to 8 PM) (42 27
71 11 (night) (42 26 29 30.

Car rental: Avis (42 21 64 16 (also rents bikes
and scooters); **Budget** (42 38 37 36; **EuropCar** (42
27 83 00; **EuroDollar** (42 21 42 09; **Hertz** (42 27 91
32; **Lubrano** (42 21 44 85 (open Sundays).

Bus tours: the **CAP** bus company at 10 Avenue
de Lattre-de-Tassigny offers day trips to Cassis
and the *calanques*, Les Baux-de-Provence, the Lubéron and other places in Provence (42 23 14 26.

**Medical emergencies: Hospital (Centre Hos-
pitalier)** (42 33 50 00; **SOS Médecin** (42 26 24 00.

Aix's daily food market at the Place Richelme.

FESTIVALS

The **Festival d'Art Lyrique et de Musique**, generally known as the **Festival d'Aix**, is an opera and
classical music festival that takes place from early
July to early August. It is one of France's oldest
and most prestigious festivals, created in 1948.
After a period of experimentation in which it lost
some of its following, it appears to be returning to
its traditional Mozartian roots. For information,
contact the Tourist Office.

WHAT TO SEE AND WHAT TO DO

Aix is a compact city with almost everything of
interest within walking distance of the Fontaine
de la Rotonde and the adjoining Cours Mirabeau.
Fontaine de la Rotonde is the most un-Aix-like
of Aix's many fountains, foisted upon the city by
Napoléon III and his heavy-handed public works
czar, Baron Haussmann (the pained looks on the
faces of the lions around the base seem to mirror
the feelings of the Aixois, disdainful and slightly
embarrassed).

Vieil Aix, the medieval city where the Cathedral and markets are, lies directly to the north of

the Cours, and the aristocratic seventeenth century Quartier Mazarin (for which the Cours was built in 1651 as the carriage promenade) to the south.

Cours Mirabeau

The broad, café-lined street of the Cours Mirabeau is sheltered by majestic old plane trees in four parallel rows that give one the feeling of being inside a great cathedral, but more ethereal because of the sunlight filtering in through the canopy of leaves. And better yet, in this cathedral you can have a drink.

The cafés, shops and restaurants are all on the north side. At Nº 55, notice the sign for Cézanne's father's hat business, Chapellerie du Cours Mirabeau. The south side is lined by honey-colored limestone *hôtels particuliers* (private mansions), most now banks or public buildings. The **King René Fountain** is at one end, the **Fontaine de la Rotonde** at the other, and between them, amid the four auto lanes that run the Cours's four-block length, there are two other fountains — squat, lumpy brutes caked with moss and sprouting weeds that are much loved by the Aixois. One is called "**Moussue**" (mossy) or "**Fontaine Chaude**," because the water is hot, and the other is **Neuf Canons** (Nine Canons). At the top of the Cours is the King René Fountain with a nineteenth century statue of the "Good King" holding a bunch of muscat grapes, and facing it is "Les 2 G," **Les Deux Garçons**, one of the most famous cafés in France. For many travelers, their happiest memory of southern France will be of lingering over a drink at one of the cafés on the Cours Mirabeau watching the bright-looking, mostly young people of Aix parade by.

Vieil Aix

To explore **Old Aix** start at the mossy fountain and walk up Rue Clémenceau to little Place Saint-Honoré, where the elegant seventeenth century Hôtel Boyer d'Eguilles at 6 Rue Éspariat is now the **Musée d'Histoire Naturelle** and has a famous collection of Provençal dinosaur eggs. It is open daily from 10 AM to 12 PM and 2 PM to 6 PM, closed Sunday morning. At nearby **Place d'Albertas** with its three-winged *hôtel particulier* and fountain (one of supposedly two hundred in Aix), turn right and follow Rues Aude and Maréchal Foch to **Place Richelme**, where a **food market** has been held every morning since the Middle Ages. The **Hôtel de Ville**, an Italian baroque building with handsome wrought iron balconies and gates, is in the next square, along with the **flower market** and the **Tour de l'Horloge**, an elaborate clock tower built in 1510 on the foundations of a Roman gate. The large, open **Place des Cardeurs** is popular with students because of the numerous modestly-priced cafés and eating places on it.

Saint-Sauveur Cathedral was built piecemeal from the twelfth to the seventeenth centuries, but incorporates elements that are even older. On the front wall facing little **Place de l'Université**, you can see sections of Roman, Romanesque and Gothic stonework side by side. This spot was also the crossroads of the highways that made Aix important in the days of Provincia Romana — the Aurelian Way (the street in front of the cathedral) and the Decumanus Way to the Mediterranean (now Rue du Bon Pasteur).

Inside the cathedral is Nicolas Froment's gentle **triptych of the Burning Bush**, with portraits of King René (to whom the painting was long attributed) and Queen Jeanne at prayer on the side panels, one of the finest works in the South of France. The main panel presents a mystical vision of the Virgin and Child in the middle of Moses's burning bush. To see it, you must ask the guardian to open the protective cover and turn on the light, a chore he is sometimes less than eager to do. The main door of the church secretes another masterpiece, carved walnut figures of the **Four Prophets** by early sixteenth century Provençal sculptor Jean Guiramand. Again you must get the guardian to open the protective panel. In the **Baptistry**, which dates from the fourth or fifth century, six of the eight Corinthian columns are from the Roman forum that formerly stood on this site. The little **cloister** dates from the twelfth century. Some Festival d'Aix concerts are held here, but operas and other big events are presented in the courtyard of the adjoining **Palais de l'Archevêché**, the grand seventeenth and eighteenth century archbishops' palace. Upstairs the excellent **Musée des Tapisseries** has seventeen delightful Beauvais tapestries from that period, including nine based on Don Quixote. It is open 10:30 AM to 6 PM, closed Tuesday.

L'Établissement Thermal, the eighteenth century baths on the site of Caius Sextius's 122 BC baths west of the cathedral, is under renovation and is expected to reopen in 1996.

Across the Cours Sextius on Rue Célony in its own park is the **Pavilion Vendôme**, one of the epitomes of Aix's particular Baroque style, with twin Atlantes, colossal sculpted bodybuilders, straining to hold up the central balcony. Open 8:30 AM to 12 PM and 2 PM to 6 PM, closed Tuesday.

Two lively **markets** are held on the east side of Vieil Aix on Tuesday, Thursday, and Saturday mornings. A **Provençal market** is held at **Place des Prêcheurs** near the Église de la Madeleine and an **antiques and *brocante* (bric-a-brac) market** at the adjoining **Place de Verdun**. Chocolate lovers can satisfy their craving at the **Puyricard** chocolate factory's retail outlet nearby at 7 Rue Rifle-Rafle.

Quartier Mazarin

The Quartier Mazarin is the six block grid starting on the south side of the Cours Mirabeau and running down to the Boulevard du Roi René that Archbishop Mazarin laid out in the mid-seventeenth century. Over the century that followed, a remarkable concentration of elegant *hôtels particuliers* went up. At 38 Cours Mirabeau is the **Hôtel Maurel de Pontevès**, now the Court of Appeals, eight windows wide and three-stories high with colossal twin Atlantes from Pierre Puget's studio in Toulon straining on either side of the front door to support a fancy wrought iron balcony. Go inside and admire more fancy wrought iron, much prized in Aix, on the staircase.

Hôtel de Caumont, now the **Darius Milhaud Music School**, at 3 Rue Joseph Cabassol (named for the banking partner of Cézanne's father) was

and one of his scenes of Montagne Sainte-Victoire from his so-called Synthetic Period, 1886 to 1906, when he planted the seeds that would soon grow into Cubism. The paintings are on loan to the museum by the French Government. To the eternal shame of Aix, the Aixois scorned Cézanne as the dilettante son of a rich banker and nobody bought his work. The feeling was mutual. Cézanne never painted a single picture of his native city. Be sure to go down to the basement of the museum to see the Celto-Ligurian sculptures from the archaeological digs at Entremont. The grim-faced heads of warriors are particularly fascinating. The Greek stylistic influence is clear, but they have personalities of their own that are disturbingly

designed by Robert de Cotte, the architect of the chapel at Versailles. It too has handsome wrought iron exterior balconies and a great sweeping stairway in the main hall, all open and airy, with delicate wrought iron balustrades.

About the **Fontaine des Quatre Dauphins** at the intersection of Rue Cardinale and Rue du Quatre Septembre writer M.F.K. Fisher says, "Four of the merriest dolphins ever carved by man spout into the graceful basin under its stone needle, topped by a stone pine cone, and it seems unlikely that anyone can pass by this exquisite whole without feeling reassured in some firm way."

The **Musée Granet** just down Rue Cardinale from the Fontaine des Quatre Dauphins at Place Saint-Jean de Malte has eight small paintings by Cézanne. Among them are "Bathsheba" from his impressionist period, "Portrait of Madame Cézanne" from his middle period, and "Baigneuses"

real. The museum is open from 10 AM to 12 PM and 2 PM to 6 PM, closed Tuesday except in July and August.

As you walk around the Quartier Mazarin, keep an eye out for Aix's most famous food product, the little flat biscuits made from almonds, honey and melon called *calissons d'Aix*. **Maison Béchard** at 12 Cours Mirabeau, **Confiserie Brémond** at 16 Rue d'Italie and **Léonard Parli** at 33 Avenue Victor Hugo make delicious calissons. They are especially tasty when eaten fresh.

Aix is also known for its *santons de Provence* (little saints), the sculpted figures of Provençal country people used in Christmas crèches. **Paul Fouque** at 65 Cours Gambetta is the acknow-

ABOVE LEFT: One of the estimated two hundred fountains in Aix. ABOVE RIGHT: A butcher shop in Aix.

ledged master of this craft. *Santons* by **Lise Berger** and **Simone Jouglas** are sold at **Au Petit Bonheur**, a crafts shop at 16 *bis* Rue d'Italie. It also carries *faïences* (china) from Moustiers and cheerful yellow bowls from Aubagne.

WHERE TO STAY

There are 75 hotels in Aix and environs and many furnished flats. The Tourist Office helps visitors find accommodations.

Expensive

The **Villa Gallici****** at 18 *bis* Avenue Violettes, a short walk from the Cathedral (42 23 29 23

FAX 42 96 30 45, is one of the loveliest hotels in southern France. All 17 rooms have canopied beds, and the use of Provençal fabrics is delightful. It is set in a secluded private park on a hillside above town, and its pool and gardens have a flavor of ancient Rome. No restaurant, but the neighboring Clos de la Violette, the best in town, caters the hotel. The **Pullman Roi René****** at 24 Boulevard Roi René (42 37 61 00 FAX 42 37 61 11, is on the southern edge of the Quartier Mazarin, a five-minute stroll from the Cours Mirabeau. It has 134 tasteful, modern sound-insulated rooms, a small pool in the interior garden, indoor garage, and friendly, efficient service.

Moderate

The **Mercure Paul Cézanne***** at 40 Avenue Victor Hugo (42 26 34 73 FAX 42 27 20 95, a few minutes walk to the Cours Mirabeau, is a charming

antique-furnished hotel with 55 comfortable, fully renovated rooms and use of the pool at the Pullman Roi René right down the street. It is my favorite place to stay in Aix. The **Hôtel des Augustins***** 3 Rue Masse, a few steps from the Cours (42 27 28 59 FAX 42 26 74 87, is a fifteenth century convent with a soaring stone-walled entrance hall and 29 large, attractive rooms. Martin Luther holed up here with his Augustinian brothers after being excommunicated in Rome by the Pope.

Inexpensive

The **Hôtel Cardinal**** occupies two eighteenth century townhouses in the Quartier Mazarin at 22 and 24 Rue Cardinale (42 38 32 30 FAX 42 21

52 48. It has a warm ambiance and attentive personnel, some rooms with kitchenettes. There are three modern **Campanile*** hotels and motels in and around Aix, spotless and good for a family. The closest to the center of town is the 60-room motel on Route de Valcros in the Jas de Bouffan section (42 59 40 73 FAX 42 59 03 47. Rooms go for 275 francs. The **Hôtel des Arts*** at 69 Boulevard Carnot (42 38 11 77 is a modest, well-kept hotel on the fringe of Vieil Aix.

Camping

The largest camping ground and the closest to town is the **Chantecler** on the Route de Nice in **Val Saint-André** five kilometers (three miles) from Aix, reached by Cours Gambetta from the center of the city. It has 250 to 300 places on its well-shaded eight hectares (20 acres) of land with a clear view of Montagne Sainte-Victoire and is open all year (42 26 12 98. You must reserve early for the period from May to the end of August. A smaller camping grounds, **Arc-en-Ciel**, is nearby at **Pont des Trois-Sautets**, also on the Route de Nice, open all year (42 26 14 28.

WHERE TO EAT

Expensive

The **Clos de la Violette** in a discreet garden setting at 10 Avenue Violette (42 23 30 71 FAX 42 21 93 03, features the sophisticated Provençal cuisine of youthful Jean-Marc Banzo, the only chef in Aix who can boast of a Michelin star. Closed on Sundays and on Mondays at lunch. Reserve long in

closed on Sundays and Monday lunchtime. **Côté Cour** at 21 *bis* Cours Mirabeau (42 26 32 39 is in a trellised interior courtyard a few steps in from the Cours. This is young Aix's favorite luncheon spot, for *gazpacho glacé* or shrimp and mango salad followed by a Provençal *plat du jour*. Closed Sunday night and Mondays, the month of May and first two weeks of June. The **Cour de Rohan**, 10 Rue Vauvenargues at Place de l'Hôtel de Ville (42 96 18 15, is an airy tea room with a courtyard and large open fireplace serving light luncheons. For solid brasserie fare in the heart of the Provençal and bric-a-brac markets, try the busy **Brasserie la Madeleine** at 41 Place des Prêcheurs (42 28 38 02.

advance. The **Table du Roi**, at the Pullman Roi René (42 37 61 00, serves the cuisine of talented Dominique Frérard, rich with the savors of Provence, in the spacious dining room or in the quiet courtyard. Open daily. **Les Frères Lani** at 22 Rue Leydet in Vieil Aix (42 27 76 16 is a cool, elegant restaurant where brothers Joël and Lucien Lani serve refined regional cuisine. Luncheon menus start at 130 francs. Closed Sunday and Mondays and the first two weeks of August.

Moderate

The **Bistro Latin** is just what its name indicates, a lively eatery serving hearty Provençal fare. I like everything about it. The tasty three-course Bistro luncheon keyed to the fresh products in the market that day is an outstanding value at 90 francs, and the ambiance is relaxed and friendly. It is at 18 Rue de la Couronne in Vieil Aix (42 38 22 88,

Inexpensive

Good prices are to be found at bistros and cafés on the Place des Cardeurs, where the clientele is mostly students. **Hacienda** at 7 Rue Merindol (42 27 90 82, on a tiny tree-shaded square at the lower end of the Place des Cardeurs, serves a very good fixed-price lunch of hors d'oeuvre, hot main course, quarter-carafe of wine and dessert for 57 francs. **Dolce Vita** on Place des Martyrs, the square in front of the Archbishop's Palace (42 64 04 70, serves *carpaccios* (razor-thin slices of raw beef or salmon seasoned with herbs and olive oil) and salads. The best pizza in the world is to be had at **Pizzeria Capri**, a

OPPOSITE: A café on Aix's Cours Mirabeau and the Fontaine de la Rotonde. ABOVE: Cézanne's beloved Montagne Sainte-Victoire east of Aix.

hole-in-the-wall on Rue Fabrot up from the Cours Mirabeau. No phone.

Cafés

The famous **Les Deux Garçons**, "Les 2 G" (pronounced lay-duh-zhay), at 53 Cours Mirabeau dates from 1792 and was named for the two waiters named Guerin and Guion who bought it in 1840. You can sip where Cézanne, Zola, Picasso, Cendrars, Milhaud, Piaf, Sartre, Mauriac, Churchill and many other famous clients sipped before you, either on its regally situated terrace near the Fontaine du Roi René or in its grand gilt-framed-mirrored salons inside.

At the **Café du Cours** at N° 45 there are live

bands in the evening, and the music spills out onto the terrace where the tables are packed with students having a good time. If you study the menu carefully, as they do, and stick to the wine in carafes, you can eat here surprisingly cheaply, given the location and ambiance, for 70 to 100 francs.

NIGHTLIFE

The best fun is hanging out on the Cours. But if you like to gamble, Aix has a **Casino** near the Fontaine de la Rotonde. For jazz, **Le Scat Club** on Rue de la Verrerie (42 23 00 23, gets big name artists from time to time, as does **Hot Brass** on Chemin de la Plaine des Verguetiers (42 21 05 57. The top disco as of this writing is **Le Mistral** at 3 Rue Frédéric Mistral (42 38 16 49. But this can change rapidly. For the latest update, ask a hip-looking student.

HOW TO GET THERE

The closest airport to Aix is Marseille-Provence. There are buses from the airport to Aix's Gare Routière every 45 minutes, a 30-minute ride that costs 40 francs. To come by train, you have to connect at Marseille. Aix's train station is centrally located, a five-minute walk to the Rotonde. By bus, there are frequent connections from Avignon, Marseille and Nice. By car it is 80 km (50 miles) from Avignon by the N 7 or the A 7 and A 8 autoroutes, 176 km (110 miles) from Nice by the A 8, and 31 km (19 miles) from Marseille by the N 8 or the A 51. If you arrive by car,

I suggest that you park at the municipal parking garage (marked by a big "P") at either the Casino, which is convenient to the Tourist Office and the Cours Mirabeau, or at Place des Cardeurs in the heart of Old Aix.

AROUND AIX

Montagne Sainte-Victoire and "Cézanne Country"

The Tourist Office has designed a walking tour called "In the Footsteps of Cézanne" that points out all the places in Aix that were important in Cézanne's life — L'Église de la Madeleine where he was baptized, the school where he and his boyhood friend Émile Zola were classmates, and so forth. But as a grown man, Cézanne had a hostile relationship with his native city and spent as little time in town as possible, preferring to be in his studio in his home on the outskirts of Aix or in the countryside that we now think of as "Cézanne Country." Route D 17 to the east of Aix is a lovely tree-lined road well marked with "Route Cézanne" signs that leads to **Le Tholonet**, **Château Noir** and the **Bibemus Quarries**, all of which he painted many times, through red earth countryside dotted with scrub pines. Before us looms fabled **Montagne Sainte-Victoire**, named for the victory of Marius over the Teutons in 102 BC, lying 15 km (9 miles) east of Aix. This massive, elongated ridge of limestone with myriad planes and ever-changing patterns is a natural kaleidoscope that endlessly fascinated the painter who Renoir called

Alpes-de-Provence, vegetables from the Durance and a fine selection of local Palette wines (see WINE TASTING below). The rooms are moderately priced, the restaurant, which is closed Sunday nights and Mondays, is expensive.

Vasarély Foundation

The Vasarély Foundation on Avenue Marcel-Pagnol in **Jas-de-Bouffan**, four kilometers (two and a half miles) west of town, is one of op-art pioneer Victor Vasarély's two big installations in Provence. This one in Aix is a huge space for the Hungatian-born optical art pioneer's "architectural" environments, ensembles of murals, wall hangings and large paintings among which

"the master of all of us." Cézanne painted it about sixty times. Shame on anyone who visits Aix without making the effort to see Montagne Sainte-Victoire.

Outdoors-types who can handle the 945 m (3,100 ft) hike up Montagne Sainte-Victoire will be rewarded with a vast panorama from the **Croix de Provence** at the top. The hike normally takes three to four hours round-trip. The trail starts at **Les Cabassols** on Route D 10 on the north side of the Montagne near the **Château de Vauvenargues**, where Picasso is buried.

If you want to dine or stay in the Montagne Sainte-Victoire area, the **Relais Sainte-Victoire***** in **Beaurecueil** immediately southwest of the Montagne ℂ 42 66 94 98 is ideal. It is a friendly 10-room inn with a delightful outdoor terrace where noted chef René Bergès serves fish straight from the Vieux Port de Marseille, lamb from the

the spectator wanders and "feels" the artist's bold manipulations of geometric patterns. Open from 9:30 AM to 12:30 PM and 2 PM to 5:30 PM, closed Tuesday except July and August. Vasarély's other museum, the so-called "didactic" one, is in Gordes.

Cézanne's Studio, Entremont and Puyricard

North of Vieil Aix, **Cézanne's Studio** in the last house he lived in has been lovingly restored to the way he left it when he died in 1906, complete with apples and bottles and a statue of Cupid he used in still-lifes. The house is set in a wooded garden on a hillside overlooking the city at 9 Avenue Paul Cézanne, about 500 m (550 yards) north of the

The Vasarély Foundation in the Jas-de-Bouffan suburb of Aix, where Op Art master's Victor Vasarély's large "architectural" works are displayed.

Cathedral Saint-Sauveur via Avenue Pasteur. It is open from 10 AM to 12 PM and 2:30 PM to 6 PM, closed Tuesday.

Continue out Avenue Paul Cézanne and you will come to the **Oppidum d'Entremont**, a four hectare (10 acre) field of ruins on a plateau north of the city, which was the thriving Celto-Ligurian community the Romans destroyed in 124 BC. The artifacts from here, powerful and well worth seeing, are attractively displayed in the Musée Granet in Aix. Unless you are an archaeology buff, this site its likely to be disappointing. It is two and a half kilometers (about a mile and a half) north of Aix on D 14. Open 10 AM to 12 PM and 2 PM to 6 PM, closed Tuesday and holidays.

A few kilometers to the north on D 14 in **Puyricard**, you can visit the **Chocolaterie Puyricard** factory and watch their yummy candies being made. Better yet, you can taste them. Open weekdays.

For those who, like Cézanne, like their privacy, the **Mas d'Entremont****** is in a large wooded park on the plateau of Entremont. It has a tennis court, swimming pool and respected restaurant. Its 18 rooms are spacious, medieval in decor, with heavy wooden furniture, beamed ceiling and wrought iron grills, and there are isolated bungalows on the grounds. It is in **Célony**, three kilometers (two miles) northwest of Aix on N 7 at the junction of RN 96 (42 23 45 32 FAX 42 21 15 83. It is expensive.

Wine Tasting

The principal wine of the area is **Côteaux d'Aix-en-Provence**, known mainly for its light, dry rosés, but also making some reds and whites. The **Syndicat de Défense des Vins des Côteaux d'Aix-en-Provence**, the producers' association, furnishes information on the *appellation* and a list of vineyards you can visit. Their office is at the Maison des Agriculteurs on 22 Avenue Henri-Pontier, up the hill from the north side of Vieil Aix (42 23 57 14.

To the northeast of Montagne Sainte-Victoire in **Rians**, **Château Vignelaure** is a top producer of the Côteaux d'Aix-en-Provence *appellation* with a large cellar open to the public daily and a modern art gallery with works by Miro, Hartung, Arman, César and others. Two other Côteaux d'Aix-en-Provence vineyards of the highest quality that are gorgeous old *châteaux* to visit are **Château de Fonscolombe** (42 61 68 62 and **Château La Coste** (42 61 89 98, north of Aix in **Le Puy-Sainte Réparade** by the Durance River.

One of the most prestigious wine-growing areas in southern France lies just off the road from Aix to Saint-Victoire on D 58. **Palette**, around the village of **Meyreuil**, is a miniscule *AOC* with only two vineyards. Long-respected

Château Simone ((42 66 92 58) makes richly scented deep purple reds, along with whites and rosés. **Château Crémade** ((42 66 92 66), the other Palette vineyard, is also highly appreciated by wine connoisseurs.

How to Get There

There are local buses to Montagne Sainte-Victoire, Cézanne's Studio, the Oppidum d'Entremont, Puyricard, and the Vasarély Foundation. Ask for bus schedules at the Tourist Office. If you are driving from the center of Aix, to get to Montagne Sainte-Victoire, take Boulevard des Poilus and Route D 17 east. For Cézanne's Studio, the Oppidum d'Entremont and Puyricard head north

on Avenue Pasteur, and the signs will lead you to your destinations. To get to the Vasarely Foundation from the Rotonde in Aix, take Avenue des Belges and Avenue de l'Europe away from the center of town four kilometers (two and a half miles) to Avenue Marcel-Pagnol in Jas-de-Bouffan.

AVIGNON

The hulking Papal Palace and the medieval ramparts that encircle Avignon make this city on a bend in the Rhône a dramatic sight from any approach. In the Middle Ages, when the walls were ringed by deep moats, the effect would have been even more potent.

The Rhône River at Avignon.

Avignon today is a city of 100,000, with most of its residents living in modern neighborhoods outside the five kilometers (three mile) circle of ramparts. Inside the walls, old Avignon is quiet, even somber, off-season. But in July and early August when the Festival d'Avignon attracts outstanding theater troupes, dance companies and orchestras from all over the world, it becomes the most animated city in France. Crowded, yes. But exciting. Full of life. Musicians in the broad square in front of the Papal Palace, buskers on the Place de l'Horloge. Avignon in July gives a sense of what it must have been like to be at a medieval fair.

Avignon is also the capital of the Vaucluse, an area made up mostly of the Comtat Venaissin, the lands that belonged to the Popes of Avignon in the Middle Ages and did not become French until 1791. It is bounded by France's largest river, the swift-flowing Rhône on the west, the Durance on the south and the east, and by Provence's protective ring of mountains, the Dauphiné Alps, in the north. The whole area is easily explored from Avignon.

BACKGROUND

The Rocher des Doms, a steep spur of rock overlooking the Rhône is a natural fortress that has made Avignon attractive to settlers since prehistoric times. Traces of habitation go back to 4000 BC. The town had a name, Avenio, and was the capital of the Gallic Cavares tribe by the time the Greeks from Marseille established a river port and trading post there in the fifth century BC. Avignon flourished under the Romans, but was destroyed by successive waves of invaders that swept up and down the Rhône, Germanic tribes, the Saracens, the Franks and the Burgundians, until peace was re-established by the Counts of Toulouse and Barcelona in the twelfth century.

In 1309, Pope Clement V (1305–1314), a Frenchman, fed up with Rome at a time when Italy was in virtual anarchy, accepted King Phillip the Fair's offer of protection and moved to the Church-owned Comtat Venaissin, apparently viewing it as a temporary relocation. A pious man, Clement V lived in rural monasteries in the Comtat. His more worldly successor John XIII (1316–1334), a former Bishop of Avignon, moved back into his old bishop's palace in Avignon and set up his court there. His successor Benedict XII (1334–1342) felt that the seat of the Roman Catholic Church needed more impressive quarters and built what is now known as the Old Palace. Clement VI

The twelfth century Pont Saint-Bénézet, exalted in the song *Sur le Pont d'Avignon*, and the fourteenth century Papal Palace of Avignon.

(1342–1352) added the even more impressive New Palace. He also bought Avignon from Queen Jeanne of Naples, the Countess of Provence, in 1348. The vast wealth of the Church stimulated the arts, but also attracted all sorts of scoundrels and debauchés. Petrarch, who worked for a cardinal in Avignon, called the City of the Popes "a sink-hole of vice." In 1376, Saint Catherine of Siena convinced Pope Gregory XI to move back to Rome. But when he died the next year, cardinals loyal to the King of France elected a pope in Avignon and cardinals in Rome elected another one there. They promptly excommunicated one another, and the Great Schism was on. It was a period of unparalleled venality in the Church, with the rival popes in Rome and Avignon outdoing one another to market pardons for sins. This went on until 1409, when the last anti-Pope in Avignon, Benedict XIII, lost favor with the French king and had to leave town. The Church of Rome regained its uncontested title to Avignon and the Comtat de Venaissin and held it until the French Revolution, when the former Papal holdings became one of the richest and most intriguing parts of the patrimony of France.

GENERAL INFORMATION

The **Tourist Office** is at 41 Rue Jean-Jaurès (90 82 65 11, a short walk up the main street from the railway station. The staff is helpful and well-informed and has mountains of intriguing brochures about Avignon, trips on the Rhône and excursions into the Vaucluse. They can also help you with Festival of Avignon reservations. For reservations for accommodations —hotel rooms, apartments and house rentals, **Vaucluse Tourisme Hébergement**, a service of the tourist authority of the Vaucluse, will make bookings for you in Avignon and the Vaucluse. Their counter at the Tourist Office is open during the summer, and their main office at the Comité Départemental de Tourisme on Place Campana near the Hôtel de Ville is open all year (90 82 05 81 FAX 90 86 54 77.

The following information might prove useful:

Airports: The **Avignon-Caumont Airport** is eight kilometers (five miles) east of town on N 7) (90 81 51 15. The **Marseille-Provence International Airport** is 75 km (47 miles) away (42 78 21 00.

The **railway station, Gare SNCF**, is on Boulevard Saint-Rôch, outside the main gate of the city, the Porte de la République (90 82 50 50.

The **bus station, Gare Routière**, is on Boulevard Saint-Rôch near the train station. For information on **regional buses** (90 82 07 35. The **international bus lines, Eurolines** (90 85 27 60 and **Iberbus** (90 86 88 67, also stop here. **City buses** and buses for Villeneuve-lès-Avignon leave from the main Post Office and Place Pie (90 85 44 93.

Car rental: **Avis** (90 87 17 55; **Budget** (90 87 03 00; **Europcar** (90 82 49 85; **Hertz** (90 82 37 67; **Thrifty** (90 27 93 83.

Bike rental: **Masson**, Place Pie (90 82 32 19; **Velomania**, 1 Avenue de l'Amelier (90 82 06 98; **Dopieralski**, 80 Rue Guillaume Puy (90 86 32 49.

Taxis: 24 hour radio taxis, Place Pie (90 82 20 20.

There are **boat trips** on the Rhône that you can get by the Pont d'Avignon (90 85 65 54. The **boat restaurant**, Mireio, offers lunch or dinner cruises on the Rhône, Allées de l'Oulle (90 85 62 25.

The little **Tourist Train** makes a circuit of the old town from April to the beginning of

October. It leaves every half-hour from the Tourist Office and the square in front of the Papal Palace.

Bus tours: Lieutaud Voyages offers full-day and and half-day trips to Roman Provence, the Camargue, the Lubéron, Les Baux and the Alpes and wine roads. They leave from the Cours de la Gare by the railway station (90 86 36 75.

The **Comité Interprofessionel des Vins des Côtes du Rhône**, two blocks from the main Tourist Office at 6 Rue des Trois Faucons (90 27 24 00 FAX 90 27 24 13, offers a free booklet laying out seven different Côtes du Rhône wine routes with the names and addresses of caves that can be visited.

Medical emergencies: SAMU (emergency medical service), (15. **SOS Médecins** (90 82 65 00.

FESTIVALS

The **Festival d'Avignon**, created by Jean Vilar in 1947, is held from early July to early August and puts on 300 theatrical, dance and musical events in 12 locations including the Grand Cour of the Papal Place. 120,000 spectators attend. The plays are in French. For information, contact their office at 8 bis Rue de Mons, 84000 Avignon (90 82 67 08. Book well in advance for the main events. The **Festival Off** is a spin-off from the main festival offering productions by new and avant-garde theater companies, often more exciting than those of Big Brother. They are at 1 Rue Victor Hugo, 84000 (90 85 79 62.

WHAT TO SEE

Everything you will want to see in Avignon is within walking distance. If you arrive by train, you are ten minutes from the center of town. If you are traveling by car, park near the train station on the south side of the city, just outside the peripheral road that skirts the ramparts. Rue Jean-Jaurès, the main street, takes you from the station to the heart of town. Just past the Tourist Office at 41 Rue Jean-Jaurès, the street changes its name to Rue de la République and leads to tree-shaded, café-lined **Place de l'Horloge**, the main square of Avignon for more than 2,000 years. This was the site of the Roman forum when the town was called Avenio. There are no traces left of the Romans, but you can admire the fifteenth century **Gothic clock tower** after which the place is named and two

handsome nineteenth century neoclassical buildings, the **Hôtel de Ville** and the **theater**.

A few steps farther is the larger **Place du Palais**, dominated by the vast bulk and relentless austerity of the fourteenth century crenelated fortress-cum-palace the **Palais des Papes**, one of the best preserved structures of the medieval period. Its 50 m (160 ft) tall battle towers are a striking reminder of the insecurity of those times, for even so exalted a personage as a Pope. The **Cour d'Honneur** inside the main portal becomes the main stage for theatrical and dance performances during the Festival.

Inside, the Papal Palace is as austere and imposing as it is on the outside. The rooms are vast, most of the walls bare stone. In the days of the popes, they were covered with frescoes or hung with rich tapestries, and every corner of the palais was lavishly furnished. While there are a few frescoes by Simone Martini and Matteo Giovanetti, and the Papal bed chamber has fanciful blue walls and a ceiling with hundreds of painted birds, little else remains. In the vast banquet hall (Grand Tinel) four huge eighteenth century Gobelins tapestries hint at its former sumptuousness, and the museum has plans to create virtual reality imagery that will show visitors exactly how it looked when the Popes lived here. The Papal Palace is open daily from at 9 AM to 7 PM most of the year, but closes at lunchtime in the winter.

The **Musée du Petit Palais** is a fourteenth century cardinal's mansion at the north end of the Place du Palais that houses an excellent collection of medieval and early Renaissance painting and sculpture from Italy and the School of Avignon. Some artists represented here are Taddeo Gaddi, Paolo Veneziano, Botticelli and Ghirlandaio, and there is a fifteenth century School of Avignon altarpiece by Enguerrand Quarton, whose masterpiece, the *Coronation of the Virgin*, is worth a trip across the Rhône to Villeneuve-lès-Avignon to see. The Petit Palais is open from 9:30 AM to 12 PM and 2 PM to 6 PM, closed Tuesday.

The **Rocher des Doms**, now a park, was the original settlement of Avignon. The panorama from the observation point at the top is tremendous — the Papal Place and all of Old Avignon, the Rhône, the Pont d'Avignon, Villeneuve-lès-Avignon across the river with its Tower of Philippe-le-Bel, Charterhouse of the Val de la Bénédiction and mighty Fort Saint-André dominating the whole valley, while to the northeast, Mont-Ventoux commands the horizon.

Pont Saint Benedict, the famous bridge of the song *Sur le Pont d'Avignon*, was completed in 1190 and spanned 900 m (2,925 ft) between Avignon and the Île de la Barthelasse. It was built, legend

In the Papal Palace, the Chapel of Saint-Jean OPPOSITE, decorated in 1346 by Matteo Giovanetti, and ABOVE a contemporary art exhibit of works by Botero.

has it, because angels commanded a shepherd boy named Bénézet to construct a bridge across the Rhône at this spot, and to prove it was Heaven's wish, gave him the strength to lift an impossibly heavy stone. A brotherhood formed to build the bridge, raised the money and completed the project in eleven years. The bridge is narrow, suitable only for pedestrians and horses. Originally it had 22 arches, but by the seventeenth century, after it had been broken by floods and repaired time and again, the city abandoned it. Only four arches remain, along with its little Romanesque chapel. The bridge can be visited daily from 9 AM to 6:30 PM April through September, to 5 PM off-season.

Histoire d'Avignon, a wide-screen audio-visual fresco of the history of Avignon with narration in seven languages, is shown every 20 minutes at the **Espace Saint-Bénézet** at the foot of the Pont d'Avignon (90 85 00 80.

Avignon is a fascinating city to stroll in, with many corners to explore. **Rue des Teinturiers**, the cloth dyers' street, is a tree-shaded, cobblestone alley that runs alongside one of the little fingers of the Sorgue. A few mossy water-wheels the Indian dyers used in the nineteenth century to rinse their fabrics remain in place. Petrarch's beloved Laura, who died in the Plague of 1348, was buried by the Sorgue at the Convent of the Cordeliers, whose bell tower remains. At the **Chapelle des Pénitents Gris** (Grey Penitents Chapel), proceed deep into the interior to see a strange altarpiece, a large gilded bas-relief sunburst, a seventeenth century work from Peru.

Photo Allesandri, 11 *bis* Rue des Teinturiers, has a dazzling collection of original photo postcards of Avignon and Provence.

Les Halles, the town's lively covered food market is at Place Pie, between Rue des Teinturiers and Place de l'Horloge, open Tuesday through Saturday mornings. This is the best place to find the makings for picnics, and there are modestly-priced restaurants around it.

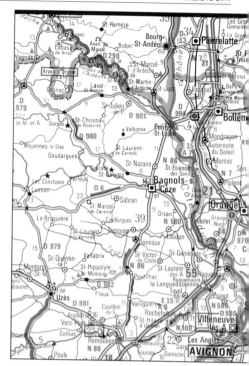

WHERE TO STAY

For a population area of modest size, Avignon and its immediate vicinity boast an extraordinary number of good hotels in all categories.

Expensive

The **Hôtel d'Europe****** at 12 Place Crillon (90 82 66 92 FAX 90 85 43 66, is a sixteenth century nobleman's home that has been a luxury hotel since the eighteenth century and has hosted the likes of Napoléon and the Brownings. There are Aubusson tapestries in the public rooms and 44 guest rooms furnished with antiques. **La Mirande****** at 4 Place Amirande, (90 85 93 93 FAX 90 86 26 85, is a splendid seventeenth century mansion near the Palais des Papes meticulously restored and converted into an aristocratic 19-room hotel. The Europe and the Mirande are lovely places to visit and have tea. The **Auberge de Cassagne****** is an old Provençal estate a five minute drive from town with 19 deluxe guest rooms, a beautiful garden, a pool and tennis courts. It is five kilometers (three miles) northeast of Avignon via N 7 at 450 Allée de Cassagne in Pontet (90 31 04 18 FAX 90 31 04 18.

Moderate

The **Mercure Palais des Papes***** Quartier de la Balance, near the Petit Palais (90 85 91 23 FAX 90 85 32 40, has 87 attractive rooms convenient to the center of town. For a more rural hotel experience, **La Ferme**** is a 20-room inn with a swimming pool amid woods and farm fields on an island in the middle of the Rhône, at Chemin des Bois on the Île de la Barthelasse (90 82 57 53 FAX 90 27 15 47. It is inexpensive off-season, moderate in the summer. It is reached by the Pont Edouard Daladier.

Inexpensive

Médiéval** 15 Rue Petite Saunerie (90 86 11 06 FAX 90 82 08 64, has 20 rooms, spacious but somewhat somber, in a seventeenth century townhouse near the Palais des Papes. The **Angleterre**** 29 Boulevard Raspail (90 86 34 31 FAX 90 86 86 74, is a Logis de France member with 40 simple rooms a short walk from the train station. The 15 room **Mignon*** at 12 Rue Joseph Vernet (90 82 17 30 FAX 90 85 78 46, is a pleasant centrally located hotel.

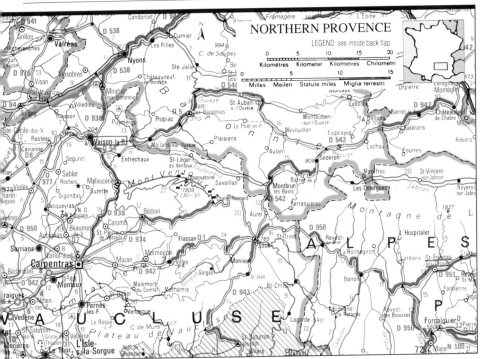

Camping

The camping grounds are on the Île de la Barthelasse, easily reached by the Pont Edouard Daladier. The **Camping Municipal Saint Bénézet** (90 82 63 50 and the **Bagatelle** (90 86 30 39 are attractive sites with views of the Papal Palace and the Pont d'Avignon. The Camping Municipal has 300 places and is open from March 1 to October 31, the Bagatelle 360 places open all year. Also on the island, but less well-situated are the 175-place **Parc des Libertés** (90 85 17 73, open June 15 to September 15, and the 100-place **Deux-Rhônes** (90 85 49 70, open all year.

WHERE TO EAT

Expensive

In an unpromising location upstairs on a main shopping street, **Hiély-Lucullus** at 5 Rue de la République (90 86 17 07 is an Avignon institution that raises hearty traditional regional cooking to gourmet level. The gratin of mussels and spinach, lobster stew and *râble de lapereau farci de son foie, sauce poivarde* (young rabbit stuffed with its liver, served with pepper sauce) are delicious, and regional wines are available by the carafe. There are fixed price menus from 135 francs. I find the relaxed ambiance of Hiély-Lucullus very appealing. But for an elegant dining experience, try **Christian Étienne** at 10 Rue de Mons to the right of the Papal Palace (90 86 16 50. Amid the contemporary art decor of his thirteenth and fourteenth century townhouses, chef Christian Étienne re-reinterprets traditional Provençal cuisine with dishes such as roast rougets (red monkfish) with melted apples and garlic, or fennel sherbet with saffron sauce. There's a luncheon menu at 160 francs on weekdays, otherwise it is very expensive. Both Hiély-Lucullus and Christian Étienne have earned one prestigious Michelin star. So have the restaurants of all three expensive hotels mentioned above. **La Vieille Fontaine** at the Hôtel d'Europe is known for its presentation of *coquilles Saint-Jacques* and roast baby lamb, while at **La Mirande** you can dine on lobster ravioli and roast squab with pistachio butter, and at the **Auberge de Cassagne** Provençal classics are featured, such as stuffed zucchinis and tomatoes, *rougets* with fresh lime and fennel sauce, and breaded strips of lamb and young rabbit with *légumes farcis*. The wine of preference at all these top restaurants is, naturally, Châteauneuf-du-Pape.

Moderate

Fourchette II near the Place de l'Horloge at 17 Rue Racine (90 85 20 93 has a plain decor, relaxed ambiance and savory Provençal food at low prices. Fixed-price menus start from 110 francs. It is very popular, so reserve in advance. **Les Trois Clefs**, close to the Tourist Office at 26 Rue de Trois Faucons (90 86 51 53, is a cozy inn-like restaurant with turn-of-the-century photos of Avignon on the walls and menus keyed to the market, 140 francs, wine included.

Inexpensive

At the **Tache d'Encre**, 22 Rue des Teinturiers (90 85 79 71, you'll find simple, nourishing fare in a big, lively restaurant with music on the weekends. **Port de Barques**, 25 Place Pie (90 82 63 82, is a brasserie on the market square serving fresh fish and shellfish platters, with fixed-price menus starting at 85 francs.

NIGHTLIFE

Outside the Festival period, this is not an exciting city for night life. The best place to look for it is along the **Rue des Teinturiers**, where a young crowd gravitates to its bars and inexpensive restaurants.

HOW TO GET THERE

There are four flights a day from Paris to Avignon-Colmont Airport on AirInter and about a dozen high-speed *TGV* trains, a trip of approximately four hours. There are also frequent trains from Nîmes, Arles, Montpellier, Marseille and other main southern cities. Eurolines has buses from London and other European cities, and a number of regional bus lines service Avignon. The only direct public transportation between Aix and Avignon is by bus. By car, take the A 7 *autoroute* down the Rhône Valley from the north or up from Marseille 95 km (59 miles) to the south. From Aix take the A 8 and the A 7. The distance is 80 km (50 miles).

VILLENEUVE-LÈS-AVIGNON

Avignon is the City of Popes, Villeneuve-les-Avignon the City of Cardinals. It lies directly across the Rhône from Avignon and was easily reached in the Middle Ages by the Pont Saint-Bénézet to the Île de la Barthelasse, then a short bridge over the western branch of the river to Villeneuve. In the fourteenth century, cardinals crossed the bridge and set up their residences in Villeneuve to maintain a bit of independence from the Popes. Villeneuve was in France, Avignon in the Holy Roman Empire.

There are **two tourist offices**. The main one is at 1 Place Charles-David (90 25 61 33, open all year. The other is at 58 Rue de la République by the entrance to the Chartreuse (90 25 61 55, open only in the summer.

WHAT TO SEE

The **Tour Philippe-le-Bel** was part of the French fortifications at the Villeneuve end of the bridge, and in the late fourteenth century, formidable **Fort Saint-André** went up on Villeneuve's highest hill. There are panoramas of Avignon from both places.

On the hill below Fort Saint-André are the moody ruins of a huge Carthusian monastery, the **Chartreuse du Val de Bénédiction**, founded in 1356. It became an important way-station on the medieval pilgrimage route to Compostela. Concerts are held here in the summer.

A few **cardinals' residences** remain on Rue de la République. The finest, that of Pierre de Luxembourg, is now the **Musée Municipal**. It houses one of the great paintings of the medieval period, *The Coronation of the Virgin* by Enguerrand Quarton (sometimes spelled Charanton). Quarton was a native of Picardy, but worked for years in Aix and Avignon and became fascinated by the Mediterranean light. This brilliantly luminous, hard-edged

work looks like it could have been painted in the 1980's instead of 1453, when it was. On the theological level, an unusual feature is that God the Father and God the Son, seen placing a crown on the head of the Virgin, are represented as twins. Among many other works to see in this rich collection are a remarkable fourteenth century Virgin painted on sculpted ivory and a death mask of Jeanne de Laval, the second wife of Good King René. Open from 10 AM to 12:30 PM and 3 PM to 7:30 PM from the April 1 to the end of September, 10 AM to 12 PM and 2 PM to 5 PM the rest of the year. Closed the month of February and national holidays.

WHERE TO STAY AND WHERE TO EAT

The **Hostellerie le Prieuré****** at 7 Place du Chapitre, (90 25 18 20 FAX 90 25 45 39, is a fourteenth century priory in the Cardinals' District with

26 antique-furnished rooms and 10 apartments, lush gardens, a pool and tennis court. The rooms are quite expensive (520 to 1,200 francs), as is its excellent Provençal restaurant, which rates one Michelin star. The hotel is a Relais & Châteaux member. **La Magnaneraie***** is an elegant fifteenth century residence on the heights of Villeneuve at Camp de Bataille (90 25 11 11 FAX 90 25 46 37. It has a large swimming pool and sun deck, tennis court, and 25 comfortable rooms in the expensive range (500 to 950 francs). Its lovely garden restaurant serves noted chef Gérard Prayal's Provençal cuisine. **L'Atelier**** is a charming moderately-priced small hotel in a sixteenth century house in the center of Villeneuve-lès-Avignon at 5 Rue Foire (90 25 01 84 FAX 90 25 80 06.

Camping

Camping Municipal de la Laune is a spacious, well shaded camping ground with a pool, on Chemin Saint Honoré, near Fort Saint-André (90 25 76 06.

HOW TO GET THERE

To get to Villeneuve-lès-Avignon by bus, take the N° 10 from the Avignon train station (Gare SNCF), Place Pie or from Porte de l'Oulle on the Avignon end of the Pont Edouard Daladier. It leaves every half-hour. Driving, take the Pont Edouard Daladier across the Rhône and the Île de la Barthelasse and go right on the opposite side of the river on Avenue Gabriel Péri to get to the center of Villeneuve.

CHÂTEAUNEUF-DU-PAPE

This hilly town 18 km (11 miles) north of the Papal City is where the Popes of Avignon chose to establish their vineyards. With the tower of a castle built by wine-loving John XXII in 1316 overlooking it, Châteauneuf-du-Pape continues to produce southern France's most prestigious wine. The vineyards are unusual. They are covered by a thick bed of *galets*, rounded stones deposited by the Rhône in the Ice Age, that heat up in the sunlight and stay warm at night, making the vines feel good so that the grapes make especially delicious wines.

GENERAL INFORMATION

The **Tourist Office is at Place du Portail in the center of town** (90 83 71 08. It will provide a map and a list of wine estates and their visiting hours.

WINE TASTING

Châteauneuf-du-Pape wines belong to the overall family of Côtes du Rhône wines. This family

of wines is grown on both sides of the Rhône River, and the ones grown in the areas south of the Drôme River are known as Côtes du Rhône Méridionales (southern Côtes du Rhône). The wines are predominantly reds. Generally speaking, they are lighter, more clear and more fruity in the northern areas — the Drôme, the Papal Enclave and the northern part of the Gard — and more full-bodied and earthy in the Vaucluse, where other famous wine villages such as Gigondas and Vacqueyras are located, and where Châteauneuf-du-Pape makes the deepest-hued, most robust reds of all.

The system of *Appellation d'Origine Contrôlée* (*AOC*) began here. In 1923, the wine-growers of

Châteauneuf-du-Pape agreed on a rigid set of standards governing every aspect of the growing of the grapes and the making of the wine, an idea that spread to other wine regions. Thirteen kinds of grapes are blended to make red Châteauneuf-du-Pape, and each vineyard has its own secret recipe. Reds account for 95 percent of the production. The remaining five percent are whites, normally made from six varieties of grapes. The reds should be kept three to five years for full maturation. The whites can be drunk in the first two years.

The most beautiful wine *château* to visit and among the most highly respected is **Château la Nerthe**, an elegant mansion in a tree-shaded park that was taken by the Nazis as their regional HQ

OPPOSITE: Villeneuve-lès-Avignon, with Fort Saint-André on top of the hill. ABOVE: Working in the vineyards at Châteauneuf-du-Pape.

during World War II. Its big, atmospheric cellar is open weekdays from 8 AM to noon and 2 to 6 PM (90 83 70 11. Other prestigious estates one can visit are **Domaine du Vieux Télégraphe** (90 33 00 31, **Clos des Papes** (90 83 70 13 and **Château de Mont Redon** (90 83 72 75. The wines of Châteauneuf-du-Pape tend to be quite expensive, especially those of glamorous estates such as these. Much more affordable Châteauneuf-du-Pape, but of very high quality, is made by the **Domaine de Nalys**, an up-to-date operation that spurns glamour and tries to keep prices down. They were among the first to market whites, in the 1960's. They are on the Route de Courthezon (D 92) west of town (90 83 72 52.

In general, the caves are open weekdays and by appointment only on Saturdays.

WHERE TO STAY AND WHERE TO EAT

The **Hostellerie des Fines Roches****** is an ivy-covered mock-medieval *château* on a hill, reached by a private road through its vineyards (90 83 70 23 FAX 90 83 78 42. It has seven antique-furnished guest rooms all with views of Avignon and the Rhône Valley. It also boasts one of the area's top restaurants (Michelin one-star), featuring chef Philippe Estevenin's gastronomic Provençal fare and local wines. It is expensive. The **Verger des Papes** is a casual eating place by the ruins of the fourteenth century Château des Papes with a large

The statue of Emperor Augustus, the town's patron, at the first century AD Théâtre Antique in Orange.

open terrace and grand panoramic view, serving hearty Provençal cuisine — *escargots, daube, bourride* (snails, beef stew, fish stew) — at moderate prices (90 83 50 40.

HOW TO GET THERE

By car, Châteaneuf-du-Pape is 18 km (11 miles) north of Avignon on N 7 and D 17. There are three buses a day from Avignon's Gare Routière.

ORANGE

This bustling town of 30,000 lies 28 km (18 miles) north of Avignon and six kilometers east of the Rhône. It is a main distribution center for the area's big peach, pear and apple orchards, market gardens and vineyards and is home to a military air base and a Foreign Legion post. But to the world, it owes its fame to its Roman Arc de Triomphe and especially its huge Roman Théâtre Antique, still in regular use after almost 2,000 years.

BACKGROUND

Orange's name has nothing to do with the fruit or the color. It comes from Arausio, its Celtic-Liguarian name. With the support of Octavius, veterans of Caesar's Second Gallic Legion colonized the town in 35 BC, and their patron's largesse continued when he became Augustus in 27 BC. Orange prospered under the *Pax Romana* until 412, when it was sacked by the Visigoths.

In the twelfth century, the town gained the status of an independent principality under the rule of the troubadour-prince Raimbaut of Orange. In 1530, through a complicated series of marriages, the Dutch branch of the German house of Nassau came into possession of Orange. Its leader, William the Silent, began the Netherlands' war of independence against Spain, and he made Orange a bastion of Protestantism during the Wars of Religion. It became a refuge for dissenters persecuted in arch-Catholic Avignon and the Comtat Venaissin. In 1713, after the War of the Spanish Succession, Orange's Dutch rulers ceded the principality to France. They kept the name of the House of Orange, however, which they had adopted, and it remains the name of the Dutch royal family to this day.

GENERAL INFORMATION

The **Tourist Office** is opposite the Théâtre Antique at Cours Aristide Briand (90 34 70 88.

The **train station, Gare SNCF**, is on Avenue Frédéric Mistral (90 82 50 50.

The **bus station, Gare Routiére**, is nearby on Avenue Frédéric Mistral (90 34 15 59.

FESTIVALS

Since 1902, Orange's Théâtre Antique has been the site of one of Europe's most important opera and orchestral music festivals, **Les Chorégies d'Orange**, held in July and early August. For information, contact Chorégies d'Orange, BP 205, 81017 Orange (90 34 24 24. The box office is at the Théâtre Antique.

WHAT TO SEE

The **Théâtre Antique**, built in the first century AD, is the best preserved Roman theater anywhere. Its huge brick scenic backdrop stands 38 m (125 ft) high and is 103 m (338 ft) wide. In Roman times it was decorated with 76 columns in three tiers with dozens of statues in niches. Only a few columns and one statue remain, that of Augustus striking a suitably imperial pose. The auditorium's steep semicircle of stone risers can seat up to 10,000. The acoustics are excellent, but if you go to a performance, be sure to bring cushions. The stone slabs are a killer.

The theater can be visited daily except Christmas, New Years and May Day. The best overall view is from the high hill in back of the auditorium, the **Parc de la Colline Saint-Eutrope**. This is where the Princes of Orange had their castle. It was demolished in 1672 by the Count of Grignan, Mme. De Sévigné's son-in-law, during one of Louis XIV's many wars.

The **Arc de Triomphe** from 20 BC is also well preserved. It has a vivid bas-relief of the Second Gallic Legion doing battle against the Gauls on the top central panel, naval emblems and other decorative elements and handsome Corinthian columns. At 22 m (72 ft) high and 21 m (68 ft) wide, it is the third largest Roman triumphal arch standing.

Harmas is the museum and botanical garden of J.H. Fabre (1823–1915), a world-renowned entomologist from the area, who spent the last thirty-six years of his life at his big farm near Orange amassing a vast collection of butterflies, insects, shells, fossils and minerals and painted a series of 700 astonishingly life-like watercolors of mushrooms of the Vaucluse. Harmas is in **Serignan-du-Comtat** eight kilometers (five miles) northeast of Orange on the N 7 and D 976. It is open from 9 AM to 11:30 AM and 2 PM to 6 PM, to 4 PM in the winter, closed Tuesday, the month of October and national holidays.

WHERE TO STAY AND WHERE TO EAT

The **Hôtel Arène***** at Place de Langes (90 34 10 95 FAX 90 34 91 62, has 30 large, pleasant, moderately-priced rooms on a quiet square in Old Orange, a

Relais de Silence and Logis de France member. For truffle omelets, zucchini blossoms, guinea fowl and other Provençal treats, try **Le Parvis** at 3 Cours Pourtoules (90 34 82 00, where you dine on the shaded terrace or in the wooden-beamed dining room. The three-course fixed-price menu at 98 francs is an excellent value.

Camping

Camping is at **Le Jonquier** on Rue Alexis-Carrel northwest of the city, open mid-March to the end of October (90 34 19 83.

HOW TO GET THERE

The *TGV* (high speed train) does not stop at Orange. Coming from Paris, you have to get off at Valence and switch to a local train. There are frequent trains from Avignon and regular bus connections with Avignon, Carpentras, Séguret and Vaison-la-Romaine. The tourist office and bus stations have the schedules. If you are driving, Orange is reached by the A 7 *autoroute* from the north or the south and the A 8 from Nîmes, Montpellier and the southwest, and there are good direct roads from Carpentras and Vaison-la-Romaine.

SUZE-LA-ROUSSE AND LA DRÔME PROVENÇALE

North of Orange lies a sunny wedge of land known as "La Drôme Provençale." It is shielded from frigid northern air by the mountains of the Dauphiné, making it the northernmost area in France where the olive tree will grow, thus Mediterranean in climate. It is also is an important truffle-producing area and makes Côtes du Rhône and Côteaux du Tricastin wines. This area lies in the *départment* of the Drôme, which is north of the current political boundaries of Provence, but is climatically and historically Provençale. And as it is a bit off the main tourist track, it offers the traveler a chance to discover this "admirable land of happy hills and light," as Jean Giono called it, in a relatively untrammeled state.

Suze-la-Rousse 20 km (12.5 miles) directly north of Orange is an important town for students of wine — literally, because it is the home of the **Université du Vin**. This respected institute founded in 1978 offers a full range of courses about wine, from professional programs for wine-makers and *sommeliers* to weekend wine-tasting sessions for the serious amateur. For information, contact the Université du Vin, Le Château, 26790 Suze-la-Rousse (Drôme) (75 04 86 09 FAX 75 98 24 20.

The university is housed in the **Château de Suze**, a twelfth century castle, once the property of the Princes of Orange, that dominates the pretty

Provence

village and the vine-covered countryside from a hill in the center. It was remodeled in the sixteenth century and has an elegant arcaded Renaissance courtyard and richly painted and stuccoed Renaissance and Baroque rooms. The architecture of the *château* makes it worth visiting in its own right, and the University's state-of-the-art wine-tasting laboratory in a former chapel is a marvel of function and beauty.

The *château* is open from 9:30 AM to 11:30 AM and 2:30 PM to 5:30 PM, 6 PM in the summer, open every day in July and August, closed Tuesdays and Wednesday mornings the rest of the year.

The **Tourist Office** is in the *château* (75 04 81 44.

HOW TO GET THERE

Suze-la-Rousse is easily reached by car from Orange, a lovely drive on D 11 and D 117. Traveling through this part of the country is particularly enjoyable, because grape-growers have the happy custom of planting rose bushes at the ends of their rows of vines. There is no public transport to Suze-la-Rousse.

GRIGNAN

Grignan is a graceful old northern Provençal town built around the handsome hilltop *château* of the powerful Adhémar family. As in Suze-la-Rousse, the *château* was a medieval stronghold first and was expanded and turned into a Renaissance showplace in the sixteenth century. It owes its everlasting fame to Mme. de Sévigné, whose letters to her daughter written in the late seventeenth century and published in 1726 became popular thanks to her sharp observations of the life of her period. Her daughter was the wife of the Count of Grignan, the Viceroy of Provence, and Mme. de Sévigné loved Grignan, spent a good deal of time here and died at the Château. It was looted and badly damaged during the Revolution, but heirs of the Adhémar family restored it early in the twentieth century.

GENERAL INFORMATION

The **Tourist Office** is next to the Château (75 46 56 75.

The **Caveau des Côteaux du Tricastin** next door to the Tourist Office has wines of all the producers of the *appellation* and makes them available for free tasting, and it sells them at the same price as the vineyards themselves. Knowledgeable personnel are there to help you with your choices and direct you to vineyards you may want to visit (75 47 55 54.

WHAT TO SEE AND WHAT TO DO

In the richly furnished and decorated 25-room **Château de Grignan**, the main attraction is Mme. de Sévigné's apartments, restored to the style of her period with Louis XIII and Louis XIV furniture and Aubusson tapestries of mythological scenes. Classical music **concerts** are held at the *château* in the summer, and there are fine views of Mont-Ventoux to the southeast. The *château* can be visited daily from April 1 to the end of October from 9:30 AM to 11:30 PM and 2 PM to 5:30 PM (6 PM in the summer), and it is closed Tuesdays and Wednesday mornings the rest of the year.

WHERE TO STAY AND WHERE TO EAT

For deluxe lodging in Grignan, the **Manoir de la Rosaire*** on the Route de Valréas (75 46 58 15 FAX 75 46 91 55, is an elegant mansion in a large private park with a beautiful pool and a view of the Château. It has 12 spacious, tastefully decorated rooms in the upper-moderate to expensive range and a gourmet restaurant.

For an inexpensive lunch of lamb and fresh vegetables or other simple, savory Northern Provençal fare, seek out **L'Eau à la Bouche**, a flowery little restaurant on Rue Saint-Louis in the heart of the old village (75 46 57 37.

For a real country experience and a chance to get to know Côteaux de Tricastin wines, the **Domaine Saint-Luc*** rents five cozy guest rooms, all with private baths, in Eliane and Ludovic Cornillon's big eighteenth century farmhouse. For dinner, guests feast on Provençal products fresh from the farm and sample the Domaine Saint-Luc's prize-winning wines. A double room costs 290 francs, breakfast included, and dinner is 130 francs. Reserve early. It is in **Baume-de-Transit** halfway between Grignan and Suze-la-Rousse (75 98 11 51 FAX 75 98 19 22.

Camping

Grignan has two camping grounds, **Les Truffières** (75 46 93 62, which has 35 places, a restaurant, bar, washing machines and a pool, and the 30-place municipal facility, **Le Rochecourbière** (75 46 50 06, which has a pool, but none of the other conveniences. Both are open from April 1 to the end of October.

HOW TO GET THERE

For those motoring down from Northern Europe, the closest exit to Grignan from the A 7 *autoroute* is **Montélimar-Sud**, which is about a six-hour drive from Paris. That's where I get off when I'm heading for my little retreat in the Vaucluse, and for anyone who's not in hurry, I recommend leaving the A 7 at this point and taking the well-maintained secondary roads through the lovely olive groves and vineyards of La Drôme Provençale and the Vaucluse. This is a much more pleasant way of getting into the mood of Provence than driving past the Centrale Nucléaire du Tricastin, the huge nuclear power plant you will see if you keep driving south on the *autoroute*.

Grignan is 18 km (11 miles) east of the *autoroute* on D 541.

There are five buses a day to Grignan on the Teste bus company's regular route between Montélimar and Nyons.

VALRÉAS AND THE PAPAL ENCLAVE

The Papal Enclave is an anomaly of history, a little island of land acquired by the Popes of Avignon and owned by the Papacy until 1791 that is now part of the Vaucluse, but lies within the borders of the Drôme. Valréas is the chief town of the Papal Enclave. It has a handsome, mostly eighteenth century **Hôtel de Ville** and a jewel of a Romanesque church, the twelfth century **Église de Notre-Dame-de-Nazareth.**

On June 23 Valréas enacts the medieval pageant of the **Nuit du Petit Saint-Jean** in which a four-year old boy is crowned Little Saint John, blesses the crowd in a procession and protects the town for the rest of the year.

Market days are Wednesday mornings at the Place de la Mairie and Place de la Poste and Saturday at the war memorial. On Wednesdays in November, there is a truffle market.

The **Tourist Office** is at Place Aristide Briand, Valréas (90 35 04 71.

WINE TASTING

The Papal Enclave is prime Côtes du Rhône wine country, and there are outstanding wine cooperatives in **Valréas** and **Visan**, nine kilometers (five and a half miles) to the south. Two exceptional individual wine makers in the Papal Enclave are **Domaine du Val des Rois** (90 35 04 35 and **Domaine de la Prévosse** (90 35 05 87 in Valréas.

HOW TO GET THERE

The Teste line's Montélimar–Nyons buses stop at Valréas five times a day in either direction, and Cars Mery has five buses a day from Avignon's Gare Routière via Orange, a trip of one hour and thirty minutes. By car, Valréas is nine kilometers (five and a half miles) east of Grignan and 14 km (9 miles) west of Nyons on D 541, and 35km (22 miles) northeast of Orange on D 976.

NYONS

Nyons is the olive capital of La Drôme Provençale. Chef Alain Ducasse calls the black olives of Nyons the best in the world, and in 1994, "the Black Pearl," as it is known here, and the olive oil of Nyons were the first to be awarded an AOC in this newly created agricultural *appellation controlée* category.

Lest you think this is some quaint little business, the Cooperative du Nyonsais has 260,000 trees and presses 65,000 tons of olive oil per year. And there are private producers as well. From late November to late February, the oil mills are in full swing, and the public is invited to watch the process.

But all is not olives in Nyons. Truffles ("black diamonds"), fruit jams and jellies and honey are also important products of the region, and this town of 6,000 is the center of it all.

The **Tourist Office** is on the broad main square of town, Place de la Libération (75 26 10 35.

FESTIVALS

Les Olivades, the big olive festival, takes place the second Sunday in July.

WHAT TO SEE AND WHAT TO DO

To savor cured olives of all kinds and olive preparations such as *tapenade*, a purée of black olives flavored with herbs of Provence and capers, which is also made in a green olive version, or *anchoïde*, made with anchovies, vinegar and olive oil, there are three excellent choices in town. The bright, modern **Cooperative du Nyonsais** at Place Olivier de Serres, a few blocks from Place de la Libération, offers the full range of products, including their *AOC* olive oil, as well as wines of the region that you can buy by the glass, by the bottle or *en vrac*, in 28-liter plastic containers. **Moulin Ramade** on the Impasse du Moulin off Avenue Paul Laurens is another distinguished mill. The colorful **Vieux Moulin** by the Pont Roman, is part mill, part shop and part museum of traditional processing techniques. It has been owned and operated by the Autrand family since 1725, and genial owner Jean-Pierre Autrand will show you the operation. During pressing season from November to February, you can watch the process at all three mills.

The town has a medieval section, the **Quartier des Forts**, an arcaded old square, **Place Docteur Bourdongle**, and a fourteenth century donkeyback bridge called the **Pont Roman** over the River Eygues. Nyons has a busy **market** Thursday mornings on Place de la Libération, one of the best in Provence. For marvelous cheeses from the nearby mountains, **La Halle aux Fromages** on Place de la

Libération is open Tuesday through Sunday, with a delicious selection of breads to go with them.

WHERE TO STAY AND WHERE TO EAT

The **Auberge du Vieux Village**** on the Route de Gap three kilometers (two miles) east of town in the village of **Aubres** (75 26 12 89 FAX 75 26 12 89, is a charming 19 room country inn with rustic decor, modern bathrooms and balconies overlooking a peaceful valley, a swimming pool, gym and restaurant. Prices are moderate. La Picholine*** on the Promenade de la Perrière, one kilometer from Nyons via the Promenade des Anglais (75 26 06 21 FAX 75 26 40 72, has 16 attractive, moderately-priced rooms, a pool and a garden shaded with ancient olive trees, a restaurant and a view of the town from its hillside. For a hotel on the main square in town, try the **Colombet**** at 55 Place de la Libération (75 26 03 66 FAX 75 26 42 37, with 29 pleasant rooms and a cheerful restaurant, with room and food prices inexpensive to moderate. For restaurants, my top choice in town is **Le Petit Caveau** at 9 Rue Victor Hugo (75 26 20 21, for its offbeat culinary combinations, such as lamb with honey and linden-blossom tea, or stuffed rabbit with *tapenade*, and good local wines. The prices are moderate, with fixed-price menus starting at 95 francs. Another fine restaurant with lots of culinary surprises and moderate prices is **La Charrette Bleue** in **Condorcet**, seven kilometers (four miles) to the east of town on the Route de Gap (75 27 72 33.

Camping

There are two camping grounds in Nyons. The deluxe **Camping des Clos** on the Route de Gap (75 26 29 90, open all year, has 150 places and a pool. The **Camping Municipal de Nyons** on the Promenade de la Digue near the center of town (75 26 22 39 is a more modest grounds with 97 places and no pool, open April through early November. There are a dozen camping grounds in nearby communities. For information contact the Nyons Tourist Office.

HOW TO GET THERE

Lieutaud Voyages has three buses a day from Avignon via Vaison-la-Romaine. By car, Nyons is 14 km (9 miles) east of Valréas and 16 km (10 miles) north of Vaison-la-Romaine on D 938, a pretty drive through peach orchards, vineyards and rolling hills. It can also be reached by D 976 and D 94 from Orange, a distance of 42 km (29 miles).

VAISON-LA-ROMAINE

Vaison-la-Romaine is three towns in one. As its name indicates, Provence's Roman heritage figures strongly in one of them, but you will also have a restored medieval town and a lively "modern" one to explore. Attractively situated at the foot of Mont-Ventoux, this town of 7,000 is the commercial and cultural hub of the upper Vaucluse. The good selection of hotels and restaurants in and around Vaison make it the best base for exploring the northern reaches of Provence.

BACKGROUND

The earliest inhabitants were Bronze Age Ligurians, conquered in the fourth century BC by the Celtic Voconces tribe, who set up their capital at Vaison. In 123 BC, the same year the Romans established Aix, they defeated the Voconces and took over Vasio Vocontiorum, as they called it. As Rome integrated Provence into its economy, especially after Caesar's defeat of Massalia in 49 BC, the Roman landowners of Vaison became rich on wine, fruit and vegetables, the area's most important products to this day, and Vaison became a thriving town of least 10,000 inhabitants.

As the Empire collapsed, the Church took the lead in Vaison's direction, installing a bishop as early as the fifth century. In 1125, the great lords of the South, Counts Alphonse of Toulouse and Raimond Bérenger III of Barcelona agreed to settle their claims in Provence, with Toulouse getting the lands north of the Durance. When the Count built Vaison's *château* on the hill to the south of the Ouvèze River, people started to build their houses on the slope below the castle for protection, and Haute Ville, the medieval city, developed. In the next century, because of his support of the Cathars during the Albigensian Crusade, the Count of Toulouse was stripped his lands, and in 1274, King Philip III of France and his uncle Count Charles of Provence gave Toulouse's lands in Provence to the Pope. As part of the Papal Comtat Venaissin, comprising most of the present department of the Vaucluse, Vaison remained a possession of the Church until the Revolution.

In the eighteenth and nineteenth centuries, people abandoned the Haute Ville and moved the town back across the river to its modern site between the Roman and medieval cities.

GENERAL INFORMATION

The **Tourist Office** is on Place du Chanoine Sautel between the Roman sites of Puymin and La Villasse (90 36 02 11. It also handles tourist information for Séguret and the Mont-Ventoux area.

FESTIVALS

From mid-July to mid-August, Vaison has its **Festival d'Été** (summer festival), with music, dance and theater performances at the Roman theater practically every night. For information, get in touch with the Tourist Office.

WHAT TO SEE

To either side of the **Place du Chanoine Sautel**, named in honor of the abbot who led the excavations, lie 12 hectares (30 acres) of **Roman archaeological sites**, open daily except Christmas and New Years Day. The **Puymin** quarter lies to the east on a slope planted with cypress and oaks and contains foundations of villas and copies of statues found during excavations. The originals can be seen in the **Museum** in the middle of the site, which also has delightful mosaics of birds

and flowers. The **water cistern** is on the eastern edge, and to the north there is a 6,000-seat **Roman Theater** where concerts of the **Festival de Vaison** are held.

At **La Villasse** to the west of the Place Sautel are the central shopping streets of the Roman city, the baths, the House of the Silver Bust (where a silver bust on display in the museum was found) and the Dolphin House, the luxurious villas of wealthy Roman families of the first century AD.

The excavations date from 1907, when Abbé Sautel began his digs. In 1924 Vaison added "la-Romaine" to its name.

A few steps to the west of La Villasse is the former **Cathedral of Notre-Dame-de-Nazareth**, a Romanesque church built mainly in the twelfth and thirteenth centuries, but containing elements from earlier Christian churches and

even a Roman temple that stood on the site. It has an unusual cloister from the eleventh and twelfth centuries with groups of three small arches supported by double rows of pillars, with large vaulted arches above.

A short walk along Avenue Jules-Ferry takes you to the heart of the "modern" town, centering on pleasant cafe and restaurant-lined Place Montfort. The **market** there Tuesday mornings is very festive. Cross the **Roman Bridge** over the Ouvèze River. During the flood in 1992, this 2,000 year-old structure withstood 1,000 tons per square meter of water pressure, with the raging waters washing over the top of it. Up the hill is the **Haute Ville**, where the houses and churches date mainly from the thirteenth to the sixteenth century. Since World War II, Haute Ville has been restored and massively gentrified, and its narrow cobble stone streets, tiny squares with fountains, and shops of crafts people are very pleasant to explore. The hike up the hill to the **Château of the Counts of Toulouse** is quite a work-out. Only part of the shell of the donjon remains, but there is a superb panorama of Mont-Ventoux, the Barronies range and the Valley of the Ouvèze.

WHERE TO STAY AND WHERE TO EAT

The **Beffroi*** in Haute Ville, the medieval part of town (90 36 04 71 FAX 90 36 24 78, has 20 antique-furnished rooms in adjoining sixteenth and seventeenth century residences with a garden overlooking the modern and Roman towns. Doubles go for 630 francs. **Logis du Château**** in Les Hauts de Vaison above Haute Ville (90 36 09 98 FAX 90 36 10 95, is an attractive, medium-priced 40-room modern hotel with a pool and panoramic view. Both hotels have restaurants, but you would better off eating at the **Auberge de la Bartavelle**, Place sus Auze, near Place Montfort (90 36 02 16, where you can feast on the savory Southwest specialties such as *foie gras* and *magret de canard* (breast of fattened duck) or Provençal dishes at very affordable prices in a cheerful atmosphere. Closed Mondays and Saturday lunch. **Le Bateleur**, a well-established restaurant at Place Aubanel near the Roman bridge (90 36 28 04, serves honorable Provençale fare at moderate prices. **Auberge d'Anais**, Route de Saint-Marcellin, just west of Vaison (90 36 20 06, has 12 modest rooms, in a friendly inn amid vineyards and olive trees with a clear view of Mont-Ventoux. There is also a swimming pool. 280 francs for a double room, breakfast included, and a restaurant with tasty Provençale menus from 85 francs. **Restaurant Saint-Hubert** a few kilometers farther along in

A 43 AD portrait of Emperor Claudius in the museum at Vaison-la-Romaine, excavated from the ruins in the Roman quarter of Puymin.

Provence

Entrechaux (90 46 00, is noted especially for its game dishes during hunting season.

Camping

There are two camping grounds in Vaison-la-Romaine, both open from Easter to the end of October. They are the 55-place **Camping du Théâtre Romain** (90 28 78 66 across the street from the Roman theater and the somewhat larger **Carpe Diem** 800 m (half a mile) from the center of town on the Route de Malaucène (90 36 02 02. For other camping grounds in the surrounding countryside, contact the Tourist Office.

HOW TO GET THERE

There are three buses a day from Avignon and Orange, two from Carpentras and seven from Nyons. The Tourist Office can give you the schedules. By car, it is 27 km (17 miles) northeast of Orange on D 975, 16 km (10 miles) south of Nyons on D 938, and 27 km (17 miles) north of Carpentras, also on D 938.

MONT-VENTOUX

"The Giant of Provence," Mont-Ventoux, looms over Vaison-la-Romaine, only 18 km (11 miles) from the domed peak of the mountain. Bald at the top, it looks perpetually snow-covered. But in fact, what you see in the summer are fields of light-colored stones. There is snow only in the winter, normally at altitudes above 1,200 m (4,000 ft), and the skiing is good from December to April. The mountain is 1,912 m (6,265 ft) high.

Francesco Petrarch, the poet and pioneer of Humanist thinking, who has been called "the first modern poet" and "the first modern man," lived for many years in Provence and climbed Mont-Ventoux in 1336. For this he has been called "the first mountain climber," in that he is the first individual on record to climb a mountain just for the pleasure of it.

As you climb to the top, you pass from from Mediterranean vegetation, to pine forests to bare pebbles above the tree line. The view from the top is vast — the Cévennes, Montagne Sainte-Victoire, Marseille and the Mediterranean — and on a very clear day, you can see all the way down to Mount Canigou in the Pyrénées. The best time to be up here is at dusk, to see the lights coming on in towns all over Provence and the beacons lighting up along the coast. The clearest visibility is right after a mistral. But a word of warning: the mountain is not called *ventoux* for nothing. In fact, the early inhabitants of the area believed that the god of the wind lived here and that Ventoux was the source of the mistrals. If it is windy below, it will be very uncomfortable on the top, even unbearable on the top.

HOW TO GET THERE

To get to Mont-Ventoux, take D 938 from Vaison-la-Romaine to Malaucène, then D 974 along the north slope 21 km (13 miles) to the observation point at the Col des Tempêtes. There are no organized tours to Mont-Ventoux from Vaison-la-Romaine, but you can hire a taxi for the trip for 300 francs (90 36 00 04.

SÉGURET AND THE DENTELLES DE MONTMIRAIL

The Dentelles de Montmirail is a chain of limestone hills topped by a jagged filigree of white rock that looks something like lace (*dentelles*) from a distance. They run 16 km (10 miles) north-south from just below Vaison-la-Romaine on their northern end to Beaumes-de-Venise on the south. Few of the peaks top 400 m (1,300 ft), but their cragginess makes them impressive. They are a favorite place of rock climbers. Flat and gently rolling vineyards lie to the west, lovely with the Dentelles as a backdrop. This is some of the finest wine country in the South, and the wines of Gigondas, Vacqueyras and Beaumes-de-Venise have gained international renown.

Séguret, 10 km (six miles) south of Vaison on D 23, is a charming town of 714 inhabitants that clings to the western face of the Dentelles and looks like Bethlehem in a Christmas crib — which is just what it becomes in December, a living *crèche* with townspeople in costume, when it puts one of the most colorful Christmas pageants in Provence. The village is closed to cars. Its narrow pedestrian streets are lined with up-scale shops, winding up to the top of the hill, and there are good restaurants (see below).

Beaumes-de-Venise (*beaume* is the word for cave in Provençal and "Venise" is a contraction of Venaissin) has an unusual Romanesque chapel, **Notre-Dame-d'Aubune**, on a lonely hill outside town. Its tall, square bell tower has windows, cornices and moldings treated with classical motifs.

GENERAL INFORMATION

The **Tourist Office** in Beaumes-de-Venise is on Cours Jean Jaurès (90 62 94 39.

WHERE TO STAY AND WHERE TO EAT

In Séguret, the **Domaine de Cabasse***** Route de Sablet (90 46 91 12 FAX 90 46 94 01, is a peaceful 12-room inn on the grounds of a vineyard at the foot of the Dentelles, with a pool. The top priced double rooms are 650 francs. They have inventive Provençale cuisine (lots of truffle dishes in season) at modest prices, with a 70 franc luncheon menu, wine included, on weekdays. It's open from March to November. **La Table du Comtat***** (90 46 91 49 FAX 90 46 94 27, at the top of the old village with a marvelous view of the plain, is the deluxe address of the Dentelles. It has eight tasteful, moderately expensive rooms and a gourmet restaurant, excellent, but very expensive, except for the 150 franc luncheon menu during the week. Open late March to November. A favorite of mine is **Le Mesclun**, a very good medium-priced restaurant in the village on Rue Poternes (90 46 93 43, serving seasonal specialties and its delicious house Côtes du Rhône from the Roaix-Séguret cooperative. Very popular, reserve early. In summer, dine on

the terrace overlooking the vineyards. Off-season, ask for a table by the window. Open mid-April through October.

In Gigondas, the **Montmirail***** Route de Vacqueyras (90 65 82 50 FAX 90 65 81 50, has 46 neat rooms, moderately priced, and a pool amid prestigious vineyards at the foot of the Dentelles.

In Beaumes-de-Venise, **Auberge Saint-Roch**, in the village (90 62 94 29, is a quaint little inn with fresh, well-prepared local fare at moderate prices and four pleasant rooms, 240 francs for a double.

Camping

Camping Municipal Roquefigueur is an attractive, newly renovated shaded site with 40 places on the Route de Lafare at the entrance to Beaumes-de-Venise (90 62 95 07. It is next to the town swimming pool. Open April 1 to the end of October.

WINE TASTING

There are outstanding **wine cooperatives** in **Roaix-Séguret**, **Sablet**, **Gigondas**, **Vacqueyras** and **Beaumes-de-Venise**, all making *AOC* Côtes du Rhône wine, and the Beaumes-de-Venise cooperative also sells its delicious Muscat de Beaumes-de-Venise, a sweet aperitif wine. Some outstanding individual producers whose caves you can visit are **Domaine du Pesquier** (90 65 86 16 in Gigondas and **Domaine de la Monardière** (90 65 87 20 and **Château de Montmirail** (90 65 86 72 in Vacqueyras. For an especially beautiful drive through the Dentelles de Montmirail wine country, take the road from Beaumes-de-Venise in the direction of Malaucène and follow the signs for the **Château Redortier** (90 62 96 43 in **Suzette**. Motor 15 minutes up into the hills to the De Menthon family's vineyard that nestles amid white limestone crags at the top of the Dentelles. The Château itself is not fancy, but it makes outstanding Gigondas and Beaumes-de-Venise Côtes du Rhône wines, and the view is spectacular.

CARPENTRAS

All roads in the middle of the Comtat lead through Carpentras. And since you are bound to get lost trying to find your way through it, the signs being amazingly hard to follow, you may as well stop and look around. It is a big, busy town of 26,000, the hub of the central Vaucluse. Carpentras was the administrative center of the Papal Comtat Venaissin from 1320 until the French Revolution, and it had an important place in Jewish history in France. From 1342 onward, Jews were offered special protection here, as in other localities in the Comtat, where quarters called "carrières" (from the Provençal word meaning street) were set aside for them. After the expulsion of the Jews from the Kingdom of France in the late Middle Ages, the Papal properties of Avignon and the Comtat became their only safe haven on the territory that is now France.

This was not all done out of Christian charity, however. Along with the special protection came some very special taxes.

GENERAL INFORMATION

The **Tourist Office** is at 170 Allée Jean-Jaurès across from the marketplace (90 63 57 88.

There is a fair in mid-July, **Corso de Nuit**, with theater, song and folk arts.

The main gate and shady fountain of the medieval village of Séguret in the Dentelles de Montmirail.

WHAT TO SEE

The **Porte Juive** (Jewish Portal), built in the 1470's, is the richly decorated Gothic Flamboyant south door of **Saint-Siffrien Cathedral**. It got its nickname at the end of the fifteenth century, when Jews entered it to be baptized as Christians in order to escape discrimination and persecution, which were widespread despite the "special protection." The cathedral itself was started in 1404 and completed in 1519. Its interior is elaborately decorated, and there is a glorious gilded wood Baroque altarpiece by the sculptor Jacques Bernus, a native of the area, whose work can also be seen in the **local museum**.

The **Synagogue**, the oldest in France, was first built in the fifteenth century, but was rebuilt in the eighteenth century and has the look of that period, full-blown Baroque. Some fourteenth century ritual baths remain. It fronts on the **Place de la Mairie** and is open weekdays from 10 AM to 5 PM, closed to the public on Saturdays, Sundays and Jewish holidays.

There is a large **market** Friday mornings extending from Les Halles in the heart of the old city out to the long, plane tree-shaded Allée Jean-Jaurès.

Carpentras is famed for its *berlingots*, a caramel sweet. You will not regret trying **Confiserie Daussy's** version. They can be found at Rue Porte-de-Mazin. The **Confiserie Villeneuve-Hardy's** at 288 Avenue Notre-Dame-de-Santé are also delicious.

WHERE TO STAY AND WHERE TO EAT

Le Fiacre** 153 Rue Vigne (90 63 03 15, is a little hotel of great charm with 20 inexpensive to moderately-priced rooms right in the center of the old town. No restaurant. For that, try **Le Vert-Gallant** at 12 Rue de Clapies (90 67 15 50, where imaginative Jacques Méjean knows how to make the most of the fresh products of Carpentras's market. The three-course weekday luncheon menu is 95 francs, more ambitious menus are 160 francs and up.

Camping

There are no camping grounds in Carpentras itself, but a number of attractive ones in the countryside nearby. **Camping Le Ventoux** is a deluxe site at **Mazan** seven kilometers (four miles) east of town with 49 places and a pool, open all year (90 69 70 94. **Camping le Brigoux** is another upscale site with 197 places in **Aubignan**, five kilometers (three miles) north of town (90 62 62 50, open March 15 to the end of October. **Camping Le Bouquer** is a modest 35-place site, open from mid-May to mid-September; it is in **Caromb**, five kilometers (four miles) northeast of town (90 62 30 13.

HOW TO GET THERE

Carpentras is the transportation hub of the central Vaucluse. There are bus connections ever hour from Avignon, less frequently from the other directions. For schedules, contact the Tourist Office. If you are driving, the main roads are D 942 from Avignon 25 km (16 miles) away, D 950 from Orange 23 km (14 miles) away, and D 938 from Vaison-la-Romaine to the north and Isle-sur-la-Sorgue and Cavaillon to the south.

ISLE-SUR-LA-SORGUE

As you drive south from Carpentras, you will see that the River Sorgue branches out into little fingers and irrigation canals, some dating from the time of the Popes, that wend their way to the Ouvèze and the Rhône. One branch filled the moat that encircled the ramparts of Avignon. The water of the Sorgue is cool. It creates a micro-climate that is very different from that of most of Provence — moist and green, with market gardens rather than vineyards — one of the richest vegetable growing areas in France. Long rows of old cypresses protect the fields from the mistral.

Isle-sur-la-Sorgue is called "the Venice of Provence," but looks more like a canal town in northern Europe — shady streets, cafes alongside canals, mossy water wheels, relics of the town's once-thriving silk industry, all in Manet-like tones of dark green. This is a graceful, sophisticated town of 13,000 with many art galleries and antique shops at the **Village des Antiquaires de la Gare** near the trains station, open Saturday, Sunday and Monday. There is a **flea market** on Sundays on the **Avenue des Quatre-Otages**, and dealers come from all over Europe for the big **antique auctions** twice a year, at Easter and August 15.

The **Tourist Office** is on the central square, Place de l'Église (90 38 04 78.

WHERE TO EAT

La Guinguette, on the canal at Partage-des-Eaux (90 38 10 61, is an old-fashioned cafe-dance hall with an outdoor terrace under the plane trees by the edge of the Sorgue with fresh, tasty Provençal menus starting at 85 francs.

HOW TO GET THERE

Isle-sur-la-Sorgue is 17 km (10.5 miles) from Carpentras on D 938, and 26 km (16 miles) from Avignon on N 100. There are buses from Avignon practically every hour.

FONTAINE-DE-VAUCLUSE

The Fontaine-de-Vaucluse is a mysterious natural fountain in a valley 10 km (six miles) east of Isle-sur-la-Sorgue that is the source of the River Sorgue. The Latin *vallis clausa* (closed valley) is the origin of the name Vaucluse.

Petrarch lived here for sixteen years and sat by the river writing sonnets about Laura de Noves, a young woman he first saw at church in Avignon on April 6, 1327. He was overwhelmed by her beauty, but she was married and, luckily for the development of lyric poetry, a virtuous lady, attainable only in flights of verse.

series of costly high-tech probes in the early 1980's.

Le **Monde Souterrain de Norbert Casteret** (the Underground World of Norbert Casteret) is a collection of rock formations brought together by the renowned speleologist from his thirty years of explorations under the earth, with stalagmites and stalactites, subterranean rivers and waterfalls that have been imaginatively reconstructed in caves, and there are audio-visual displays on the attempts to find the source of the Fontaine. Open daily from 10 PM to 6 PM in June, July and August; closed Tuesdays the rest of the year from November 15 to the end of February.

Unfortunately, the tranquillity that attracted the poet is shattered in the summer, when tens of thousands of tourists ride into the valley every day and are bombarded with tacky souvenirs. Come here off-season if at all possible. The **Tourist Office** is on Chemin de la Fontaine, the walkway leading to the fountain (90 20 32 22.

WHAT TO SEE

From a clear, perpetually self-renewing pool at the foot of a 200 m (650 ft) rock cliff in a narrow valley in the Vaucluse Plateau, the cool water of the **Fontaine-de-Vaucluse** rushes downhill with impressive force to form the River Sorgue. The source of this water is a mystery that has defied all attempts to locate it. Commander Cousteau failed in three separate explorations, as did a

Next door is the big water wheel and machinery of **Vallis Clausa**, a paper mill that demonstrates how paper was made in the fifteenth century. It has an attractive gift shop.

The **Musée de la Résistance**, opened in 1990, is devoted to France during World War II, with absorbing displays on the collaborationist Pétain government and on the Résistance, which was very active in the town of Fontaine-le-Vaucluse and in the nearby Lubéron. Open daily except Tuesdays from 10 AM to 12 PM and 2 PM to 6 PM from Easter to All Saints Day and weekends only the rest of the year.

Fontaine de Vaucluse, site of the mysterious source of the Sorgue River, where the poet Petrarch lived... .

WHERE TO EAT

Two fine restaurants with dining terraces over-looking the river and luncheon menus at 125 francs or less are **Le Parc (90 20 31 57** and **L'Hostellerie du Château (90 20 31 54.**

CAMPING

There are good camping grounds in the area of Fontaine-de-Vaucluse. **Camping Municipal les Prés** is a pleasant 42-place site in town (90 20 32 38, open all year. Caping La Coutelière in Galas two and a half kilometer (about a mile and a half) south of town on the banks of the Sorgue has 80 places and is open mid-March to the end of October (90 20 33 97. It has a pool and tennis court.

HOW TO GET THERE

Fontaine-de-Vaucluse is 33 km (21 miles) east of Avignon, seven kilometers (four miles) east of Isle-sur-la-Sorgue. There are eight buses a day from Isle-sur-la-Sorgue, four from Avignon.

THE LUBÉRON

The Lubéron is a discreet rural retreat of chic Parisians that became famous in the English-speaking world when Peter Mayle's tongue-in-cheek narrative of his adventures renovating his house in the area, *A Year in Provence*, became a best-seller in 1989. The British arrived, much to the annoyance of the Northerners who got there before Mr. Mayle.

The Lubéron comprises the wooded range of the Montagne du Lubéron and a lovely farm valley with the little Coulon River flowing through it. The Lubéron starts about 25 km (15 miles) east of Avignon and runs east-west some 50 km (30 miles), with Route N 100 running straight down the middle. On the north it is bounded by the Vaucluse Plateau and the south by the Durance River. Much of the Lubéron is part of a 130,000 hectare (312,000 acre) natural preserve, the Parc Naturel Régional du Lubéron, created in 1977, with 51 towns and villages included in it.

The most interesting towns to visit are in the western half of the Lubéron — **Gordes, Roussillon, Bonnieux, Lacoste** and **Oppède-le-Vieux.** Lovers of the great outdoors should head for eastern half, where there are plenty of camp sites and hiking trails through this heavily forested part of the Montagne du Lubéron. The Lubéron is a restful area with few sites of real cultural importance,

ABOVE: Gordes, the most luxurious town in the chic Lubéron. OPPOSITE: The Abbey of Sénanque near Gordes, one of the exquisite twelfth century Cistercian monasteries known as "The Three Sisters of Provence."

a nice breather for those who have over-done it in Aix or Avignon. But a word of warning: accommodations are very limited. If you want to stay here in the summer, you must book months in advance. For assistance, contact Vaucluse Tourisme Hébergement in Avignon (see GENERAL INFORMATION, page 196).

Since the area is close to Avignon to the west and Aix to the south, day-trips can be made from either city by coach or private vehicle.

GORDES

The hilltop town of Gordes, whose dramatic profile has been seen on many a travel poster, was the

first town in the Lubéron to undergo full-scale gentrification in the 1960's, thanks to the support of Minister of Culture André Malraux. There are good **crafts shops,** and for those who want to stay in the Lubéron, Gordes has the most hotels and restaurants. But they are expensive.

The **Tourist Office** is in the Château (90 72 02 75.

What to See

The **Château** dominates the town, an eleventh century fortress replaced in the sixteenth century by a Renaissance palace. Inside there is a magnificent Renaissance fireplace. The two upper floors house the **Vasarély Didactic Museum,** showing the development of Victor Vasarély's work from his intriguing early realistic and Surrealist efforts to the full-blown Op-Art for which he became world famous. Open 10 AM to 12 PM and 2 PM to 6 PM, closed Tuesdays except in July and August.

Dry-masonry huts called *bories*, igloos made of flat stones, abound in the area around Gordes. They look prehistoric, but most date from the seventeenth century or later. Some were shepherds' huts, others apparently refuges from town in times of plague. There is a heavily promoted **Village of Bories** off Route D 2 a few kilometers outside of Gordes. If you are traveling with kids, they can have fun romping from *borie* to *borie*. But for adults this pseudo-historical tourist-trap is not worth the 25 francs. With 3,000 *bories* in the area, you can see all you want as you drive around.

Dramatically set in a deep, narrow valley three kilometers (two miles) north of Gordes, the **Abbaye de Sénanque** is the most beautiful of the twelfth century Cistercian abbeys known as the "Three Sisters of Provence." All were built on the same pattern, but unlike its uncompromisingly austere sisters of Le Thoronet and Silvacane, Sénanque has allowed a slight touch of roundness to creep into its design. Without diminishing its purity in the least, the bay of the church adds an appealing softness to the overall effect.

Sénanque is a working monastery occupied by a Cistercian monastic community, and part of the complex is reserved to them, but the original twelfth century parts are open to the public. They include the scriptorium, where the monks copied manuscripts, the only room that was heated; the chapter house; the church, with its purity; the cloister; and the refectory. The buildings have been kept in exactly the state they were in when they were built eight hundred years ago. Sénanque is especially attractive in July when the field of lavender in front of it is in flower.

The abbey is open to visitors from 10 AM to 12 PM and 2 PM to 6 PM April through September except on Sunday mornings, and open afternoons only the rest of the year. In the summer religious music is performed in the church.

Le Thoronet, Sénanque's sister abbey in the Var is described on page 158. The third sister, **Silvacane**, lies on the south bank of the Durance, about halfway between Gordes and Aix. It is used in the summer for concerts of the prestigious International Piano Festival of La Roque d'Anthéron.

Saint-Pantaléon five kilometers (three miles) south of Gordes on D 104, is the smallest community in Provence, with a surface of 78 hectares (190 acres). The core of its tiny Romanesque **church of Saint-Pantaléon** dates from the fifth century. Little **sarcophagi** are cut into the rock outcropping upon which the church is built, put there for children who died before being baptized. The child would be laid in a sarcophagus, a Mass would be said, the child would be considered to have come back to life long enough to be baptized, then to have died again in a state of grace. The church is kept locked. To see it, get the key from the innkeeper down the street.

The village of **Roussillon** 10 km (six miles) east of Gordes is so-named because of the reddish color (*rousse*) of the earth of the sheer-cliffed plateau it sits on. The material is ochre. It was mined by the people of the area and used as pigment for paint, bringing prosperity to the village until synthetic pigments came along. This is a quiet village noted mainly for its tranquillity and unusual site. It was also the place where Samuel Beckett spent the dark years of the World War II Occupation and served as a courier for the Résistance. The **Tourist Office** is at Place de la Poste (90 05 60 25.

Where to Stay and Where to Eat

On the expensive side, the **Bastide de Gordes****** in Gordes (90 72 12 12 FAX 90 72 05 20, is a noble Renaissance residence on the hillside of town, now a refined 18-room hotel with a pool cut into the rock and a grand view of the Lubéron. **Les**

Bories**** on the Route de Sénanque, two kilometers out of Gordes (90 72 00 51 FAX 90 72 01 22, is a picturesque hotel on eight hectares (20 acres) of private park, with some of its 17 deluxe rooms in authentic bories, indoor and outdoor pools, a tennis court and a view of Gordes. The restaurant is small, mainly for hotel guests; non-guests must reserve well in advance. **Mas des Herbes Blanches****** Route des Murs in **Joucas**, eight kilometers (five miles) east of Gordes (90 05 79 79 FAX 90 05 71 96, is an elegant country house in the middle of 10 hectares (24 acres) of sweet-smelling *garrigue* (wild herbs, flowers and grasses) with 16 pretty guest rooms. There's a pool, tennis court and the top restaurant in the northern Lubéron, serving sophisticated Provençal cuisine (brochettes of grilled prawns with rosemary, slices of young pigeon breast with *tapenade*). One Michelin star. A Relais & Châteaux member.

Provence

The **Ferme de la Huppe**, five kilometers (three miles) east of Gordes on D 2 (90 72 12 25 FAX 90 72 01 83, is an eighteenth century farm with eight moderately-priced guest rooms, swimming pool and an expensive restaurant that serves some of the area's best Provençal country cuisine.

Auberge de Carcarille** is an 11 room inn in the countryside in **Les Gervais** four kilometers (two and a half miles) south of Gordes on D 2 (90 72 02 63 FAX 90 72 05 74. It has a swimming pool and peaceful location, and its room rates are at the lower end of the moderate range (310 to 360 francs), quite reasonable for the quality and the location. It is a Logis de France member.

The dramaticaly hued cliffs of the village of Roussillon in the Lubéron, where ochre for paints was once mined.

CAMPING

Camping des Sources is a well-shaded 200-place site with a swimming pool two kilometers from Gordes on the Route de Murs (90 72 12 48. It is open from April 1 to the end of October.

How to Get There

There are three buses a day to Gordes from Cavaillon, which has frequent bus connections with Avignon. By car, Gordes can be reached via N 100, the road through the center of the Lubéron, and D 2. Coming from Fontaine-de-Vaucluse, take D 100 through the hills, a distance of 16 km (10 miles).

THE COLORADO DE RUSTREL

For more ochre and plenty of it, drive east to **Rustrel** about 20 km (12.5 miles) past Roussillon and follow the signs for the carrières d'ocre, the ochre quarries. Known as the Colorado de Rustrel, this 15 sq km (10 sq miles) expanse of open-pit mines was exploited between 1871 and 1930, when it was abandoned. The wind and the rain have sculpted strange natural forms, and the 22 shades of color, from bright yellows to deep reds are truly amazing. For the best color for photographs, come in the late afternoon.

APT

Plunked square in the middle of the valley, Apt is the commercial center of the Lubéron with a

population of 11,500. It has been famed for centuries for its candied fruit, as beautiful as they are sweet. Mme. de Sévigné loved them. The **Aptunion** candied fruit factory skillfully follows the old tradition, and you can watch them at work in the Quartier Salignan, two kilometers out of the center of town on the Route d'Avignon. Aptunion is especially noted for its magic with cherries. They also sell nougat, *callisons*, unusual jams and jellies and fruits preserved in alcohol at low factory prices.

Apt is also the gateway to the nearby **Parc Naturel Régional du Lubéron** (Lubéron regional nature park), and the **Maison du Parc** has an information center and exhibits on the plants and wildlife of the Lubéron. They publish a brochure *20 Promenades et Randonnées dans le Parc Naturel Régional du Lubéron* (20 Walks and Rambles in the Lubéron Nature Park) that suggests walking, bicycling and horseback itineraries. It is at 1 Place Jean-Jaurès in the heart of the old town (90 74 08 55.

For ambience and quality, Apt's Saturday morning **market** that winds through the town from Place de la Bouquerie to Place de la Mairie is one of the most authentic in all of Provence. If you find yourself anywhere near Apt on a Saturday, it is well worth the effort to get here for it.

The **Tourist Office** for the Pays d'Apt (Apt Country) is located on Place de la Bouquerie at the entrance to the old part of town (90 74 03 18.

Where to Stay and Where to Eat

There are clean, comfortable, moderately-priced little inns scattered throughout the Lubéron, most with pools and tennis courts, and there are even a few inexpensive ones. Logis de France has 24 member hotels in the Lubéron. **Lou Caleu**** in **Saint-Martin-de-Castillon** north of Apt near the Colorado de Rustrel (90 75 28 88 FAX 90 75 25 49 is an example, with 16 tasteful rooms, a restaurant serving French and Provençal dishes, pool and tennis court. The **Saint-Paul**** in **Viens** (90 75 21 47 FAX 90 75 30 80 is a handsome old farm in wooded hills 12 km (seven and a half miles) east of Apt converted with care into a 21-room hotel, with a pool and tennis court and farmhouse-style restaurant with traditional French and Provençal cuisine. Prices are moderate at both these hotels. Reserve long in advance.

CAMPING

There are two camping sites in Apt, the modest 50-place **Camping Municipal Les Cèdres** 300 m outside of town on the Route de Rustrel (90 74 14 61, open all year, and the more luxurious 100-place **Camping du Lubéron** on the Route de Saignon, open from Easter to October 30 (90 04 85 40. For a list of sites in more remote areas, contact the Tourist Office.

How to Get There

There are five buses a day from Avignon, a trip of somewhat over an hour, depending on the route the bus takes. For details, contact the Tourist Office. By car, take N 100 from Avignon.

Le Grand Lubéron

The Lubéron range stretches out from east to west "like a big blue whale," as writer Jean Giono called it. To the southeast of Apt, the tallest and most heavily forested part of it centers on the Mourre Nègre, at 1,125 m (3,700 ft) the highest point in the range, with a tall telecommunications tower at the top. Hikers will find a vast panoramic view,

with humpbacked Mont-Ventoux looming to the north and Montagne Saint-Victoire, a white whale, to the south.

Fort de Buoux south from Apt is another high point hikers will enjoy climbing to. Here you will find the hilltop ruins of a medieval fortress destroyed in the seventeenth century by Louis XIV because it had become a Protestant stronghold. It was the successor to Roman and Ligurian fortresses, whose stones can be seen among the ruins. There is a view of the narrow valley of the Aigue Brun, the stream that separates the Grand Lubéron from the Petit Lubéron.

Where to Stay

The **Auberge des Seguins**, reached by D 113 up the hill from the town of **Buoux** (90 74 16 37, is a Logis de France inn with 27 rooms in a colorful complex of rustic stone houses built into the hillside

Provence

below the fort. It has a swimming pool and a restaurant serving hearty meals featuring fresh local products, such as trout from the mountain streams, and something that is extremely rare in these parts — low prices. Rooms go for 190 to 250 francs demi-pension, and a meal will cost you about 100 francs.

Le Petit Lubéron

The southwestern part of valley is known as "Peter Mayle country" to the English, the "Petit Lubéron" to the French. In the late nineteenth and early twentieth centuries, most of the population of this area migrated to the cities, and many of

these towns started to fall into ruin. But in the late 1950's artists, craftsmen and *le Tout-Paris* discovered the area, and it became fashionable to buy a house here and fix it up, all the more so in the affluent decades that followed. Anti-snob snobs may sneer at the palpable chic of these villages. On the other hand, if it weren't for gentrification, most would be ghost towns today. Some are still partly abandoned.

The most picturesque spots in the Petit Lubéron are the perched villages of **Bonnieux, Lacoste, Ménerbes,** and **Oppède-le-Vieux,** which are pleasant to stroll in. The **Marquis de Sade's Château** on the hilltop in Lacoste may be interest-

The Pont Julien across the Coulon River OPPOSITE on the Roman Empire's Domitian Way, leading to the ochre-toned village of Roussillon ABOVE LEFT. ABOVE RIGHT: A café in Gordes.

ing to visit some day, but at the snail's pace its private restoration project is moving, it will be years before it is ready. This is the place where the divine Marquis orchestrated the monster debauch during the winter of 1774–1775 that landed him in the Bastille for twelve years. The book he wrote in prison, *The 120 Days of Sodom*, made him a household name. The *château* was destroyed during the Revolution and is closed to the public. To see it, make an appointment with owner André Bouer (90 75 80 39.

At the **Musée de la Boulangerie**, 12 Rue de la République, Bonnieux (90 75 88 34, you can see the ancient process of bread-making, in a woodburning stove built in 1844, and study the history of the staff of life. Open 10 AM to 12 PM and 3 PM to 6:30 PM June through September, except Tuesdays; open weekends September through May; closed January ad February. The **Tourist Office** is at Place Carnot (90 75 91 90.

Where to Stay and Where to Eat

The **Hostellerie du Prieuré***** the Village, Bonnieux (90 75 80 78, is a seventeenth century priory with a garden, at the foot of the ramparts of the old village, with 10 antique-furnished rooms, a fireplace and good country cooking. **Le Fournil** is a pretty restaurant in the heart of the village of Bonnieux with a dining terrace by the fountain at 5 Place Carnot (90 75 83 62, serving bright luncheon menus at 90 francs.

CAMPING

The modest **Camping Municipal du Vallon** on Route de Ménerbes is open from March 15 to the end of September (90 75 86 14.

How to Get There

There are three buses a day from Avignon to Bonnieux, a one-hour ride, and three from Apt, a 20-minute ride. By car, Bonnieux can be reached

by N 100 and D 36 from Avignon, or by a number of possible roads from Aix about 40 km (25 miles) to the south.

AVIGNON TO NÎMES

In the heyday of the Roman Empire, Nîmes was one of the key cities of Provincia Romana, the link between the road to Rome and the road to Spain, and it has retained the most impressive architectural ensemble from that period of any city in France. This Roman heritage links Nîmes closely with the Roman cities of Provence — Orange, Vaison-la-Romaine, Saint-Rémy and Arles. So, for reasons of historical and cultural continuity as well as the ease of visiting Nîmes from Avignon or Arles, short drives or train rides away, we include Nîmes and its surrounding area in our itinerary of Provence, even though it lies west of the

Rhône in the modern political region of Languedoc-Roussillon rather than Provence-Alpes-Côte d'Azur.

Using Avignon as our starting point, we head for the Pont du Gard, the famous bridge of Nîmes's aqueduct system. It sits 26 km (16 miles) straight west of Avignon via Route N 100.

PONT DU GARD

The Pont du Gard is one of the engineering masterpieces of classical antiquity. Built by Agrippa in 19 BC, this beautifully preserved aqueduct bridge spans a gorge over the Gardon (or Gard) River about 20 km (12.5 miles) northeast of Nîmes. It is part of a 50 km/30 mile-long system

The Pont du Gard aqueduct, a masterpiece of Roman engineering, provided the water for the city of Nîmes.

that brought water down to the city from the source of the Eure River in the hills near Uzès. The bridge is 275 m (900 ft) long and 49 m (160 ft) high with three tiers of rounded arches that are wide on the bottom and middle levels and narrow on the upper level, and you can walk along the top. Boats and kayaks are available for rental along the river, and the river is suitable for swimming. The best time is at sundown.

A word of warning: don't leave anything you can't afford to lose in your car in the parking lot. This is one of the most visited sites in France, and there is a great deal of thievery.

There is a Tourist Office on the right bank of the river about 200 m from the bridge (66 37 00

02. It is open from April 1 through the end of September.

Where to Stay and Where to Eat

The **Vieux Castillon****** in **Castillon-du-Gard** (66 37 00 77 FAX 66 37 28 17, is a delightful 33-room Relais & Châteaux hotel with tennis courts and a large swimming pool in a tiny medieval village perched on a rock near the Pont du Gard, with superb truffle-laced Provençal cuisine in its restaurant. The rooms and meals are expensive, but the 200 franc luncheon menu is an excellent value.

It is four kilometers (two and a half miles) from the Pont du Gard on Route D 228. Another ensem-

ble of old stone buildings converted into a lovely inn is the **Hostellerie Le Castellas*****on Grande Rue, the tiny main street of **Collias** a few kilometers west of the Pont du Gard (66 22 88 99 FAX 66 22 84 28. This friendly hotel has 14 artistically renovated rooms, a pool and flowery garden and a restaurant with savory regional cuisine. Rooms run 440 to 590 francs, fixed-price menus from 165 francs. **Collias**, reached by D 981 and D 112, is a sweet little village, once a haven for hippies, where you can rent kayaks and paddle on the river.

CAMPING

Camping International des Gorges du Gardon, Chemin de la Barque Vieille (66 22 81 81, is a large, well-shaded camping ground with 180 places, a snack bar and swimming pool, on the bank of the river by the Pont du Gard, open March 15 to October 15. Reserve long in advance. The more deluxe **Camping le Barralet** is in **Collias**, seven kilometers (four miles) to the west along the river (66 22 84 52. It has 90 places and is open from Easter to the end of September.

How to Get There

There are six buses per day from Avignon, ten from Nîmes and Uzès. For schedules, check with the Tourist Office. By car, it is 26 km (16 miles) from Avignon via N 100 to Remoulins and D 981 to the Pont du Gard. From Nîmes, it is 23 km (14 miles) via N 86 to Remoulins and D 981.

UZÈS

"O, little Uzès! If you were in Umbria, tourists would run from Paris to see you!," wrote André Gide. Uzès is an aristocratic hill town of exceptional charm, the seat of the Dukes of Uzès, the highest-ranking noble family of France in the seventeenth century. It sits on a little plateau 15 km (nine miles) northwest of the Pont du Gard above treeless countryside covered with scrub brush, wild herbs and grasses known as garrigue. Rosemary, thyme, sage, lavender, iris and orchids are among the plants that create its powerful aroma. The scents in the Spring make it an especially pleasurable time to visit.

GENERAL INFORMATION

The **Tourist Office** is on Avenue de la Libération (66 22 68 88, next to the large public parking area at the western entrance to the old town. The bus station is next door (66 22 00 58.

WHAT TO SEE AND WHAT TO DO

The main square is the **Place aux Herbes**, tree-shaded and framed by arcaded houses. The **weekly**

ABOVE: The Palace of the Dukes of Uzès.
OPPOSITE: A back street in Uzès, one of the most elegant towns in Southern France, and one of the most pleasant to stroll in.

market centers here and spills out all over town. It is one of the liveliest, most colorful, best-provisioned of all Provençal markets. There are oysters from Bouzigues, sausages from Arles, cheeses from Haute Provence and the Cévennes, wine from the Rhône Valley, lavender honey and a fine selection of regional crafts and fabrics. If you have time for only one market on your trip, this is the one I would recommend. It is held on Saturday mornings.

The **Palace of the Dukes of Uzès** began as a fortress in the eleventh century, and new sections were added regularly up to the time of Louis XV. As a result, it is a living catalogue of French *château* architecture. It can be visited from 9:30 AM to 12 PM and 2:30 to 6 PM from April 1 to the end of Septem-

noons in the summer, afternoons and weekends the rest of the year). Another literary great with links to Uzès was Jean Racine. His family sent him here as a youngster in hopes that he would forget the theater. He is said to have meditated at the **Pavillon Racine**, a belvedere near the Cathedral that overlooks a wide expanse of *garrigue*. Young Jean enjoyed Uzès and wrote to his friends in Paris, "Our nights are more beautiful than your days." But the first chance he got, he went back to Paris.

WHERE TO STAY AND WHERE TO EAT

The **Hôtel d'Entraigues***** Place de l'Évêché (66 22 32 68 FAX 66 22 57 01, is a fifteenth century

ber and closes at nightfall the rest of the year. Seventeenth century **Cathédrale Saint-Théodorit** has an imposing organ from the period of Louis XIV that is played at the **Nuits Musicales d'Uzès**, the classical music festival in July (for information, call the Office de Tourisme). The twelfth century **Tour Fenestrelle** is a rounded Lombard-style campanile of six storeys with many windows, the only one of its kind in France, and the sole remains of the medieval cathedral destroyed by the Protestants in the Wars of Religion. The **Municipal Museum** in the former Episcopal Palace next to Cathedral has a collection of André Gide memorabilia; his family was from Uzès, and he spent a good deal of time here (open mornings and after-

mansion across from the Archbishop's Palace with 19 restful rooms, swimming pool and the best restaurant in town, the **Jardins de Castille**. Room and food prices are moderate. For an elegant *château* in the country, try the **Hôtel Marie d'Agoult***** in **Arpaillargues**, five kilometers (three miles) west of Uzès on D 982 (66 22 14 48 FAX 66 22 56 10. This seventeenth century *château* has 26 tasteful rooms, a swimming pool and tennis courts, a large private park and fine restaurant with a 140 franc luncheon menu. Rooms are in the 750 to 850 franc range. A Relais de Silence member, open mid-March to mid-November. Another good place to eat in the area is the charming, rustic **Auberge Saint-Maximin** in the village of **Saint-Maximin** on D 891, the road to Pont du Gard, five and a half kilometers (three and a half miles) from Uzès, serving flavorful country cooking at modest prices (66 22 26 41.

At a Provençal-style market, such as the one at Uzès ABOVE LEFT and RIGHT, all manner of local products is sold, crafts items and fabrics as well as foods.

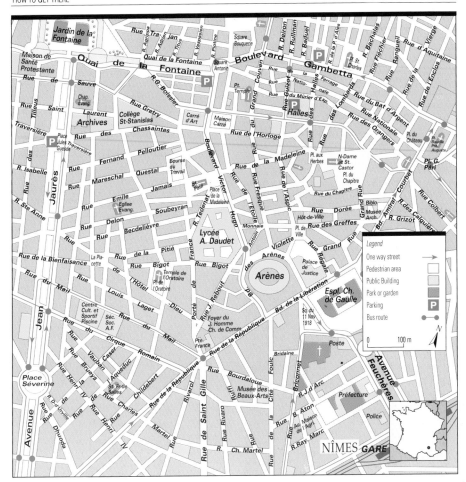

Camping

The **Camping Municipal du Val de l'Eure** has 70 places by the river with the municipal pool and tennis courts nearby, open June 15 to September 15. It is on the road to Bagnols-sur-Cèze (D 982), 500 m from the center of Uzès (66 22 11 79. The 50-place **Camping La Paillote** is just up the the road in Quartier Grezac (66 22 38 55. It has a pool and is open from March 20 to October 20. **Camping Le Moulin Neuf**, three and a half kilometers (two miles) north of town on the road to Saint-Quentin-la-Poterie (66 22 17 21, is a spacious 100-place site in the *garrigue* with a swimming pool and tennis courts, open April 1 to the end of September. There are several others in the vicinity. The Tourist Office has a list.

HOW TO GET THERE

There are 10 buses a day from Nîmes. If you are driving, Nîmes is 25 km (16 miles) to the south on D 979.

NÎMES

After decades of slumbering on its Roman laurels, this city of 125,000 known as "the Rome of France" woke up in 1983 and elected Jean Bousquet Mayor, a post he held for 12 years. Mayor Bousquet came into office with a passion for modern architecture, a vision of how to blend it with Nîmes's past, and the wherewithal to bring it to fruition. The result is an array of public buildings and monuments by famous modern artists, designers and architects such as Jean Nouvel, Philippe Starck and Martial Raysse. Norman Foster's elegant art exhibition center and library the Carré d'Art opened in 1993 facing the first century AD Maison Carrée. Unlike the provocatively ultra-modern Centre Georges Pompidou built in Paris in 1977, which many people still consider an affront to good taste, the new buildings in Nîmes counterpoint rather than clash with the city's architectural heritage.

Incongruously, Nîmes is also the bullfighting capital of France. Only Madrid and Seville have more *corridas* than Nîmes.

BACKGROUND

Nemausus was the name of a water spirit worshiped by the Ligurian Volcae Arecomici tribe. He lived in the spring that is now part of the Jardin de la Fontaine, around which the tribe settled. In 121 BC, the Romans took control of the area, and with its key position on the road between Italy and Spain, the town of Nemausus started to grow. When the original spring proved too small for the Romans' large water needs, they

built the aqueduct of which the Pont du Gard is part to bring water down from the Cévennes, providing 44 million gallons a day. Nîmes grew to a population of more than 20,000 and became one of the most prosperous cities in Gaul. After the fall of Rome, Nîmes was overrun by the Visigoths, Saracens and Franks before coming under the rule of the Counts of Toulouse. As supporters of the Cathars, Nîmes suffered during the Albigensian Crusade, and as one of the principal cities of Protestantism, it was caught up for centuries in ravages of the Wars of Religion. Nevertheless, under the direction of its Protestant bourgeois, a prosperous cloth manufacturing industry developed. In the seventeenth century,

A café on the Place aux Herbes in Nîmes ABOVE. OPPOSITE: The Roman arena in Nîmes, is used regularly for bullfights TOP, circuses and pop concerts BELOW.

they invented a new way to make sturdy fabric from Egyptian cotton that they dyed blue and sold to be made into shepherd's capes, skirts for farm women, and workers' clothes. It sold well in Europe and eventually made its way to America, where, in 1848, a San Francisco clothing manufacturer named Levi Straus started using it to make sturdy pants for gold miners. The label on the shipment from France said "*de Nîmes.*" The Americans called it "denim." In the late twentieth century, when every young person in the world was wearing the product it invented, "The Rome of France" joined the modern world and transformed itself into one of the economic and cultural centers of the New South.

GENERAL INFORMATION

The city of Nîmes has **two Tourist Offices**. The main one is on 6 Rue Auguste, near the Maison Carrée (66 67 29 11. The other is at the Gare SNCF (66 84 18 13. They have excellent free brochures in several languages, including English, and a particularly helpful staff who will make hotel reservations for you in Nîmes and the surrounding area. They also run guided tours of the city in English.

For more information about the Département du Gard, contact the **Comité Départemental du Tourisme du Gard** at 3 Place des Arènes (66 21 02 51.

The following information might be helpful: **Nîmes-Garons Airport** (66 70 06 88. The **train terminal, Gare SNCF**, is on Boulevard du Sergent Triaire, a ten minute walk east of the Arena, (66 23 50 50. The **bus terminal, Gare Routière**, is on Rue Sainte-Felicité, behind the train station (66 29 52 00.

Taxis (66 29 93 33 or (66 29 40 11.

Bike rental, at the baggage room of the train station.

Car rental: **Avis**, 1 *bis* Rue de la République (66 21 00 29; **Budget**, 6 *bis* Avenue du Général Leclerc (66 29 88 08; **Hertz**, 39 Boulevard Gambetta (66 76 25 91; **Rent-a-Car**, 14 Avenue Georges Pompidou (66 62 30 40.

Medical emergencies, SAMU (15.

FESTIVALS

Nîmes has three major **bullfighting** festivals a year. In February, there is the **Feria du Carnaval**. In May, the **Feria de Pentecôte** (Pentecost), a ten-day festival. In the third week of September, **Feria des Vendanges**, the harvest festival.

Bullfighting is pursued with a passion in the area from the lower Rhône Valley to Spain. Two styles are practiced, Spanish style, with its pomp and colorful costumes, where the bulls are killed in the ring, and Provençal style, *à la cocarde*, where

nimble young men in white try to pluck a rosette from between the horns of the bull without getting gored, and the bulls are not put to death. Nîmes is the capital of *la tauromachie*, as Spanish-style bullfighting is known. But most people who go to the *ferias* are not *aficionados*. They go to party. They dance in the streets, frolic all night and drink wine at *bodegas*, informal bars that spring up everywhere. The meat of the bulls killed in the ring is sold to butchers and can be eaten in restaurants, the ultimate homage or the ultimate insult, depending on your point of view.

From the second week of July to the third week of August, **L'Été de Nîmes**, the summer cultural festival, puts on an ambitious program of dance,

classical folk, pop and rock music and street performances.

WHAT TO SEE

Les Arènes, Nîmes's 24,000-seat arena, is the best preserved of the seventy Romans amphitheaters in the world. Like the Roman theater in Orange, it owes its survival to the fact that it was converted into a fortress in the Middle Ages, and it later became a walled village. In the days of *Provincia Romana*, the arena was used for combats of gladiators and animals and could be flooded for aquatic events. In hot weather, it was covered by a huge awning. The holes for its support poles can be seen in the rock of the upper facade. Now it is converted to a 7,000-seat indoor theater from October to April by covering it with a huge translucent textile membrane and heating the interior space. Otherwise the arena is open-air and is used for pop, rock, and classical music concerts, operas, circuses and bullfights. It can be visited from 9 AM to 7 PM in the summer, 9 AM to 12 PM and 2 PM to 5:30 PM the rest of the year.

One block from the Arènes, in the café-lined **Place du Marché**, look at the fountain designed by Martial Raysse of a life-sized crocodile in chains, the emblem of the city, commemorating

the defeat of Antony and Cleopatra by Octavius in Egypt. **G. Courtois**, the Pâtissier-Confiseur-Glacier-Salon de Thé at 8 Place du Marché near the fountain is a good spot to pause for a delicious pastry or chocolates and coffee.

The **Maison Carrée**, the central landmark of the city, was built in 5 AD and is the best preserved of all Roman temples. Though "*carrée*" is French for "square", it is a rectangle, 26 m (85 ft) long by 15 m (50 ft) wide. Until the late Middle Ages, the term *carrée* was used to describe any figure with four right angles. It stands 17 m (56 ft) high, has 32 perfect Corinthian columns supporting its roof and sits on a pedestal 15 steps high. The Maison Carrée looks like the vastly larger Madeleine in Paris, for which it served as a model. It is used for temporary art exhibits, open from 9 AM to 7 PM in the summer, to 5:30 PM the rest of the year.

Directly across the square is the **Carré d'Art**, Norman Foster's homage to the Maison Carrée. The cool, airy, classically ordered glass and steel pavilion opened in 1993 and is the city's major art exhibition center, contemporary art museum and library. It is open from 11 AM to 6 PM, closed Monday.

One block up Boulevard Alphonse Daudet, named for the Nîmes-born author, is Martial Raysse's 1989 assembly of fountains and sculptures at **Place d'Assas**, which interprets the story of water in Nîmes with elegance and a modern sense of humor.

The nearby **Jardin de la Fontaine** is the eighteenth century re-working of Nîmes's original *raison d'être*, the spring of Nemausus, and the Roman baths, turned into an ornate public garden with canals lined with stone balustrades, statuary and shade trees. To the left of the spring are the ruins of the so-called Temple of Diana, which was more likely the library of the Roman baths. It was destroyed during the Wars of Religion. Brides and grooms traditionally have their pictures taken in the Jardin de la Fontaine. On a Saturday in June, as you look around, you can see half a dozen festively dressed wedding parties striking poses at the same time.

Take the stone staircase up the wooded hill overlooking the garden and follow the paths to the top of Mont Cavalier, 114 m (374 ft) high, where the **Tour Magne** stands. The ruins of this octagonal tower stands 30 m (almost 100 ft) tall and was obviously an important monument when the Romans built it in 15 BC, but nobody knows for sure what it was for. The panorama from the top of Mont Cavalier is the best in the city.

The Museums of Nîmes

The **Musée du Vieux Nîmes** (Museum of Old Nîmes), housed in the seventeenth century former bishop's palace, is the city's most interesting museum, covering the history of Nîmes and its surrounding area from the Middle Ages to the present, including the tragic Wars of Religion. It has a fascinating collection of textile patterns from the nineteenth century and furniture from the seventeenth century on. The museum puts on two special exhibits per year, always worth seeing. It is on the Place aux Herbes, near the Cathedral.

The **Musée Archéologique** has a rich collection of statues, ceramics and other finds from Gallo-Roman antiquity through the middle ages, with an outstanding collection of ancient coins. It is in a large seventeenth century Jesuit school at 13 *bis* Boulevard Amiral Courbet on the east side of town. The **Musée Taurin**, the bullfighting museum, and the **natural history museum** are also located here.

The **Musée des Beaux Arts** has old masters of the sixteenth and seventeenth centuries, principally from France, Germany and the Netherlands, some from Italy and Spain, and Roman mosaics. It is on Rue de la Cité Foulc to the south of the Arènes.

The **Musée d'Art Contemporain** at the Carré d'Art puts on ambitious exhibitions of contemporary art in its vast, airy galleries.

The museums are open from 11 AM to 6 PM, closed on Monday.

WHERE TO STAY

Expensive
Imperator Concorde**** Quai de la Fontaine (66 21 90 30 FAX 66 67 70 25 is a lovely old mansion on the Jardin de la Fontaine with 62 rooms decorated in Provençal style. **Le Cheval Blanc****** Place des Arènes (66 76 32 32 FAX 66 76 32 33, is a 26-room luxury hotel fronting on the Arena recently modernized by Jean-Michel Wilmotte.

Moderate

The **New Hôtel La Baume***** 21 Rue Nationale (66 76 28 42 FAX 66 76 28 45, is a tastefully modernized seventeenth century mansion in the heart of old Nîmes with 34 comfortable rooms at 380 francs. **Plazza**** 10 Rue Roussy (66 76 16 20 FAX 66 67 65 99, is a favorite of bullfighting *aficionados*, with 28 rooms in 1930's style. It's near the arena, with a top price of 420 francs.

Inexpensive

The **Listia**** 2 *bis* Boulevard des Arènes (66 67 66 20 FAX 66 76 22 30, is a much less expensive hotel favored by fans of the *corrida*, 24 of its rooms with private bath. The **Royal**** 34 Boulevard Alphonse Daudet (66 67 28 36 FAX 66 21 68 97, is a 31-room Art Deco hotel with lots of atmosphere. Favored by artists.

Camping
Camping du Domaine de la Bastide is an attractive 240-place site five kilometers (three miles) south of Nîmes on the Route de Générac near the Costières stadium (66 38 09 21. It is open all year. There are eleven other camping grounds in the vicinity of Nîmes and several others further afield. Ask for a list at the Tourist Office.

WHERE TO EAT

L'Enclos de la Fontaine at the Imperator Concorde is one of the city's top restaurants, and its flowery dining terrace is a good, though expensive, place to try *brandade de morue*, the garlic-fla-

vored codfish dish that is a specialty of Nîmes. **Le Cheval Blanc**, at the hotel of the same name, is an elegant gourmet restaurant serving top-rated Mediterranean (one Michelin star) cuisine, quite expensive. In the same hotel is the moderately-priced **Bistro des Costières**. **Le Caramel Mou** at 5 Rue Jean Reboul off Boulevard Victor Hugo (66 21 27 07, offers local specialties and fresh market cuisine in an amiable atmosphere, about 200 francs à la carte. A place I enjoy greatly is **Le P'tit Bec** at 87 *bis* Rue de la République (66 38 05 83, a pretty little garden restaurant with tasty regional fare and a good choice of Languedoc wines with menus starting at 90 francs. The

OPPOSITE: Nîmes's 5 AD Maison Carrée and its 1993 Carré d'Art, a library and art exhibition center. ABOVE: A bird handler at the medieval show at Beaucaire.

cabillaud à l'infusion d'estragon (fresh codfish in tarragon sauce) is excellent here. For wildly inventive gourmet dishes, such as a floating island of truffles on a sauce of wild mushrooms or *fricassée* of quail and sweetbreads with licorice, head out to Chef Michel Kayser's restaurant **Alexandre**, nine kilometers (six miles) from the center of town in **Garons** (66 70 08 99. This Michelin one-star establishment has an outstanding list of Costières de Nîmes wines.

WINE TASTING

Costières de Nîmes, formerly known as Costières du Gard is a one of the new *appellations* of Languedoc that has made great strides in improving quality. Its vineyards cover a large area of pebbly ground between the hills north of Nîmes and the edge of the Camargue. They make dry *rosés* and some whites, and are building a good reputation for their reds, which are similar to Côtes-du-Rhône, but less expensive.

At the **Château de la Tuilerie** on Route de Saint-Gilles next to the Golf de Campagne golf course you can sample the wines from their own estate and those of many other producers of Costières de Nîmes in their Jardins des Vins boutique. It is open Monday through Saturday (66 70 07 52.

HOW TO GET THERE

Air Inter has four flights a day from Orly to Nîmes-Garons Airport, eight kilometers (five miles) south of the city. There are eight TGV's from Paris, a four-and-a-half-hour trip, and many trains from Avignon and Arles (a 20 minute trip from each) and from Montpellier and points south, and Carcassonne and points west. There is **international bus service** on Iberbus from Spain ((66 29 50 62) and on Eurolines from many places in Europe ((66 29 49 02) and frequent **regional bus service** to and from Uzès, Pont du Gard, Aigues-Mortes, La Grande Motte and other towns of the Languedoc coast. All bus service is from the **Gare Routière** (66 29 52 00. By car, Nîmes is easily reached by a web of highways converging from every direction, including the A 9, La Languedocienne, the through route from the north that branches off from the A 7 at Orange and continues south to Spain.

BEAUCAIRE

In the days of the Roman Empire, Beaucaire was a key point on the route between Rome and Spain. 24 km (15 miles) east of Nîmes on the west bank of the Rhône, it was the port where you crossed the river to or from Tarascon on the other side. The

Roman road stayed in use long after the collapse of Empire, and in the Middle Ages, strategically situated Beaucaire became the site of a huge, tremendously colorful fair to which as many as 300,000 traders and merchants came from all over Europe during the month of July to do business and have fun. Streets were named for the products they specialized in — wool, cotton, silk, jewelry, weapons, saddles. Traders in foodstuffs had their stands by the river, and the fairground spread out across the plain between the river and the castle. There were troubadours, jugglers, clowns, acrobats and performing animal acts. It remained active from the thirteenth century to the nineteenth century, when the railroad made it obsolete.

Beaucaire was also a key military position for the Kingdom of France on the Rhône, which was the border with Provence in the Middle Ages. For centuries, two mighty castles, France's Château of Beaucaire and Provence's Château of Tarascon

menaced each other across the Rhône. The Count of Provence was a vassal of the Holy Roman Emperor, and boatmen still referred to the two banks of the river as "Kingdom" and "Empire" as late as the nineteenth century.

The **Tourist Office** is at 24 Cours Gambetta (66 59 26 57.

WHAT TO SEE AND WHAT TO DO

The **Château of Beaucaire** was built in the eleventh century by the Count of Toulouse and dismantled in the seventeenth century by Richelieu, and only the outer shell of remains. But it is impressive nevertheless, and its view of Tarascon, the Rhône Valley and the Alpilles is exceptional. The Château of Beaucaire puts on a medieval costume show called **Les Aigles de Beaucaire** (The Eagles of Beaucaire) with free-flying eagles, vultures and falcons every afternoon from Easter

to the end of October) at 3, 4, 5 and 6 PM. It costs 35 francs for adults, 20 francs for children under 13. For information call (66 59 58 33. If you are traveling with children, this is one of the most unique and exciting events you can take them to. But it is a thrill for people of any age.

Beaucaire is also the place where the **Canal du Rhône à Sète** begins, the boat canal that cuts to the west of the Camargue and connects the Rhône River with the Canal du Midi. Those who fantasize about cruising the canals of southern France may want to look at the houseboats. Two companies rent them in Beaucaire, Ancas Away at Quai du Général de Gaulle (66 58 66 71 and **Connoisseur Cruisers** at 14 Quai de la Paix (66 59 46 08.

The Eagles of Beaucaire, a medieval birds of prey show at the Château de Beaucaire on the Rhône.

WHERE TO STAY AND WHERE TO EAT

The place to stay and to eat is **Les Doctrinaires***** on Quai du Général de Gaulle (66 59 41 32, a seventeenth century residence of the Doctrinaire religious order tastefully converted into a hotel with 34 very comfortable rooms at moderate rates and a restaurant in a pretty courtyard with fixed-price menus from 110 francs.

Camping

Camping le Rhodanien is a well-equipped site with a swimming pool on the fairground, the Champ de Foire, by the river (66 59 25 50. It has 100 places and is open from March 20 to October 20.

HOW TO GET THERE

There are regularly schedules buses from Nîmes and Avignon, and frequent service from Tarascon just across the bridge. By car, from Nîmes take D 999, a distance of 24 km (15 miles), or from Avignon N 570, which connects with D 970 to Tarascon, where you cross the bridge to Beaucaire. It is 24 km (15 miles) too.

TARASCON

Massive Tarascon Castle on the east bank of Rhône halfway between Avignon and Arles is the very image of the medieval storybook castle. The town's name comes from the Tarasque, a legendary man-eating monster tamed by Saint Martha, Mary Magdalene's sister. Its name is also associated with Tartarin de Tarascon, the Provençal braggart hunter-warrior hero of Alphonse Daudet's mock epic novel.

The **Tourist Office** is at 59 Rue des Halles, in back of the Church of Saint Martha (90 91 03 52.

WHAT TO SEE

The **Château de Tarascon**, begun in the twelfth century and completed in the fifteenth, was the alternate principal residence of Good King René. Its mighty exterior walls soar to 150 ft (45 m) above the river, and from the upper battlements, there is a grand panorama of the lower Rhône Valley. Inside you will find a marvelous collection of eighteenth century ceramic apothecary jars, elaborate painted wood ceilings and a dramatic series of seventeenth century tapestries on the life of Scipio Africanus. It is open from 9 AM to 7 PM in the summer, from 9 AM to 12 PM and 2 PM to 5 PM the rest of the year.

The mostly fourteenth century **Église Sainte-Marthe**, across the street from the *château*, has a sarcophagus that supposedly contains the remains of the Saint.

La Maison de Tartarin is a reconstruction of the home of Daudet's fictional hero, including the wildly overgrown exotic garden in which Tartarin wove overblown tales of his exotic adventures. The people of Tarascon hated the book when it came out, feeling that Daudet, a native of Nîmes, had ridiculed their town. Now, since it keeps their town on the tourist map (like Cézanne in Aix, Van Gogh in Arles), they love it.

The Maison de Tartarin is at 55 *bis* Boulevard Itam, open from 9:30 to 12 PM and 2 PM to 7 PM in the summer, and closes at 5 PM off-season.

WHERE TO STAY AND WHERE TO EAT

The top hotel in town is the **Provence***** at 7 Boulevard Victor Hugo (90 91 06 43 FAX 90 43 58 13, with 11 large, very comfortable rooms, but no restaurant. The best eating is up the street at the **Hôtel-Restaurant Saint-Jean**** 24 Boulevard Victor Hugo (90 91 13 87 FAX 90 91 32 42, which serves generous portions of tasty regional fare at very modest prices and rents 12 spacious, pleasant, inexpensive rooms.

HOW TO GET THERE

There is frequent regular bus service from Nîmes, Arles and Avignon, some 25 km (16 miles) away, and from Beaucaire directly across the bridge.

ARLES

With its sun-baked hues and terra-cotta tiled roofs stradling a wide bend in the Rhône, Arles is the Provençal city par excellence. Though half the size of Nîmes, it is even more loaded with historical attractions, having been a great Roman port, the capital of Provincia Romana, the seat of a Christian archbishopric from the third century, even the capital of the Roman Empire for a moment in the early fifth century, and the most important center of Christianity in southern France throughout the Middle Ages. For more than a thousand years, thanks to its strategic position near the mouth of the Rhône halfway between Italy and Spain, Arles was the crossroads of Western civilization. Much of its interest today comes from that glorious millennium.

And as if all that weren't enough, the ghost of Vincent Van Gogh hovers over Arles too.

BACKGROUND

In the sixth century BC the Greeks from Marseille established a Rhône port and trading post in a marshy place they called "Arlate" — "the town in the swamp." Arles broke from the mother city and sided with Julius Caesar in his civil war against

Pompey, and when Caesar triumphed in 49 BC, Arles was rewarded with a large part of Marseille's shipping business. Its position at the junction of the Rhône and the Aurelian Way made Arles a natural center for trading. From the beginning of the Pax Romana well into the Middle Ages, with periodic interruptions by the barbarians, Franks and Saracens, Arles was the most important and prosperous city in the region. Its markets drew traders from all over Europe and the Middle East.

Christianity established itself early in Arles. Saint Trophime became the first bishop early in the third century, and Emperor Constantine called the first council of bishops at his palace in Arles in 314. The Church of Saint-Trophime was begun at

the beginning of the seventh century, and the monastery of Montmajour became one of the most powerful in Europe. Arles's necropolis of Les Alyscamps was the most revered in Christendom. Being buried there was a virtual guarantee of getting into heaven.

The re-emergence of Marseille as the main port during the Crusades and establishment of Aix as the political capital by the Counts of Provence sent Arles into a slow, steady decline. Its geographic position kept the barge traffic alive, but in the nineteenth century, the railroad came down the Rhône and took away the most profitable north-south traffic.

Culturally, Arles became the capital of Frédéric Mistral and the Félibrige movement, which revived the Occitan language and the region's pride in its culture. When Mistral won the Nobel Prize for Literature in 1904, he invested his prize

money in establishing the Arlaten Museum of Provençal folk arts and traditions.

In the twentieth century Arles has made itself a crossroads once more, not of empires or kingdoms, but of its own local area, and has become prosperous from agriculture and tourism.

GENERAL INFORMATION

There are **two Tourist Offices** in Arles. The main one is on the Esplanade Charles de Gaulle, on the south side of Boulevard des Lices (90 18 41 20. main street of Arles. The other Tourist Office is at the railway station, the Gare SNCF on Avenue Paulin Talabot (90 49 36 90. These Tourist Offices

sell a pass to all museums in Arles, all of which are open daily except national holidays. The pass costs 40 francs They also offer a two-hour Van Gogh walking tour Tuesdays and Fridays, leaving at 5 PM from the main Tourist Office.

Other information which may be of use:
Nîmes-Garons Airport (66 70 06 88.

The **train station, Gare SNCF**, is on the north side of town on Avenue Paulin Talabot (90 82 50 50.

The **bus terminal, Gare Routière**, is just across from the train station (90 49 38 01. **City bus line: S.T.A.R.**, 16 Boulevard Clémenceau (90 96 87 47.
Taxis: (90 96 90 03; (90 49 69 59; (90 93 31 16.

RIGHT: A photography exhibit at the Van Gogh Foundation, part of the annual Rencontres Internationales de la Photographie. LEFT: The twelfth century Romanesque facade of Arles's Church of Saint Trophime.

Car rental: Arles Auto Service, 84 Avenue de Stalingrad (90 96 82 82; **Avis**, 12 *bis* Avenue Victor Hugo (90 96 82 42; **EuropCar**, 2 *bis* Avenue Victor Hugo (90 93 23 24; **Hertz**, 4 Avenue Victor Hugo (90 96 75 23.

Bicycle rental: Gare SNCF baggage counter (90 96 43 94; **Collavoli**, 15 Rue du Pont (90 96 03 77.

Bus tours of Arles and the region, **Arles Voyages**, 12 Boulevard Georges Clémenceau (90 96 88 73.

Medical emergencies: S.M.U.R (mobile emergency service) (90 49 29 99; **hospital (Centre Hospitalier)** (90 49 29 29.

FESTIVALS

The **Feria Pascale** (Easter Fair), with bullfighting and related activities, is held on Easter Saturday, Sunday and Monday.

The **Fête des Gardians**, a rodeo of Camargue cowboys, takes place the last Sunday of April.

The Festival of Tradition, **Fête d'Arles**, features a parade with more than 1,000 people in period dress, with music, song, and dance. At the same time there is **La Course Royale de la Cocarde d'Or**, which is the running of the bulls and Provençal bullfighting. It all takes place the last weekend of June and first week of July.

Rencontres Internationales de Photographie is a major international photography exhibition with seminars. It is held during the month of July.

The Rice Harvest Festival, **Prémices du Riz**, is held in mid-September, with bullfighting on the second Sunday of that month.

Much music and literature has been inspired by the beauty of the women of Arles. They are typically tall and proud of carriage with pale skin and dark eyes and hair. In their traditional long dress with lace shawl and cap that they wear at festivals, they make a fiery and elegant appearance.

WHAT TO SEE

Arles's first century AD **Roman Arena** is slightly larger than Nîmes's, but less well preserved. Most of the stonework of the upper level was removed for other uses over the years. Luckily, as in Nîmes, the coliseum was converted into a fortress during the Middle Ages and a village built inside. Otherwise, there would have been a good deal less of it standing today. Like the arena of Nîmes, it hosts bullfights, concerts and other events. It has a seating capacity of up to 12,000 in its 34 rows of bleachers. It can be visited daily from 9 AM to 12:30 PM and 2 PM to 7 PM, May through September, shorter hours in different months the rest of the year.

Only one small section of Arles's 25 BC **Roman Theater** remains, but in its day it was larger than that of Orange, with a capacity of over 12,000, and more elaborately decorated. In the summer it is equipped with wooden risers for theatrical productions.

After seven years when first one half, then the other was boarded over for restoration, the main portal of the **Church of Saint-Trophime**, one of the masterpieces of Provençal Romanesque sculpture, was unveiled fully in October 1993. On the tympanum, a stern Christ oversees the Last Judgment surrounded by the symbols of the four Evangelists. To the left, the saved are being welcomed into Heaven by an angel (we know they are good because they have their clothes on) and to the right the damned (no clothes on) are being dragged to Hell in chains by a devil, a pitiful scene that must have struck fear into the beholders' hearts when it was created in the twelfth century.

The capitals of its little pillars of the **Cloister of Saint-Trophime** are decorated with sculptures of biblical scenes and the pillars themselves with the lives of saints and apostles. The north and east arcades of the cloister are twelfth century Romanesque, the south and west fourteenth century Gothic.

The **Muséon Arlaten** (Museum of Arles, in Provençal), founded by Mistral, has a large, well-displayed collection of Provençal folk arts, farm and craftsmen's tools and interesting historical documents, such as warrants to arrest nobles and seize their property during the French Revolution. Open from 9 AM to 12 PM and 2 PM to 7 PM June through August, afternoons only the rest of the year. Closed Monday.

The **Musée Réattu** has 57 Picasso drawings donated by the artist in 1972 in appreciation for the many *corridas* he enjoyed attending in Arles. Most date from 1971 and deal with such favorite motifs as the artist and his model, harlequins and monsters. The museum also has paintings, drawings and watercolors by Gauguin, Vlaminck, Dufy, Marquet and Vasarély, sculptures by Germaine Richier, César and Pol Bury and a large photography collection, including prints by Lartigue, Karsh and Man Ray. Open daily, 9 AM to 12:30 PM and 2 PM to 7 PM, May to September, somewhat shorter hours in different months the rest of the year.

Espace Van Gogh, a cultural center, is a former hospital where Van Gogh stayed during the winter of 1888–1889 after he cut off part of his ear. The wide central courtyard's flower garden has been planted to match his famous painting. The space is now used for art exhibits.

From the welter of tee-shirts and post cards and other Van Gogh memorabilia on sale by souvenir hawkers in Arles, you would think he was their local sports hero. But Arles snubbed and rejected the troubled Van Gogh and never bought any of the 200 paintings and 100 drawings he did in the incredibly productive fifteen months he spent here. The two houses he lived in, which would have been worth millions in any currency as tourist attractions, were destroyed by Allied bombs in 1944.

Les Alyscamps (Elysian fields) was a Roman, then early Christian necropolis. Its long alleyway lined with great trees and a double row of stone sarcophagi leads to the ruins of the twelfth century **Church of Saint-Honorat**. In the Middle Ages, when it was an important place of pilgrimage, there were sarcophagi by the thousands. Most have disappeared, but fortunately, the Musée de l'Arles Antique has some good exam-

Arles now can display many fine pieces it had to keep in storage before. Most of the works of art from the Roman period sculptures, mosaics and sarcophagi were created in Arles and its region. They include the exquisite mosaics of "The Rape of Europa" and "Orpheus and the Venus of Arles," a famous statue found in digs at the Roman Theatre; a copy is on display here, the original being in the Louvre. There is a remarkable collection of third to fifth century Christian sarcophagi carved with scenes from the Old and New Testaments and touching images of the deceased in white marble. Open daily from 9 AM to 12:30 PM and 2 to 7 PM, May through September, shorter hours in different months the rest of the year.

ples. Les Alyscamps has long been a favorite scene for artists. Van Gogh and Gauguin painted side by side here during a period of relative harmony. Open daily, the same hours as Roman Arena.

From any of these places, you are likely to end up on the **Boulevard des Lices**, the main street of Arles, which is fine. It has wide sidewalks shaded by big plane trees and numerous cafes in lining the north side for you to relax and refresh yourself in. If you are here on Saturday morning, this is where the **market** is held.

Arles's spacious new **Musée de l'Arles Antique** (Museum of Ancient Arles), opened in 1995, brings together the large collections of the **Musée d'Art Païen** (Museum of Pagan Art) and the **Musée d'Art Chrétien** (Museum of Christian Art) that were previously housed in two colorful, but very cramped, decommissioned Baroque churches. With 3,000 sq m (28,000 sq ft) of exhibition space,

WHERE TO STAY

Expensive
The **Jules-César******* Boulevard des Lices (90 93 43 20 FAX 90 93 33 47, is a seventeenth century Carmelite convent, now a deluxe 49 room Relais & Châteaux hotel with gardens and a swimming pool. **Nord-Pinus******* on the Place du Forum (90 93 44 44 FAX 90 93 34 00, is a legendary hotel with wrought iron and bullfighting posters decor. Picasso, Cocteau, Piaf and Montand were guests here and matadors like to stay during the *corridas*. Prices for its 18 rooms range from 500 to 1,500 francs.

The restaurant-lined Place du Forum in Arles, where modestly-priced food can be found.

Moderate

D'Arlatan*** 26 Rue Sauvage (90 93 56 66 FAX
90 49 68 45, the former residence of the Counts
d'Arlatan de Beaumont, is a 34-room hotel of
authentic charm on a quiet side street near the
Place du Forum with an interior garden and
private garage. **Mas de la Chapelle***** on D 35,
five kilometers (three miles) north of town (90
93 23 15 FAX 90 96 53 74, is a sixteenth century
chapel with 14 rooms, swimming pool and tennis
courts.

Inexpensive

The **Musée**** 11 Rue Grand-Prieuré (90 93 88 88
FAX 90 93 34 00, is a pleasantly renovated 20-room
hotel with a quiet patio across from the Musée
Réattu. **Le Cloître**** 18 Rue du Cloître (90 96 29
50 FAX 90 96 02 88, is a friendly, well-maintained
old 33-room hotel on a side street by the Cloister
of Saint-Trophime.

Camping

Camping City at 67 Route de Crau (90 93 08 86,
a 100-place camping grounds about two kilometers (one and a half miles) south of town is open
March through the end of October. **Les Rosiers**,
Pont-de-Crau (90 96 02 12, also with 100 places,
is open from Easter through the end of October.
Other nearby camp sites are the 70-place **Le
Gardian** (90 98 46 51 and the 66-place **La Bienheureuse** (90 98 35 64 on Route N 113 in **Raphèle-les-Arles** about eight kilometers (five
miles) to the southeast, both open all year.

WHERE TO EAT

Expensive
The **Restaurant Lou Marques** in the Hôtel Jules-
César is the first choice for traditional Provençal
cuisine in *Grand Siécle* surroundings, with a
luncheon menu at 150 francs, dinner 195 francs
and up. The Jules César's pretty **Restaurant du
Cloître** serves light Provençal luncheon menus at
98 francs and wine by the *carafe* (90 93 43 20. I
enjoy the atmospheric **Brasserie du Nord Pinus**,
now under the direction of Jean-André Charial
of the Oustaù de Baumanière, which offers
bright Provençal menus at 120 francs for lunch,
140 francs for dinner, with wine from Château
Romanin by the *carafe*. At **L'Olivier**, 1 *bis* Rue
Réattu (90 49 64 88, you can sample the cuisine of
another resourceful Provençal master chef, Jean-
Louis Vidal, in a delightful sixteenth century stone
house with a glassed-over interior garden.

Moderate

The **Café Van Gogh**, 11 Place du Forum (90 49
83 30, an exact reproduction of Van Gogh's 1888
Café de la Nuit, is a cheerful café-brasserie, lit just
the way Van Gogh saw it.

Inexpensive
At the popular **Hostellerie des Arènes** by the
arena at 62 Rue du Refuge (90 96 13 05, you will
eat well-prepared Provençal home cooking (duck
in green pepper sauce, beef stew, seafood puff
pastry) in generous portions at remarkably low
prices. **Poisson Banane**, another lively spot,
serves Caribbean-flavored dishes at very affordable prices. It is at 6 Rue du Forum (90 96 02 58.

NIGHTLIFE

The cafés along the Boulevard des Lices cater to
the tourists trade, and therefore are the most expensive in town. For livelier, less expensive cafés,
go to the **Place du Forum**, where the Poisson
Banane and the Café Van Gogh are, and colorful
Place Voltaire north of the arena, where live jazz
or pop music is played Wednesday nights.

HOW TO GET THERE

The closest international airport is Marseille-
Provence 65 km (40 miles) away. The closest domestic airport is Nîmes-Garons 23 km (14 miles)
away, to which there are four regular flights a
day from Orly in Paris. By train, there is frequent
service from Paris, a trip of about four and a half
hours. There is also frequent train service from
Avignon or Nîmes, a 20-minute ride, and from
Aix, Marseille and Montpellier. Les **Cars de
Camargue** provides daily bus connections with
Nîmes, Aix, Marseille and Les Saintes-Maries-de-
la-Mer (90 96 36 25. **Les Cars Verts** provides
service between Arles and Avignon, Nîmes Airport, Aix, Marseille and the Camargue (90 93 74
90. Driving from Paris by the autoroutes, take A 7
to Orange, A 9 to Nîmes and A 54 to Arles.

THE ALPILLES

From the outskirts of Arles as you look across the
flat plain to the northeast, you see a chain of mountains off in the distance — at least, that's what it
appears to be. But in fact, it's an illusion. The
craggy white limestone peaks are mere hills, few
of which reach even 300 m (985 ft), and they are
closer to Arles than they look. They start only
10 km (six miles) away. This chain of would-be
mountains is known as the **Alpilles** (pronounced
aahl-pee), or "Alpettes" in English. Yet small as
they are, these mini-Alps exercise a powerful appeal. They are indelibly associated with Alphonse
Daudet, whose famous windmill is in Fontvieille
and whose hero Tartarin hunted in these hills, and
Van Gogh spent a year at the asylum in Saint-
Rémy. Today "Saint-Rem" has become every bit
as chic as "Saint-Trop," and the Alpilles is an "in"
place for celebrities and international princesses.

There are chic wines here too — *AOC* Baux-de-Provence.

ABBAYE DE MONTMAJOUR

The first sight that greets you as you head northeast from Arles on D 17, the road to Fontvieille, is the brooding ruins of the Benedictine **Abbey of Montmajour**, founded in the tenth century and a power in the Middle Ages. Its monks drained the swamps to create farm land, and with their revenues from agriculture and from pilgrims, Montmajour rose to national influence. After a period of decline in the seventeenth century, new constructions were undertaken in the late eighteenth century, but when the abbot, Cardinal Rohan, was implicated in the scandal of Marie Antoinette's necklace, Louis XVI closed the abbey.

The medieval church, cloister and other early structures of the abbey have been restored and can be visited. The Baroque wing has been left to the elements. The abbey offers a panoramic view of the Alpilles, the plain of the Crau, Arles and the Cévennes.

The **Chapelle Sainte-Croix**, a twelfth century Romanesque gem, sits on a field to the right of the road 200 m to the north of the abbey. Like Saint-Pantaléon near Gordes, it has child-sized sarcophagi hewn out of the slab of stone it rests on.

FONTVIEILLE

The **Moulin de Daudet**, the windmill made famous by Daudet's delightful collection of Provençal stories, *Lettres de Mon Moulin (Letters from My Windmill)*, is in Fontvieille, five kilometers (three miles) north of Arles. It is one of the South's most popular attractions for French tourists. Daudet did not live or write in the mill. He stayed at the home of friends when he came to Fontvieille, and the stories were written in Paris. But he loved the country around the mill and often meditated on the hillside. A small **Daudet Museum** has been installed in the mill with phonographs, documents and memorabilia. It is open daily from 9 AM to noon and 2 to 7 PM April through September, to 5 PM the rest of the year. Closed the month of January.

The **Tourist Office** is at 5 Rue Marcel Honorat in the center of Fontvieille (90 54 67 49.

Where to Stay and Where to Eat

At the **Auberge la Regalido****** on Rue Frédéric Mistral in the center of Fontvieille (90 54 60 22 FAX 90 54 64 29, Jean-Pierre Michel, representing the sixth generation of chefs in his family, serves savory dishes of the Alpilles in the flowery terrace of his ancient former olive oil mill. There is a light luncheon menu at 150 francs, others at 250 and 400 francs. This delightful restaurant, a favorite of mine, richly merits its Michelin star. The inn has 14 tranquil rooms tastefully decorated *à la Provençale*. A Relais & Châteaux member. Closed the month of January.

LES-BAUX-DE-PROVENCE

This desolate, foreboding valley surrounded by barren white rocky crags is believed to have inspired Dante's description of Hell. It lies 10 km (eight miles) east of Fontvieille.

The name of Les Baux derives from the Provençal *li baus* — the rocks. The rocks turned out to have a valuable mineral in them, and rich de-

posits of it were discovered in 1821. The ore, used to make aluminum, was named after Les Baux — "bauxite."

High above the valley is the uninhabited **Upper Town**, the medieval seat of the powerful lords of Baux. This town had a violent history, particularly under Raymond of Turenne, "The Scourge of Provence," who delighted in making prisoners jump to their deaths off the sheer cliffs. The Upper Town may have been abandoned by residents, but certainly not by tourists, who swarm over the place in July and August, nor by merchants who service their craving for arts and crafts items and souvenirs. There is plenty of mass-produced junk, but also a good deal of high-quality handicrafts for sale in the

ABOVE: Les-Baux-de-Provence, a town with a particularly violent history.

better boutiques. The views from Les Baux are sensational in all directions — Arles and the Camargue, the Rhône Valley, Mount Ventoux, Aix, and the Lubéron. For good photography, go early in the morning or late in the afternoon; at mid-day the intense sun burns everything out. You will find the **Tourist Office** at the Hôtel de Manville a sixteenth century mansion that also houses the town hall and a contemporary art museum. It is halfway up the hill from the parking lot (90 54 34 39.

Where to Stay and Where to Eat
The **Oustaù de Baumanière******(90 54 33 07 FAX 90 54 40 46, is a 500 year-old farm in the wild beauty

of the Val d'Enfer at the foot of Les Baux, with 24 supremely comfortable rooms and suites, pool, tennis and a nearby golf course. Under the direction of owner-chef Jean-André Charial, it has one of the great restaurants of southern France, with two Michelin stars. At 900 to 1,100 francs for a room and menus at 400 and 700 francs, it is very expensive. But if you feel like a splurge, this is the place to do it. Closed mid-January to the beginning of March. The **Cabro d'Or******, the Oustaù's sister inn a few kilometers away, is a delightfully soothing 22-room hotel amid flower gardens and cypresses, with a pool and tennis courts and an outstanding restaurant (one Michelin star) (90 54 33 21 FAX 90 54 38 88. Prices are one-third lower

ABOVE: Provençal horsewoman. OPPOSITE and PAGE 238: Saint Rémy-de-Provence is the liveliest town in the Alpilles for festivals and special events.

than at the Oustaù. Closed mid-November to mid-December. Both establishments are Relais & Châteaux members. In a setting of comparable charm with a view of the upper town, a pool and a top quality, very convivial restaurant, the **Mas d'Aigret**** is an exceptional value. It offers a luncheon menu at 90 francs, wine included, and its 15 cheerful rooms rent for 500 to 850 francs. It is on Route D 27 A(90 54 33 54 FAX 90 54 41 37. Closed Wednesdays at lunch, the month of January and most of February.

How to Get There
Bus service is minimal. There are two buses per day each from Arles, Avignon and Saint-Rémy. The best way to explore the Alpilles is by car, which you can rent in Avignon or Arles: If you are biker who doesn't mind climbing a few hills, you could rent in bikes Arles or Saint-Rémy. By car, Les Baux is nine kilometers (five and a half miles) northeast of Fontvieille on D 17 and D 78.

SAINT-RÉMY-DE-PROVENCE

Saint-Rémy is the liveliest town in the Alpilles, the crossroads of the area, with an outstanding Provençal market, lots of festivals and important Roman and pre-Roman ruins to tour. It is also remembered as one of the key places in Van Gogh's troubled life.

General Information
The **Tourist Office** is at Place Jean-Jaurès (90 92 05 22, about 100 yards south of town via Avenue Durand-Maillane or Avenue Pasteur. It provides good maps, brochures and advice about what to do in Saint-Rémy and the Alpilles, including itineraries of places painted by Van Gogh. It also runs guided tours in English and several other languages.
Bike rental: Florélia, 35 Avenue de la Libération (90 92 10 88.
Horseback riding: Club Hippique des Antiques, Rue Astier (90 92 30 55.

Festivals
Saint-Rémy is a town of many festivals and events, a dozen a month in the summer — music, sports, bulls, goats, horses — a rural version of Monaco or Cannes. The main ones are the **Fête de la Transhumance**, the shepherds' festival, on Pentecost Monday in late May or in June, in which thousands of sheep are driven through the streets. **Organa**, an international festival of organ music, is held from July to September. From August 13 to 15, **Feria**, a festival of bullfights and farm-related events, is held. It culminates with the Carreto Ramado, a procession featuring fifty horses and a huge carriage laden with flowers and farm products.

What to See

Two beautifully preserved Roman memorials called **Les Antiques** are located without an easy walk south of the Tourist Office on D 5, the road to Les Baux. The more unusual one is the **Mausoleum**, so-called because that is what it was long thought to be. But in fact it is a memorial to Emperor Augustus's two favorite grandsons, and their statues can de seen inside the circle of columns in the uppermost level of the 18-m (60-ft) white stone tower. There are fine bas-reliefs of hunting and battle scenes on the lower level. The second of the Antiques is a **commemorative arch**, also from Augustus's reign.

Glanum, across the road, is an extensive archaeological site that has been under excavation since 1921. It is named for a Celtic-Ligurian tribe called the Glani, and evidence of three different civilizations, one on top of the other, has been unearthed — Celtic-Ligurian, Greek and Roman. The site is open daily from 10 AM to 12 PM and 2 PM to 7 PM.

Also across the road from Les Antiques and through a grove of olive trees is the former **Monastery of Saint-Paul-de-Mausole**, the mental hospital where Van Gogh had himself committed in May 1889 to try to tame his self-destructive demons. He spent a full year here and painted twisted olive trees, cypresses, hay fields and starry nights, 150 painting and drawings in all. In the alleyway leading into the hospital he painted his famous irises the day after his arrival. The monastery dates from the twelfth century and has a charming little cloister and Romanesque church that you should not overlook.

In town, the sculptures and mosaics excavated from Glanum are on display at the **Archaeological Museum** at the Hôtel de Sade on Place Favier in the heart of old Saint-Rémy, open daily from 10 AM to 12 PM and 2 PM to 5 PM. Nearby, the **Église Saint-Martin** has a magnificent organ with 5,000 stops that went back into service in 1993 after a long restoration. It is used for the Organa concert series.

A large Provençal **market** is held in the main squares of the Old Town Wednesday mornings and a smaller one Saturday mornings.

Where to Stay and Where to Eat

For the height of discreetly elegant living, the **Château des Alpilles****** two kilometers west of town on D 31 (90 92 03 33 FAX 90 92 45 17, is a nineteenth century mansion in a large private park shaded by huge trees with 15 very spacious rooms, tennis courts and a pool. The **Hostellerie du Vallon de Valrugues****** on Chemin Canto Cigalo (90 92 04 40 FAX 90 92 44 01, is a 41 room luxury hotel also with pool and tennis courts, whose gourmet restaurant is one of the

finest in the Alpilles, with one Michelin star. These hotels are expensive. For a pleasant little hotel in the country at moderate rates, try **Canto Cigalo**** also on Chemin Canto Cigalo (90 92 14 28 FAX 90 92 24 48, with 20 rooms at 260 to 330 francs, no restaurant. Also in the moderate price range, the **Auberge de la Reine Jeanne**** at 12 Boulevard Mirabeau (90 92 15 33 FAX 90 92 49 65, is a comfortable, convivial 10-room inn in a seventeenth century house in heart of old Saint-Rémy. For lunch, try the popular, modestly-priced **Bistrot des Alpilles** at 15 Boulevard Mirabeau, (90 92 09 17, serving tasty local dishes, such as roast lamb or *brandade de morue*, the Provençal-style codfish, with a luncheon menu at 60 francs. Closed Sunday.

CAMPING

Le Mas de Nicholas (Camping Municipal) is a well-shaded deluxe camping ground with 140 places, a pool and view of the Alpilles on Avenue Théodore Aubanel (90 92 27 05, open from March 15 to the end of October. 105-place **Camping Pegomas**, Route de Noves (90 92 01 21, also has a pool, open March 1 to the end of October.

Wine Tasting

The towns of the Alpilles make wines of the recently established Baux-de-Provence *appellation*. They produce mainly light, dry rosés, but its reds have gained a great deal of respect in recent years. A few of the prestigeous vinyards you can visit are **Château Romanin** in Saint-Rémy (90 92 45 87, with huge wine caves cut into the rock near the ruins of a castle and **Domaine des Terres Blanches**, also in Saint-Rémy, (90 95 91 66 and **Mas de la Dame** (90 54 32 24 in Les Baux.

How to Get There

There is frequent daily bus service to Saint-Rémy from Avignon, and some daily service from Arles, Tarascon and Aix, but little from Les Baux. All buses stop at Place de la République, the large square across from the Église Saint-Martin. For bus schedules, contact the Tourist Office. By car, it is nine and a half kilometers (six miles) north of Les Baux on D 5, 24 km (15 miles) northeast of Arles via Les Baux, and 19 km (12 miles) south of Avignon on D 571.

THE CAMARGUE

The Camargue is the wide, flat delta of the Rhône, made up of salt marshes and mud flats, lagoons with flamingos, long sandy beaches, rice and wheat fields and grass lands for cattle and horses herded by Camargue cowboys called *gardians*, and is the scene of big Gypsy pilgrimages twice a year. It is one of the most haunting places in all of France.

The delta starts below Arles, where the Rhône forks: the Grand Rhône flowing to the southeast and the Petit Rhône to the southwest. In the winter of 1993–1994, dikes along the Petit Rhône gave way, and 24,280 hectares (60,000 acres) of Camargue ranch and farmland ended up under water, causing $10 million in property damage and havoc for the wildlife.

At the center of the Camargue is the 13,500 hectare (32,500 acre) **Réserve Nationale de Camargue**, established in 1927, one of the oldest national wildlife preserves in France. Essentially consisting of the **Étang de Vaccarès** (Pond of Vaccarès)

and the marshlands along its shores, it is closed to the public, but its bird life can be observed from the road around its periphery and from the **Digue de la Mer** (sea dike) that runs between the Étang and the Mediterranean. There are more than 400 species of birds, and the pink flamingo is the symbol of the Réserve. In summer, there can be as many as 300,000 flamingos in residence.

Surrounding the Réserve is the 85,000 hectare (204,000 acre) **Parc Naturel Régional de Camargue (Camargue Regional Natural Park)**. This is mainly privately-owned land covered by environmental controls to protect the flora and fauna, and there are plenty of trails that allow you to explore it. Besides the wetlands, here you will also find rice and wheat fields, small vineyards and ranches known as manades that breed bulls for bullfighting à la cocarde (where they don't get killed) and the little white wild horses of the Camargue that aren't really wild any more, policed by the gardians. There are extensive salt pans at **Salin de Giraud** on the east side of the Camargue where the Grand Rhône flows into the Mediterranean and on the west side at the **Salins du Midi** near Aigues-Mortes. These are diked-off marshes where salt is evaporated from sea water, and mountains of it wait to be carted away.

LES SAINTES-MARIES-DE-LA-MER

The Camargue has only one real town, Les Saintes-Maries-de-la-Mer, whose large Romanesque church can be seen across the flatlands from miles around.

Background

The reason this little town of 2,000 has so impressive a church is the Provençal legend of the Boat of Bethany. According to this legend that developed early in the Middle Ages, Mary Magdalen, her brother Lazarus (he who was raised from the dead), her sister Martha, two other Marys (Mary Jacobé, the Virgin's sister, and Mary Salomé, the mother of the apostles James and John), their Black servant Sara, and Maximinus and Sedonius were set adrift in a boat from Jerusalem by Jews and washed up on the shore at les Saintes-Maries-de-la-Mer in about 40 AD. Mary Magdalen retired to the hills of La Sainte-Baume and became a hermit, and Lazarus, Martha, Maximinus and Sedonius proceeded inland to spread the Word. The two other Marys and Sara stayed in Les Saintes-Maries-de-la-Mer, tended the shrine they built to the Virgin, and when they died were buried there. Their tombs became a place of pilgrimage, and in the ninth century, the original shrine was replaced by a fortified church incorporated into the ramparts that the Archbishop of Arles ordered built to protect the town from Saracen pirates. Unfortunately for him, he was kidnaped from the construction site by the Saracens and died in their custody. In the twelfth century, the ninth century church was replaced by the larger fortified church we see today.

There is no evidence that authenticates the legend of the Boat of Bethany. Furthermore, the participation of Mary Magdalen in this voyage seems to have been based on the confusion in the medieval mind between the identities of Mary of Bethany, who was the sister of Lazarus and Martha, and Mary Magdalen, who was not. Nevertheless, the worship of all the Saints Mary continues to this day at the places associated with them in Provence, and the Gypsies have adopted Saint Sara as their patron saint.

General Information

The **Tourist Office** of Les Saintes-Maries-de-la-Mer is at 5 Avenue Van Gogh near the town beach (90 97 82 55.

The **Fondation du Parc Naturel Régional de Camargue**, Centre de Gins, Pont du Gau, 13460, Saintes-Maries-de-la-Mer (90 97 86 32, provides information about the **nature reserve**. At the **Parc Ornithologique du Pont du Gau**, Route D 570, 13460 Saintes-Maries-de-la-Mer (90 97 82 62, you'll find information about birds and a short **nature trail** with blinds for bird-watching. Another wildlife information center is located at **La Capelière** on Route D 36B on the east side of the Étang de Vaccarès. It has one and a half kilometers (one mile) of **nature trails** with observation points.

Bikes can be rented in Les Saintes-Maries-de-la-Mer at **Delta Vélos**, Rue Paul Peyron (90 97 84 99 (open all year), or **Le Vélociste**, 1 Place des Remparts (90 97 83 26.

For information on renting **horses**, see the section on horseback excursions that follows.

Binoculars are highly recommended in the Camargue, and mosquito repellent is a must.

parades, cattle-branding and horse races. In the fall, there is a smaller pilgrimage in honor of Mary Salomé on the Sunday closest to October 22.

What to See and Do

Like other medieval churches along this coast, **L'Église des Saintes-Maries** has thick stone walls, tiny windows, crenelated battlements and the brutal look of the fortress, which it became when pirates invaded. Inside the somber building there is a well that provided water during sieges, a chapel with the relics of the two Saint Marys, a model of the boat that supposedly brought the saints to Provence, and in the crypt, relics of Saint Sara and the black statue that the Gypsies carry in

The phrase used to ask for it is, "*de la créme anti-moustique, s'il vous plaît.*"

Festivals

There are two annual pilgrimages to Les Saintes-Maries-de-la-Mer, one in May the other in October. They are officially dedicated to the two Marys, (Jacobé and Salomé) and there are elaborate processions in their honor, but the Gypsies' homage to Saint Sara on May 24 is the highlight of the year. Gypsies come from all over Europe, and though there are plenty of tourists among the 25,000 people who attend, the fête has a real Gypsy flavor. There is Gypsy music everywhere, and in the afternoon, they carry the effigy of Saint Sara from the church to the sea. The pilgrimage continues on May 25, and on the 26th, the *gardians* put on a celebration in honor of Marquis Baroncelli, a popular figure in the culture of the Camargue, with

the procession in May. For a small charge, you can climb the 53 steps to the roof for a splendid panorama of the Camargue and the sea.

For those who get swept up in the mystique of the Camargue, a trip down the street to the **Musée Baroncelli** on Rue Victor Hugo is in order. Marquis Folco de Baroncelli, born in 1869 of a wealthy Florentine family in Avignon, became a *gardian* in the Camargue as a young man and, inspired by Mistral, devoted his long life to reviving the Camargue's traditions and developing it for ranching and agriculture. There are interesting displays on local history and archaeology from the days of the Romans onward, on the animal and plant life of the delta, and on the life of the

OPPOSITE: In Camargue-style bullfighting, the bull gets to go home after the fight. ABOVE: The church of Les Saintes-Maries-de-la-Mer, fortified to defend against Saracen pirates.

extraordinary Marquis Baroncelli himself. It is open from 10 AM to 12 PM and 2 PM to 6 PM, closed Tuesday from October to May.

The **Musée Camarguais** is a huge nineteenth century barn on the main road between Arles and Les Saintes-Maries-de-la-Mer that has been imaginatively converted into a museum of the Camargue's geology, history and culture, with a special emphasis on farm and ranch life. There is a three-and-a-half-kilometer (two-mile) Camargue farm trail. It is on Route 570 at **Mas du Pont de Rousty** nearly halfway between Arles and Les Saintes-Maries-de-la-Mer (90 97 10 82. It is open from 9:15 AM to 6:45 PM June through August, 10 AM to 4:15 PM the rest of the year. Closed Tuesday.

EXCURSIONS

There are more than fifty stables and dude ranches in and around the Camargue where horses can be rented. Some simply send you off with a guide, but many of the big *manades* — ranches that raise bulls for the ring — offer demonstrations of cattle roping and branding, stunt riding, and bullfighting *à la cocarde*, along with **horseback excursions** into the Camargue. One of these is the 600 hectare (1500 acre) **Domaine Paul Ricard**, a dude ranch and experimental farm in Méjanes on the north side of the Étang de Vaccarès. They have exhibitions of bull roping and branding (Sundays and holidays from Easter through mid-July), a narrow-gauge train that takes you along the edge of the Étang de Vaccarès and bullfights on the 14th of July.

Their rates for renting a horse are 200 francs for a half-day, 320 francs for a full day (90 97 10 60 or 62. For information on other stables and *manades*, contact the Office de Tourisme in Les Saintes-Maries-de-la-Mer or the Association des Loueurs des Chevaux, Mas-des-Lys, Route d'Arles (90 97 86 27.

La Digue de la Mer is a dike built in the nineteenth century between L'Étang de Vaccarès and the sea. It runs 20 km (12.5 miles) eastward from Les Saintes-Maries-de-la-Mer to connect with the road to Salin de Giraud, the next town. The roadway on top of the dike has been closed to vehicular traffic for several years, but it is open to people on foot, bicycle or horse-back — a boon to nature lovers.

The **Tiki III excursion boat** makes four trips per day up the Petit Rhône in July and August, less often the rest of the year. The trip takes 75 minutes and allows you to observe the cattle and horses and wildlife along the shore. The pier is at the mouth of the Petit Rhône west of Les Saintes-Maries. 48 francs (90 97 81 68.

THE BEACHES

The Camargue has 60 km (40 miles) of fine sand beaches, much favored by naturistes and other sun-worshipers. The **Plage de Beauduc** has two rustic restaurants, **Chez Juju et Manu** and **Chez Marc et Mireille**, good for fresh grilled fish, moderate to expensive. The large **Plage de Piémanson**, also known as the **Plage d'Arles**, on the east side of the Camargue is the only beach with life guards throughout the summer. The main nudist beach is four kilometers (two and a half miles) east of Les Saintes-Maries at **Pertuis de la Comtesse** near the Gacholle lighthouse. Nudists and non-nudists co-exist on the **Plage de Piémanson**, and there is a small nudist stretch at **Le Golue** on the Salin de Giraud beach.

WHERE TO STAY AND WHERE TO EAT

While many people prefer to camp in the Camargue, there is no dearth of hotels, including 19 three-star establishments and five four star.

The most luxurious is the **Mas de la Fouque****** on Route du Bac du Sauvage, off D 38, four kilometers (two and a half miles) north of Les Saintes-Maries (90 97 81 02 FAX 90 97 96 84. Serenity is guaranteed at this 13-room luxury resort in a private park deep in the Camargue, with swimming pool, tennis courts, golf practice holes and regional food. Very expensive.

L'Estelle*** in the same area as the Mas de la Fouque, is an attractive modern ensemble of bungalows with 17 rooms, tennis court, pool and horses, with room rates in the 500 to 600 franc range (90 97 89 01 FAX 90 97 80 36. The **Lou Mas du Juge** is an easygoing inn with seven cheerful, moderately-priced rooms, and you can rent horses. The excellent, but expensive restaurant specializes in seafood and boeuf gardian, bull meat stewed in red wine, the Camargue specialty. It is on D 85 in the Quartier Pin-Fourcat northwest of town (66 73 51 45. The **Pont du Gau**** Route 570 (the main road to Arles) five kilometers (three miles) north of Les Saintes-Maries (90 97 81 53, is good Camargue-style restaurant with moderate prices that rents nine pleasant guest rooms at 240 francs. The **Longo Mai**** in **Le Sambuc** (90 97 21 91 has 16 inexpensive rooms, hearty regional food and horses for rent. It is

HOW TO GET THERE

Les Cars de Camargue has five buses a day from Arles in the summer, leaving from 24 Boulevard Clémenceau or from the Gare Routire. In Les Saintes-Maries-de-la-Mer, the stop is at the intersection of Rue Jean Jaurs and Avenue d'Arles at the entrance to town (get there a half-hour early to be sure of a seat). In the summer, there are daily buses from Nîmes and a few buses per week from Montpellier. Tour operators run excursions from Arles (Arles Voyages) and Avignon (Lieutaud Voyages). For schedules, contact the tourist office. Driving from Arles to Les Saintes-Maries-de-la-

24 km south of Arles via D 36, on the west bank of the Rhône. For the tops in Camargue cuisine in downtown Les Saintes-Maries-de-la-Mer, try **Hippocampe** on Rue Camille-Pelletan (90 97 80 91, or **Brûleur de Loups** on Avenue Gilbert-Leroy (90 97 83 31, which has a terrace overlooking the sea. Both offer good value. Be sure to try the tellines, tiny succulent shellfish offered as hors d'oeuvres.

Camping

La Brise is a huge camping ground by the beach on the east side of town (90 97 84 67, open all year. It has 1,610 camping places on its 44 hectares (106 acres), a large swimming pool and a wading pool for little children. **Le Clos du Rhône**, D 38, two kilometers from town (90 97 85 99 is a comfortable site with 450 places and a pool, open Easter through the end of September.

Mer, take the bridge across the Rhône (Pont de Trinquetaille) and follow the Route de Camargue (D 570) all the way. It is 38 km (14 miles) from Arles. To get to the east side of the Camargue (Le Sambuc, the Plage d'Arles), branch off to the left from D 570 onto D 36 two and a half kilometer (about a mile and a half) south of the bridge and take it south, parallel to the Grand Rhône.

Alternatively, take D 35 south from Arles and the little ferry, the Bac de Barcarin, across the Rhône. But be aware that in the summer, there can be a long wait for the ferry.

OPPOSITE: The Monastery of Saint Paul-de-Mausole in Saint Rémy, where Van Gogh spent one astonishingly productive year. ABOVE: Exploring the Camargue by horseback. Don't forget your mosquito repellent.

Languedoc

THE LANGUEDOC of history, the huge medieval realm of the powerful Counts of Toulouse, was the cradle of Occitan culture, the land of troubadours, courtly love and religious toleration that was crushed by the Albigensian Crusade. Today's Languedoc covers only half the territory of old. When the new administrative regions were drawn up in 1981, Languedoc's historical capital of Toulouse was made the capital of another region, Midi-Pyrénées, and Montpellier was made the capital of modern-day Languedoc, with culturally Catalan Roussillon tacked on to form the region of Languedoc-Roussillon. As a result, Languedoc and Roussillon tend to get lumped together in people's minds the way Alsace and Lorraine used to be. But in fact, they are every bit as different as Alsace is from Lorraine, or as Provence is from the Côte d'Azur.

Languedoc is the only part of France named for a language. The language of Oc was suppressed by the Edict of Villers-Cotterêts in 1539, which established French as the state language. Southerners still resent the high-handed treatment they have received from Paris over the centuries, but the Félibrige movement in the nineteenth century set the area on the recovery of its cultural identity, and the economic rise of Montpellier and the Modern South since the 1960's has made the South — Montpellier especially — a very attractive place to young people. The cultural inferiority complex of the past has evaporated. Paris is no longer seen as the only place where one can do important things. Now even the casual traveler will find many a bright young ex-Parisien who has chosen to live in Languedoc, for the ease of living and for the career opportunities in the dynamic new South.

All this modernity enlivens Languedoc and improves creature comforts, but it also creates the seemingly inevitable curses that go along with it — urban sprawl, commercial centers, *hypermarchés* (super supermarkets) and fast food chains that kill the special ambiance of a place and deface once-lovely coastal areas.

Nevertheless, compared to Provence and especially to the Côte d'Azur, Languedoc is a fresh place for the traveler to explore. There are wide open spaces, magnificent medieval abbeys and fortresses, interesting cities and surprising art treasures, 160 km (100 miles) of sandy beaches on the Golfe du Lion from the Camargue south to Argelès-Plage, and practically all Mediterranean Languedoc makes wine. And finally, for the budget-minded traveler Languedoc is noticeably easier on the wallet and credit card than its more touristically established neighbors to the east.

Readers who have been following our itinerary through Provence will approach Languedoc from Arles or the Camargue. Travelers motoring from the north on the A 9 *autoroute (La Languedocienne)* should exit at Nîmes. It is actually in Languedoc, though for historical and archaeological reasons we have included it in our look at Provence (see AVIGNON TO NÎMES, page 219). Visitors can either explore this "Rome of France" or head south to Saint-Gilles on the Languedocian fringe of the Camargue.

SAINT-GILLES

BACKGROUND

Saint-Gilles, three kilometers (two miles) west of

the Petit Rhône, is named for another saint who washed up on these shores, this one in the eighth century. The tomb of Saint-Gilles at the abbey he founded became an important place of pilgrimage in the middle ages, and in the twelfth century the modest original church was replaced by a much more magnificent one.

It was an incident at Saint-Gilles that set off the Albigensian Crusade. In 1208 the papal legate Pierre de Castelnou was murdered at the door of the church by a follower of the Count of Toulouse, and Pope Innocent III seized on this rash act as his pretext for unleashing a crusade to crush the Cathars.

ABOVE: The old choir of the twelfth century Church of Saint-Gilles. OPPOSITE: Celebrating Saint-Louis, the king who established a permanent French presence on the Mediterranean coast at Aigues-Mortes.

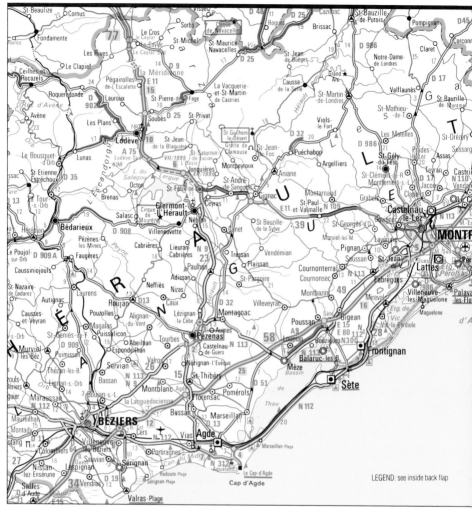

LEGEND: see inside back flap

GENERAL INFORMATION

The **Tourist Office** is at Place Frédéric Mistral (66 67 33 75.

WHAT TO SEE AND DO

The splendid western facade of the **Église Saint-Gilles** has three Romanesque arched doorways with decorative columns and stone sculptures depicting the life of Christ. The ensemble dates from the same period as the tympanum of Saint-Trophime and is similar in style. The sculptures were the first to represent the Passion of Christ in full. For the best light, come in the late afternoon. Unfortunately, the Wars of Religion and the Revolution destroyed the rest of the building.

The town of Saint-Gilles is on the Canal du Rhône à Sète, and you can rent houseboats or take cruises. *La Salicorne* is a 164 passenger restaurant-cruise boat that makes **day-trips through the Camargue** to Aigues-Mortes and Les Saintes-Maries-de-la-Mer, operating all year. It is at the Quai du Canal (66 87 33 29. For **houseboat rental**, contact **Blue Line** at 2 Quai du Canal (66 87 22 66.

WHERE TO EAT

For *petite friture* (fried whitebait), *rougets grillés* (grilled red mullet), *entrecôte gardianne* (steak from Camargue bulls) and other local dishes, stop in at **Saint-Gillois** at 1 Rue Neuve (66 87 33 69. It is unpretentious and modestly priced, with a 55 franc lunch weekdays, 139 francs tops.

HOW TO GET THERE

There are frequent buses from Arles and Nîmes. By car, Saint-Gilles is 16 km (10 miles) west of

EASTERN LANGUEDOC

0	5	10	15	20
Kilomètres	Kilometer	Kilometres	Chilometri	

	5		10		15
illes	Meilen	Statute miles	Miglia terrestri		

Arles on N 572, 23 km (14 miles) north of Les Sain-tes-Maries-de-la-Mer on D 570 and D 37, and 19 km (12 miles) south of Nîmes on D 42.

AIGUES-MORTES

The walled town of Aigues-Mortes ("dead waters" in Occitan) on the western edge of the Camargue was the Kingdom of France's first foothold on the Mediterranean coast. King Louis IX (Saint Louis), bought the land from the monks of the Abbey of Psalmody in 1240 and had a port built for Crusaders on their way to the Holy Land. By the mid-fourteenth century, Aigues-Mortes was a thriving town of 15,000. But its port silted up and eventually went dry and the fortunes of the town with it. The town now finds itself five kilometers (three miles) from the Mediterranean, and its population is one-third of its glory

days. But what remains from that period is very impressive.

GENERAL INFORMATION

The **Tourist Office** is at Porte de la Gardette, to the left just inside the gate (66 53 73 00.

WHAT TO SEE AND WHAT TO DO

High **crenelated stone ramparts**, completely intact, surround the town, with ten gates and fifteen round towers interspersed. The 500 m (1,640 ft) **southwestern wall**, where the medieval docks used to be, is especially formidable. So is the massively thick, 40 m (130 ft) tall circular **Tour Constance**. It was used as a political prison from the late Middle Ages to Napoléon's time. Protestant leaders spent long years of incarceration here during the Wars of Religion. From the top of the tower, there is a grand panorama: the town with its Roman-style grid pattern, the Camargue and the Salins de Midi salt pans to the east, the bulky resort of La Grande-Motte to the south and the Cévennes Mountains to the northwest.

Behind the stern walls, the town is surprisingly pleasant to stroll in, especially on Wednesday and Sunday mornings, which are the **market days**, and there are good crafts shops.

Le Pescalune, a converted barge, makes a two-and-a-half-hour circuit of the canals of the western Camargue, passing through wildlife areas, ranches, salt pans and vineyards. It leaves its pier by the Tour de Constance daily at 10:30 AM and 3 PM in the summer (66 53 79 47.

WHERE TO STAY AND WHERE TO EAT

The most attractive hotel inside the town walls is the **Templiers***** at 23 Rue de la République (66 53 66 56 FAX 66 53 69 61, a seventeenth century mansion with 11 expensive guest rooms. The **Saint-Louis***** is a tastefully furnished 22-room hotel with a quiet patio at 10 Rue Amiral Courbet near Place Saint-Louis (66 53 72 68 FAX 66 53 75 92. Its rooms are moderate in price. The **Croisades**** is a pleasant newer hotel with 14 rooms in the 240 to 300 franc range. It is outside the walls of the town at 2 Rue du Port to the west of the maritime channel (66 53 67 85 FAX 66 53 72 95.

The **Arcades** at 23 Boulevard Gambetta (66 53 82 77, offers sophisticated treatment of local farm, ranch and sea products in a sixteenth century mansion with stone walls, beamed ceilings, decorated in violet and rose, expensive overall, with a 125 franc menu at lunch. It also rents six pleasant medium-priced rooms.

The **Camargue** at 19 Rue de la République (66 53 86 88, is a solid old family-style eatery under the trees serving local fare at moderate

LA GRANDE-MOTTE, LE GRAU-DU-ROI AND PORT-CAMARGUE

prices — fresh shellfish, grilled lamb chops, *gardiane* stew from the meat of Camargue bulls, and *vin des sables* (wine grown in the sands), a local specialty (see WINE) below.

Camping

Camping **La Petite Camargue** in the Quartier Le Mole is a deluxe 420-place site with a swimming pool, tennis courts and restaurant, open from Easter to the end of September (66 53 84 77. **Camping de Port Vieil** is a few kilometers north of Aigues-Mortes on D 46 in Saint Laurent d'Aigouze (66 88 15 42. It is a 100-place site with a pool and restaurant open April 1 to the end of October. Camping Bellevue in **Aimargues** is open all year

is 48 km (30 miles) from Arles by D 570/D 58 through the Camargue, 37 km (23 miles) from Nîmes by N 113 and D 979, and 29 km (18 miles) from Montpellier by D 66 and D 22.

LA GRANDE-MOTTE, LE GRAU-DU-ROI AND PORT-CAMARGUE

Developed in the late 1960's as part of the de Gaulle government's master plan to create affordable vacation places for French families, La Grande-Motte (which literally means "the big lump") was the first of many modern beach and

(66 88 63 75. This is an attractive, shaded area with 180 places and a pool, about 12 km (seven and a half miles) north of Aigues-Mortes on D 979. Otherwise, head for La Grande-Motte or Port-Camargue on the coast.

WINE TASTING

Listel's **Domaine de Jarras** on D 979 between Aigues-Mortes and Le Grau du Roi offers free tasting of its pale amber vin des sables, wine made from grapes that grow in the sand, a real thirst-quencher on a hot summer day. Open daily all year (66 53 63 65.

HOW TO GET THERE

There are numerous buses daily from Arles, Nîmes and Montpellier. Driving, Aigues-Mortes

marina complexes to be built on this coast. Its cluster of bloated white concrete pyramids rises up out of nowhere on the flatlands to the west of the Camargue. It now accommodates 100,000 vacationers in the summer. You may not like La Grande-Motte's looks, but it does have a certain quirky flare, which is more than can be said for most of the *habitation à loyer modéré* or *HLM* (middle income housing) vacation complexes farther down the coast. With so many French people with vacation money to spend, you can be sure there is good eating in these parts.

The resort has absorbed the neighboring old fishing port of **Le Grau-du-Roi** and spawned a

ABOVE: The completely walled Crusaders' port town of Aigues-Mortes, where the Mediterranean once lapped at its walls. OPPOSITE: Italian flag throwers at the Feast of Saint-Louis at Aigues-Mortes.

new marina, **Port-Camargue**, now the largest yacht harbor in Europe, with 4,500 berths. If you like to look at big sailboats, this is definitely the place.

La Maison des Vins et des Produits du Gard sells fresh fruit, wine, honey, olive oil, crafts products and fabrics of the Gard *départment*, open daily all year. It is east of Port-Camargue on Route de l'Espiguette (66 53 07 52.

For an excursion into the dunes, drive another seven kilometers (four miles) east to the lighthouse, **Le Phare de l'Espiguette**. Those with the urge to shed their clothes may do so. *Naturistes* and wearers of bathing suits mingle unabashedly on this beach.

and swimming pool, and it fronts on the vast pleasure boat port. The restaurant serves Jean-Pierre Cazals's savory specialties such as roast fillets of red mullet in olive oil and fillet of Camargue *toro* with anchovies and nuts. This is a Michelin one-star restaurant, very expensive. The rooms are in the moderate category, 460 to 680 francs. It is open from April to the beginning of October. The other gourmet restaurant of the area, one of the most distinguished in Languedoc, is **Restaurant Alexandre** in La Grande-Motte, serving the sophisticated regional cuisine of Michel Alexandre. Here you can treat yourself to a little *bouillabaisse* as an appetizer, fresh cod with *tapenade* (black olive paste) or pork baked with juniper berries

GENERAL INFORMATION

Tourist Offices: Place de la Mairie, Grande-Motte (67 29 03 37; Boulevard Front-de-Mer, Le Grau-du-Roi (66 51 67 70; Port Camargue, Carrefour 2000 (66 51 71 68 (open Easter to September).

WHERE TO STAY AND WHERE TO EAT

There are dozens of resort hotels on all levels of price and quality in this area, and my top choice as both a hotel and a restaurant is **Le Spinaker******** at Pointe du Môle in Port-Camargue (66 53 36 37 FAX 66 53 17 47. It has 21 bright, cheerful rooms opening onto private sun terraces, with a garden

and Provençal vegetables and an outstanding regional wine list. Alexandre is on the Esplanade de la Capitanerie in front of the Casino (67 56 63 63. It is expensive. Another good restaurant in Port-Camargue, though not very atmospheric, is **L'Amarette** at the Centre Commercial Camargue 2000 (66 51 47 63, for fresh shellfish and fish dishes, somewhat expensive. It is closed most of the winter. In Le Grau-du-Roi, **Le Palangre** at 56 Quai Charles de Gaulle (66 51 76 30, is a pleasant restaurant with outdoor tables on the old port serving excellent grilled meat and fish with fixed-price menus starting at 80 francs.

For information on other hotels in the area and help with reservations, the Tourist Offices will be happy to be of service.

Camping

This is an active area for camping. Port-Camar-

ABOVE: La Grande-Motte, the first modern resort complex built on the Languedoc coast. OPPOSITE: A charming *Languedocienne*.

gue has thirteen camping grounds on the beach along the Route de l'Espiguette including the deluxe 1,440-place **Camping Elysée Residence** (66 53 54 00, which has a swimming pool, and the more modestly equipped **Camping de l'Espiguette** (66 51 43 92, which has 2,250 places. La Grande-Motte has seven camping grounds with 1,511 places. For details, contact the Tourist Offices.

HOW TO GET THERE

There are frequent buses from Montpellier and Nîmes. Driving, take the same roads as for Aigues-Mortes.

LA GRANDE-MOTTE TO MONTPELLIER

Heading west from La Grande-Motte on D 59, the shore road to Palavas-les-Flots, neighboring **Carnon-Plage** has an eight-kilometer (five-mile) stretch of open sandy beach where no construction is allowed, very popular with people from Montpellier a mere 10 km (six miles) away. Continue south along the beach past the turn-off to Montpellier and drive through the modern resort of **Palavas-les-Flots** accross the bridge to **Maguelone**, where a big fortified former cathedral from the twelfth century sits alone in the middle of nowhere, the sole survivor of another important Languedoc town left high and dry, not by the sea like Aigues-Mortes, but by the Church of Rome, when the Pope transferred the bishopric to up-and-coming Montpellier in

the sixteenth century. The church is austere on the outside, but inside its great rounded Romanesque vaults soften the austerity. It can be visited any day, but is best appreciated during the many concerts of religious choral music they have in the summer. The acoustics are perfect. The church fronts on the coastal lagoon where you often see flamingos and other waterfowl. In the summer Maguelone can be a problem for people with sensitive noses. The stagnant water in the area gives off a stench of rotten eggs.

MONTPELLIER

Like Nîmes, Montpellier is a city that woke up after a long period of somnolence. In this case the awakening started earlier, in the 1960's, when IBM (International Business Machines) moved to Montpellier and other high-tech companies followed suit, the prestigious university acting as a magnet. Montpellier's contemporary architecture reflects its new dynamism.

This is a city that takes itself very seriously. It has even created its own grandiose vocabulary for the areas of economic activity (or pôles as they like to call them) it is focusing on: Pôle Héliopolis (tourism, culture, festivals, and leisure activities), Pôle Agropolis (agricultural technology for hot climates), Pôle Antenna (communications), Pôle Informatique (computers) and Pôle Euromédecine (medicine and medical technology). Montpellier's overall term for itself is "Le Surdoué:" "the highly gifted one."

This is a young persons' city. Of its 200,000 inhabitants, 50,000 are students.

BACKGROUND

Montpellier is a relatively new city for this part of the world. It celebrated its 1,000th birthday in 1985. Created by the Lords of Guilhem and originally a dependency of Maguelone, it benefited from its proximity to three important roads and had access to the Mediterranean by the then-navigable River Lez. From the beginning, Montpellier's merchants imported herbs and spices from the Middle East, including medicinal plants, and the town quickly became one of the main conduits in Europe for the medical secrets of the Arab and Jews, then far ahead of the West. By the eleventh century, Montpellier had fortifications with twenty-five towers. The line of its walls had the shape of a shield, or écusson, a term by which Old Montpellier is still known.

In 1204 the marriage of King Pedro of Aragon and Marie of Montpellier, the daughter of Guilhem VIII, brought the town into the Catalan sphere, and it prospered for a century and a half under the Kingdoms of Aragon and Majorica. Montpellier's University was founded in the early thirteenth century and, thanks to its Arab and Jewish contacts, became one of Europe's leading medical schools (Rabelais studied medicine there in 1530). In 1349 King Philip VI of France bought Montpellier, and it became France's main Mediterranean port. In the fifteenth century Jacques Coeur, the fabulously wealthy financial advisor to King Charles VII, set up his southern headquarters here. The city's thriving sea trade collapsed, however, when Provence was annexed by France in 1481, and Marseille took over the bulk of the shipping. As a Protestant stronghold during the Wars of Religion and

Richelieu's and Louis XIII's invasions, Montpellier took a terrible beating. But somehow its cloth manufacturers and traders survived, and the evidence of that is the fifty or so mansions from the seventeenth and eighteenth century in the Écusson district.

Though the River Lez silted up long ago, Montpellier has not given up on being a Mediterranean port. One of Mayor Freche's dreams is the Port-Marianne project, which envisions a link from the foot of the Antigone Center via a widened River Lez to the sea at Palavas-les-Flots some 10 km (six miles) away. This dream has been deferred for the moment because of financial problems.

The Promenade du Peyrou on the heights overlooking Montpellier.

GENERAL INFORMATION

The central **Tourist Office** for the Montpellier area is in the Passage du Tourisme at the north end of the Place de la Comédie (the Triangle) (67 58 67 58. There are other offices at: 78 Rue de Pirée (to the right of D 66 from the *autoroute* as you approach Antigone from the east) (67 22 06 16; Rond Point des Prés d'Arènes at the southern approach from the *autoroute* (67 22 08 80; and the railway station, the Gare SNCF (67 92 90 03. The Tourist Office makes bookings for hotels and country guest houses, runs cultural tours, sells tickets for festivals and shows, exchanges currency, sells products of the region and offers an array of free booklets, including one on the old mansions in the Écusson that are open to visitors. It provides literature and verbal assistance in several languages.

For additional travel information on the outlying areas in the hills above Montpellier and the Languedoc shore, contact the **Maison de Tourisme de l'Hérault**, BP 3067, Avenue des Moulins, 34034 Montpellier (67 84 71 70. It is located three-and-a-half kilometers (two miles) west of downtown Montpellier at the Rond-Point d'Alco.

The following numbers may be helpful:

Montpellier Mediterranée International Airport (67 20 85 00.

The **train station, Gare SNCF**, is at Place Auguste-Gilbert (67 58 50 50.

The **bus station, Gare Routière**, is attached to the train station and fronts on Place du Bicentenaire (67 92 01 43. Sodétrhé, the agency that oversees bus transportation in the Hérault department, also provides information on buses (67 84 67 85, but they only speak French. Non-French-speakers should contact the Tourist Office.

Taxis: Radio Taxis, Gare SNCF (24 hours) (67 58 74 82; **T.R.A.M. Taxi** (67 92 04 55; **Taxi Radio 2000** (67 41 37 87.

Car rental: Alcoloc (67 92 07 50; **Avis** (67 92 92 00; **Hertz** (67 58 65 18; **Someloc** (67 92 35 97.

Bike rental: at the reception desk of the **Gare SNCF**.

Coach tours: Courriers du Midi runs day trips in the summer to Marseille, Arles and the Alpilles, the Camargue, the Gorges du Tarn, Saint-Guilhem-le-Désert, the Canal du Midi and other places. For information and reservations, contact the Tourist Office or Courriers du Midi (67 06 03 74.

Medical emergencies: SOS Médecin (67 72 22 15.

FESTIVALS

Printemps des Comédiens is a French and European theater festival held in early June. The **Montpelier International Dance Festival**, a tremendous event featuring all kinds of dance with top companies

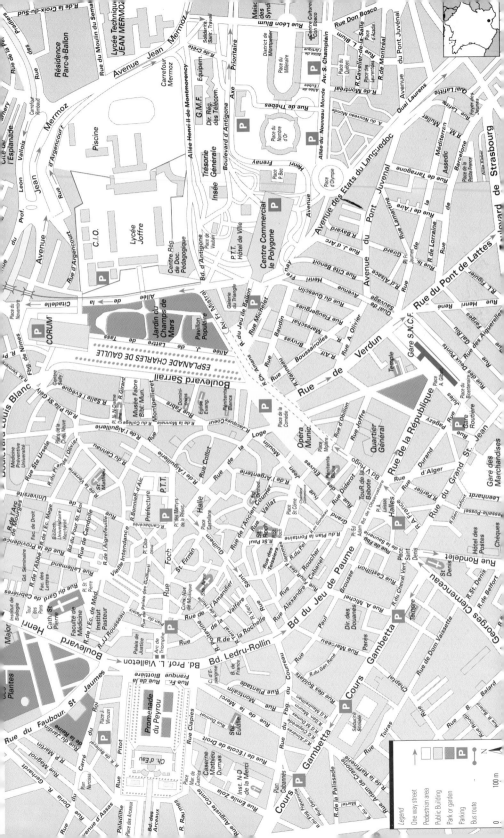

from all over the world, takes place in late June and early July. The **Festival de Radio-France et de Montpellier,** running from mid-July to mid-August, presents leading French and international ensembles performing opera, symphonies, chamber music and jazz at the Cathedral, Opéra Comédie, Corum, Château d'O, and other sites in an around town. For information, contact the Tourist Office.

WHAT TO SEE AND WHAT TO DO

Named for the nineteenth century opera house at the south end of the square, **Place de la Comédie** is the social center of the city and the link between the boldly modern areas of Polygone and Antigone to the east and discreet old Écusson to the west. The Place itself is wide and lined with large cafés, with several rows of tables spreading out into the square, and the pretty **Fountain of the Three Graces** is in the middle. The tree-shaded Esplanade branches off its northern end, and many of the streets that run off the Place are walking streets.

Vieux Montpellier

Head up into the **Écusson** district (with your free booklet of the Tourist Office in hand) to explore one street after another lined with seventeenth and eighteenth century mansions, about 50 still standing, in Vieux Montpellier. Especially noteworthy are the **Hôtel des Trésoriers de France**, originally Jacques Coeur's mansion, updated in the seventeenth century, at 5 Rue des Trésoriers-de-France, the elegant **Hôtel de Varennes** at 2 Place Pétrarque (named for the poet, who studied at the University from 1316 to 1319) and **Hôtel des Trésoriers de la Bourse** at 4 Rue des Trésoriers de la Bourse, designed by the city's leading early eighteenth century architect, Jean Giral. The work of a later Giral, Jean-Antoine, can be admired up the hill in the **Promenade du Peyrou,** on the other side of the big **Arc de Triomphe** dedicated to Louis XIV. This is a gem of a park on a plateau overlooking the city, marred only by an equestrian statue of the Sun King that is pompous even by his standards.

Jean-Antoine Giral's masterpiece is the **Château d'Eau** at the far end of the park, a hexagonal pavilion of classical proportions designed to mask the reservoir for water arriving from the 800 m (2,600 ft) long, 22 m (72 ft) high **Aqueduc Saint-Clement,** longer but lower than the Pont du Gard after which it was patterned. The Promenade du Peyrou is a pleasant spot for a picnic with views of the Cévennes, the Mediterranean and, on days when the *tramontane* has cleared the air, Mont-Canigou in the Pyrénées.

A **flea market** is held at Place des Arceaux beneath the aqueduct's arches on Saturdays.

The **Musée Fabre** has an outstanding collection of nineteenth century French paintings, especially strong on Courbet and Bazille, also three Delacroix and works by David, Ingres and Géricault. The most important works were donated Alfred Bruyas, a would-be painter whose hobby was having his portrait painted—32 times in all. Nineteen likenesses of the sad-eyed narcissist with the bright red beard are on display at the Fabre, including four by Gustave Courbet, the father of French realism. One is "La Rencontre," nicknamed "Bonjour Monsieur Courbet," in which the black-bearded painter is seen taking a stroll in the Languedoc countryside, where he happens to run into a red-bearded gentleman (guess who). The museum also has nine paintings by Montpellier-born Frédéric Bazille, one of the founders of Impressionism, who painted side by side with Renoir and Monet, but was killed at 29 in the Franco-Prussian War. His "La

Vue du Village" and "Les Remparts d'Aigues-Mortes" are drenched in the sunlight of Langue-doc. There is also a gentle Berthe Morisot portrait, "L'Éte," from the Impressionist period, and from the twentieth century, there are lesser works by Matisse, Bonnard, Delaunay, Dufy and de Staël, the bright, lively "Les Joutes à Sète" by François Desnoyer and a charming landscape of Collioure by André Lhote. The museum is on the east side of the Écusson on Boulevard Bonne Nouvelle, fronting on the Esplanade. It is open from 9 AM to 5:30 PM Tuesday through Friday, 9:30 AM to 5 PM Saturday and Sunday, and closed Monday.

Modern Montpellier

Modern Montpellier, built in the 1980's and 1990's, starts on the east side of the Place de la Comédie with the **Polygone** business center, dominated by the multi-terraced pyramid of the Sofitel hotel.

To Polygone's east is **Antigone**, architect Ricardo Bofill's vast, grandiose neo-neo-classical business and residential complex that may soften with age as trees grow in and human beings make their presence known, but for the moment has a cold, Mussolini-like quality, except for the part by the River Lez, where a graceful row of **restaurants** fronts on the stream. Another star of the modern architectural line-up is the **Corum**, a huge dark brown, bunker-like complex of concert and assembly halls designed by Claude Vasonti at the far end of the Esplanade. Overall, Montpellier's new architecture is too stark for my taste, but it may age well, and it has certainly made the city far more interesting to look at than it was twenty years ago.

Place de la Comédie, Montpellier's café-lined main square, a popular spot for this university town's 50,000 students.

The *Folies* of Montpellier

In the early eighteenth century, the rich of Montpellier built extravagant summer residences known as *folies* (follies) in the countryside around the city. The city has now gobbled up most of that countryside, but about thirty of them remain, and some have been restored and furnished in the style of the period and can be visited. **Château de la Mogère**, designed by Jean Giral, and **Château de Flauguergues** in the style of an Italian villa, lie to the east of the city and have been well maintained. **Château de la Mosson**, once the most sumptuous of them all, lies to the west. Today only its handsome shell remains standing, but its grand park is magnificently

melancholy. **Château d'O** to the northwest of the city is used in the summer for festival performances. Its park is decorated with statues from Mosson. Check with the Tourist Office for visiting hours and ask for their brochure on the folies that can be visited.

WHERE TO STAY

Montpellier has 3,600 hotel rooms, an over-supply for a city of its moderate size, which puts the traveler in a good bargaining position. Rates are lower in Montpellier (and Languedoc generally) than they are to the east of the Rhône for hotels of comparable quality. Here is a selection of the many other good hotels in this city.

ABOVE: *Pétanque* players in Montpellier.
OPPOSITE: Anitgone, Montpellier's vast modern business and residential complex.

The **Alliance-Métropole****** 3 Rue Clos René (67 58 11 22 FAX 67 92 13 02, located between the railway station and the Place de la Comédie, is the palatial hotel of the city with 81 luxurious rooms and rates in the 580 to 640 franc range. The **New Hôtel du Midi***** 22 Boulevard Victor Hugo (67 92 69 61 FAX 67 92 73 63, has 47 tastefully modernized rooms in a *belle époque* style on a corner of the Place de la Comédie, very reasonable at 380 francs. The **Noailles***** at 2 Rue des Ecoles-Centrales (67 60 49 80 FAX 67 66 08 36, near the Musée Fabre has 30 well-equipped rooms in a landmark seventeenth century mansion with doubles at 440 francs. **Le Guilhem***** at 18 Rue Jean-Jacques Rousseau (67 52 90 90 FAX 67 60 67 67, is a former seventeenth century coach inn with a great deal of character. Its 33 rooms are furnished with antiques, and it has a large flowery sun terrace. It is near the Promenade du Peyrou and the Cathedral. Doubles here run from 350 to 470 francs. For a delightful hotel in a lush private park slightly outside of town, try the **Demeure des Brousses***** an eighteenth century estate on the Route de Vauguières (67 65 77 66 FAX 67 22 22 17. It has 17 rooms in the 450 to 600 franc range. It is four kilometers (two-and-a-half miles) southeast of the city by D 21 and D 172, toward the airport.

At more moderate prices, **Les Arceaux**** at 33 Boulevard des Arceaux by the Aqueduct (67 92 03 03 FAX 67 92 05 09, has 18 rooms at 250 to 320 francs. **Palais**** at 3 Rue du Palais (67 60 47 48 FAX 67 60 40 23, is nicely situated in the Écusson and has 26 pleasant rooms in the 230 to 360 franc range. The **Campanile** chain has four of its pleasant, modern two-star motels on the outskirts of town with rooms at 275 francs. They are the 82-room **Montpellier-Est** in the ZAC (commercial zone) du Millénaire, 1083 Rue Henri-Becquerel (67 64 85 85 FAX 67 22 19 25; the 46-room **Montpellier-Nord**, Centre Commercial Carrefour, Route de Ganges, Saint-Clément-de-Rivière (67 04 45 25 FAX 67 41 22 80; the 59-room **Montpellier-Sud**, Avenue du Mas d'Argelliers (Route N 113) (67 58 79 80 FAX 67 92 51 81; the 50-room **Montpellier-Ouest**, Parc d'Activités la Peyrière, off Route N 116, in Saint-Jean-de-Védas (67 47 99 77 FAX 67 47 99 15. For a very inexpensive hotel, try the cheerful **Le Plantade*** at 10 Rue Plantade, south of the Promenade du Peyrou (67 92 61 45, with 12 rooms in the 125 franc range.

Camping

The closest camping grounds are in **Lattes** directly south of the city, which has eight sites ranging from the deluxe 302-place **Eden Camping** (67 68 29 68, open June 1 to the end of September, to the modest 78-place **Le Camarguais** (67 50 60 05, which is open all year. Both are on the Route de Palavas. For information contact the Tourist Office.

WHERE TO EAT

As with hotels, Montpellier has a good selection of restaurants, starting with the Pourcel brothers' **Jardin des Sens**, arguably the finest restaurant in Languedoc, where you can feast on little squid (*encornets*) stuffed with *ratatouille*, fried oysters from Bouzigues, lamb with its sweetbreads, soufflé of bitter chocolate and a fine selection of regional wines. This is a two Michelin star restaurant, quite expensive, with a weekday luncheon menu at 165 francs. It is a small place. You must reserve in advance. It is at 11 Avenue Saint-Lazare off Avenue de Nîmes (N 113) to the north of the city (67 79 63 38. Other noteworthy gourmet restaurants are **Le Chandelier** for traditional French cuisine at 3 Rue Albert Leenhardt not far from the train station (67 92 61 62 and **Le Mas** at the Demeure des Brousses on Route de Vauguières (67 65 52 27, a little paradise five minutes from the center of town with an outstanding regional kitchen, both of them expensive. A restaurant I enjoy greatly is **Le Ménestrel**, a former grain warehouse from the thirteenth century that has excellent regional fare at reasonable prices, with a luncheon menu at 90 francs. It is on Place de la Prefecture in Vieux Montpellier (67 60 62 51. Reservations are a must. There are modestly priced restaurants of all nations on and around the lively Rue des Ecoles Laïques a few blocks west of the Corum. There is even a French one, **Le Vieil Écu**, serving hearty local fare in a cheerful ambiance.

NIGHTLIFE

The big cafés of Montepllier front on the wide open spaces of the **Place de la Comédie**. If you prefer a cozier ambiance, walk down the Place staying to the right of the opera house, turn right at its rear corner and walk up Rue du Cygne to little **Place Saint-Côme** or **Place Saint-Roch** just up the street, where you will find a number of easy-going cafés and restaurants. For live music try **Mimi la Sardine**, 1317 Avenue de Toulouse (67 69 27 90, a fun club with rock, jazz, and other sounds from Languedoc and all over the world, or **Le Sax-a-Phone**, 24 Rue Ernest Michel (67 66 80 90. **Macadam Pub** at 1 Rue des Deux Ponts by the train station (67 64 37 09, is a friendly bar that starts to get lively around midnight and stays open till dawn, with a D.J. and many kinds of beer.

WINE TASTING

The Hérault is the largest wine-making *départment* in France.

In the past it was known mainly for plonk, but as the demand for such low-grade wine dried up in the decades following World War II, wine makers here moved more and more into quality wines. **Côteaux du Languedoc**, an *appellation contrôlée* since 1985, is the most widely produced *AOC* wine, with 50,000 hectares (120,000 acres) planted in its approved vines, producing 45 million liters per year. It is a rising star in the firmament of French wines. Included are 12 different terroirs, specific wine-growing areas whose names are added to the *appellation* on the label. It extends over a large area from the southern edge of the Costières de Nîmes area to the northern edge of the Corbières and produces mostly robust reds, some rosés and a little white — **Picpoul de Pinet**, excellent with shellfish.

This is a vast wine lake to plunge into, and one way to do it without drowning in confusion would be to visit the big, modern wine information center, the **Maison des Côteaux du Languedoc** (67 06 04 44, in the seventeenth century **Mas de Saporta** in **Lattes** just south of Montpellier's city limits. It has a huge wine shop, a restaurant with 70 different Côteaux du Languedoc sold by the glass and people to help lay out an itinerary for visits to vineyards.

The **Syndicat des Producteurs de Vins de Pays d'Oc** (67 92 23 33), has an office in another building in the complex with information on *vin de pays* producers. Most wines produced in Languedoc are not the prestigious *AOCs*, but modestly labeled *vins de pays* (wine of the country). Do not let this discourage you. These wines can be remarkably good. The wines are generally labeled either *Vin de Pays d'Oc* or *vin* *de pays* from a specific locality. Wines made from a single variety of grape — Cabernet Sauvignon, Merlot, Syrah, Sauvignon and Chardonnay in particular — are becoming increasingly popular.

The **Mas de Saporta** is less than fifteen minutes by car from the heart of Montpellier. It is immediately south of the Montpellier Sud (south) exit of the autoroute, or on Route de Palavas if you are coming from town. There are signs pointing the way.

Other *AOC* wine areas in the Hérault are **Faugères** to the north of Béziers, **Saint-Chinian** to the northwest, and part of the large **Minervois** area to the west of Béziers. The aperitif wines

Muscat de Mireval and **Muscat de Frontignan** are also made in the Hérault, and **Noilly-Prat** is located in Marseillan.

The **Club des Grands Vins de Châteaux du Languedoc**, a group of eight high-quality vineyards from the magnificent Abbaye de Valmagne near the Bassin de Thau down to the Château de Lastours in the Corbières, sets up wine-tasting tours of their Châteaux. This is strictly first class. A three-day tour with all hotels, meals and ground transport included costs 3,480 francs, four days 4,415 francs. For information, contact Jean Viennet, Château de Raissac, Route de Murivel, 34500 Béziers (67 28 15 61 FAX 67 28 19 75.

Medieval Saint-Martin-de-Londres ABOVE and OPPOSITE TOP and the Valley of the Vis OPPOSITE BOTTOM, one of many spectacular natural sites in the foothills of the Cévennes.

HOW TO GET THERE

There are 10 flights a day from Paris on Air Inter and a few flights a week from London on Dan-Air and Air Littoral. There are 10 *TGV*'s a day from Paris, a four-hour and 40-minute ride, and frequent trains from Marseille, Avignon, Nîmes, Carcassonne and Perpignan and stops in between. There is also good regional bus service in the department of the Hérault with frequent service to Aigues-Mortes, Béziers and the towns of the coast and some service to towns in the hills north of Montpellier. The Tourist Office can give you the schedules. By car, Montpellier is easily reached by the A 9 *autoroute* from the north or the south.

THE HÉRAULT RIVER VALLEY

Short drives north or west of Montpellier take you into the wide open countryside in the foothills of the Cévennes. Vineyards are practically everywhere, fragrances of the wild herbs, flowers and grasses known as *garrigue*, long stretches of road lined by poplars, just like in the old French movies — and there is little traffic compared to the roads of Provence and especially the Côte d'Azur. It is worth renting a car, even for a day's outing.

SAINT-GUILHEM-LE-DÉSERT

In the foothills of the Cévennes, Saint-Guilhem-le-Désert is less than an hour's drive west of Montpellier. It is a picturesque medieval village at the entrance of the dramatic gorges of the Hérault River, built around its Romanesque abbey. Its founder Guilhem was a warrior and trusted confidant of Charlemagne who gave up the life of wealth and power and retired to this secluded spot to lead life of prayer and austerity. A **festival of religious music** is held in the village throughout the summer.

The **Centre de Canoë-Kayak** by the river in Saint-Guilhem-le-Désert rents boats for rides down the rushing Hérault River and arranges guided hikes to upland sites (67 57 44 99. You can also visit the **Grotte de Clamouse** near the river just south of Saint-Guilhem-le-Désert, which is an impressive cave with a labyrinth of vast galleries and tortured stalagmites coaxed out of the limestone by the action of water. It is open all year.

SAINT-MARTIN-DE-LONDRES

Thirty six kilometers (22 miles) east of Saint-Guilhem-le-Désert lies Saint-Martin-de-Londres, a lovely medieval town with an eleventh century **church** built by the monks of Saint-Guilhem. The

ensemble is a classified historical site. This is also a good starting point for hikes into the garrigue covered countryside or to climb or hang-glide from **Pic Saint-Loup**, the 658 m (2,160 ft) peak that rises sharply to the east. The name Londres, by the way, has nothing to with the one in England. It is strictly of local origin.

Another attraction of the area is the **Grottes des Demoiselles** 17 km (11 miles) north of Saint-Martin-de-Londres on D 896. It has vast galleries 50 m (165 ft) high and astounding stalagmites and stalactites, including the "Virgin and Child," a limestone statue sculpted by water.

THE GORGES OF THE VIS AND THE CIRQUE DE NAVACELLES

The pleasant little tree-shaded town of **Ganges**, a former silk-manuacturing center eight kilometers (five miles) north of the Grotte des Demoiselles, is the starting point for an excursion to the west on D 25 along the picturesque Gorges of the Vis to the even more picturesque Cirque de Navacelles. This is a gigantic crater cut deep into the limestone by an abandoned course of the Vis River. It zeros in on a perfect circle of flat farmland at the bottom with an island of limestone in the middle. This is one of many bizarre topographical features of this area that look like messages to extraterrestrial civilizations. The view from the top is extremely impressive, and for hikers the descent into the valley makes for an exhilarating outing.

GENERAL INFORMATION

It's best to get your information about the Hérault River Valley at the Tourist Office in Montpellier before starting off. But if you don't, there is a **Centre d'Accueil**, or welcome center, for the area at Place Général Claparède in **Gignac** (67 57 58 83, about 10 km (six miles) south of Saint-Guilhem-le-Désert. The **Tourist Office** of Saint-Guilhem-le-Désert is at the **Mairie** (town hall) (67 57 42 50. In Saint-Martin-de-Londres, the little Tourist Office is open in the summer (67 55 09 59. Otherwise go to the Tourist Office at Ganges 19 km (12 miles) to the north (67 73 66 40. It also has information on the Gorges of the Vis and the Cirque de Navacelles.

WHERE TO STAY AND WHERE TO EAT

Your best bet for accommodations in the Saint-Guilhem-le-Désert area (and there are not many choices) is the **Hostellerie Saint-Benôit** ** in **Aniane**, six kilometers (four miles) south of Saint-Guilhem-le-Désert (67 57 71 63 FAX 67 57 47 10. This is a pleasant 30 room Logis de France inn with a pool and a good restaurant, open all year. Rooms are in the 255 to 310 franc range, and fixed price

menus start at 99 francs. For a real culinary treat in this area, go to the **Mimosa** in nearby **Saint-Guiraud**, a restaurant favored by wine connoisseurs because of owner David Pugh's exceptional knowledge of the wines of the region, which he is most generous about sharing. They also rave about Brigit Pugh's imaginative cooking, inspired by what's fresh in the market and in her own garden that day. Open March to the beginning of November, closed Sunday night and Monday at lunch except in the July and August. It is expensive. To get there from the Grotte de Clamouse, take the D 141 about eight kilometers (five miles) to the west. Mimosa is on Route D 130 in Saint-Guiraud (67 96 67 96.

In Saint-Martin-de-Londres, **Les Muscardians** at 19 Route Cévennes (67 55 75 90 FAX 67 55 70 28, serves delicious and generous regional lunch that is a bargain at 120 francs. The most beautiful hotel in the Hérault Valley area is the **Château de Madières***** in **Madières**, 20 km southeast of Ganges on D 24 (67 73 84 03 FAX 67 73 55 71. Built within the walls of a fourteenth century fortress on a remote hillside overlooking the Gorges of the Vis, this thoroughly comfortable 10-room Les Relais de Silence hotel has a large pool, a fitness center and serves fine regional cuisine in magnificent vaulted dining rooms. It is expensive. Open March 26 to November 2.

For an inexpensive hotel near the Cirque de Navacelles, try to get into the five-room **Auberge de la Cascade**** (67 81 50 95. It is open from March to December. Another inexpensive option is the 14-room **Gorges de la Vis*** in **Gornies** on D 25, the road between Ganges and the Cirque de Navacelles. It has a restaurant that serves hearty regional fare (67 73 85 05.

Camping

Camping de la Muse (67 57 92 97, on Chemin de la Muse in Gignac has a pool, tennis court, food shop and bar and 61 places, open June to September. The well-equipped 36-place **Camping du Pont** on Boulevard du Moulin in Gignac is open all year (67 57 52 40. In the Saint-Martin-de-Londres area, **Camping Pic Saint-Loup** on the Route du Pic Saint-Loup has 80 places, a pool, miniature golf, restaurant, food shop and bar, open April 1 to the end of September (67 55 00 53. There are no camping grounds near the Cirque de Navacelles, but if you ask their permission, farmers will generally let you camp on their land for a night.

WINE TASTING

Mas de Daumas Gassac in Aniane is a newly established vineyard that sold its first wine in 1978 and became a star three years later, when its deep, flavorful reds were hailed by *Gault Millau Magazine*. They have been getting rave reviews from the wine critics ever since. The vinyard now makes highly praised whites and rosés as well. Their wine is a *vin de pays de l'Hérault* that sells at the prices of top Bordeaux wines — ten times the standard price of *vin de pays* from Languedoc. The special soil and microclimate of the vineyard, unusual choices of vine stocks, careful attention to the winemaking process and owner Aimé Guibert's astute sense of publicity have made this little miracle possible. Open daily except Sunday from 10 AM to 12 PM and 2 PM to 6 PM (67 57 71 28. In **Montpeyroux** on Route 141 west of the Grotte de Clamouse, **Domaine d'Aupilhac** (67 96 61 19, and **Les Vignerons de Montpeyroux** (67 96 61 08, make highly praised Côteaux du Languedoc. You must call for an appointment. In **Jonquières**, a little village a few kilometers farther to the west on D 141, Olivier Jullien, a passionately dedicated young oenologist who is a native of the area, operates **Mas Juillen**, a cluster of tiny Côteaux du Languedoc vineyards. He is committed to expressing the character of each of his little parcels of land in the wine he makes. His two blends of red and two blends of white are all richly flavorful, and each one is truly unique. Mas Jullien is open daily, from 10 AM to 12 PM and 2 PM to 6 PM in the summer, afternoon only off-season (67 96 60 04.

The Pic Saint-Loup area east of Saint-Martin-de-Londres is another outstanding Côteaux du Languedoc area. Top winemakers to visit here are **Mas Bruguière** (67 55 20 97, open daily from 5 PM to 8:30 PM, **Château La Roque** (67 55 34 47, open daily except Sunday from 9 AM to 12 PM and 4 PM to 6 PM, and **Domaine de l'Hortus** (67 55 31 20, open weekdays from 5 PM to 8 PM and Saturdays from 9 AM to 8 PM. Closed Sundays.

HOW TO GET THERE

There is frequent daily bus service to Gignac, Saint-Martin-de-Londres and Ganges, but to see the countryside around them, you need a car. Gignac is 30 km (19 miles) west of Montpellier on N 109 and Saint-Guilhem 10 km (six miles) farther to on D 32 and D 27 via Aniane. To Saint-Martin-de-Londres 27 km (17 miles) north of Montpellier, take the Route de Ganges (D 986). Ganges is 46 km (19 miles) from Montpellier.

THE BASSIN DE THAU

The Languedoc shore is one nearly-unbroken sandy beach extending 160 km (100 miles) along the Gulf of Lion from the Camargue down into Roussillon, to the start of the rocky Côte Vermeille. Directly to the back of it are big salt water lagoons called *étangs* or *bassins*. These lagoons were once open bays, but were sealed in by sands washed down by the Rhône over the centuries. Access to

the sea is kept open by a few narrow channels that are constantly dredged. The sanding-up of the shore line has been a curse because it has ruined once-busy sea ports, but also a blessing, because the beaches attract tourists and the lagoons are rich breeding grounds for shellfish.

The largest of these lagoons, the Bassin de Thau, lies 30 km (19 miles) southwest of Montpellier. It is known throughout France for its mussels and oysters of Bouzigues.

GENERAL INFORMATION

Tourist Offices: Rue Massaloup, Mèze (67 43 93 08; 6 Avenue du Port, Balaruc-les-Bains (67 48 50 07.

WHAT TO SEE

The Bassin de Thau is 20 km long by four kilometers wide (12.5 by one and a quarter miles), and as you look out over the water, you see row after row of rectangular platforms that look like they're floating in the air. They are frames for the nets in which the shellfish are raised and are supported by stilts in the water. This is France's largest shellfish breeding ground. The towns of the **Bassin de Thau** — **Mèze**, **Marseillan** and several others — produce a quarter of France's oysters and mussels, all marketed under the name of the little town of **Bouzigues**. Fresh,

Frames for oyster culture in the Bassin de Thau, the coastal lagoon that is France's leading shellfish producer.

inexpensive seafood can be found there and in simple eateries all around the Bassin de Thau.

The **Musée de l'Étang de Thau** on the port in Bouzigues has a videotape program showing the whole process of mussel and oyster farming, or *conchyliculture* as they call it. The program is in French, but for non-French speakers, the visuals are easy to follow, and there are displays of the tools of the trade. It is open daily from 10 AM to 12 PM and 2 PM to 6 PM, closed November to February (67 78 33 57.

WHERE TO STAY AND WHERE TO EAT

Côte Bleue*** on the port in Bouzigues (67 78 31 42 FAX 67 78 35 49, is a very comfortable 32-room hotel with a swimming pool and one of the top restaurants in the area, my first choice for sea food on this side of the Bassin de Thau. The rooms are moderately priced and the restaurant expensive. Closed January. **La Palourdière** is a rustic family style eatery run by a shellfish producer with very fresh seafood at modest prices. Reserve in advance, because it's always full (67 43 89 19. It's about two kilometers south of Bouzigues on the little road that runs alongside the Bassin de Thau. It is open from April to October. Fronting on the colorful port of Marseillan, the **Château du Port**** is a *belle époque* mansion with lots of character and 16 spacious rooms at moderate prices (67 77 65 65. The **Restaurant du Château du Port** next door is a cheerful eatery serving hearty food at modest prices (67 77 31 67. The best and most beautiful restaurant in Marseillan is the **Table d'Emilie** at 8 Place Couverte near the market, a delightful thirteenth century stone house with a garden serving inventive regional cuisine at moderate to expensive prices (67 77 63 59. Try the Bouzigues oysters in Noilly from the local Noilly-Prat aperitif wine company. Six kilometers (four miles) north of Marseillan in the heart of Picpoul de Pinot wine country is one of the finest restaurants in Languedoc, **Léonce**, at 2 Place de la République in **Florensac** (67 77 03 05. Young Jean-Claude Fabre, in the third generation of chefs in his family, serves *supions à la Provençale* (cuttlefish), squab, sea bass and other regional specialties and has a huge cave of Languedoc and Roussillon wines. For a Michelin one-star restaurant, the prices are remarkably modest. There is a weekday luncheon menu at 120 francs, and the à la carte prices for food and wine are very reasonable. Léonce also rents 11 rooms at 220 to 250 francs.

Camping

Camping Beau Rivage in **Mèze** is a well-equipped camping ground with 234 places, a restaurant, bar and pool by the edge of the Bassin de Thau on N 113. It is open from the beginning of April to the middle of October (67 43 81 48. In Bouzigues, the more modestly equipped **Camping Lou Labech** on Chemin du Stade by the edge of the Bassin has 40 places and is open from the beginning of July to the end of September (67 78 30 38. Balaruc-le-Vieux and its resort suburb of Balaruc-les-Bains have five camping sites. For information, contact the Tourist Office at Balaruc-les-Bains.

WINE TASTING

One visit you are sure to enjoy if you like either wine or medieval architecture and you will rave about if you like both is to the **Abbaye de Valmagne** eight kilometers (five miles) north of

Mèze on D 161 (67 78 06 09. The huge church of the defunct Abbey is one of the rare examples of Gothic architecture in the South, and it now serves as a spectacular cellar for Abbaye de Valmagne wines, a prestigious *AOC* Côteaux du Languedoc grown on land first planted in vines by monks in the twelfth century. The village of **Pinet** lies 10 km (six miles) west of Mèze on D 18E, and dry white Picpoul de Pinet of high quality can be tasted at **Les Vignerons de Pinet** in Pinet (67 77 03 10, and **Hugues de Beauvignac** in the next-door town of Pomérols (67 77 01 59. The *cave* of the Vignerons de Pinet is open daily except Sunday, but you must call ahead to visit the Abbaye de Valmagne or Hugues de Beauvignac. **Noilly Prat**

A water-jousting contest in the harbor of Sète, "the Venice of Languedoc," OPPOSITE and ABOVE. Sète is France's largest fishing port on the Mediterranean.

is on the port in Marseillan (67 77 20 15, and you can tour their large aperitif-making plant every day except Sunday.

HOW TO GET THERE

There are more than a dozen buses a day from to Montpellier to Mèze, Bouzigues and other main towns of the Bassin de Thau. The trip takes less than half and hour by express bus from Montpellier to Bouzigues, ten minutes longer on the local bus. The easiest way to get there by car from Montpellier is by N 113, which goes directly to Bouzigues and Mèze. This is a very rural area, and the best way to explore it is by car or bike.

of water, and its houses run up the slopes of Mont Saint-Clair, the only high ground for miles around.

Adding to Sète's Italianate flavor is its large population of descendents of Calabrian fishermen who emigrated here in the early twentieth century. Of the 2,000 families in Sète that support themselves on fishing, the majority are of Italian descent. *Tielle*, the local squid and tomato pie, is of Italian origin.

GENERAL INFORMATION

The **Tourist Office** is at 60 Grande Rue Mario-Roustan (67 74 71 71, the main street paralleling the west side of the Canal de Sète. This is a

SÈTE

Sète calls itself "the Venice of Languedoc," and unlike most would-be Venices, Sète delivers. This is not the touristy Venice of the Piazza San Marco, though. More the workaday Venice of, say, the Stazione Marittima. Sète is a real port with its rough and tumble side, but has its picturesque spots too, like the wide Canal de Sète leading to the Vieux Port, where the houses are all painted in different shades of pastel.

Sète, then called "Cette," was created in the late seventeenth century as the port for the Mediterranean end of the Canal du Midi. Now a city of 42,000 and the largest French fishing port on the Mediterranean, it sits on the thin isthmus of Onglous between the Bassin de Thau and the sea with a complex of canals that link the two bodies

very well-run office with excellent maps and brochures.

The **train station, Gare SNCF**, is on the Quai Maréchal Joffre (67 58 50 50. The **bus station, Gare Routière**, is at Place de la République (67 74 66 90.

Taxis: **Gare SNCF** (67 48 62 98; Quai de Lattre de Tassigny (67 74 05 61.

Car Rental: **Europcar**, 23 Quai Noel Guignon (67 74 98 74; **Languedoc Location**, 5 Rue Longuyon (67 74 60 76; **Wallgren**, 11 Quai de la République (67 74 85 67.

Nautical sports: Société Nautique at the Môle Saint-Louis (67 74 98 97, rents sail boats and windsurfers and organizes scuba-diving trips.

Boat trips: Sète Croisières at the Quai de la Marine (67 46 00 10, offers frequent tours of the port and Bassin de Thau daily in season, cruises to Aigues-Mortes twice a week and a cruise on the

Canal du Midi on Sundays. They also run two fishing trips per morning and offer night fishing twice a week.

Sète Croisières also operates **little tourist trains** from the Quai de la Marine that take you around the town and the port and up Mont Saint-Clair.

Health emergencies: Hôpital Générale, Boulevard Camille Blanc (67 46 57 57.

FESTIVALS

Hardly a day goes by without some festival or special event. The main ones are the **Festival de Saint-Pierre** the first weekend of July and the **Fête de Saint-Louis** around the August 25. They feature nautical jousting, a sport in which youngsters stand on the elongated prows of competing galleys try to knock each other into the water with big sticks, like Punch and Judy.

WHAT TO SEE AND WHAT TO DO

Walk along the **Môle Saint-Louis**, the sea wall that protects the Vieux Port and has the training base for France's America's Cup challengers at the far end of it. From here you get the best view of the busy port, the Venice-like Canal de Sète with the pastel houses and the town rising up Mont Saint-Clair.

Calling a peak of 175 m (575 ft) a mountain might seem presumptuous, but if it happens to be the only elevation whatsoever for dozens of miles around, as **Mont Saint-Clair** is, you can get away with it. From its observation platform at the top, "the Venice of Languedoc" lies at your feet and grand vistas spread out before you: the Mediterranean, the beaches and beach towns up and down the shore, the Bassin de Thau, vineyards, Montpellier, and the foothills of the Cévennes.

Sète is the birthplace of the great modern poet Paul Valéry, who is buried in the Cimetière Marin, the Sailors' Cemetery, overlooking the Mediterranean on the slope of Mont Saint-Clair, about which he wrote some of his most famous lines. The modern **Musée Paul Valéry** directly above the cemetery has a room devoted to the life and work of the poet, who was a talented artist as well. The museum also has exhibits on the history of Sète, an interesting modern art collection and a room devoted to songwriter Georges Brassens, who also wrote about his native Sète. It is open from 9 AM to 12 PM and 2 PM to 6 PM, closed Tuesdays from October to the end of May. Georges Brassens is buried in the Cimetière le Py on Boulevard Camille Blanc facing the Bassin de Thau. **L'Éspace Brassens** at 67 Boulevard Camille Blanc has more exhibits on this modern troubadour.

The **Plage de la Corniche** is a 20 km (12.5 mile) strip of fine sandy, non-built-up Mediterranean beach that runs south from Sète to Cap d'Agde along the narrow isthmus between the Bassin de Thau and the sea.

WHERE TO STAY

The glamorous *belle époque* **Grand Hôtel***** has a delightful atrium winter garden four-storeys high and 43 very comfortable guest rooms and four suites. Here you can experience *le luxe* at a maximum double room rate of only 480 francs. It is at 17 Quai Maréchal de Lattre at the junction of two main canals (67 74 71 77 FAX 67 74 29 27.

For a charming and peaceful little hotel near the beach, **Les Terrasses du Lido***** on the Corniche at the Rond-Point Europe has nine moderately-priced rooms and a pool (67 51 39 60 FAX 67 53 26 96. **Le Saint-Clair**** is a modern hotel with 10 pleasant rooms, a pool and a garden in a quiet side street 200 m from the beach at 9 Avenue du Tennis la Corniche (67 53 78 27. Its rooms range in price from 200 to 350 francs. **Les Sables d'Or**** also on the Corniche at Place Edouard Herriot (67 53 09 98 FAX 67 53 26 96, has 30 rooms with a top rate of 310 francs.

Camping

Camping in Sète is at the deluxe 856 place **Le Castellas** at the beach seven kilometers (four miles) south of town on N 112, the Plage de la Corniche (67 53 26 24, open mid-May to the end of September, or the modest **Le Philippe** at

6 Boulevard Joliot Curie (67 53 08 64 by the Plage de la Corniche on the south side of Mont Saint-Clair, open April to the end of September. The adjoining beach area to the south, **Marseillan Plage**, has a vast complex of 22 camping grounds offering almost 4,500 places. For information contact the Tourist Office of Mèze, Sète or Cap d'Agde.

WHERE TO EAT

At **Saveurs Singulières** at 5 Quai Charles-La-Maresquier across the Canal de Sète from the Quai de la Marine (67 74 14 41, you can dine on the imaginative, strictly local cuisine of young

local squid pie, go to **Paradiso** at 11 Quai de la Résistance (67 74 26 48.

WINE TASTING

Le Vignerai, a museum built in a long chain of caves in the south side of Mont Saint-Clair, presents the history of Sète, its maritime tradition and the wines of the region, with free wine tasting. It is on Boulevard Camille Blanc, open daily from March to November (67 51 17 12. **Fortant de France**, Robert Skalli's big, gleaming modern blending and bottling plant for varietal vins de pays represents an important new direction in wine-making and marketing in Languedoc.

Valérie Sabatino, a native of Sète with the emphasis, naturally, on fish. It is expensive. Open evenings only (to 11 pm) in July and August, and open for lunch and dinner the rest of the year, except Sunday evening and Monday. You must reserve. **Palangrotte** at 1 Rampe Paul Valéry (Quai de la Marine) near the Tourist Office (67 74 80 35, a highly respected seafood restaurant, is the best place for fresh shellfish platters, Sète's style of *bourride de baudroie* (monkfish stew), and *bouillabaisse*. Fixed price menus start at 130 francs. Open daily, closed Sunday night and Monday from September 30 to June 30. Reservations are recommended. For inexpensive fish and shellfish in a bustling workaday ambiance, try **Chante-Mer** (67 74 03 10, or the **Hostal** (67 74 33 96, on the Promenade J.B. Marty overlooking the modern Criée aux Poissons, the wholesale fish market and the Vieux Port. To sample the best in tielles, the

There is free wine tasting and a modern art gallery. It is at 278 Avenue Maréchal Juin, on the north side of the port, open Monday to Friday all year (67 46 70 23.

HOW TO GET THERE

Sète is 30 minutes from Montpellier Airport. By rail it is half an hour from Montpellier or Béziers, and there are frequent buses from both those cities. By car, Sète is reached by the A 9 *autoroute* and N 300 to the shore or more colorfully by N 112, the shore road from Montpellier to Béziers.

The waterfront of Agde at the eastern end of the Canal du Midi, on which boats can travel across France from the Mediterranean to the Atlantic.

AGDE AND CAP D'AGDE

Agde at the southern end of the Bassin de Thau is the second oldest city in France after Marseille, founded 2,500 years ago by the Phocean Greeks. They called it *Agathé*, "the beautiful one." It became a prosperous colony trading in wine and olive oil, and it remained an important port until the late Middle Ages when Montpellier and Aigues-Mortes and later Sète took its business away. Today it is a somber-looking town of 13,000 at the junction of the Hérault River and the Canal du Midi dominated by a large twelfth century fortified church made of black lava, the former **Cathedral of Saint-Étienne**. But this town's not nearly as somber as it appears at first glance.

GENERAL INFORMATION

The **Tourist Office** of Agde is at the Espace Molière on Rue Roger ℂ 67 94 29 68; in Cap d'Agde at the main traffic circle at the park-like entrance of the town ℂ 67 26 38 58.

WHAT TO SEE AND WHAT TO DO

Agde is known as "the Black Pearl of Languedoc" because much of the **old town** is built of lava from the nearby extinct volcano, Mont Saint-Loup. Its web of twisting old streets lined with cafés, restaurants and boutiques is lively and makes for pleasant strolling, as does the riverfront. Bateaux du Soleil at 7 Quai du Chapitre in front of the cathedral offers afternoon **cruises** on the cool, tree-shaded Canal du Midi in the summer.

The **Musée Agathois** on Rue de la Fraternité near the town market has numerous amphoras from the ancient Greek port and other archaeological finds and an eclectic collection of models of ships, *ex-voto* (thanksgiving) paintings, costumes, apothecary jars and other interesting exhibits. It is open daily from 10 AM to 12 PM and 2 PM to 6 PM, closed Tuesday.

Mont Saint-Loup is a few kilometers east of Agde. An easy walk to its 111 m (365 ft) peak gives you an excellent 365 degree panorama of the Bassin de Thau, the Mediterranean, Cap d'Agde, Agde and the Cévennes.

Cap d'Agde on the coast five kilometers (three miles) east of Agde at the foot of Mont Saint-Loup, is a modern resort complex developed entirely since 1970 that now accommodates upwards of 100,000 people in the summer. It is a neatly laid-out development with curving drives and rows of red-ochre bungalows. If you blink your eyes, you might think you were in California. The resort is built around a yacht harbor with docks for 1,750 boats, and there are numerous sailing and windsurfing schools. Cap d'Agde boasts of the

some of the best sports facilities in Europe, including the **Club Pierre Barthes**, the largest tennis training center in Europe, where you can rent one of their 43 courts by the hour or stay at their hotel, take lessons and play tennis every day. It is on Avenue de la Vigne ℂ 67 26 00 06. **Golf du Cap d'Agde** is one of the best courses in Mediterranean France ℂ 67 26 54 40.

The **Musée d'Archéologie Sous-Marin** (Museum of Underwater Archaeology) has a number of objects from Greek antiquity found in underwater explorations of the harbor of Agde. The most important piece is an exquisite Hellenistic bronze statue of a nude youth, Ephèbe, found in 1964. Open from 9 AM to 12 PM and 3 PM

to 6 PM, from 2 PM to 7 PM in the summer, closed Monday.

To get naked yourself, go to the *naturiste* quarter of **Port Ambonne**, which occupies the beach on the north side of town. This is a complete nudist community with nudist hotels, camping grounds restaurants, banks and supermarkets, and on a typical midsummer day 25,000 to 30,000 nudists can be found on the beach here. The office is at the Rond-Point du Bagnas ℂ 67 26 79 69, open in season. Otherwise contact the Cap d'Agde Tourist Office.

WHERE TO STAY AND WHERE TO EAT

La Tamarissière*** at 21 Quai Thèophile Cornu at the mouth of the Hérault River, four kilometers

ABOVE: Languedoc farmer.

(two-and-a-half miles) from the center of Agde on D 32E, is a very comfortable 27-room hotel in a peaceful waterfront setting with a flowery garden and pool that has one of the most distinguished restaurants in the Hérault. Seafood is Chef Nicholas Albano's specialty, and I recommend the grilled *loup de mer* (sea bass) or the flavorful *coquilles Saint-Jacques* (sea scallops). Fixed-price menus run from 145 to 355 francs and rooms are in the 450 to 620 franc range (67 94 20 87 FAX 67 21 38 40. There are numerous small modern hotels at all prices, and the Tourist Offices of Agde and Cap d'Agde will book one for you. For an unusual hotel, look into **La Galiote**** at 5 Place Jean Jaurès next to the cathedral in Agde (67 94 45 58 FAX 67 94 14 33. This former residence of the bishops of Agde has 16 antique-furnished rooms, some overlooking the Hérault River, a cozy bar and an attractive, moderately-priced restaurant. Double rooms go for 190 to 400 francs. In Cap d'Agde the top restaurant is **Les Trois Sergents** on Avenue des Sergents (67 26 73 13, specializing in seafood.

Camping

There is a vast array of camping facilities, nudist and non-nudist, in the area. There are 20 camping grounds in Agde and Cap d'Agde and 27 in **Vias**, Agde's neighbor to the east. Between them they have several thousand camp places, most of them on or near the beach. For information on camping in Agde or Cap d'Agde, contact their tourist offices. Vias has its own Tourist Office at Boulevard de la Liberté (67 21 68 78.

HOW TO GET THERE

There are seven trains a day to Agde from Paris via Montpellier, a five-and-a-half hour trip. From Séte or Béziers, it is a fifteen minute train ride. If you are driving, Agde and Cap d'Agde lie 20 km (12.5 miles) south of Sète by the coast road (N 112), and Agde is eight kilometers (five miles) south of the A 9 *autoroute*.

PÉZENAS

The delightful town of Pézenas has a tangle of seventeenth century streets so storybook-perfect that they are often used as a location for *Three Musketeers*-era movies. It was an important place in the career of Molière, and there are many reminders of his presence here. It is 22 km (14 miles) north of Agde.

BACKGROUND

In the seventeenth century, Pézenas was the co-capital of Languedoc with Montpellier, and it was bursting with social activity when the Estates

General were in session. From 1650 to 1656, Molière enjoyed the patronage of Prince Armand de Bourbon-Conti, the Governor of Languedoc, and Pézenas became his base during that part of his thirteen year self-imposed exile in the provinces. Molière enjoyed spending time in the shop of his friend Gély the barber, where he eavesdropped on the dialogue of the nobles.

GENERAL INFORMATION

The **Tourist Office** is on Place Gambetta in the former barbershop of Gély (67 98 35 45. Be sure to pick up their excellent brochure on the historical buildings of the town, laid out as a walking tour.

WHAT TO SEE AND WHAT TO DO

Pézenas today is a quiet town of 7,600, except when it comes alive for its **Scène d'Été**, a theater, art and music festival that goes on all summer. But even off-season, Vieux Pézenas is well with a visit to stroll through its perfectly preserved *Grand Siècle* streets. The **Musée de Vulliod-Saint-Germain** is a beautiful sixteenth century mansion with a fine collection of sixteenth to eighteenth century furniture, Aubusson tapestries and exhibits on Molière. It is open from 10 AM to 12 PM and 3 PM to 6 PM, closed Tuesday all year and Wednesdays off-season. **Hôtel d'Alfonce**,

ABOVE: The old Languedoc capital of Pézenas has a wealth of elaborate mansions from the seventeenth century, when Molière spent several years there.

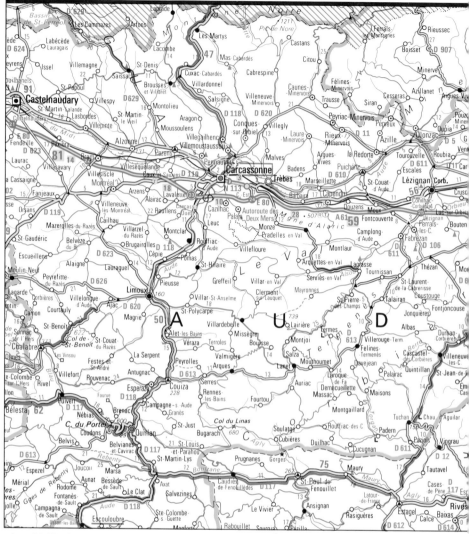

where Molière's company performed in 1655 and 1656, can be visited on Tuesdays and Fridays.

Be sure to try the local specialty, *petits patés de Pézenas*, little tubular pies filled with meat, brown sugar, suet and lemon rind, a sort of mince meat pie. They were supposedly introduced by Lord Clive in 1768 during a leave he was taking from India. **Pâtisserie-Confiserie B. Quatrefages** on Rue Conti is the grand master of this savory specialty.

WHERE TO STAY AND WHERE TO EAT

Oddly, downtown Pézenas does not have much to offer in the way of hotels and restaurants, but if you head out to the **Hostellerie de Saint-Alban***** five kilometers (three miles) south of Pézenas at 31 Route d'Agde in the village of **Néz-**

ignan-l'**Évêque**, you will find a handsome nineteenth century mansion with a large swimming pool, tennis court, peaceful, shaded grounds, restaurant and 14 tasteful rooms (67 98 11 38 FAX 67 98 91 63. Double rooms run 350 to 520 francs. A Relais de Silence member. **Genieys**** at 9 Avenue Aristide Briand in Pézenas (67 98 13 99, is a 28-room Logis de France inn, a bit outside the old part of Pézenas, but a comfortable place with a restaurant esteemed for its seafood. Prices are moderate. For the best gourmet cuisine in the area, **Léonce** in Florensac is only 10 km (six miles) south of Pézenas (see page 264 for details).

HOW TO GET THERE

Pézenas is 20 km (12 miles) inland from the Bassin de Thau. There are frequent buses from Montpel-

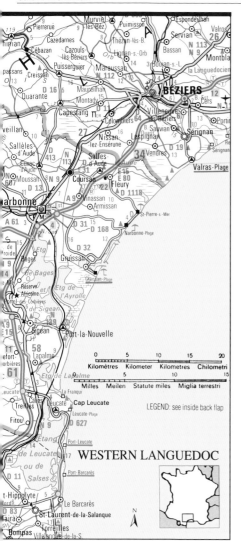

Kilométres Kilometer Kilometres Chilometri

Milles Meilen Statute miles Miglia terrestri

LEGEND: see inside back flap

WESTERN LANGUEDOC

lier, Séte, Agde and Béziers. By car it is 10 km (six miles) north of the A 9 *autoroute*.

BÉZIERS

Unlike Pézenas, which reflects its time, not its place, in Béziers you know exactly where you are in the South. Its central esplanade, the **Allées Paul-Riquet**, 600 m (almost 2,000 ft) long, shaded by four rows of huge plane trees and enlivened by outdoor cafés, will remind you immediately of Las Ramblas in Barcelona. Béziers is the first place where you sense that you are approaching Spain, only 121 km (75 miles) to the south.

When it comes to bullfighting, "The French Seville," as it is known, is out-done only by Nîmes and Arles in Mediterranean France in

number of *corridas*. For rugby also, a sport in which Béziers has long been a top international competitor, the passion of its fans for the home team is fierce.

With 80,000 people, Béziers is the Hérault's second largest city, and it is the most important city for wine in this hugely productive wine-growing department.

BACKGROUND

During the *Pax Romana*, Béziers was a wealthy wine-producing colony and a main stop on the Domitian Way. In 1209, it became the tragic scene of the first military action of the Albigensian Crusade, when the Northern army laid siege to the city. "Nearly twenty thousand were put to the sword, regardless of age and sex," Papal Legate Arnaud Aumary reported to the Pope. In the seventeenth century, Béziers native Pierre-Paul Riquet's brilliant engineering feat, the Canal du Midi, spurred major growth in the local wine trade and farm exports, and the city finally came back fully from the utter devastation of the Crusade. The Canal du Midi was the greatest engineering feat of its time — a 245 km (153 mile) long canal linking the Atlantic, via the Garonne, and the Mediterranean. It has 64 sets of locks, seven bridges that take the canal over natural obstacles and a tunnel under the Ensérune plateau. The brainchild of Baron Riquet (1604–1680), it was begun in 1666 and took 10,000 to 12,000 workers 14 years to complete it. The strain wiped out Riquet physically and financially in the process. But the result, which Riquet did not live to see, was a tremendous boon to the economy of the region. Rail and highway transport eventually took away the cargo hauling business, and today *le tourisme fluvial* (floating tourism) accounts for all the traffic, with houseboats and cruise barges plying the peaceful, tree-shaded ribbon of water.

GENERAL INFORMATION

The **Tourist Office** is at 27 Rue du 4 Septembre on Place Gabriel Péri between the Cathedral and the Allées Paul Riquet (67 49 24 19.

For **airport information, Béziers-Agde Airport** (67 90 99 10.

The **train station, Gare SNCF** (67 62 50 50.

The **bus station, Gare Routière,** (67 28 23 85.

Taxis: Place de la Victoire (67 28 49 90; **Gare du Midi** (67 28 49 91; **Place Jean Jaurès** (67 28 49 92.

Car rental: **Avis** (67 28 65 44; **Budget** (67 49 38 81; **Europcar** (67 62 09 89; **Hertz** (67 49 02 02: **Locabest** (67 76 41 00; **Wallgren** (67 76 57 46.

Boating on the Canal du Midi: Port Neuf (67 76 26 38.

Wine information: Béziers-Oenopole, Maison des Arts, 3 Rue Paul Riquet (67 28 88 94.

Medical emergencies, Centre Hospitalier, Boulevard Ernest Perreal (67 35 70 35; **S.M.U.R.** (67 35 73 69.

FESTIVALS

In July the **Festival de Béziers** puts on an all-star program of classical, pop music and jazz, and in the first two weeks of August this normally tranquil city goes wild during the **Feria**, the big bull-fighting festival. For details contact the Tourist Office.

WHAT TO SEE AND WHAT TO DO

The fortified **Cathedral of Saint Nazaire** sits on a steep hill above the River Orb. The best view is from below, on the south bank of the river by the end of the Pont Vieux. This is a blocky church, not graceful at all, but impressive, even intimidating — a reflection of the mentality of the Church at the end of the thirteenth century when it built this cathedral to replace the one destroyed in the Albigensian Crusade. Inside, other than a number of handsome stained glass windows, the church has little to recommend it. But the view from its belvedere has a great deal to offer — the river, a vine-covered plain across which the table-top plateau of Ensérune stands out clearly to the southwest.

The **Musée des Beaux Arts** near the rear of the cathedral has a heterogeneous collection of European paintings and sculpture from the fifteenth century to the present, including works by Delacroix, Géricault, Corot, Dufy, Soutine, De Chirico and Utrillo. It is open daily except Monday from 9 AM to 12 PM and 2 PM to 6 PM most of the year, from 10 AM to 7 PM in July and August.

But the most enjoyable thing in Béziers is observing real life along the colorful promenade and in the cafés of the **Allées Paul-Riquet**.

The most dramatic locks on the **Canal du Midi** are the **Écluses de Fonséranes**, better known as the **Neuf Écluses** (Nine Locks), in Béziers's western suburb of Fonséranes. It is reached by D 113 and D 9 south in the direction of Narbonne. This staircase-like series of nine locks was designed to overcome a 25 m (82 ft) drop in level. A modern water slope parallel to it has replaced the old locks.

Small **boats** can be rented all along the canal for little rides, and a number of companies rent **houseboats** for cruises. **Rives de France** in **Colombiers** near Ensérune (67 37 14 60, has modern houseboats that sleep four, six or eight people, no permits required. **Les Bateaux du Soleil**, based in Agde, runs half-day luncheon cruises from Béziers on Sundays (67 94 08 79.

WHERE TO STAY

The **Château de Lignan*** in **Lignan-sur-Orb** seven kilometers (four and a third miles) north of Béziers via D 19 is the most attractive hotel in the area (67 37 91 47 FAX 67 37 99 25. This handsome eighteenth century *château* now an elegant 49-room hotel, sits in a large private park with the River Orb flowing through it. It has a swimming pool, hammam (Turkish bath), Jacuzzi and a gourmet restaurant, **L'Orangerie**, under chef Antoine Anclin, a protégé of Alain Senderens from Lucas Carton, known for its discriminating selection Languedoc wines. The hotel and the restaurant are moderate to expensive. The most stylish downtown hotel is the **Imperator***, moderately priced and ideally situated at 28 Allées Paul Riquet (67 49 02 25 FAX 67 28 92 30. The nearby **Splendid** ** at 24 Avenue du 22 Aout

(67 49 23 82 FAX 67 49 94 32, is a solid, inexpensive alternative. Both have garages, important in this town, because parking is a real headache.

Camping
You can camp by the Canal du Midi at the 75-place **Berges du Canal** a few kilometers east of Béziers in **Villeneuve-lès-Béziers** (67 39 36 09, open all year. The beach town of **Sérignan-Plage** has 17 camping grounds with 4,000 places, and **Valras-Plage** has eight with 1,400 places. They are both about 15 km (nine miles) southeast of Béziers. For information, contact the Tourist Office of Sérignan (67 32 42 21, or Valras-Plage (67 32 36 04.

WHERE TO EAT

Le Framboisier, 12 Rue Boeildieu (67 49 90 00, a few steps to the east of the Allées Paul Riquet,

features hot oysters with sorrel, pan-fried sea scallops with wild mushrooms, fricassee of monkfish with little squid, and roast fillet of salt cod with potatoes in olive oil. With specialties such as these, chef Angel Yagues has earned his restaurant one Michelin star. It is expensive, with fixed-price menus at 140, 200 and 330 francs. Reservations are a must. Le Framboisier is closed Sunday and Monday, the month of February and the last half of August. Another fine restaurant is **Le Jardin** at 37 Avenue Jean Moulin (67 36 41 31, which offers a delicious three-course luncheon special of oyster casserole, salmon and *dorade* (sea bream) with flavored rice, and home-made sherbet at 130 francs. At the **Bistrot des Halles** at 3 Rue Porte Olivier (Place de la Madeleine) (67 28 30 46, you may feast on a variety of simple and tasty

The bridge carrying the Canal du Midi over the River Orb at Béziers.

dishes such as platters of shellfish, fried mussels and smoked salmon, and there are fixed-price menus at 62 and 106 francs, wine included.

HOW TO GET THERE

There are four flights a day from Paris to Béziers-Agde Airport. Béziers is on the main line from Paris to Barcelona, and there are several trains a day, via Montpellier, Sète and Agde. There are also frequent bus connections from Montpellier, the towns of the Bassin de Thau, and Pézenas. By car, Béziers is on the A 9 *autoroute* and several other main national and *départmental* routes.

THE OPPIDUM D'ENSÉRUNE

The Oppidum d'Ensérune is a table-top plateau that rises 120 m (394 ft) above the flat plains 13 km (eight miles) southwest of Béziers. The oppidum was a settlement of the Greeks from Marseille dating from the fourth Century BC. A natural fortress, it quickly grew into a sizable town (estimates run up to 10,000), peopled mainly by newly emigrated Gauls. The Oppidum d'Ensérune was destroyed in the third century BC, most likely by Hannibal, but was rebuilt by the Romans when they established their colony at Narbonne. When the Pax Romana made life on the lowlands safe, the impractical hilltop was abandoned forever.

Extensive ruins of dwellings have been excavated, and since it was an important necropolis

for several centuries, digs have yielded many fine ceramic pieces. They are on display in the **museum** on the site, open daily in the summer, closed Tuesdays off-season.

There are panoramas from the oppidum's four observation points of the Cévennes, Béziers, the coastal plain, the Canal du Midi, which runs just south of the oppidum and Mont-Canigou off in the distance. Looking toward Béziers, on the plain just below the oppidum is the curious **Étang de Montady,** a huge former marsh that was drained and turned into a farm field by an order of monks in the thirteenth century. It is shaped like a gigantic pie chart with dozens of narrow wedges of many different shades zeroing in on a disk in the

center. Extraterrestrials must be scratching their heads over this message.

For tourist information, stop at the **Syndicat d'Initiative**, 17 Avenue d'Espignan, Nissan-lez-Ensérune (67 37 14 12. The Oppidum is reached by N 113 from Béziers to the town of Nissan-lez-Ensérune and D 162E to the site.

NARBONNE

At first glance, only Narbonne's powerful cathedral, one of the three loftiest in France, testifies to this city's former importance in the world. But even with that, it is hard to imagine that this pleasant inland city of 47,000 with a secondary

At the Feria in Béziers in mid-August, the whole town comes alive for the big annual bullfighting event.

branch of the Canal du Midi flowing through it was once a booming Mediterranean port, the capital of Provincia Romana Narbonensis, and the most important city west of Rome itself.

BACKGROUND

Founded by the Romans in 118 BC as their first full-fledged colony between Italy and Spain, Colonia Narbon Martius quickly became a major port and transportation center on the Domitian Way. In 45 BC, Julius Caesar rewarded veterans of his Tenth Legion with properties there, and in 27 BC, it became the capital of Provincia Gallia Narbonensis, ranking with Lyon as the most popu-

lous city in Gaul. At the collapse of the Roman Empire, the Visigoths took Narbonne and made it their capital. One warring race after another followed — the Franks, the Saracens, the Franks again under Pepin the Short. Stability returned with the reign of Charlemagne, and under its powerful viscounts and archbishops, Narbonne steered clear of the Cathars and prospered as a port and center of commerce in the early Middle Ages, greatly aided by a productive Jewish colony that the city welcomed.

But in the fourteenth century, everything went wrong: the Plague, invasion by the English during the Hundred Years War, the expulsion of the Jews by the Kingdom of France, the silting up of Narbonne's harbor due to a shift in the course of the Aude River and the closing of the Étang de Bages, Narbonne's passage to the sea, by sand bars. Like Aigues Mortes, Montpellier and other towns along this coast, Narbonne was left high and dry.

With the bulwark of its economy gone, Narbonne faded from the world scene. Its cathedral

ABOVE: The archaeological museum at the Oppidum of Ensérune has displays dating from the Greek settlement in the fourth century BC. OPPOSITE: Narbonne's graceful walkway along the Canal de la Robine and its soaring Southern Gothic Cathedral of Saint-Just.

was never finished. The Canal de la Robine, its connection to the Canal du Midi, was blocked from completion for a century by powerful interests in Béziers and did not reach Narbonne until three years before the French Revolution, by which time, only a few thousand inhabitants remained.

Only in the twentieth century, after the vineyards recovered from the phylloxera epidemic, did Narbonne start to come back, and in the period since World War II it has done very well. It is the main distribution center for the huge winegrowing areas of the Aude, and with its strategic rail and highway connections, has made itself a main transshipment center for manufactured goods. In recent years, it has attracted manufacturing to its modern suburbs as well. Since World War II, Narbonne has edged out Carcassonne as the most populous city in the department of the Aude.

GENERAL INFORMATION

The **Tourist Office** is at Place Salengro near the front of the Cathedral (68 65 15 60.

The **train station, Gare SNCF**, is on Avenue Carnot, to the north of the center of the city (67 62 50 50.

Bus information: call the Tourist Office. Intercity buses stop at train station and at the Quai du Victor Hugo.

Car hire: A.D. Loc Auto (68 33 56 63; **Avis** (68 32 43 36; **Budget** (68 90 74 64; **Europcar** (68 32 34 54; **Eurodollar** (68 32 42 27; **Hertz** (68 32 04 27; **Spanghero** (68 32 04 65.

WHAT TO SEE AND WHAT TO DO

The **Cathedral of Saint-Just** is Narbonne's claim to architectural fame. The only Gothic cathedral in Languedoc, it was begun in the thirteenth century after the Albigensian Crusades as a manifestation of the power of the Church, but the completion of the cathedral was blocked by a law suit by the City of Narbonne in 1340, preventing the Church from knocking down a section of the city walls, and the cathedral was never finished. Nevertheless, truncated as its nave is, it boasts of the third highest vault of any Gothic cathedral in France, 41 m (135 ft) in height, surpassed by one meter by the Cathedral of Amiens, and by seven meters by Beauvais Cathedral. This is fortress-like Southern Gothic, massive and sturdy, not the lacy flamboyant style so familiar in the North. Its flying buttresses are block-like, not flute-like. The **Treasury**, a subterranean vault reached by a small door between the Cathedral and the Chapel of the Annunciation, contains a strange early sixteenth century Flemish tapestry on the Creation and part of an allegory on prosperity and adversity. It also has a fine collection of illuminated manuscripts and

silver religious vessels. It is open daily from 9 AM to 12 PM and 2 PM to 6 PM from May 15 to October 15.

The fourteenth century gothic **Cloister**, which has marvelously gruesome gargoyles, connects the cathedral and the **Passage de l'Ancre**, the medieval alley between the two buildings of the **Archbishops' Palace**, the **Palais Vieux** (Old Palace) on the side next to the cathedral and the **Palais Neuf** (New Palace) across the passage. In the **Cour de la Madeleine** of the Palais Vieux stands the bell tower of the long-disappeared Church of Saint-Théorodat, its ninth century rectilinear austerity contrasting with the maze of flying buttresses on the cathedral beyond.

The excellent **Musée Archéologique** is in the Palais Vieux, but is entered through the courtyard of the Palais Neuf. Unfortunately, all Narbonne's Roman building were torn down over the centuries and their stones recycled into other buildings, but pieces of them have survived and are displayed here. They include bas-reliefs from triumphal arches and sarcophagi, and there are models of Roman Narbonne. The museum also has artifacts from as far back as the Paleolithic era. It is open from 10 AM to 11:30 AM and 2 PM to 6 PM, closed Mondays in the winter, and national holidays.

The larger Palais Neuf, dating mainly from the fourteenth century, contains the sumptuous apartments of the archbishops, re-done in the seventeenth and eighteenth centuries, that now house the **Musée d'Art et d'Histoire**. Most of the art collection belonged to the archbishops. There are interesting paintings by Pieter Brueghel the Younger, Canaletto and Salvatore Rosa, a large number of Montpellier apothecary jars and an outstanding collection of ceramic tableware from Moustiers, Marseille and Montpellier from the golden age of French *faïences* (glazed, painted earthenware) in the eighteenth century. It keeps the same hours as the Musée Archéologique.

If you are willing to walk up the 179 steps to the top of the massive thirteenth century **Donjon Gilles Aycelin**, you will be rewarded with an excellent view of the cathedral, the red tile-roofed city, the hills of the Clape, the Corbières and the Pyrénées. It is open daily in the summer from 10 AM to 11:50 AM and 2 PM to 6 PM. Entrance is free.

Wedged in between the Palais Vieux and the Palais Neuf on the Place de l'Hôtel de Ville is the nineteenth century neo-Gothic **Hôtel de Ville** designed by Viollet-le-Duc.

Narbonne is a very pleasant city to stroll in, especially along the plane tree-shaded park on both sides of the **Canal de la Robine**. The **Pont des Marchands** just below the Hôtel de Ville is lined with little shops. Just south of the canal on the Cours Mirabeau is the **Halles de Narbonne**, a big cast iron, stone and mostly glass pavilion from the year 1900 that is one of the most attractive and highest quality covered markets in all of France. There are plenty of cafés where you can have an inexpensive lunch and sample the wine of the region.

Excursions

In July and August, the passenger barge *Tramontane* cruises down the Canal de la Robine and out into the Étang de Bages et de Sigean, ending up at Port-la-Nouvelle on the Golfe du Lion. The boat leaves the Cours Mirabeau at 10 AM daily and arrives at Port-la-Nouvelle at 5 PM. The fare is 85 francs. For those who wish to return to Narbonne, there is a bus for 35 francs. Food and drink prices on the boat are reasonable (68 48 35 48.

You can **rent houseboats** and cruise on the Canal du Midi, or if you have ten days to spare, cruise up through the Camargue via the Canal du Rhône à Sète and turn in the boat in at Beaucaire. **Connoisseur Cruises** at 7 Quai d'Alsace can arrange this (68 65 14 55.

Weekends and holidays from July through September, the *Autorail Touristique du Minervois* makes a daily trip from Narbonne to **Bize-Minervois** 20 km (12.5 miles) away, with stops at **Salles d'Aude** to tour **The Museum of Gallo-Roman Pottery,** to taste regional foods at the highly respected **Oulibo olive oil cooperative** at **Cabazec** and at **Bize** to see a **seventeenth century textile mill** created by Colbert. The train leaves Narbonne at 2:30 PM and gets back at 7 PM. The fare is 56 francs. The station in Narbonne is on Rue Paul Vieu near the Gendarmerie. For reservations and information call (68 27 05 94.

WHERE TO STAY AND WHERE TO EAT

The most glamorous and expensive hotel in the Narbonne area is the **Château de Villefalse****** 16 km (10 miles) south of the city in Sigean. It is a luxurious health-oriented resort in a nineteenth century mansion in the middle of a vineyard with 15 sumptuous rooms and suites with canopy beds and ten modern duplex suites in a new annex, a large pool, tennis courts and a state-of-the-art fitness center. Room rates range from 640 to 1,800 francs. It also has a first-rate restaurant serving gourmet regional cuisine (68 48 54 29 FAX 68 48 34 37. The **Relais du Val d'Orbieu***** in

the village of **Ornaisons** 14 km (nine miles) west of the city on N 113 is a delightful country inn with gardens, a large pool, tennis court, golf practice hole and 13 spacious rooms at rates of 390 to 650 francs. Its restaurant is the finest in the area, with fixed-price menus starting at 145 francs (68 27 10 27 FAX 68 27 52 44. In town, **La Résidence***** at 6 Rue 1er Mai (68 32 19 41 FAX 68 65 51 82, a pretty nineteenth century town house on a quiet street in the center of the city, has 26 tasteful rooms at moderate rates, with 420 francs the top price for a double. The big pink **Grand Hôtel de la Dorade**** at 44 Rue Jean-Jaurès in the heart of the city overlooking the Canal de la Robine is a Narbonne institution, founded in 1648. It has 40 comfortable, modernized rooms at remarkably reasonable rates — 270 francs for the average double room, 300 francs tops. Its **Toque d'Or** restaurant serves good regional food at honest prices,

and its piano bar, the **Black Bull**, is a lively spot in the evening (68 32 65 95 FAX 68 65 81 62. At the **Hôtel de France**** at 6 Rue Rossini near the market you will find 11 neat rooms for 100 to 220 francs (68 32 09 75. All the in-town hotels mentioned have garages.

The top restaurant in town is **L'Alsace** at 2 Avenue Pierre Sémard across the street from the train station (68 65 10 24, serving excellent fish and shellfish dishes, with a luncheon special weekdays at 110 francs. Closed Monday night and Tuesday.

Le Léonard down the street at 34 Avenue Pierre Sémard (68 65 29 36, is a friendly restaurant with shellfish, grilled fish and meat at

modest prices. Closed Sunday night and Saturday at lunch.

Camping

The camping grounds of the region are mainly at the beach. There are three at **Narbonne Plage**: the deluxe **Camping Municipal La Falaise** with 336 places (68 49 80 77; **Camping Le Soleil d'Oc** with 212 places (68 49 86 21; and the large 808 place **Camping Municipal Côtes des Roses** on the Route de Gruissan (68 49 83 65. They are open from April to the end of September, very crowded in mid-summer. In **Gruissan**, **Camping les Ayguades** has 350 places and is open from March 1 to the end of October (68 49 81 59.

Narbonne's Archbishop's Palace LEFT, covered food market CENTER, and a quiet downtown street RIGHT.

At **Sigean**, the best equipped camping grounds is the 65-place **Camping Grange Neuve** (68 48 58 70, on the Route Réserve Africaine, open all year.

WINE TASTING

Narbonne is the commercial center of a huge wine-making area with *appellations* that include Corbières, Minervois, La Clape and Fitou along with non-*AOC* wine sold mostly as *Vin de Pays d'Oc*. In the past this area was known almost exclusively for cheap table wine it produced for the French working man (with the exception Fitou, an *AOC* since 1948), but it has made giant steps in

HOW TO GET THERE

The Béziers-Agde Airport is 36 km (22 miles) to the north and has four flights a day from Paris. Narbonne is a main railway interchange, where the line between Paris and Barcelona connects with the line between Narbonne to Toulouse, and there are frequent train connections with Montpellier, Béziers, Carcassonne, Perpignan and other cities of the area. Courriers du Midi has regular bus service to Narbonne via Pézenas and Béziers, continuing on to Perpignan. However there is very little bus service between different parts of the Aude. To get around, you need your

quality in the past twenty years, and today is one of the most dynamic wine-growing areas in France. The large modern **Palais du Vin** just south of central Narbonne represents 2,500 wine makers and offers free wine tasting, literature and help on planning wine routes. It is on the Route de Perpignan (N 9) (68 41 47 20, open daily.

Serious students of wine should take a run out to **Lézignan-Corbières** 20 km (12.5 miles) west of Narbonne on Route N 113 to visit the **Musée de la Vigne et du Vin**. It is a large nineteenth century wine-making estate that was converted into a museum in 1973 with old tools and machinery, a big vat for crushing grapes by feet, wagons, storage cellars and the family's home. There is free wine tasting and abundant literature. It is at 3 Rue Turgot opposite the Lézignan-Corbières railway station (68 27 07 57. Open daily all year.

own transportation. Coming by car, Narbonne is at the junction of the area's two main thruways, the north-south A 9 and the east-west A 61.

AROUND NARBONNE

Narbonne is the gateway to the *départment* of the Aude. The Corbières starts immediately to the southwest, and the Minervois and Carcassonne are less than an hour's drive to the west. But there are some unusual drives to be made in the vicinity of Narbonne itself too.

La Montagne de la Clape and Gruissan

The Montagne de la Clape is valuable wine country, and the growers cultivate little parcels far up into the piney hills between Narbonne and the coast 12 km (seven and a half miles) away. Its highest peak, 214 m (700 ft) **Pech Redon**, towers over the lagoons and flat vineyard-covered plains. Among the best known makers of *AOC* Côteaux du Languedoc La Clape and the most picturesque to visit are **Château Pech-Céleyran** ((68 33 50 04) in **Salles d'Aude** at the northern end of la Clape and **Château de Pech Redon** (68 90 41 22, off D 32, the road to Gruissan.

The fishing village of **Gruissan** on the sea side of La Clape, inhabited since the dawn of history, has managed to retain much of its charm. Its little ochre-roofed houses form concentric circles around the hilltop ruins of its **Tour Barberousse**. Amid the bland modern beach resorts that have sprung up along the Languedoc coast in the past twenty years, this old village is a gem. Flamingos can often be seen wading in the **Étang de Gruissan**. There is no problem finding good seafood here. Two tried-and-true choices are **L'Estagnol** (68 49 01 27, with a flowery terrace overlooking the Étang, and **La Marée** (68 49 16 26, in the heart of the village. Both are moderately priced.

On June 29 Gruissan celebrates the **Fête de Saint-Pierre** (Feast of Saint Peter) with vespers, blessing of the fishing fleet, wreaths of flowers cast into the water to commemorate sailors lost at sea, and at night there is a popular ball.

The **Tourist Office** in Gruissan is at Boulevard du Pech Maynaud (68 49 03 25.

To get to La Clape and Gruissan from Narbonne, take D 32, the Route de Gruissan. Gruissan is 17 km (11 miles) from Narbonne.

La Réserve Africaine de Sigean

The African Reserve of Sigean has more than 2,400 animals living in nature on its 200 hectare (500 acre) simulated African range. There is a four mile drive through the African savanna where you can see families of lions and elephants, rhinos, giraffes, zebras, monkeys, ostriches, 157 species in all. The park attracts over 300,000 visitors a year. It is opens at 9 AM daily all year. 80 francs for adults, 60 francs for children four to 14 years old (68 48 20 20. A sure-fire attraction if you are traveling with kids.

It is 15 km (nine miles) south of Narbonne via N 9.

L'Abbaye de Fontfroide

The large, beautifully restored Abbey of Fontfroide 14 km (nine miles) southwest of Narbonne is an oasis of greenery amid the parched limestone hills of the Corbières. Set in a little wooded valley with cypresses all around it, the place has a distinctly Tuscan air. The abbey was founded by Benedictines at the end of the eleventh century and prospered immediately. It affiliated itself with the Cistercians in 1146. Fontfroide became a bastion of Catholic orthodoxy against the Cathar movement. In fact, the murder of one of its monks, papal legate Pierre de Castelnau at Saint-Gilles in

1208, set off the Albigensian Crusade. The abbey's main buildings, made of pink and ochre sandstone from the Corbières, date from twelfth and thirteenth centuries — the church with its 18 m (60 ft) barrel-vaulted nave, the lovely cloister with double rows of marble columns and capitals sculpted in floral motifs, along with the **chapter hall**, **refectory**, **kitchen**, **dormitory** and **cellars**. The abbey owned vast farms and vineyards and was a power in the region. One of its members became Benedict XII, Pope of Avignon from 1334 to 1342. From the fifteenth century on, the abbey declined, and it was abandoned in 1791. In the late nineteenth century, Cistercians from Sénanque tried to revive it, but gave up in 1901. Luckily, a philanthropic

family of the area, the Fayets, bought the deteriorating abbey in 1908 and started its tasteful restoration. There is a **rose garden** with more than 3,000 bushes. Concerts are held at the abbey from June through September. Open all year (68 45 11 08.

THE CORBIÈRES

If we were to think of Languedoc as a living organism, its brain would be Montpellier, its stomach the Carcassonne to Castelnaudary *cassoulet* belt, its sex glands presumably Cap d'Agde, and its heart and soul the Corbières. This sun-blasted range of rugged limestone hills in the center of the Aude *département*, famed for its potent red wines, is also a land of savage beauty with historical sites that are unbelievably dramatic — the "citadels of vertigo," the cliff-top fortresses, that were the last refuges of the Cathars during the Albigensian Crusade, where the "perfects" serenely, even cheerfully, plunged into the bonfires rather than give up their faith.

OPPOSITE: The grape harvest in Languedoc, where winemakers have greatly improved quality in the past few decades. ABOVE: The African Reserve of Sigean has 2,400 African animals living in natural habitats.

The hills of the Corbières start immediately to the southwest of Narbonne. They are bounded on the east by the narrow plain along the Gulf of Lion that runs 50 km (30 miles) south from Narbonne to Salses. On the south, the border is formed by the Agly River and the Fenouillèdes, foothills of the Pyrénées. The western and northern borders are defined by the Aude River, which flows north from the Pyrénées to Carcassonne, then elbows eastward to the Mediterranean above Narbonne, with the Canal du Midi, the Autoroute des Deux Mers and N 113 running along its valley.

In the Corbières, we have scenery, wine, history, and adventure — the chance to drive, ride bikes or horses, or hike miles and miles along *garrigue* scented back-country roads without seeing another car or person and explore magnificent sites that only serious travelers get to. It is an area that has yet to be corrupted by mass tourism, perhaps because the spirit of the Cathars lives on. However, since there are so few tourists, there are also few tourist facilities. Hotels, restaurants and — be warned — service stations are few and far between. If you are exploring the Corbières by car, keep your eye on the fuel gauge and tank up frequently.

Most travelers dip into the Corbières from the cities on three of its corners — Narbonne on the northeast, Carcassonne on the northwest and Perpignan on the southeast. Narbonne has a good range of hotels and restaurants, and Carcassonne and Perpignan offer creature comforts that should please even the most sybaritic of softies.

A good place to plunge into the Corbières is the **Château de Lastours** in **Lastours** a few kilometers west of the African Reserve of Sigean via D 611 A, just past Portel-des-Corbières. It is one of the region's most highly-rated vineyards, making a wide range of wines from robust aged *AOC* Corbières reds and bright *blanc de blancs* to this year's pale pink *vin gris*, a life-saver when served chilled in the oven-like summers around here. Besides its award-winning wines, the Château deserves high praise for its far-sighted employment policy of providing work at fair pay in a stable community framework for mentally handicapped people, enabling them to lead independent lives. The village has become a cultural center for the area with concerts and art exhibitions the year round, and racing teams train for the Paris to Dakar cross-Sahara auto race in the 600 hectares (1,400 acres) of canyons and *garrigue* that surround the *château*'s 160 hectares (385 acres) of vines. The *château* has a good, moderately priced restaurant (68 48 29 17.

According to Corbières folk wisdom, vines must "suffer" to produce grapes that make good wine. If there ever was a place for that, it is this arid, rocky, sun-blasted terrain swept often by the *tramontane*, a wind that can blow for days at a time. Only two things will grow here, the fragrant tangle of scrub brush, rosemary, thyme, lavender and wild flowers known as *garrigue* for one, and the grape vine for the other. Science has yet to resolve the mystery of how the flavors and aromas of other plants in the vicinity get into the grape, but they do it somehow, and the proof is found in the wine.

DURBAN-CORBIÈRES

This old fortified village lies 12 km (seven and a half miles) west of Lastours via D 611. Part of its fourteenth century ramparts remains, as does one wall of its eleventh century **Château des Seigneurs de Durban** on the hill in the center of town, very impressive nonetheless.

As noted, creature comforts in the Corbières are rudimentary. So people who are passionate about gourmet food should plan their day around lunch or dinner at **Le Moulin**, a converted mill on a hill amid vineyards with a view of the Château, where you can sample David Moreno's imaginative Mediterranean concoctions that have earned him one of the few Michelin stars in Languedoc. Fixed price menus start at 158 francs. There is a superb selection of local wines. This is a very popular restaurant. Be sure to reserve. It is on Route D 611 in Durban (68 45 81 03.

For **wine**, drive down to the **Cave Pilote de Villeneuve-les-Corbières** (68 45 91 59, four kilometers (two and a half miles) south of Durban on D 611. This pioneering cooperative with 82 member vineyards was formed in 1948 to experiment and improve quality, and has become one of the region's most consistent producers of fine wines. They make five blends of Fitou reds, Corbières reds, whites and rosés, Muscat de Rivesaltes and *vin de pays*. The *cave* is open daily except Sundays from 8:15 AM to 12 PM and 2 PM to 6 PM.

VILLEROUGE-TERMENÈS

As usual around here, this little village in the heart of the Corbières is dominated by a medieval castle. What's unusual about Villerouge-Termenès is the big **medieval pageant** it puts on in the summer. The pageant is based on the tragic story of Guilhem Bélibaste, the last Cathar "perfect" in Villerouge to be burned at the stake in 1321. It is held every Saturday in mid-summer, and there are **medieval-syle feasts**. For information and schedules, contact Estival Médiéval (68 70 06 24.

The eagle's nest Cathar fortress of **Termes** is 12 km (seven and a half miles) west of town via D 613 and D 40. Its setting overlooking the Gorges of the Terminet is dramatic, but the fortress itself is in a state of utter ruin. Be careful if you decide to climb up there: the terrain is very rough and is considered dangerous. The fortress of Termes resisted the army and siege engines of Simon de Montfort for four months in 1210, but finally fell because of lack of water. It is one of the so-called "Five Sons of Carcassonne," described on pages 290 to 292.

What little lodging there is in the area is in *chambres d'hôtes* (bed and breakfasts) and *gîtes* (country cottages). For information and bookings, call ADHCO in the nearby village of **Mouthoumet** (68 70 04 45. In the pretty village of **Davejean** seven kilometers (four miles) south of Villerouge-Termenès, **Madame Tavard** rents

they owned most of the Corbières. In the fourteenth century, the Black Plague and the Black Prince Edward put an abrupt end to the prosperity. In the seventeenth century, the Saint-Maur order took over the abbey and restored it spiritually and financially, but during the Revolution, it was split in two and sold off. While it is no match architecturally for Fontfroide, the Abbey of Lagrasse has handsome buildings from both its prosperous times, and the village has two ancient bridges, one a "donkey back" from the twelfth century, the ruins of its ramparts, old houses and a good market. The Abbey can be visited daily from 10 AM to 12 PM and 2 PM to 6 PM, to 7 PM in summer.

twopleasant *chambres d'hôtes* with private baths, at 140 francs for a double, breakfast included, and meals are 60 francs (68 70 01 85. The nearest hotel and camping grounds are in Lagrasse 13 km (eight miles) to the north.

The most interesting route from Durban-Corbiéres to Villerouge-Termenès is via the small but perfectly adequate D 40, a distance of 20 km (12.5 miles) due west from Durban.

LAGRASSE

The **Abbey of Lagrasse** in Lagrasse on Route D 3 in north-central Corbières is even older than the Abbey of Fontfroide. Founded by Charlemagne himself around the year 800, it became rich thanks to gifts and privileges, and by the twelfth century owned lands as far afield as Béziers and Toulouse. Between the abbeys of Lagrasse and Fontfroide,

The **Tourist Office** is at the Place de la Halle (68 43 10 05.

The **Auberge Saint-Hubert** at 9 Boulevard des Promenades has nine clean, simple rooms at 130 to 260 francs and a modestly priced restaurant serving regional fare (68 43 15 22. It is a Logis de France member. The **Auberge des Trois Grâces** at 5 Rue du Quai rents four modest rooms at inexpensive rates (68 43 18 17.

Camping Municipal Boucocers is a few kilometers south of town in **Bachandres**. It is an attractive site with 40 places, open all year (68 43 10 05.

To get to Lagrasse from Narbonne, take N 113 west to Lézignan-Corbières (where you can visit the Musée de la Vigne et du Vin, see WINE TASTING,

The sun-blasted hills of the Corbières, a land of wine, history, adventure and savage beauty.

page 280) and D 611 and D 212 southwest to La-grasse, 38 km (24 miles) in total. From Villerouge-Termenès, take D 613, D 23 and D 3 to the north, a distance of 13 km (eight miles).

CARCASSONNE

Carcassonne is the largest medieval fortress city in Europe. Its twin rings of tall, massive crenelated walls measure three kilometers (nearly two miles) in circumference, and there are 52 mighty towers. It is one of the Old Continent's most unforgettable sights. Legend has it that when Edward the Black Prince arrived with his army in 1355, he took one look at the fortress and decided to move on (after sacking and burning the unwalled lower town first, naturally). Until the advent of the canon, it was considered impregnable. Hence its nickname, the "Maid of Languedoc."

La Cité, as the walled city on the hill is called, looks down on the flat, grid-patterned **Ville Basse**, the lower city on the left bank of the Aude. The Lower City dates from the thirteenth century and prospered after the opening of the Canal du Midi, which runs through it. Today virtually all of Carcassonne's 43,500 people live in the lower city. It is the center of the area's wine trade, agro-industries and light manufacturing and is the capital of the Aude department. Less than 100 people actually live year-round in the Cité. The medieval Cité is particularly dramatic on summer nights, when it is illuminated, and even more so on the 14th of July, when there is a tremendous fireworks display.

BACKGROUND

The earliest inhabitants of Carcassonne were Iberians whose traces date from the sixth century BC. They were supplanted by Germanic Volcae Tectosages in the fourth century BC. The Romans took it over and built their first fortress here in 122 BC, the year after they conquered Vaison-la-Romaine and established Aix-en-Provence and four years before they founded their colony at Narbonne. Their objective was to control the pass between the Montagne Noire and the Corbières, the strategic bottleneck on the only trade route between the Atlantic to the Mediterranean. Carcasso, as the Romans called their new *oppidum*, prospered for five centuries under the Pax Romana. But in the middle of the fifth century, as the Empire crumbled, the Visigoths overran Languedoc and Spain. They held

Carcassonne until the Saracens swept up from Spain in 725, took it and renamed it Karkashuna. In 759, Pepin the Short, the King of the Franks and father of Charlemagne, descended from the North and chased them back to Spain. After the breakup of Charlemagne's empire, the Trencavel family ruled Carcassonne as vassals of the Counts Toulouse, and it became a thriving merchant town. Being Viscounts of Albi, Béziers and Nîmes in addition from 1082 to 1209, the Trencavels became very rich, and their court in Carcassonne was one of the brightest of the Age of the Troubadours. But all this changed abruptly in the early thirteenth century, when 24 year-old Viscount Raymond Roger Trencavel stepped forward to defend the many Cathars in his domains, defying Pope Innocent III. In August, 1209, after the fall of Béziers, Simon de Montfort and his army laid siege to Carcassonne. Violating a safe conduct for negotiations, de Montfort took Raymond Roger prisoner, and Carcassonne surrendered. Three months later, Raymond Roger died in his cell, and Simon de Montfort became Viscount of Carcassonne. After De Montfort was killed at the siege of Toulouse in 1218, his son Amaury was unable to maintain control of the lands and turned Carcassonne over to King Louis VIII in 1223. From then on, except when the Wehrmacht took it over during World War II, it has been under French rule.

Though there are some parts of Roman walls and extensive sections built by the Visigoths, most of what we see today dates from the thirteenth and fourteenth centuries, when Saint Louis, Philip the Bold and Philip the Fair made the Cité a paragon of medieval defensive architecture. But the development of artillery made all medieval fortifications obsolete. And when the Treaty of the Pyrénées in 1659 made the Pyrénées the frontier between France and Spain, Carcassonne lost its strategic importance. The Cité deteriorated, and by the time of the Revolution had become a virtual ghost town, with the whole social and economic life taking place in the lower city, where, thanks to the Canal du Midi, the linen and wine trades were booming. By the 1830's, all the roofs of the fortress had caved in and the walls had become dangerously dilapidated, and the government ordered it to be demolished. But local archaeologist Jean-Pierre Cros-Mayrevieille, writer Prosper Mérimée, then Inspector of Public Monuments, and architectural restorer Viollet-le-Duc mounted a successful campaign to save it.

About thirty percent of the Cité as it stands today, mainly the roofs and upper levels, is the work of Viollet-le-Duc. It has been controversial right from the start. Too medieval story-book romantic say the purists, especially the treatment of the roofs and turrets. The original roofs,

OPPOSITE: Carcassonne, Europe's largest medieval fortress city, was saved from demolition in the early nineteenth century by pioneering landmark conservationists.

it seems, were red tile, not slate. Such inaccuracies are easy to forgive, though, when you consider that if it hadn't been for those men, La Cité de Carcassonne would no longer exist. It was just in the nick of time that they managed to convince the Louis Philippe government to save it. Some of the demolition work had already begun.

GENERAL INFORMATION

The main **Tourist Office** of Carcassonne is at 15 Boulevard Camille-Pelletan at Square Gambetta in the lower town (68 25 07 04. From Easter through November, a sub-office in the Cité is open just inside the Porte Narbonnaise (68 25 68 81. For information about hiking, horseback riding, sports and accommodations in other parts of the Aude, contact the Comité Départemental du Tourisme de l'Aude at 57 Rue d'Alsace, Carcassonne (68 11 42 00, also in the lower city.

The following numbers may prove useful during your stay:

Airport information, Carcassonne-De Salvaza Airport (68 25 12 33.

Train information, Gare SNCF, at the northern end of Rue Maréchal Joffre (68 47 50 50.

The **bus station, Gare Routière**, is on Boulevard de Varsovie on the west side of town (68 25 12 74.

Car rental: Avis (68 25 05 84; **Budget** (68 72 31 31; **Europcar** (68 25 05 09; **Hertz** (68 25 41 26; **Spanghero** (68 47 52 76.

Bicycle rental: at the baggage room of the **Gare SNCF** (68 71 79 14 or **Fun Sports**, 14 Rue J. Monet (68 71 67 06.

Taxis: (68 71 50 50.

Health emergencies: SAMU: (15, or the **Hospital Center** on Route Saint-Hilaire (68 24 24 24.

Tourist train: *Le Petit Train de la Cité* makes a 20-minute circuit of the Cité from May 1 to September 30.

FESTIVALS

The **Festival de la Cité** is a month-long program of music, theater and dance events held during the month of July. On the **14th of July** there is a spectacular fireworks display.

During the first two weeks of August, **Les Médiévales**, a grand costume pageant, takes over the city.

For more information contact the Tourist Office.

WHAT TO SEE AND WHAT TO DO

The view of the **Cité** standing out against the skyline can't help but impress even the most jaded of travelers. But for a full appreciation of the

massive **stone walls and 52 towers** and the ingenuity of their design, I suggest taking the *Petit Train de la Cité*'s 20-minute **circuit of the walls**, which leaves from the main gate, the Porte Narbonnaise. The trip will take you through the **Lices** (the Lists), the fortress's most effective defensive feature. This is a wide, barren space between the outer and inner rings of walls in which any attacker who managed to make it over the outer wall would have no place to hide from the projectiles rained down on him by defenders atop the inner wall. In times when the city was not under attack, the Lices were used for jousting. About 500 m to the right of the Porte Narbonnaise you will see a section of wall dating from late Roman Empire (fourth century AD), identifiable by its small grey stones broken by courses of red bricks, in contrast to the large rectangular stones of the medieval period. If you have the time to explore the walls on foot, all the better.

The **Porte Narbonnaise** is so-named because it faces east toward Narbonne. Built at the most vulnerable point of the fortress, it has two massive round bastions flanking a drawbridge and a portal, which was barred in the old days by a heavy chain and two iron portcullises. It dates from the time of Philip the Bold and was the only entrance wide enough for a carriage. Inside the gate, the narrow, cobblestone main street, **Rue Cros-Mayreveille**, picturesque, but overloaded with souvenir shops, leads directly to the **Château Comtal**. This nine-towered castle was built by the Counts of Trencavel in the twelfth century and is surrounded by mighty walls and a moat of its own. The Château is open daily from 9 AM to 7:30 PM in July and August, shorter hours off-season. The Château is visited by guided tour only, and it is well worth taking, even if you don't speak French. It leads you through the **Lapidary Museum**, which has sculptures and carved stones from the Roman and medieval periods, out through courtyards and up along the top of the walls of the city, which adjoin the Château's walls at one point. The view of the Cité and the countryside is spectacular from here.

The **Basilique de Saint-Nazaire** (Basilica of Saint Nazaire) started as a Romanesque cathedral, built between 1096 and 1130, and a barrel-vaulted nave supported by two side aisles with semi-circular vaults remain from that period, but the transept and choir are Gothic, built after the Albigensian Crusade. So is the church's most glorious feature, its fourteenth century **rose windows**. **Simon de Montfort's tombstone** can also be seen in the church, but his body was removed from the cathedral in 1224 and buried in the North to prevent desecration. The Basilica lost its cathedral status in 1803 when the bishopric was transferred to the Lower Town, where the church of Saint Michel became the cathedral.

As for the **Lower Town**, despite its importance as a commercial and transportation center and capital of the Aude department, it is a remarkably dreary place. Other than visiting the tourist offices, taking a train or bus, or looking for a hotel or restaurant, which are generally much less expensive than in the Cité, there is little reason to come here. The city was laid out in a rigid grid pattern in the mid-thirteenth century (like Aigues-Mortes, also laid out at the time of Louis IX), and the utter regularity of the streets adds to the feeling of monotony.

Carcassonne is one of three cities famous for *cassoulet*, a rich, very filling casserole of

WHERE TO STAY

The Carcassonne area has more fine hotels than all the rest of the Aude put together.

In the **Cité**, the **Hôtel de la Cite****** at Place de l'Eglise (68 25 03 34 FAX 68 71 50 15, is the Gothic-style former episcopal palace transformed into an exquisite hotel with 23 rooms fully furnished with antiques and equipped with modern bathrooms in grey marble, with a small swimming pool and a lovely French garden looking out at the ramparts. Rooms run 870 to 1100 francs. The **Hôtel du Donjon***** at 2 Rue Comte Roger (68 71 08 80 FAX 68 25 06 60, is a tasteful, pleasant

white beans and preserved meats baked in an earthenware pot. The other two cities are Castelnaudary and Toulouse. All use as their base the white beans (*haricots blancs*) grown in the Lauragais countryside surrounding Castelnaudary. Essentially the differences between them have to do with the meats that are used — various combinations of goose or duck parts conserved in their own grease, sausages, mutton, lamb or pork. In Carcassonne's style, you will find mutton, and sometimes partridge during the hunting season. A war of words has raged for centuries as to which of the three styles is the superior. This is a debate I steer clear of. They are all delicious when prepared well. So let your own taste be your guide. But you certainly should give cassoulet a try in either Carcassonne or Castelnaudary, or, if you have an enormous appetite, make a comparison in both towns.

and very comfortable 36-room hotel in a medieval residence with rooms in the 290 to 490 franc range. **Les Remparts**** at 3 Place du Grand Puits (68 71 27 72, is the best choice in the lower price range, with 18 rooms at 280 to 330 francs. All have garages for guests' cars.

My choice, however, because I like a bit more space around me, is the **Mercure Le Vicomté***** outside the walls of the Cité, a five minute walk from the Porte Narbonnaise at 18 Rue Camille Saint-Saëns (68 71 45 45 FAX 68 71 11 45. This relaxing hotel has 58 attractive, modern rooms at 440 francs, a good-sized garden with a pool that you can really swim in and a poolside luncheon patio with a marvelous view of the Cité.

The elegant Hôtel de la Cité within the walls of the medieval city.

In the **Lower City**, the finest hotel is the **Montségur*****, at 27 Alée Iéna (68 25 31 41 FAX 68 47 13 22, a nineteenth century town-house furnished with antiques, with 21 very comfortable rooms at 390 to 510 francs. The **Royal Hôtel**** at 22 Boulevard Jean-Jaurès (68 25 19 12 FAX 68 47 33 01, has 18 neat rooms equipped with showers. There are no bathtubs in the hotel. Rooms run 280 to 330 francs. Up the street at 27 Boulevard Jean-Jaurès, the **Central**** has 20 clean, recently renovated rooms at the remarkably low rates of 160 to 200 francs for a double (68 25 03 84 FAX 68 72 46 41.

On the **outskirts of the city**, the **Domaine d'Auriac****** is a gorgeous 13-room Relais & Châteaux inn in a country mansion set in a three hundred year-old park with ancient cedars, magnolias and flower gardens, a pool, tennis court and private nine hole golf course. Rooms here go for 660 to 1,300 francs in the summer, 500 to 900 francs off-season. It is on the Route de Saint-Hilaire, four kilometers (two and a half miles) southwest of the Cité (68 25 72 22 FAX 68 47 35 54.

Camping

The Carcassonne Tourist Office guide to lodging and restaurants lists seven camping grounds within an eight kilometer (five mile) radius of Carcassonne and five more within a 28 km (17.5 mile) radius. The closest to the Cité is **Camping de la Cité**, a few kilometers to the south on the Route de Saint-Hilaire, a well-equipped 200-place site with a restaurant, bar, food shop, swimming pool and tennis court (68 25 11 77. It is open from March 1 to the end of October. For a full list, get in touch with the Tourist Office.

WHERE TO EAT

There are very good restaurants here, starting with the **Barbacane** at the Hôtel de la Cité, a gorgeous dining room worthy of a medieval banquet. Here you may sample the subtle Languedocien-Provençal cuisine of Michel Del Burgo, featuring puff-pastry with vegetables and foie gras, brochette of squab with risotto, veal cutlets braised in Banyuls wine sauce and a myriad of other mouth-watering inventions that have earned him a Michelin one-star. There is a fixed-price luncheon menu weekday at 250 francs, wine included. The evening menu is 400 francs.

The **Domaine d'Auriac** also sports a Michelin star, thanks to owner-chef Bernard Rigaudis's *foie gras*, *cassoulet*, knuckle of veal in Chardonnay wine from Limoux and for dessert, cinnamon ice cream with a warm pear and almond tart, among other culinary treats. Here the luncheon menu is 170 francs, 350 francs in the evening.

At the **Château Saint-Martin "Logis de Trencavel,"** a sixteenth century *château* in a wooded park, noted chef Jean-Claude Rodriguez makes a classic cassoulet that is highly esteemed by Carcassonne natives. The cost of the dish, a meal in itself, is 95 francs. Sea bass with a mousse of scallops, sole in tarragon and other specialties have earned this restaurant a Michelin star also. Fixed-price menus run 160 and 280 francs, and there is a fine selection of Corbières and Minervois wines. The Château Saint-Martin is in the hamlet of **Montredon**, four kilometers (two and a half miles) northeast of town (68 71 09 53.

Two other excellent restaurants in the Cité are the **Brasserie Le Donjon** at the hotel of the same name (see above) and **Dame Carcas** at 15 Rue Saint-Louis (68 71 37 37. So is the **Auberge du Pont-Levis**, which is outside the Porte Narbonnaise with a superb view of the Cité (68 25 55 23. They are less expensive than the first three mentioned, and all make a very good *cassoulet*. In the Lower Town, talented young chef Didier Faugeras has made a name for himself at his restaurant **Le Languedoc** at 32 Allée d'Iéna (68 25 22 17, across the street from his parents' hotel, Le Montségur. Here you will find an excellent *cassoulet* also, along with other cuisine of the region and original creations.

HOW TO GET THERE

There are two flights a day from Paris's Orly Airport on Régional Airlines and several high-speed *TGV* trains daily from Paris via Montpellier, a six-and-a-half-hour trip or via Toulouse or Bordeaux, a seven-hour trip. There are trains from Montpellier about every hour, a one-and-a-half-hour ride, as well as from Narbonne. Occasional local trains run down the Aude River Valley to Limoux, Quillian and Perpignan. Regional bus service is minimal in the Aude, except between the main cities. Driving to Carcassonne, the fastest way is by the A 61 *autoroute* from Narbonne or Toulouse. If you are coming from Lagrasse, take D 3 west through the dramatic gorge of the Alsou and on to Carcassonne 35 km (22 miles) away. To get to the Cité by bus from the Lower Town, take the N° 4 local bus.

CASTELNAUDARY

Cassoulet lovers may want to make a pilgrimage to Castelnaudary, acknowledged by one and all as the birthplace of the dish. The white beans known as *lingots* (ingots) that are the basic ingredient are grown here. Their virtue is that they remain firm while at the same time becoming saturated with the juices of the meat as they bake in the clay pot.

Castelnaudary is a low-key provincial town of 11,000 with many fine seventeenth and eighteenth century homes, and its **Grand Bassin**, formed by a series of four locks on the Canal du Midi, is an important center for canal boating.

GENERAL INFORMATION

The **Tourist Office** is at Place de la République (68 23 05 73.

Train station, Gare SNCF (68 23 01 46.

Houseboat rental: Crown Blue Line, Grand Bassin, 11400 Castelnaudary (68 23 17 51 FAX 68 23 33 92.

LIMOUX

Limoux is a delightful old hill town south of Carcassonne famed for its sparkling white Blanquette-de-Limoux wines, like champagne, but with its own unique taste. The so-called *méthode champenoise*, the method for putting bubbles in wine, was developed in Limoux in the sixteenth century, well before it got up to Champagne.

Limoux's wide boulevards are lined with large plane trees, and pretty **Place de la République** has arcaded buildings around it and a fountain in the middle. There is a good **regional**

WHERE TO EAT AND STAY

You can hardly go wrong finding a good cassoulet in this town. But the one I recommend is that of the restaurant of the **Hôtel du Centre et du Lauragais****. Here it is made with *confit de canard* (duck parts conserved in their own grease). A regional menu of warm salad with poultry livers, *cassoulet*, a green salad and desert will run you 120 francs. The hotel also has 16 neat, spacious, recently renovated rooms with at a top price of 220 francs. It is at 31 Cours de la République (68 23 25 95 FAX 68 94 01 66. A Logis de France member.

HOW TO GET THERE

Castelnaudary is 37 km (23 miles) west of Carcassonne on N 113.

Languedoc

market on this square and on the Promenade du Tivoli on Friday morning.

This is a town that likes to have fun. In a tradition that comes down from the middle ages, **Carnival** lasts from January through March, when it is celebrated every Sunday with three frolics on the Place de la République at 11 AM, 5 PM and 9 PM.

The **Tourist Office** is on the Promenade du Tivoli (68 31 11 82.

WHERE TO STAY AND WHERE TO EAT

The handsome 19-room **Grand Hôtel Moderne et Pigeon***** at 1 Place Général Leclerc (68 31 00 25

ABOVE: Limoux, where the secret of putting bubbles in wine was discovered, and is still very much in use.

FAX 68 31 12 43, started as a nunnery, then became a private mansion, then a bank before becoming a hotel at the beginning of this century. Rooms here rent for 290 to 470 francs. It has a solid, old-fashioned dining room that features *canard à la Limouxine*, a local duck dish prepared with saffron, and has an excellent cellar of local wines. For lunch, my favorite place is the **Maison de la Blanquette** on the Promenade du Tivoli (68 31 01 63, a wine shop in the front and a bright, cheerful, very good restaurant in the rear. It serves hearty local dishes such as *fricassée*, Limoux's own *cassoulet*-like dish made with white beans, but substituting pork for goose or duck. Fixed price menus run from 65 to 200 francs, wine included. It is owned by the Caves du Sieur d'Arques, the big local wine cooperative.

WINE TASTING

Blanquette de Limoux is clean, bright, easy-to-drink champagne-like wine. **Caves du Sieur d'Arques** makes excellent Blanquette de Limoux and the slightly less bubbly Crémant de Limoux, both wines in degrees of dryness up to extra-brut. Try the Blanquette de Limoux labeled Blaners. They also make a several highly-rated varietal *vins de pays d'Oc*. They are on Avenue du Mauzac (D 118) as you enter Limoux from the north (68 31 14 59. Open daily from June to the end of August, closed weekends the rest of the year.

HOW TO GET THERE

Limoux is 25 km (16 miles) south of Carcassonne on D 118.

THE CATHAR FORTRESSES

The sheer-cliffed hilltop forts of Puilaurens, Peyrepertuse, Quéribus, Aguilar and Termes had been built in the eleventh century by Catalan lords to defend themselves against the Trencavels, but eventually fell into the hands of Trencavel allies who put them at the disposal of the Cathars in their time of need. The Treaty of Corbeil between France and Spain in 1258 after the defeat of the Cathars gave these "citadels of vertigo" to France, and Puilaurens became France's southernmost stronghold. The vestiges we see at Puilaurens and the other fortresses in this group date mainly from the late thirteenth century, when France reinforced them to protect its new southern border with Spain. After the Treaty of the Pyrénées in 1659, which pushed the frontier down to the Pyrénées, these fortresses lost their military purpose, and the sites were eventually abandoned.

PUILAURENS

The fortress of Puilaurens 43 km (27 miles) south of Limoux, one of the "Five Sons of Carcassonne," as the Albigensian Crusaders called these hilltop forts, that became, along with Montségur to the west, the principal refuges of the Cathars after the Battle of Muret in 1213. Puilaurens sits on a sheer peak dominating its valley and can be seen from afar. It is the one Cathar fortress that the Albgensian Crusaders failed to take.

What to See and What to Do
From the parking area, a steep walled pathway zig-zags up to the remarkably well-preserved fortress. Its large *donjon*, four round towers and high walls with their crenels and merlons are fully intact, everything bleached as white as the great lump of limestone its sits upon. There are sheer cliffs virtually the whole way around. From the top, 697 m (2,300 ft) high, you can see Mont-Canigou, the mythic mountain of the Catalan nation, snow-capped most of the year.
Do not try to climb to these ruins without sturdy hiking shoes.

Where to Stay and Where to Eat
The **Hostellerie du Grand Duc**** five kilometers (three miles) south of Puilaurens on D 22 in **Gincla** (68 20 55 02 FAX 68 20 61 22, is a handsome old manor house in a quiet, woodsy setting that is an inn of exceptional charm with 10 inexpensive rooms, 280 francs tops. It has a moderately-priced restaurant with food of high quality. In the summer meals are served on the outdoor terrace, off-season in the cozy dining room with a fireplace and wood-beamed ceiling. A Logis de France member, open March 15 to November 15.

How to Get There
Puilaurens is 68 km (42 miles) south of Carcassonne. To get there, head down the Aude River Valley on D 118 to **Quillian**, then take D 117 west for 17 km (11 miles) along the narrow, twisting road through the Défilé (gorge) de Pierre-Lys along the Aude River. As you emerge from the gorge, turn right (south) at **Lapradelle** onto D 22 and wind up two kilometers (one and a quarter miles) to the parking lot of the fortress.

PEYREPERTUSE

Peyrepertuse is the most dramatic of the Cathar strongholds and the largest purely military fortress in Languedoc, with outer walls measuring two and a half kilometers (over one and a half miles) around. The massive bleached stone ruins are perched high on a sheer rock outcrop with breathtaking views of the Corbières from a height of almost 800 m (2,600 ft). The ruins themselves and the panorama of the rugged Corbières countryside make Peyrepertuse one of the most spectacular sites in all of Mediterranean France.

Peyrepertuse fell to the Northerners in 1240. Like the rest of the fortresses in the southern Corbières, it lost its military importance after Roussillon became French, and was finally abandoned in 1789.

Access by road is from the village of **Duilhac-sous-Peyrepertuse**. Drive to the parking lot at the base, and hike up the rocky path a grueling 15 to 20 minutes to the **Lower Fortress**, built on the site of the original medieval fortress (though recent finds of pottery shards place the site's earliest occupation at the time of the Romans). Continue upward to the newer sections built under Louis IX and his successors in the late thirteenth century: the *donjon*, the **lower courtyard**, and climbing upward to the pinnacle 100 ft above the courtyard, the round towers and crenelated walls of **Château Saint-Georges** with its vast panorama of the Corbières, the Château of Quéribus and the Mediterranean in the distance.

Where to Stay and Where to Eat
The **Auberge du Vieux Moulin** is a quaint old inn in Duilhac-sous-Peyrepertuse with 14 rooms with bath or shower at 200 francs and light luncheon menus at 45 francs, copious full meals at 95 and 135 francs in the rustic dining room or the tree-shaded dining patio in good weather (68 45 02 17 FAX 66 45 02 18.

Wine Tasting
The little **Domaine du Trillol** with 11 hectares (26 acres) below Peyrepertuse in **Rouffiac-des-Corbières**, open daily (68 45 01 13.

How to Get There
The quick way from Puilaurens or Gincla to Peyrepertuse is to go north on D 22 to D 117 and eastward on that.

The scenic route, which adds 24 km to your trip, all twists and turns, and offers the chance to see some very different scenery — grey granite stone of the Pyrénées, primeval forests and innumerable little streams — a contrast to the parched white limestone of the Corbières, loops around to the south on D 22 through the hilly back country of the Fenouillèdes, a small range north of the Pyrénées. From **Sournia**, the only real town of this area, a 10 km (six mile) detour to the south on D 619 takes you to the 1,026 m (3,365 ft) **Pic du Baou**, which has a magnificent vista of Mont-Canigou, the Conflent and Prades, with a huge field of yellow flowers in the foreground if you go in the spring. Heading north now on D 619, pause

at **Ansignan** to admire the 168 m (550 ft), 29-arch **Aqueduct** of an irrigation system built by the Romans that is still watering the vineyards to this day, then proceed to Saint-Paul-de-Fenouillet a few kilometers away.

At **Saint Paul-de-Fenouillet**, reached by either D 619 or D 117, take D 7 through the **Gorges de Galamus** and turn right onto D 14, where the best views of Peyrepertuse are to be had from **Rouffiac-des-Corbiéres**.

Peyrepertuse can also be reached from Narbonne about 60 km (38 miles) away via D 611 through Durban-Corbières or from Perpignan about 40 km (25 miles) away via D 117 to Maury and D 19 to Cucugnan.

QUÉRIBUS

The eleventh century fortress of Quéribus eight kilometers (five miles) southeast of Peyrepertuse was the last Cathar stronghold to fall to the Crusaders, in 1255. Smaller than Peyrepertuse, Quéibus is mostly in ruins, though the donjon is impressive. What merits the rough climb of at least 20 minutes to the top of the sharp peak 730 m (2,400 ft) high is the magnificent panorama of the plain of Roussillon and the panorama of the Pyrénées, giving us a preview of our last region to visit on this trip.

Quéribus lies two kilometers (one and a quarter miles) south of Cucugnan on D 123. **Cucugnan**

The fortress of Quéribus, one of the "Five Sons of Carcassonne," Cathar strongholds in the southern Corbières during the Albigensian Crusade.

is a charming village that is the scene of one of the most popular tales in Daudet's *Letters from My Mill*, *The Curate of Cucugnan*. From Easter to the end of the year, the Théâtre de la Poche acting company presents an 18-minute audio-visual rendering of the story at the **Théâtre Archille Mir**, named for a collaborator of Daudet. It is narrated in French, in a flavorful Southern accent, but there is a brochure in English for those whose French is not up to par. The program starts automatically every 20 minutes. The theater is also the place to get information about Cucugnan and assistance with lodging in the area (68 45 03 69. Cucugnan is four kilometers (two and a half miles) east of Duhilac-sous-Peyrepertuse on D 14.

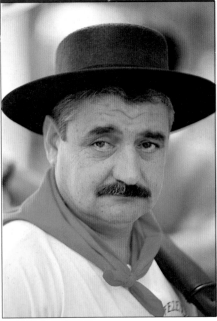

Where to Stay and Where to Eat
The **Auberge de Cucugnan** at 2 Place de la Fontaine (68 45 40 84 FAX 68 45 01 52, serves the best in regional cooking in its dining room in a old stone barn. It is noted for its *coq au vin*, Catalan sausage, guinea hen, rabbit and wild boar stew. There are fixed-price menus at 95, 150, 170 and 240 francs, wine included. The inn rents seven inexpensive rooms. It is closed the first two weeks of September and Wednesdays from January 1 to the end of March.

The **Auberge du Vigneron****, a Logis de France inn, also offers seven simple, inexpensive rooms in the 200 to 230 franc range and good country cooking in its rustic restaurant, with menus at 80 and 150 francs. It is at 2 Rue Achille Mir (68 45 47 78 FAX 68 45 03 08.

In **Maury**, eight kilometers (five miles) south of Cucugnan, **Les Oliviers** is a modest 36-place

camping ground open from mid-June to mid-September (68 59 15 24.

Wine Tasting
Highly respected red *AOC* Corbières wines come from **Domaine du Révérend** in Cucugnan, with 20 hectares (48 acres) of vines at the foot of Quéribus (68 45 01 13, which can be visited daily.

AGUILAR

The fourth of the "Five Sons of Carcassonne" is 16 km (10 miles) northeast of Cucugnan in **Tuchan**. It survived a siege by Simon de Montfort in 1210, and the French did not take it until 30 years later. It is the least dramatic of the five fortresses, but has a well-preserved square *donjon* in the center of a hexagonal array of ramparts with six round towers. They date from the time of Louis IX. There are fine views of the vineyards of Tuchan.

The **Ferme Équestre de Saint-Roch** in Tuchan offers half-day, full-day, or more extended horseback tours of the Cathar sites, an exhilarating way to see them. Rates are 160 francs for a half day, 280 francs for a full day. The farm also rents modest accommodations (68 45 47 91.

Camping
Domaine la Peirière is a 20 place camp site in the countryside near Tuchan, about 12 km (seven and a half miles) east of Cucugnan (68 45 49 64. It is open from May 1 to the end of September.

Wine Tasting
In Tuchan, **Château de Nouvelles**, a short walk from the ruins of Aguilar, is a leading maker of *AOC* Fitou wines (68 45 40 03. The wine cooperatives of Cucugnan, Tuchan and the village of **Padern** midway between them are also respected producers and welcome wine-tasters daily.

How to Get There
Tuchan is reached by D 14 from Cucugnan.

The fifth of the "Five Sons", the fortress of Termes, is in the middle of the Corbières near Villerouge-Termenès (see page 282).

As he moves southward through Languedoc, the traveler notices more and more Iberian features in people he meets ABOVE AND OPPOSITE.

Roussillon

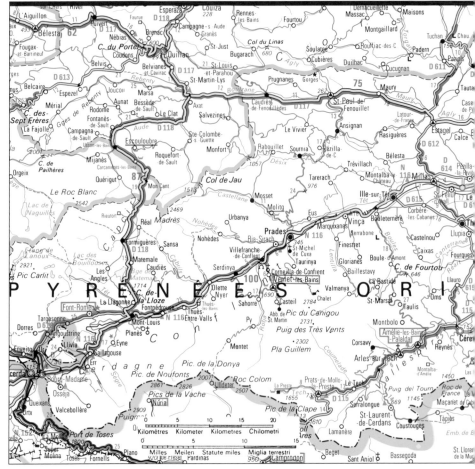

ROUSSILLON is the southern corner of Mediterranean France and the perfect place to wrap up this journey, because in many ways, the two extremities of our region are like bookends. Both have huge ranges of mountains that plunge dramatically into the sea, the Alps and the Pyrénées. Both have strong ethnic flavors, Italian and Catalan. It's a toss-up as to which has the sunnier weather, though Roussillon may have a slight edge, with 325 days of sunshine a year. Nice has its *Train des Pignes* (Pine Cone Train) to the Alpes-de-Haute-Provence, Roussillon its *Petit Train Jaune* (Little Yellow Train) into the Catalan heartland of the Cerdagne in the Pyrénées. We even find the same artists in both places. Besides their better-known stays on the Côte d'Azur, Matisse, Picasso, Chagall, Dufy and Cocteau all spent important periods in their careers in Roussillon. Travelers who are put off by the ultra-sophistication of the Côte d'Azur should consider taking a run down to Roussillon. Here they will find a place that combines sun, sea, magnificent mountain scenery and first-rate cultural attractions, from tenth century Romanesque abbeys to the masters of twentieth century art. It is 467 km (296 miles) by highway from Nice to Perpignan, a perfectly manageable one-day drive.

On the other hand, if gourmet cuisine and luxury living are high on your list of priorities, you will not find much of that in Roussillon. By comparison, the Alpes-Maritimes area (Nice, Cannes, Antibes, Vence, Monaco, etc.) boasts more than two dozen Michelin-starred restaurants (several of which sport two stars, one with three), but Roussillon, an area of roughly the same geographical size, has only four, with one star each. Don't worry, though, you will eat well in Roussillon — this is still France, after all — but on simply prepared dishes such as grilled anchovies, red mullet and other sea fish, trout from Pyrénées streams, fresh vegetables and fruit, of which Roussillon is an important producer. There are far fewer hotels than on the Côte d'Azur too, and only a handful that attain the level of luxury that is commonplace east of the Rhône.

Roussillon

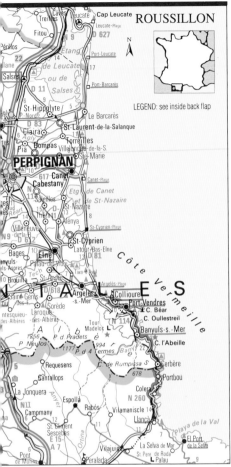

Wilfred the Hairy of Cerdagne to make himself Count of Barcelona in the tenth century. In the twelfth century, his successors made themselves Counts of Provence and Kings of Aragon, and in 1172, Counts of Roussillon. This was the golden age of Catalan power, when the Counts of Barcelona rivaled the Counts of Toulouse as supreme lords of the South, and Barcelona ranked with Venice and Genoa as one of the greatest sea trading powers in the world. The Western Mediterranean became a "Catalan lake."

For a brief, but artistically memorable period from the late thirteenth through the mid-fourteenth century, the Kingdom of Majorca came into existence. It was created in 1276 by King Jaime the Conqueror of Aragon to give his younger son Jaime a kingdom, the elder son Pedro inheriting the throne of Aragon. It was made up of Roussillon, the Balearic Islands and Montpellier, with Perpignan as its capital. Sixty-eight years and two kings later, the ephemeral Kingdom of Majorca was reabsorbed by the Kingdom of Aragon, in 1344, but left an impressive architectural heritage.

In the late fifteenth century, with the marriage of Ferdinand of Aragon and Isabella of Castile, Catalonia fell under Spanish rule. In 1659, after a series of wars, Spain ceded Roussillon to young Louis XIV, and the border was moved south to the Pyrénées. As it had done earlier in the Occitan areas of Provence and Languedoc, Paris imposed the French language and culture on Roussillon and vigorously suppressed everything Catalan.

Today, all people in Roussillon speak French. But a third of them also speak Catalan. And while there is none of the violence that marks Basque nationalism at the other end of the Pyrénées, the Catalans are a proud, independent-minded people whose sense of national identity is strong. Street signs are in Catalan as well as French, and the red and yellow flag of Roussillon—blood and gold — is seen as often as the French red, white and blue. When Picasso, Dali, Miro, Casals and other Catalan artists wanted a taste of Catalonia without going back to Spain, they found it with no difficulty in Perpignan, Collioure, Céret, or Prades. In Roussillon, as in Alsace and parts of the French Basque Country, the traveler often finds himself amazed to realize that he is still in France.

The good news is that everything is much cheaper in Roussillon, even the handful of Côte d'Azur-quality restaurants and hotels. Another advantage for Roussillon is that it has vineyards — interesting ones such as Collioure, Banyuls, Rivesaltes, Côtes du Roussillon — whereas the Alpes-Maritimes has practically none. And as in Languedoc, but even more so, here the traveler has the chance to get off the beaten track and explore a splendidly scenic part of France, one that has managed to hold onto its unique Catalan identity.

BACKGROUND

Though most of historic Catalonia now lies on the Spanish side of the Pyrénées, the birthplace of the Catalan nation is in France. It is the high plateau of the Cerdagne deep in the Pyrénées by Andorra, which is predominantly Catalan too. The Catalans made their fortune in iron ore and metal forging here in the early middle ages, enabling Count

PERPIGNAN

Perpignan is the capital of Roussillon, its only real metropolis, the center of the area's big fruit and wine trade and in recent years, a mecca for computer businesses and high-technology research. It is a clean, vivacious, attractive city of some 105,000 people that lies eight kilometers

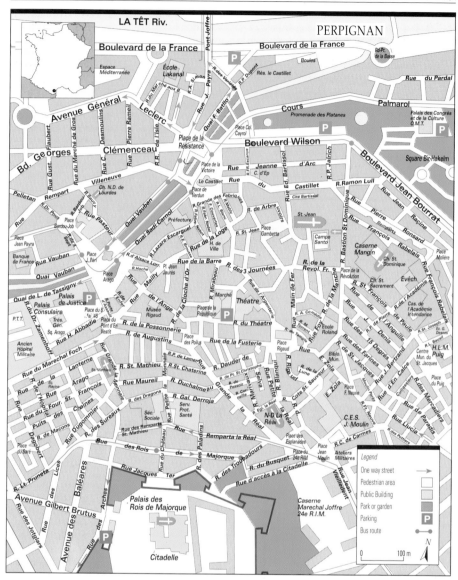

(five miles) inland from Mediterranean with the non-navigable Têt River running through it. The Pyrénées loom up to the south, and Mont-Canigou, the symbol of Catalan nationhood, exerts its magical presence from 100 km (60 miles) away. It is snow-capped most of the year. Like its Catalan big sister-city of Barcelona, Perpignan is a lively place, delightful to stroll in.

GENERAL INFORMATION

The **Tourist Office** is located in at the Palais des Congrès at the far end of the Promenade des Platanes (68 66 30 30, and also there is an office at the airport. They provides information about the

city and some help on the rest of Roussillon. But for complete information on both the city and the outlying areas, contact the **Comité Départemental du Tourisme Pyrénées-Roussillon** at 7 Quai de Lattre-de-Tassigny (68 34 29 94 FAX 68 34 71 01. They are extremely helpful, and their maps and brochures are excellent. If you plan to explore the outlying areas, be sure to pick up their listing of all the hotels, restaurants and camping grounds in Roussillon.

Airport information, Perpignan-Rivesaltes Airport (68 61 28 98.

The **train station, Gare SNCF**, is on the west side of the city at the end of Avenue du Général de Gaulle (68 35 50 50.

The **bus station, Gare Routière**, is on Avenue du Général Leclerc to the west of Place de la Résistance (68 61 28 98. For **buses to towns along the coast**, call **Car Inter 66** at (68 35 29 02.

Car rental: Avis, 13 Boulevard du Conflent (68 34 26 71; **Citer**, 44 Avenue du Maréchal Juin (68 67 31 05; **EuropCar**, 28 Avenue du Général de Gaulle (68 34 65 03.

Bike rental: Cycles Mercier, 1 Rue du Président-Doumer (68 85 02 71.

Taxis: Accueil Perpignan Taxis (68 35 15 15; **Taxis-Radio Catalan** (68 55 55 05; 68 67 40 52.

Medical emergencies: SAMU (68 61 06 66 or 68 61 66 66.

FESTIVALS

The **Procession of the Penitents of Sanch** on Good Friday is a colorful, if rather macabre, expression of faith by the Brothers of the Holy Blood (*sanch* in Catalan), who parade though the streets in red robes with sharp-pointed hoods and bare feet carrying an effigy of Christ. The **Festival Mediterranéen de Musique**, for classical music, is held in July and August with concerts at the Palace of the Kings of Majorca. A photojournalism festival, **Visa pour l'Image**, is held in early September, and in mid-September, **Aujourd'hui Musiques** is a two-week festival of new orchestral and operatic compositions and jazz.

WHAT TO SEE

The **Castillet** is a tall, sturdy fortress that was built as the main gate of the city in the fourteenth century, when it was completely walled, and it is now the dividing mark between the old town and the new. It houses the **Museum of Catalan Popular Arts and Traditions**, also known as the **Casa Pairal**, or "ancestral home" in Catalan, which offers an engaging introduction to Catalan culture. From the roof, there is a vast panorama of the city, the sea, the Corbières, Mont-Canigou and the Pyrénées. It is open in the summer from 9:30 AM to 11:30 AM and 2:30 PM to 6:30 PM, the rest of the year from 9 AM to 11:30 AM and 2 PM to 5:30 PM. It is closed Tuesday and national holidays. Entrance is free.

The **Loge de la Mer** is the most elegant building in the city, a fourteenth century meeting hall for sea traders that is now occupied by a Quick fast food franchise, adapted in reasonably good taste. It fronts on the **Place de La Loge**, where the cafés are popular gathering places for the Perpignanais. On Tuesday and Thursday nights in the summer, people get up and do the stately Catalan dance, the sardana, in the square. Here you can also admire one of Maillol's most famous cast bronze nudes, "La Mediterranée." **Place Arago** a few blocks to the west is another square with a number of lively cafés.

The **Cathèdrale Saint-Jean** on Place Gambetta a short walk to the east of the Place de la Loge is an impressive structure with a surface of red brick and pebbles that has a single nave 48 m (158 ft) long. It was started in 1324 during the reign of Sanche, the second of the three Kings of Majorca, whose death effigy can be seen in a side chapel, but the church was not consecrated until 1509 and work on it continued into the seventeenth century. Nevertheless, it is the most coherent example of Gothic church architecture in the south of France. Inside, there are many art treasures to admire, including the marble main altar and a number of altarpieces from the sixteenth and seventeenth centuries in side chapels, particularly

those in the chapels of Saint Peter and of Saints Eulalie and Julie off the left-hand aisle. As you are leaving the church by the right side, look for the leather-covered door to the corridor that leads to the chapel containing the "Dévôt Christ." This is a painfully realistic wooden sculpture of Christ crucified, a German work from the early fourteenth century. According to local legend, the Christ's bowed head is tilting very slowly closer to His chest — it is only a fraction of an inch away now — and when it touches, the world will end.

The **Musée Hyacinthe-Rigaud** in a seventeenth century mansion at 16 Rue de l'Ange down the street from Place Arago is named for the leading portrait artist of Louis XIV's court, and it has two excellent portraits by him, one of the elegant

ABOVE: Le Castillet, the medieval fortress that is Perpignan's ground zero.

Cardinal de Bouillon and other a self-portrait of the amiable-looking painter. But this is an amazingly eclectic art museum whose collection ranges from the magnificent fifteenth century Catalan altarpiece "La Retable de la Trinité," which allegorically depicts the Loge de la Mer, which commissioned it, with the sea at its doorstep, to work by contemporary Catalan painter Antoni Tàpies. It includes three sketches by another noted Catalan, Pablo Picasso. One is of the Countess de Lazerme, his mistress in the mid-1950's, whose home this building was, and who still lives in another wing of it. Among the other works are a delightful pointilist painting by Maillol, "Portrait de Jeune Fille," nine oils and

numerous drawings by Dufy, along with works by Ingres, Brueghel, Marie Laurencin, Calder and others. This museum is full of surprises. It is open from 9:30 AM to 12 PM and 2:30 PM to 7 PM from mid-June to mid-September, and it opens at 9 AM and closes at 6 PM the rest of the year. Closed Tuesdays and holidays. Admission is free.

The **Palace of the Kings of Majorca** is inside the medieval **Citadel**, which dominates the city from its highest point. It was started in 1276 by King Jaime I to house his court and was completed by the Kings of Aragon when they re-absorbed the Kingdom of Majorca. You can visit the apartments of the king and the queen, the chapel and public rooms, which are handsome spaces with grand walk-in fireplaces, but they are practically empty and give little sense of how people lived and worked here. The most attractive part of the palace is the wide courtyard in which concerts are

held in the summer (check at the Tourist Office for the program). The palace can be visited from 9:30 AM to 12 PM and 2:30 PM to 6 PM in the summer, from 9 AM to 12 PM and 2 PM to 5 PM off-season. Closed Tuesday and national holidays.

WHERE TO STAY

Perpignan is the only place in Roussillon that offers a large choice of hotels, and there are many good choices indeed. A number of hotels participate year-round in a two-nights-for-the-price-of-one program on weekends. The Tourist Office has a list.

Villa Duflot**** in a luxuriant private park slightly south of the city is Perpignan's deluxe

address, and my personal choice. It has 24 sunny rooms done in updated 1930's style, some opening directly onto the pool. For a hotel of its quality, the rates are remarkably reasonable, with doubles at 540 and 640 francs. It is at 109 Avenue Victor-Dalbiez (68 56 67 67 FAX 68 56 54 05. The **Park***** at 18 Boulevard Jean Bourrat (68 35 14 14 FAX 68 35 48 18, is a local institution with 67 cushy, traditional-style rooms, 280 to 500 francs for a double, and the best restaurant in town (see WHERE TO EAT). The **Mercure***** is a tasteful modern hotel with 60 up-to-date rooms, with doubles at 470 to 540 francs. It is at 5 Cours Plamarole near the Castillet (68 35 67 66 FAX 68 35 58 13. The **Athéna**** at 1 Rue Queya near the Musée Hyacinthe Rigaud (68 34 37 63 FAX 68 51 07 25, is a fourteenth century residence with a great deal of character. Its 39 rooms are somewhat small, but they are quiet and modestly priced, in the 250 franc range.

The **Poste et Perdrix**** at 6 Rue des Fabriques-d'En-Nabot (Place de Verdun) (68 34 42 53 FAX 68 34 58 20, is another hotel of character, this one dating from 1832, with 38 neat, clean rooms at a top rate of 260 francs.

A luxury hotel I include here because I have no other place for it is **L'Île de la Lagune****** a small modern resort hotel on a little island in an inlet of the Mediterranean, the lagoon of **Saint-Cyprien**, 19 km (12 miles) to the east of Perpignan. It has a swimming pool and a private beach, 18 tasteful multiple-level rooms and four suites, all with sea views, and one of the finest restaurants in Roussillon (see WHERE TO EAT). The rate for a double room is 750 francs (68 21 01 02 FAX 68 21 06 28.

Catalan ceramics and has a bright Mediterranean ambiance. It serves *tarte de saumon*, roast scallops in sea urchin sauce and other inventive dishes, seafood primarily, and has an eminent cellar of Collioure and Côtes du Roussillon wines. It is the only restaurant in town with a Michelin star. The Chapon Fin is expensive, with menus at 180 and 450 francs, but the **Bistro du Park**, also under the direction of chef Eric Lecerf, offers a three-course luncheon at 98 francs, wine included. The other gourmet restaurant to look into is the **Festin de Pierre** in a fifteenth century residence at 7 Rue du Théâtre (68 51 28 74, noted for its inventiveness with local food products and its astute choice of wines. For a

Camping

There is a great number of camping grounds along the beaches to the east of Perpignan. The closest are in **Canet-en-Roussillon**, which has nine of them with 2,500 places. It is 11 km (seven miles) straight east of Perpignan. **Argelès-sur-Mer** 20 km (12.5 miles) southeast of Perpignan has no less than 56 camping grounds with thousands of places. Other beach towns with a number of camping grounds are **Le Barcarès** with thirteen, **Saint-Cyprien** with five, **Sainte-Marie-la-Mer** and **Torreilles** with six each. For information, contact the Comité Départemental du Tourisme Pyrénées-Roussillon.

WHERE TO EAT

The **Chapon Fin**, the gourmet restaurant of the Hôtel Park (*see* WHERE TO STAY), is decorated with

more popular style of eating, try the **Casa Sansa** at 3 Rue Fabriques Couvertes near the Castillet (68 34 21 84, a place I enjoy enormously. It is a big, bustling eatery with a *bodega* atmosphere serving strictly Catalan specialties. Here you may sample *esqueixada de bacalla* (marinated codfish) and *pollastre amb gambas* (chicken and shrimp in Rivesaltes wine sauce) and local wines at moderate prices. For a gastronomic change of pace — the cool, bright taste of Atlantic shellfish and a chilled glass of Muscadet — **La Huitrière** serves fresh oysters trucked down on ice from Brittany. It is 12 Rue Pierre Ramiel (68 35 56 42, west of the Castillet off Boulevard Georges Clémenceau.

The medieval Loge de la Mer, now a fast-food outlet, and one of the many open-air restaurants near the Castillet OPPOSITE LEFT and RIGHT. ABOVE: Catalan sculptor Aristide Maillol's *"Mediterranée"* at City Hall.

The **Brasserie Vauban** at 29 Quai Vauban (68 51 05 91, serves honest brasserie fare. The **Grand Cafe de la Bourse** at 2 Place de la Loge is the best place to take in the *sardana* dancing on Tuesday and Thursday nights. For *tapas* and a true Barcelona atmosphere, try **La Bodéga Pescador** on Rue Fabriques Couvertes, open till 2 AM.

For gourmet dining by the sea, take a jaunt to **L'Almandin**, the restaurant of **L'Île de la Lagune** (see WHERE TO STAY page 301). Here you may feast on Collioure anchovy blinis with *tapenade, bouillabaisse* of cod and monkfish in crayfish sauce, and other compositions of chef Jean-Paul Hartmann that have earned him a Michelin star. Fixed price menus

price menus start at 170 francs. Open daily June 15 to September 15, closed Sunday night and Monday off-season.

WINE TASTING

If you want to visit a vineyard, but don't have much time for exploring the countryside, visit the **Domaine Sarda-Malet** at Mas Saint-Michel, 12 Chemin du Sainte-Barbe, on the south side of Perpignan, actually within the city limits. They make red and white Côtes du Roussillon, the principal *AOC* table wine of Roussillon, and Rivesaltes and Muscat de Rivesaltes *doux naturel* (sweet aperitif wine), all to perennial critical raves. Their cellar is open weekdays from 8:30 AM to 12:30 PM and 2 PM to 7 PM, on weekends by appointment (68 56 72 38.

HOW TO GET THERE

There are four flights daily from Paris's Orly Airport to Perpignan-Rivesaltes Airport. By train, Perpignan is on the main lines from Paris and Geneva to Barcelona. By bus, Eurolines has service from London and many other cities in Europe, Iberbus has buses from Spain, and Courriers du Midi has daily buses from Montpellier. By car,

Perpignan is on the A 9 *autoroute* and is the hub of all the other main roads of Roussillon.

EXCURSIONS FROM PERPIGNAN

Perpignan is the jumping-off point for a number of fascinating trips in Roussillon — one to the north, one to the south, and two following the river valleys into the Pyrénées. The distances are short. The northern points of Salses-le-Château, Rivesaltes and Tautavel are less than half an hour's drive from Perpignan. To the west, Prades, the main town of the Conflent, is only 43 km (27 miles) away. Short distances to the southwest lie the art village of Céret, Amélie-les-Bains, and the Vallespir, the southernmost part of in France. And to the south of Perpignan are the ancient capital of Elne and the rugged Côte Vermeille (Vermillion Coast), with its charming ports of Collioure and Banyuls-sur-Mer, an easy day-trip by car. If time is short, a trip combining Céret and Collioure could be done in a day.

The only part of Roussillon that is not interesting from a scenic point of view is the Côte Sablonneuse, the 32 km (20 mile) stretch of flat, sandy coast between Port-Bacarès and Argelès Plage, which has one banal new beach resort after another, along with vast expanses of camping grounds. Otherwise, Roussillon is as intriguing as any other part of Mediterranean France, and the least "spoiled" by mass tourism. The Carinter 66 bus network can take you to all parts of Roussillon, and there is train service to some of these areas. But unless you are a serious hiker or biker, you will have no means of getting out into the countryside once you get there. A car is the best bet, if it is within your means. And as in Languedoc, the roads in Roussillon are excellent.

SALSES LE CHÂTEAU

As you whip along the A 9 *autoroute* between Narbonne and Perpignan, you could easily fly past the Fortress of Salses without even noticing it. Yet this massive, low-lying fort — which is completely intact — was once one of the most important military structures in Europe. It sits in the middle of the narrow plain between the marshes of the Étang de Salses and the rugged slopes of the Corbières that was the only flat, firm land between the Atlantic seaboard and the Mediterranean that an army could easily cross to get to or from the Iberian Peninsula. Its strategic significance became clear in 218 BC when Hannibal convinced the local Gallo-Iberian tribe that controlled it to give his army and 37 elephants free passage on their way north from Spain, and they went on to nearly bring Rome to its knees.

The squat red-ochre stronghold we see today was built in 1497 by King Ferdinand of Spain to defend the then-Spanish border from the French. The walls are 15 m (almost 50 ft) thick at the base, built low to the ground with rounded contours to deflect the fire of the newly perfected cannon. The fortress could billet up to 1,500 troops and there were stables for 300 horses. It proved its worth against Richelieu's invading armies, but lost its usefulness when the Pyrénées became the border in 1659. Vauban is said to have wanted to demolish the fortress, but dropped the project as too difficult and expensive. When you see the bulkiness of the walls, you will understand why.

The Fortress of Salses is 16 km (10 miles) north of Perpignan. It can be reached by car via the *autoroute* if you are traveling in either direction. Park in the Aire de Salses rest area and walk to the fort, a five minute stroll. However there is no exit ramp for vehicles to Salses. So unless you are continuing north or south on the *autoroute* you should take the N 9 to get there. The fortress is open all year from 9 AM to 6:30 PM, to 7:30 PM in the summer, closed on national holidays.

For information call (68 38 60 13.

TAUTAVEL

In 1971, the skull of the oldest known European was found in a limestone cave in the sheer-cliffed Arago valley 30 km (18 miles) northwest of Perpignan. Tautavel Man lived 450,000 years ago and hunted buffalo, rhinoceros, wild boar and other game in the plains below. The **Centre Européen de la Préhistoire** in Tautavel, opened in 1992, is a modern museum of pre-history with geological exhibits, reconstructions of the Tautavel Man's habitat, bones of the animals he hunted, and the skull of the Man himself, with an audio-cassette in English that leads you through it (68 29 07 76. Open daily from 10 AM to 12:30 PM and 2 to 6:30 PM.

The **Grotte d'Arago**, the cave where the Tautavel Man was found, can also be visited in July and August when archaeological digs are in progress. For information, contact the **Tourist Office** at the Tautavel town hall, the Mairie (68 29 12 08.

If you are coming from Salses, take D 12 through the hauntingly bleak landscape east of the village of Vingrau and take the local roads to Tautavel, a distance of 27 km (17 miles) in all. It is about the same distance from Perpignan via D 117 through the *vin doux naturelle* capital of Rivesaltes to Cases-de-Pène and D 59 north through rolling vineyards to the valley of Tautavel.

Where to Eat

The Dauré family's **Château de Jau** directly south of Tautavel in **Cases-de-Pène** is a winemaking estate that serves a Catalan feast at lunchtime in the summer — *fougasse* (flavored Mediterranean bread), tomatoes and Serrano ham, lamb cutlets

and sausage grilled on a fire of dried grape vines, Roquefort cheese, and cinnamon ice cream, served with a different wine at each course — all for 135 francs. The meal is served in a shaded rustic courtyard of the handsome red-ochre eighteenth century estate house, daily from June 15 to the beginning of October. Seating is limited, and you would be wise to reserve in advance (68 38 91 38. You can also visit the contemporary art exhibits put on by the *château* every summer, which are of a very high level, and independently of the lunch, taste their wine (see below). The Château de Jau is a few kilometers west of Cases-de-Pène on a private road off D 117. It is about 10 km (six miles) west of Rivesaltes.

Wine Tasting

At the **Château de Jau** (see above), you can sample their highly esteemed wines, covering a wide range of different types made in Roussillon, from *AOC* Côtes du Roussillon red, *blanc de blanc* (white wine made only from white grapes) and rosés to Vin d'Été, their popular *vin de pays*, as well as Muscat de Rivesaltes, a white *vin doux naturel* (sweet aperitif wine), a very dark Rivesaltes, and *AOC* Collioure red table wine and the Robert Doutres label of *AOC* Banyuls *vin doux naturel* from the Clos de Paullilles on the Côte Vermeille. The cellar is open weekdays from 8 AM to 5 PM. While visiting the land of the Tautavel Man, you

The massive Fortress of Salses OPPOSITE, built in 1497 by King Ferdinand of Spain. ABOVE: The 450,000 year-old Tautavel Man, the oldest human skull discovered in Europe.

could stop in at the village's excellent wine cooperative, **Les Maîtres Vignerons de Tautavel** at
24 Route de Vingrau, which makes the full range
of wines of the area. Try their Côtes du Roussillon
"Cuvée Professeur Henry de Lumley," named in
honor of the man who discovered the Tautavel
Man — 1986, if they still have any — to find out
how rich, smooth and flavorful Côtes du Roussillon can be. They are open daily from 9 AM to 12 PM
and 2 PM to 6 PM (68 29 12 03.

Another top winemaker in this area is the
century-old **Domaine Cazes** at 4 Rue Francisco-
Ferrer in Rivesaltes, where the Cazes brothers,
Bernard and André, make 15 different types of
Rivesaltes, Muscat de Rivesaltes, Côtes du Roussillon and *vin de pays* on their 160 hectare (384 acre)
estate, a very large spread for this region. Their
wines get consistently high grades in blind tests
by wine experts. Open weekdays from 8 AM to
12 PM and 2 PM to 6 PM (68 64 08 26.

THE ASPRES

Immediately to the west of Perpignan's plain on
a straight line with Mont-Canigou rises a strange,
sparsely-populated range of Pyrénées foothills
called the Aspres. Its craggy terrain is covered by
scrub oaks, wild asparagus, herbs and berry
patches, and flocks of goats graze in the shadow
of the ancient watch towers, chapels and abbeys
that abound in the these hills. The main points of
interest here are the medieval town of Castelnou
and the Prieuré de Serrabone.

To get to Castelnou from Perpignan, take D 612
for 14 km (nine miles) to **Thuir**, where you might
want to stop at Pernod-Ricard's **Caves Byrrh** to
see what is billed as the largest oak vat in the
world, with a capacity of more than a million
liters, and taste their aperitif wines. Open daily in
July and August, weekdays in spring and autumn
(68 53 05 42.

CASTELNOU

This is a beautifully preserved walled village in
the heart of the Aspres with the golden stone
houses of its 152 people clustered at the foot of an
eleventh century fortress of the Counts of Cerdagne and Besalu. It is noted for its pottery, ironwork and other handicrafts, and its steep, narrow
streets, which offer the chance to work up an
appetite for another good reason to come here, a
meal at l'Hostal.

L'Hostal is one of the few restaurants in Roussillon that still prepares *cargolade*, the traditional
Catalan dish of snails, pork chops and sausages
grilled on an open fire of dried vine clippings, a
complicated meal to make that must be ordered
in advance. This feast costs 220 francs, wine and

dessert included. Normal fare is offered too, with
fixed-price menus from 120 and 230 francs, wine
included. You dine on the a big, festive outdoor
terrace in fine weather, in the cosy dining room
otherwise. It is closed January 1 to March 15 and
Mondays and Wednesday evenings, except in
mid-summer (68 53 45 42.

To get to Castelnou from Thuir, drive six kilometers (nearly four miles) to the west on D 48.

PRIEURÉ DE SERRABONE

Serrabone is the oldest Augustinian priory in
Europe, started in 1082. At first glance, the ex-
treme austerity of its dark grey schist exterior may
give you a chill. But surprises await you inside.
First, the entry way, a lovely colonnaded balcony
on the edge of a ravine with carvings of monsters
on the capitals.

But this is a mere hint of what awaits you
inside — an amazing ensemble of sculpted capitals atop the rose marble columns of the tribune
representing eagles, lions, griffins, and other
fantastic beasts from the *Book of the Apocalypse*, one
of the true master-pieces of Romanesque art. The
priory also has a 42 hectare (100 acre) botanical
garden with more than a thousand specimens
of Mediterranean plants. As from many points
around here, there is a marvelous view of Canigou only 16 km (10 miles) to the west. Open
daily except public holidays from 10 AM to 6 PM
(68 84 09 30.

To get to Serrabone from Castelnou, drive
west on D 48, heading toward Canigou. Marvelous vistas are revealed by every twist and turn
in the circuitous roads though the Aspres. As
you mount, the view becomes more and more
open. From the little Romanesque chapel of **Fontecouverte** by the junction with D 2 you can see
the Mediterranean. Go six kilometers (three and
a half miles) south on D 2 to **Caxias**, then right
another six kilometers on the road to Col de Four-
tou. Turn right there onto D 618 and follow it
10 km (six miles) to the north. The access road to
Serrabone is on your left.

Serrabone can also be reached more directly
from Perpignan via N 116 west to **Bouleternère**
and D 618 south.

THE CONFLENT

Named for the confluence of streams flowing into
the River Têt from the Fenouillèdes, the Canigou
Massif and the Cerdagne, the peaceful valley of
the Conflent is noted for its peach orchards and
market gardens, its access to Mont-Canigou, its
two Romanesque abbeys, the Pablo Casals Music
Festival and the walled city of Villefranche-de-
Conflent. It is reached by N 116.

PRADES

The commercial hub of the Conflent is Prades, a quiet town of 6,500, known to the outside world as the adopted home of the great Catalan cellist Pablo Casals in the 1940's and 50's during his self-imposed exile from Franco's Spain and for the renowned **Casals Festival** held from late July to mid-August. For tourist and festival information, contact the **Syndicat d'Initiative**, BP 24, Rue Victor Hugo, 66502 Prades (68 96 27 58 FAX 68 96 50 95.

The main concert site is the tenth century **Abbey of Saint-Michel-de-Cuxa** in a little valley just

adding its touch of menace from the hills above it, Villefranche-de-Conflent might look unwelcoming at first glance. Wrong. This little town of less than 300 year-round residents is one of the friendliest places in Southern France, and one of the most active in the summer, thanks in large part to the initiative of the bright, dedicated young team that runs its tourist and cultural programs. In June, July and August, potters, wood carvers and iron workers open their boutiques, the cafés are in full swing, and a rich program of musical and other cultural events gets under way.

The town lies six kilometers (nearly four miles) south of Prades on N 116 in a narrow valley

outside town. It has a handsome four-story rectangular bell tower and especially lovely cloister, despite the fact that half the capitals of its columns are in New York, at the Metropolitan Museum's Cloisters.

The seventeenth century **Église de Saint-Pierre** in the center of otherwise uninteresting Prades features a huge 1699 baroque altarpiece by Catalan master wood carver Joseph Sunyer. Forty statues and bas reliefs of angels, saints, men and animals in leafy and flowery settings, all gilded and painted, surround a majestic Saint Peter on a throne. Put a one-franc coin into the automatic timer to light up this "sculpted opera."

VILLEFRANCHE-DE-CONFLENT

With its stern military ramparts completely surrounding the town and hilltop Fort Libéria

at the confluence of the Têt and Cady rivers, strategically important in the past because it is the only passage between the Cerdagne and the Conflent, via the Têt River Valley. Villefranche-de-Conflent was founded in 1092 by the Count of Cerdagne, who built the original fortress. It was enlarged by the King of Aragon in the late thirteenth century after the Cathar fortresses to the north fell to the French, but it was destroyed by the French in the war with Spain in the 1650's. After the Pyrénées frontier was established, the indefatigable Vauban came to town (twice, in 1669 and 1679), and laid out the system of ramparts we see today. Seeing that the town was vulnerable to sniping from the hills above it, he

Streets scenes ABOVE LEFT and RIGHT in the fully walled town of Villefranche-de Conflent, one of liveliest spots in Roussillon in the summer.

ordered **Fort Libéria** to be built up there. In the nineteenth century, Napoléon III had a thousand-step tunneled stairway built up to it from town (you don't have to climb it; there is an off-road vehicle to take you up there).

Inside those seventeenth century walls, Villefranche remains a medieval town. The twelfth century **Église-Saint-Jacques** has a dark, haunting mood and a blend of artistic styles from Romanesque austerity to Spanish gilded baroque.

The **Association Culturelle** at 38 Rue Saint-Jean (68 96 25 64 is open all year, and Guy and Lydie Durbet, the directors, are more than happy to share their vast fund of knowledge about everything about the region. The **Tourist Office**

net-les-Bains, a favorite of Rudyard Kipling, where a clear view of **Mont-Canigou** greets you. Continue south on the same road to **Casteil** and park. The abbey is not accessible by car. Hikers can reach it by a steep, rugged trail, about half an hour each way. Once up there, you will fall under the spell of Romanesque purity of the church and the cloister and even more, the magnificent site on the slope of Canigou. Stairs to the left lead up the hill above the abbey for the best view. It is open all year except in bad winter weather (68 05 50 03.

Garage Villaceque in Vernet-les-Bains provides **jeep rides** to the abbey for 150 francs per person (68 05 51 14.

is at Place de l'Église (68 96 22 96, is open in the summer, and Anne-Marie Diaz and her staff will find you hotel or guest house accommodations.

Villefranche-de-Conflent is also the place where you connect with the *Petit Train Jaune* to the Cerdagne (see page 307), and information about that is available at either office.

ABBAYE DE SAINTE-MARTIN-DU-CANIGOU

The eleventh century abbey lies eight kilometers (five miles) south of Villefranche-de-Conflent. To get there, take D 116 to the old spa town of **Ver-**

The **Tourist Office** in Vernet-les-Bains is at Place de la Mairie (68 05 55 35.

WHERE TO STAY

There are 29 hotels in the Conflent, half of them concentrated in the spa towns of Vernet-les-Bains, which has two three-star and five two-star hotels, and Molitg-les-Bains, which has one of the few four-star hotels in Roussillon (the Château de Riell, see below), one three-star and two two-star hotels. Prades and Villefranche-de-Conflent have two perfectly acceptable two-star hotels each. For information and help getting rooms, contact the Tourist Offices in the above-mentioned towns. They can also find you *chambres d'hôtes* (bed and breakfasts) and *gîtes*, rural cottages.

The luxurious **Château de Riell****** is a nineteenth century mansion in the style of a medieval

ABOVE: Lively wrought iron restaurant signs in Villefranche-de-Conflent. The *Sardana*, the stately Catalan dance, seen OPPOSITE in Collioure, is also done in many other towns and villages in Roussillon.

castle with two swimming pools, two tennis courts and 24 hectares (60 acres) of private park with a view of Mont-Canigou, fireplaces in all 22 antique-furnished rooms and the only gourmet restaurant in the area (see WHERE TO EAT, below. Double rooms run 950 to 1,200 francs. It is a Relais & Châteaux member. Open from April 1 to November 1. It is in **Molitg-les-Bains**, six kilometers (four miles) from Prades (68 05 04 40 FAX 68 05 04 37. The hotel will arrange thermal treatments at the local spa.

In **Prades**, there are two neat, pleasant modern hotels. The moderately-priced 39-room **Pradotel**** (68 05 22 66 FAX 68 05 23 22, has its own swimming pool and is open from April 1 to the end of October. The less expensive 30-room **Hexagone**** is next to the Prades's large public pool and tennis courts, which visitors are free to use. It is open all year (68 05 31 31 FAX 68 05 24 89. This is a very friendly little hotel.

In **Villefranche-de-Conflent**, the **Vauban**** in the center of town at 5 Place de l'Eglise (68 96 13 03, has 16 rooms and is open from July 1 through the first week of October. The **Auberge du Cèdre**** is a 10-room Logis de France inn, open all year (68 96 37 37. It is outside the town walls, a five-minute walk along the river.

Camping

The best camping grounds in the Conflent are to be found in **Vernet-les-Bains**, which has three, including the **Camping L'Eau Vive** by a mountain stream on the Chemin Saint-Saturin (68 05 54 14. This is a well-equipped 58-place park with a swimming pool, restaurant, bar, washing machines and rental of tents and campers, open all year. The more modest 100-place **Camping del Bosc** at 68 Avenue Clémenceau is open from March 1 to the end of October (68 05 54 54. In Prades, the simple **Camping Municipal** on the Plaine Saint-Martin has 60 places and is open from April 1 to the end of September (68 96 29 83.

WHERE TO EAT

Château de Riell's restaurant excels in sophisticated Catalan-French fare such as anchovy puff pastry, lamb roast with thyme and pimentos, filet of sole with poached oysters and caviar, and ice cream with fresh apricots and figs. It rates one Michelin star and is expensive. In the hill village of **Eus**, one of the prettiest in France, the **Grangousier** (68 89 28 32, is a small, cheerful restaurant with a delightful dining terrace looking out at Mont-Canigou that serves delicious, but expensive, regional menus at 185 and 280 francs. Closed the last two weeks of October. Eus is five kilometers (three miles) north of Prades on D 35. In Villefranche-de-Conflent the leading restaurants are the **Auberge Saint-Paul** at 7 Place de l'Eglise

(68 96 30 95, expensive, closed part of November, most of January and the first two weeks of February, and **Au Grill** at Rue Saint-Jean (68 96 17 65, serving simple, well-prepared fare of the region at moderate prices, with fixed-price menus from 78 francs. Closed November 15 to February 15.

HOW TO GET THERE

There are six trains a day from Perpignan to the Conflent, a 45-minute trip to Villefranche. There are also six buses a day, a one-hour and fifteen minute trip. By car take N 116, which follows the valley of the River Têt.

THE CERDAGNE

THE ROUTE OF *LE PETIT TRAIN JAUNE*

Villefranche-de-Conflent is the starting point for a 63 km 40 mile) excursion on *Le Petit Train Jaune* to the plateau of the Cerdagne deep in the Pyrénées, the cradle of the Catalan nation. In the summer, open cars are added to enhance the experience. The complete trip southwest from Villefranche to La Tour de Carol, at the end of the line at the Spanish border, takes a bit under three hours, but you can get off at any of the 21 stops if you don't want to go all the way. The section between **Olette**, about 10 km (six miles) from Villefranche, and **Mont-Louis**, 28 km (17.5 miles) away, is the most dramatic. The train crosses a 16-arch viaduct far above the Têt, another bridge 80 m (283 ft) high, and emerges from a long tunnel to reveal the wide, verdant central valley of the Cerdagne and mile-high **Mont-Louis**, the highest fortified city in France, built by Vauban in 1681. The trip from Villefranche to Mont-Louis takes 80 minutes.

The Cerdagne is a ski area, and the next two stops, **Bolquère-Eyne** and especially **Font-Romeu** have major resorts. It also has more sunny days than any other place in France, which is why the government built its solar energy research centers at **Font-Romeu** and **Odeillo**, site of the *four solaire*, a gigantic solar oven with 2,000 sq m (21,528 sq ft) of mirrors, the largest in Europe. The next stop is **Estavar** on the border of **Llivia**, a Spanish enclave within the boundary of France. It remained Spanish because of an oversight in the Treaty of the Pyrénées in 1659.

If you want to really get away from it all, get off the train at **Saillagouse**, the next stop, and go to the pretty village of **Llo** three kilometers (two miles) away and check into the **Auberge Atalaya***** (68 04 70 04 FAX 68 04 01 29, a charming wood and stone inn with 12 delightfully decorated rooms (Mme. Toussaint, the owner is a former decorator), a good restaurant, its own swimming pool and golf, tennis and horseback riding nearby. The Auberge Atalaya is moderate to moderately expensive in price. It is a Relais de Silence member.

In Saillagouse itself, the Planes Family's rustic **Vieille Maison Cerdane** restaurant and 18-room **Planes Hotel**** offers a cheerful, well-run, modestly-priced alternative. It is at Place des Contes de Cerdagne (68 04 72 08 FAX 68 04 75 93. They also have a 20-room modern annex, the **Planotel****, which has a pool.

Bourg-Madame and **La Tour de Carol**, the last two towns on the line, are on the Spanish frontier.

Tourist information about the Cerdagne can be had from the following Tourist Offices: Villefranche-de-Conflent, Place de l'Église (68 96 22 96; Mont-Louis, Rue du Marché (68 04 21 97; Font-Romeu, Avenue Emmanuel Brousse (68 30 68 30; Saillagouse (68 04 72 89.

If you want to drive to the Cerdagne, take N 116 southwest from Villefranche-de-Conflent.

THE VALLESPIR

The **Tech River Valley** winds to the southeast of Mont-Canigou to the Pyrénées pass of the Col d'Ares at the Spanish border. The Vallespir, as the area is known, is the southernmost place in France. It is much appreciated by the rest of the nation because it brings the first cherries to the market in the spring. As the early-ripening cherries indicate, the Vallespir is an exceptionally sunny place. Fruit orchards blanket the valleys, and pastures and chestnut forests run up into the hills. Practically any back road you choose to explore in this as-yet-little-discovered area will be a dramatic one, and you will always have Mont-Canigou as a reference point to keep you from getting lost.

CÉRET

This lively hill town 32 km (20 miles) southwest of Perpignan was a favorite retreat of Catalan artists and their friends in the early twentieth century and came to be called "The Mecca of Cubism" because of the work Picasso and Braque did here in 1911 and 1912, when they were collaborating so closely that their paintings were virtually indistinguishable. Gris, Chagall, Kisling, Masson, Soutine and Manolo, Picasso's Catalan sculptor friend who "discovered" Céret, also spent substantial periods here — which accounts for the astounding collection this town of 7,200 has in its **Museum of Modern Art**. There are first-rate works by all these artists and by Matisse (17 sketches he did in Collioure), Maillol, Dufy, Cocteau, Miro, Dali and such present-day names as Arman, Ben, Tàpies, Viallat and Jean and Jacques Capdeville. The core of the collection is 53 works by Picasso. Twenty-eight are terra-cotta bowls painted with bullfighting scenes that he made specially for this museum. The building was enlarged and entirely renovated in 1992 and is a model of how modern art works should be displayed. It is open every day from 10 AM to 7 PM from mid-July to the end of August, 10 AM to 6 PM and closed Tuesdays the rest of the year.

Céret has a wide, lively main street that changes names every block from Boulevard du Maréchal Joffre, to Jean-Jaurès, to Place Picasso, to Lafayette, but is known here simply as "Le Boulevard." It is shaded by huge plane trees and lined with cafés and boutiques, and off it, there are old squares with fountains. A market is held every Saturday for foods of the region — anchovies, oysters, ham, honey, *paella*, roast chicken, grilled fish — and local arts and crafts work.

Be sure to pause and look at fourteenth century **Pont du Diable** (Devil's Bridge) at the entrance to town. Its single arch 45 m (174 ft) wide spans the River Tech at a height of 22 m (72 ft). Cherry orchards cover the hills around town, and Mont-Canigou looms benevolently to the west.

The **Tourist Office** is at 1 Avenue Clémenceau, just off "the Boulevard" (68 87 00 53.

Festivals
Céret has numerous festivals and special events. The main ones are the **Easter procession**, the **cherry market** in April and May, **Feria** (bullfighting, fireworks, street dances) on the weekend closest to the 14th of July and the **Sardana Festival**, a big Catalan traditional dance event held the second to the last weekend in August. For details, contact the Tourist Office.

Where to Stay
The **Terrasse au Soleil****** on the Route de Fontfrede (68 87 01 94 FAX 68 87 39 24, is a rambling old farmhouse in the cherry tree-covered hills above town once owned by Charles Trenet, now a cheerful 27-room hotel with a swimming pool, tennis

courts and golf practice hole. The young owners, Pascal and Brigitte Levielle-Nizerolle, have both worked in America. The hotel has rooms in the moderate and expensive ranges. It is a Relais de Silence member, open the first week of March through New Years Day. The **Arcades**** at 1 Place Pablo Picasso in the heart of Céret (68 87 12 30 FAX 68 87 49 44, has 26 neat, simple rooms, moderately priced to inexpensive, in the heart of town. The **Vidal*** is an old-fashioned, inexpensive 11-room Logis de France inn at 4 Place du 4 Septembre, just off Place Picasso (68 87 00 85.

Camping

Céret has four camping grounds, the best-equipped being the 100-place **Camping Saint-Georges** (68 87 03 73, open all year. It has a pool and tennis court. If you can't find a space in Céret, there are four regular camping grounds and one nudist establishment in neighboring Mauriellas-las-Illas.

Where to Eat

Les Feuillants, 1 Boulevard la Fayette, Céret (68 87 37 88, in a big, elegant Art Nouveau mansion under the huge plane trees of old Céret, is one of the few gourmet restaurants in Roussillon, serving the inventive Mediterranean cuisine of Didier Banyols and wines of the region selected by one of Roussillon's top *sommeliers*, his wife Marie-Louise. Expensive, but there is a 120 franc fixed-price luncheon menu on weekdays. The restaurant has one Michelin star. The **Terrasse au Soleil** has, as its name indicates, a large sunny terrace, where fine local dishes such as duck with cherries are featured. The **Vidal** offers generous portions of home cooking at modest prices.

How to Get There

Line 35 of the Carinter 66 bus network runs frequent service between Perpignan and Céret and the other towns of the Vallespir. There are about fifteen buses a day. Coming by car from Perpignan, a distance of 32 km (20 miles), the easiest thing is to take the A 9 *autoroute* south to Le Boulou and D 115 west to Céret. From there the D 115 runs southwest along the Tech River and reaches the Spanish frontier at the Col d'Ares.

AMÉLIE-LES-BAINS AND PALALDA

The ancient spa of Amélie-les-Bains, eight kilometers (five miles) to the southwest of Céret on D 115, has been drawing people for cures since at least the days of the Romans, and today its waters are prescribed for rheumatism and respiratory problems. The lovely **Gorges du Mondony** begin only a 15 minute walk south of town, and the medieval Catalan village of Palalda, its steep narrow streets all decorated with flowers, is three kilometers

(two miles) to the east. It has a little **Museum of Tradition and Popular Arts** with a reconstituted Catalan kitchen and bedroom from the turn of the century. It is open daily from mid-February to mid-December from 2 PM to 6 PM, to 7 PM in the summer.

Like most spa towns, Amélie-les-Bains has a casino.

The **Tourist Office** in Amélie-les-Bains is at Quai du 8 Mai 1945 (68 39 01 98.

Where to Stay and Where to Eat

Because of the spa, Amélie-les-Bains has an inordinate number of hotels for a town of 3,300 — one three-star hotel, nine two-star hotels, and 18 one-star or non-rated. The **Castel Émeraude**** a Relais de Silence member, is a big, rambling white hotel with medieval-style twin turrets in a quiet country setting on the bank of the Tech River. It has 59 recently renovated rooms at 240 to 360 francs and a well-reputed restaurant with menus from 95 francs. It is one kilometer west of town on the Route de la Corniche (68 39 02 83 FAX 68 39 03 09. The best restaurant in the area is the **Mas Pagris** in Montalba d'Amélie (68 39 38 73, reached by a five kilometer (three mile) drive or walk along the Gorges du Mondony. It serves savory dishes made from local products such as wild mushrooms, brook trout and country sausage. Be sure to try the *boules de picolat*, meatballs cooked in wine and wild mushroom sauce and served with white beans. A meal costs about 100 francs. In the summer, you dine outsides, where the only sound to disturb you will be that of a nearby waterfall.

THE SOUTHERN VALLESPIR

Arles-sur-Tech

Another town of note in the Vallespir, Arles-sur-Tech is known for the lovely **cloister** of its medieval abbey and its Romanesque **Église Sainte-Marie**, which contains a strange tomb, the **Sainte-Tombe**, that keeps filling with a mysterious liquid in a manner that defies scientific explanation. The nearby **Gorges du Fou** is remarkable too. In places it is no more that three meters (10 ft) wide and more than 100 m (330 ft) high. **Corsavy** is a tiny, picturesque hill village near Arles-sur-Tech with narrow medieval streets leading up to the ruins of its **castle** and splendid views of Mont-Canigou, whose peak is only 12 km (7.5 miles) away.

Arles-sur-Tech's **Tourist Office** is on Rue Barjau (68 39 11 99. There is only one hotel, but it is pleasant and inexpensive, **Les Glycines**** at 32 Rue du Jeu de Paume (68 39 10 09, a well-maintained old-style establishment from the late nineteenth century with 32 neat, clean rooms and the best restaurant in town.

The largest and best-equipped **camping grounds** in the southern Vallespir is **Le Vallespir** in Arles-sur-Tech. It has 296 places, a restaurant, bar, washing machines, a swimming pool and tennis court and is open from April 1 to the end of October (68 39 05 03. The pleasantly situated, but modestly equipped 150-place **Camping Riuferrer** is open all year (68 39 11 06.

Prats-de-Mollo

Built on the slopes of an open valley of the Tech 19 km (12 miles) southwest of Arles-sur-Tech, Prats-de-Mollo was a favorite holiday spot of the Kings of Aragon. It has a **Romanesque church**, **medieval ramparts** and the inevitable Vauban fortress, **Fort Lagarde**, on a rocky spur above the town, built to defend the border with Spain, only 14 km (nine miles) to the south. Neighboring **La Preste** is a spa noted for treatment of urinary problems. Napoléon III had a road built to it so he could go for a cure, but the Franco-Prussian War permanently disrupted his plans.

There are 12 hotels in Prats-de-Mollo and La Preste and three modest camping sites, open from April through October. For information about this area, contact the Prats-de-Mollo Tourist Office at Place le Fioral (68 38 70 83.

PERPIGNAN TO THE CÔTE VERMEILLE

The Côte Vermeille (Vermilion Coast) is a string of crystal clear Mediterranean inlets and sheer cliffs etched by the Mediterranean into the eastern end of the Pyrénées. The reddish color of the rock gives the coast its name. The cliffs twist along the coast for 20 km (12.5 mile) from Collioure to Cape Cerbère at the frontier of Spain, and the terraced vineyards of the Banyuls and Collioure *appellations* run up the steep hillsides most of the way. The Côte Vermeille starts 24 km (15 miles) southeast of Perpignan. As you head down there, try to make time for a stop at Elne, which is on the route, half-way between Perpignan and Collioure.

ELNE

Thanks to its steep hill dominating the rich farm plains around it, Elne has been inhabited since time immemorial, and continuously since the sixth century BC. It was the local capital of the Iberians, then the Romans, who made it the capital of Roussillon. Its name derives from Helene, the mother of Emperor Constantine. From 568 to 1602 Elne was an episcopal see, and its large Romanesque **Cathédrale Sainte-Eulalie et Sainte-Julie**

dates from the eleventh century. The cathedral's marble **cloister**, built between the twelfth and the fourteenth centuries, is one of the high points of medieval Catalan art, and its imaginative sculptures of fabulous animals, biblical figures and floral patterns show how the style evolved.

In 1276, Elne lost its status as capital of Roussillon when the King of Majorca moved his court to Perpignan. Today it is a quiet town of 6,000 that makes its living from the fruit and wine trade.

The **Tourist Office** is in the town hall, la Mairie (68 22 05 07.

Elne is 13 km (eight miles) south of Perpignan and can be reached by frequent trains and Carinter 66 buses. By car, take N 114.

COLLIOURE

This town ranks with Cassis and Saint-Tropez as the most beautiful of Mediterranean France's small ports. It has a large thirteenth century fortress jutting out into the harbor, brightly colored little fishing boats, a church on the water, three beaches, the red-roofed Vieux Quartier, green hills surrounding the ensemble, fortresses atop them, and bright sun and deep blue skies almost every day. "There is no sky more blue in France than in Collioure," said Matisse, who came here in 1905 and fell in love with the light. It was in Collioure that he finally shucked his last formal constraints: "I worked as I felt, only by color," and out of that breakthrough came "Bonheur de Vivre" and "Fenêtre Ouverte." Derain, who came with Matisse in 1905, painted his dazzling "Phare de Collioure." When the artists came back in 1906, Dufy, Gris and Marquet joined them, and as a result, Collioure became known as the "Cradle of Fauvism."

Collioure's beauty has not been lost on the tourists, be warned. Armies of them arrive in midsummer, swelling the little town to several times its normal population of 2,700.

General Information

The **Tourist Office** is at Place 18-Juin, one block in from the central beach, the Plage Boramar (68 82 15 47.

Train station, Gare SNCF (68 82 05 89. Get **bus information** at the Tourist Office. The buses stop at the main parking lot of the town.

For **scuba diving, windsurfing** or **bike rental**, contact **C.I.P. Collioure**, 1 Rue du Puits Saint-Dominique (68 82 07 16.

Festivals

On Good Friday evening, the candlelight **procession of the Brotherhood of the Sanch** is held. On August 16, the **Feast of Saint Vincent** has bullfights, fireworks and a procession up into the hills to Notre-Dame-de-Consolation. A *sardana*

OPPOSITE: The medieval port of Collioure on the Côte Vermeille, a favorite of Matisse, Derain and many other leading artists of the twentieth century.

dance competition is held the first Sunday of September.

What to See and What to Do

The **Château Royal**, the bulky fortress dominating the harbor, was built by the Knights Templar in the thirteenth century, when the Catalan fleet ruled the Western Mediterranean, and Collioure was a major commercial port as Perpignan's outlet to the sea. People in Collioure still refer it as the Château des Templiers. The royal designation came in the fourteenth century, when the Kings of Majorca summered here. The fort was reinforced by Charles V and Philip II of Spain in the sixteenth century to protect Col-

wood-carved altarpieces, five of them by the Catalan Baroque master Joseph Sunyer, including the huge three level triptych in back of the main altar.

Narrow streets wind up the hill of the **Vieux Quarter du Mouré**, and at the top sits seventeenth century **Fort Miradou**.

One place you should not miss is the **Hostellerie des Templiers** on the Quai de l'Amirauté, a hotel, bar and restaurant with an huge collection of art works. The many artists who came to Collioure from the time of Matisse and Derain onward became friends of René Pous, the owner of a local café, and they lavished paintings and drawings on him. Sadly, works by some of the big-name artists, Matisse and Picasso among them, were

lioure from the French, and it took its final shape when Vauban made his inevitable modifications, adding the ramparts that jut out into the harbor. In summer, the Château is used for art exhibitions and concerts. It is open from 10 AM to 7:30 PM in summer, afternoons the rest of the year ☎ 68 82 06 43.

Across the little fishing harbor from the Château Royale at the end of the pebbly **Plage Boramar** is the seventeenth century **Église Notre-Dame-des-Anges** with its bullet-shaped bell tower, converted from an old lighthouse. The interior is murky, especially when you step in from the dazzling sunshine, but let your eyes adjust, and take a look at the nine remarkable gilded

stolen several years ago. But with 2,000 original works on the walls of the hotel, bar and restaurant, there is no lack of art to peruse. The establishment is now run by René Pous's genial son Jo and his children, and its bar remains the place to plunge into the life of this town.

If you want to see more artworks, the **Musée d'Art Moderne de Collioure** at the Villa Pams on the Route de Port-Vendres has a contemporary art collection and puts on temporary exhibits run by the Musée d'Art Moderne de Céret. For information about their programs, call the museum at ☎ 68 82 10 19, or check at the Tourist Office.

For an inspiring walk into the hills, climb to the **Ermitage Notre-Dame-de-Consolation**, a hermitage with a number of sailors' ex-votos (offerings made in pursuance of a vow). There are fine views of Collioure, the sea and the mountains throughout the eight kilometer (five mile) hike

The Côte Vermille is famed for its anchovies and other seafood OPPOSITE, that are brought in daily by the fishing fleet of Port Vendres ABOVE.

up and back, for which you should allow an hour and a half.

Collioure is famed for its anchovies, and they are grilled outdoors for you along the Plage Boramar. You can also buy delicious fillets of anchovies in jars, marinated in a variety ways. The leading specialists in this ancient technique are **Roque Salaisons** on Route de la Démocratie (N 114) (68 82 04 99, or **Desclaux & Cie** at the Carrefour du Christ, the intersection of N 114 and Rue de la République, the main street down to the port (68 82 05 25. They have retail outlets at their workshops.

Where to Stay and Where to Eat

Collioure is the big resort of the Côte Vermeille, but its hotels are minuscule by Côte d'Azur standards. It has one four-star hotel, five three-star hotels and six two-star hotels with 281 rooms total in those categories — less than the Carlton or the Martinez alone in Cannes. And prices are relatively low too. The **Relais des Trois Mas****** on the Route de Vendres (68 82 05 07 FAX 68 82 38 08, high overlooking Collioure's harbor, has 19 elegant rooms with luxurious baths at 660 to 860 francs and four suites, a pool, health center and a restaurant, **La Balette**, with menus at 165 and 345 francs. Closed mid-November to mid-December. **Casa Pairal***** on the Impasse des Palmiers, 150 m from the beach (68 82 05 81 FAX 68 82 52 10, has 26 big, beautifully furnished rooms in a hundred year-old Catalan mansion with a palm-shaded garden and swimming pool. A Relais de Silence member, open April 1 to November 2. Its rooms run from 370 to 820 francs. **Hostelrie des Templiers**** at 12 Quai de l'Amirauté (68 98 31 10 FAX 68 98 01 24, has 52 neat rooms in the hotel and its annex. They have been recently renovated, and original art is everywhere. Fresh local fish is the restaurant's forte, served in the dining room with a mural by Claude Viallat or on the outdoor terrace facing the port and the Château. The restaurant is closed Sunday evenings and Mondays, the hotel and restaurant the month of January. Room and meal prices range from inexpensive to moderate.

CAMPING

Collioure has two modest camping sites, **La Girelle** (68 81 25 56, and **Les Amandiers** (68 81 14 69, both by the Plage de L'Ouille a short walk north of town, open from April to the end of September. If you can't get into one of them, the next town to the north, **Argelès-sur-Mer**, has 56 camping grounds with thousands of places. **Les Criques de Porteils**, the closest, is a well-equipped 200-place camp on a cliff overlooking the Plage de L'Ouille one kilometer north of the Collioure train station, open April 1 to the end of September (68 81 12 73.

How to Get There

There is frequent train service from Perpignan on the Port Bou line (the main line from Paris to the Spanish border) and Carinter 66 bus service from Perpignan's Gare Routière. If you are driving down N 114, traffic is especially bad around Collioure in the summer. Stop-and-start conditions are not unusual. A new bypass around Collioure that runs from Argelès to Port-Vendres is a help. But given the volume of traffic in the summer, be prepared for slow going.

Wine Tasting

The vineyards you will see terraced up the steep, rocky slopes running the whole length of

the Côte Vermeille make two *apellation contrôlée* wines — Collioure and Banyuls. The Collioure wines are deep-colored, exceptionally aromatic dry reds and bright, aromatic rosés, and Banyuls are *vins doux naturels*, sweet aperitif wines. It is common for the vineyards of the four communities authorized to make them — Collioure, Port-Vendres, Banyuls-sur-Mer and Cerbère — to make both. The Collioure *appellation* is small, only 330 hectares (792 acres) of vineyards producing a million liters of wine (as compared to 30 million for Côtes du Roussillon or 45 million for Côteaux du Languedoc). The **Maison de la Vigne et du Vin** on Place du 18 Juin (68 82 49 00, across from the Tourist Office, is open from June to September and provides literature on Collioure wine in several languages and arranges wine-tasting visits. **Domaine la Tour Vieille**, one of the most acclaimed producers of both Collioure and Banyuls wines, operates a *cave* in town from Easter to the end of September. It is centrally located on Rue Berthelot. Otherwise, visit the Domaine la Tour Vieille's 10 hectare (24 acre) vineyard in the hills above town at 3 Avenue Mirador. Call ahead for an appointment (68 82 42 20. (For information on *AOC* Banyuls wines, see the next section on Banyuls-sur-Mer).

PORT-VENDRES

From Collioure, an exciting drive to make is a loop that follows the coast to **Banyuls-sur-Mer** and swings up into the hills to return to Collioure on the spectacular **Route des Crètes**, the Crest Road along the foothills of the Pyrénées overlooking the Mediterranean.

The town directly south of Collioure is Port-Vendres, the only deep water port in Roussillon. Ancient Greek mariners used it, and the Romans gave it its name, Portus Veneris, Port Venus. It took its present shape in the seventeenth century, when it became French, and Louis XIV's finance minis-

ter Colbert decided to make it a commercial port, and Vauban built his customary forts to protect it. The handsome ensemble of eighteenth century buildings to the north of the port reflects the prosperity that resulted. And here on the **Place de l'Obelisque** you can see the only monument in France that celebrates Louis XVI — a 29 m (95 ft) **marble obelisk** that the king gave the town shortly before the French Revolution. Prosperity continued through the nineteenth and early twentieth century, when Port-Vendres boasted of "the shortest distance in the calmest waters between France and Algeria," and it became a main port for cargo and passenger traffic with North Africa. The loss of Algeria in 1962 dealt a death blow to its large-scale port activities. Today Port-Vendres, population 5,370, has a faded, B. Traven-like atmosphere, like Tampico in *The Treasure of the Sierra Madre*. It is a cargo port of modest activity, a year-round yacht harbor and a fishing port with the most active fleet on the Roussillon coast. The **Criée aux Poissons** (fish auction) is held at 4:30 PM

at the Quai du Fanal, the fishing fleet's dock at the northern entrance to the harbor. For vacationers Port-Vendres offers numerous little beaches and good access to all water sports. But unfortunately its dramatic landscape is badly marred by too many tasteless modern buildings.

The **Tourist Office** is at Quai Pierre Forgas in the center of town (68 82 07 54.

Continue down the coast to Banyuls-sur-Mer, six kilometers south of Port-Vendres.

BANYULS-SUR-MER

This pleasant beach town on a long palm-lined crescent of sandy shore framed by a sweep of the Albères foothills is famous for two reasons: it is the home of Banyuls *vin doux naturel*, a delicious sweet aperitif wine, and it is the birthplace of sculptor Aristide Maillol (1861–1944), who lived and worked here in the summers for much of his life and is buried at his farm outside of town. Banyuls is an excellent place for sailing, scuba diving and all water sports and has a good selection of hotels and restaurants. In summer its normal population of 4,662 quadruples.

Since 1991 the local celebrity has been Dolphy, a vivacious lady dolphin who has staked out this stretch of coast as her habitat and pops in along the beach from time to time.

The **Tourist Office** is at Avenue de la République, on the beach across from the Hotel de Ville (68 88 31 58, a very helpful and efficient operation that can give you all the information you need about hotels, restaurants, sailing, scuba diving and other activities in the area. They also have a long list of furnished rooms and apartments for rent.

What to See and What to Do

Maillol's **Tomb** is at his farm in a little valley amid hills covered by olive and fig trees a few kilometers from the center of town. The tomb is in the garden, watched over sorrowfully by one of Maillol's hefty nudes, a copy of his War Memorial in Perpignan. There are plans to convert Maillol's house and studio into a museum, but that has not happened yet. Get precise road directions at the Tourist office. The tomb is downhill from the road, and you can easily drive right past it without noticing it.

Another Maillol nude, **Harmonie,** is in the little garden in back of Banyuls's Hôtel de Ville.

The **Aquarium of the Laboratoire Arago**, one of the oldest and most important marine biology laboratories in France, has 39 display tanks containing 250 species of creatures from the Gulf of Lion. It is on Avenue du Fontaulé on the south side of the pleasure-boat port (68 88 73 73. It is open daily all year from 9 AM to 12 PM and 2 PM to 6:30 PM, and to 10 PM in July and August.

ABOVE: The tomb of Catalan scupltor Aristide Maillol in his native Banyuls-sur-Mer.
OPPOSITE: Port Vendres, Roussillon's only deep water port, has been used by mariners since the time of the ancient Greeks.

Where to Stay

If you decide to stay overnight in Banyuls, I recommend **Les Elmes**** on the Plage des Elmes just north of town (68 88 03 12 FAX 68 88 53 03, a bright, cheerful 31-room hotel on the beach, very popular with scuba divers. Rooms here are in the moderate range, 280 to 480 francs for a double. **Le Catalan***** on the Route de Cerbère (68 88 02 80 FAX 68 88 16 14, is a moderately-priced modern hotel-restaurant on a hill above town, all 36 rooms with a sea view and a big terrace pool.

CAMPING

The well-shaded 33-place **Camping du Stade** on the Route du Stade (68 88 31 70, is open April 1 to the end of October. **Camping Municipal** is on Avenue Guy Malé (follow the signs for the Cellier des Templiers). It has 227 places and is open all year except for the month of November and the first two weeks of December (68 88 32 13.

Where to Eat

Le Sardinal on Place Paul Reig (68 88 30 07, is the gastronomic restaurant of town, serving Catalan dishes and seafood. Very popular, be sure to reserve. It is expensive. **La Littorine**, the restaurant of Les Elmes, serves imaginative seafood at reasonable prices, with fixed-price menus at 90 and 150 francs. **Al Fanal** on Avenue du Fontaulé across from the aquarium (68 88 00 81, offers well-prepared Catalan specialties at modest prices.

Wine Tasting

As in Collioure, wine makers in Banyuls-sur-Mer make both *AOC* Collioure and Banyuls *vin doux naturel*. This natural sweet wine is drunk as an aperitif or after dinner. A properly aged Banyuls is considered the only wine that goes with chocolates, and it is good with cigars. You will have no trouble finding it here. It is sold by the glass or the bottle at stands along the beach, or you can visit producers' *caves* and taste it for free. The Grande Cave of the **Cellier des Templiers**, the largest producer, is right outside town on Route du Mas du Reig (D 86). The visit consists of a 20-minute film and a 45-minute guided tour of the vast cellars with their gigantic oak vats and stainless steel tanks and the wooden barrels of wine aging outside in the sun. The wines are aged from three to fifteen years before being sold. There is free wine tasting at the end of the tour. The cave is open daily 9 AM to 7 PM April through October, 9 AM to 12 PM and 2 PM to 6 PM and closed Sundays the rest of the year (68 88 06 74.

The smaller **Cave Cooperative de l'Étoile** in the center of town, another fine producer, has a shorter tour of its cellars, also with free wine tasting. It is at 26 Avenue du Puig Dalmas (66 88 00 10. Open daily except Sunday in summer, weekends in the

off-season. Both of these companies also make *AOC* Collioure wine of very high quality.

The young Parcé brothers accomplish wonders with their little vineyard, producing extraordinarily delicious and highly acclaimed Banyuls and Collioure wines from their **Domaine de la Rectorie's** 30 hectares (72 acres) of vines. Try their red Collioure from 1991, which received the highest rating on a recent year's respected Hachette wine testing program. They are at 54 Avenue du Puig-del-Mas (68 88 18 55. Call ahead for a *rendezvous*.

ROUTE DES CRÊTES

From Banyuls, you have two choices of roads, the coast road that winds along 10 km (six miles) of bleak cliffs to the dreary rail terminus town of **Cerbère** by the Spanish border, or the Route des Crêtes. On the coast road, the cliffs are dramatic

at a couple of points, especially **Cap Réderis**, and you might want to drive to the frontier just for the sake of having done it, but frankly, the time it takes doing that would be better spent taking in the scenic pleasures of the Route des Crêtes. To get to the Route des Crêtes, swing up into the hills in back of Banyuls and take steep, winding D 86 northward for spectacular vistas of the Mediterranean from many points. You will pass the ruins of several medieval towers that were part of an elaborate signal network from the time of the Kings of Majorca and Aragon. They allowed watchmen overlooking the Mediterranean to flash signals deep into Roussillon in a matter of minutes. Park your car below the **Tour Madeloc** about 10 km (six miles) north of Banyuls and walk 15 minutes up to the tower. From its height of 652 m (2,140 ft), it surveys the whole coast from Cap d'Agde in the north well down the Costa Brava in Spain.

Two kilometers north of the Tour Madeloc is the **Ermitage Notre-Dame-de-Consolation**, the hermitage with sailors' *ex-votos* on a hill overlooking Collioure.

The road now descends to Collioure, where you can order a glass of Collioure wine and take one more look at the delightful old port with its *château* and church and brightly painted little fishing boats that so many artists have painted, a fitting way to end our journey through Mediterranean France.

For the resourceful traveler, there are many unspoiled inlets to be found amid the red cliffs of the Côte Vermeille.

Travelers'
Tips

GETTING TO MEDITERRANEAN FRANCE

BY AIR

Nice-Côte d'Azur International Airport, the third busiest in France after De Gaulle and Orly in Paris, serves six million passengers a year in its two big modern terminals. There are nine flights a day from London (Air France, British Airways, British Midland, Air UK), and Delta has one flight a day from New York and one from Atlanta. There are more than 40 flights a day from Paris (Air Inter, Air Liberté, AOM) and direct flights from 33 other airports in France, from 40 in other European countries and 16 in Africa and the Middle East. There is bus service every 20 minutes from the airport to Nice's Gare Routière (a 20-minute ride, 21 francs), every hour to Cannes (45 minutes, 70 francs), Monaco (45 minutes, 80 francs) and Menton (75 minutes, 85 francs). There is also frequent helicopter service to Monaco, Sophia Antipolis, Cannes and Saint-Tropez.

Marseille-Provence International Airport at Marignane is the second largest airport in Mediterranean France, with three flights a day from London on British Airways and one on Air France and about 20 flights a day from Paris on Air Inter, TAT and AOM. **Montpellier Airport** has 10 daily flights from Paris and a few flights per week from London on Air Littoral and Dan-Air. Other airports with daily flights from Paris are **Toulon-Hyères** (convenient to Saint-Tropez) with five, **Avignon-Caumont** with four, **Nîmes-Camargue** (convenient to Arles) with four, **Béziers-Agde** with four, **Carcassonne** with two and **Perpignan** with four. Until recently internal flights were very expensive in France, but as European rules against protection have come into play, other French airlines have been able to challenge Air Inter's former monopoly, and prices fell drastically in 1995 and 1996. The Paris–Nice round trip dropped to 690 francs.

enter the market in the spring of 1997, prices may drop even more. The best bet is to check with a travel agent. The airlines also offer reductions for students, senior citizens and off-season travel.

BY TRAIN

The *TGV*, the *Train à Grande Vitesse* (Very Fast Train), travels on high-speed rails from Paris as far south as Valence, about 80 km (50 miles) south of Lyon, and on normal tracks from there to the south. The SNCF (Société Nationale des Chemins de Fer), the French national railroad company, is planning to extend the high-speed rails to Marseille, Montpellier and beyond, perhaps by the end of the century, but environmental

challenges have delayed the project. For the moment, the TGV gets you from Paris to Avignon in three hours and 45 minutes, to Marseille in four hours and 45 minutes, Montpellier in about five hours, Perpignan six and a half and Nice in seven.

If you can book you trip a month or more in advance, great savings are to be had thanks to the SNCF's Joker programs. Joker 8 gives you up to 40 percent off if you book eight days or more in advance, Joker 30 up to 60 percent off you book at least 30 days in advance. There are also reductions of up to 50 percent for passengers 12 to 25 years of age or over 60 and for people traveling with children under 16. The low-priced France Rail Passes give you three days of unlimited travel

within a one-month period and you can add up to six days at a supplemental daily charge. The present cost in the United States is $145 for the first three days and $30 per additional day and there are substantial reductions for two persons traveling together. To qualify for these fares, you must purchase the tickets outside of Europe. If you buy them inside Europe they are more expensive. Any established North American travel agency can issue French Rail Passes. The Eurailpass, which offers unlimited rail travel throughout Western Europe (except for the United Kingdom), is not a good idea for travelers who want to explore so small and area as Mediterranean France. You have to do a great deal of traveling to make it cost-effective. To save the effort of long distance driving, you can ship your car by rail from either Paris or Calais to Avignon, Narbonne or Nice, ride in comfort on a *TGV* and pick up your car in the sunny South.

For information in the United States about rail travel in France call ℂ 1-800-4-EURAIL. For information in Canada call ℂ 1-800-361-RAIL. In Great Britain contact French Railways, 179 Piccadilly, London W10V 0AB ℂ (information) (0891) 515-477; (reservations) ℂ (035) 300-003.

OPPOSITE: The red rocks of the Esterel Corniche west of Cannes. ABOVE: Ferry to the Îles d'Hyères.

By International Bus Lines

The cheapest way to get to Mediterranean France from London is by Eurolines, the big European bus line. At current rates, a round-trip ticket between London and Marseille is 920 francs for adults, 680 francs for children four to 12 years of age. In London the buses leave from Victoria Coach Station (05 82 40 45 11. Travel agents can give you Eurolines's schedules and sell you tickets.

By Car

To drive in France, you must be 18 or over. Drivers licenses from other European Union countries, the United States and Canada are accepted in France. People bringing their own cars to France must have proof of ownership and insurance.

The Routes

Most people driving to Mediterranean France from Paris take the **A6 Autoroute du Soleil** from Paris to Lyon, a distance of 461 km (288 miles), then the **A 7** (still called the Autoroute du Soleil) down the Rhône Valley. The A 7 ends in Marseille, 313 km (196 miles) south of Lyon. For the Côte d'Azur, the **A8 La Provençale** branches east from A 7 just north of Marseille and cuts straight through the center of the Var to Cannes, Antibes, Nice, Monaco and on to Italy.

For Languedoc-Roussillon, the **A 9 La Langue-docienne** branches off from A 7 at Orange and runs southwest past Nîmes, Montpellier, Béziers, Narbonne and Perpignan and down into Spain.

For Carcassonne, the **A 61 Autoroute des Deux Mers** branches westward from the A 9 a few miles south of Narbonne.

These toll roads (*autoroutes à péage*) are expensive. To save money, you could take the **Nationale 7** south from Paris through the Massif Centrale to Lyon, then down the Rhône Valley, paralleling the A 6 and A 7, and cut east through the Var to the Côte d'Azur. It is free, but very slow.

A colorful alternate route to the Côte d'Azur is the **Route Napoléon (N 85)** from Grenoble through the Alpes-de-Haute-Provence to Cannes.

CAR RENTAL

There are a dozen or more auto rental services operating in the region, large and small, and prices vary widely depending on the time of year, the level of competition and so forth. For Americans, the rates of international companies are considerably cheaper if you make your reservation in advance via an 800 (toll-free) number. The major ones are: **Avis** (800-331-1084, **Budget**

(800-472-3325, **Dollar (EuroDollar)** 800-800-4000, **Hertz** (800-654-3001, **National (EuropCar)** (800-CAR-EUROPE, **Thrifty** (**800-367-2277**. Avis and Hertz are generally more expensive than the others.

CAR LEASING

For tourists from outside the European Union who plan to rent a car for 23 days or more, the best price you can get is by a lease-purchase arrangement whereby you pay in advance a fixed rate based on the period of time you plan to use the car and sign a promissory note to purchase the car if you do not return it to the dealer at the end of your trip. For the lowest-priced car, the Renault Twingo, the cost is under US$25 a day for a 23-day period, less for longer periods. Complete insurance coverage is included. The cars can be picked up and returned in many cities in France, includ-

ing Nice, Marseille and Perpignan. In the United States, contact **Renault Eurodrive**, 650 First Avenue, New York NY 10016-3214 ((212) 532-1221, 1-800-221-1052 (1-800-477-7116 in the Western states) FAX (212) 725-5379.

VISAS

No visas are required by France or the Principality of Monaco for holders of valid United States, Canadian, European Union, Australian or New Zealand passports visiting France as tourists for up to three months. By law, visitors wanting to stay longer than that should obtain long-term visas before coming to France. Tourists in France who decide they want to stay longer than three months and be perfectly legal about it can simply pop across the Italian or Spanish border, get their passports stamped and come back into France

for another three months. But in fact, holders of any of the above-mentioned passports who don't break any laws in France are unlikely to be bothered by any French authorities.

French law requires everyone to carry proof of identification at all times. If you lose your passport, contact your consulate or embassy to get a temporary replacement.

CONSULATES AND EMBASSIES OF PRINCIPAL ENGLISH-SPEAKING COUNTRIES

United States Consulate   12 Boulevard Paul Peytral, 13286 Marseille (91 54 92 00 FAX 91 55 09 47; 31 Rue du Maréchal Joffre, 06000 Nice (93 88 89

The Cirque de Mourèze, one of many strange natural formations in the Cévennes above Montpellier.

55 (no FAX). United States Embassy in Paris ((16-1) 42 61 80 75.

British Consulate 24 Avenue du Prado, 13006 Marseille (91 53 43 32 FAX 91 37 47 06. They have a 24-hour emergency service. British Embassy in Paris ((16-1) 42 66 38 10.

Irish Consulate 152 Boulevard J-F Kennedy, 06600 Antibes (93 61 50 63 FAX 93 67 96 08, and Villa les Bruyères, 1 Place Sainte-Devôte, Monte-Carlo, Monaco (93 15 70 00 FAX 93 22 72 47. Irish Embassy in Paris ((16-1) 45 00 20 87.

The Canadian, Australian, New Zealand and South African governments have no consulates in the Mediterranean France region. For inquiries, call their embassies in Paris:

Canadian Embassy ((16-1) 44 43 29 00.
Australian Embassy ((16-1) 40 59 33 00.
New Zealand Embassy ((16-1) 45 00 24 11.
South African Embassy ((16-1) 54 55 92 37.

TOURIST INFORMATION

FRENCH NATIONAL TOURIST INFORMATION OFFICES OUTSIDE FRANCE

The French government has travel information offices known as "Maisons de France" in many foreign countries. The main ones in the English-speaking world are as follows:

ABOVE: Perpignan is a city of numerous convivial little squares. OPPOSITE: The village square in Châteauneuf-du- Pape, Southern France's most distinguished wine center.

IN THE USA:
Beverly Hills: 9454 Wilshire Boulevard, CA 90212 ((310) 271-6665 or 2661. The central phone number is (900) 990-0040.
Chicago: 676 North Michigan Avenue, Suite 3360, IL 60611 2819 ((312) 751-7800.
New York: 444 Madison Avenue, 16th Floor, NY 10022 ((212) 838-7800.
IN CANADA:
Montreal: 1981 McGill College Avenue, Suite 490, QUE H3A 2W9 ((514) 288-4264.
Toronto: 30 Patrick Street, Suite 700,ONT M5T 3A3 ((416) 593-4723.
IN GREAT BRITAIN:
London: 178 Picadilly, W1V 0AL ((071) 629-2869.
IN IRELAND
Dublin: 35 Lower Abbey Street, Dublin 1 ((353) 1 877 18 71.
IN AUSTRALIA:
Sydney: BWP House, 12 Castlereagh Street, NSW 2000 ((612) 231-5244
IN HONG KONG c/o Air France, 21st Floor, Alexandra House, Charter Road, Central ((852) 2524-7584.

NATIONAL TOURIST INFORMATION OFFICES IN PARIS

Maison de Tourisme de France 8 Avenue de l'Opéra, 75001 Paris (42 96 10 23.
Office du Tourisme de la Principauté de Monaco 9 Avenue de la Paix, 75002 Paris (42 96 12 23.

REGIONAL TOURIST OFFICES

Comité Régional du Tourisme Provence-Alpes-Côte d'Azur 2 Rue Henri-Barbusse, 13241 Marseille (91 39 38 00.
Comité Régional du Tourisme du Languedoc-Roussillon 20 Rue de la République, 34000 Montpellier (67 22 81 00.
Office du Tourisme de la Principauté de Monaco 2A Boulevard des Moulins, MC 98030 Monaco (93 50 60 88.

DÉPARTEMENTAL TOURIST OFFICES

France is divided into 96 administrative districts called départements, rather like counties in the United States or Great Britain. The tourist authorities of the départements are excellent sources of written information about hotels, camping grounds, sports, cultural activities, cuisine and wines in their areas. Many of their brochures are in English. There are ten départements that are wholly or partially in Mediterranean France, and I strongly recommend your contacting them:
Comité du Tourisme Riviera-Côte d'Azur (Alpes-Maritimes) 55 Promenade des Anglais, 06000 Nice (93 44 50 59, for the area from Menton

to Cannes, including Nice, the hill towns around Vence, Antibes, and Grasse.

Comité Départemental de Tourisme du Var 5 Avenue Vauban (BP 51 47), 83000 Toulon (94 09 00 69, for the Esterel coast, the Maures, the Saint-Tropez peninsula, the Îles de Hyères, Toulon and Bandol.

Comité Départemental du Tourisme des Alpes-de-Haute-Provence 19 Rue du Docteur Honnorat, B.P. 170, 04005 Digne-les-Bains (92 31 57 29, for the Grand Canyon of the Verdon and the "Lavender Alps" of Haute-Provence.

Comité Départemental de Tourisme des Bouches-du-Rhône 13 Rue Roux de Brignole, 13006 Marseille (91 13 84 13, for Cassis, Marseille, Aix-en-Provence, Arles, the Alpilles and the Camargue.

Comité Départemental de Tourisme de l'Aude, B.P. 862, 57 Rue d'Alsace, 11012 Carcassonne (68 11 42 00, for Narbonne, the Corbières, Carcassonne and Cathar Country.

Comité Départemental du Tourisme des Pyrénées-Roussillon, B.P. 540, 7 Quai de Lattre de Tassigny, 66000 Perpignan (68 34 29 94, for Perpignan and the eastern Pyrénées.

TOURIST INFORMATION AND ASSISTANCE ON THE SCENE

All cities and towns have their own *Office de Tourisme*, and in smaller localities, it is often called the *Syndicat d'Initiative*. Local tourist offices are

Comité Départemental de Tourisme du Vaucluse 84008 Avignon (90 86 43 42, for Avignon, Châteauneuf-du-Pape, Orange, Vaison-la-Romaine, Mont-Ventoux, the Dentelles de Montmirail and the Lubéron.

Comité Départemental de Tourisme de la Drôme, 1 Avenue de Romans 26000 Valence (75 82 19 22, for Nyons, Grignan and "La Drôme Provençale."

Comité Départemental du Tourisme du Gard, 3 Place des Arènes, 30000 Nîmes (66 21 02 51, for Nîmes, the Pont du Gard, Uzès, Aigues-Mortes and La Grande-Motte.

Comité Départemental du Tourisme de l'Hérault, Avenue des Moulins, B.P. 3067, Avenue des Moulins, 34034 Montpellier (67 84 71 70, for Montpellier, the foothills of the Cévennes, Sète and the Bassin de Thau, Agde, Béziers and the Canal du Midi.

stocked with free maps and brochures on food, accommodations, sports, outdoors and cultural activities in their area, and the staffs are generally well-informed and very helpful. Some tourist offices will book rooms for you, and many offer guided tours of the principal cultural attractions in their town or city, including tours in English, German and other languages. Tourist offices I have found to be especially helpful in Mediterranean France are those of Menton, Monaco, Nice, Annot, Digne-les-Bains, Cannes, Castellane (for the Grand Canyon of the Verdon), Saint-Tropez (town and peninsula), Toulon, Marseille, Aix, Arles, Saint-Rémy, Avignon, Carpentras, Nyons, Grignan, Nîmes, Uzès, Montpellier, Sète, Cap d'Agde, Carcassonne, Limoux and Villefranche-de-Conflent. As a general rule, I'd suggest making the *Office de Tourisme* your first stop when you arrive in a city or town. If you want to write away for tourist information about any town or city you're interested in, simply address an envelope to OFFICE DE TOURISME, the name of town or city and, if you are writing from another country, obviously, FRANCE. If there is specific information you want, but you don't know French, you can write a note in English. Someone will be able to read it.

WHAT TO TAKE

You can buy just about any type of product in France that you can in North America, Great Britain or Australia, but, with the happy exception of

French wines, it is likely to cost you a good deal more. Clothes are very expensive in France, and other than the one or two items they may want to buy to prove that they went there, cost-conscious travelers should bring any clothes they'll need with them. The same goes for over-the-counter pharmaceuticals (aspirins are ridiculously expensive), vitamins, suntan and other lotions, film, mosquito repellent, generally anything you would buy in an American drug store. English language books cost two to three times as much in France as in Britain or America, and though English language books can be purchased in Nice, Cannes, Aix and Montpellier, the range of titles is not extensive. In the summer, you will not needed a pullover in the evening if you stay near the shore, but in the mountains it can sometimes gets chilly. In the winter, you will be wise to bring some good warm clothes, especially is you will find yourself

in the path of the *mistral* in Provence or the *tramontane* in Languedoc.

THE CLIMATE

There is rarely any rain in the summer, and temperatures rarely drop below 30°C (87°F) in the daytime. From mid-September to November, there can be rain and occasional storms along the Rhône Valley. Winter is generally dry and sunny. Spring is mild, and there will some rain. In Provence, the mistral, the powerful wind that sweeps down the Rhône Valley can arrive at any time of the year, as can the *tramontane* winds in Languedoc.

TRAVELING IN MEDITERRANEAN FRANCE

AIR

Given the short distances between the cities in Mediterranean France and the infrequency of flights, it doesn't make a great deal of sense to fly unless you are on urgent business. However, if you are in a hurry, Air Littoral has one flight a day each way between Nice and Marseille (40 minutes), one each way between Nice and Montpellier (50 minutes), and two flights a week connecting Nice and Perpignan (70 minutes). Air Littoral's phone number in Nice is (93 18 95 15.

TRAINS

The train service along the Mediterranean coast is excellent, particularly on the Côte d'Azur, where the local Métrazur service runs trains about every half-hour between Saint-Raphaël and Menton. The only coastal area that is not served by rail is the section between Fréjus and Hyères, including the Saint-Tropez Peninsula. Toulon, Marseille, Arles, Avignon, Montpellier, Béziers, Narbonne, Carcassonne and Perpignan are also well served by rail. Getting inland by rail is another story.

From Nice, there is the Cuneo line into the Alpes-Maritimes and the *Train des Pignes* (the Pine Cone Train) into the Alpes-de-Haute-Provence, a line from Marseille along the Durance River into the Alpes-de-Haute-Provence, a train from Narbonne to Carcassonne, and a train from Perpignan to Villefranche-de-Conflent, then the *Petit Train Jaune* (the Little Yellow train) into the Cerdagne region of the Pyrénées.

Distances are short. From Nice to Marseille, for example, it is about a two-and-a-half hour train ride.

BUSES AND URBAN TRANSPORT

There is good bus service between the main towns and cities — Nice, Antibes, Cannes, Fréjus-Saint-Raphaël, Saint-Tropez, Marseille, Aix, Avignon, Arles, Montpellier, Sète, Béziers, Narbonne, Carcassonne and Perpignan — but service to the interior is infrequent and requires a great deal of patience. The tourist offices have the timetables for the bus services, but you usually have to ask for them. They don't necessarily have them on display.

Public bus systems in the main cities are good, and Marseille has a modern subway system.

DRIVING IN FRANCE

One rule of the road you must be extremely careful to obey at all times is *priorité à droite* — priority of the car on the right coming into an intersection, unless you are in a traffic circle. But even in an intersection, watch out for cars trying to cut in from the right (French drivers are extremely competitive). Drive defensively, in other words.

Seat belts must be buckled in the back seat as well as the front, subject to hefty fines for violators.

Driving under the influence of alcohol carries very heavy fines.

Roads are labeled A for *autoroute*, N for *route nationale* and D for *route départementale*. The latter generally have good surfaces, but are narrow, especially for American drivers, who are used to wide roads. The speed limit on *autoroutes* (toll highways) is 130 km (81 miles) per hour. On the *routes nationales*, non-toll national highways (marked in red on most maps), it is 110 km (68 miles) per hour, 90 km (56 miles) per hour on lesser country roads and 50 km (30 miles) per hour in the city.

Toll roads are marked *péage*.

MAPS

Kümmerly+Frey/Blay Foldex maps 1:250 000 (1 cm: 2,5 km), Sheet 14 for Provence–Côte d'Azur, Sheet 10 for Languedoc–Roussillon and Sheet 5 for South-West–Pyrenees are widely available in book stores, stationery shops and service stations in France.

SPORTS

Mediterranean France has superb facilities for water sports and practically any other sport you can think of. For an overview, see SPORTING SPREE, page 25.

Travelers' Tips

GOLF

There are thirty-two 18-hole golf courses in the Provence–Alpes–Côte d'Azur region and eleven in Languedoc-Roussillon. Some of the most important ones are:

Golf de Monte-Carlo in Monaco (93 41 09 11.
Golf de Cannes-Mandelieu in Mandelieu (27 holes) (93 49 55 39.
Golf de Cannes-Mougins in Mougins (93 75 79 13.
Golf Club Opio Valbonne in Valbonne (93 12 00 08.
Grasse Country Club in Grasse (93 60 55 44.

Golf de Barbaroux in Brignoles (94 59 07 43.
Golf Country Club de la Salette in Marseille (91 27 12 16.
Golf Club de Nîmes-Campagne in Nîmes (66 70 17 37.
Golf de La Grande-Motte in La Grande-Motte (36 holes) (67 56 05 00.
Golf de Montpellier-Massane in Baillargues (67 87 87 87.
Golf du Cap d'Agde in Cap d'Agde (67 26 54 40.
Golf de Saint-Cyprien in Saint-Cyprien (27 holes) (68 37 63 93.

The **Fédération Française de Golf** lists all the courses Mediterranean France. They are at 69 Avenue Victor-Hugo 75783 Paris (44 17 63 00

OPPOSITE: A field of sunflowers in Languedoc. ABOVE: *Pétanque* was invented in Mediterranean France and is played in every village, town and city.

FAX 44 17 63 63. For more information about playing golf in the regions, see SPORTING SPREE, page 25.

ACCOMMODATIONS

A full range of accommodations is available in Mediterranean France, and in vast numbers from some of the most sinfully de luxe hotels in the world in Monte-Carlo, Cannes and Saint-Tropez to a sleeping bag in a farmer's field. There are tourist hotels of all levels of quality and price, furnished apartments, houses and cottages, rooms in private homes, nudist colonies and camping and caravaning grounds galore. Unlike some

parts of the world where you have to scrounge for a decent place to stay, the problem here is one of an embarrassment of choice.

HOTEL CATEGORIES

The French Ministry of Tourism has a rating system for hotels, with (theoretically) five levels **** L (luxury), **** (first-class), *** (very comfortable), ** (comfortable), * (simple, but adequate). I say "theoretically," because lately, the hotels in the four-star-L category have been lumped together with the four-star hotels in the tourist office listings. To find out which is which, just look at the prices. The luxury hotel will be considerably more expensive than the first-class one. Some hotels have no stars. This is not necessarily because they don't merit them. The hotel may be too small to be rated, or the owner may not have felt like filling

out the many forms required. The rating system is very complicated, and the differences between hotels of one category and the next may not matter to some clients. For instance, whether the elevator goes to the third or the fourth floor, or the percentage of rooms that have private baths can account for the difference between a three-star and a two-star classification. In terms of service, all hotels three-star and above are required to have reception personnel who speak two foreign languages, one of which must be English, and to serve breakfast in the rooms. Unless you demand considerable luxury, a three-star will normally be perfectly satisfactory. For most people, *un bon petit deux étoiles* — a good little two-star hotel — should be quite adequate in a room with a private bath or shower, which more than 40 percent of the rooms in two-star hotels are required to have. Lower than two-stars, clean, simple places can be found, but less than 20 percent of the rooms are required to have private bath or showers. On this level, price rather than comfort is uppermost in the client's mind.

HOTEL PRICES

Generally, the closer to the Mediterranean, the higher the prices, the highest being on the Côte d'Azur, where Very Expensive/Luxury hotels are common, and declining as you move westward. Prices also tend to decline as you move inland, though not always (the Alpilles, for instance, is an expensive area). It is possible to find good, reasonably priced hotels on the Côte d'Azur, but you have to look for them. To the west of the Rhône in Languedoc and Roussillon, there are few hotels in the "Very Expensive "category and prices are considerably lower in general.

The categories of hotel room prices are calculated on the cost of a standard double room:
VERY EXPENSIVE = 1,500 francs and up
EXPENSIVE = 650 to 1,500 francs
MEDIUM = 300 to 650 francs
INEXPENSIVE = 300 francs and under

It should be noted that hotels often have rooms in two different price categories, depending on the location of the rooms in the hotel (with a view or without a view), the furnishings, etc. In our price categories, we are referring to the better quality double rooms in a given hotel.

It is not absolutely accurate but is a good rule of thumb to say that the average price of a room in a given city will drop to half as much as you go down to the next category. For example, in a town where a four-star (****) hotel room goes for 1,200 francs, a three-star (***) will be 600, a two-star (**) 300, a one-star (**) 150.

It should also be noted that the room prices we mention may not correspond exactly to the ones you are quoted when you make your reservation.

Prices are subject to change. But they probably will not change by too much.

HOTEL CHAINS AND GROUPS

Relais & Châteaux is an association of prestigious independently-owned and operated small-to-moderate-sized country inns, superb residences and sumptuous hotels of great character, generally in magnificent settings, mostly in the four-star category. The restaurants range in quality from very good to fabulous. For the beautiful Relais & Châteaux catalogue, which is worth getting just to read and look at the pictures, write, call or fax them at one of the following locations:

ism. Most are modern building with attractive contemporary decor and soothing color schemes (purples, pastels, coral), but some, such as the Paul Cézanne in Aix and the La Vicomté in Carcassonne, are elegant older hotels furnished with antiques. The rooms are quiet and very comfortable (excellent beds, very firm), and well-equipped (mini-bar, TV with Canal Plus (the French cable or satellite channel), touch-tone phone, modern bathrooms), and the staff is bright and attentive. They have a sumptuous all-you-can-eat breakfast buffet for 50 francs. Most have restaurants, and they are quite good. Prices vary from city to city, but except for a few very short periods throughout the year, they are

FRANCE: 15 Rue Galvani, 75017 Paris, (45 72 90 00 FAX 45 72 90 30
USA: 11 East 44th Street, New York NY 10017, ((212) 856-0015 FAX (212) 856-0193
GREAT BRITAIN: 7 Cork Street, Mayfair, London W1X 2AB, ((071) 287-0987 FAX (071) 437-0241
AUSTRALIA: Mary Rossi Travel, Suite 3, The Dennison, 65 Berry Street, North Sydney 2060, ((02) 957-4511 FAX (02) 929-6326.

The catalogue is free if you come to the office. There is a charge of 60 francs (US$10) if you want it mailed to you.

The **Mercure** chain has 173 hotels in France, most of them in the three-star category, with 22 in Mediterranean France. Though the chain is part of the Accor mega-group (2,000 hotels worldwide) and most of their guests are business travelers, Mercure hotels are far from cold or impersonal and tend to be well-located for tour-

generally in the Moderate category, from 350 to 650 francs. Their catalogue can be picked up in any of their hotels or ordered from: Mercure-Altea, 7 Allée du Brevent, 91021 Evry (60 77 93 83 FAX 60 77 21 08. For reservations in France (33-1-60 77 22 33; United States (1-800-MERCURE; United Kingdom (44-0181-741-3100.

Campanile is a chain of 350 cheerful, modern two-star hotels and motels in France, England and the Benelux countries, with 35 in our Mediterranean area. The typical Campanile is an American-style double-decker motel with less than 50 rooms run by a hard-working young couple. The standards of comfort and cleanli-

OPPOSITE: La Grande-Motte on the Languedoc Coast. ABOVE: One of the many inns in the Camargue oriented to exploring the wildlife-rich region by horseback.

ness are very high. The beds are firm and the bathrooms modern, and there is a TV, coffee-maker and touch-tone phone in every room. The decor is rustic, almost to the point of kitch, and the fare in the restaurants is very simple — grills and buffets are heavily featured (the 35 franc all-you-want breakfast buffet is excellent value). Most Campaniles are in ZACs (Zones d'Actvité Commerciale), modern commercial parks away from the center of town, quiet, but rarely with any local atmosphere. They are especially practical for families and offer a children's menu at 39 francs. At the current room rate of 270 francs, the quality-price ratio is hard to beat (at their 170-room hotel across the Promenade des Anglais from the Nice–Côte d'Azur Airport, the rate is 370 francs, an exception). For the guide to their hotels, call, fax or write to Campanile Europe, 31 Avenue Jean Moulin, Marne-la-Vallée, 77200 Torcy ((33-1) 64 62 46 46 FAX (33-1) 64 62 46 61. The same numbers can be used to make reservations.

Logis de France is an association of 4,200 small and medium-sized family-owned and operated hotels and inns in the three-, two- and one-star categories, in the inexpensive to moderate price ranges. There are hundreds of them in Mediterranean France, many in off-the-beaten-track places, each different, each reflecting the personality of its owners. Their motto is L'hôtellerie à visage humain (hotel-keeping with a human face). The hotels range from fairly elegant to quite modest, but the standards of cleanliness are good at all levels. The Logis de France guide, which has good maps that show you where all the logis are located, is sold by news dealers everywhere in France (70 francs). The départemental tourist offices often distribute free pamphlets on the Logis de France in their areas, and there is a Logis de France counter at the Gare Routière (bus terminal) in Nice. The central address is: Fédération Nationale des Logis de France, 83 Avenue d'Italie, 77013 Paris (45 84 70 00 FAX 45 83 59 66.

FURNISHED APARTMENTS

Local tourist offices provide lists of furnished apartments, rented by the week, often much cheaper than a hotel if you are vacationing with the family or a group of friends. Ask for the list of appartements meublés.

GÎTES

Gîtes ruraux are furnished rural houses you can rent by the week or the weekend at modest rates, from 500 to 2,000 francs a week, depending on size and location. A booklet with photos and details can be obtained from Maisons de France overseas, from Offices de Tourisme in the different

localities or from the Fédération Nationale des Gîtes de France, 35 Rue Godot-de-Mauroy, 75009 Paris (49 70 75 75. The booklet covers the whole of France. It is in French with an explanation of the symbols in English. 90 francs. Reserve as early as possible. The most popular Gîtes are booked a year in advance.

BED AND BREAKFASTS

For information on Bed and Breakfasts in the region, see BACKPACKING, page 35.

YOUTH HOSTELS

For details on youth hostels, see BACKPACKING, page 35.

CAMPING

For details on camping, refer to BACKPACKING, page 34.

RESTAURANTS

For information on Mediterranean French cuisine and wine, see GALLOPING GOURMETS, page 50. For information on the top restaurants in the region, see LIVING IT UP, page 36.

RESTAURANT PRICES

Our price categories are based on the average cost of a meal per person, not including drinks. VERY EXPENSIVE = 600 francs or more. EXPENSIVE = 300 to 600 francs. MEDIUM = 125 to 300 francs. INEXPENSIVE = 125 francs or less.

In many cases, we give specific prices of fixed-price menus or certain dishes. It should be understood that these prices are subject to change at any time.

TIPPING

IN RESTAURANTS

At the bottom of the menu you will see the phrase service 15 % compris (15 percent service charge included). This means that the price of every item listed on the menu has the tip included in it. The prices of the items you order will be added up just as they appear on the menu, and that total is all you are required to pay. In practice, people usually leave a little something if they are happy with the service — an extra five percent, or a 10 franc piece. But they have no obligation to do so if they don't want to.

IN HOTELS

It is customary to give porters 10 francs per piece of luggage and to leave the chambermaids 10 francs a day.

TAXIS

A 10 percent tip is generally sufficient, but you can give more if the service is particularly good.

POST OFFICES

Post offices are open from 8 AM to 6 PM Monday through Friday and 8 AM to noon on Saturday. Post offices have bright yellow signs with the words *La Poste* or *PTT*. Stamps can also be purchased in *tabacs* (tobacco shops), large hotels and some newsstands.

TELEPHONES

France has one of the most modern telephone systems in the world, and it is quite easy to use. For pay phones, there are still a few old-fashioned coin-operated instruments on the street or in bars or cafes (normally using a one-franc piece), and in some bars or cafés, you make your call first and pay the barman after. But most pay phones now operate on Télécartes, and if you plan to use the phone much, you would be wise to buy one. A Télécarte is a credit card-sized piece of plastic with a computer chip in it that entitles you to a certain number of message units. They can be bought in any tabac (tobacco shop) or post office and cost from 40 to 96 francs. Télécartes can be used for calls to foreign countries as well as domestic.

For local calls, dial the phone number without any prefix. From any place in Mediterranean France to any other place in France other than Paris and the Île de France, you don't need any prefix either. Just dial the number. For calls to Paris from outside the Île de France, you must dial **16**, listen for the tone, then dial **1**, then the eight digit phone number. But when you call from Paris to any number in France outside the Île de France, you only dial **16** and the phone number.

For direct dial international calls, dial **19** (tone), then the country code, area code and number. For example, to call Boston, you dial **19**, **1** (for the United States), 617 (Boston's area code), then the phone number. For Great Britain, dial **19**, the country code **44 1**, followed by the city code without the "0." The country code for Ireland in **353**. For overseas directory inquiries, dial **19-33-12 plus the country code**. If you don't know the country code, call 12 for it. To place a call through an international operator, dial **19-33 plus the country code**. But note that for operator-assisted calls to the United States, you use **11** as the country code (rather than **1**, which you use for direct-dial calls).

NEW 10-DIGIT DIALING

In October 1996, a ten digit telephone system will be introduced in France. Two digits will be added infront of the existing numbers which are otherwise unchanged. They are **01** for Paris and the Île de France, **02** for the Northwest, **03** for the Northeast, **04** for the Southeast (including the area covered by this book) and **05** for the Southeast. The

prefix **16** is eliminated. For overseas calls the currently used prefix 19 will be replaced by **00**. For more detail on dialing procedures, look in the front of the Yellow Pages (*Pages Jaunes*), where there are explanations in English and several other languages. To find city codes, look in the front of the yellow pages under *États-Unis* for United States and *Royaume-Uni* for the United Kingdom. For a more complete list of city codes, get the little booklet called *Le Guide du Téléphone International*, available in offices of France Télécom.

France Télécom has many advanced services, including the Minitel computer information system, which you will want to find out about if you plan to stay in France for a long time. But one service travelers may find useful is Téléphone Interprète, in which two people speaking

A café in Béziers.

different languages can communicate through France Télécom interpreters in 72 languages. It's not cheap (27 francs a minute for English, German, Italian, Spanish or Portuguese, higher for other languages), but it could be a life saver. You can charge it on your Master, Visa or several other bank cards (but not Diners Club or American Express). France Télécom also has a service for written translations. For information, call toll free (05 219 319.

EMERGENCY PHONE NUMBERS

Directory inquiries (12;
SAMU (24 hour ambulance service) (15;
Police (17; Fire (18.

BANKING HOURS

Generally banks in the provinces are open Tuesday to Saturday from 9 AM to 4:30 PM and closed Sunday, Monday and the afternoon before holidays.

CHARGE CARDS

The most widely accepted charge card is the Visa, and if you plan to be charging a lot, you would be wise to get one from a bank in your own country before leaving home. MasterCard is accepted almost as frequently. American Express and Diners Club cards are generally accepted in large or deluxe establishments, but modest hotels and restaurants often refuse them because of the high service charges the seller has to pay. Another virtue of having a Visa card is that it enables you to get cash advances in French francs from banks that honor them.

TAXES AND TAX REFUNDS

Americans or other non-Europeans purchasing 2,000 francs or more worth of goods in a single store are eligible for a refund of the value-added tax (the *TVA*, or *taxe sur la valeur ajoutée*). The discounts can range from 10 to 22 percent, depending on the nature of the goods. You must show your passport to the store staff and ask them to fill out the French customs *TVA* refund form. To get the refund, you have the form processed by French customs (*la duane*) at the airport, on the train or at the frontier post when you are leaving the country. Be prepared to show them the items you purchased, because sometimes they ask. The refund will be either mailed to you or credited to your credit card if you purchased the items on it, which is a lot quicker and easier.

WEIGHTS AND MEASURES

Units of distance:
1 km = .625 (5/8) mile
1 meter = 3.28 feet

Units of weight:
1 gram = .035 ounces
1 kilogram (kilo) = 2.2 pounds

Units of volume:
1 liter = 2.1 US pints = 1.76 UK pints

Temperature:
Temperature in France is measured in degrees Celsius (Centigrade). 0°C is freezing, 100°C is boiling, room temperature (68°F) is 20°C, body temperature (98.6°F) is 37°C. For a rough approximation, multiply the temperature Centigade by two and add 32.

ELECTRIC CURRENT

Current in France is 220 volts AC, 50 cycles. You cannot use American standard appliances without a transformer. If you want to use your portable computer in France, it would be wise to get a multi-standard power supply in the United States before leaving on your trip.

DATES AND TIMES

In France, the date is expressed as follows: 1 June 2000, or 1/6/2000 (not 6/1/2000). The time is generally expressed by the 24-hour clock. Thus 8 AM is 8 h or 8 h 00 (*huit heures*) and 8 PM is 20 h or 20 h 00 (*vingt heures*). Noon is *midi* (12 h) and midnight is *minuit* (24 h).

CRIME

In France, the South has a reputation for crime and corruption. The flight of ex-mayor Jacques Médecin to Uruguay, the 1994 murders of Deputy Yann Piatt of Hyères, the apparent double suicide of two politically-connected brothers the Var, the bribery scandal involving the Olympic de Marseille football team and other evil doings certainly have kept that image alive. But as far as serious crimes against persons or property are concerned, any American city would be delighted to exchange crime rates with any town or city in Mediterranean France. There is plenty of purse-snatching, pick-pocketing and breaking into cars, and occasional physical violence to tourists, but the sensible precautions you would take at home should stand you in good stead here — namely, stay out of rough neighborhoods and don't leave anything of value in your car.

If you are traveling overnight on trains, be sure to hide your valuables well. Skillful thieves are known to prey on sleeping passengers in the sleeping compartments.

FRENCH NATIONAL HOLIDAYS

New Years Day, January 1
Easter Sunday and Easter Monday
Labor Day, May 1
Victory in Europe Day (1945), May 8
Ascension Thursday (mid-May)
Pentecost Sunday (late May)
Bastille Day, July 14
Assumption Day, August 15
All Saints Day (*Toussaint*), November 1
Armistice Day (1918), November 11
Christmas Day, December 25

MAJOR FESTIVALS AND EVENTS IN MEDITERRANEAN FRANCE

CÔTE D'AZUR

LATE JANUARY **Monte-Carlo Rally**
FIRST WEEK OF FEBRUARY **International Circus Festival**, Monaco
FIRST TWO WEEKS OF FEBRUARY **Fête du Citron**, lemon festival, music, parades with lavish floats sculpted with lemons, Menton; Mardi Gras period Carnaval in Nice, France's biggest, with parades, music, dancing in the streets.
APRIL **Monte-Carlo Open**, international tennis matches.
MID-MAY **Cannes Film Festival; Bravade de Saint-Torpes**, Saint-Tropez.
SECOND WEEKEND IN MAY Fête de la Rose, Grasse.
LATE MAY **Grand Prix de Monaco**, Formula-1 car racing.
Month of June **Festival de la Danse et de l'Image**, Toulon.
JUNE 15 **Bravade des Espagnols**, Saint-Tropez.
JULY **Festival de Musique Classique**, Vence.
EARLY TO MID-JULY **Nice Jazz Festival**
LATE JULY **Jazz à Juan**, Juan-les-Pins.
FIRST SUNDAY OF AUGUST **Fête de la Lavande** (lavender festival), Digne-les-Bains; **Fête du Jasmin**, Grasse.
AUGUST **Chamber music festival**, Menton; **Festival International des Feux d'Artifice** (international fireworks festival), Monaco.
END OF SEPTEMBER **Nioulargue**, a huge international sailing event, Saint-Tropez.
DECEMBER **Fête du Vin**, Bandol.

PROVENCE

FEBRUARY 2 **Fête des Chandelles**, Marseille; **Mardi Gras, Feria du Carnaval**, Nîmes.
GOOD FRIDAY TO EASTER **Corrida**, Arles.
APRIL 25 **Wine Festival**, Châteauneuf-du-Pape; **Fête de Saint-Marc** (patron saint of wine), Villeneuve-lès-Avignon.
LAST SUNDAY OF APRIL **Fête des Gardians** (cowboys), rodeo, Arles.
PENTECOST **Feria de la Pentecôte** (ten-days bullfighting festival), Nîmes; **Fête de la Transhumance** (shepherds' festival), Saint-Rémy-de-Provence.
24 TO 25 MAY **Gypsy pilgrimage**, les Saintes-Maries-de-la-Mer.
ALL SUMMER **Pop, rock, and classical music concerts** in the Arena in Nîmes; **bullfights** at the Arena in Arles.
SECOND HALF OF JUNE **Jazz and chamber music**, Aix-en-Provence.
ALL OF JULY **Festival de la Sorgue** (music, theater and dance festival), Fontaine-de-Vaucluse and Isle-sur-la-Sorgue.
JULY, AUGUST **L'Été de Vaison** (dance, music and theater festival), Vaison-la-Romaine; **Music Festival**, Villeneuve-les-Avignon; **Medieval Music**, Abbaye de Sénanque, near Gordes.
JULY TO SEPTEMBER **Organa** (organ concerts), Saint-Rémy-de-Provence.
FIRST HALF OF JULY **Festival International de Folklore de Château-Gombert**, Marseille; **Festival Populaire** (folk and popular music, dance and theater), Port-de-Bouc, near Martigues.
EARLY JULY TO EARLY AUGUST **Festival d'Avignon**, (a huge official theater festival), and the **Festival-Off**, Avignon; **Festival International d'Art Lyrique et de Musique**, Aix-en-Provence; **Offenbach et Son Temps**, lyric art, dance and theater festival, Carpentras.
WEEKEND BEFORE JULY 14 **Fête Internationale de l'Olivier**, Nyons.
MID-JULY **Soirées Musicales de Saint-Maximin**, Saint-Maximin-la-Sainte-Baume.
SECOND HALF OF JULY **Rencontres Internationales de la Photographie** (major photography exhibitions), Arles.
LAST TWO WEEKS OF JULY **Chorégies d'Orange** (opera and lyric music in the Roman Theater), Orange; **Festival des Nuits Musicales**, Uzès.
THIRD WEEK OF JULY **Jazz festival**, Salon-de-Provence.
JULY 21 AND 22 **Fête de Sainte-Marie-Madeleine** (with midnight masses celebrated in the grotto), Sainte-Baume.
LATE JULY, EARLY AUGUST **Concours de Boules** (a big *pétanque* tournament organized by *Le Provençal* newspaper), Parc Borély Park, Marseille.
LAST SUNDAY OF JULY **Fête de la Tarasque**, Tarascon.

FIRST THREE WEEKS OF AUGUST **Festival International de Piano**, La Roque-Athéron; **Music and Theater festival**, Gordes.

THIRD WEEK OF AUGUST **Provençal Wine Festival** (with parades, bravades, theater), Séguret.

SECOND WEEK OF SEPTEMBER **Fête des Prêmices du Riz** (rice harvest festival), Arles.

THIRD WEEK OF SEPTEMBER **Feria des Vendanges** (bullfights and related events), Nîmes.

SUNDAY CLOSEST TO OCTOBER 22 **Fête de Sainte-Marie-Jacobe** (procession and blessing of the sea), Saintes-Maries-de-la-Mer.

Month of December **Music festival**, Marseille.

DECEMBER 24 Provençal midnight mass throughout the region. Among the most noted are the shepherds' masses at Allauch east of Marseille, Fontvieille, Les Baux, the grotto at La Sainte-Baume, the Arena at Nîmes and at Séguret.

LANGUEDOC-ROUSSILLON

JANUARY TO MARCH **Traditional carnival processions** every Sunday, Limoux.

GOOD FRIDAY **Procession des Pénitents de la Sanch** (Penitents of the Blood), Perpignan and other processions at Collioure and Arles-sur-Tech.

EARLY JUNE **Printemps des Comédiens**, Montpellier.

JUNE 24 TO 25 **Fête de Saint-Jean** (the Catalan patron saint, dancing, fireworks), Perpignan, Céret, Villefranche-de-Conflent.

LATE JUNE, EARLY JULY **Festival International de Danse** (a huge international dance festival) Montpellier.

LATE JUNE TO LATE AUGUST **Scene d'Été à Pézenas** (crafts, music, theater, traditional dancing), Pézenas.

FIRST WEEKEND OF JULY **Fête de Saint-Pierre** (fishermen's festival), Sète.

EARLY JULY **Music Festival**, Carcassonne; **Festival de la Côte Languedocienne**, Béziers.

MID-JULY TO MID-AUGUST **Festival International de Radio France** (orchestral music, opera, chamber music, jazz), Montpellier; **Côtes du Roussillon Wine Festival**, Perpignan; **Joutes Nautiques** (nautical jousts), Agde; **Festival Médiéval** (medieval costume pageant and feasting), Villerouge-Termenès.

JULY 14 **Bastille Day** (fireworks, lighting up of the City), Carcassonne.

MID-JULY **International Music Festival** (Casals Festival), Prades.

MID-JULY TO MID-AUGUST **Nuits Musicales du Palais** (classical music), La Grande-Motte; **Festival Mondial du Folklore** (world folklore festival), La Grande-Motte.

LATE JULY, Early August **Fête de la Mer** (sea festival), Agde, Cap d'Agde.

JULY 30 **Festa Major** (religious processions), Arles-sur-Tech.

AUGUST **Tournoise de Joutes** (nautical jousting), all month, Sète.

FIRST TWO WEEKS OF AUGUST **Les Médiévales** (medieval costume pageant with jousts, crafts and music), Carcassonne.

AUGUST 9 TO 11 **Feria** (bullfighting festival), Collioure.

AUGUST 14 TO 15 **Feria** (running of the bulls, bullfights, parades, and fireworks), Béziers.

LATE AUGUST **Festival de la Sardane** (traditional Catalan dancing, 400 dancers in costume), Céret.

ABOUT AUGUST 25 **Fête de Saint-Louis** (historical pageants), Aigues-Mortes; **Fête de Saint-Louis** (nautical jousts, fireworks, and swimming contests), Sète.

EARLY SEPTEMBER **Visa pour l'Image** (international photojournalism festival).

MID-OCTOBER **Fête Votive** (Provençal bullfighting), Aigues-Mortes.

THIRD SUNDAY OF OCTOBER **Fête du Vin Nouveau**, Béziers.

FRENCH FOR TRAVELERS

When you're traveling, local people appreciate it if you make an effort to use even a few words in their language. Luckily, everyone already knows the essential phrases to use to greet people in France — "*Bonjour, monsieur*" for men, "*Bonjour, madame*" for women and "*Bonjour, mademoiselle*" for young women. Always use those phrases, even if they are the only ones you know.

It is considered rude not to preface a request with "Monsieur" or "Madame."

Here are some other words and expressions you may find useful or encounter often in your travels in Mediterranean France:

yes *oui*
no *non*
good morning/afternoon *bonjour*
good evening *bon soir*
goodbye *au revoir*
please *s'il vous plait*
thank you *merci*
you're welcome *je vous en prie*
it's all right *ça va*
OK *OK*
yesterday *hier*
today *aujourd'hui*
tomorrow *demain*
tomorrow morning *demain matin*
tomorrow afternoon *demain après-midi*
day *jour*
week *semaine*
month *mois*
Sunday *Dimanche*
Monday *Lindi*

Tuesday *Mardi*
Wednesday *Mercredi*
Thursday *Jeudi*
Friday *Vendredi*
Saturday *Samedi*
January *Janvier*
February *Février*
March *Mars*
April *Avril*
May *Mai*
June *Juin*
July *Juillet*
August *Août*
September *Septembre*
October *Octobre*
November *Novembre*
December *Décembre*
one *un*
two *deux*
three *trois*
four *quatre*
five *cinq*
six *six*
seven *sept*
eight *huit*
nine *neuf*
ten *dix*
twenty *vingt*
fifty *cinquante*
one hundred *cent*
five hundred *cinq cent*
one thousand *mille*
how much? *combien?*
what's the price? *quel est le prix?*
what? *quoi?*
who? *qui?*
where? *où?*
when? *quand?*
I don't understand *je ne comprends pas*
speak slowly, please *parlez lentement, s'il vous plait*
do you speak English? *parlez-vous Anglais?*
excuse me *excuzez-moi*
how are you? *comment allez-vous?*
what's your name? *comment vous appelez-vous?*
what's that? *qu'est-ce que c'est?*
I'm hungry *j'ai faim*
I'm thirsty *j'ai soif*
I'm tried *je suis fatigué*
a beer, please *une bière, s'il vous plait*
a draft beer *un pression*
red wine *vin rouge*
white wine *vin blanc*
rosé wine *vin rosé*
coffee *café*
tea *thé*
rare (meat) *saignant*
medium *â point*
well done *bien cuit*
open *ouvert;* closed *fermé*
expensive *cher;* cheap *bon marché*

hot *chaud;* cold *froid*
large *grand*
small *petit*
a little *un peu*
a lot *beaucoup*
all *tout*
nothing *rien*
up *en haut;* down *en bas*
right *droit;* to the right *à droite*
left *gauche;* to the left *àâ gauche*
straight ahead *tout droit*
before *avant;* after *après*
waiter *serveur;* waitress *serveuse*
the menu *la carte*
the bill (check), please *l'addition, s'il vous plait*
the toilet *la toilette*
one moment, please *un moment, s'il vous plait*
TGV, for *train à grande vitesse* high speed train
TVA, for *taxe sur la valeur ajutée* value-added tax
Some words you will encounter in the South:
oppidum pre-Roman hill settlement
mas large farm complex
bastide large country estate
beffroi bellfry, bell tower
calanque Provençal fjord
cirque a deep, circular depression in the earth
made by a previous course of a river
col mountain pass
garrigue rough, treeless lands covered with
grasses, wild herbs and wildflowers
maquis scrub brush
étang pond or swamp
gardian Camargue cowboy
appellation d'origine controlée, or *AOC* government
standards for the growing and production of top
wines
côte coast or, when referring wine, hills (also
called *côtes, coteaux* or *costières*
cave cellar
créche a Christmas crib
santons "little saints" in Provençal, small sculpted
figures used in *créches*
mistral strong wind that blows down the Rhône
Valley
tramontane strong wind off the Massif Central
that blows across Languedoc
For the vocabulary of Mediterranean cuisine,
see GALLOPING GOURMET, page 50.

GUIDES TO HOTELS AND RESTAURANTS

There many specialized guides to help you select
hotels and restaurants. The *Guide Michelin France*
is the bible. 1996 is its 87th edition, it is the best-
selling book in France — more than 600,000 copies
a year. (Only the Paris phone directory is distributed in greater numbers, and that is free). The
squat little red tome's 1,300 pages are loaded with

valuable information, starting with its widely trusted ratings of hotels and restaurants. To be in the book at all is good. One star designates a restaurant of very high quality, two stars means it is tremendously good, and the famous three Michelin stars portends gastronomic nirvana. There are fine little maps of the main towns and cities indicating the location of the hotels and restaurants they have selected, the tourist offices and main tourist attractions. It also lists addresses and phone numbers of automobile dealerships and tire shops, phone numbers of airports and golf courses, and gives distances from other towns and cities. Michelin's dozens of funny little symbols (explained in English as well as French) take a while to get used to, but it is well worth the effort to learn how to use this book. No traveler in France should be without it. 135 francs.

Maisons Coté Sud magazine puts out its annual *Guide Bonnes Adresses* at the beginning of the summer. It has a fine selection of hotels, restaurants, vineyards and boutiques for food, fabrics, clothes, art, crafts and home furnishings in Mediterranean France, with capsule descriptions of each establishment. Available in newspaper shops throughout the area (98 francs, in French only).

Semaine des Spectacles Provence/Côte d'Azur (5 francs) is a pocket-sized weekly guide to entertainment, sports, the arts and outings in the Alpes-Maritimes, Var and Bouches-du-Rhône, and it has a good selection of restaurants. It is in French only.

Le Petit Futé publishes a series of bright, up-to-date guides on the main cities and areas of Mediterranean France (Nice–Côte d'Azur, Marseille, Provence-Bouches-du-Rhône, Nîmes, Montpellier, Perpignan), covering just about everything (in French only, 30 to 40 francs).

Cap d'Agde journalist Georges Renault puts out a discriminating little annual guide to restaurants in Cap d'Agde and vicinity called *Le Panse Pas Bête*, with a text in French, English and German. It is available at news stands in Agde, Cap d'Agde and the area (12 francs).

Le Guide du Routard's *Hôtels et Restos en France* concentrates on food and accommodations in the lower price range. In French only.

Recommended Reading

ARDAGH, John, *The South of France*, Mitchell Beazley, London 1983, and *France Today*, Penguin 1987 (updated 1993)

BERRY, Liz, *The Wines of Languedoc-Roussillon*, Ebury, London 1992

BLUME, Mary, *Côte d'Azur, Inventing the French Riviera*, Thames and Hudson, London 1992

BRAUDEL, Henri, *The Mediterranean and the Mediterranean World in the Age of Philip II*, HarperCollins, New York 1986

BROMWICH, James, *The Roman Remains of Southern France*, Routledge, London and New York 1993

CHARIAL-THUILIER, Jean-André, *Bouquet de Provence*, Pavilion, London 1990 (seasonal recipes from owner-chef of the Oustaù de Baumanière in Les Baux-de-Provence)

COOPER, Bill and Laurel, *A Spell in Wild France*, Mandarin, 1993 (about cruising through the Camargue)

DAUDET, Alphonse, *Letters from my Windmill*, Penguin

FISHER, M.F.K., *Two Towns in Provence* and *Map of Another Town*, Little Brown and Company, Boston Toronto 1964

FITZGERALD, F. Scott, *Tender is the Night* (many editions)

FORTESCUE, Winifred, *Perfume from Provence*, Black Swan 1993 (reprint of the aristocratic English lady's 1935 account of living in Grasse)

GIONO, Jean, *The Man who Planted Trees*, Peter Owen, London 1969

HARRIS, John P., *An Englishman in the Midi*, BBC Books 1991, and *More from an Englishman in the Midi*, BBC Books, 1993

JOHNSON, Hugh, *The Story of Wine*, Mandarin, London 1991

JOHNSTON, Mireille, *The Cuisine of the Sun*, Penguin 1992

MAYLE, Peter, *A Year in Provence*, Pan 1989, and *Toujours Provence*, Pan 1991

MORE, Julian and Cary, *A Taste of Provence*, Pavilion Books, London 1988

OLNEY, Richard, *Lulu's Provençal Table*, Harper Collins, 1994

PAGNOL, Marcel, *Jean de Florette* and *Manon of the Springs*, Pan 1987 (or any other book by Pagnol)

PILKINGTON, Roger, *Small Boat in the Midi*, J.M. Pearson, London 1989 (cruising on the canals of the South)

ROUQUETTE, Yves, *Cathars*, Editions Loubatières, Toulouse 1992

SMOLLETT, Tobias, *Travels through France and Italy*, Oxford University Press 1981

STENDHAL, *Travels in the South of France*, trans. Elizabeth Abbott, Calder and Boyers, London 1971

VAN GOGH, Vincent, *Collected Letters*, Thames and Hudson 1958

WYLIE, Laurence, *Village in the Vaucluse*, Harvard University Press 1974.

Quick Reference A–Z Guide
to Places and Topics of Interest with Listed Accommodation, Restaurants and Useful Telephone Numbers

A

environs
  Entremont *193*
  Puyricard *193*
  Vasarély Foundation *191*
festivals 184
general information
  airport:
    Marseille-Provence International
      Airport, (42 89 09 74 *184*
  bus station:
    Gare Routière, (42 27 17 91 *184*
  bus tours:
    CAP, (42 23 14 26 *184*
  car rental:
    Avis, (42 21 64,16 *184*
    Budget, (42 38 37 36 *184*
    EuroDollar, (42 21 42 09 *184*
    EuropCar, (42 27 83 00 *184*
    Hertz, (42 27 91 32 *184*
    Lubrano, (42 21 44 85 *184*
  medical emergencies:
    Hospital, (42 33 50 00 *184*
    SOS Médecin, (42 26 24 00 *184*
  railway station, (91 08 50 50 *184*
  taxis:
    Les Artisans, (42 26 29 30 *184*
    Mirabeau, (42 21 61 61 *184*
    Taxi-Radio Aixois, (42 27 71 11 *184*
  Tourist Office, (42 16 11 61 *183*
history 183
restaurants
  Bistro Latin, (42 38 22 88 *189*
  Brasserie la Madeleine, (42 28 38 02 *189*
  Clos de la Violette, (42 23 30 71 *189*
  Côté Cour, (42 26 32 39 *189*
  Cour de Rohan, (42 96 18 15 *189*
  Dolce Vita, (42 64 04 70 *189*
  Hacienda, (42 27 90 82 *189*
  Les Frères Lani (42 27 76 16 *189*
  Mas d'Entremont (in Célony), (42 23 45 32
  Relais Sainte-Victoire, (in Beaurecueil)
    (42 66 94 98 *191*
  Table du Roi, (42 37 61 00 *189*
Alpes-Maritimes
camping information in
  L'Hôtellerie de Plein Air des Alpes-Maritimes
    (93 20 91 91 *96, 119*
Amélie-les-Bains *302, 309*
accommodation
  Castel Émeraude** (68 39 02 83
    FAX 68 39 03 09 *309*
attractions
  Gorges du Mondony *309*
  medieval Catalan village (Palalda) *309*
  spa *309*
general information
  Tourist Office, (68 39 01 98 *309*
restaurants
  Castel Émeraude (68 39 02 83 *309*
  Mas Pagris (in Montalba d'Amélie),
    (68 39 38 73 *309*
Aniane *262–263*
accommodation and restaurant
  Hostellerie Saint-Benôit**, (67 57 71 63
    FAX 67 57 47 10 *262*
attractions
  wine tasting: Mas de Daumas Gassac,
    (67 57 71 28 *263*

Annot *52, 100*
accommodation
  Hôtel de l'Avenue** (92 83 22 07
    FAX 92 83 22 07 *100*
attractions
  medieval walled town and caves *100*
general infomation
  Tourist Office, (92 83 23 03 *100*
where to eat 100
Ansignan *291*
Anthéor *146*
Antibes *25, 38, 44–45, 126–132*
  – see also Cap d'Antibes
access 132
accommodation
  Auberge Provençale*, (93 34 13 24 *128*
  Mas de la Pagane**, (93 33 33 78
    FAX 93 74 55 37 *128*
  Royal***, (93 34 03 09 FAX 93 34 23 31 *128*
attractions
  Cathedral *127*
  Château Grimaldi *127*
  Musée Picasso *127*
  Provençal market *128*
  sailing *25*
  wine tasting, Domaines Ott, (93 34 38 91 *128*
general information
  bike rental:
    Holiday Bikes, (93 74 50 25 *127*
  bus station (Gare Routière), (93 34 37 60 *127*
  car rental:
    Avis, (93 34 65 15 *127*
    Budget, (93 34 36 84 *127*
    Côte d'Azur Auto, (93 67 81 81 *127*
    EuropCar, (93 34 79 79 *127*
    Fun Location, (93 67 66 94 *127*
    Hertz, (93 61 18 15 *127*
    Midi Location, (93 34 48 00 *127*
  taxis, (93 33 93 97 *127*
  Tourist Office, (92 90 53 00 *126*
  train station (Gare SNCF),
    (93 99 50 50 *127*
restaurants
  Aux Vieux Murs, (93 34 06 73 *129*
  Le Bacon, (93 61 50 02 *129*
where to eat 129
Apt *30, 216–217*
access 217–218
accommodation
  Camping du Lubéron, (90 04 85 40 *216*
  Camping Municipal Les Cèdres,
    (90 74 14 61 *216*
  Lou Caleu**, (in Saint-Martin-de-Castillon)
    (90 75 28 88 FAX 90 75 25 49 *216*
  Saint-Paul**, (in Viens) (90 75 21 47
    FAX 90 75 30 80 *216*
attractions
  Parc Naturel Régional du Lubéron *216*
general information
  Maison du Park, (90 74 08 55 *216*
  Tourist Office, (90 74 03 18 *216*
restaurants
  Lou Caleu, (in Saint-Martin-de-Castillon)
    (90 75 28 88 *216*
  Saint-Paul, (in Viens) (90 75 21 47 *216*
archaeology, museums of *42*
architecture *see* Mediterranean France,
  architecture

Drôme River *171*
Duilhac-sous-Peyrepertuse *29, 331*
  access 291
  accommodation and restaurant
    Auberge du Vieux Moulin, (68 45 02 17
      FAX 66 45 02 18 *291*
  attractions
    Cathar fortress of Peyrepertuse *33, 290*
Durance River *193, 214*
Durban-Corbières *282*
  attractions
    Cave Pilote de Villeneuve-les-Corbières,
      (68 45 91 59 *282*
  restaurants
    Le Moulin, (68 45 81 03 *282*
E eagle's nest villages *20*
electricity *332*
Elne *78, 310*
  access 310
  attractions
    Cathédrale Sainte-Eulalie et Sainte-Julie *310*
  general information
    Tourist Office, (68 22 05 07 *310*
embassies
    Australian (Paris), ((16-1) 40 59 33 00 *324*
    British (Paris), ((16-1) 42 66 38 10 *324*
    Canadian (Paris), (16-1) 44 43 29 00 *324*
    Irish (Paris), ((16-1) 45 00 20 87 *324*
    New Zealand (Paris), ((16-1) 45 00 24 11 *324*
emergencies
    ambulance: SAMU, (15 (24-hours) *332*
    fire, (18 *332*
    police, (17 *332*
Entrechaux *207*
  restaurant
    Restaurant Saint-Hubert, (90 46 00 05, *207*
Entremont *191*
Entrevaux *100*
  attractions
    massive medieval ramparts and
      fortifications *100*
equestrian sports, information *27*
    Association Nationale de Tourisme Equestre,
      ((1) 46 48 83 93 *27*
Estavar *307*
Étang de Montady *275*
Eus *307*
  restaurants
    Grangousier, (68 89 28 32 *307*
Èze *13, 102, 104–105*
  access 106
  accommodation
    Château de la Chèvre d'Or****, (93 41 12 12
      FAX 93 41 06 72 *105*
    Château Eza****, (93 41 12 24
      FAX 93 41 16 64 *105*
    Hermitage du Col d'Èze**, (93 41 00 68 *106*
    Les Romarins (camping) *106*
  attractions
    Jardin Exotique *105*
    White Penitents' Chapel *105*
  general information
    Tourist Office, (93 41 26 00 *105*
  restaurants
    Borfiga, (93 41 05 23 *106*
Èze-Bord-de-Mer *104*
F festivals *46, 48–49*
  listing *333–334*

fishing, fresh water *25*
Florensac *264*
  accommodation and restaurant
    Léonce, (67 77 03 05 *264*
Font-Romeu *307–308*
  attractions
    skiing *307*
  general information
    Tourist Office, (68 30 68 30 *308*
Fontaine-de-Vaucluse *211–212*
  access 212
  accommodation
    Camping La Coutelière (in Galas),
      (90 20 33 97 *212*
    Camping Municipal les Prés,
      (90 20 32 38 *212*
  attractions
    Le Monde Souterrain de Norbert Casteret *211*
    Musée de la Résistance *211*
    Vallis Clausa paper mill *211*
  restaurants
    L'Hostellerie du Château, (90 20 31 54 *212*
    Le Parc, (90 20 31 57 *212*
Fontecouverte *304*
Fontvieille *235*
  accommodation
    Auberge la Regalido****, (90 54 60 22
      FAX 90 54 64 29 *235*
  attractions
    Daudet Museum *235*
  general information
    Tourist Office, (90 54 67 49 *235*
Fos-sur-Mer *25*
Fox-Amphoux *158*
  accommodation
    Auberge du Vieux Fox**, (94 80 71 69
      FAX 94 80 78 38 *158*
    International Camping, (94 70 06 80 *159*
France, general information
    driving, advice and regulations *327*
    Maisons de France *324*
    central number, ((900) 990-0040 *324*
    visa requirements *323*
Fréjus *146–147*
  accommodation
    Auberge du Vieux Four**, (94 51 56 38 *147*
    Camping de Saint-Aygulf (in Saint-Aygulf),
      (94 17 62 49 FAX 94 81 03 16 *147*
    Excelsior*** (in Saint-Raphaël), (94 95 02 32
      FAX 94 95 33 82 *147*
    Holiday Green (camping), (94 40 88 20 *147*
    L'Aréna***, (94 17 09 40 FAX 94 52 01 52 *147*
  attractions
    Archaeological Museum, (94 17 09 40 *147*
    La Villa Romaine *147*
    Quartier Episcopal *147*
  general information
    bus station, Gare Routière (Sodétrav),
      (94 95 24 82 *147*
    Tourist Office, (94 17 19 19 *146*
    train station, Gare SNCF, (94 91 50 50 *147*
  history 146
  restaurants
    Auberge du Vieux Four, (94 83 10 50 *147*
    L'Equipe, (94 51 12 62 *147*
    L'Orangerie, (94 83 10 50 *147*
    Lou Calen, (94 52 36 87 *147*
French language courses *see* language courses

accommodation
  pilgrims hostel (42 04 50 21 *167*
attractions
  La Sainte-Baume cave and chapel *167*
Plan-du-Castellet *166*
attractions
  wine tasting: Domaine Tempier,
  (94 98 70 21 *166*
Pomérols *265*
  wine tasting: Hugues de Beauvignac,
  (67 77 01 59 *265*
Pont de Rousty *242*
Pont des Trois-Sautets *189*
Pont du Gard *219–220*
  – *see also* Castillon-du-Gard, *and* Collias
  access 220
  accommodation
  Camping International des Gorges du
  Gardon, (66 22 81 81 *220*
Pont-de-Soleils *143*
Porquerolles *25, 162*
  access 164
  accommodation
  Auberge des Glycines***, (94 58 38 36
  FAX 94 58 35 22 *163*
  Mas du Langoustier***, (94 58 30 09
  FAX 94 58 36 02 *162*
  Sainte-Anne**, (94 58 30 04
  FAX 94 58 32 26 *163*
  attractions
  Fort Sainte-Agathe *162*
  sailing *25*
  general information
  ferry service, TLV, (94 58 21 81 *164*
  tourist office, (94 58 33 76 *162*
Port Ambonne (nudist beach) *55, 268*
  nudist community, (67 26 79 69 *268*
Port Grimaud *153*
  restaurants
  Port Diffa, (94 56 29 07 *155*
Port-Barcarès *38*
Port-Camargue *25, 252*
  attractions
  sailing *25*
  access 253
  accommodation
  Camping Elysée Residence, (66 53 54 00 *253*
  Le Spinaker***, (66 53 36 37
  FAX 66 53 17 47 *252*
  environs
  nudist beach, Le Phare de l'Espiguette *252*
  general information
  Tourist Office (66 51 71 68 *252*
  restaurants
  L'Amarette, (66 51 47 63 *252*
  Le Spinaker, (66 53 36 37 *252*
  shopping
  La Maison des Vins et des Produits du Gard,
  (66 53 07 52 *252*
Port-Cross *162*
  access
  ferry service, TLV, (94 57 44 07 *164*
  accommodation
  Le Manoir**, (94 05 90 52
  FAX 94 05 90 89 *163*
  general information
  Tourist Office (for Îles d'Hyères)
  (94 65 18 55 *162*

attractions
  calanques (fjords) *172*
Port-Grimaud *154*
  accommodation
  La Giraglia****, (94 56 31 33 *154*
Port-Vendres *25, 314*
  attractions
  fish auction *314*
  scuba diving *25*
  yacht harbor and fishing port *314*
  general information
  Tourist Office, (68 82 07 54 *314*
postal services *331*
Prades *34, 302, 305, 307*
  access 307
  accommodation
  Hexagone**, (68 05 31 31
  FAX 68 05 24 89 *307*
  Pradotel**, (68 05 22 66 FAX 68 05 23 22 *307*
  attractions
  Abbey of Saint-Michel-de-Cuxa *305*
  Église de Saint-Pierre *305*
  festivals
  Casals Festival, (68 96 27 58 *305*
  general information
  Syndicat d'Initiative, (68 96 27 58
  FAX 68 96 50 95 *305*
  restaurants
  Grangousier (in Eus) (68 89 28 32 *307*
Pramousquier *159, 160*
  access 160
  accommodation
  Camping les Mimosas, (94 05 82 94 *159*
  Parc-Camping de Pramousquier,
  (94 05 83 95 *159*
Prats-de-Mollo *310*
  accommodation 310
  attractions
  Fort Lagarde *310*
  medieval ramparts *310*
  Romanesque church *310*
  general information
  Tourist Office, (68 38 70 83 *310*
Prieuré de Serrabone (Priory of
  Serrabone) *33, 304*
public transport *36*
Puget-Théniers *100*
Puilaurens, Cathar fortress of *32, 290*
Puyricard *193*
  access 193

Q **Quéribus**, Cathar fortress of *33, 291–292*
  attractions
  panoramic view of plain of Roussillon and
  Pyrénées *291*
Quillan *290*
  attractions
  fortress of Puilaurens *290*

R **Ramatuelle** *154*
  attractions
  jazz festival in July
  perched village
  accommodation
  Château de la Messardière****, (94 56 76 00
  FAX 94 56 76 01 *154*
  Hostellerie le Baou***, (94 79 20 48
  FAX 94 79 28 36 *154*
  La Ferme d'Augustin***, (94 97 23 83
  FAX 94 97 40 30 *154*

Les Bergerettes***, (94 97 40 22
　FAX 94 97 37 55　*154*
festivals 154
restaurants
　Château de la Messardière, (94 56 76 00　*154*
rambling *see* hiking
Raphèle-les-Arles 234
accommodation
　La Bienheureuse (camping), (90 98 35 64　*234*
　Le Gardian (camping), (90 98 46 51　*234*
Remoulins 220
Réserve Nationale de Camargue 240
restaurants, general　*37–38, 330*
　general information and prices　*330*
　gourmet　*37–38*
Rhône River 170
Rians 193
attractions
　wine tasting　*193*
Rivesaltes 302
Roaix-Séguret 209
rock climbing, information, Comité du Tourisme
　Riviera-Côte d'Azur, (93 50 60 88　*28*
Roquebrune-Cap-Martin 13, 20, 116
acess 116
accommodation
　Vista Palace Hôtel****, (92 10 40 00
　　FAX 93 35 18 94　*116*
　Westminster**, (93 35 00 68 FAX 93 28 88 50　*116*
attractions
　castle　*116*
festival 116
general information
　Tourist Office, (93 35 62 8　*116*
history 116
restaurants
　Le Piccolo Mondo, (93 35 19 93　*116*
　Le Vistaero (92 10 40 00　*116*
Rouffiac-des-Corbières 291
wine tasting:
　Domaine du Trillol, (68 45 01 13　*291*
Roussillon (Luberon)　*30, 212, 214*
Roussillon (Region of Languedoc-Ruissillon)
　295–317
history 297
Route des Crêtes 316
attractions
　Cap Réderis　*317*
　Ermitage Notre-Dame-de-Consolation　*317*
　Tour Madeloc　*317*
Roya Valley 117
Rustrel 216
attractions
　carrières d'ocre (ochre quarries)　*216*

S **Sablet** 209
sailing *see also* watersports　*25*
information,
　Fédération Française de Voile (FFV),
　　((1) 44 05 81 00　*25*
Saillagouse 308
accommodation
　Planes Hotel**, (68 04 72 08
　　FAX 68 04 75 93　*308*
　Planotel**, (68 04 72 08 FAX 68 04 75 93　*308*
general information
　Tourist Office (68 04 72 89　*308*
restaurants
　Vieille Maison Cerdane, (68 04 72 08　*308*

Saint-Cyprien 25, *301*
accommodation
　camping　*301*
　L'Île de la Lagune****, (68 21 01 02
　　FAX 68 21 06 28　*301*
attractions
　sailing　*25*
restaurants
　L'Île de la Lagune, (68 21 01 02　*301*
sport
　Golf de Saint-Cyprien, (68 37 63 93　*327*
Saint-Gilles 247
access 248
attractions
　cruises on Canal du Rhône à Sète　*248*
　houseboat rentals, Blue Line,
　　(66 87 33 29　*248*
general information
　Tourist Office, (66 67 33 75　*248*
restaurants
　La Salicorne (restaurant-cruise),
　　(66 87 33 29　*248*
　Saint-Gillois, (66 87 33 69　*248*
Saint-Guilhem-le-Desert 26, *260, 262*
accommodation and restaurant
　Hostellerie Saint-Benôit**, (in Aniane)
　　(67 57 71 63 FAX 67 57 47 10　*262*
attractions
　canoeing and kyaking: Centre de
　　Canoë-Kayak, (67 57 44 99　*260*
　Grotte de Clamouse　*260*
festivals 260
restaurant
　Mimosa, (in Saint-Guiraud),
　　(67 96 67 96　*262*
Saint-Guiraud 262
restaurant
　Mimosa, (67 96 67 96　*262*
Saint-Jean-Cap-Ferrat 103
accommodation
　Belle Aurore***, (93 76 04 59
　　FAX 93 76 15 10　*104*
　Brise Marine***, (93 76 04 36　*104*
　Costière*, (93 76 03 89　*104*
　Voile d'Or****, (93 01 13 13
　　FAX 93 76 11 17　*104*
general information
　Tourist Office, (93 76 08 90　*103*
restaurants
　Le Provençal, (93 76 03 97　*104*
　Le Sloop, (93 01 48 63　*104*
Saint-Laurent-d'Aigouze 250
accommodation
　Camping Port Vieil, (66 88 15 42　*250*
Saint-Martin-de-Canigou Romanesque
　abbey　*34*
Saint-Martin-de-Castillon 216
accommodation and restaurant
　Lou Caleu**, (90 75 28 88 FAX 90 75 25 49　*216*
Saint-Martin-de-Londres 32, *260–262*
access 262
accommodation
　Camping Pic Saint-Loup, (67 55 00 53　*262*
attractions
　Grottes des Demoiselles　*262*
　hang-gliding on Pic Saint-Loup　*262*
general information
　Tourist Office, (67 55 09 59　*262*

LÉGENDE • LEGEND • ZEICHENERKLÄRUNG • LEGENDA • LEGGENDA

plus de 500 000/more than 500,000/über 500 000/
meer dan 500.000/più di 500.000

PARIS

100 000 - 500 000

BREST

50 000 - 100 000

PAU

10 000 - 50 000

Rodez

5 000 - 10 000

Nangis

1 000 - 5 000

Sancerre

moins de 1 000/under 1,000 inhabitants/weniger als
1 000 Einwohner/minder dan 1.000 inwoners/
meno di 1.000 abitanti
Saissac

Hameau, Hamlet, Weiler, Gehucht, Frazione
Brès

Autoroute avec nom et numéro d'échangeur
Motorway with interchange name and number
Autobahn mit Name und Nummer des Autobahnkreuzes
Autoweg met naam en nummer verkeerswisselaar
Autostrada con denominazione e numero di svincolo

Incarville
19
A 13

Autoroute en construction
Motorway under construction
Autobahn im Bau
Autoweg in aanbouw
Autostrada in costruzione

Autoroute en projet
Motorway projected
Autobahn in Planung
Autoweg projet
Autostrada in progetto

Route à chaussées indépendantes
Dual carriageways
Zweibahnige Straße
Weg met twee banen
Strada a doppia carreggiata

Route à chaussées indépendantes en construction
Dual carriageways under construction
Zweibahnige Straße im Bau
Weg met twee banen in aanbouw
Strada a doppia carreggiata in costruzione

Route à chaussées indépendantes en projet
Dual carriageways projected
Zweibahnige Straße in Planung
Weg met twee banen projet
Strada a doppia carreggiata in progetto

Route express à une seule chaussée
Single carriageway express road
Einbahnige Schnellstraße (2-spurig)
Snelweg met een enkele rijbaan
Strada rapida ad una sola carreggiata

Route express à une seule chaussée en construction
Single carriageway express road under construction
Einbahnige Schnellstraße in Bau (2-spurig)
Snelweg met een enkele rijbaan in uitvoering
Strada rapida a una sola carreggiata in costruzione

Route de transit international
International throughroute
Internationale Fernstraße
Internationale hoofdroute
Strada di transito internazionale

Route de transit régional
Regional throughroute
Regionale Fernstraße
Regionale hoofdroute
Strada di transito regionale

Route de communication principale
Main connecting road
Hauptverbindungsstraße
Interlokale verbindingsweg
Strada di comunicazione principale

Autres routes
Other roads
Übrige Straßen
Overige wegen
Altre strade

Sentier, chemin muletier
Footpath, mule-track
Fußweg, Saumpfad
Voetpad, karrespoor
Sentiero, strada mulattiera

21%

Route à forte montée (plus de 15 %)
Road with steep gradient (more than 1 in 7)
Straße mit starker Steigung (Über 15 %)
Sterk stijgende weg (meer dan 15 %)
Strada con forte salita (oltre il 15 %)

Parcours pittoresque
Scenic road
Malerische Wegstrecke
Schilderachtig weggedeelte
Percorso pittoresco

F

Bac pour automobile
Car ferry
Autofähre
Autoveer
Traghetto per automobili

Ligne maritime
Shipping route
Schiffslinie
Bootdienst
Linea di navigazione

Route à trafic limité
Road with trafic restrictions
Straße mit Verkehrsbeschränkung
Weg met verkeersbeperkingen
Strada con limitazioni di tràffico

Route à péage
Toll road
Straße mit Gebühr
Tolweg
Strada a pedaggio

XII/1996

Date de mise en service
Date opened to traffic
Verkehrsübergabedatum
Datum indienststelling
Data della messa in esercizio